Pomponio Leto

Eight Months at Rome, during the Vatican Council

Impressions of a Contemporary

Pomponio Leto

Eight Months at Rome, during the Vatican Council
Impressions of a Contemporary

ISBN/EAN: 9783744782012

Printed in Europe, USA, Canada, Australia, Japan

Cover: Foto ©ninafisch / pixelio.de

More available books at **www.hansebooks.com**

EIGHT MONTHS AT ROME

DURING THE

VATICAN COUNCIL.

IMPRESSIONS OF A CONTEMPORARY.

By POMPONIO LETO.

TRANSLATED FROM THE ORIGINAL.

LONDON:
JOHN MURRAY, ALBEMARLE STREET.
1876.

LONDON:
PRINTED BY WILLIAM CLOWES AND SONS,
STAMFORD STREET AND CHARING CROSS.

PREFACE BY THE TRANSLATOR.

The Memoirs of the Vatican Council which are here presented to the public, are the work of a sincere and liberal Roman Catholic, and are inspired by a genuine desire to promote the welfare of that religion. The book is marked by a spirit of frankness and moderation, and there is abundant internal evidence to show that the writer had peculiar means and opportunities of closely observing the incidents which he depicts, and of recording them with accuracy. When to these recommendations it is added that the subject is one of universal and enduring interest, enough has been said to justify the attempt that is made to render the work accessible to the generality of English readers by this translation.

The Translator is however sensible, that some injustice may have been done to the original, in a version which has been undertaken by one who is little acquainted with the metaphysical arguments in which the Author frequently engages; and with the technical language in which those arguments are embodied. The general meaning of the original has, it is hoped, been invariably preserved; but there are refinements and distinctions in the Italian, which may not have been always rendered with perfect accuracy, and which the English language is, perhaps, scarcely fitted to reproduce. To errors of this nature, for which the Translator must be held responsible, the Author and the reader will, it is hoped, alike extend their indulgence.

NOTICE BY THE EDITORS.

This manuscript, containing a sort of chronicle of the Vatican Council, having been placed in our hands, we have deemed its publication advisable on account of the great national importance for Italy, of all that concerns the time and the subject; both in itself, and in its connection with the past, the present, and the future. Moreover because, excepting in so far as the question has been dealt with by the periodical contemporaneous press, very few works have appeared in Italy with the view of enlightening the public, and recalling their attention to that memorable event, particularly in its relations, direct and indirect, with the reviving civil and political life of the country.

This object being especially aimed at in the present work, it seems the better adapted for filling a gap much felt in our current literature, since the prorogation of the Vatican Council.

The book is well suited for general readers, because, as the Author himself explains, it has no kind of theological aim or pretension; but treats rather of the influence likely to be exercised by the Council on the condition of our people, and their religious state, a consideration which renders it especially important to Italians; while the narration is made with an absence of party spirit and an impress of truth which may cause it to be useful and instructive for all.

We present it to our readers as we ourselves have received it, leaving untouched even the anachronism inscribed on the title-page, where it is stated that the book is the work of a contemporary, and yet it bears the name of Pomponio Leto. That the former statement is correct is undeniable, that the Author was an eye-witness of all he relates is beyond doubt, as the book itself proves; whereas the name of Pomponio Leto can no more be accounted that of a contemporary at the Vatican Council, than it was at the Council of Trent. Still there has always been, and there will be at least for a long time to come, a Pomponio Leto in Italy. That name embodies a type which arose at the time of the Renaissance, especially in Rome, and was produced by the combination of the genius of classical antiquity with Christian sentiment, and by the Latin spirit of inquiry, in contact with the first source of the principle of authority. It represents resistance, opposition, and investigation slowly progressive, but yet compatible with Catholic feelings and institutions.

Pomponio Leto was a philosopher who taught in one of the Italian schools of thought and learning at the period of the Renaissance; and was on that account regarded with much suspicion, and even persecuted by Paul II., but subsequently numbered Paul III. among his pupils, and became himself the friend of two later Popes, Sixtus IV. and Innocent VIII.

Our readers must not suppose that we desire to deal in fables, or to set their imagination to work in regard to our manuscript; for the conditions to which we have referred, were more frequently met with in the fifteenth, than they are in the nineteenth century.

We only wish to point out that as Italy is morally and intellectually, if not politically, the product of the two great movements of world-wide interest evolved in her and by her, to which we have already alluded— Catholicism, and the questions pertaining to it, must ever have a part in the political combinations of the nation, as philosophy and the old classics have deeply modified her religious feelings. For that reason philosophers are bound to attach great weight to spiritual influences, and a Pomponio Leto will always be forthcoming to indite the history of a Council.

INTRODUCTION.

THESE impressions, recorded during the Vatican Council at Rome, as the events occurred, were originally intended for a periodical Review; but owing to certain difficulties having arisen, their publication in that form was suspended, and the work itself might have been laid aside, had not some friends who regarded it with favour, encouraged the Author to persevere in his design. He then continued to collect, as he had done before, in their proper sequence, the most notable particulars of that important period of contemporary history; not only those which of right belonged to the public, but others which by good fortune were rescued from the official secrecy in which they should have been lawfully shrouded. In so doing he had no other purpose but that of endeavouring to fix in the memory of all those interested in these transactions, a true image of that great event, rendering its external features, so to speak, as impressive and familiar as possible.

To make an exhaustive study of such a complex subject as a Council, would involve a far greater effort than either the limits of the present work or the powers of the Author allow, and to this accordingly he has not aspired. Some one placed in more favourable circumstances may be enabled, before long, worthily to satisfy the desires of those who are intent upon the study of the religious and political history of our age. These pages contain a simple chronicle, or rather they embody the fugitive recollections and impressions retained by the memory of the Author, or the memory of others (where such could be usefully invoked), mingled with the reflections which occurred to him, and which were recorded at the same time.

In collating these slender notes, little method has been observed. The narrative was originally commenced at the end of each successive month, so as to form an article : the same plan has been followed here, therefore every chapter bears the name, and describes the proceedings of the month just elapsed; and preserves the form which the current development of events produced; each chapter moreover carries with it the impress of the opinions prevailing at the moment, and of the actual condition of affairs. Passing under review the impressions of those earlier months, after the lapse of all the phases which culminated in the declaration of Infallibility, how many mistaken opinions appear! how many antecedents which failed to produce the results expected from them! Nevertheless, with the exception of some slight re-touches, rather affecting the form than the substance, and indispensable to preserve a certain unity in the composition, it has been thought preferable to alter nothing that was committed to writing under the force of first impressions. It will consequently not be surprising if the arrangement in which the materials are disposed is defective, and the materials themselves are sometimes disconnected or reiterated. But if for such reasons the present book does not pretend to be a history, nor a work of literary merit, it yet possesses a certain stamp of reality which, consistently maintained during the eight months of the duration of the Ecumenical Council, may, perhaps, help others in forming an opinion on this notable period of Ecclesiastical history when it shall belong to the distant past; and may enable the book even now, in the living present, to direct upon the events it records an amount of light which, though cast here and there in scattered rays from contemporary publications, has not been as yet combined in any other quarter to exhibit them comprehensively and at once.

After this preamble, it is hardly necessary to add that the Council is here regarded, not in its bearing on theology and canon law, but in its relation to civil life; and that it is studied, not from within, which was, indeed, impossible for common spectators, but from without, as the title-page is intended to indicate.

It only remains for us to assure the reader that, though these sketches may be wanting in the depth and research which so grave a subject demands, yet by way of compensation they are strictly conformable to truth; for there is very little related of which the Author was not a personal witness, or which he did not receive on authority of equivalent value.

TABLE OF CONTENTS.

	PAGE
PREFACE BY THE TRANSLATOR	iii
NOTICE BY THE EDITORS	v
INTRODUCTION	ix

DECEMBER.

I.—OPENING OF THE COUNCIL 1

    1. Announcement of the opening of the Council.—2. Its first meeting.—3. Procession.—4. Entrance into St. Peter's.—5. Description of the Council Hall.—6. First Session.—7. The Fathers do homage.—8. Benediction by the Pope.—9. The Council is opened.

II.—THE IMPORTANCE OF THE ASSEMBLY 7

    1. Importance of the Assembly.—2. Condition of Christendom.—3. Causes of its divisions.—4. Present state of affairs.—5. The longest interval without an Ecumenical Council.—6. Character of this meeting.—7. Causes that brought about the Council.—8. The Catholic party.—9. Reasons for the convocation of the Council.—10. Bull of Convocation.

III.—THE MEETING OF THE COUNCIL 13

    1. First official document.—2. Impression it produces.—3. Invitation to Protestants and schismatical bodies.—4. Proceedings of foreign ambassadors.—5. Objects of the Council.—6. Further remarks on the same matter.—7. Hospitality

III.—THE MEETING OF THE COUNCIL—*continued.*

offered to the bishops.—8. Nomination of the Commissions.— 9. The *Civiltà Cattolica.*—10. Its article of February 6th.— 11. The Fulda proclamation and Padre Giacinto's letter.— 12. Pastoral of the Archbishop of Paris, and publications of the anti-Infallibilist party. — 13. The programme of the Council is unfolded.—14. The Archbishop of Westminster.

IV.—THE RULES AND CONDITIONS OF THE ASSEMBLY 22

1. Jubilee and preliminaries. — 2. First Papal allocution. — 3. Order of the Council.—4. The same subject.—5. The same subject.—6. Nomination of the presidents and other officials. —7. Objections to the Order.—8. Objections to the nominations.—9. Position of parties.—10. Their description.— 11. Considered with regard to their nationality.—12. The French episcopate.—13. French Opposition.—14. Opportune declaration.—15. German episcopate.—16. The other Catholic bishops.—17. Italian episcopate.

V.—FIRST SESSION 31

1. Papal allocution at the first Session. — 2. First meeting of the Congregations.—3. Judges of excuses and complaints.— 4. Bull for the election of the Pope.—5. Bull for the limitation of censures.—6. Election of persons to serve on the Commissions for amendments.—7. The great questions under discussion in the Council.—8. The first question.—9. The second question.—10. The third question.—11. The Papacy essentially Italian.—12. The Roman Curia in regard to the Church.—13. Interests of the Papacy and of Italy.—14. One question should not prejudice another.—15. Predictions.— 16. Importance of these events.

JANUARY.

I.—THE SECOND SESSION 42

1. Aspect of the Church of St. Peter's on a feast-day.—2. The same.—3. Second Session.—4. Aspect of the Council Hall. —5. Defects of the same.—6. Profession of faith.—7. Description of the ceremony.—8. Reasons for its taking place.

II.—THE ARRANGEMENT OF THE WORK.—FIRST SCHEME 46

    1. Classification of subjects.—2. Ecclesiastical policy is omitted from the Commissions.—3. Distribution of the schemes.—4. Duty of the Commissions.—5. Nomination of the same.—6. Method observed in the debates.—7. The Assembly sanctions the scheme.—8. Difference between an Ecclesiastical Council and an assembly of laymen.—9. On Papal approbation.—10. On the proposals of the bishops.—11. Composition of the Council.—12. Addresses against its Order.—13. The Opposition declares itself.—14. The scheme "De Fide."—15. Observations on the same.—16. Debate on the same.—17. On the Opposition.—18. Its composition.—19. The Italians.—20. Admonitions of the presidents.—21. Other provisions.—22. The scheme "De Fide" sent back.

III.—FIRST STEP TOWARDS INFALLIBILITY.—OTHER SCHEMES 57

    1. Petition for Infallibility.—2. The predominant question.—3. The promoters of the address.—4. Its contents.—5. Its arguments.—6. Manner of its publication.—7. Number of signatures.—8. Undignified supposition.—9. Promoters of the address.—10. Addresses against Infallibility.—11. Singular situation.—12. Division of parties in the Assembly.—13. Efforts to promote Infallibility.—14. Revelations of the *Unità Cattolica.*—15. Distribution of new schemes.—16. Their form is displeasing.—17. The scheme "De Episcopis."—18. Discourse of the Bishop of Cologne.—19. Speech of the Bishop of Orleans.—20. General features of the schemes.—21. The bishops ask for more information on the subjects of debate.—22. The scheme "De Catechismo."

IV. THE SCHEME "DE ECCLESIA" 67

    1. Distribution of the scheme "De Ecclesia."—2. On Infallibility.—3. Arguments to be brought forward.—4. Continuation of the Congregations without much result.—5. The number of bishops diminishes.—6. Opinions on the duration of the Council.

FEBRUARY.

I.—THE FIRST RESULTS OF THE SCHEME "DE ECCLESIA" 72

1. Summary of the proceedings of the three previous months.— 2. On the Canons contained in the scheme "De Ecclesia."— 3. Summary of their contents.—4. Fate of the addresses of the Opposition.—5. Letters of the Bishop of Orleans.— 6. Tactics of the Opposition.—7. Explanation of the tardiness in the deliberations of the Council.—8. Attempt to obviate this defect.—9. Italian addresses.—10. Project for shortening the speeches.—11. Project of reconciliation.—12. Failure of the same.—13. Other plans for bringing about an agreement. —14. New diplomatic intervention.—15. The amended schemes.—16. Affairs of the East.—17. Debate on the scheme "De Catechismo."

II.—THE SCHEME "DE ECCLESIA" 83

1. The twenty-one Canons of the scheme.—2. Summary of the same.—3. Their probable effect on the world.—4. Means of escape.—5. Temporal power before Infallibility.—6. Remainder of the scheme.—7. Its application.—8. Conclusion.

III.—CONDITION OF THE CATHOLIC NATIONS 91

1. Displeasure caused by the publication of the Canons.— 2. Questions for the consideration of the Council.—3. Questions regarding France.—4. Catholicism and modern society. —5. The Revolution.—6. Dilemma.—7. Exceptions to preceding observations.—8. Responsibility of Institutions.—9. Excessive authority.—10. Intolerance and indulgences.—11. Asceticism.—12. Centralisation.—13. Rebellion.—14. Conclusion.

IV.—THE NEW ORDER 105

1. Objections to preceding arguments.—2. Address of the Catholics of Coblentz.—3. Infallibility sole object of attention.— 4. Close of the first phase of the Council.—5. The new Order.—6. Judgment of the majority.—7. Holidays.— 8. Anecdotes.—9. Different *postulata*.—10. Various publications.—11. Speech at the opening of the Exhibition.— 12. Diplomatic interference is aroused.—13. Predictions.— 14. Conclusion.

MARCH.

I.—APPENDIX TO THE SCHEME "DE ECCLESIA" 118

   1. Distribution of Appendix to the scheme "De Ecclesia."—
   2. Foreign influence.—3. Plans for leaving the Council.—
   4. Great discouragement.—5. More on politics.—6. Recall
   of the French ambassador.

II.—A TRUCE 123

   1. Death of Count de Montalembert.—2. Funeral service in his
   honour.—3. More petitions by the bishops.—4. Article by
   Döllinger.—5. Suspension of the scheme "De Ecclesia."

III.—THE FIRST SCHEMES AGAIN BROUGHT FORWARD 126

   1. The first schemes again brought forward.—2. Stormy sitting.
   — 3. Protest of the Bishop of Bosnia and Sirmio. —
   4. Speech of the Pope.—5. Incidents relating to the Eastern
   bishops.—6. Theme for a speech at the Roman University.
   —7. Withdrawal of some amendments.—8. Reasons for the
   same.—9. Despatches of Count Daru and of Cardinal Antonelli. — 10. Ambassadors. — 11. Relations between France
   and the Vatican.—12. The scheme "De Fide" voted in
   part.—13. Catholic Art Exhibition.—14. The same.

APRIL.

I.—THE SCHEME "DE FIDE" FOR THE SECOND TIME 137

   1. Cessation of diplomatic intervention.—2. Definitive voting on
   the scheme.—3. Result of the voting.—4. Easter Festival.
   —5. The public Session fixed.—6. Third Session.—7. Impression it produced.

II.—THE FIRST SCHEME "DE FIDE" 141

   1. Comparison of the first and second schemes.—2. The same.—
   3. Description of first scheme. — 4. The same. — 5. The
   same.—6. Considerations. — 7. Further reflections.—8. On
   faith.—9. The connection of faith and science.—10. Dogmatic Theology.—11. Close of observations on first scheme.
   —12. Annotations.

III.—THE SECOND SCHEME "DE FIDE" 149

1. The scheme as a whole.— 2. First and second chapters.— 3. Third chapter.—4. Fourth chapter.—5. Observations of the bishops.— 6. Their influence.— 7. Continued observations.—8. Difficulties that beset the scheme.—9. Reasons for describing the scheme.—10. Note of the North-German Confederation.

MAY.

I.—THE SCHEME "DE ECCLESIA" FOR THE SECOND TIME 155

1. The scheme "De parvo Catechismo" for the second time.— 2. The scheme "De Ecclesia" sent back.— 3. Returns modified.—4. The scheme "De parvo Catechismo" is voted. —5. Its amendments are voted, and the scheme is laid aside. —6. The debate on the scheme "De Ecclesia" is opened. —7. It is continued.—8. Speech of the Pope on giving the Prizes at the Exhibition of Catholic Art.—9. Speech against Infallibility.

II.—FOREIGN POLICY 160

1. Despatch by Ollivier.—2. 'Ce qui se passe au Concile.'— 3. Disquietude at the Vatican.—4. Speech by Monsignor Kettler.—5. Infallibility publicly promoted.—6. Address of the Roman parish priests.—7. Unfortunate position of affairs.—8. Duke of Saldanha.—9. Feast of St. Peter.

JUNE.

I.—CLOSE OF THE GENERAL DISCUSSION 167

1. Close of the general discussion on the scheme "De Ecclesia." — 2. Speech of Monsignor Maret. — 3. New protests. — 4. Proposal for secret voting.—5. Resistance to be kept up to the last.—6. Feast of Pentecost.—7. Objections to proposal of the Archbishop of Malines.

TABLE OF CONTENTS. xix

                                                                    PAGE

II.—SUMMARY OF THE QUESTION OF INFALLIBILITY 173

    1. Summary of the question.—2. The scheme "De Ecclesia" is reduced.—3. First and second chapters.—4. Third chapter, and its quotation from St. Gregory the Great.—5. Doctrines of the scheme "De Primatu."—6. The time for presenting observations upon personal Infallibility limited to ten days. —7. Text inserted in the first draft of "De Ecclesia."— 8. No special Canon for Infallibility.

III.—DEBATE ON INFALLIBILITY 179

    1. Prognostications and state of parties.—2. Processions, prayers, and addresses.—3. Opening of the debate on Infallibility.— 4. Approach of summer. — 5. Speech of the Pope on the Festival of Corpus Domini. — 6. The fight begins. — 7. History of the question of Infallibility. — 8. The same. —9. The same.—10. Continuation and ending.—11. Speech of Cardinal Guidi.—12. Speech of Valerga.—13. Speech of the Archbishop of Osimo.—14. Predictions.—15. A third party.—16. The Opposition pray for a prorogation of the Council.

JULY.

I.—CLOSE OF THE DEBATES 195

    1. Effects of the climate. — 2. Weariness of the assembly. — 3. The bishops begin to leave Rome.—4. The first heads of the scheme "De Ecclesia" are voted. — 5. Close of the discussion. — 6. Reasons of the Opposition for accepting it.—7. The same.—8. Discussion on the amendments.— 9. The Opposition consider their future course.—10. Formula of Infallibility.—11. After the proposal.—12. The third chapter is voted.—13. The fourth chapter is voted.— 14. The vote on Wednesday, July 13.

II.—FOURTH SESSION 206

    1. Calculations well founded, but disappointed.—2. The Opposition send a message to the Pope.—3. Adjunct to the formula

II.—FOURTH SESSION—continued.
PAGE
of Infallibility.—4. Protest of the assembly.—5. Last attempts of the Opposition.—6. Fourth Session.—7. Reflections on the vote.—8. Protests of the Opposition.—9. After the event.—10. Text of the Canons that promulgate Infallibility.—11. The future.—12. Mnemosynon.

CONCLUSION 223

APPENDIX OF DOCUMENTS.

DOCUMENTS.
I. Bull of Convocation of the Council 259
II. French Correspondence from the 'Civiltà Cattolica' 262
III. Proclamation of the Bishops at Fulda 263
IV. Letter of Padre Giacinto 266
V. Pastoral of the Archbishop of Paris 268
VI. Pastoral of the Bishop of Orleans 273
VII. Promulgation of the Jubilee 294
VIII. Allocution of the Sistine Chapel 296
IX. Bull "Multiplices inter" 298
X. Allocution at the First Session 303
XI. Bull for the Pope's Election 304
XII. Bull for limiting Censures 306
XIII. The Canons published in the 'Allgemeine Zeitung' and the 'Süd-Deutsche Presse' 311
XIV. Statistical Extract from Franscini 320
XV. Last Letter of Montalembert 321
XVI. Address of the Catholics of Coblenz to the Bishop of Treves .. 321
XVII. New Order of the Council, &c. Article by Döllinger 326
XVIII. The Scheme "De Fide" 332
XIX. Formula of Adhesion to the Dogma of Infallibility given by the 'Italie,' at the end of June 1870 337
XX. The Scheme "De Ecclesia," from the 'Giornale di Roma' .. 337

EIGHT MONTHS AT ROME.

DECEMBER.

I.—OPENING OF THE COUNCIL.

1. Announcement of the opening of the Council.—2. Its first meeting.—3. Procession.—4. Entrance into St. Peter's.—5. Description of the Council Hall.—6. First Session.—7. The Fathers do homage.—8. Benediction by the Pope.—9. The Council is opened.

1. AT nine in the morning of December the 8th 1869, the salutes from Monte Aventino and the bells of all the churches in Rome, announced to the world the opening of the Twentieth Ecumenical Council, fifteen centuries after the first so recognised by history—that of Nicea; eighteen after that of Jerusalem, and three after the last Council—that of Trent.

2. At the same hour, all those called to attend the Council were assembled in the great hall above the portico of the Vatican Basilica, which on this occasion was arranged as a chapel; though it is generally used for the functions of the Papal Benediction and of the Last Supper.

The Pope, who on ordinary occasions never leaves his own apartments till all is prepared and ready for his reception, was to-day one of the first to enter the hall, as if to show that he desired to place himself on an equality with those present; and remained quietly seated till the long cortége was complete which was to pass before him in solemn procession to the Church of St. Peter. There were 47 cardinals present out of the 55 in Rome; more than 700 bishops out of the 1000 supposed to form the entire Catholic episcopate; more than 20 mitred abbots, five abbots *nullius*, and about 30 Generals of Orders; this being the computation given by the Official Index published in Rome, of those who were present, and had the right of sitting at the Council.

The *Civiltà Cattolica* gave the complete list of names as 723, the *Unità Cattolica* at 720—both differing from the Official Index, which declared them to be over 760; but, in truth, it was difficult to make the calculation with perfect accuracy, this only being certainly known, that the polling papers gathered at the first sitting of the Council amounted to 678.

Nine of the Bishops present were Patriarchs, four of the Western Church, and five Oriental. There were five Primates, and above 130 Archbishops; these, however, had not all the charge of a diocese, and among the Patriarchs were some who had never in their lives left Rome. There were also a considerable number of Archbishops and Bishops *in partibus*, who were not diocesans, and scarcely knew the geographical situation of the territories whence they derived their designations; all these, however, were equally admitted to the Council and allowed to vote. Abbots and Generals of Orders had also a seat, together with the power of voting, although without any real claim to that privilege.

The result of all these concessions was very materially to affect the action of the Council by admitting to its assemblies a numerous body of dignitaries holding no cure of souls; and consequently, though equal in dignity to the other ecclesiastics, inferior to them in that practical knowledge and sense of responsibility which was required to render their vote disinterested and valuable; they availed, however, to swell the numbers present, and to make the Vatican Council the largest ever witnessed in the Catholic Church. While the hierarchy were assembled in the upper hall, the rest of the Roman clergy, both regular and secular, arranged themselves along the great staircase, the portico, and the church, and formed two long lines through which the procession passed.

3. When all were assembled, the Pope rose, prostrated himself before the altar, and began, with his singularly clear and distinct voice, to intone the hymn to the Holy Spirit, the choir

took up the strain, and the procession moved onward in the following order: first, the chamberlains and private chaplains, who headed the cortége, then the consistorial advocates, the promoters of the Council, and the singers; next to them, the "Abbreviatori di Parco Maggiore," the "Votanti di Segnatura," the "Cherici di Camera," and the "Auditori di Rota," two prelates in each of the four classes last mentioned having the duty of scrutinising the votes of the Council; then came the Head of the "Sacro Ospizio," and two chaplains carrying the Pope's mitre and tiara. The abbots in ordinary, the abbots *nullius*, the bishops, archbishops, prelates, patriarchs, and cardinals according to their order then followed, preceded by an incense-bearer, and the apostolic sub-deacon carrying the Papal cross between two acolytes, the bishops and cardinals being each accompanied by a chaplain or train-bearer.

Close to them were the senator and the "conservators" representing the municipality of Rome, the vice-chamberlain of the Church, and the Prince of the Pontifical Throne; then two protonotaries, the cardinal-deacon, the masters of ceremonies, and finally the Pope himself, carried on his chair of state under a canopy; the generals of religious orders, various other officials and persons in the service of the Council, secretaries, notaries, and lastly, shorthand-writers, who completed the procession.

4. This long line of dignitaries of the highest grade then passed down the lines formed by the humbler ecclesiastics, and leaving the great hall above the portico, advanced through that which gives access to the Sistine Chapel; then descending the grand staircase of Bernini, they turned to the right through the portico and solemnly entered the Church of St. Peter, which now appeared to be filled for the first time within the memory of man.

The Pope and the bishops were vested in white, the day being the Feast of the Immaculate Conception; and the Pope, who usually wears a tiara or a mitre of plates of gold, now had on a costly mitre made especially for the occasion. These particulars have some significance, as they were intended to indicate a certain equality with all the other bishops, which, however, did not extend beyond the minor accessories of ceremonial.

At the entrance of the Church, the Pope descended from his

Throne and, uncovering his head, proceeded to the Papal altar, where he took up his station.

5. The Council Hall is situated in the right transept of the Church of St. Peter, in the area in which the ceremony of the Washing of the Feet is held on Maundy Thursday; it lies between the two pilasters which support the cupola of Michael Angelo, and the space above is filled in by an attic and a tympanum, under which is a great door that remained open to satisfy the curiosity of the public during the ceremony and, indeed, during all the public sittings of the Council, only being shut when the private Congregations were held. The guardianship of this door belonged, of ancient right and usage, to the Knights of Jerusalem, and they hastened to avail themselves of the privilege by placing their services at the disposal of the Council, showing a natural eagerness to follow the deliberations from so favourable a position, rather than to hear them by report from afar.

As, however, it is the special duty of the "guardie nobili" to accompany the Pope on all occasions, it was found necessary to commit the keeping of the great door equally to them and to the Knights of Jerusalem. Above the door was inscribed in large letters the appropriate text, "Go ye, and teach all nations: I am with you always, even unto the end of the world."

The hall itself, though simply arranged, presents an imposing appearance, due to its own grand proportions; at the further end is placed the Pope's throne, next to it the benches for the patriarchs and cardinals, and then the seats for the bishops, descending gradually in seven rows till they reach the level of the floor. Every seat bears a number corresponding to the ticket given to each of the bishops, according to which they were inscribed in the printed catalogue distributed to all members of the Council. The hall is adorned with various paintings, representing the Doctors of the Church, and the Popes who have convened Ecumenical Councils, and above the throne hangs a picture of the Descent of the Holy Spirit; everything is simple but striking.

There is, however, one serious defect in the building with reference to public speaking, namely, its want of acoustic properties. The immense height of the vaulted roof, and the grand arches of the nave, seemed to favour the desires of that portion of the Council which was accused of being inimical to discussion, by swallowing up the most learned propositions and the wisest sayings in their vast depths before they could be heard. Indeed, this inconvenience was found to be so serious, that many people believed that the Vatican Hall, prepared with such care, would only be used for public sittings and for the promulgation of decrees, and that the closed meetings would be held in the "Sala degli Svizzeri," or some other of the great courts or churches of Rome.

6. Towards eleven o'clock all were seated in the Council Hall—the Pope on his throne, the cardinals and patriarchs in their places, and then the bishops, Latin, Greek, Melchitic, Russian, Roumanian, Bulgarian, Syrian, Chaldean, Maronite, Copt, and Armenian, all vested in their pontifical attire. They presented one of the most remarkable spectacles ever witnessed by human eyes, especially in our days, when such grand displays of pomp are rare.

No spectator, however little inclined to sympathise with the assembly, could do otherwise than marvel, not so much at its outward magnificence, as at the moral power inherent in the Papacy which could still avail, after the lapse of centuries, to draw together by a simple letter of invitation multitudes from the furthest corners of the world, men of all nations, united by a discipline almost without perceptible authority; yet many of them devoted to a degree unknown in any other assembly, even to the furthering of their own abasement, and ready to contend with public opinion, not for the extension, but for the restriction of their own prerogatives. Such a spectacle enables one to comprehend the sense of indomitable power with which the Popes have always acted; no other rulers have ever reached such a pitch of authority and grandeur in dealing not only with their own subjects, but with human society at large.

7. As soon as the Pope entered, the Cardinal-Vicar intoned the mass; after which, the Secretary of the Council having placed a copy of the Gospels on a superb lectern, the Bishop of Iconium, standing before it, delivered a Latin oration, and the Pope, in his pontifical vestments, received the allegiance of all the members of the Council. This consisted in the bishops

kneeling before him, one after the other, and kissing his knee. What an effort must it have cost him, who bears the humble title of "Servant of the Servants of God," to keep in memory that modest designation during such a ceremony!

8. This being ended, the Pope bestowed his solemn benediction on the assembly three times, and pronounced the opening allocution; after which there was a movement of deep emotion among all present. Every one who knows the Pope is aware how peculiarly sensitive he is, and how liable to strong excitement: at that moment he seemed inspired by the deepest faith and enthusiasm, which supported him, notwithstanding his age, through all that long and fatiguing ceremony, and the whole assembly shared his enthusiasm; for it is in the nature of earnest conviction and intense feeling to find a ready response in the breasts of others.

The Pope, after pronouncing his allocution, invoked the Holy Spirit and the Virgin, and then rising, extended his arms towards Heaven, when the whole assembly simultaneously rose; it was a solemn sight. None of the differences which were afterwards to cool that enthusiasm and divide those hearts were yet apparent; and all the fears, the hopes, and the affections of the Catholic world were agitating the breasts of those who formed its universal assembly.

9. After other prayers, and the hymn to the Holy Spirit, the decree for the opening of the Council was read, and the consent of the assembled bishops being asked, they responded with the liturgical "Placet"; a thanksgiving followed, and then the first Session closed; the second being fixed for the 6th of January. Such was the opening of the Vatican Council called together eighteen centuries after Christ, to consider and influence the fate of the Catholic Church, and to decide whether the Western nations of Europe, with their present social and political institutions, have or have no longer a religion.

II.—THE IMPORTANCE OF THE ASSEMBLY.

1. Importance of the assembly.—2. Condition of Christendom.—3. Causes of its divisions.—4. Present state of affairs.—5. The longest interval without an Ecumenical Council.—6. Character of this meeting —7. Causes that brought about the Council.—8. The Catholic party.—9. Reasons for the convocation of the Council.—10. Bull of Convocation.

1. Thus far we have treated of the Council externally, and in this respect it was indeed splendid, and surpassed all expectations. It was a marvellous sight to behold so many dignitaries from all parts of the world assembled at the Pope's invitation, ready to bend before him, and to encounter on the threshold of the Vatican (as a French writer has observed) the Patriarch of Babylon and the Bishop of Chicago, representatives of bygone ages and of ages yet to come, met together at a period of highly-developed civilisation, with intentions and purposes of such vast importance.

But if one turns from these thoughts to bare matters of fact— from the contemplation of externals to that of the subject in itself—the Bishop of Chicago does not represent a Catholic Chicago, any more than the Patriarch of Babylon represents a Catholic Babylon.

It is no wonder that these two extreme examples do not represent Catholic societies; but how many of the other bishops are in the same position! Leaving out of the question all the prelates *in partibus infidelium*, what do the American bishops really represent in connection with the titles of their dioceses? What, for instance, does the Bishop of New York represent in face of the Catholic or universal Church? or, not to take the countries known to be anti-Catholic, how many are the French bishops able to feel themselves pastors of the whole or the greater part of their flock, or who really represent a Catholic society, or even a true Catholic majority? Among the great nations of Europe such a state of things could only be found in Italy, or more probably in Spain; in Ireland and Poland, if they be reckoned as nations; and lastly, less universally, yet more really in some parts of Germany.

2. If the West has remained Christian, nevertheless, since the

eighth century, when, with but transitory exceptions, the Catholic or universal Christian faith reached its culminating point, many great nations or races have detached themselves by degrees, and according to their separate tendencies and characteristics, from that faith, and no Councils have been able to prevent their secession. Neither the fourth Council of Constantinople, nor later, the Council of Florence, could hinder the schism of the East, which was the first stage of disunion; nor could the Council of Trent bring back the German races to the fold, and restrain the advance of Protestantism, which was the second stage of disunion, and cost the Catholic Church the loss of Germany, England, Scandinavia, and through them of America and Australia.

The third phase, which for nearly a century has menaced Catholicism in the countries still remaining to it, is that which, having as yet no other designation, we may call by the generic name of Revolution. What attitude would the Vatican Council assume with respect to this new phase—how would it face this danger? Such was the great problem which every one, from the opening of the Council, was endeavouring to solve.

Would the Council proceed on a principle of selection or of elimination? Would it take a wide limit, so as to embrace the greater portion of mankind within the Church, or would it choose a narrow limit, and thus throw numbers into revolution? Such thoughts occupied all earnest minds, because for them both the moment and the subject were most serious, far more so than was apparent to superficial observers. We repeat, the question at stake was to decide whether the Catholic nations of Europe are, or are not to have a religion—not a nominal or outward form merely, but a real religion in common, which should be manifest in their actions, and be in harmony with their customs and institutions.

3. If the Council of Constantinople did not prevent the schism of the East, or the Council of Trent the Reformation in the West, yet undoubtedly other Councils have, with more or less difficulty, finally triumphed and accomplished the end for which they were convened. Thus, the Councils of Nicea, Ephesus, and Chalcedon really conquered, not indeed at once but eventually, the errors they condemned, and no traces of those errors remain at the present day. And the reason for this success is, that every time

the Catholic Church had to oppose a mere error of judgment, arising simply from differences of opinion, she conquered it with more or less ease, according to its greater or less importance, because in such a case the principle of authority embodied and represented the interests of the great majority of Catholics, who were ready to sacrifice purely speculative differences for the sake of unity.

When, however, the Church had to confront great interests, and the general or partial, yet weighty tendencies of a race or nation, which either gave rise to some error, or by furnishing a pretext for it, manifested it to the world, then those tendencies strengthened the error which finally triumphed through their instrumentality. Who does not recognise in the two great schisms that have rent the Christian world the manifestation of those sentiments, old as the human race, pride in the past and impatience for the future? Who does not see in the one, intolerance of the old yoke, and in the other, opposition to the new?

If to all this be added the consideration of the other great interests and secondary combinations also at work, a just view may be obtained of the different powers fighting in the camp of Theology, in those ages especially when they could find expression in no other way.

4. To which of these two cases does the present state of things appertain? Under what external and internal conditions has the Vatican Council assembled to meet the difficulty, and how will its deliberations affect the progress of society and of the Church?

To find the first answer is not difficult, because there is no doubt that behind every inquiry suggested in the Council there lies a great social question of deep moment at the present day, involving an immense amount of living interests.

The second answer was not so easily perceived at the opening of the Council; and in order to form some conjectures and make an approximate judgment, it was necessary to review all that had preceded it, and to observe the present course of its deliberations.

5. From the foundation of the Church up to the present time there never had been so long a period without the assembling of an Ecumenical Council. Many reasons can be adduced for this, to be sought principally in the calm which followed the stormy crisis of the Reformation, in the religious apathy which

prevailed in the latter centuries, as also in the great difficulty of calling together a General Council, after the last experiment at Trent, which resulted in the position of the bishops being strengthened as regards their flocks, though weakened in other respects; and in the fact that the authority of the Pope having been secured on this occasion, he had no wish to expose it to another trial. But (without going into further particulars) the main reason is that the Church, which had hitherto formed a sort of constitutional monarchy, emerged from the Council of Trent by virtue of constant and progressive explanation and discussion as a monarchy, only slightly tempered; and from this came the unwillingness, and even dislike, subsequently shown to the assembling of her States-General.

If, by a further process of discussion, the Church should become an absolute monarchy, the Vatican Council might prove her last deliberative assembly; and her meetings, changing their character, might become simply consultative, and therefore, like the consistory of cardinals, rather a solemn ceremony than a real event in the economy of the Church.

6. It is undeniable that the spontaneous act of the Pope in calling together the Council, when nothing obliged him to do so, and when the episcopate generally was attached and subservient to his wishes, was an act of liberal tendency—a step backwards in the path of absolutism, and a step in advance towards a larger and more complete restoration of the ecclesiastical constitution, because that is founded in the combined opinion of many rather than in the absolute power of one.

Whoever doubted the good effects of the Council, must logically have doubted also the character and disposition of the episcopate, the good-will of the Pope in the matter being apparent. Indeed, in summoning this assembly his action was entirely free and spontaneous, though up to a certain degree he may have been influenced by the force of circumstances.

7. In the year 1859-60, when troubles in Italy seemed to threaten her political existence, Rome, finding her territories slipping from her grasp, and without the means of retaining them, turned for help, as she has always done in similar perils, to the other Catholic nations. But the political condition of Europe being such as to prevent her obtaining assistance from

the various Governments, Rome addressed herself (with her peculiar power of adaptation to the exigencies of the moment) to public opinion, instead of to the Cabinets of Europe. In that appeal she availed herself of the press, of public meetings, and of all other means of influence; in fact, she adopted the policy of partisanship instead of diplomacy. From this beginning there sprung, or rather rose again, the so-called Catholic party, which rapidly increased till it presented a well-organised body, with a strong will, and a clear and definite programme.

This party was then moulded, disciplined, and kept in constant communication with Rome by means of the different gatherings held there on various occasions, such as the promulgation of the dogma of the Immaculate Conception, the centenary of St. Peter, and the canonizing of new saints. Its consolidation was also assisted by the institution of "Peter's pence" for replenishing the Papal finances, by the enrolling of the Zouaves for a short period of service, which was renewed every year, by the issue of different publications and newspapers, by civil and religious festivities, and by many other means; in fact, the traditional policy of the Church of Rome, though remaining essentially the same, shifted its ground, and created for its service, instead of the Holy Alliance, a cosmopolitan Catholic party, which combined the strongest interests and passions, and fought with good success against the adverse march of the times.

The Society of the Jesuits was an excellent instrument in the cause, on account of its unique and extraordinary discipline, and of its authority and extension in all parts of the world, which enabled it to work in the matter with a unity of aim and action, otherwise difficult to obtain.

8. All this could not be accomplished without quitting the field of politics and entering upon that of principles, since in the Papacy the two powers are so nearly connected as necessarily to act on one another. The Catholic party, which naturally personified the principle of absolute authority, had drawn most of its adherents from the world that was past, and was no sooner arrayed for the combat than it found itself in collision with the world as now existing; the shock was soon felt, and was as violent as the toleration of the present age admitted.

Rome was unable to moderate the ardour of this conflict, nor could she, being placed at the mercy of her defenders, maintain the equanimity in action which, notwithstanding her authoritative position, or perhaps even on account of it, she had hitherto preserved.

While the religious movement was in its first stage and only showed itself in the pages of the *Civiltà Cattolica*, the *Univers*, and the pastoral letters of some of the French bishops, the Encyclical and the Syllabus came to light, and no one in the Church either raised objections or suggested doubts, all minds being occupied with the peril that threatened the temporal power. Only the Bishop of Orleans seemed to view the course of events with some anxiety, which he indicated in his sibylline treatise on the Encyclical; but it was of little avail, for the impetus being now given, it was too late to check the progress of events.

9. The retrograde step embodied in the declaration of the Encyclical,—that the Pope could not follow the spirit of the times,—and the results of the unfortunate battle of Mentana, both combined to render the Pontiff more than ever desirous of finding in the episcopate a real help and support, not only privately and officially, but formally and solemnly, and of obtaining the aid and advice of the whole Church for the purpose of lightening the responsibility that weighed so heavily upon him. Moreover, on several occasions he had already been brought into contact with great assemblies of the bishops, had become familiar with them, had studied their opinions and dispositions, and was aware of the important help to be drawn from them in the present difficulty; besides which, he had found many of the prelates favourably inclined towards an Ecumenical Council.

10. On the 29th of June, 1868, a few months after Garibaldi had reached the gates of Rome, when revolution had penetrated beyond the walls of the city even to the doors of the Vatican, and the barracks of the Zouaves were blown into the air, the apostolic letter for the assembling of the Council was published; the Pope, showing wonderful reliance in his own destiny, having chosen this most grave and dangerous moment for its convocation.*

* See Appendix, Document I.

III.—THE MEETING OF THE COUNCIL.

1. First official document.—2. Impression it produces.—3. Invitation to Protestants and schismatical bodies.—4.—Proceedings of foreign ambassadors.—5. Objects of the Council.—6. Further remarks on the same matter.—7. Hospitality offered to the bishops.—8. Nomination of the Commissions.—9. The *Civiltà Cattolica*.—10. Its article of February 6th.—11. The Fulda proclamation and Padre Giacinto's letter.—12. Pastoral of the Archbishop of Paris, and publications of the anti-Infallibilist party.—13. The programme of the Council is unfolded.—14. The Archbishop of Westminster.

1. We now come to the public and official acts of the Council, and from them it is easy to judge of the intentions and aim of the assembly, and also to form some conjectures —though in these caution is necessary—as to the direction in which it would probably move.

2. The idea of the Council sprang naturally in the Pope's mind from the desire of finding some shelter from the storms which beset him, and of lightening the burden of his heavy responsibilities. The Catholic party easily acceded to the plan, thinking that the bishops, who were in some places harassed, and in others found their powers diminished, would readily meet the wishes of the party, on account of the work they had done, and the energy with which they had successfully fought for the interests of the Church; besides, the present seemed a favourable occasion for inducing the entire episcopate either to accept their views, or at least to become participators in their responsibility.

It is true that some viewed with unfavourable eyes the calling together of any assembly that could possibly be dispensed with; but these were a few incorrigible members of the "Curia," or a still smaller body of "prudent" men, the larger number inclining to the other opinion.

The rest of the Church having for the last eight years heard but one note of alarm, that which was sounding the dangers that threatened the temporal power, turned for help to the Ecumenical Council, and trusted that it might devise some remedy for the evils which had been so long impending. Public opinion is slow in these days to concern itself with matters not of immediate consequence, and did not trouble itself with any far-sighted reflections on the subject of the assembly.

3. An invitation to join the Council was then sent to the Protestant and schismatical bodies, rather with the pretence of including all Christian denominations in its assembly, than with any expectation that they would come; for the letters were couched in terms which presupposed entire submission to Rome in all who should attend. The invitations were declined with more or less courtesy, as was to be expected. Further negotiations were carried on for a time with some hope of success, but these also proved in the end abortive.

An attempt was made to obtain from the Russian Government permission for the Polish bishops to attend the Council, but this attempt failed; and, if the story be true, its only result was to victimise an innocent person, a Polish priest, who happened to be obnoxious to the Russian Government, by whom his expulsion from the Roman States was demanded as one of the conditions preliminary to the grant by the Czar of his "exequatur." The priest was banished; but, nevertheless, the permission was not granted by Russia, nor did the bishops ever arrive.

From these preliminaries it gradually became evident that the great questions which divide Christendom would meet with no solution in a Council, from whose deliberations they were excluded one after the other.

4. One of the first discussions that took place, was on the propriety of admitting the ambassadors of Christian Sovereigns to the meetings of the Council; but as the Pope had very little desire for their presence, and the several Governments had no wish to meddle in the matter, it was easy to come to an agreement on this point. A Congregation of cardinals was held, in which it was decided that the ambassadors should not be present at the Council, but that the Secretary of State should keep them informed of all the business that was transacted. A great interchange of notes and despatches followed; and it was finally determined that at the public Sessions a particular tribune, as was customary at all great ceremonies, should be reserved for the diplomatic body, who were obliged to rest satisfied with this amount of participation in the deliberations of the Council; and the publications of the *Libro giallo* (yellow book) confirmed the acceptance of these conditions by the two parties reciprocally interested in the liberty of Church and State.

5. The Papal Bull, published on the 29th June, 1868, in the vestibule of the Vatican Basilica, enumerates (in its liturgical compilation) the reasons for assembling the Ecumenical Council as follows:—" The horrible tempest (*horribili tempestate*) threatening society and the Church;" "the authority of the Apostolic See trodden under foot;" "the abolition of religious corporations;" "the confiscation of ecclesiastical property;" "the insults offered to the clergy;" "the perversity of the press;" "the increase of Sectarianism;" "the secularisation of education;" and, finally, "the corruption and impiety of manners, and the unbridled license of thought." Further on it also alludes to the discipline and instruction of the clergy.

6. If it be borne in mind that the Council was convened on the day dedicated to the Immaculate Conception of the Virgin, so as to be under her patronage, as the Pope had announced in his first allocution on the subject addressed to the bishops assembled for the Centenary of St. Peter, 30th of June, 1867, it will be obvious how he viewed the matter with regard to dogma, and to what end the Council was directed as a means of discipline.

7. At the same time the Pope addressed a circular to the bishops, offering them hospitality; this was accepted by some entirely; by others, in part; and by others, again, courteously refused, as being able to dispense with it without thereby suffering inconvenience. At the opening of the Council it was reckoned that about three hundred bishops were guests of the Pope, half of them living entirely at his expense, the others being indebted to him for lodging only. It was calculated that this hospitality cost the Pope's private exchequer about 2500 lire a day; but as such a contingency had been foreseen, a short while before the opening of the Council some of the faithful had imagined a way of meeting the expense. This was by instituting a festival on the fiftieth anniversary of the first mass celebrated by the Pope; and the immense amount of money collected on the occasion, amounting to several million francs, served to defray the heavy expenditure occasioned by the Council.

8. Before the meeting of the assembly, the Pope instituted a Congregation of cardinals to undertake all the preliminary work, and placed at its head the Cardinal-Vicar of Rome; the

members of the body being eight—Reisach, Bernabo, Panebianco, Bizzarri, Bilio, Caterini, and Capalti. Six of these were themselves presidents of other Commissions branching out from it, whose duty it was to classify the matters to be treated of in the Council in the following order:—Commission on Dogma, under the presidency of Cardinal Bilio (to whom, in great measure, though perhaps wrongly, the compilation of the Syllabus was attributed); Ecclesiastical Policy, under Cardinal Reisach; Affairs of the East, under Cardinal Bernabo, Prefect of the Congregation "De Propaganda Fide;" Religious Orders, under Cardinal Bizzarri; Ceremonial, under the Cardinal-Vicar; Ecclesiastical Discipline, under Cardinal Caterini. Besides these, the Pope appointed a Commission on Biblical Studies and the Revision of the Index, under the presidency of Cardinal de Luca, but he was not included in the Directive Congregation, and his commission remained on one side, and was not integrally connected with the others. It attracted, however, a good deal of public attention by reason of the important nature of its subjects, and was commonly reckoned among the six principal Commissions, that on Ceremonial being omitted as of little moment. The fact is, that the management of this Commission seemed, from the first, displeasing to the authorities, as the affairs relating to the Index were treated of in a large and liberal spirit, and the result was that after a few meetings it entirely dropped. It remained in public opinion as one of the six Congregations, but had no status, and all mention of it was omitted in the official organs. It was thus consigned to oblivion, notwithstanding that its members had already commenced much business, important both in matter and in the manner of its transaction.

The members of these Commissions were theologians and counsellors chosen by the Pope and the Committee of cardinals in Rome and in different Catholic countries. They, of course, received, under the strictest seal of secrecy, information as to the matters to be treated of in the Council, either fully or by degrees, according as they were prepared in Rome.

Together with the creation of these Commissions, notice was sent to the bishops of a fixed and limited number of subjects to be discussed in the Council, that they might have the opportunity of studying them beforehand; but, saving these, the Vatican maintained absolute silence towards the bishops with regard to the matters for debate. The result of this was to place the bishops at a disadvantage with reference to those theologians who were admitted to a more intimate knowledge of the concerns of the Council than fell to their own lot, these latter being also officially their inferiors. Much was said both in Rome and in Germany against this system of concealment, which kept the bishops in ignorance of matters on which they had a right to give their opinion, and regarding which they would shortly be called to pass judgment; but the reply from the Vatican was, that these being subjects on which the Pope voluntarily consulted the bishops, the manner and time of the communication must be left entirely to him, and that the greatest reserve was necessary for fear of any interference from the press in Europe.

9. Meanwhile, the *Civiltà Cattolica* exercised great influence in the Church, and especially in the Vatican; this paper was a periodical compiled by the Jesuits, which ever since the recent Italian troubles had fought valiantly for the Papacy, and was able, being under a favourable ægis, to discuss sundry persons and things without fear of contradiction, notwithstanding the restrictions imposed on the press; consequently, it took an active part in preparing and directing the preliminaries of the Council. Having reached this point, the *Civiltà Cattolica* determined to pursue its advantage, and commenced a series of articles under the heading of "Matters pertaining to the Council," in which, without fear of opposition, and fortified by the official "imprimatur," it set forth a full exposition of its own views on all the subjects that were to be treated of.

The Jesuits had, indeed, found some difficulty in making the ideas of their organ acceptable to the preparatory Commissions, though many of their order were among the members; but by reason of this, and of their authority in those assemblies, they felt confident of ultimate success, and began openly to manifest their intentions, and to show, without circumlocution, what in their opinion, should be the programme of the future Council.

10. For some time past, a spirit of opposition to this sort of dictatorship had arisen in the Church, and a portion of the

Liberal Catholics who, between the absolutism of the so-called Catholic party on the one hand, and the general carelessness of Freethinkers on the other, had hitherto dragged on a painful existence, and had been reduced to silence by the events of the last ten years, now again showed signs of life. The articles of the *Civiltà Cattolica*, as emanating from Rome, had caused serious apprehensions, and tended to increase this feeling of mistrust wherever it existed, till at length, on the 6th of February, 1869, an article was published, under the heading of " French Correspondence," giving clearly and exactly the whole programme of the Vatican Council, and announcing that its principal objects were the declaration of the Syllabus, of the Infallibility of the Pope, and of the Assumption of the Virgin ; and a further notice caused yet more astonishment, which announced that the work being all arranged, and the opinion of the Church so evident, the Council would have little further to do, and would be of short duration.* At this, the Catholic Opposition broke forth openly ; the Bishop of Orleans among the first, as is well known, openly refuting those ideas as injurious to the episcopate, and the dispute was from that moment carried on by the press with an eagerness very unusual in such matters. The *Civiltà Cattolica* endeavoured, in the April number, to excuse itself by saying that the letter in question was only the production of a French correspondent; but being entirely in accordance with the well-known opinions of the paper, this reply was of no avail, and the article remained as the signal of assault. No one could imagine the reason of such an indiscreet and inopportune because premature attempt on the part of the *Civiltà Cattolica;* and it was said, in extenuation of the mistake, that the party represented by that periodical had become uneasy as to the ultimate success of the Council, and, fearing that it might not coincide with their wishes, had adopted this means of—as it is sometimes expressed—forcing the situation. However that may be, it is certain that hitherto there had prevailed in Rome full confidence in the power of the Vatican to obtain a unanimous consent, or a large majority, for all its propositions, so that the intelligence of these differences of opinion was most unexpected.

* See Appendix, Document II.

11. The strength of the Opposition increased; letters, articles, pamphlets, and pastorals succeeding one another with great rapidity, but the first ecclesiastical document in a moderate sense of any importance, as emanating from a reunion of the higher orders of the Church, was the pastoral or proclamation of German bishops dated from Fulda.* It was signed by the bishops of all the principal sees in Germany, and was the only protest which had hitherto appeared bearing a local, and not merely a personal character. This document, drawn up in a broad and liberal spirit, was the expression, not of individual opinion, but of the majority of those Catholic populations who, by natural disposition, neither think lightly nor act rashly, and, fortunately for them, are not afflicted either with the levity of the French, or the indifference of the Italian character.

The number and nature of the signatures bore testimony to this opinion, as it was evident that some of them were affixed to the document only by reason of the strong force of public opinion in their country; and the pastoral itself was in every respect so well and forcibly framed, that by reason of the authority of its subscribers it was considered entirely beyond the reach of censure, by those even who disliked it most.

On the other hand, the first document emanating from France was of a noisy and personal character. It was a letter written by a Carmelite friar, Father Giacinto; and, for that very reason, it attracted the attention of the profane.† It was not acceptable to the ecclesiastical world, being the fragment of an animated disquisition, in which the subjects, instead of being calmly argued, were treated in a hasty manner, and from its nature was only adapted for publication in the newspapers. Rome, acting with magnanimity and shrewdness, took no notice of the work. Dupanloup sharply but courteously disapproved it; the French Catholic Liberals were silent on the matter; and Father Giacinto, by the advice of influential friends, went off to America.

12. Next in order comes the pastoral letter of the Archbishop of Paris, and this, though somewhat intricate and diffuse, is the ablest among the French documents, and carries the most weight;‡ its language and style were displeasing at Rome, but

---

* See Appendix, Document III.   † Ibid. Document IV.   ‡ Ibid. Document V.

next to the pastoral from Fulda, it was of great importance, from its moderate spirit, from its subject, and from the distinguished position of its author.

Shortly after appeared the publications of the Bishop of Orleans—his pastoral,* his pamphlet, and his letter to Veuillot. The fiery defender of the temporal power, in his pastoral, envelops his repugnance to the doctrine of personal Infallibility with many expressions of devotion to the Holy See; in the other document he is more explicit, and becomes once more the ardent apologist; in fact, he constitutes himself the head or official champion of Liberal Catholic opinions in the Latin world. What a grand office might that be, if only the Western nations had a more lively feeling of religion! and, on the contrary, how characteristic is it of the times, that the bishop should find the exercise of his championship so difficult.

The book by the Bishop of Sens, Monsignor Maret, entitled, 'The General Council and Religious Peace,' next appeared; and then a publication in Germany, under the assumed name of Janus, entitled, 'The Pope and the Council,' besides many other works of a Liberal Catholic tendency, in France, Italy, and Germany. The two books above mentioned are, however, the most complete exponents of the plan of Opposition, and the latter really sets forth the programme of Catholic resistance in Germany, where alone the Opposition has held its ground and maintained a constant and local character.

The question was more hotly debated every day; and in addition to these clear and decided expressions of public opinion, special organs of the Press opposed with great vigour that paper which had for so long held possession of the field. All sorts of stories were circulated, such a religious excitement had not been seen for years, and Rome, which had hitherto remained quiescent, now seemed fully aroused. "Janus" was put in the Index, and the sale or circulation of Maret's work was prohibited; the Secretary of the Index declaring that, though the Congregation did not consider its tenets reprehensible, they were not conformable to Roman doctrine. We may observe, for it is worthy of notice, that the two works thus severely reprobated, were not only written on the subject of the

* See Appendix, Document VI.

Council, but were in a certain sense addressed to it. The *Civiltà Cattolica*, the *Univers*, and the *Unità Cattolica* sufficed to confront the other minor publications of the Opposition.

13. The result of all these polemics was to lift in some degree the thick veil which ecclesiastical secrecy had so closely drawn over the mysterious work of the Committees, and the public began openly to discuss the questions of the Syllabus, of the Pope's personal Infallibility, and of the Assumption of the Virgin in soul and body—that being the series of propositions announced on the 6th of February by the *Civiltà Cattolica*. To these was added a scheme of clerical reformation, with a view of modifying the authority of the different orders of the hierarchy, and with the intention of promoting the advance of the Church from the possession of a limited to that of an absolute sovereignty. There may have been exaggeration in this belief; but whether the prevalent rumours were true or false, public attention, casting aside all secondary considerations, fastened on the questions of " personal Infallibility," and of " the Syllabus."

14. Nevertheless, by reason of the secrecy imposed, and at first maintained beyond all expectation, the work of the Committees was shrouded in profound darkness from the gaze of the outer world. Anecdotes and opinions were circulated, but without any certainty of their accuracy.

The principal support of the Syllabus lay in the fact that it was a Papal act, and once brought before the Council by public opinion, it could scarcely be afterwards invalidated, without the risk of seriously affecting the authority of the Holy Father. As to the question of " Infallibility," its only exposition had hitherto been carried on in the pages of the *Civiltà Cattolica*; but Monsignor Manning, Archbishop of Westminster, wishing to supplement this deficiency, wrote a pamphlet, in which he supported the doctrine most vehemently. His opinions on the point were already known, and by reason of his rank in the Church, carried considerable weight, if not for the ideas themselves, at least for the way in which they were brought forward, and the opportune moment chosen for their expression. Indeed, by his activity and energy he became the principal champion of the supporters of Infallibility, as the Bishop of Orleans was of those who opposed it.

Manning was not long since a Protestant, and not only joined the Catholic Church, but became Archbishop of Westminster: none are so devoted as converts; and the fact of having been in error the first half of his life did not hinder his becoming in the latter an ardent advocate of Infallibility. At any rate, as his antecedents justified the supposition that he was lacking in the traditional ecclesiastical spirit which is seldom acquired save by early habit and long usage, a presumption further supported by his own immoderate restlessness, it seemed likely that his authority would be somewhat diminished in the estimation of that portion of the clerical world whose principles, being conservative, are best able to exercise a calm and impartial judgment.

IV.—THE RULES AND CONDITIONS OF THE ASSEMBLY.

1. Jubilee and preliminaries.—2. First Papal allocution.—3. Order of the Council. —4. The same subject.—5. The same subject.— 6. Nomination of the presidents and other officials.—7. Objections to the order.—8. Objections to the nominations.—9. Position of parties.—10. Their description.—11. Considered with regard to their nationality.—12. The French episcopate.—13. French Opposition.—14. Opportune declaration.—15. German episcopate.—16. The other Catholic bishops.—17. Italian episcopate.

1. On the 11th of April appeared the second Papal document which concerns the Council—the apostolical letters announcing the Jubilee * to be enjoyed by all Catholics during its Session. The bishops thronged in greater numbers to Rome; and as the day for the solemn opening of the Council drew near, the Cardinal-Vicar issued an edict on November 18th, ordering the public prayers which are usual on great occasions; and lastly, the municipality invited the citizens to hail the auspicious event with rejoicings and festivities. On the 2nd of December the Pope convened a preparatory meeting of all the fathers in the Sistine Chapel, as a preliminary to the opening of the Council, and on this occasion the third public document was published.

2. When the bishops were assembled, the Pope made an allocution, in which he again reverted, though more vaguely,

* See Appendix, Document VII.

and with fewer details, to the aim of the Council, saying it was "to supply a remedy for the many evils which disturbed the Church and society." * On this occasion, the fathers received copies of the apostolic letter, "Multiplices inter," which is dated November 27th, and is the fourth official document of the Council, containing all the regulations for its management.†

3. Foremost among these is that which orders "all the Fathers, officials of the Councils, theologians, doctors of the sacred Canons, and all others who in any way assist the Fathers and the aforesaid officials in the work of the Council, not to divulge or manifest to any outside the Council, the decrees or other matters to be examined, or the discussions or opinions of any that are present." Further on, the same injunction is repeated to those who, not possessing the episcopal dignity, are either servants of the Council, or, by reason of some office, attend at its meetings; and from such is required the further obligation of an oath.

4. In the same list of rules, the power of proposing questions is conceded to the Fathers, but with the following stipulations: —

1st. That they be previously communicated in writing to a Congregation of cardinals and bishops specially deputed for this purpose.

2nd. That they be of general importance.

3rd. That they can be shown to be opportune.

4th. That they be in harmony with the mind and traditions of the Church.

The appropriation of seats then followed, according to which, by reason of a singular prerogative peculiar to the Roman Curia, the cardinals, not themselves bishops, who being without the right, yet enjoy the privilege of a seat and the power of voting in the Council, occupy the first places.

The patriarchs, primates, archbishops, bishops, the abbati *nullius*, and lastly, the abbati *generali* and Generals of Orders followed in succession; and thus seven tiers of seats were arranged in the Council Hall corresponding to the same ranks in the hierarchy.

* See Appendix, Document VIII. † Ibid. Document IX.

5. The Fathers were forbidden by the regulations to leave Rome during the sittings of the Council, and were therefore released from the obligation of residing in their dioceses for that time.

6. In the same act the following cardinals were appointed presidents of the Council:—Bilio, De Luca, Capalti, Reisach, and Bizzarri, and along with them the other officers of the Council, beginning with the Secretary, the Bishop of Sant Ippolito; Monsignor Fessler, a German professor of Canon Law in Vienna; and with him, the sub-secretary, the clerks, the assistants, the notaries, advocates, examiners of voting papers, promoters of the Council, masters of the ceremonies, shorthand-writers, and the guardians of the Council, who were the two Roman princes assisting at the Pontifical Throne, Colonna and Orsini.

All the officials swore to fulfil their obligations and to maintain the secrecy prescribed in the apostolic letter; and thus terminated the preparatory meeting which preceded the opening of the Council.

7. The Order produced a most unfavourable impression on the greater part of the bishops in Opposition; they especially distrusted the article by which the power of initiating a question was to be subordinated to a Congregation of cardinals, and that one which prohibited their absence from Rome during the Council. They said that the Order left no way open for legal opposition; and it was reported by tale-bearers in the city, that the dominant party would use it for their own advantage, and were determined, not only to adhere to their programme, but to maintain it to the end, the Pope being with them, and that they would take every means of subduing the Opposition. Above all, the prohibition against leaving Rome was interpreted as an attempt to shorten the duration of the Council—a suggestion for which the *Civiltà Cattolica* had been much blamed—and as an endeavour to prevent any actual protest against the work of the Vatican. Some, who took exaggerated views, went still further; they added to the vigour both of the resistance and of the attack, and predicted that scandals would arise in the Church in consequence.

8. The power of initiative given to the bishops, though subject to the control of a Congregation, was an unexpected

concession, but its value was greatly diminished and the feeling of mistrust, already existing, increased by the fact that the persons composing this Commission as well as all the others were almost exclusively drawn from the ranks of the majority, and were, in consequence, little inclined to favour the proposals of the Opposition.

A little later, the members of the Congregations were declared. There were twelve cardinals: Patrizi, Di Pietro, De Angelis, Corsi, Riario Sforza, De Rauscher, Bonnechose, Cullen, Barili, Moreno, Monaco, and Antonelli; and besides these, Manning, Archbishop of Westminster, the Archbishop of Tours, Archbishop of Baltimore, Archbishop of Malines, the Bishops of Valenza and Paderborn, a bishop from Chili, and two Oriental Patriarchs; the rest of the Commissions being composed of Italian bishops—making, in all twenty-six Fathers. Of these by far the greater number represented the Roman Curia, and the Opposition were scarcely represented at all; some of the bishops clearly inclined to the Catholic party, and others were of no particular shade of opinion.

In fact, it was evident that this Congregation, in virtue of the number and rank of its members, constituted an assembly which, pretending only to be of secondary consideration, in reality had the power of determining, without appeal, most of the matters to be brought before the Council, even those of serious importance, such as the propositions of the bishops, who, from their pastoral office and practical knowledge of the needs of their people, might often bring forward questions well worthy of consideration.

The Congregation, which had the power of allowing or preventing discussion on these proposals, really judged them *à priori* in a more absolute manner than the Council itself.

All this did not escape the notice of the Opposition; and the appointment of so many cardinals, and of the most strenuous supporters of the prerogative of the Vatican to serve in the Congregation, caused great alarm among those who were already apprehensive.

9. The fears and hopes of the different parties grew stronger day by day, and the strength of the contending factions was anxiously reckoned up. The Opposition were fully aware of their small number, which, taking also into account the disfavour

showed them in the Order of the Council, rendered it very difficult for them to carry out their designs.

Glancing at the assembly, it appeared that, taking it as a whole, the Opposition might be reckoned as one-fourth or one-fifth; but if considered only with regard to those who decidedly opposed them, they would be as one to two, leaving out of the calculation all the bishops of undetermined opinion, and those who though nominally adherents of the majority were still susceptible to the influences exercised by the other side.

10. The Catholic party, properly so called, or the Infallibilist, as it tried to designate itself, predominated with different gradations in the Spanish episcopate; as also among most of the French and Italians, in the small body of English bishops, but more strongly among the Irish. The same opinions prevailed among all the South American bishops, but scarcely among the North American; among the Orientals with but slight exceptions; among the bishops *in partibus;* and almost all the representatives of the small Catholic nationalities, excepting the Portuguese, shared the like views.

The opinions of the rest were of a less decided character, and the more determined among them constituted the Opposition. One of its members reckoned that if they had been able to draw over to their opinions fifty Italian or Spanish prelates they might have held their own in the contest; but it was not easy to obtain that number, as the Spanish bishops could not be counted on in this respect, and only twenty of the Italian favoured the Opposition. All these estimates were, however, immature, for as yet it was very difficult to form any with accuracy.

11. In making these reflections, it is well to remember how the bishops were massed together, for it was their habit from the time of their arrival in Rome to group themselves in their meetings according to their nationality, and thus by their separate action they indicated their views and their dispositions.

12. The French bishops have certainly a leaning towards Rome, in consequence of all they have suffered from the effects of the revolution; they are drawn towards it as a person stumbling in darkness, and doubting which way to go, turns eagerly to the light that shines from afar to guide him, and owing to this inclination the strength of Gallicanism has been weakened.

However, this decided proclivity of the French Church is not the result of a pure and simple abdication of her autonomy, but a change in its direction. The bishops, feeling their powers diminishing at home, turned not unnaturally towards Rome for two reasons; first, on account of the preponderating authority which their numbers and importance would give them there among the rest of the Catholic episcopate; secondly, because France, always desirous of increasing her influence, was more likely to support them abroad than at home; and that they judged rightly is proved by the military occupations in Italy effected by the various French Governments, whereby they have anticipated rather than followed the Ultramontane movement afterwards developed in the French Church. This also accounts for the great docility shown of late by the French prelates towards the Holy See in all disputed matters, even in those of which traditionally they had reason to be jealous, and of the solicitude they manifested for the Papacy in its recent reverses, instead of endeavouring to curtail its prerogatives still further, after the example of their predecessors before the French revolution. Only the Archbishop of Paris, being consistently moderate in his opinions, stood firm; and partly from his individual qualities, partly from his dignified position, he became the centre and rallying-point of all that yet remained of the old Gallican Church.

13. While, however, the bishops were thus drawn towards Rome, they could not forget that they lived in France; considering their own interests, as well as their ministerial office, they could not afford to lose any of the influence they possessed there, and so were restrained from directly opposing the tendency of the age and the general spirit pervading their country. The exaggerations of the Catholic party have too often the result of exposing its ecclesiastical adherents to the danger of witnessing the gradual diminution of their flocks.

Owing to the compact and peculiarly Italian nature of the Roman Curia, it is very exclusive, and could not, without radical modification, yield to the wishes of the French prelates. Accordingly, those bishops who were influenced by the considerations we have indicated, formed a sort of confederation, a party distinct from the others, though more in form than in substance, and they constituted the French Opposition; of which Dupanloup, by reason of his unlimited devotion to Rome, the bent of his mind, and the obligations imposed on him by his literary and social proclivities, naturally became the chief. He was better adapted for the position than Darboy, who remained in a sort of isolation, serene and unmoved even by the prospect of a cardinal's hat.

14. It is unnecessary to remark that in discussing these various tendencies we refer only to such differences of thought and opinion as the force of circumstances necessarily produces among men, and we do not allude to those deliberate individual purposes which it would be unwise to canvass, and which have little bearing on great and important questions.

15. The most clear, sincere, disinterested, serious opposition was that of the German bishops, among whom the Ultramontanes bore the same proportion as the Liberals among the Spaniards. Their opposition was the most clear, because they made no secret of their wishes, which were well known; the most sincere, because they pretended no change of opinions, but simply remained as they always had been, moderate; the most disinterested, because by reason of their antecedents and small numbers, as well as the state of Germany, they could never hope to exercise much influence in the government of the Church; and the most serious, because they embodied and represented the real opinions of the majority of their flocks. The German bishops derived this character of moderation from the fact of their representing a people whose religion had felt the influences of cultivation and progress, and also to the Protestantism which, prevailing so extensively in Germany, considerably modified the working of Catholicism in that country.

16. The same state of things does not, as a rule, appear in England, where many of the bishops, with Manning at their head, being more Catholic than the Pope himself, make themselves famous for their Ultramontane opinions; but there is a reason for this. The German bishops are surrounded by Protestants, but their people are Catholic, and thus Protestantism only works as a rival religion; whereas in England, Protestantism has the ascendency, and therefore the bishops would hold an isolated and difficult position were it not for the liberty they enjoy,

which much exceeds that to be found in France. They are surrounded by Protestants, and consequently they are more strongly attracted towards the Vatican, the universal centre of their faith, than towards that branch of their Church which exists in England only by toleration.

Indeed, it was sometimes remarked that the Irish bishops showed themselves less inclined to the doctrine of Infallibility than the English. The Belgians in this matter followed the French ; Monsignor de Mérode trod in the steps of Dupanloup, and both having been champions of the temporal power, became afterwards adversaries of Infallibility, *et tu quoque Brute, fili mi !* The constitution and liberal tendencies of Belgium naturally influenced its representatives.

As for the Spaniards, imbued as they are with the traditions of Torquemada, it is so much gained for humanity when they are satisfied with being simply Ultramontanes. The South Americans are merely Spaniards who have crossed the sea ; and the Portuguese, for the most part, are Liberals.

The bishops from the United States have a character of greater simplicity and individuality, and are little accustomed to ecclesiastical politics, the result of the society in which they live, which is entirely different from that of Europe. This disposition, and the fact that many of them were educated for clerical life in the colleges of Rome, as well as the small amount of consideration they enjoy in a country so little Catholic as America, rendered them more favourable to the ideas predominating in Rome than was expected. Still even they never forgot their country; they concealed the independence of citizens of the United States under their ecclesiastical dignity, and sooner or later, in greater or less measure, the most reasonable and liberal ideas prevailed among them.

As to the Orientals, living isolated in heathen countries, or surrounded by schismatical Greeks in the midst of wretched and untaught populations, they naturally looked to Rome as their one object of existence ; and provided there was no question of their privileges, of which they are extremely jealous, showed themselves most subservient to the Vatican. They made a grand display with their splendid vestments, and gave the surest votes to the Ecumenical Council.

The bishops *in partibus* were still more devoted to Roman interests; for having no dioceses and no flocks in connection with the titles conferred upon them by the Pope, they formed together with the Orientals a nucleus directly dependent on the Congregation " De Propaganda Fide," and were, with few exceptions, naturally subservient to the " Curia Romana."

17. There remain, then (leaving out small fractions), simply the Italians, and they being very numerous, were the only body able to set themselves against the French. The Italian episcopate, which, beyond any other, was concerned in many of the questions at stake, could also, when it chose, carry the most weight.

We have already alluded to the saying attributed to one of the bishops of the Opposition, that if they could reckon fifty Italian and Spanish prelates on their side, they might have hoped to prevail: but no reliance could be based on the Spaniards; and as to the Italians, it was impossible (for such an end) to count on the support of more than twenty among them.

If this estimate be incorrect, it is nevertheless true that the Italian episcopate might have been the arbiter of the question, and that those who inclined to the opinions of Maret and of Dupanloup were very few in number. The reason for this is to be found in the nature of the traditional education which prevails among the Italian clergy, and in the little experience they had had up to this time of the questions to which modern civilisation had given rise. Various other reasons might also be adduced, but the principal one must on no account be forgotten, which is that they were Italian. Nor is it so only because the irritation resulting from recent events so worked on their minds as to render them more devoted adherents of Rome, for that result could only be of a transitory nature; and even though it occasioned a feeling of displeasure, could never have accounted for the uniform and coherent line of action which they subsequently adopted. The real reason of the conduct of the clergy is found in the fact that the Papacy itself is Italian, not politically, which would be difficult to prove, but essentially.

What is the authority which has for centuries commanded the obedience of kings and of nations, which at the present day has subjects in the most remote corners of the earth, and can assemble round its throne the dignified representatives of distant churches for the purpose of acknowledging its supremacy? By whom has this authority for many centuries been wielded, not occasionally, but according to an invariable tradition? By an assembly of Italian prelates.

This is the reason why the Opposition of Dupanloup, which touches the Pope's authority, found but few followers among the Italian bishops; neither did the Syllabus, that cherished formula of the Catholic party, meet on the whole with any warm support. It seemed, therefore, that if the Italian episcopate were up to a certain point in accordance with the " Catholic party " on the matter of Papal authority, it was not prepared to follow its determination to set at open defiance the exigencies of modern society, and, indeed, contrary dispositions began to show themselves in some of the bishops. In the midst of all these conflicting opinions, the Pope, the cardinals, and a few Roman prelates, remained inflexible, prepared to defend the Church from the aggressions of society, and on behalf of the Curia to resist the resumption by the Church of her own proper authority.

V.—FIRST SESSION.

1. Papal allocution at the first Session.—2. First meeting of the Congregations. —3. Judges of excuses and complaints.—4. Bull for the election of the Pope. —5. Bull for the limitation of censures.—6. Election of persons to serve on the Commissions for amendments.—7. The great questions under discussion in the Council.—8. The first question.—9. The second question.—10. The third question.—11. The Papacy essentially Italian.—12. The Roman Curia in regard to the Church.—13. Interests of the Papacy and of Italy.—14. One question should not prejudice another.—15. Predictions.—16. Importance of these events.

1. In this state of affairs we come to the ceremony described at the beginning of this narrative, the opening Session of the Vatican Council. In the allocution then held, which was the fifth public act of the Council, the enemy against which it would contend was again specified :* " Illa impiorum conjuratio

* See Appendix, Document X.

fortis, opibus potens, munita institutis, et velamen habens malitiæ libertatem, acerrimum adversus sanctam Christi ecclesiam bellum omni scelere imbutum urgere non desinit." An indication vague certainly, but of which the application, under a "velamine," was not difficult.

The style is expansive and full of confidence, as is shown by the expression, " Ecclesia est ipso cœlo fortior," and the dignity of the Papal See is maintained by calling the Council " Unio sacerdotum Domini cum supremo gregis ejus pastore." Particular mention of the City of Rome is also made in the allocution, " Quæ Dei munere tradita non fuit in direptionem gentium." Nothing else was said which could throw more light on the subject.

2. After the first Session, commenced the Congregations, or ordinary assemblies, from which the public were excluded, and in these was unfolded the whole work of the Council. Ecclesiastical secrecy was maintained here as well as in the Commissions, the barest formalities only being officially known, though it was impossible to prevent something transpiring to the public of what occurred in an assembly of seven or eight hundred persons.

3. In the first and second Congregations, held on the 10th and 14th of December, after mass and the usual ceremonies, there followed the voting for the election of the five judges of excuses, and as many of complaints, "judices excusationum," and "judices querelarum." According to Conciliar discipline, the duty of the first is to receive and examine the procurations and excuses of the absent bishops, and the applications for leave of absence on just grounds, during the Council, on which, however, they do not decide themselves, but refer the matter to the assembly ; and the second have to judge any controversies arising between those who are gathered together. All these judges are chosen by the votes of the Fathers in Council.

4. The most important event in the first Congregation was the publication and distribution of the Papal constitution in the form of a Bull, by which the Pope, alluding to the reasons that guided him, and citing the examples of Julius II. and Pius IV., ordained that, in the event of his death during the Council, the

new Pontiff, should be elected as usual by the Cardinals, without any intervention on the part of the Council, which should from the moment of his death be *ipso facto* prorogued.*

From this document it is clear that some apprehension was felt lest the ancient rights and privileges enjoyed by the Curia at the election of a Pope should be disputed and called in question. In his allocution the Pope provides for the Church in her relations to society, and in the Bull he provides for the privileges of the Curia in its relation with the Church. This Bull had been compiled in November, but was only now published.

5. The second Congregation was occupied by another Bull on the limitation of censures, and under this title ecclesiastical censures were again published.† Every one knows, or, rather, every one does not know, how great in number and how various in character these may be. The Pope being well aware of this, abrogates them entirely in the constitution, "Apostolicæ Sedis," with the exception of certain titles which virtually include them almost all, so that the whole penal ecclesiastical system is maintained intact.

These censures are preserved in their ancient style, beginning with "heretics," their abettors, and those that give them shelter. This last would furnish a good moral theme for young students in theology, for how would it apply to the Roman hotel keepers and to the Pontifical Government, who not only give shelter to heretics, but a church in which to celebrate their worship outside the Porta del Popolo? These censures refer to the cases of those who possess prohibited books—of schismatics —of those who appeal to a future Council—of those who injure ecclesiastical dignitaries—of those who obstruct ecclesiastical jurisdiction—of laity intermeddling with the judgment of ecclesiastical things or persons—of those who falsify apostolic letters: then comes a special censure against the unauthorised bestowal of absolution in confession; and, finally, one against all those who either invade, destroy, or retain, for themselves or others, the cities, territories, places, or rights that appertain to the Roman Church, or who disturb, usurp, or retain the supreme jurisdiction therein. It is useless to give here the long index

* See Appendix, Document XI.   † Ibid. XII.

which all may examine for themselves. This act is one of apparent moderation, in that it limits or contracts the cases liable to punishment, but it must be observed that although certain titles are abrogated, those that remain include the whole penal ecclesiastical code in full force. It is obvious that the Pope in abolishing some censures, while he confirms others, exercises supreme authority in matters of discipline, and it should be remarked that he thus acts *proprio motu* in the face of the Church assembled in the plenitude of her power, for the very purpose of exercising it, and of judging all matters touching ecclesiastical discipline, and consequently, many of those contemplated in the Bull.

What if the Council had not deemed all those acts worthy of punishment, or at least had not thought well to inflict it in some cases? But we must leave such questions to the bishops, as we freely confess ourselves unable to arrive at their solution.

6. In the Brief that regulates the proceedings of the Council, four Commissions are instituted instead of the six that undertook the preparatory work. These four are composed of ninety-six bishops in all, twenty-four for each Commission, corresponding to the four parts into which the matters to be treated in the Council are divided—namely, Faith, Discipline, Affairs of the East, and Religious Orders. In the second Congregation, the names of those who should compose these commissions were settled, beginning with that on Faith ; the same subject was discussed in the Congregations held on the 20th and 28th, and with such matters the year 1869 drew to a close.

7. From all that has hitherto occurred, it is evident that there are three grand questions of principle before the Council, on the solution of which very important results depend, though careless observers might pass them over. The first is the ancient conflict always going on in the Church from the earliest ages, between those who maintain a direct supernatural agency in all matters, and those who, without rejecting it, believe also in secondary causes.

The infallibility of a single man is a more striking miracle, and a greater infraction of the laws of nature, than the infallibility of a large and well-organised assembly under the security of a strong and severe discipline; it is much more so, because the infallibility of a society with regard to itself is by its very nature relative, while that of an individual towards society cannot be other than absolute. It is reasonable to believe that God protects the Church, as we believe that God protects the world, and that the Church in her own office should be infallible, may be in a certain sense reasonable; but that God should take away from an individual man the liability to error, which is characteristic of humanity, would be an absolute and standing miracle. In the first case Faith allies herself with reason, in the second she subdues it.

In the various cases in which, under one form or another, the conflict between these two opinions has been waged in previous Councils, the decision has always been in favour of the absolute miracle. Thus far, we have considered the matter as regards Faith, that is to say, the speculative question.

The second question is the position of the modern world, and the greater part of its institutions as confronted with the Syllabus; and as this concerns Discipline, or the practical part of the matter, it is the social question.

The third touches the position of the hierarchy of the Church, relatively to the Roman Curia, and this I may call the political question.

8. The first matter, considered as a principle, enters into the region of dogma, and as such, its discussion is neither useful nor desirable for us; but in its practical application at a certain point it approaches the third question.

9. As to the second, the social question—those who can rightly interpret public opinion, will find (notwithstanding the prevalent religious indifference) this to be its clear and emphatic expression. It is the ardent longing of society (looking beyond the narrow limits of party to the wide interests of nations) for the cessation of that antagonism between the claims of civil and religious authority upon conscience among Catholic populations, which in its results has gone far towards depriving them of any conscience whatever.

Indeed, all who belong to Christian or merely civilised nations, will readily agree in the desire for peace, and in the hope that some settlement of these social and political questions may be found other than the alternative of absolutism and rebellion, which seems at our day to be the lot of most Catholic countries. The strength of the Latin nations is exhausted by their constant oscillations between the theories of the *Univers* and those of the *Rappel*, between the dogmas of the *Unità Cattolica* and those expressions of opinion, or rather unbridled instincts for which nothing is sacred; oscillations which sway backwards and forwards between revolutionary barricades on the one hand and *coups d'état* on the other.

This was the momentous question now before the Vatican Council, most serious because the displacement of the material aims of great societies, regarded merely in its philosophical aspect, is fraught with serious risk to their moral perceptions, and must, therefore, be considered as dangerous by all of whatever shade of opinion. Besides this, it is undeniable that matters of faith which do not influence practice, and practices which do not spring from faith, are especially repugnant to the spirit of the age. Everything at this time seemed to strengthen the desire that the discipline of the Church, which is by nature flexible, should meet the new wants of society by extending itself to as large a number of adherents as it could embrace, rather than that in narrowing its limits it should cast out into uncertainty many of those still in heart adhering to their ancient faith.

10. As to the third question, that which regards the internal policy of the Church, it presents itself to Italians under a special form, unlike that in which it appears to other Catholic nations. The bishops assembled in Rome might be of different opinions on the various questions proposed to them; but there is one point on which they would all, Infallibilists or Anti-Infallibilists, be inclined to agree, so far as ecclesiastical discipline allowed, viz., in the preservation and aggrandisement of their own prerogative, and consequently in resisting and modifying, if not diminishing, the authority of the Roman Curia. Indeed, notwithstanding the marvellous power of the ecclesiastical institutions of the Church, almost every time that a Council has been convened to consider her organisation and interests, this strife between the bishops and the Curia has been renewed.

When, on the other hand, we consider the external dealings

of the Church in her contact with civil society, we find that the differences between Rome and the episcopate were never very serious, and of late have been less than ever, and for this reason; that on whichever side the balance of power inclined, the interests of the "Curia" and the episcopate being here identical, no strife would ensue between them, and consequently no important change could be effected by the Council.

On the contrary, in the internal question, the tendency of the episcopate to enlarge or simply to guard its own rights, and that feeling which may be termed the instinct of self-preservation that has always existed with varying fate and intensity, and from time to time has shown itself in the Church; this feeling, though often subdued and vanquished, has again appeared involved in the question of Infallibility.

There is, however, a barrier to this tendency, and that is represented by the Pope and the cardinals, who for many centuries have stood firm as personifying the best organised institution in the world; and, wonderful to relate, owing to their own strength and power, they were followed in the recent struggle by many of the bishops. The only portion of the episcopate to which this observation does not altogether apply, and which has not the same interests as others in this question, is the Italian; and, as we have already observed, the Italian prelates showed little inclination to join the Opposition.

11. The Papacy is an institution by nature profoundly and entirely Italian, and in a certain way the most ardent defenders of the Papacy render back with one hand to Italy, regarded as an abstraction, what they take away with the other. If Italy had not always had the art of ruining her own productions, and if her sons of all ranks had not been influenced by the spirit of intestine divisions, what profit might she not have drawn from such a combination! Every day this fact becomes clearer to the Papacy and to Italy; and perhaps in the future, when of less importance, it will be plainer still. Would that both one and the other could comprehend—what, indeed, seems easy to understand—that all power which is inevitable should be so directed as to effect the greatest good, or, at any rate, the least evil! But we must leave these almost retrospective reflections, and turn to those facts which may enlighten us on the

special affinity of the internal policy of the Church with the Italian nation.

12. As long as the Papacy existed by its inherent strength, derived from the principle of its traditions, the practical application of its authority, and the place which it held in the political organisation of Europe, it never permitted its decrees to be subjected to discussion; but since it has resorted to the means of help furnished by modern society, that is, to parties, and has received from them the aid of men and money, the force of circumstances has given to those very auxiliaries a new and powerful influence on the Papacy. They, for the most part, were strangers to Italy and to the Curia, properly so called, and up to the meeting of the Council they had supported the cause of the Pope unanimously, and had fought valiantly for him in his recent reverses; but having reached the cross roads opened before them by the Council, they branched off in two divisions, though Dupanloup and De Mérode, the leaders of the Opposition, continued as ardent champions of the temporal power of the Pope, as Manning and Deschamps, who were the principal upholders of his spiritual supremacy. These particulars must be borne in mind, because it is by no means certain that all parties, even the most devoted to Rome, would invariably consider it their duty to strive for the greater glory of the Italian prelates; and that, in the course of events, they would never desire to take part themselves in the supreme direction of the Chûrch. This is a point that has nothing in common with the doctrine of Infallibility, indeed, events have proved the contrary; the interests, both of the supporters and the antagonists of Infallibility, being here very much the same. Still, this question of the relations of the foreign episcopate to the Roman Curia is in many ways owing to the complex nature of human interests mixed up with that of Infallibility, this latter being the ground and the pretext on which the tendencies above alluded to, enter into the contest with the Roman Curia; which has always maintained a firm and inexorable policy, and notwithstanding all the dangers to which it has been exposed by the course of recent events, and the appeal made to all Catholic nations, has never admitted the slightest change among its members, or the least modification in its institutions.

But how long could such a state of things last? Whatever solutions the other great questions at issue have already found, or are to find, in the Council, will the conditions of the Roman Curia remain as they have been till now, when the course of this religious movement is accomplished?

13. This contingency is not an unimportant one for Italy, or for the rest of the Catholic world. If we could imagine a fundamental change in the economy of the Church, affecting not her temporal power only, but the manner in which she so actively interferes directly and indirectly, in all the most important social and political questions, in such a case, Italy would be as disinterested as other nations. But as that is not probable, it follows that the Papacy, remaining as firmly rooted as ever in the Church, but ceasing to be Italian, and losing thereby that birthright of indigenous tradition which is natural to it and guides it, would change its character as an active agency in the world, and become a problem for all, and Italy could not remain indifferent to such a vicissitude.

But to resume—omitting the consideration of what is convenient for the Church—a question which it is not our object to discuss, Italy would neither derive any advantage herself, nor benefit the world in general, by surrendering the Papacy, with or without modification, into the hands of foreigners. On her own account such a course would be prejudicial, because the national preferences that foreigners bring with them would make an intrenched position in the very heart of Italy, of which all countries by turn would try to hold the keys; and with regard to the world at large, the change would be detrimental, because if once the Papacy ceased to be Italian, it would lose the traditions that animate it, that are identified with it as its second nature, and would enter upon a new and untried course, of which no one as yet could predict the end. Perhaps, on more than one occasion, Italy has already committed the mistake of endeavouring (more than was either necessary or advisable) to thrust the Papacy into the hands of foreigners; and that these mistakes have not as yet produced the evil that was to be expected, is due to the cohesion and tenacity of the Roman Curia.

14. However, such secondary considerations must not distract us from those of a more important character; which prove

how desirable it is, that on every subject and under every aspect, the decisions and the policy of the Church should be as broad, as reasonable, and as conciliatory as possible ; and that her aim should be to connect the religion of the great majority of the Latin race with the increase of their civilisation and the spread of their greatness, rather than to make it a religion fit only for bigots.

, We should learn to be very cautious in the means we adopt for promoting the good, both of the Church and of Italy ; we must avoid the vulgar oratory of declamation, and the enunciation of grandiloquent and foregone conclusions; and also especially resist that cynical indifference, which counsels an equally cynical resignation to events which it was unable to anticipate. In order to reconcile conflicting interests, Italy should strive to maintain the initiative of all that is useful in secular concerns, to place herself at the head of the religious movement of our day ; and to carry out the needful reforms in the discipline of the Church ; functions for which her peculiar position renders her well fitted, though in truth she seems too little disposed to take the task upon herself.

15. At the opening of the Vatican Council it would have been presumptuous to prognosticate its success ; for, putting aside unforeseen contingencies, no one could predict the course of an assembly of about 1000 persons. It was only known that the great majority, speaking in parliamentary language, were Conservative ; so that the promoters of absolutism had more followers in the Council than those who were in favour of a comparatively Liberal policy, and exercised a predominant authority. The Liberal Catholics had to contend with the smallness of their own numbers, and the general constitution of the Council, which was so arranged as to prove a great bar to the initiative of the Opposition. According to various estimates, the strength of the Opposition, embracing different gradations of opinion, was about 150 or 200 ; and, reckoning on the influence which might be exercised on the wavering, it seemed probable that they might suffice to neutralise the efforts of the partisans of Infallibility, though not to take the initiative themselves, or still less to imprint a character of liberal reform on the Council.

Certainly the state of affairs was unpromising for the Opposition, though some hope was derived from the general acknowledgment of the needs of modern civilisation, and from the longing for reconciliation which extended on all sides and to all classes.

Would this longing suffice to prevent the execution of those programmes of absolutism now circulating in the higher spheres of the Vatican? Optimists answered this question hopefully: but as for the prospect of obtaining any real change in matters of discipline long rooted in the Church, all were fully aware that neither the desire, nor the conditions necessary for such a result existed.

16. At any rate, if it was then impossible to form a correct judgment as to the future, it was at all events very useful to follow the course of events so important, and, for Italy especially, fraught with such momentous results; and that is what we propose to do in writing the present work.

JANUARY.

I.—THE SECOND SESSION.

1. Aspect of the Church of St. Peter's on a feast day.—2. The same.—3. Second Session.—4. Aspect of the Council Hall.—5. Defects of the same.—6. Profession of faith.—7. Description of the ceremony.—8. Reasons for its taking place.

1. EVERY one who has been at Rome knows the peculiar physiognomy of the Church of St. Peter on a day of festival: a mixture of the sacred and the profane; of the majestic and the vulgar; of the sublime and the grotesque—such as Shakespeare, perhaps, first dared to depict with congenial energy—is the characteristic of the scene, a mixture which, running through all the varieties of style from Michael Angelo to Pinelli, presents a complete image of Catholic society, from the splendour of a Pope to the squalor of a boor—from the faith of St. Peter to the faith of the Magdalene.

2. The motley crowd moves under those immense arcades with the easy freedom of men who feel themselves at home, and to whom by long usage the most solemn and mysterious acts of worship have become familiar. Cardinals, peasants, princes, beggars, favourites of fame, followers of fashion, in garments of every shape and colour, sweep past one another with an incessant movement that reminds one of the description given by Dante (Inf. xviii.)—

> "Come i Roman per l'esercito molto
> L'anno del Giubileo, su per lo ponte
> Hanno a passar la gente modo tolto,"

and of a public thoroughfare. From time to time a single group, preceded by an official from the palace, forces its way with difficulty through the surging crowd—probably a king, or one of the great of the earth—while every now and then you may find a wayworn traveller with flowing hair, prostrate in devotion in some corner of the church—a pilgrim who has come from the depths of Galicia to kneel at the shrine of the Apostles.

3. Such was the aspect presented by the Church of St. Peter on the 6th of January in this year, when the second Session of the Vatican Council was held. There was nothing, however, on this occasion to indicate that any special event occupied the public mind; the general concourse was smaller, but, owing to the arrival of more bishops, the Council Hall was better filled than at the first Session, and presented a striking appearance.

4. Unfortunately, the grandeur of the effect was somewhat marred by the necessity of placing the seats very close together, owing to the number of Fathers present; and as each seat was marked with a figure of large dimensions, it will easily be understood that the appearance presented by the hall when filled (though in one sense imposing) was rather that of a closely packed and numbered multitude, than, as it should have been, a venerable assembly of distinguished persons.

5. It had been decided to change the hall for the Congregations, on account of the serious acoustic defect we have already mentioned, for it was related that in one of the first meetings, when the bishops were interrogated on some proposition, that they answered "Nihil intelleximus," instead of "Placet;" but this plan was soon abandoned, and an attempt was made to remedy the defect, by stretching awnings across so as to reduce the size of the area about one-third, and to crowd the bishops more closely together round the throne. These awnings, being only used for the Congregations, were removed during the public Sessions, and the same hall served for both assemblies, but at the cost of much inconvenience and without a satisfactory result, as it was still very difficult if not impossible to hear, a serious embarrassment in the long discussions carried on in an unfamiliar language with every variety of pronunciation.

6. The procedure of the Council of Trent was followed and imitated on this occasion, though with a different intention. The third Session of that Council was occupied in drawing up

the confession of faith which is contained in the Creed of the Roman Church, as, owing to the tardy arrival of the bishops, no important business could be transacted.

At the Vatican Council the confession of faith served to occupy the second Session; because on account of the shortness of the time, and of the unexpected resistance evoked by the first matters proposed, no other work was ready, and no decree prepared for promulgation.

It was a common practice in all Councils, especially the more ancient ones, on account of the great divisions within the Church which drew people away in all directions, that the assembly, in order to give proof of fellowship, should commence its deliberations by reciting a creed or common profession of faith; in our days, when such divisions are either much lessened or no longer exist, showing themselves, when they do occur, without, not within the Church, such a profession of faith, like many other old traditions, becomes a mere ceremony.

With this view, the enlarged and precise formula of Pius IV. was selected, because it contains the additions made at the end of the Council of Trent on account of the Reformation, and because it is the one used in all public acts, and obligatory at the University for those who wish to obtain their degrees at the end of the scholastic course.

7. On the 6th of January, after the Fathers had taken their places in the hall, and the Pope, surrounded by his court, was seated on his throne, the solemn mass, used on such occasions, was celebrated, after which the Secretary of the Council placed the book of the Gospels upon the altar. The prayers followed, and the Pope, crossing himself six times, blessed the assembly. The reading of the Gospel and the invocation of the Holy Spirit took place, and then the ritual being completed, the two " *avvocati promotori* " of the Council approached the Pope's throne, praying him to allow the profession of faith to be made by the Fathers.

This being complied with, the Pope first recited the formula himself, and after him the Bishop of Fabriano, ascending the ambo, read it aloud; then all the Fathers, one by one, according to their rank, approached the throne, and kneeling with the right hand on the Gospels repeated in turn, " spondeo, voveo et juro juxtaformulam prelæctam." Each one repeated this phrase in the language of his own ritual, so that it was heard in six or seven different tongues, and the ceremony lasted over two hours. When it was completed, the two "promoters" of the Council requested the apostolic protonotaries to draw up the record of the proceedings, and with a hymn of thanksgiving the second Session was closed, having, like the first, consisted merely in ceremonies.

8. The reason for having recourse to this expedient to occupy the second Session, which had been fixed beforehand, but for which nothing was ready, was certainly the shortness of the time; but also in making the arrangements, no doubt had been entertained as to the celerity with which they could be carried through.

The first propositions contained only matters of dogma which did not admit of doubt; so it is no wonder that having reckoned six months as long enough to spend on the questions most open to dispute, it was supposed that one month would amply suffice for the consideration of the others, and that the decrees relating thereto might be published in the first Session after the public opening.

Matters, however, went contrary to the expectation: the first subjects provoked unlooked-for discussion; and as the public Session was announced for that day, no other way was found of occupying the time save in having recourse to the profession of faith. But the better to understand this, before proceeding further we will call to mind the rules that guided the progress of the assembly.

II.—THE ARRANGEMENT OF THE WORK.—FIRST SCHEME.

1. Classification of subjects.—2. Ecclesiastical policy is omitted from the Commissions.—3. Distribution of the schemes.—4. Duty of the Commissions.—5. Nomination of the same.—6. Method observed in the debates.—7. The assembly sanctions the scheme.—8. Difference between an Ecclesiastical Council and an assembly of laymen.—9. On Papal approbation.—10. On the proposals of the bishops.—11. Composition of the Council.—12. Addresses against its Order.—13. The Opposition declares itself.—14. The scheme "De Fide."—15. Observations on the same.—16. Debate on the same.—17. On the Opposition.—18. Its composition.—19. The Italians.—20. Admonitions of the presidents.—21. Other provisions.—22. The scheme "De Fide" sent back.

1. The matters to be treated of in the Council were classified in five sections—Faith, Discipline, Religious Orders, Eastern Affairs, and Ecclesiastical Policy (omitting the section on Ceremonial as less important), and were prepared in the Commissions corresponding to these titles, which were named by the Pope at the convocation of the Council. Consequently, up to the present time these subjects were nothing but propositions set forth by the Pope in order to obtain the opinions of the bishops, whereby the primary object of the Council was very much restricted; and instead of being a general discussion on the wants and condition of the Church, it was limited to an inquiry from the bishops of what the Pope desired to know.

2. The section for Ecclesiastical Policy, which naturally included the relations between Church and State, was subsequently set aside; owing, probably, to diplomatic considerations and their results. There remained then the four first, and among these the subjects of the fifth section were divided, the section on Discipline receiving the chief accession.

Accordingly, when the Council selected by vote the five Commissions to take the place of those previously nominated by the Pope, that on Policy no longer appeared, any more than that on Ceremonial.

The Commissions chosen by the Pope for the preparatory work, no longer existed officially at the opening of the Council; having completed their duty of compiling all the subjects to be discussed in a series of schemes (*schemata*), each of which comprised one set of subjects.

3. These schemes were only communicated separately by the Secretaries to the Council, as the time of their discussion arrived; and thus it was impossible for the bishops to know *à priori* their number and contents. Neither could they learn whether they would all be preserved, and in their original form; or if, according to the progress of the deliberations, some might not be laid aside or modified otherwise than was indicated by the Bull—"Multiplices inter"—which declared that they should be maintained in their integrity.

Such a method of proceeding left the bishops in complete ignorance of what would be the next subject, and prevented their forming a just opinion of all on which they had ultimately to judge. It also followed that the order in which the different subjects were presented to the Fathers greatly influenced their reception by the assembly, as sometimes the mere collecting and placing together an assemblage of laws may suffice to prove their value and desirability.

This was, in fact, one of the chief complaints of the Opposition, of that portion especially, which, belonging to free countries like America, was accustomed to subject all matters to the fullest investigation. They could not understand such mysterious proceedings, and, generally speaking, the entire Opposition viewed this part of the arrangement as derogatory to their dignity, and injurious to the success of the Council.

4. As the Pope at the beginning had named the first Commission to prepare his propositions, so now the Council chose an equal number to undertake the amendments. Not five, but four only were named, corresponding to the classification explained at the beginning of this chapter; indeed, only three were chosen at first, that on Eastern Affairs remaining suspended, till finally nominated in the Congregation of January 19th.

The gravity and the delicate nature of this subject, together with the international questions it involves, and the difficulties experienced by the Oriental bishops—the only competent judges in such matters—all, perhaps, contributed to this suspension; and ought to have had great weight in the progressive treatment of the Eastern question. In fact, the only business of these Commissions was to receive at second-hand the schemes which, having met with partial or entire disapproval in the

Council, they then amended according to the views of the assembly ; so that the same schemes which had failed on being presented as the Pope's initiative, might return again to the Council as the proposals of its own Commissions, and modified according to what was believed to be its own opinion.

5. This part of the arrangements might have been sensible enough, but that which diminished its good effect on the Opposition was the choice of the individuals elected on these Commissions, which provoked much comment.

It was said that tickets bearing the names of candidates were photographed in large numbers and distributed to the bishops, many of whom on their arrival, knowing nothing of the persons in question, were likely to accept them at once ; and it was added, that these tickets were actually found in the urn, when the polling papers were scrutinised, having been placed there by some of the Fathers who wished to avoid the trouble of copying them. It was also said, in proof of the moral violence exercised, that some of the Fathers, feeling that it was impossible to contend against this sort of electoral influence, placed blank polling papers in the urn from a feeling of disdain. However that may be, it is undoubted that the names drawn, the first especially, proved to be exactly such as the *Civiltà Cattolica* would have chosen.

Without overlooking the part that the contending forces in Council might take in the matter, it is certain that the opinions prevailing among the majority of the Fathers, especially at the beginning, contributed greatly to bring about the election of those Commissioners.

6. By the Bull, " Multiplices inter," was established the order to be followed in the discussion of matters already arranged and settled. The proposed scheme is communicated to all the Fathers, who may then study it with the assistance of one or more theologians, chosen by themselves, and bound to secrecy. Those who intend to speak, either for or against the matter, inscribe their names by turns in a register ; and in one or more Congregations the speakers are heard on every question, after which comes the real debate, the discussion properly so called.

If the scheme is either universally accepted, or meets with few objections, it is put to the vote, agreed on, and promulgated in the next public Session; but if it meets with serious resistance, it is sent back to the Commission to which it belongs, to be modified, and then again brought before the assembly.

A few copies of the speeches and discussions, as reported by the shorthand-writers, are printed at the private office of the Council for the use of the presidents only, all other persons having to depend on their memory for the impressions received in the Congregations.

7. The schemes approved and compiled in the form of decrees are then put definitively to the vote in the public Sessions; this is done orally by the scrutineers, who interrogate the Fathers one by one, and having received their answers—"Placet" or "Non placet"—inscribe the answers and the names in a book, and thus ascertain the majority, and the issue of the vote.

8. According to the ideas of laymen on the constitution of an assembly, the matter is here decided, as the opinion of the majority being ascertained, the point is settled. But in this assembly the vote of the majority, however deliberate, does not constitute the decision, unless approved by the Pope, to whom it is then submitted, and who may either give or withhold his sanction. Only when the vote of the assembly is approved by the Pope does it become law, although the decree speaks of the number or unanimity of the consenting bishops, which shows that the Council is a deliberative, and not simply a consultative one. This rule has generally prevailed in great assemblies of the Church, and on this occasion full advantage was taken of it by Rome; indeed, the canons of the Vatican Council begin with the formula, "Pius Episcopus, servus servorum Dei, sacro approbante Concilio, ad perpetuam rei memoriam," a title which gave rise to no small complaint on the part of the Opposition.

According to the very extended application thus made of the principle, not only does the vote of the majority require the Pope's sanction in order to become a binding decree, but the "Curialisti" maintain that the vote of the minority, with the Papal approbation may be of equal value; although even they allow that prudence would never permit the use of such a power.

9. Without, however, further entangling ourselves in these questions, one thing is certain, namely, that according to canon-

E

ical theory and the practice of Catholic institutions, the approbation of the Pope alone gives the authority of a canon to the decision of a general Council. This distinguishes the nature of a Conciliar assembly from that of a civil or political one, as whatever weight may be attached to the vote of a Council, it is still really of a consultative character, since the power of the Pope, instead of being subject to it, actually outweighs it.

In forming a judgment on these points, this fact must be borne in mind, because it follows, that if in ecclesiastical assemblies the majority lose the authority they possess in meetings of the laity, the minority, on the other hand, obtain it; for as the reason of a decision may, in the Pope's mind, proceed from expediency and not from numbers, it follows that some minorities may, for special reasons, carry more weight with them than is warranted by their numerical composition. These grounds afforded a reasonable hope of success to the Opposition in the present Council, because, though few in number, they represented populations, societies, and interests of far more importance than did most of the Infallibilists.

10. It will now be apparent, from the explanations we have given, how many difficulties the Opposition had to contend with. All propositions proceeded from Commissions nominated by the Pope, and when they did not meet with a favourable reception, returned to other Commissions composed almost entirely of the same elements as the first. By the Bull, the bishops possessed the right of initiating questions, but these could not come before the assembly until they had received the sanction of a special Congregation nominated by the Pope (and containing twelve cardinals), and finally of the Pontiff himself. After all this preparation, they passed into the category of Papal propositions; but as according to the provisions of the schemes they were only communicated separately to the bishops, it became a very difficult matter for the latter to bring forward any subject themselves. Being left in ignorance of the questions to follow, how could they make propositions that might not be in accordance with the course of deliberations? Who can tell what is wanting without knowing what already exists? How is it possible to prejudge a question which may be reserved for future deliberation? According to this plan, the bishops would only

know at the end of the proceedings many things on which they might wish to deliberate; and then, how could they take up again matters already discussed, and connect questions that had been considered separately, or would now be most difficult to modify by reason of their previous treatment. The Commission nominated by the Pope to examine the proposals of the bishops met for the first time on Sunday, the 23rd of January; but the Opposition asked, with reason, what proposals would be accepted for discussion in the Council in the state of affairs just described?

11. The same cardinals who presided over the first Commissions, which prepared the schemes, presided also over the second, whose duty it was to modify them when they proved unacceptable; and three of these cardinals were, at the same time, legates or presidents over the five, who directed the whole procedure of the Council. If to this it be added that (in the present condition of the Church) a great proportion of the bishops present at the Council were simply nominees of the Pope, and not the representatives of the opinions of their dioceses, if we consider the numbers of the bishops *in partibus* who are all subject to the Curia, of the Vicars-Apostolic, who are dependants of the *Propaganda Fide*, of the Generals of Orders, who form a sort of Papal army; and remember, moreover, that the half of these, including men who, from their dignity and position, might be expected to be independent (as, for example, the French cardinals) were guests of the Pope, it will easily be understood how much suspicion was awakened among the Opposition, and how everything concerning the Order of the Council was received by them with greater mistrust than the propositions in themselves seemed to warrant. To all this was added another consideration, of no small consequence, which contributed to keep up the feeling of irritation and suspicion.

The work of the Council of Trent was settled in its second Session in a sort of Order by which the whole procedure was fixed; but this Order, like a simple decree, was submitted in the accustomed manner to the "Placet" of the Fathers, discussed and approved by the whole assembly.

The corresponding act to this in the Vatican Council was a Papal Bull, by which the whole Order of the Council was settled à priori without discussion, and by the sole authority of the Pope, the assembly having no voice whatever in the matter.

12. In consequence of this, the Opposition began to concentrate their efforts on certain principal points; and in order to guard against the dangers threatened by the superior numbers of the majority, they insisted especially on the necessity of unanimity for any declaration of dogma, and upheld the importance of this maxim to the end. Some of the wisest bishops were of opinion that the modification of the Order should at once be insisted on, as without it, all resistance would be impossible, and could be put down almost as soon as it appeared. With this view two addresses were made to the Pope: the one signed by twenty-eight bishops, praying for the reform of the whole Order; the other, asking for its partial modification, being signed by a great part of their number. A small number of the French also presented a petition in the same sense, but these addresses produced no effect, and did not even receive an answer. Perhaps, if the Opposition had insisted further, and had shown themselves firmly united from the beginning, they might have been spared great trouble in the end.

13. The discontent occasioned by the difficulty of hearing in the hall, by the names of the Commissioners, and, above all, by the regulations of the Council having been disregarded, it increased and strengthened the Opposition, by attracting to it some of the uncertain and irresolute, and as soon as it could be legally manifested, it became very formidable.

14. The scheme "De Fide" was the first published, and it was discussed in the last Congregations in December. It contained a sort of dogmatic decree against every modern error, and, indeed, every ancient error as well. It condemned Materialism, Pantheism, and all kinds of philosophical systems under a series of heads, which, beginning with the creation of the world, and continuing to the present day, set forth and affirmed the whole body of Catholic doctrines. The compilation of this scheme was attributed to the Jesuits, and especially to Father Franzelin, Professor of Theology in the Roman College.

15. Now it is clear that in a Catholic assembly no doubt could arise on these matters, and therefore such declarations

can only concern those who are beyond the pale of the Catholic Church and of Christianity, but here a dispute arose. A Catholic assembly, said some, is called together to legislate for those who recognise it and, in some measure, depend upon it, but those who are out of the Church are already condemned by their own act; with regard to these denunciations the Council might just as well condemn Buddhism or Islamism.

Then, as to philosophical systems and opinions, they added —the Catholic Church may, if it pleases, oppose its own philosophy to that of the Rationalists, or confront Rosmini with the German philosophers; that would be to fight on the same ground; but to condemn is not to discuss. We can condemn those who hear us or are subject to us, but we either argue with, or are silent, regarding those with whom we have nothing in common, and who cannot hear us. Every unauthorized condemnation is useless, and injures, rather than enhances, the dignity of him who pronounces it. Such were the principal arguments of those who opposed the first scheme. Besides, they took exception to other things, and especially to the title that headed the scheme, which began with "Pius Episcopus" instead of "Sacrosancta Synodus," as was usual in the principal Councils, especially that of Trent. Of this title we shall speak hereafter, when we come to discuss the scheme "De Fide;" but as soon as it appeared it gave rise to vehement objections on the part of the Opposition, as it implied a solution of the whole question which divided the Council before it had been discussed.

Moreover, the manner in which the scheme was compiled was obnoxious to the assembly, being mean, invidious, trifling, and likely to render its contents anything but acceptable to the ears and the intellects of the nineteenth century. Only conceive the impression produced by the mournful lucubrations of the Fathers of the *Civiltà Cattolica*, and of a few theologians, little versed in the ways of the world, on all those bishops who, being either themselves highly cultivated, or understanding, even if not sharing, the great movement of modern society, are aware of its importance, and can estimate the great value of the questions it involves. The effect of all this was, that on account of the vehemence of the Opposition, the scheme, instead of being promulgated in the second Session, as had been intended, was sent back in its entirety to the "Congregation on Faith," to which it belonged, in order to be revised.

16. This discussion occupied six Congregations, that of December 28th being the first and the most important, because in it the Archbishop of Vienna, and the Archbishops of San Louis and of Nisibi, spoke extremely well. The Archbishops of Sorrento, Smyrna, and Malta, all unanimously opposed the scheme for the reasons before specified, and the Archbishop of Halifax also spoke against it with great effect. On the 30th the discussion was continued by Strossmayer, Genouhilhac, Caixal y Astrade, and a Roumanian Greek bishop. The same subject was under deliberation on January 3rd; but from that date the publication of the names of the orators in the Official Gazette, which had hitherto taken place, was prohibited, most probably on account of the interest they had excited in the public mind since the preceding Congregations. On the 4th, 8th, and 10th of January the scheme was discussed without interruption, and then, the debate being closed, it was sent back for revision.

17. This fact rendered it evident that the Opposition, in which people had hitherto been slow to believe, had really acquired importance, and showed that matters would not progress as easily as was pretended by the *Civiltà Cattolica*. Indeed, though it was impossible yet to judge of the final result, it was clear that the vague and uncertain divergences of opinions which had but hitherto prevailed were now concentrated in a real opposition, not as yet very unanimous and well organised, but far more serious than was expected. Above all, that which gave it weight and constituted its importance was the elements of which it was composed, as we shall now proceed to point out.

18. The German bishops, being almost unanimous, were foremost in the Opposition, their leaders being such men as the Archbishop of Vienna, Cardinal Schwarzemberg, and Monsignor Hefele, Bishop of Rottenburg, a prelate profoundly versed in ecclesiastical learning. The German episcopate standing very high both in intellectual culture and in social condition,

and being firmly united, had drawn together into a common line of action even those members of their body the least disposed towards it, such as the Archbishops of Mayence and of Cologne, the former a most remarkable man, and others. The German bishops gave proof, moreover, of the greatest aptitude and vigour in discussion. The Archbishop of Vienna in one of the recent debates showed such vivacity, and caused the president so much embarrassment, that to him was attributed by the public, the substitution of De Angelis for De Luca in the direction of the debates; the change being effected after that stormy meeting, though it may have been only in consequence of ecclesiastical regulations.

The eldest of the five presidents usually conducted the proceedings; and on account of the death of Cardinal Reisach, which had recently occurred, that office fell to Cardinal de Luca; but he in turn had to cede the place to Cardinal de Angelis, on his nomination to the post of president as being the senior. Schwarzemberg was highly distinguished on account of his birth, his courteous manners, and the decision of his language, and almost all the other bishops were for some reason or other highly esteemed and remarkable men.

The Bishops of Hungary and Croatia, led by the Primate of Hungary (Strossmayer), the Bishop of Bosnia and Sirmio, and the Archbishop of Colocza, formed one group with the Germans; Monsignor Strossmayer being universally considered the most splendid orator, the best Latin scholar, and the person of highest authority. The Archbishop of Colocza, Monsignor Haynald, was much esteemed for his learning, and considered liberal in his opinions, and the final decision regarding the unlucky scheme was attributed to a speech of his. The rest of the Opposition was made up as follows:—About one-third of the French bishops, who followed with various gradations the steps of the Archbishop of Paris; the Bishop of Orleans and Maret, author of the book, 'On the General Council and Religious Peace;' almost the whole of the American episcopate, about twenty Italian bishops, and other small parties. These taken together formed a body which, on account of the learning of its members, the illustrious names it contained, and the nations it represented, made up in importance the weight it lacked in numbers.

19. Monsignor Tizzani, Bishop of Nisibi *in partibus*, made some stir among the Italians by the speech already mentioned; and although blind and aged, he was able to exercise considerable influence in the assembly by his eloquence, and the strength of his arguments. The Bishops of Casale, Biella, and Salerno, showed themselves able orators in the succeeding discussions, but with slight success; because, as we have already explained, the Italians who joined the Opposition were few and timid, though at the same time they made but little stir in the opposite camp. It was very difficult to judge correctly of the disposition of the Italian bishops; as a rule, they inclined towards Rome, but they were by no means inclined to surrender themselves blindly into the hands of the so-called Catholic party, and on many occasions a spirit of moderation seemed gradually gaining ground among them.

20. A more rigorous observance of the Order of the Council was the consequence of the vote of mistrust which sent back the first scheme for revision, and of the clearer perception of the situation which prevailed after the public Session of January 6th. In one of the first Congregations that followed, the presidents warned the Fathers against the length of speeches, and the useless repetition of things already discussed by others; and admonished them solemnly on the necessity of secrecy, adding to the simple injunction given in the Order the further threat that those who transgressed it would be considered *rei gravis culpæ*, that is to say, guilty of mortal sin. The effect caused by this last admonition varied according to the different shades of opinion prevailing among the Fathers. Those who considered the Council a sovereign assembly depending only on itself, asked how such an obligation could possibly be made binding upon them; and declared that although this secrecy was a just and mutual obligation for convenience sake, it could never so fetter the conscience as to render those who infringed it guilty. Nevertheless, we must allow that notwithstanding these opinions, secrecy as to the Council was, especially at first, very well preserved, considering that more than a thousand persons were present, and the little that did transpire was gathered from the few words indiscreetly dropped by many, rather than by the revelations of one.

21. The bishops were forbidden to print their speeches, even for the use of their colleagues; just as the 'Diario di Roma' was not allowed to publish the names of the orators, as had been done for the first Congregations. It really seemed that those who guided the Council were trying to justify the apprehensions to which the first appearance of the Order had given rise, and to foment the prevailing discontent by pushing it to its extreme limits at the expense of the Opposition, against whom every sort of moral violence was adopted; all of which, as might naturally be expected, ended by bringing about results very different from those intended.

22. Meantime, the scheme, having been returned to the Commission on Faith, was studied anew; and if we are correct in believing that this work was entrusted to its original compilers, and among them to Father Franzelin, its opponents could hardly expect any such modification as was likely to content them.

III.—FIRST STEP TOWARDS INFALLIBILITY.—OTHER SCHEMES.

1. Petition for Infallibility.—2. The predominant question.—3. The promoters of the address.—4. Its contents.—5. Its arguments.—6. Manner of its publication.—7. Number of signatures.—8. Undignified supposition.—9. Promoters of the address.—10. Addresses against Infallibility.—11. Singular situation. —12. Division of parties in the assembly.—13. Efforts to promote Infallibility.—14. Revelations of the *Unità Cattolica*.—15. Distribution of new schemes.—16. Their form is displeasing.—17. The scheme "De Episcopis." —18. Discourse of the Bishop of Cologne.—19. Speech of the Bishop of Orleans.—20. General features of the schemes.—21. The bishops ask for more information on the subjects of debate.—22. The scheme "De Catechismo."

1. The Infallibilists continued their work outside the doors of the Council. A notice was circulated by the Archbishop of Westminster, and the Fathers of the *Civiltà Cattolica*, along with a letter addressed to the bishops, soliciting the Council to proclaim the personal Infallibility of the Pope in faith and morals.

2. There was abundant excitement on other matters, but this was the important point, the dominant question of the

Vatican Council; all else was of minor consequence, and turned on this. Every individual in his own way, and according to his own ideas and interests, felt that here was the *to be or not to be* of the matter.

3. The letter was signed by eighteen bishops from different countries, but scarcely any of them Italian. The address was headed by the signature of the Archbishop of Westminster; and it was said also by that of the Archbishop of Baltimore, one of the few American Infallibilists.

4. The address was with much subtlety addressed to the Commission, whose duty it was to receive the proposals of the bishops, and was the first episcopal document of importance presented with the view of obtaining leave for its discussion; and was all that the Infallibilists had been able to carry out of the programme announced by the *Civiltà Cattolica*, which said that the Council at its first sitting would proclaim Infallibility by acclamation.

5. The address was based on what it declared to be the universal opinion of the Church, as previously manifested, and insisted on the necessity of the dogma in order to preserve her unity, citing other Councils in which it had to a great extent been recognised. But the most learned of the Opposition affirmed that these examples were neither exact, nor to the point, because such an explicit and personal declaration as the Infallibilists required, had only up to the present time met with the sanction of a Provincial Council (recently held in Holland, if I mistake not) which, from its inconsiderable numbers, could carry no weight whatever. Who can explain the reason why Holland, the classic ground of Protestantism and Positivism, has, as far as its microscopic proportions would allow, filled the Roman State with Zouaves, and the Council with Infallibilists? Perhaps it is owing to the strength and energy which characterise the movements of robust and determined nations. The contents of the address were calculated to impress very deeply all who considered them calmly, and reflected that they were the expressions of men in whose hands are deposited the religious interests of multitudes, and who act as the guides of whole nations; the tone of indifference, or we might almost say of disdain, with which the writers regard the separations and schisms likely to

ensue from their address is most striking, being so entirely at variance with their mission.

6. It was remarked that this notice or pamphlet was circulated without bearing any sort of licence; and in Rome, as is well known, nothing can be printed without an "approbation," and all sorts of addresses are absolutely forbidden. Of course this second restriction could not apply to the Fathers in Council; but with regard to the first, the omission was evidently intentional, in order to avoid what would have been unbecoming if the Papal authorities had directly sanctioned such a request.

7. The promoters of this address took much pains to obtain signatures, but the precise number of those subscribed was never ascertained. One of them had affirmed that they could count on 500 bishops, but this was perhaps rather the expression of an arithmetical venture than of certain and individual knowledge.

On subtracting from the whole number of bishops sitting in the Council those 200 who formed the Opposition, there remained certainly about 500,.and the person in question apparently assumed that all these would consent to sign the address ; or perhaps he founded his hypothesis on the numbers who had done homage to the Pope, particularly on the festival of the centenary of St. Peter, though between that act of respect, and the declaration of Infallibility, a very wide distance intervened. Later on, when the address had been circulated, the signatures were with greater accuracy calculated at 400, with the prospect of additions, and the best-informed individuals and those above suspicion were satisfied as to the correctness of this total. Any one judging only from the external aspect of opinions in the Council would have considered this number exaggerated, and some tried to reduce it to 200, or even 100; but on the whole the most probable calculation was the second one, already stated, as made by the promoters of the address, though there never was entire certainty on the matter.

8. Some tried to point out to the compilers that the address was not only questionable in itself, but actually inopportune, as tending to preclude a discussion that should have taken place when the question of the Prerogatives of the Roman See were under deliberation, and that therefore it should not have been

mooted beforehand; but they met with the answer that the assent of the presiding Cardinals had been obtained to the step. The only result of so indiscreet a proceeding was to expose the Curia Romana to the imputation of having sought, without any sense what was becoming, to bring about its own apotheosis.

9. The more moderate among the clergy were much dissatisfied with these proceedings, which, as they truly observed, did more harm than good to the cause they were intended to defend. For the Jesuits, the question of Infallibility was a complex one, involving much that concerned their own existence; and many reasons, too numerous to analyse, induced them by a sort of fatality to declare retrospectively Infallible both Clement XIV., who annulled their order, and Pius IX., who did much the same, and left them to seek a new formula for interpreting the judgment of any Pope who should take a like step hereafter.

The persistence of the Archbishop of Westminster was perhaps the logical result of his own antecedents. Having been a priest and a Protestant at the outset of his career, he knew his own religion from within and not from without, and the Catholic religion from without but not from within. He was well acquainted with the many divisions and sub-divisions of Protestantism, and admired the majestic unity of Catholicism. He did not appreciate the good effects of allowing a moderate degree of liberty, and the constant exercise of the conscience and reasoning powers; neither did he understand the dangers arising from the excessive authority exercised by United Catholicism. In fact, he was enamoured of the principle of authority as the slave adores the idea of liberty; and this want of discrimination and of real Catholic perception in his dealings with the Council was a matter of reproach to him even by the most faithful and devout clergy at Rome. As for all the other Infallibilist bishops, we can only again remark that the ardour they manifested in following out their end was a phenomenon beyond the comprehension of the very Council itself.

10. The reason adduced by the Infallibilists for the publication of this address was that the Opposition having first done the like, it was impossible for them to be behindhand; but the comparison was inexact. The addresses of the Opposition

which preceded the publication of this one, only concerned the Order of the Council, and in no way prejudged matters that were to be brought forward for discussion, but after the address of the Infallibilists was published, appeared the addresses of the bishops of the Opposition in a contrary sense. They were signed by about forty-five out of fifty-seven of the German and Austrian bishops, while others declared that they reserved themselves to oppose the Infallibilist address whenever the occasion should present itself.

The Primate of Hungary was at first among these latter; but he afterwards signed an address, and between twenty and thirty of the French did the like. Some of the French, especially the cardinals, joined that portion of the Germans who held back from making a protest.

A third address which was prepared by the Italians had twenty or twenty-five signatures. Taking all into consideration, the number of representatives of different nations who signed addresses against Infallibility amounted to more than 160. The Infallibilists had directed their document to the Council, thus giving it the form of an episcopal proposal, and so the Opposition were obliged to address theirs directly to the Pope. As all proposals after being accepted by the Congregation, like the other acts concerning the Council, had to receive the approbation of the Pope, it was absolutely necessary that their addresses should be directed personally to him, because where his sanction was withheld, no discussion was possible.

11. Can anything be imagined more singular than the position of a man who receives in his house a vast concourse of people assembled with the intention of proclaiming his apotheosis, and at the same time listens to their earnest prayers beseeching him to forego that honour?

12. After the appearance of these addresses, it was possible to divide the assembly with tolerable accuracy, assuming that the figures of the Infallibilists were correct, and the result was as follows. The Infallibilists numbered about 400, the Opposition reached 160 or 200, and there remained about 100 of the timid and irresolute, who preferred to watch the combat rather than take part in it themselves. If the figures of the Infalli-

bilists were incorrect, the numbers taken from them would swell the sum of those who had not yet made up their minds, and of these a large proportion were Italians.

13. The Infallibilists, on their part, left no means untried in propagating their doctrines outside the walls of the Council. The Feast of the Epiphany was celebrated early in January, and at that time, owing to some old custom, it was usual to exhibit in the church of St. Andrea della Valle a representation of the Grotto of Bethlehem, with the Holy Family, and the adoration of the Magi, in memory of the extension of Christianity to all nations, which that event prefigured; this representation lasted for a week, and during that time long discourses were made in the church in different languages. The Infallibilists availed themselves of this ceremony to make during those eight days a series of addresses, all bearing directly or indirectly on their favourite subject, the style being a concentration of that of the *Civiltà Cattolica*, and sometimes even eclipsing it. Monsignor di Ginevra, Bishop of Ebrun *in partibus*, in a speech, asserted so strong a likeness between the Grotto of Bethlehem, the Shrine, and the Vatican—and so close an analogy between the Infant adored in the one and the old man venerated in the other — that the audience, though well disposed to judge him favourably, considered his language quite extravagant. Such flights of imagination seemed exaggerated even to the most vehement Infallibilists present; and one of the clever descendants of the old "Pasquins," remarked, in allusion to the recent death of several cardinals, that fifteen hats were visibly hovering in the air, and that possibly some Father of the Council, being much excited in his mind, might mistake them for tongues of fire, and speak accordingly, as if inspired.

Father Gallerani, a Jesuit, was especially violent, making his sermon a vehicle for politics quite after the style and fashion of the *Unità Cattolica*. The Bishop of Thule, one of the most ardent Infallibilists, about whom many stories were already circulated, and who was noted for the rudeness with which he had received Maret at his arrival in Rome from France, made a long speech to prove the importance of proclaiming Infallibility, in order that the world, worn out with vacillation and uncertainty, might find at length a place in which truth resided, and a person by whom truth could be proclaimed whenever it was sought, and thereupon promised universal peace and rest for the conscience. That such a consummation would be very convenient is undeniable, but this kind of argument is akin to those which in political matters, and treating of the sort of peace following on one of the numerous experiments made with that view upon mankind, was expressed in the well-known words, *L'ordre règne à Varsovie.* The orator then proceeded to point out that the present was a suitable time for the proclamation of Infallibility; and being very bold in this part of his argument, was loudly applauded by part of the audience, which was on that day almost exclusively French, the reason for such an outburst of joy being probably none other than the old habit which causes the public to show transports of delight when some sort of yoke is to be put about its neck.

14. In the meantime, the *Unità Cattolica* commenced a new campaign. Wishing to profit by the enthusiasm of the last few years, it promised to its readers, and began to publish, the whole repertory of the protestations and addresses put forth by the various bishops under the pressure of recent political events, using for this purpose extracts from letters, chance phrases, and matters of a private nature, comparing them so as to compromise their authors, and thus to bring the pressure of public opinion to bear on the timid and uncertain.

15. In this condition of affairs, the second scheme was published; the first had occupied six Congregations before it was sent back, and the second seemed destined to meet with a like fate. Three or four schemes instead of one, were distributed at the same time to the Fathers as subjects of the next discussion, all concerning matters of discipline. The titles were three, because the fourth pamphlet was merely an appendix to the others, "De Episcopis—De Moribus Clericorum—De Catechismo." Each of these was divided into several chapters; the first, for example, containing the following headings:—" De Synodis—De Vicariis Generalibus—De Sede Episcopali Vacante —De Officio Episcoporum—De Residentia—De Visitatione—

De Obligatione Visitandi sacra Limina—De Conciliis Provincialibus—De Synodis Diœcesanis—De Vicario Generali, &c."

16. The Congregation of January 12th began to consider these new matters, which occupied it during several sittings; for this scheme also, though its subjects were such as pertained to the ordinary ecclesiastical law, met with much resistance. That which generally irritated the Opposition in these projects of decrees—beyond the manner in which the subject was treated—was the shape or form in which they were brought forward, as this always implied that they must be accepted in their entirety as presented, and not otherwise, and this irritation, combined with that caused by the impossibility of in any way shaking off the yoke of the Order of the Council, was shown on every opportunity.

17. The scheme "De Episcopis" touched several questions of vital concern for the episcopate, and tended to circumscribe their rights with reference to vacant benefices, the appointment of vicars, and other matters of great importance. Paoli Sarpi had said of the bishops who attended the Council of Trent, that they entered the Council bishops, to come out simple priests; so now the bishops attending the Vatican Council, or a part of them at least, were much alarmed at the idea of finding themselves further despoiled of their dignity, and therefore strenuously opposed every measure tending to diminish their authority within their own dioceses. Six persons spoke in the Congregation of January 15th, and as many on the 19th. On the latter occasion, the Archbishop of Paris made a most eloquent discourse, in which he insisted on the necessity of restoring to the bishops the consideration and dignity due to their office, and thus vindicated the position of the General Assembly of the Church; but his views by no means resembled those of the proposed scheme. His language was very severe: addressing himself to the partisans of Infallibility, he reproached them with walking in darkness, while he and those who shared his opinions followed the light; alluding to the mighty power of the age which makes itself felt by all who co-operate in its movement, either by active labour or mental work. Monsignor Darboy had only to stretch out his hand to secure a cardinal's hat, but he preferred the simple satisfaction of doing

his duty. The torrent, whose impetuous course he so accurately described, has swept him away into its eddying depths, an elect and noble victim. This speech was, perhaps, his last cry to warn the Church of the danger that threatened her, and then his voice was drowned for ever in one of those terrible convulsions by which society is from time to time degraded, and he disappeared unregretted and unwept, like a stranger from a world that was unworthy of him.

18. The deepest impression was made that day by a stirring speech of the Archbishop of Cologne, who, of all the Germans, was considered one of the most Roman in opinion. The views of Darboy had long been patent to all; but as the Archbishop of Cologne was not supposed to favour the Opposition, his speech struck very deeply as an indication of the general state of opinion.

19. In the meeting of the 21st, after several Fathers had spoken, the Bishop of Orleans arose; the greatest attention prevailed, and many prelates left their seats in order to surround him. It was impossible, however, to obtain an accurate report of his words, owing to the difficulty of hearing in the Council Hall, which was very trying to orators not possessed of strong voices.

20. It appears that the bishops of the Opposition found great fault with the authors of the schemes for the narrowness of their ideas, and it was reported that one of them compared the City of Rome to an enchanted island, the inhabitants of which, having been asleep for three centuries, were quite astonished on awakening to find that the habits and customs of the world had considerably altered. This story, if not true, is at all events well calculated to describe the effect produced by these schemes (the first especially) on the most enlightened and intelligent part of the Opposition. On another occasion, an eminent English statesman, when speaking of the political constitution and traditions of Rome, observed that their consideration produced the same sort of effect on the mind as is felt on raising the marble slab that covers an ancient monument.

21. Meantime, the bishops never ceased demanding fuller communications on the subjects to be discussed during the Council. Some amount of concession was determined on, in

order to calm these disturbances ; and it was finally announced that the Pope, seeing that present arrangements were not likely to lead to any conclusion, was disposed to order the compilation of a general index to be distributed to the bishops for their information. It was also said that Cardinal de Angelis, the senior president, was about to circulate some project of adjustment on the question of Infallibility, which might be acceptable to both parties, and might, at any rate, avail to divide those dissentients who were united by the pressure exercised by the majority ; but the accuracy of all these reports, though emanating from trustworthy sources, could of course only be proved by time.

Meanwhile, the fifth scheme was promulgated (being the sixth since the beginning of the Council), although two of the four last were not yet completed ; but as no remedy, though so urgently needed, had been found for the very involved state of affairs, it seemed probable that all the subsequent schemes would follow the first, to the office of the Commissions for amendment.

22. Even the scheme "De Catechismo," which from its nature was closely allied with the daily life of the Catholic populations, appeared likely to share the fate of the others. We must remember that the Catholic catechism has different formulas— though the substance of all is the same—sanctioned by long and constant use in the various churches ; now the question arose of modifying that catechism, and every one is aware how difficult it is to interpolate changes in matters of tradition, which are identified with feelings and habits contracted at an early age.

The tendency towards concentration and equalisation in all laws and institutions, which prevails at the present day, is often repugnant to and vehemently resisted by human nature, which rather seeks unity in an allowable variety ; a certain measure of liberty affording the only hope of obtaining an agreement between different races and nations on any one subject.

IV.—THE SCHEME "DE ECCLESIA."

1. Distribution of the scheme "De Ecclesia."—2. On Infallibility.—3. Arguments to be brought forward.—4. Continuation of the Congregations without much result.—5. The number of bishops diminishes.—6. Opinions on the duration of the Council.

1. The sixth scheme, which was distributed at the sitting of the 21st January, came into the hands of the Fathers scarcely dry from the press, a fact which suggested the surmise that it was a fresh edition made under the impression caused by the bad success of the first, and consequently revised and reprinted. As it was better written, this opinion was in some measure corroborated, but with regard to its spirit, the essential point, that, as we shall see, gave little reason to believe that any such considerations had influenced its compilation.

Under the heading "De Ecclesia," it really contained all the most serious questions before the Council; it was a purely dogmatic scheme, treating especially of the Pope's authority, "De Primatu Pontificis," &c., and was said to contain a chapter entitled, " De Potestate Temporale ;" it was, in fact, the battleground on which the character and fate of the Council were to be decided, and on that decision depended the solution of all those questions which the volition of men and the force of circumstances had brought before its tribunal.

2. In this scheme the question of Infallibility, the pivot on which all else turned, was again brought under discussion. A question of the gravest import from its own nature, it assumed still larger proportions from the fact that it involved most of the decrees of the Church, especially the more recent ones, as, for instance, the Syllabus ; and great part of the political and religious system developed in these latter years. If the question of Infallibility were settled in the affirmative, not only would the conclusions of the past receive a solemn confirmation, but any future modification through the united action of the episcopate would be rendered very difficult; and yet this latter course was surely the most legitimate and constitutional expression of Catholic opinion. Indeed, after careful observation, it appeared that the question, so far as it treated of absolute

dogma, was already won by the minority, because even the partisans of Infallibility were well aware of the difficulty and danger that exists in forcibly proclaiming a dogma in the face of an intelligent minority amounting to a fourth of the whole assembly. Meantime, the address of which we have spoken had already so far prospered, that if the Council (or the Commission for receiving proposals) had accepted the petition in favour of Infallibility, said to carry 400 signatures, the promoters of that doctrine might well have been satisfied with such a favourable result, in default of the unanimity they desired.

A rumour also prevailed, that in order to make a sort of compromise, the Pope had accepted the address as an act of homage, and not wishing the question to be formally proposed, had enjoined silence on the matter. But as no bishop was likely to bring forward a counter-proposition in favour of fallibility, the result of all these proceedings in days to come would certainly be this: that to posterity, ignorant of the details of the matter, it would appear that the great majority of the Vatican Council was in favour of the personal Infallibility of the Pope. Future generations would imagine that the Pope, from considerations easily understood, had declined the expression of that wish, but that the fact remained recorded by the Curia Romana, as what is called *proxime fidei*; and if, at the time of which we write, the Opposition did not believe in the full and decisive success of the dogma of personal Infallibility, they had no defence against its being declared *proxime fidei*.

3. The most singular part of the whole proceeding is that, on probing the opinion of Catholics, even of those who in the recent troubles had manifested the greatest zeal for the Papal cause, they showed a great amount of indecision, if not of repugnance, towards a dogmatic declaration of personal Infallibility; and the like sentiments prevailed even among the clergy up to a certain rank in the hierarchy. But on entering the Council Hall, it was found that between the defenders of the dogma, those who adhered to it, and those who simply submitted to it, there was a large majority in favour of Infallibility. This phenomenon can only be explained by taking into consideration the present constitution of the episcopate, for the conditions that regulate the nomination and election of bishops naturally induce them

to turn more readily to the source from which their authority is derived, than to the people among whom they exercise it; and thus they reflect the ideas that prevail in the Curia, rather than the public opinion of their flocks. Beyond all doubt, there existed in the very centre of Catholicism a certain spirit of opposition, prepared, not only to hold its own against the aggressions of the so-called Catholic party, but also to exact the reforms so urgently needed by the age; and this opposition was not only constantly engaged in the conflict, but was actually, though slowly, gaining ground.

It was impossible, on account of the weighty reasons we have already mentioned, to form any conjecture as to the length to which this opposition might be carried; because it had opposed to it all the strength and vigour inherent in an ancient and well-disciplined institution, which had been gradually moulded by the lapse of centuries, and which possessed not only a complete system of education and legislation, the habit of authority with the greatest power and means of enforcing it, but what is of still greater consequence, a familiarity with ecclesiastical policy, and the prerogative of dispensing all the honours and dignities of the hierarchy.

4. Congregations were held on the 24th and 25th of January, which, including the public Sessions, made fifteen meetings in all since the Council was opened two months previously; and as no conclusion had yet been arrived at, it was evident that the hope of its short duration would be disappointed. Moreover, as events had turned out so differently from what had been expected, the interests of the Catholic party and of the Opposition became in some cases identical; for if the latter desired that matters should go slowly, in order to avoid being overcome by superior numbers, so, on the other hand, whenever a strong resistance was made, the former were willing to temporise, and sometimes even to prorogue an assembly so little amenable to their wishes, as to threaten destruction to the edifice which for the last twenty years they had been carefully constructing.

5. The words attributed by the *Constitutionnel* to Ollivier, the new French minister, " that it was impossible to treat with Italy for the removal of the French army of occupation while the Council was sitting," tended considerably to strengthen these

considerations, and to reconcile the Catholic party to the longer duration of the Council. On the 19th the election by vote of the Commission for Affairs of the East took place, and it became apparent, by the polling-papers collected, that the number of bishops present had diminished by seventy. Of these the greater part had left Rome; four were dead; and it was reported that others had absented themselves owing to some concealed discontent, thus rendering very bad service to their own cause. Moreover, some of the French prelates had been obliged to return to their dioceses on account of political disturbances. From these facts it became evident, that as the summer drew on, the number of absentees would increase, and some persons consequently advised the prorogation of the Council; but if this course were once adopted all would be uncertainty in the future; for during the prorogation changes might take place. The bishops, who on returning to their respective dioceses, escaped from the authoritative atmosphere of Rome, would be able to consult the feeling of their flocks; public opinion, once aroused, must necessarily exert some influence over them, and nothing would in that case have remained of all that had been proposed, save the fact that the Council had been opened. The Catholic party were assured of the permanency of the French occupation —no small thing, seeing that politics were, after all, at the bottom of the affair—and Catholicism secured this advantage, that it could emancipate itself from a rapid and summary fulfilment of the programme of the *Civiltà Cattolica*, and gain time, which in cases of difficulty is the best remedy and the best counsellor.

6. As these opinions gained ground, they coincided with an increasing desire for the prolongation of the Council. The Opposition desired it openly, the Curia acquiesced; only the most resolute Infallibilists were against it, although neither did their tactics point to its being of short duration.

They maintained a passive demeanour in the Council before the Opposition; few, if any of them spoke; and they did not conceal their hope that, when the spirit of opposition had exhausted itself on these first matters of common interest, the *furia francese* would calm down, and they would triumph more quickly and easily than was at first supposed. But they forgot that they had also to deal with the unimpassioned German nature, and with the tenacity of the Italians, who possess traditionally a more intimate acquaintance with the battle-field than any other nation. At the same time the Italians, in order to profit by their advantages, should have clearly recognised the influence they might exercise with regard to the Papacy and the other questions agitating Catholicism and their own great responsibility, of which they must render an account to history.

FEBRUARY.

I.—THE FIRST RESULTS OF THE SCHEME "DE ECCLESIA."

1. Summary of the proceedings of the three previous months.—2. On the canons contained in the scheme "De Ecclesia."—3. Summary of their contents.—4. Fate of the addresses of the Opposition.—5. Letters of the Bishop of Orleans.—6. Tactics of the Opposition.—7. Explanation of the tardiness in the deliberations of the Council.—8. Attempt to obviate this defect.—9. Italian addresses.—10. Project for shortening the speeches.—11. Project of reconciliation.—12. Failure of the same.—13. Other plans for bringing about an agreement.—14. New diplomatic intervention.—15. The amended schemes.—16. Affairs of the East.—17. Debate on the scheme "De Catechismo."

1. THE Ecumenical Council had now been sitting three months without arriving at any result. One of the Fathers, on being asked how soon it would finish, answered by inquiring when it would begin; and in this story we have a true picture of the state of affairs which prevailed last month, which still existed, and which to all appearance would continue in future. The scheme "De Episcopis" had, like that "De Fide," been sent to the Commission on amendments, and had been closely followed by those "De Moribus Clericorum" and "De Catechismo."

Up to this time the subjects under consideration were such as did not touch any serious question, at least directly, or any on which the opinions of the Council were substantially divided. But decided resistance was expected when the scheme "De Ecclesia" came under discussion; it had been distributed in the Congregation of January 21st, and was full of the most difficult questions, such as vehemently stir up the members of the Church, and are of more or less importance to society, according as Catholic feeling is exercised thereon.

2. Through some indiscretion, for which we should be grateful, the canons of the scheme "De Ecclesia" were published in

the *Augsburg Gazette,* and also in a more detailed form, together with the doctrinal part of the scheme, in the *Süddeutsche Presse.* In the part of the scheme entitled " De Romano Pontifice," were the rules briefly yet fully expressed, by which not only the most unlimited power was attributed to the Papacy, but in which the temporal power was also indirectly sanctioned, and in the doctrinal part were all those designations such as *doctorem et judicem supremum,* which, having been for long used regarding the Pope in official documents, have prepared the way for the declaration of his supreme Infallibility.

3. But as the explicit declaration of the personal Infallibility of the Pope was not, and could not be, inserted in a scheme which emanated directly from himself, the Infallibilist bishops had last month prepared an address to the Council, in which that declaration was formally demanded. This address followed very closely on the distribution of the scheme " De Ecclesia," so as to complete it, and was addressed to the Commission on " Postulata," as an amendment to be added to the propositions of the scheme itself, in order that the Council, as that document expresses it, "apertis omnemque dubitandi locum excludentibus verbis sancire velit supremam, ideoque ab errore immunem esse Romani Pontificis auctoritatem, quum in rebus fidei et morum, ea statuit ac præcipit, quæ ab omnibus Christi fidelibus credenda et tenenda, quæque rejicienda et damnanda sunt."

Thus were brought to light in a scheme to be afterwards converted into a decree, the doctrine or doctrines which have agitated the Catholic world of late years, viz. the exaltation of Papal authority, the principles of the Syllabus, and, though much more indirectly and in a less absolute form than these, the Temporal power, the first being at the same time cause and effect of the other two, the very doctrines in fact which settle and define the practical action of the Vatican Council on civil society.

4. It was not difficult to predict how the assembly would receive the other propositions, as the respective opinions of the Fathers on these points were known (though nothing was certain); but, with regard to Infallibility, the number and strength of those who opposed it *a viso aperto* were patent to all, by means of the various addresses which they had signed. The Opposition, not wishing to make a positive proposal, but only to put forth a negative opinion in reply to the decided " postulatum " of their

adversaries, and desirous to make their views known before the debate commenced, were obliged to address themselves directly to the Pope, his approbation being necessary for every matter to be brought forward in the Council, though it had previously been accepted by the Commission. They had done this immediately on hearing a report of the address of the Infallibilists, giving as a reason for inducing the Pope to grant their request and withhold his approbation from the "postulatum," the great diversity of opinions on the matter, and praying him to use his authority to impose a dignified silence on so dangerous a subject.

The Pope sent all the addresses in this sense to the identical Commission on "Postulata," which had already received the address in favour of Infallibility. However difficult it be to comprehend the organisation of the Council, it is plain that this action of the Pope was equivalent to a distinct refusal, for those documents were addressed to him, and not to the Commission, and it was obviously impossible for the latter to entertain a negative demand—a demand which asked them not to make their own petition. It was, of course, open to the Commission to accept or reject a proposal once made; but if in accepting a proposal they received also the observations in opposition to it, the general discussion would have been insensibly diverted from the subject in itself to the question of its expediency, and its consideration transferred from the general assembly, to the Commission on " Postulata," which would have overturned the order of Conciliar treatment, and have displaced and prejudged the question. This refusal, though conveyed with all legal formality, was displeasing to the bishops who had subscribed the address, as they considered that being 137 in number, and representing about one-third of the Catholic populations, besides including in their body the most illustrious men in the Church, and the pastors of the principal Congregations both in Europe and America, they had a right to expect that the respectful expression of their wishes should meet with a better reception.

5. However, owing to that great ally of the Curia Romana, the fear of scandal, a feeling that generally governs all its dependants —the most remote as well as the nearest (sometimes really from motives of Christian charity)—the discontent of the Opposition was kept under control outside the Council Hall, and only manifested itself from time to time by small explosions, as in the case

of the letters of the Bishop of Orleans, which were published in the newspapers, and fully expressed his discontent, and which, notwithstanding their vivacity, were never repudiated by their author.

In his answer to the Archbishop of Malines, in which he treats of the *reimprimatur* refused by the censorship, so that he was obliged to publish the letters himself, the Bishop of Orleans points to that very fact as a proof of the treatment to which bishops were subjected in Rome; and in writing to his Chapter, seems to lament the persecutions falling on him after having given such numerous and undoubted proofs of his devotion to the Church and the Apostolic See.

6. Within the Council however, this discontent showed itself openly by a systematic and continued opposition, which was no longer a simple diversity of opinion, but had taken such a definite form as alone answered to the position in which the minority were placed. Being only a small body under pressure of rules by which everything was definitively submitted to the action of the legates and the Pope, there remained for them no resource but so far as possible to temporise. To this end they occupied the time with lengthy orations, in which they undoubtedly had the advantage of their adversaries, from the learning and eloquence of most of their body, many of them being well acquainted with public life, and some, as, for example, the Hungarians, acquainted with parliamentary procedure, from experience gained in their national Diets.

Even their adversaries admired the *mira venustas* of these speeches. They awaited the beneficial results of time, the awakening of public opinion; they looked to the future and the unknown. Would such tactics render applicable to them the words said of Fabius, that "*cunctando restituant rem?*"

7. These considerations gave a significance to three months of unproductive labour and vain expectation, although nothing remarkable occurred during that time. Every one knows the length of the Council of Basle and its vicissitudes. The Council of Trent lasted eighteen years; and it is evident that months and years were necessary for the full consideration of the important matters brought before the Vatican Council in such different circumstances, and after the lapse of three centuries.

But that was exactly what many wished to avoid. They pretended that a work so important as the reform, or even simple revision of the Catholic legislation, with the view of bringing it into harmony with the new wants and conditions of modern society, could be accomplished in the same short space of time as would suffice for voting a budget; and they desired that the Council should be merely a grand ceremony for the solemn fulfilment of a pre-arranged programme, and not an event of real importance. Therefore the fact that the proceedings assumed the character of an actual discussion was in itself a notable circumstance, to which it was impossible not to attach importance when the cause of it was known.

8. Of course this strategy was very displeasing to the majority, who complained of the waste of time, and the length of the speeches, which occasionally occupied entire "Congregations," as many Fathers spoke on the same subjects, and the same arguments were frequently repeated. Indeed, but for the reasons above given, such laments were worthy of consideration, because, if the time squandered in useless words is to be regretted in all assemblies, in this it was more especially so; on account of the loss occasioned to those who composed it, by a protracted absence from their Sees and their duties at home. Moreover, on this point one disadvantage attending this Council as compared with others, and influencing its duration, was, that no distinction of parties being recognised, there could be no collective expression of opinion, and the orators only spoke their individual mind; so that any number might speak on the same subject and in the same sense.

Yet one becomes tolerant of such an abuse, and even grateful for it, on considering how few were the means allowed to the Opposition for defending themselves, and preventing the influence of the dark traditions of the Middle Ages from gaining the upper hand in Catholicism. Such, however, was not the opinion of the majority, and of the legates, who began to seek some means of providing against this, as yet unforeseen, danger.

9. In the English Parliament, in order to obviate this consumption of time, speeches are not read, but delivered *vivâ voce;* a rule which limits the number of orators, and also controls their length. It was proposed, in imitation of this practice, that in the

Vatican Council written speeches should be prohibited, and that the orators should depend only on memory; having, at the same time the permission of placing their manuscript, if they wished, on the president's desk, for the fuller information of the legates.

It was said that this project was brought forward by some of the Italian bishops, with the hope of obtaining certain reforms in the Order of the Council, in a restrictive sense; and that it would thus form an answer by the Infallibilist party to the first addresses of the French and German bishops of the Opposition, who, on their part, had sought for a liberal and extended reform of the same Order. A short while before this, certain Italian bishops, belonging for the most part to the southern provinces, had prepared a petition in favour of Infallibility, interspersed with quotations drawn from the writings of St. Thomas Aquinas and St. Alphonso di Liguori; and these proceedings would by no means have conduced to imprint the stamp of liberality on the opinions of the Italian episcopate; the project, however, went no further, but dropped out of notice.

10. Although the attempt to modify the Order of the Council, with regard to the method of discussion, did not take exactly the intended shape, yet another proposal to the same effect was soon made, which caused great apprehension among the bishops of the Opposition, who saw themselves threatened in their last means of defence; and those of them who held the highest position prepared to take more definite and determined measures to avert the peril. They endeavoured to procure a protest by the laity from such a quarter as would best insure its being heard, and thereby to defeat the plan which, if successful, would deprive the Opposition of the greater part of its means of action, and leave it merely the empty consolation of offering the fruit of its reflections in writing to the Cardinal legates, for their particular information. These precautions did, in fact, stop the matter from being carried further, though the idea was not entirely laid aside.

The *Augsburg Gazette* published a telegram from Rome, in which a similar project was set forth, with this difference, however, that the manuscripts were to be consigned to the respective Commissions, according to the subjects of which they treated. This was a less radical innovation than consigning them to the presidents; but at the same time, it hindered them from being publicly known, and made it impossible to maintain a strict control over the most important matters—those contained in the written speeches—which are of course fuller and more detailed than such as are made from memory only. This last project, like the other, included a proposition for resolving questions by silence where unanimity was impracticable.

L'Unità Cattolica, a journal usually well-informed in these matters, did not entirely contradict the truth of this last hypothesis, and though it was not carried into effect, no doubt was entertained that every way was tried which might serve to limit the discussions. The Sunday Congregations, on which devolved the duty of examining the petitions of the previous month, also took up the subject, and a special meeting was held for its consideration. A last project, which met with greater favour, as being more conciliatory, prohibited the reading of speeches, but allowed them to be given in writing to the Commissions (as in the case of the second project we have mentioned), with this difference, however, that they were to be condensed, printed, and distributed to the Fathers. Afterwards, the oral discussion and the voting were to take place. It was said that a clause was added to this project, which provided that the observations and objections of the Fathers could not be simply negatived, but must have appended to them the affirmative opinion of their opponent on the matter in question; and though this condition was not ultimately brought forward, the party predominating in the Council continued to seek for some solution of the difficulty.

11. Meanwhile it was necessary to remove the existing mistrust, to divide the Opposition, which, though quite in the minority, greatly embarrassed the proceedings of the Council; and to endeavour to bring over some part of its members to the opinions of the majority. With this view, a new kind of " postulatum " was circulated, to serve like the first-mentioned (or instead of it) as an appendix to the matters contained in the scheme, " De Romano Pontifice "; its aim being to obtain the signatures of the less resolute dissentients to a formula in favour of Infallibility, but more moderate in tone than that which had provoked so much resistance.

This new project contained three principal points: First, the condemnation (but without an anathema) of those who appeal from the sentence of the Pope to a future Council; secondly, the condemnation of the opinion of those who say that only apparent, and not real obedience, is due to the judgments of the Pope; thirdly, the condemnation of those who affirm that there may be such a real discordance between the episcopate and the Pope as to render it necessary to judge which of them is the greater; as such a discordance could not occur, and therefore should not be considered at all by the Church. This project was followed by a long commentary on its utility; and it was declared to be more convenient than a pure and simple declaration of Infallibility, which would always afford ground for innumerable discussions among theologians as to the conditions required for proving a case *ex cathedrâ*, that being, according to its own promoters, the only way in which the matter must be considered as " of faith." It was observable, also, how by this plan such a solution of difficulties would be arrived at, as would obviate the trouble of solving many historical questions very embarrassing for those who desired to reconcile them with personal Infallibility; and ultimately it was strongly urged as the best means of obtaining such a measure of unanimity as was requisite for attaining grave decisions with any safety. It was, indeed, a real attempt at conciliation, the only one, perhaps, then possible. It was so worded as to be in favour of blending (up to a certain point) the Infallibility of the Pope with the Infallibility of the Church, and was a return to the ancient Roman theological opinions, which are far more moderate and less definite than the new, for the latter, being produced by the mingled enthusiasm and terror of the Catholic party, are as absolute and exclusive as the sentiments from which they have sprung.

12. As is usually the case, the idea of a third party did not please either one side or the other; the Opposition only saw in it an attempt to divide them; and the Infallibilists, feeling that if it were successful they would be considered beaten, regarded it with no sort of satisfaction. The project was certainly welcomed by those who in all assemblies seek for peace and agreement; but these quiet spirits are never possessed of much authority,

nor can they settle great questions; and though the plan obtained the support of a few active members of the Opposition, it failed in regard to the end for which it was designed, and the difficulties remained the same as ever.

13. Whilst the eager desire to overcome the obstacles that hindered the consummation of their plans, continued to occupy the minds of those most deeply engaged in the impenetrable recesses of ecclesiastical politics, the assembly, which had already been sitting a considerable time, began to divide itself into different parties; intrigues were formed, and all sorts of reports and projects were spread abroad, the origin and the truth of which it was most difficult to ascertain. Among others, a proposal attracted considerable attention, said to have been originated by one of the most illustrious, if not the most influential persons in the Council; this was a method of accommodation founded on the acceptance by both parties of the formula of the Council of Florence, with some slight modification. As the reputed author was one of the heads of the Opposition, this plan would have been on his part equivalent to an abdication, and therefore the report, whether true or only circulated from party spirit, acquired particular value. The most violent Infallibilists declared that they must remain firm, without admitting any idea of accommodation; that as a last resource the utmost pressure of authority would be used, and the dogma defined on the strength of a simple numerical majority, leaving the minority out of the question; as in their opinion it would melt away on meeting with such firm and vigorous resistance, and find itself finally constrained to submit to the "riverenza della somme Chiavi." *

14. The ever-increasing rumours indicating that some check, at any rate, must be placed on the liberty of discussion, augmented the fears of the Opposition to such a pitch, that they (the French especially) turned for succour to diplomacy, which seemed at length inclined to emerge from that state of supine neutrality hitherto observed in all matters concerning the Council. The Catholic Governments instructed their ambassadors to strengthen the anti-Infallibilist bishops with their authority, and to assist them with some arguments which might prove

---

* " The reverence for the keys superlative."
LONGFELLOW's Dante, *Inf.* xix. 101.

sufficiently convincing to calm the enthusiasm of their adversaries.

15. The third point on which the Opposition were agitated, besides the Order of the Council, and the proposal of Infallibility, was the desire of finding out what became of the schemes once sent back; as by this only could they measure the real value of their own resistance. It was already known that in the Commissions for emendation the schemes were revised either by the persons who had originally drawn them up, or by others of like opinions; but even supposing that they were amended in this way, what came of it? According to the Order, they could be put to the vote "si nihil obstiterit." The universal opinion was, that they ought not to be again subjected to partial discussion, but put to the vote as entire schemes; for once amended according to the opinions of the Council, there remained nothing but to submit them to the definitive vote. In this case would the judgment of the majority suffice to change those schemes into decrees? If that was so, the Opposition would be utterly defeated. Then again, was this judgment sufficient in matters of discipline of great importance, and of dogma? Was it entirely free from danger, and if this course was not adopted, what other criterion would be thought sufficient? Such were the speculations, the result of which the Opposition awaited with little satisfaction, considering the temper of the party predominant in the Vatican. The next Session was to make known openly what they had to expect.

16. Meantime, as usually happens when men's minds are excited, every little incident that would otherwise have passed unnoticed, becomes of immense importance, it is at such moments that "Poca favilla gran fiamma seconda."*

One of the fixed ideas that the Church and the Propaganda, in that zeal for unity which is now so much felt, have been indefatigably working out in these latter years, is the uniting of the different Oriental rites; not their liturgies, which would be an impossible work, but their laws and privileges, particularly those regarding episcopal elections, of which the Orientals are exceedingly jealous, and other special matters of jurisdiction and discipline. Rome had long been able to count for support on two

* "A little spark is followed by great flame."—LONGFELLOW's Dante, *Parad.* i. 34.

of the Oriental Patriarchs who were her sworn lieges, the Latin and the Armenian. The first, Monsignor Valerga, before his promotion to the episcopal dignity, was simply a Roman ecclesiastic; the second, Monsignor Hassoun, was as devoted to Rome as a Roman ecclesiastic could be. But the Propaganda had never been able to induce the old Chaldean Patriarch to further its designs, as he remained a firm supporter of the privileges of the Oriental churches, and was followed by a considerable and influential portion of the Eastern clergy, both regular and secular.

The Pope could not suffer such resistance; and in the presence of Valerga, who was the interpreter and only witness of his interview with the Chaldean, he one day invited the old Patriarch either to submit or to resign his office. Being reduced to this extremity by his imperious brother, the Patriarch chose rather to resign than bend to the Pope's authority, and this episode, which was reckoned as the herald of a new schism long threatening in the East, created a great sensation.

The rumour of certain retrospective processes to be carried on at the same time by means of the Propaganda before the Holy Office against some bishops under its own immediate jurisdiction, who had manifested a want of docility in seconding its projects, also excited much notice, and provoked very undesirable analogous recollections of the detested name of the Holy Inquisition. Events of this nature are of common occurrence in ecclesiastical administrations, and might be repeated a thousand times without acquiring great weight or attracting much notice; but in such a moment as the present, and under prevailing circumstances, they acquired exceptional importance.

17. Altogether, the state of affairs was most complicated, and betokened no sort of approach to a conclusion. The Infallibilists on their part held that a defeat would be followed by very disastrous consequences for the Pope's authority; and, on the other hand, the Opposition were so entangled by public opinion and the wishes of their flocks that they could not recede from their position. While events were in this stage, the scheme "De Catechismo" came under deliberation in the Congregations, and the large numbers who inscribed their names as orators on the subject awoke some displeasure.

The matter in question was no less than an attempt to abolish the catechisms in various forms in the words of which different nations had been ever accustomed to lisp their religious belief, and to substitute for all, one common catechism, probably the Roman. It happened that some bishop, in the heat of discussion, ventured to take exception to the pattern thus set forth as a type to be universally adopted; but for an individual at Rome to object to the Roman Catechism was a liberty which the Holy City, *par excellence*, though accustomed to every vicissitude of fortune, could scarcely have expected.

II.—THE SCHEME "DE ECCLESIA."

1. The twenty-one Canons of the scheme.—2. Summary of the same.—3. Their probable effect on the world.—4. Means of escape.—5. Temporal power before Infallibility.—6. Remainder of the scheme.—7. Its application.—8. Conclusion.

1. The moment for the discussion of the scheme "De Ecclesia" was approaching. Very serious reflections arose from a study of its propositions, as reported by the *Augsburg Gazette* and the *Süddeutsche Presse*, especially those parts which refer to the primacy, the temporal dominion, and the other points which, more or less, directly touch on the Pope's authority.*

The scope of the twenty-one Canons given by the *Augsburg Gazette* is partly to reaffirm ancient beliefs and traditions, and partly to sanction certain opinions in their most absolute form, and in the sense of what would be called on the other side of the Alps the purest "Ultramontanism." If there is anything new in them, it is the precise, and I might almost say geometrical form of the system to which these points are all reduced, and the way in which not only many of the most cultivated and flourishing nations of the world are condemned as dissentients from the Church, but even a great part of the customs and institutions of those countries actually in connection with her are included in the same condemnation.

As to the first point, it was observed by many irreproachable Catholics that all these differences having been already condemned

* See Appendix, Document XIII.

in their own day, it was useless, even for reasons of ecclesiastical policy, to offend and irritate great and powerful nations by reiterating a judgment which there was no hope of their accepting, and that the only result of such a course would be to give them a most unfavourable idea of a religion thus intolerant and aggressive. Then, as to the second point, many asked of what avail could be the endeavour to cast Governments and nations out of the Church, and to narrow and restrict her limits, instead of endeavouring to enlarge them—a duty indicated by her very name and mission?

Such were the considerations to which the publication of this document gave rise, and indeed a perusal of its contents makes one wonder with what object it was compiled and to whom the greater part of it was addressed. So far as dissentients from its doctrines are concerned, they (as we already remarked) have been long since condemned, and their position with regard to the Church has been clearly settled. Freethinkers will only class these Canons with those that preceded them, and see an additional reason for disregarding them all, so that there remain only the Catholics, rightly and properly so called. They seldom err on the side of tolerance, and all these judgments enter, more or less directly, into the habits and feelings of their religious education, which, if it needs anything, certainly requires to be deepened and enlarged rather than narrowed and restricted.

2. The first Canon, as published by the *Augsburg Gazette*, affirms the identity and autonomy of the Catholic Church; the second its immutability; the third its exterior and sensible action; and the fourth reverts to its autonomy excluding all dissentient bodies. The fifth lays down that the Catholic Church is the one only way of eternal salvation. The sixth declares, by Divine authority, that no other confession of faith can be tolerated. The seventh affirms the infallibility of the Church, and the eighth its perfection. The ninth extends its Infallibility, even to unrevealed truths, and in so doing claims for the Church unlimited and supreme power over all human society. In the tenth the Church is withdrawn from the control of the State. The eleventh establishes the supremacy of the episcopate. The twelfth authorises temporal punishments for disobedience to the law of the Church. Finally, as a corollary of all this, the

thirteenth Canon pronounces an anathema against all who say that salvation can be found out of the one holy Catholic Apostolic Church of Rome. We leave it to the authors of the scheme to consider what, in our days, such a declaration can avail to the millions of Catholics who, along with all the rest of the human race, are thereby again condemned. With the fourteenth Canon commence those declarations on the primacy of the Pope within the Church, which, by progressive steps, reach their culminating point in the sixteenth, where it is said that he has "plenam et supremam potestatem jurisdictionis in universam Ecclesiam," and also "ordinariam et immediatam in omnes ac singulas Ecclesias."

Theologians may determine what power can remain to diocesan bishops in their own churches after such a declaration as this; but it baffles the comprehension of secular persons.

The relations between Church and State are thus adjusted upon a system of gentle gradations, which the seventeenth Canon explains. The eighteenth vindicates the Divine right in all power that governs civil society. The nineteenth condemns those who uphold the supremacy of the civil right. By the twentieth all secular power is declared to be in subjection to the laws of the Church, and in the twenty-first these latter are withdrawn entirely from the cognisance of the State.

3. Now, on summing up these Canons, what do they amount to? Sole religion the Catholic—sole head the Pope—"qui habet plenam et supremam potestatem;" his laws superior to those of the State on which he exercises his judgment "de licito et de illicito," and disposes of permissions and punishments. Dante has imagined an Emperor and a Pope, who between them should direct the world; but if the idea of these Canons were fully carried out with regard to civil society, there would remain the Pope only.

It is not the aim of the present work to discuss the theological view of such decrees, so we limit our considerations to the social and civil aspect of the question. What feelings and expectations would be awakened in other religious and constituted powers, by the enunciation of an authority so complete and absolute as that set forth in these articles? This question was asked on all sides by those bishops especially who, living in civilised countries, and among liberal and cultivated nations of different religious professions, are obliged to form an opinion on these points. It was said that an American prelate, having this in mind, expressed his feelings in the apposite quotation from Tacitus: " non obtrectari a se urbanas excubias, sibi tamen apud horridas gentes e contuberniis hostem aspici."

4. It would appear that it was intended in some degree to mitigate the condemnations of the doctrinal part of the scheme; for instance, a distinction is made with regard to errors of faith between invincible ignorance and that which is wilful. But how are we to define invincible ignorance? for immediately, and it would seem as a commentary on this distinction, there follows the condemnation of liberty of conscience. This term has many meanings, and the only one which is true, and should be agreeable to all, pleases no one, and for that reason is accepted neither by its eulogists nor by its enemies. Its condemnation, thus simply expressed, answers the question we have proposed, by excluding the testimony of conscience from being the justification of invincible ignorance, which it limits to the material incapacity for acquiring knowledge, though that is a state of things rarely met with in our day, and restricted to cases which have no relation to our society.

Such a condemnation carries with it an antithesis, making the Church of Rome the point of divergence between the just and the unjust—between light and darkness—up to an absolute dualism between good and evil; between Christ and Belial, or between Rome and all that is not of Rome.

The same may be said of the civil power, to which is conceded the sanction of Divine right, in return for its submission to ecclesiastical power; but after describing the intimate union between Church and State as the source of great advantage to the latter, the scheme proceeds to assert that that union is a Divine law, and is not left free to the choice of man. If it is the duty of mankind, taken individually, to submit to the true religion, it is no less their duty, when taken collectively; and thus carrying out the syllogism to its last result, the scheme, asserts that if individual believers are to be in subordination to the Church, the State, which is a union of believers, should be the same.

In another place it adds as a corollary that, for the same reason, the State has both the right and the duty (irrespective of the obligation of maintaining public order) of inflicting penalties on persons who offend against religion.

The doctrinal portion of the scheme concludes by observing (as we have already pointed out) that to the Church belongs the supreme judgment over all questions of morals in civil society and of what is lawful in public affairs; and that as she is the guide and teacher of men in the way of salvation, those Sovereigns who have not the Church for a mother, have not God for their Father.

5. Sometimes the scheme rises above this narrow and jealous style, and delineates with vivid colours the benefits to be derived from the influence of religion upon the State; and a passage of this sort taken independently, and considered apart from the claims of unlimited power that otherwise predominate in the scheme, has an excellent effect. The one we refer to, is in these terms, "that religion teaches submission to lawful authority, not from fear, but for conscience sake; and while it inculcates obedience to kings, it also enjoins on them the care of their people, because power was given them not to satisfy the desire of dominion, but in order to exercise justice, for God has created both small and great, and has equal care of both." When, on the contrary, the scheme speaks of the temporal power, which it says " singulari divinæ Providentiæ consilio dato " to the Roman Church, it returns to the old style, which may be perhaps well adapted to the political question. It reverts to liturgical phrases on the benefits of that temporal power, and on the impiety of all " quovis insidiarum et violentiarum genere labefactare ac convellere adnitantur," and in consequence condemns those who affirm " repugnare juri divino ut cum spirituali potestate in Romanos Pontifices civilis conjungatur," and also the perverseness of those " qui contendunt Ecclesiæ non esse de hujus principatus civilis ad generale Christianæ reipublicæ bonum relatione quidpiam cum auctoritate constituere adeoque licere Catholicis hominibus ab illius decisionibus hac de re editis recedere aliterque sentire."

Now, seeing that the Pope is supreme judge, and embodies in himself the judgment of the Church under the severest penalties, it follows that, according to this proposition, it is unlawful for any one to entertain opinions on the temporal power differing from those of the Pope. It is most unlikely that the Pope should himself decree the downfall of his own power, but rather from sincere conviction promote its continuance, and therefore his decree would, in such a case, be à *priori* strengthened by the judgment issued against all those who are not of his way of thinking. That would constitute in the public law of nations a State which, in the heart of Europe, would set at defiance, as being itself superior to law, all the vicissitudes and necessities of the age, an eternal State.

Still, it cannot be denied that the formula we have just quoted was relatively moderate, though it acquired great importance from the general character of the decree in which it was incorporated. One of the greatest difficulties arising from the want of any limit to Papal authority in the constitution of the Church, is that of assigning some bounds to the matters on which the Pope has the right of judging *ex cathedrâ*, hence the danger of his making everything dogma, like the King of Phrygia who turned all that he touched into gold. And here a hypothesis presents itself: supposing that one day a Pope, either from humility or from eccentricity, should voluntarily abdicate his temporal power (though we admit such a thing is very unlikely), what would the Infallibilists who are so fond of that power, then think of the doctrine of Infallibility?

In such a case the chances are that they would not care to recognise in the occurrence a natural condition of the Church expressed by its living word, but would rather consider themselves to be suffering from the caprice and tyranny of an individual. Many similar instances might be cited to prove what, indeed, is nothing new, but old as the world itself, namely, that all absolute power is a two-edged sword that wounds both friends and enemies; whereas, liberty affords protection to both. The Infallibilists made no account of such considerations, and argued thus, Who habitually directs the Church in the absence of the exceptional and comprehensive influence of Councils? The Pope. How would the Church proceed if this guidance could be false? By this argument they showed that they were unable to appreciate the slow but collective action of society; and like all men who submit to the influence and allurements of despotism, could not relish an authority which was not distilled through the arbitrary will of one individual.

6. The rest of the scheme, if the report of it be true, was interspersed with the arguments of the Syllabus, and the favourite doctrines of the Catholic party more or less distinctly enunciated. It condemned, among other things—liberty of conscience—universal suffrage—lay teaching—the suppression of ecclesiastical immunities—the abolition of religious orders—the confiscation of the property of the clergy—the exaction of military service from ecclesiastics, and so forth. In speaking of these things the scheme, like the Syllabus, abounds too often in that sort of metaphor which, taking a part for the whole, confuses the evils of a system with the system itself, and passes judgment on a whole category of facts, only some of which are really reprehensible; as if one were to say, "thirst is wrong because it leads to inebriety."

With regard to lay teaching, the scheme certainly specifies that those only are condemned who exclude ecclesiastics from giving instruction; but with regard to universal suffrage, it seems indistinctly to condemn all those who guide their actions by public opinion or the voice of the majority; whereas, though such a criterion is not, of course, infallible, it is often the truest, and in many cases the only one to be had in modern society. There are some just remarks to be found in the scheme mixed with the most exorbitant exactions. Still the tenor of the whole document tends to enforce the ideal set forth in the formula we have described—one fold and one shepherd, by whom civil society is to be directed and guided—thus rendering it the object and instrument of the absolute and exclusive *régime* imposed by his irresponsible and unlimited will, and in so doing society carries into action the mind of the Church, and thus becomes, as it were, her embodiment and representative.

7. It is evident that all conceptions destined to become matters of deliberation in an assembly whose object it is to influence civil society should be not only specious, but opportune, and of a feasible nature ; and, therefore, the theologians, who are the authors of this scheme, in compiling the treatise

"De Monarchia," failed to render it serviceable to the living institutions and practical interests of the day, though they made it closely accord with the ideal of their own minds.

8. Of course, their programme, considered merely in its speculative part, and as an argument of faith, only concerns those who believe in it, but as its doctrines are inseparable from the working of civil institutions, with which they are substantially identified, and as their practical application is distinctly contemplated, did the theologians who drew it up in very indifferent Latin under the safe shelter of the Vatican, ever consider what its result would be? Did those theologians ever attempt to estimate the harm that must be done, and the blood that must be shed, ere this scheme could be carried into effect? The man of the greatest intellect of the age in Italy, "Cavour," well-knowing the inflexibility of the traditions of Rome, considered the separation of Church and State, the "Chiesa libera in Stato libero," as the only logical solution of the eternal and difficult problem, the conditions of which are Church and State. The scheme implicitly rejects such an idea, and explicitly condemns all those who say that the separation of Church and State is requisite for the good of society; and thus, when it is once accepted, only two hypotheses remain. The one is to consider speculatively any Catholic society active and powerful, as portrayed by the schemes, trying to carry out its ideal at the present day in the world; and you tremble at the thought of the resistance it would provoke, and the misfortunes it would entail. The other is to reflect practically on the number of adherents that such a programme would find among Catholics themselves, and you receive a very different impression from the disproportion between the grandeur of the challenge, and the poverty of the means of sustaining it. In both alternatives the mind reverts to the Bull of Convocation of the Council, which states that it was assembled for the purpose of providing a remedy for the needs and evils of society. If the first case were possible, in what would this remedy consist, but in exile, in imprisonment, in the Inquisition, in religious warfare, in schisms, and all the other evils which have already resulted from that system—sad remedies indeed? If, on the other hand (as is more probable), the second

alternative were accepted, where then is the remedy? Cruelty
or contempt, tyranny or impotence, a fatal dilemma to which
sooner or later every absolute and inexorable system is
reduced, according to its power or its object.

III.—CONDITION OF THE CATHOLIC NATIONS.

1. Displeasure caused by the publication of the Canons.—2. Questions for the
consideration of the Council.—3. Questions regarding France.—4. Catholicism
and modern society.—5. The Revolution.—6. Dilemma.—7. Exceptions to
preceding observations. — 8. Responsibility of Institutions. — 9. Excessive
authority.—10. Intolerance and indulgences.—11. Asceticism.—12. Centralisation.—13. Rebellion.—14. Conclusion.

1. The publication of the documents in the German papers
caused the greatest excitement at the Vatican; a searching
investigation was the result, and several persons slightly connected with the Council fell into trouble. Some were deprived
of their office, others were obliged to leave Rome, and punishment followed all those supposed to be the authors or accomplices of these indiscreet revelations. It is clear that one of
the principal causes of this discontent was the sensible effect
produced by these documents, in those countries especially
where such questions are of great importance; but this was
unreasonable, as it was far better for the Vatican that its
schemes should be known beforehand, than later. It was a
matter of serious import that Europe should receive, either
with indifference or with disfavour, the decrees of the Catholic
Assembly, as they were of much greater consequence than the
simple propositions of a number of theologians, even though
emanating from the Vatican. Public opinion, so severely
reprobated by the scheme, is, nevertheless, very often of the
greatest utility; and the refusal to take any account of it is
sometimes the cause of serious and irremediable mistakes.

2. If, for example, public opinion could be so far heard in
the Church, as to substitute for the Canons we have described
some other scheme treating of the subjects that now occupy
men's minds, and loudly call for a rational solution, might
not the attention of the Council be turned to matters of more
general importance, though of equal consequence to Catholicism,

than the scholastic subtleties contained in the Canons? Are there no defects in the Catholic religion save those regarding its authority? Is that the only subject worth consideration? Is the loss of the temporal power the sole evil on which we should deliberate?

Could no other matters be found worthy to occupy the attention of the Ecumenical Council, called together with such solemnity after the lapse of three centuries, to deliberate on the interests of religion?

For instance, would it not be a suitable inquiry for the Ecumenical Council of the nineteenth century, to examine into the cause of the various evils that affect the Catholic populations of our age—their abnormal condition in many ways—the slowness of their growth, and their relative inferiority, moral, civil, and political? an inferiority which is in proportion to the greater or less prevalence of the system described in the scheme.

No very profound statistical knowledge is necessary; one can see with a glance the difference in prosperity and of civilisation to be found in Spain as compared with England, and in Ireland as compared with the sister Isle—or as between Portugal and Holland; between South and North America; between Italy and Germany; between Savoy and Switzerland; and in this latter country between the Catholic and Protestant cantons?

Does not the contrast involuntarily strike the mind of any person who, sailing along the shores of the Lake of Geneva, has the opportunity of observing the relative condition of the Savoyard and the Swiss villages? Again, we must remember that in the conflict between the Austrians and the Prussians—both of the same German race—the advantage was not for the former.

Or to take another test, what progress has been made in these latter days by the first-named countries as compared with the second, in all those useful institutions by which mankind can render homage to the Creator in the pursuit of art and science, and in grand undertakings?

I say in recent times, in order to point out the epoch at which began not only the consolidation of those great differences which have divided Christendom, but also the formation of that system of Catholic Government which the Vatican Council has striven still further to enforce. We will not, however, proceed further with these comparisons, but only observe that as the scheme "De Ecclesia" asserts that the Church is a visible society of men, and exists on earth for their salvation, she cannot be entirely indifferent to the conduct of her followers.

3. The best illustration of these reflections is found on turning to France, for she presents two views to the observer, both of them well adapted to throw light on our subject. By the one she appears as the centre of life and of civilisation, by the other she affords matter for serious consideration to all who either observe her, or are influenced by her. By the first, she appears as the rival of the greatest nations; but by the second she seems to share the lot of those countries that are less prosperous, and that have before them a dark and uncertain future. To whom does France owe that part of her civilisation which enables her at the present time to rank among other great nations? I mean her culture, her science, her industry, and her material prosperity. Beginning from the encyclopedists down to the learned men of the present day, how many of the *savants*, and of those who have in any way assisted the growth of modern France, would have been recognised by Rome as her children? How many laws, how many institutions, and what an amount of learning, would have been of necessity lost to France, had the voice of Rome prevailed in that country? Imagine the consequences to France as regards culture and science, had her intellectual progress been subjected for a century to the corrections and revisions of the Roman Index? What part can the influence of Catholicism (using the terms in the very sense adopted by its own party), what part can that influence claim in the civil glory and intellectual progress of France? So far we have considered her under the aspect in which she equals the most cultivated and civilised nations of the world, but at the same time, what nation is more deeply affected than France by grave and dangerous social questions, or is in a condition less favourable for their resolution? Considered from this view, which concerns her social and political state, France affords ample material for the reflections, which we shall shortly make, on the political condition of the Catholic populations.*

* When these pages were written no one could have foretold the misfortunes so soon to fall upon France, but it seems well to leave them in their original form.

4. But turning from France, to view the matter in a more general light, how have the doctrines of absolutism—to which we have already alluded—affected the progress of the great institutions, enterprises, and discoveries of modern times, and how many of these latter—beginning even from the days of Galileo—have been carried out in spite of those doctrines?

What place can Catholicism claim for its tenets in the increase of liberty, the toleration, and the amicable and peaceful intercourse, which, after much useless destruction of humanity, seems to be the settled character of society in our days?

What part did the Catholicism of Torquemada and of Philip II. take in the grand discovery and colonisation of those new countries which are the glory of the two last centuries? Who has profited by the work of Christopher Columbus and of Amerigo Vespucci? What has Catholicism, following, though more quietly, in the same track of discovery, effected in North America; a country entirely free, in which all religions emulate one another; and, again, in Australia? These two parts of the world came into being, as it were, in a moment, through the diffusion and expansion of the European, and therefore Christian race; and what part in the miracle can be attributed to Catholicism? Has not the Catholic Church, on the contrary, reason for sad meditation on the spectacle presented by Mexico, and the other unhappy republics of the South, which are entirely under her sway? Here one would think are plenty of subjects well deserving the whole attention of the Catholic hierarchy assembled in Rome; for such facts may be more or less appreciated, may be understood in one sense or another, and attributed to this or that cause; but their existence cannot be denied, and therefore they ought to be considered.

5. Another question might also be asked, which, without entering into details—that are liable to be questioned by many —is really matter of fact. Whence comes that disordered spirit by which in our days Catholic societies exclusively are agitated — the spirit of revolution? In using this word I do not here intend to apply it in the widest sense—that which expresses a universal law felt more or less deeply, but common to all humanity. I use it in that special way which signifies the violent, brutal, and envious form of revolution, which,

from the end of the last century up to the present day, has rent and distracted the most beautiful countries of Europe. Germany, England, Switzerland, and America, have their revolutions in ideas, their modifications, their progress, their changes for the better or for the worse. But all this is carried on without anger and violence, without blows and bloodshed. They may have other evils, because humanity can never be exempt from such, but they are free from that terrible social plague—chronic revolution; the not being able to say to-day what may happen to-morrow; and what is more, these nations have not, like us, their only hope of existence in the exercise of force, which seems at the present time to have become our sole means of persuasion.

Which of the Catholic nations can live like England and America in the exercise of the greatest activity, and in a state of constant social and political agitation, without a large standing army? In how many Catholic countries has not the Government more than once collapsed during recent years; and how many of them can look forward to a more secure future? Here we have another series of inquiries which, according to the promises contained in the Papal Bull, we might expect the Council to take into consideration.

6. At first sight only two answers seem possible to these questions. Either such a state of things is the effect of the education that prevails among the populations we have mentioned, or else the form of religion in question has assimilated itself, and has prospered best among the nations that exist under those conditions.

Some try to explain away these facts by alleging the unfavourable effects of climate and the fatality of race, but they forget that the same results are met with among different peoples and in different latitudes; and even if their hypothesis were admissible as to the first alternative, they could not escape from the second. Thus from which ever side the subject is viewed, we necessarily return to one of the two parts of the dilemma, both of which are equally deserving of the most serious consideration. The partisans of the absolute prefer to accept implicitly the second solution as being the most easy, though humiliating, for humanity, and, if true, involving irreparable evil;

while generous and liberal minds are content to take the first hypothesis as the least discouraging, and affording the best hope of remedy. Those who adhere to the former opinion exonerate existing institutions from all responsibility as to the evil wrought within their range, considering it sufficient that they oppose that evil, as, indeed, they do to the uttermost. But then, they overlook the responsibility inherent in these institutions, not only as to the substance of their teaching, but as to the way in which they set about their work ; and not only as to their aims, but as the means they use for carrying out their intentions. Indeed, an excess of zeal often leads to a contrary effect ; as, for example, absolutism generates rebellion, and extreme severity in a law secures impunity to the law breaker. Events balance themselves in human affairs, the chain which begins with the inquisitor finishes with the sectary ; and the partisan of Mazzini stands at one end of the diameter, the opposite point of which is occupied by the "Sanfedista." England does not possess either the *Univers* or the *Rappel*, at least her existence is not daily threatened by similar publications; neither has she inquisitors nor revolutionary fanatics, and Fenians come only from the neighbouring shores of Ireland.

7. Of course there are exceptions to the comparisons that we have made in this chapter, but they really illustrate those comparisons more clearly, because among the Catholic populations where they are found, they correspond in very exact measure to the influence that has been exercised by large and liberal ideas, or rather to that which has been lost by the contrary ideas, and thus they from a scale which, taking the Campagna di Roma as a starting point, culminates in the prosperity of Belgium. Moreover, there is another way of measuring these exceptions, less precise, but more convincing for Catholics, as being within the bosom of the Church itself, and that is, by means of those bishops who in the Council, resisted the spirit prevailing at the Vatican.

8. At the same time it would be not only unjust but useless to fasten the responsibility of these results upon Catholicism itself, one might as well charge them upon that Christianity which has animated all modern civilisation. Up to the sixteenth century there were no effective and visible distinctions amongst

Christians in the West, and the influence of the religious movement which was formally accomplished in that century only affected the civil and political condition of Europe at a later date. Still later within the bosom of the Catholic Church herself was more decidedly manifested that spirit (called in France Ultramontanism) which, rapidly increasing after the Revolution, and as a reaction from it, reacted again upon the Curia Romana, where it had first originated. Gaining ground there by little and little, it disclosed its own desires, pressed forward its own aims, and succeeded in giving a distinct and separate existence to those political and religious conceptions which, though habitually possessed by the Curia, had always hitherto preserved an indefinite character, having been wisely shrouded in the prudent and traditional policy of that body. Now, in our day, those ideas are crudely, and with much exaggeration, asserted by the party calling itself "Catholic" *par excellence,* which has exercised so great an influence in all that concerns the Vatican Council.

This became gradually visible at every outbreak of the revolutionary spirit, first in France and then generally in the world, though the chief causes of that revolution were the very system and the very ideas which in their latent state had prepared the way for it both in France, and in the other countries (principally Catholic), where revolution seems particularly rooted; because in such cases a tardy rebellion takes the place of the reformation undergone two centuries before, by the nations of the North. Perhaps even this reformation was affected by the resistance it encountered; and it is possible that both crises might have been moderated, or even prevented, by a slow and progressive transformation moving continually round the immutable centre of eternal truth, conformably with the variations of the times and of moral conditions. This idea, which some may consider daring, is not only confirmed by the example of those countries which are the most deeply affected by the evils we have enumerated, but receives satisfactory illustration from a strict and dispassionate investigation of the spirit that generally prevails in the education of Catholic populations. It would not be difficult to specify, one by one, the laws (and very often their interpretations), the customs, the institutions, the habits, and the abuses, which have long prevailed, but more especially in the latter centuries, in Catholic education; and are the principal causes of the evils we have indicated. It is certainly neither our desire nor our business to investigate fully these grave and complicated questions, many of which have been already well discussed; but wishing to assist with a few general outlines those who study the matter in good faith, some few salient points naturally occur to the mind. When these particular evils are understood, it remains for us to judge whether they can be remedied by empirical restrictions and fresh condemnations, or whether, on the other hand, it is not more likely that such remedies only serve to increase the evil, and like the doctors of an old Italian medical school who are much addicted to bleeding, in endeavouring to cure they do not really kill the patient.

9. The principle of authority by its very nature is predominant in Catholicism, of which, indeed, it is the strength and characteristic; but this principle, owing to the natural tendency of the institutions founded upon it, has been always exaggerated to such an extent in Catholic education, that on all subjects, and in every way, it has usurped the first place, and has produced the blindest submission corresponding to the most absolute power. This thirst for authority, called forth in the first instance by the insubordination of the age, and kept up with the view of maintaining order and unity in the Church, too often results in destroying the first and impairing the second; it tends to paralyse the collective action of the hierarchy of the Church, and concentrates it in the Head, thereby isolating the clergy from the rest of society. Moreover, the excessive use of authority in relation to the masses has the result of weakening and sometimes of suppressing the working of individual consciences, by absorbing their sense of personal responsibility in the sole conscience of Church authority, and so the perception of good and evil ceases to be personal and spontaneous, and becomes reflective and obligatory. It often happens that a Catholic, unless gifted with an unusual superiority of mind, has no knowledge of good and evil other than that which he derives from the external authority, which in many cases is represented by any chance individual. Nor is this only with regard to questions of principle, where such help may be sometimes both

desirable and salutary, but the same external direction is applied on all occasions, in all contingencies, in the every-day life of the people, and is carried by simple natures into trivial details, and matters of no importance.

The consequence of such an excessive submission to authority is that the human conscience, being often illguided, is likely to go astray; at any rate, never having learned to reflect and judge for itself, it loses the capacity for so doing, grows gradually weaker, and at last becomes impotent, just as the members of the body, if never used, lose their strength. A double evil, and a very serious one, results from this state of things. In the first place, when a Catholic, brought up as we have described, is deprived of the external guidance which supports him, he has no rule or restraint to keep him straight, and the recoil from such a despotism at the present day frequently throws the pupils of the Jesuits into the wildest revolutionary excesses. In the second place, the external authority can only find expression through words spoken or written, and being unable to follow the infinite complexities of human action or to discern the secret recesses of the human heart, cannot give a rule of right and wrong to meet all contingencies; so that there must still remain many cases in which an individual being without that guidance, can only ascertain the right course by consulting the delicate and indefinable instinct of his own conscience. Hence arise the subtleties, the mental compromises, and the disingenuousness too frequently met with, among our people.

10. Another tendency much to be deplored, is the disposition of Catholics to inculcate great intolerance for all errors of the intellect, while they regard with much leniency errors of the will; yet these latter are surely infinitely more culpable than the former.

It is deplorable that a man should not know and understand what is right; but if he is guilty, he is surely less so than a man who well knowing his duty, either neglects or transgresses it. Faults of intellect do not deteriorate the character, whereas faults of the will (making every allowance for human frailty) are far less excusable.

Dante lived in an age that was certainly not given to religious indifference or to be over tolerant, yet in the 'Divina Commedia' he places heresiarchs among those who err from want of self control, apart from the abode of those who had sinned with intent, thereby showing that he regarded the guilt of the first, as distinguishable from, and less worthy of punishment than that of the latter. Besides, the working of the mind has always an ennobling effect, while the indulgence of the passions brutalises human nature. A society educated for many centuries under the stimulus of the double direction we have described, not only loses the power of exercising the individual conscience, but yields up the exercise of its own judgment to a certain set or distinct class of persons whose duty it becomes to think and to judge for the rest. Such a society becoming disinclined and inapt for the exercise of thought on account of the trouble it involves, and following only the inclinations of nature, seeks what is pleasing to the feelings and affections, and readily transgresses by yielding to the passions which appear not only attractive in themselves, but, as we have already remarked, have the promise of greater tolerance than is extended to errors of the mind. We do not mean to say that severity in principle, and charity towards frailty, are not, when united with wisdom and moderation, two marvellous characteristics of Christianity— more true to human nature than a vague indecision on the first point, and an inflexible severity on the second; but having been abused, like many other good things, they led, the one to the institution of the Inquisition, and the other to the adoption of a systematised indulgence, and such subjects are surely well worthy of deep consideration on account of their influence on Catholic populations.

11. A third point for reflection, is the tendency of Catholic education to turn aside its followers from the numerous duties of practical life, and to incline them to an ascetic and speculative existence which does not always correspond to the inexorable necessities of human nature. Two evils result from this tendency when fully developed, as often occurs among the most faithful of the Catholic populations. The first is, that this tendency, when carried into private life by a mistaken application of a sublime contempt for terrestrial matters, disposes men to go through the world with their eyes turned upwards, and their thoughts entirely abstracted from the earth. Human nature soon takes advantage of such a disposition to

justify one of its most common and pernicious propensities; industry and independence give place to idleness and mendicancy; and this disposition when coupled with an abuse of outward forms often inclines people to superstition. The second evil, and one of equal importance, is, that a Catholic, though for the most part a good subject, is not always a good citizen, because though his religious education teaches him the duty of passive obedience, at the same time it tends to absorb him, and to draw him away from the civil society in which he moves; and these conflicting attractions of the Church and of society, though sometimes useful as counterpoises, really weaken Catholic communities, which are seldom able to unite the two interests and to conciliate the two powers.

Besides those eternal moral laws on which there can be but one opinion, there are an infinity of subjects which do not absolutely represent either good or evil; and with regard to which the Catholic is often placed in a difficult position between his kinsmen, his country, his station in life, and his Church. In such cases the Church either draws him to herself by a powerful attraction, or if he resists, abandons him and casts him out. Hence, the phenomenon frequently met with in Catholic societies, though rarely, if ever, in others, that religion hinders the advancement of the nation, and that patriotism subverts religion.

12. A fourth source of great difficulty for Catholic populations is the undue centralisation which prevails in the exercise of authority. All the laws, general and particular, which inform and regulate the consciences of the Catholic world, proceed, with the weighty sanction we have mentioned, from a very small nucleus; a narrow centre of individuals, who, with the best intentions and the greatest solicitude, are yet incapable of judging and of appreciating the varying feelings and needs of populations so many and so different. This fact tends to form instead of a Catholic world a Catholic party, gradually separating it in all countries from the habits, the interests, and the affections of the rest of the nation.

13. There remains a yet greater evil than any we have spoken of, and it is this; these tendencies and impulses if developed to the highest degree might form a society *sui generis*, little dis-

posed to intellectual or material growth, and little fitted for the production of civil greatness, and the mischief would stop here. The practical result, however, is that as such a *régime* can only apply to a restricted number of people, and never to society in general, the fetters imposed on the heart and intellect by this jealous authority, and this artificial state of mind, often produce, especially among the young, a corresponding reaction, and the more intelligent such people are, the stronger is this reaction. A great proportion of the young on reaching mature age are necessarily affected by the influence of the times; and being without the safeguards of solid instruction, and such an acquaintance with practical interests as would serve to restrain, or at least to occupy their minds, they look backwards, and in so doing fall into serious errors, confounding the abuses of a system with the system itself. In their retrospection they confuse God with the priest, become equally unmindful of both, and turning their backs on religion altogether, either rush headlong into the pursuit of pleasures, burying in them all the aspirations and regrets of a wasted life, or if of too noble a nature to incur such moral suicide, they fall into another snare equally dangerous, if in some ways less deplorable. Their ardent and youthful minds endeavour to find some means of reconciling the old faith with the newly enlightened reason, of making the two compatible, but as soon as they set about it, they discover such a process to be quite impracticable; for the Church endeavours in every way to repel them, and liberty presents every attraction that can allure them. In the face of this impossibility they are driven to revolt; no rebellion is so desperate as that of a slave, and youthful multitudes of great promise, but without conscience, unused to exercise their judgment, and blinded by the heritage of hatred and of rancour that results from the moral conflicts they have experienced, are driven to swell the ranks of revolution in increasing numbers, as one generation succeeds another.

They become involved in that terrible revolution whose standard is negation, and whose aim is destruction; that cosmopolitan revolution which has already avenged, and unless restrained by Providence may yet more deeply avenge such outraged souls. Those, meanwhile, on whom devolves the responsibility of such misfortunes will learn perhaps too late, and at too dear a price, that a just balance is indispensable both in the moral and material world; and that by endeavouring to make a man grow in the swaddling-clothes of an infant, either he will become a cripple, or his bands will be rent into shreds. All that has been said of the superior and intelligent portions of society, applies equally to the less cultivated and more impulsive multitudes, who with the same defects of character and reasoning power, pass through the like moral phases unconsciously and mechanically. The defects of the lower classes may be at first sight less apparent than those of their superiors, but when they do break out openly, the consequences are more disastrous. The result of this deadly conflict between authority and reason, between the spirit and the letter, is to diminish the number of the faithful in Catholic societies, and to drive many into rebellion in will or in deed; the first class are wanting in real force, the second lack not only order and discipline, but very often morality; both are proficients in the art of destroying Governments, but are alike incapable of establishing one on a solid basis, the first for want of power, the second for want of knowledge.

The first class are immovable instead of Conservative, the second revolutionary instead of progressive: they have no common ground, and their differences instead of finding expression in changes of administration (as happens in all rational countries) find it instead in changes of Government, in which there is always a conqueror and a conquered, and therefore a triumph and a defeat with the usual consequences. The happy results of a Conservative spirit, combined with the desire of progress, are found in all well-governed and prosperous nations; but from their very nature are difficult and almost impossible of attainment in Catholic countries, especially those in which the doctrines of absolutism prevail, for such usually relapse into confusion and disorder as soon as the strong pressure which an absolute Government exercises over them is removed. Disorder and anarchy are too often the lamentable political condition of the southern nations of Europe, as compared with the state of regular and uniform progress found among the northern; and this comparison affords ample grounds for reflection on the causes why revolution is so specially rooted in Catholic countries.

14. In addition to these primary considerations suggested by the condition of Catholic populations, others of still greater importance might be cited contingent on the ordinary course of events, and leaving untouched the defects of men, which naturally have deeply affected their institutions : but we will not proceed further, and would only remark in conclusion, that the religious education of our people is negative rather than positive; and though usually sufficient in externals (though even here greater elevation is desirable), is too often lacking in substance, that is to say, in the moral and practical part.

These remarks have already led us beyond the limits we had assigned to our subject, and therefore we merely leave this outline for the consideration of those who desire to study the matter more deeply. It is a true picture of the state of things prevailing at the present day in all communities governed by the Ultra-Catholic *régime*, though of course varying in different countries according to their respective conditions. We find in them many churches, but few schools; more devotion than virtue ; more passion than judgment ; general intolerance, and scanty prosperity, with fluctuations of submission and rebellion ; they are characterised everywhere by a craving for authority, whether in a convent or a sect, but without any appreciation of the real nature of authority, which is alternately adored with servility and subjected to outrage.

IV.—THE NEW ORDER.

1. Objections to preceding arguments.—2. Address of the Catholics of Coblentz.—3. Infallibility sole object of attention.—4. Close of the first phase of the Council.—5. The new Order.—6. Judgment of the majority.—7. Holidays.—8. Anecdotes.—9. Different *Postulata*.—10. Various publications.—11. Speech at the opening of the Exhibition.—12. Diplomatic interference is aroused.—13. Predictions.—14. Conclusion.

1. Owing to the entire lack of independence in judgment, and to a determination to look on all persons either as slaves or enemies, such observations as we have just made are usually considered to bear a hostile character, and are therefore held to be injurious by those to whom they are displeasing, and by all who follow in their steps. Such persons are accustomed to relieve themselves of any responsibility as to human affairs by charging the blame on particular associations, the Freemasons, for instance; and, in recent times, on the Government of the country. But the existence of those associations affords better ground for incrimination than for apology, inasmuch as they are not produced, and have no means of affecting society except by its institutions, in which they are generated as insects in bodies, a phenomenon depending on their own decay. This is illustrated by the fact that healthy and virtuous communities which live in the exercise of liberty, are either free from such organisations, or afford them no resting-place. Freemasonry has served much the same purpose for the Catholic party as the Society of Jesuits has for the Liberals; they are respectively accused as being the cause of all the evil in the world. Then, with regard to Governments, who doubts that if they had the chance they would very soon act up to the Pope's principle, so far as they could? whereas, at the present day, they are obliged to content themselves with such a measure of authority as is permitted by the spirit of the age.

2. Even among so-called Liberal Catholics, the religious question is rarely treated on general grounds. In nearly all the publications they have issued of late years, the subject is considered only partially, and not with that fulness which alone presents it in a true light. The address of the Catholics of

Treves* to the Archbishop of Coblentz, though of a special character, seems, however, to rise to a more elevated tone; and any Catholic wishing to find a remedy within the Church for the evils we have already noticed, might well adopt the words of the address, which are as follows :—

" We cannot hide from ourselves that it is impossible for a General Council to undertake the particular examination and solution of the difficulties arising from the numerous wants of mankind which are rooted in the manifold life of the Church. The organisation of the Church ought to establish in its various parts, with freedom to develop their powers in the most salutary manner, such agencies as may best overcome evil."

The address concludes by praying for the re-establishment of those assemblies, or synods, national, provincial, and diocesan, which have always considered and provided for the different needs, both old and new, of the Church in general, and for their portion of it in particular. Taken as a whole, this address is one of the most remarkable documents produced on these subjects. It contains an answer and a remedy for all the questions and all the evils which we have pointed out; and its theory of the relations between Church and State is the most precise and reasonable commentary, on the maxim, " A free Church in a free State." In few words, the address is a full and well-arranged scheme for applying the principle of liberty, so far as is possible, to Catholic institutions.

3. Instead, however, of attending to these questions, the whole consideration of the Council was irrevocably concentrated on the question of Infallibility. The definition of this dogma weighed on the Council and hampered all its movements, the majority had no other object but this, and followed it with that intensity of purpose which is peculiar to religious sentiments and passions. Human nature alternately builds up and destroys the same things, under the sincere conviction that it is making progress; overturns with infinite labour the despotisms and the oracles it originally fabricated, and then begins to reconstruct them, always under the belief that it is accomplishing something new, and despises what is past as if that in turn had not been equally its own work.

* See Appendix, Document XVI.

Ask the Infallibilists what they think of the apotheoses of the ancients ? or of the simplicity of certain religious beliefs which are entertained by other nations with a faith as lively and sincere as their own ? and they would shrug their shoulders in compassion without deigning to answer. Again, what are the Infallibilists themselves striving for so earnestly, but to create within their own Church and country a condition of things which, if found outside their circle, they would not even condescend to discuss?

Human nature never displays such violent passions as on religious matters; and though the form of their manifestation may be milder at the present day, the intensity of feeling when applied to such subjects is always the same.

Thirty-one meetings, including the two Sessions, were held between the 16th of December and the 22nd of February, in which about 150 orators spoke, and although no mention was actually made of Infallibility, it pervaded the minds of all, on every subject. Towards the end of February, in one of the last Congregations, a French bishop named Infallibility for the first time, and proposed its speedy declaration as a mode of cutting short all difficulties; but his speech was coldly received, and the allusion allowed to drop without producing any effect. Another bishop in the same Congregation made an open and violent attack on the Opposition, but his speech met also with disfavour. In fact, this second attempt on the part of the majority was received with vehement cries of " *Sufficit,*" it is enough ; which has always been the answer to propositions that failed in gaining public favour.

4. Great part of January was occupied by the scheme regarding the episcopate, which was finally sent back in the Congregation of the 24th, after a splendid speech by the Bishop of Bosnia and Sirmio, in which he urged the re-establishment of provincial and diocesan synods, a matter which had been strongly pressed by the Catholics of Cologne in their address. He also insisted on the necessity of the intervention of the bishops in all declarations issued in the Church, and deprecated their publication on the authority of the Pope alone, in the shape of Bulls or Briefs.

In saying this, he evidently alluded to the Bull on the limitation of censures, issued by the Pope before the opening of the Council, and he concluded by observing that the attempt to reduce the bishops to the position of mere officials of the Pope was contrary to the true spirit of the Church. The Bishop of Bosnia and Sirmio (Strossmayer) also reflected in this speech on the constitution of the College of Cardinals, and complained of the difficulties which attended the admission of eminent men of different countries into its ranks.

Strossmayer spoke later on the scheme "De Moribus Clericorum," but not so brilliantly as on this occasion, when he was said to have equalled the famous speech made at the opening of the Council by which he took rank as one of the principal orators. The scheme "De Moribus Clericorum" was under discussion from the 26th of January to the 8th of February, its aim being to give the bishops unlimited power over the priests, as an equivalent to the authority asserted by the Pope over the bishops in the scheme "De Episcopis." The French and the Spaniards warmly supported the former; but among those who opposed it, Monsignor Scissmor attracted much notice by a convincing and eloquent speech, in which he pointed out the tyranny and hardships that must inevitably result from the adoption of such a system.

The rest of February was occupied with the scheme, "De Catechismo," which was finally settled in the Congregation held on the 22nd, after forty members had spoken on the subject. On this day the first phase of the Council concluded. Its time had been occupied in sending back for revision all the propositions brought before it, and in proving the utter fallacy of that part of the programme announced by the *Civiltà Cattolica*, which promised a spontaneous and unanimous agreement among members of the Council.

5. On the 22nd of February the new Order was published, the result of the deliberations carried on with the view of imposing some limit on the length of the debates. Ten days' holidays were announced, in order that the Council might rest, and start again with renewed vigour along the road in which Rome never ceases to advance, even though her progress be slackened for a while.

The opinion of the Fathers was not asked, and the assembly

was not consulted on this new Order any more than on the former one; but, like the first, it was communicated to the Council, and carried into execution by the same authority, and with the intention which had prevailed from the beginning. It contains pretty nearly all those injunctions we have noticed, as emanating from the directive body in the Council, with this difference, that in future it should be optional and not obligatory on the Fathers to present their speeches in manuscript to the Commissions; and providing that when they did so, the Commissions should print those speeches in a compendious form, and distribute them to the bishops.

Of course it followed that when the Fathers preferred simply to recite or to read their speeches, they should be allowed to do so, and therefore no real innovation was made; but the same document contained two articles, which were its " raison d'être," and contained the spirit of the new Order. The first article authorised the president to cut short an orator every time he wandered from the subject under debate; this seemed, at first sight, a simple expedient for regulating the discussion, but one of the presidents took occasion to make it severely felt on the very day on which it came into operation.

Monsignor Haynald, Bishop of Colocza, one of the most prominent bishops in the Opposition, made some historical quotation, which showed that on the occasion of the reform of the Roman Breviary, a Pope had expressed an opinion contrary to that of the present majority in the Council; and the president immediately requested him to stop, and to descend from the tribune. Such interference on a slight matter the first day that it was practicable plainly indicated to the Opposition the view that the presidents entertained of the new authority given to them. The second article was still more important, for it provided that any debate might be brought to an end when the subject had been "satis excussa," on the proposal of not fewer than ten Fathers. It declared also that when the closing was proposed it should be decided at once, and that the opinion of the majority alone was requisite on the matter. The practical result of such an arrangement was to constitute the majority sole and absolute arbiter of the debates, since it could either permit them or stop them entirely at its own pleasure.

It is true that the article says the matter must have been "satis excussa," but who was to judge of this condition? The majority again? In fact, judgment by the majority prevailed throughout the new Order, for it provided that the different parts of any scheme, and its amendments also, should be voted by the "rising or sitting" of the Fathers," and that by it "decernetur" the result of the vote of the majority.

The definitive oral vote on the whole scheme was given by saying "Placet" or "Non placet;" but nothing further was decreed with regard to it, as here the Pope's authority is touched on, an authority which will not endure the slightest diminution or qualification, and which, by its individual action can change the scheme into a decree.

6. The idea that pervades these modifications is clearly that, as it was impossible to obtain unanimity in the Council, it was necessary to be content with the vote of the majority, this last being, in fact, already so well organised and homogeneous, that full trust might be placed in it. Moreover, this was the most obvious and legal means of subduing the Opposition.

Accordingly, by the new Order everything was left to the judgment of the majority, and this arrangement gave great importance to a clause which could prejudge to the detriment of the interests of the Opposition one of the gravest questions before the Council, that, namely, of the necessity of unanimity in its decisions. The immediate danger for the Opposition, under the new Order, was that, by the aid of its provisions, the Infallibilists might, within a week, arrest the discussion on the scheme "De Ecclesia," vote its acceptance, and present it to the Pope for his approbation.

It may be inferred that they did not intend at once to avail themselves of this facility, from the fact that an injunction was inserted in the rule obliging those who objected to any measure not to be content with opposing it, but to bring forward some other proposal in its stead. This proviso would have been useless had the intention of the authorities been to impose the schemes *illico et immediate* on the minority; but it is well to point out what might have been the logical results of the new Order.

The power of the majority once established, the minority was as much at its mercy in the Council as in any secular assembly;

with this difference, however, that the judgments of the latter, if mistaken, can be revoked, whereas those of the Council, from the fact of their dealing with absolute truths, and from the mode of their enunciation, are irrevocable.

Indeed, the Papacy is an institution so well organised and established in the Church, that like the ship which is its symbolical image, it always floats, however tossed by the waves. In the scheme the Papacy condemns the majority, in the Order it approves it, without fearing to seem contradictory, since the two decisions equally rest on its own unlimited authority.

7. A new scheme, "On Religious Orders," was distributed in the Congregation of February 22nd, together, it was said, with a general index of the business before the Council, and after all these important events, began the promised ten days' vacation. This interval divides the first phase of the Council, which we have already considered, from the second now to be inaugurated on a new system, the working of which was as yet uncertain and dangerous in proportion as the pressure of the majority and consequent resistance of the minority were more deeply felt.

At first the Opposition did not make the same objections to the new Order as they did later. Most of the bishops were originally in favour of a reform, the principle of which seemed, with regard to an Assembly, natural and useful, but the danger lurking beneath it soon became apparent; and the Opposition felt that, if once accepted, their situation would become daily more difficult, and their ultimate defeat undoubted.

To reject the Order was, however, no easy matter. The Opposition felt that if sometimes the majority were wrong in pressing their opinion, the minority were certainly wrong in disregarding it. Moreover, the fate of the addresses put forth against the first Order was by no means encouraging for those who were now inclined to make a similar attempt. The prorogation of the assembly left all in doubt; the future course of the Opposition was unknown, but it was expected that, after deliberation, they would adopt some definite line of action.

8. Before closing the narration of February's events, we may mention certain occurrences which plainly indicated the popular feeling at the time. Dupanloup in one of his speeches had given the cardinals to understand that they would do well to

follow the example of their predecessors in those ages when the Sacred College manifested greater independence and firmness. Cardinal Di Pietro, in his answer, tried to turn the tables upon Dupanloup, by observing that if any strictures could be passed on the Sacred College they were due to the conduct of cardinals of old, and not to those of the present day. Perhaps the prelates were both right up to a certain point: there was nothing remarkable in the reflection, and such encounters were common between the Opposition and the majority. It happened, however, that the day on which these speeches were made, Dupanloup lost part of his manuscript between his house and the Vatican; the event in itself was entirely unimportant, but it arrested public attention, and furnished ample scope for conjecture to those who were anxiously looking out for gossip concerning the Council; in fact, it was difficult to make them believe that a bishop might lose his papers, like another mortal, without any mysterious or extraordinary results.

Some amusing incidents occurred from time to time, and served to enliven the monotony of the meetings; among these may be mentioned the speech of a Neapolitan bishop on the long coat worn by the clergy, which provoked much merriment among the venerable Fathers of the Council.

9. During the vacation, all sorts of new propositions sprang up, and the bishops spent the time in collecting fresh materials —as if there were not enough already—wherewith to put to the test the small amount of faith yet prevailing in the nineteenth century. One of these propositions on the Assumption of the Virgin had been already announced by the *Civiltà Cattolica;* and there was another brought forward by the Oriental bishops, and reported in the *Univers,* to the effect that the Church should issue some declaration to repress and limit the rights of war. It is pleasing to find this charitable thought amid so many anathemas and condemnations, but it was due to Copts and Armenians!

10. The Liberal Catholic party continued to issue publications of great interest, and among these Döllinger's article on the address of the Infallibilists holds the first place. Döllinger received the congratulations of Cologne, Bonn, Münster, Breslau, Fribourg, Tübingen, Prague, and other great intellectual centres

in Germany; of the universities and theological faculties, even those whose opinions were unlike his own; and all these addresses praised his firmness, expressed their concurrence with him, and encouraged him to persevere. On the other side of the Alps, the principal publications were Maret's defence of his own book and the letters of Père Gratry. In Italy pamphlets appeared with increasing frequency, one written with great force and accuracy, but anonymously, was entitled 'The Pretended Infallibility of the Pope.'

11. The Pope's speech, on opening the Exhibition of Art applied to Catholic worship, awoke great interest, for in it he made a declaration little expected, and which was certainly out of place on the occasion. He affirmed that it was not only wrong, but blasphemous for any to say that the Church needed reform, alluding to words recently used by a distinguished individual which had provoked his displeasure. This person was not named; but a double interpretation was put on the Pope's speech. It seems that one of the leaders of the French Liberal party, irritated by the proceedings of Rome, of which he had once been a warm supporter, had, in conversation with a friend, expressed himself openly on the matter by declaring that the Church needed an "89." The Pope cited, and condemned the phrase, and the Liberal Catholics thought that they recognised in his allusion a condemnation of their leader; the Ultramontane papers, moreover, took a malignant pleasure in pressing this meaning, in order to vex them. This is the first interpretation.

The *Osservatore Romano*, on the other hand, hastened to give a contrary view, by asseverating that the Pope had specifically attributed these words to "the great Italian demagogue"— a denomination which, though vague, certainly excluded a French Catholic. This was the second interpretation. If this latter view were the true one, the Pope had apparently mistaken the date; for though a French Catholic might naturally on such an occasion have alluded to the year '89, an Italian demagogue would rather, in the present condition of the public mind, have referred to '93.

If the Pope's speech, as appears most probable, were really directed against the French Liberal Catholics, they would only be receiving the same treatment which they tried to inflict on the

Italian Liberals; and under this aspect their punishment would be merited. If the phrase which produced such an effect be taken by itself, it is just as indefinite as most of those in the Syllabus, and, having no certain meaning, lends itself equally to the favourable and unfavourable comments made upon it. If by the word Reform, the reform of Luther be understood, the Pope could not be expected to praise it; if necessary changes only are understood, the existence of the Council proves its desirability. If there were nothing requiring change, what was the use of summoning the Vatican Council three centuries after the last that was held? But supposing there were something to change, there was something to reform; so if the Pope used the phrase in an absolute sense, he condemned himself for having summoned the Council; and this opinion would be perhaps in accordance with that of several prelates, and even of some cardinals of the Roman Curia.

12. Recent events, especially the knowledge of the maxims of public ecclesiastical law contained in the scheme "De Ecclesia," produced a change in the attitude of the Catholic Powers with regard to the Council; and according as the Church seemed indisposed to recognise the liberty of the State, they began to look with suspicion on the liberty of the Church. Up to the present time little notice had been taken of the Council except by the representatives of the smaller Catholic nations; but now the great Powers, and France in particular, instructed their ambassadors to pay closer attention to the subject, and to bring their influence to bear upon the proceedings at the Vatican. Rome, however, with her great diplomatic ability, knew how to avert their interference, and it is supposed that the fall of the Bavarian Ministry at that time was due to her influence; Bavaria was the only country that comprehended the gravity of the situation, and had acted with an amount of energy hardly warranted by the rank she held among other Catholic Powers.

Now that Rome was freed from an embarrassment by the downfall of the Bavarian Ministry, it might have been supposed that the great Powers would come forward and act in the matter. Accordingly there was some talk of ambassadors being sent to the Council by the Catholic Powers, according to ancient usage, thus renouncing the policy of abstention, from which Rome drew all the profit. Special mention was also made of an ambassador to be sent from France to Rome, in addition to the one already there accredited to the Holy See, but no name was mentioned. The Vatican, meanwhile, had so well learnt to play its part as "a free Church" that any ambassador who should succeed hereafter in taking part in a Congregation of the Council would give proof of no slight dexterity, and no common knowledge of his profession. Whatever these official intentions may have been, it is nevertheless true that the attention of Europe was now turned to the Vatican, and public opinion occupied itself with the Council more than was desired at Rome. Germany was the source of the greatest disquietude to the Vatican. Some symptoms of discussion also appeared in Italy, and none too soon, for we must admit that, though she exercises considerable influence in such matters, which are not new to her, Italy is very slow to move, and usually waits to follow the initiative of the Northern nations. The clergy of Milan thanked their Archbishop for not signing the petition for Infallibility, and besought him to uphold the rites and the dignity of the Ambrosian Church.

In the East heavy storms were gathering. The Oriental Christian communities were so irritated by the attempted abolition of their prerogatives, and by the subserviency to Rome manifested by some of their bishops at the Council, that a schism appeared probable in consequence; and schisms flourish wonderfully in the East, where many persons are quite ready to foment them to their own advantage. The danger became apparent at Rome, and some steps were taken to quell the storm, although the authorities continued to pursue the same line of conduct with regard to the East as before. On the other hand, no notice was taken of the opposition of the West, and it seemed strange that the threatened loss of a few Armenians should stir the Vatican more deeply than the representations of numbers of the most intelligent men in Europe.

13. In all respects the condition of the Council remained unchanged; the relative position of its parties, the probable results of its action, continued the same. Its duration was uncertain; but the Archbishop of Paris, in a letter to the Archdeacon of Notre Dame, said " that his return to Paris would be undoubtedly

at Easter, whether the work of the Council were already completed by that time, or whether it were to be resumed the December following." According to this calculation, there only remained to the Council six weeks of the current year in which to complete its deliberations, and therefore this opinion, notwithstanding the position of its author, was not considered to be well founded. Other people, more patient, looked for the closing, or, at any rate, the suspension of the Council at the feast of St. Peter in June—a supposition strengthened by the invariable cessation of work in Rome at that season. The real struggle in the Council remained unaltered as to its purpose— " Would the Opposition succeed in preventing absolutism from gaining supremacy in the Church ?" This was the great question on which all others depended, as they were relatively secondary and unimportant; and here three hypotheses were possible. First.—Supposing the Opposition to be vanquished and unable to control the majority, it was probable, from the prevailing temper on both sides, that most of the States, at present Catholic, would cease to be so in fact, at least in regard to the principles that govern modern civilised institutions—and with them a large number of the noble and intelligent minds, who hitherto had remained within the bosom of the Church ; and the Church herself, weakened by her losses, and finding herself at the mercy of an individual will, would be violently driven forward on a perilous course, the issue of which no human being could estimate or foresee.

Secondly. Should the Opposition succeed in modifying in any degree, more in form than in substance, the proposals of the majority, very little real change would be effected in the economy of the Church; excepting that the Curia Romana would consider the results of the Council as a new precedent to be remembered favourably for those who had sided with it, leaving the others unnoticed until a fresh opportunity should arise of resuming the interrupted work, and bringing it to an end.

Thirdly. Should the Opposition really succeed in arresting the movement towards absolutism, a reform might begin, of which this fact, and even the Council itself, would only be the prologue. But this end, though a very modest one, seemed already most difficult of attainment. A sense of alarm prevailed generally in the Opposition, and the *Augsburg Gazette*, one of its most authoritative organs, did not disguise its fears as to the final success of the great question of Reform.

14. The majority which ruled and was in its turn ruled by the Catholic party, entangled the Opposition in the confused mazes of ancient laws, traditions, and expedients, which it could handle, from long practice, with consummate art. The Opposition, while involved in these toils, were kept in good order and obedience by ecclesiastical discipline and the respect due to the Holy Keys; and found great difficulty in throwing off the yoke of a party possessing so many advantages, and striving so pertinaciously for what it considered the ideal development of the Church. Facts were, however, opposed to these just arguments, and during the three months the Council had lasted, no solution had yet been found for the principal question, or any of the others submitted to its deliberation.

MARCH.

I.—APPENDIX TO THE SCHEME "DE ECCLESIA."

1. Distribution of Appendix to the scheme "De Ecclesia."—2. Foreign influence.
—3. Plans for leaving the Council.—4. Great discouragement.—5. More on politics.—6. Recall of the French ambassador.

1. ON the evening of Monday, the 7th of March, it was discovered that an Appendix to the scheme "De Ecclesia" had been distributed to the bishops, which proposed the declaration of the personal Infallibility of the Pope, in faith and morals, on the ground that it was desired by most of the bishops in the Council. This Appendix was put forth at a moment when the Opposition had scarcely recovered from their amazement in regard to the new Order, and when many of the bishops manifested their increasing disapproval of the fact that it vested decisive power in the majority, rather than in the unanimity of the Fathers, and that it enabled the presidents to encroach on the liberty of discussion. The Appendix was, in fact, the famous "*postulatum*" contained in the address of the Infallibilists—which had aroused so much ill-will, and now reappeared with the approval of the Commission on "*Postulata*," the ground having been prepared by the new Order. This document affirmed that the Infallibility of the Pope should be considered as entirely and on every point equivalent to the infallibility of the whole Church.

This axiom was clearly expressed in a periodical published in North Italy, called *The Ecumenical Council*, by the algebraic formula: $a = a + b$, a formula which can only be verified when b, which in this case represented the episcopate, is zero. Some people might be unwilling to admit the idea suggested by this paper, and so Maret proposed another view of the difficulty; he affirmed that Infallibility was a mystery as incomprehensible as the doctrine of the Trinity. The new Appendix, of which we are treating, concluded by expressly declaring—that every one professing a disbelief in Infallibility must be considered beyond the pale of the Catholic Church.

2. This last declaration broke like a thunder-clap over the Opposition. No one expected such an assertion, and all were astonished at it; even those not immediately occupied in ecclesiastical matters. It involved a departure from the prudence and patience usually characteristic of the Roman Curia, which had never before professed doctrines either so absolute in themselves, or expressed in so absolute a form, and certainly had never employed such violent means to attain its ends. It seemed as though a northern Ultramontane blast had blown over the cautious and patient Curia, and rendered its proposals more cutting by its chilling influence. A great commotion ensued; and the Opposition were in a state of confusion, almost amounting to despair.

3. On the publication of the new Order, it was evident to the Opposition that, if they consented to continue the discussion under the conditions it established, their position would be hopeless; and they debated whether it would not be advisable to protest, and leave the Council entirely, such a course being the only one yet open to them if they did not take the road of their own dioceses. When, however, the bishops in Opposition began to reckon up the names of those who would agree to this step, their number was found to be small. At first it was said that eighty might be depended upon; but subsequently even the most ardent admitted that from thirty to fifty only would be found prepared for so extreme a measure as that of leaving the Council.

4. The publication of this new Appendix caused much alarm and disturbance in the ranks of the Opposition, for its intention was unmistakable. The new Order had already authorised the closing a debate at the judgment and desire of the majority. The proposal of Infallibility included a *monitum* of the Commission that had approved the "postulatum," and (together with the presidents) greatly influenced the direction of the Council, by which the time for presenting written observations on the

subject itself was limited to ten days. A clause was also added to the declaration of Infallibility, which distinctly affirmed that all who did not submit to the dogma were out of the Church. The Opposition saw the danger of their situation ; the majority might vote the scheme " De Ecclesia " and the Appendix in ten or fifteen days, and then they would find themselves out of the Church. If the natural timidity of persons under ecclesiastical discipline be remembered, and the intolerable position in which they are placed by being cast out of the pale of the Church, as well as all the considerations and precedents that bind them, it will easily be understood that the bold step of the majority caused the utmost dismay among the minority. The most sincere and resolute leaders of the Opposition were greatly discouraged, and it almost seemed at that moment as if the *Civiltà Cattolica* were right, and that the Jesuits had conquered.

5. According to their usual practice in moments of imminent peril, the Opposition now had recourse to the aid of diplomacy ; every one turned for help to the representative of his own country, but on this occasion with less success than before. The attention of the different Governments of Europe which had been aroused and directed to the Council had again subsided, and they returned to their former attitude of inaction.

No excuse can be found for this carelessness at a period when such important matters were under discussion—matters in many ways directly concerning those very Governments themselves. The traditional policy of Rome has always possessed the extraordinary faculty of turning its misfortunes as well as its successes to its own advantage; it has profited equally by the enthusiasm of bygone centuries, and by the indifference of the present age. Such a policy, with a settled line of action, easily adapts itself to the difficulties it meets with in order to obtain the desired end ; the Vatican party during the Council followed this course, and it succeeded. The Governments of Europe being impressed with the general decline of religious feeling, and therefore with the slight influence it would exercise on the life and interests of nations, affected great negligence for all that concerned religion. Rome had long profited by this liberty, and now the Council benefited by it likewise. The Governments laid aside the prevision and caution they usually exercised.

The Vatican was not slow to take advantage of this calm, and its adherents immediately drew up the scheme "De Ecclesia," which asserts the entire subordination of society to the authority of the Pope, with a precision never yet adopted in the formulas of the Roman Curia. Whatever opinions may be entertained on the decay of religious feeling in general, to overlook what was going on in the Vatican Council, was undoubtedly to confound the political with the historical question. Whatever may be the future relations of Church and State in conjunction with modern institutions; Catholicism is, *de facto et de jure*, the predominant, if not the sole religion of the majority of the Latin races, and therefore the manner in which it is taught and exercised, and the individuals to whom is confided its direction, cannot be indifferent to civil rulers.

All the Catholic Governments failed in discharging this duty of vigilance with regard to the Council, Bavaria only seeming to understand its importance. Some countries were by a singular chance incapacitated from exercising any influence in the matter; Spain being in a state of utter disorder, and Italy (as Visconti Venosta observed, in reply to a question on the subject in the Italian Chambers) being, from political circumstances, dissevered from all relations with Rome, and unable to influence her in any way. France held in her hands the fate of the Papacy, France guarded the doors of the Vatican Council, and though she did not respect the liberty of others, she ought at least to have respected the liberty of her own religion. France ought not to have remained deplorably indifferent while her own religion was being remoulded and modified anyhow, without endeavouring to intervene and to exercise a legitimate influence on the Council; though in her own case the sad result would be that of showing herself, according to circumstances, alternately "the Catholic nation" or the nation of "89," and as extreme in the one character as in the other.

6. The French and Austrian ambassadors had met the reiterated appeals made to them by the bishops on the publication of the new Order with the greatest official suavity. Their respective Governments had never really changed the instructions given them from the first—to maintain the strictest neutrality. The only exception to this fact (if it be considered of any

importance) may be noticed in the official and semi-official letters of Count Daru, which produced on the Court of Rome the effect already described by Monti, in referring to the *tremenda vanità di Francia*, which as he expresses it, *sul Tebro è nebbia che dal sol si doma*. It is true that the only result of the last remonstrances made by the Minister of Foreign Affairs, with a view to the reform of the Order, was, if I mistake not, the publication of the proposal of Infallibility. The bold and rapid strides of the majority, and the faint resistance of the Opposition, had for a moment aroused the French Government, which then proposed to send orators or envoys to the Council; but the result of this slight movement was to cause the hasty and unexpected distribution of the proposal of Infallibility to the bishops, and it was said that this sort of *coup d'état* once accomplished, Rome no longer objected to receive the ambassadors from France. Indeed, when the entire programme of the Council was known, and its discussion commenced, no danger was to be apprehended from any Cæsarean envoys; for it was easy to take shelter from their representations under the authority of the assembly, and in the event of their arrival their sole office would be quietly to watch the logical development of the official part of a drama, the success of which it was already easy to foretell.

France had undoubtedly proposed to exercise some interference in conjunction with the other Catholic powers, but the idea was coldly received. Spain and Italy declined to move at all in the matter of the Council, the Spanish Minister of Foreign Affairs sending a circular to that effect to his diplomatic agents, and Visconti Venosta in the speech already mentioned, declaring the opinion of the Italian Government. This attempt at combined action having failed, there was no further talk of orators being sent to the Council, either because the Pope interposed difficulties, or because the French Government, foreseeing what would be the position of its ambassador, thought well to let the matter drop, and the diplomatic movement found vent in an interchange of letters and explanations between the Vatican and the Tuileries. The French ambassador was summoned to Paris to give an account of his conduct; but this sign of displeasure was transitory, only for some days was there a talk of his definitive recall, and, in fact, the excellent Monsieur de

Banneville very soon reappeared at his post in Rome, where his influence mainly contributed to encourage the Infallibilists and reduce the Opposition to despair.

II.—A TRUCE.

1. Death of Count de Montalembert.—2. Funeral service in his honour.—3. More petitions by the bishops.—4. Article by Döllinger.—5. Suspension of the scheme " De Ecclesia."

1. The Count de Montalembert was just dead. He, like a few others, had found himself placed in so hard and painful a position by the moral condition of France and his own convictions, that after having striven all his life to sacrifice his liberal ideas for the sake of his religion, on his death-bed he found himself almost abandoned by his religion on account of his liberalism. Many lamented him as an eloquent and learned man ; only a few private friends and an inconsiderable party could follow him in his laboured mediation between the temporal power and Infallibility, and could therefore feel his loss as a politician, or as the representative of a great idea, excepting in so far as his name had strengthened the Opposition, and his great talents had helped their cause. His death, however, aroused in some measure the religious passions of the Vatican. The letter with which Montalembert closed his life, as well as his political and religious career, is well known ;* its frank and noble language is a legacy for which generous and liberal minds will ever hold him in grateful remembrance ; but it produced a very different effect on the ruling party at the Vatican. It seemed to arouse the ancient enmity against the liberal Catholic party, and the Pope went so far as to speak of M. de Montalembert before a large auditory in very unfavourable terms. The friends of the Count, however, were determined to render homage to his memory, and arranged a funeral service in his honour at the Church of Aracœli. This church was particularly connected with the Roman municipality, and Montalembert had been made a Roman patrician for the good offices he rendered to the Government on the occasion of the French expedition to Rome.

* See Appendix, Document XV.

As soon as the Pope was aware of the intended service, he prohibited its celebration, and those who were invited to attend received notice that the function would not take place on the appointed day. Notwithstanding this prohibition, a few bishops and members of the diplomatic body, along with some personal friends of Montalembert's, went to the church at the time fixed; some because they would not yield to such an arbitrary injunction, and more, because they were really unaware of the interdiction issued by the Pope. They found at the church a notice similar to that sent round to their houses, and they were obliged to depart without even being able to obtain the celebration of a low mass for the departed, at which they would have assisted without any pomp or grand solemnity. This occurrence made a deep impression on all, and was the culminating point of that phase of oppression, which commencing, with the reform of the Order of the Council, had already attained the unlooked-for proposal of Infallibility, and now ventured to forbid the celebration of a loving and pious service to one who bore the name of De Montalembert.

2. And now we come to a truce, or rather a movement which might be called a step backwards were it not to be succeeded by a bound forwards. The *Osservatore Romano* announced that the Pope, wishing to testify his recollection of all the services rendered to the Church by Count de Montalembert, had personally assisted at a service for the repose of his soul, held in the Church of the Traspontina. The truth was that the advisers of the Vatican—either of their own accord, or because they were aware of the unfortunate impression caused by the intolerance of the previous day and were desirous of making up for it—had during the night arranged this funeral celebration, at which the Pope assisted next morning unknown to all, so that the friends of the Count had no chance of being present.

Europe received by telegraph the announcement of the honours paid by the Pope to the memory of M. de Montalembert, but on those who were cognisant of this event it produced a very strange impression. The reasons adduced by the friends of the Vatican for having thus endeavoured to prevent a demonstration which, on account of the nature of Montalembert's later opinions, might seem undesirable, could not, however, avail to justify the effect produced by the intervention of the authorities, and the employment of force, in order to prevent dignitaries of the Church, Fathers of the Council, and other persons of position and eminence, from rendering to their friend what even the poorest anxiously procure for those they love—the last offices after death. And yet this happened in the case of one of illustrious name, who had deserved well of the Church.

3. The bishops, recovering from their first stupor, and seeing how little aid they could expect from diplomacy, had again adopted, after much wavering, the plans which had already proved so unsuccessful, of framing protests and petitions against the Order. In these they demanded chiefly three things:— 1st. The abolition of the limits of time imposed on the study and discussion of the schemes. 2nd. The creation of a mixed Commission, in which controverted points might be orally debated before being altered. 3rd. That all decisions should depend, invariably, not on the vote of the majority, but on the moral unanimity of the Fathers.

4. At the very time when the bishops in Opposition made these protests in Rome, an article signed by Döllinger appeared in the *Augsburg Gazette*, which set forth clearly the grounds on which the Church of Germany would be compelled to secede, unless the Council stopped short of the fatal precipice to which its course was tending.* The object of this article was to point out that no Council had ever been fettered by an Order, that the principal Councils had none at all, and that when an Order was first introduced, as in the more recent Councils, it was always voted unanimously by the Fathers themselves. The article also affirmed that no solemn declarations were ever made in the Church, otherwise than with unanimous consent, for this reason; that the Council in a certain sense cannot create new dogmas, but can only render testimony to those which rest on the universal consent of the Church. According to this principle, not only is the majority incapable of making dogmas (which is admitted by all), but it cannot even attest them; for the very ideas of a majority and a minority are at variance with the idea of universality, the latter beginning where the former ends. By this important document it appears that a Council which is sub-

* See Appendix, Document XVII.

jected to a rule not framed by itself, a Council which creates dogmas by its own authority, and in addition to this accepts the decision of the majority only, has not the characteristics necessary to make it an Ecumenical Council. This opinion, in plain words, means that the Vatican Council, under its present conditions, would not be accepted as an Ecumenical Council by those whose opinions were described in the article. Such was the language of Germany; while in the East protests and menaces increased, until an actual split took place among the Armenian Catholics on the question of the nomination of their bishops, on which point they are extremely jealous.

5. Whatever weight may be attributed to these manifestations of public opinion, or be ascribed to the influence of laymen and diplomatists, which, though slight, was yet felt, one thing is certain—the immediate discussion of the scheme, " De Ecclesia," and of the Appendix to the declaration of Infallibility, was dropped. All that we have described took place during the adjournment of the Council, which occurred on the sending back of the first schemes and the publication of the new Order. Instead of lasting ten days, as announced in the Congregation of February 22nd, this adjournment lasted twenty-five days; and when the Council met again it was not occupied with the scheme " De Ecclesia," but with the amended schemes, and thus the Opposition obtained a little respite from the severe and unexpected pressure which had reduced them to such extremities.

III.—THE FIRST SCHEMES AGAIN BROUGHT FORWARD.

1. The first schemes again brought forward.—2. Stormy sitting.—3. Protest of the Bishop of Bosnia and Sirmio.—4. Speech of the Pope.—5. Incidents relating to the Eastern bishops.—6. Theme for a speech at the Roman university.—7. Withdrawal of some amendments.—8. Reasons for the same.— 9. Despatches of Count Daru and of Cardinal Antonelli.—10. Ambassadors.— 11. Relations between France and the Vatican.—12. The scheme " De Fide " voted in part.—13. Catholic Art Exhibition.—14. The same.

1. Such was the state of affairs when, on Friday, March 18th, the Congregations were resumed after a holiday in which many important events had occurred; the sitting was occupied with the scheme " De Fide," now brought forward for the second

time, after its emendation, by the proper Commission. Notwithstanding its amended form, it met with much opposition. Five orators had inscribed their names for the debate, but three only had spoken, when the Congregation was interrupted, that the Fathers might attend one of those ceremonies which have become frequent of late years, owing to the Pope's fondness for outward display. According to an old custom, it was usual for the Pope on a Friday in March to descend from his apartments to the Church of St. Peter, in order to visit the relics which are preserved in the gallery behind the tribune; and on this occasion, the sitting of the Council was suspended, and the Fathers left the Hall to accompany him. It seems that some striking result had been expected from this Congregation, for one of the Fathers who favoured the majority suddenly endeavoured, as if by "chance," to obtain a declaration of Infallibility, but only a small number supported him; and if the Infallibilists had really pre-arranged this surprise during the recess they must have been much disappointed at its results. No other incident marked the opening of the Congregations.

2. The next sitting, on Tuesday, March 22nd, was a memorable one, as on that occasion the storm which had long been gathering under the pressure of recent events burst forth. Three orators contributed to bring it to a climax. First, Cardinal Schwarzemberg, Archbishop of Prague, then the Bishop of Grenoble, and finally Strossmayer, the effect of whose speech was such that the adjournment of the sitting was called for. The principal subjects that provoked the anger of the majority were: first, the defence of the proposals made by the Opposition for obtaining greater liberty in debate, and rejecting the judgment of the majority and all the provisions of the new Order; secondly, the continued objections to the amended schemes, as still containing excessive and useless condemnations, which the Opposition asserted were likely to produce a bad rather than a good effect on those who were not Catholics; and lastly, the exception taken to the form of the scheme, which was admitted by all to be faulty. Certain words used in attacking the judgment of the majority, offended the greater part of the bishops present; words hinting that delicate comparisons might be drawn between the votes of the Fathers according to the importance

of the flocks they represented. This question, although a difficult one, was, however, absorbed in the more important matter of determining whether the unanimity of a Council or the votes of a majority of its members should, by its decision, constitute a Canon ; and here the first storm arose.

The intolerance of the majority was further provoked by some words in which, while discussing the second subject, justice was rendered to certain Protestants by name ; and here a second outbreak occurred, more violent than any which had yet taken place. Schwarzemberg, whose speech had been the first occasion of the storm, was ordered to desist by the legate De Angelis ; and on attempting to begin again, met with so much interruption, by cries of " sileat " from the majority, that he was obliged to omit some of his discourse, and bring it to an abrupt conclusion. Strossmayer, who caused the second tempest, was three times ordered to stop by the legate Capalti, the last time in a way anything but courteous. He replied that he was tired of being thus called to order, and thwarted on every point ; that such proceedings were incompatible with freedom of debate, and that he protested against them. At this a storm broke forth, the Fathers left their seats and crowded round the tribune ; threats and menaces of every sort—" e suon di man con elle ";* cries of " Viva Pio IX. ! " " Vivan i Cardinali Legati ! " were heard in different accents in the no longer venerable assembly. One cardinal cried, " You protest against us, we protest against you ; " and other utterances equally serious and serene proceeded from every part of the hall ; in fact, the uproar was so formidable, that some confusion ensued outside, in the church itself. Certain partisans of Infallibility, on hearing the disturbance, imagined that it signified the spontaneous passing of that dogma by acclamation, as had been predicted, and were ready to add their shouts of triumph on the happy event ; others, of a contrary opinion, prepared to mock at these rejoicings ; and St. Peter's was very nearly the scene of a tumult. The ubiquitous gendarme, however, who is the last argument in every discussion, and the strongest and most effective instrument of every sort of Infallibility, here interfered, ordered off the crowd—who were

* " Sounds of hands with these."
Ford's Dante, *Inf.* iii., 27.

pressing eagerly round the door of the Council Hall, and met with no resistance save from the servants of some of the bishops, who, on hearing the cries from within, feared that their masters were threatened by some dangers in that tumultuous assembly, and tried to enter the hall to assist them.

3. The day after this storm, Strossmayer, having been admonished by his colleagues that such resistance exceeded the limits of what was lawful, took upon himself the sole responsibility of the occurrence, and presented a protest in his own name against the threats and pressure to which he had been subjected at the preceding meeting, not only with regard to the question of principle, but with regard to all that he had so energetically opposed—as the restrictions on freedom of debate, judgment by the majority, and the other points which we have mentioned.

At the first private meeting in which the leaders of the Opposition of different countries met together, Strossmayer was received with the warmest expressions of regard; and almost all, though they had not actually signed his protest, declared themselves in favour of it.

4. The Pope soon made his opinion on the matter known, in a speech he delivered when distributing to the missionary bishops the ecclesiastical vestments and ornaments sent from Belgium by a society of pious ladies, called "L'Œuvre des pauvres Églises." On this occasion he made many allusions to present difficulties, and rendered his meaning evident by the words with which he closed his speech—" be united with me, and not with revolution."

Who could possibly have predicted that these good Fathers, who, a few years back, were so strong against revolution, would now themselves be accused of revolution? Who could have told them in 1860, that in the short space of ten years the Head of the Church would have included many of them in the same class with that very Count Cavour whom they so detested, and that by a series of deductions they might find themselves at length in that bad company, actually banded with Mazzini!

Revolution! wondrous word invoked by subjects against their rulers, and levelled as a reproach against their subjects by those who govern. Rulers who endeavour to degrade Strossmayers to the level of a Rochefort not infrequently reverse the intended result, and raise a Rochefort to the height of a Strossmayer, thus rendering both equally instruments of their own ruin.

5. The Pope had directed his speech particularly against the Oriental bishops; and being alarmed at the threats of schism from the East, he employed language adapted to the crisis. He made use of many loving and considerate expressions towards them, as he had done recently on opening the Exhibition of Catholic Art, and dwelt much on his great regard for their religious rites, but strange to say, at the very time when his words were thus friendly towards the Orientals, a most inexplicable event occurred, an event which had much influence on the separation that afterwards took place in the Armenian Church. The Vicar-General of the Armenian Archbishop of Diarbekir, had severely blamed the Armenian Patriarch Hassoun, and the Latin Patriarch Valerga, both in words and in writing, for having caused by their undue servility to Rome great displeasure to the Chaldean Patriarch, of whom mention was made in a former chapter. It seems that the Pope, upon the complaint of the Armenian and Latin Patriarchs, intimated to the Vicar-General that he should retire to a monastic establishment for a short time, as a punishment for his language; but the latter, with the support of his bishop, either declined to obey this command altogether, or did not obey it exactly, whereupon his arrest was ordered, and he was seized one day while out walking. He attempted to resist, and a scandal ensued; the affair was soon known on all sides, and the Turkish Minister, resident at Florence, hastened to Rome to take the Armenians under his protection as subjects of the Ottoman Porte. It was a singular fact that brethren in Christ should find themselves reduced to seek protection against His vicar, from whom? from a Turk! The whole affair was badly managed, and though at first a matter of little consequence, was allowed to assume grave proportions, and became further involved by the fact that a community of Armenians, known as the "Frati Antoniani," were subjected to persecution of the same sort, the brothers who would not obey the injunctions of the ecclesiastical authorities ending, after many vicissitudes, by dissolving their community

and quitting Rome. Monsignor Pluym, Apostolic delegate at Constantinople, in the Pontifical Brief addressed to the Armenians of the Cilician Patriarchate a few weeks after these disturbances, was unwillingly obliged to acknowledge the unfortunate results they had produced. Speaking of those who had taken part in this affair, the Brief affirmed that " despising the laws and authority of the Church, they continued to celebrate with solemn ritual the functions of the sacred ministry, although prohibited from exercising them," and alluded to the secular clergy and many of the monks at Constantinople, to the " Mechitaristi " of the congregation of Venice, and to all the " Frati Antoniani," including those at Rome, as the persons especially compromised in the revolt. This statement was really the involuntary denunciation of an incipient schism.

6. An anecdote was circulated about this time which may be taken as an illustration of the spirit prevalent in Rome. On account of the death of Padre Modena, one of the two Dominicans who act as Censors of the Press in the office of " Masters of the Sacred Palaces," the theological chair of the Roman University was vacant. The competitors for this office had a theme given them on which to write an essay; a subject was to be selected by lot for this theme, and out of thirty the one on which the lot fell was " Papal Infallibility," a very strange coincidence.

7. But we must return to the Council. The sitting of Wednesday, the 23rd, was tranquil, as is usually the case after a storm, and the members of the Opposition who spoke that day were for the most part Armenian bishops; they upheld the views of Schwarzemberg and Strossmayer, but the legates and the majority offered no interruption. The sitting of Thursday was equally quiet; and on Saturday, the 26th, several of the objections to the scheme " De Fide," were withdrawn, and the bishops came to an agreement on part of it, so that the Optimists began again to indulge hopes of a future third Session, which up to the present time had seemed quite out of the question.

8. In order to understand this sudden calm, it must be explained that at one of the international meetings (in which all the leaders of the Opposition of different nations consulted together), after the scene of the 22nd, they had taken a new step. Finding that their petition against the vote of the majority was

of no avail, they resolved on presenting another formal protest to the effect that they rejected all dogmas declared to be such by the majority only, without the unanimous consent of the Fathers, and refused to recognise the validity of the Council as Ecumenical. This proposal met with so many supporters in the meeting, that probably, if carried into execution, it might have commanded the adhesion of a considerable portion of the Opposition; it was, in fact, the application of the principles advocated by Döllinger's article. It was also determined as a corollary to this plan that the Opposition should reserve their strength for the vital questions of the scheme "De Ecclesia," instead of wasting it in formal discussions on the scheme "De Fide." By this policy they intended to show their wish to be as conciliatory as possible, and their sincere desire for peace; twelve amendments prepared by their own party were immediately withdrawn in conformity with this plan; a period of calm succeeded to the recent tempestuous discussions, and the first almost unanimous decisions of the Council were obtained.

9. Meantime the slackening of the zeal and activity of the Infallibilists was in some measure explained by the publication of the recent note of the French Government. This note had clearly been provoked by the Canons published in the *Augsburg Gazette*, and was forced from Count Daru by the petitions of the bishops after the circulation of the new Order. The answer of Cardinal Antonelli soon appeared, and the two documents threw much light on the state of affairs. The French note remonstrated against the disquieting attitude assumed by the Church towards the State in the twenty-one Canons of the scheme "De Ecclesia." The answer of the Secretary of State was considered a chef-d'œuvre of diplomatic art; nor could it properly be otherwise, as it had to prove that those Canons which affirm that all civil society is entirely subject to the Pope were practically of no importance, and need not cause any uneasiness to Governments. This was the chief argument, which Antonelli tried to enforce. The other point on which he dwelt in his answer was more easy of demonstration, namely, that as these Canons were to be debated in the Council, no judgment could be passed on them until that discussion was over. But, after their consideration by the Council, the Cardinal

might easily protect himself against the importunities of Governments by alleging that when the Church has decided a matter, the Secretary of State cannot interfere, and he would have some foundation for the statement. The aim of Cardinal Antonelli's reply to Count Daru was to delay the mission of the proposed Imperial orator, to reassure the French Government, so as to prevent its taking any steps in the matter, and whether in consequence of the ingenuity of the note, or for some other reason, he managed to attain his end without encountering any great resistance. But being uncertain whether she would have time to secure this result, Rome delayed the discussion of the scheme "De Ecclesia" and with it that on Infallibility, and instead of these reproduced some of the old amended schemes for consideration, and this policy, together with the forbearance manifested by the Opposition, explains the truce which prevailed for some days. The respite was, however, of short duration, and the minority were soon aware that their half-measures would not lead to any result. Once reassured, the Curia and the majority resumed their former road, a road that, whatever its windings may be, has for centuries been directed towards one point, the absolute power of the Church, in herself, and over all. A policy of this nature, when unduly pressed, will often miss its mark, and unless conducted with the utmost dexterity, will be thrown back or altogether frustrated, just as it seemed certain of success.

10. The representations of France were short-lived, and the talk of a special envoy soon dropped, though at one time it was supposed that an ambassador might be sent to Rome, accredited both to the Vatican and to the Council. It was then said that, notwithstanding all the explanations which had been made, M. de Banneville's recall would be final, but this was likewise a mistake; and it appeared probable that he would return to Rome simply as ambassador to the Holy See, to resume the peaceful exercise of his duties in that capacity as heretofore.

11. The Vatican has long exercised upon France a singular influence, by which it attracts and allures her without actually winning her adhesion; and thus, although unable to work any real change in her moral condition, the Vatican, whenever it

pleases, can render France wonderfully docile to its will. By the exercise of this influence, the Vatican has of late years, without making any concession on its own part, induced France in the plainest contradiction with herself to abjure the famous principles of "89," and to reinstate and maintain in Rome a form of government which was their most explicit and conspicuous negation. The Vatican distinctly and loudly condemned those principles, as well as the whole constitution of modern France, in all the proposals hitherto brought before the Council; and in doing all this it had no other instrument than France herself, who, by her soldiers, enabled the Council to pass those judgments, and thus actually belied and condemned herself in the doctrines and actions of the Pope. Indeed, France has never ventured to assert her own free will in the face of the Vatican, a fact that is not to the credit of either party; from the date of the letter to Edgar Ney to that of the note of Count Daru, her efforts to assert her independent opinion have been confined to inefficacious words and demonstrations of such a nature as almost obliged the Roman Chancery to oppose them out of courtesy. Even with regard to the Armenian question, in which France was compelled to intervene in order to keep up her authority in the East, the same fatal spell weakened her action, and caused her to adopt very insufficient means for remedying the evil. The political effect of the disturbances arisen among Eastern Catholics, is to give greater power to Russia as the representative of Greek influence; for the Armenians, on breaking loose from Latin Catholicism, were obliged to turn to her for protection, being themselves surrounded by enemies. France, not daring to go to the root of the matter, or to exercise her authority at Rome to prevent the wrong, was content with ordering her representative at Constantinople to show kindness to the dissentient Catholics and take them under his protection, thinking thus to mend matters; but if the schism which seemed imminent actually took place, under what plea could France protect them? Not as French subjects, certainly; and not as Catholics, for they would no longer be such. In the long run, it was easier for Russia to help them. Whatever the question at issue may be, the position is the same for France as for all other nations.

Rome has an independent and separate line of action, which she expects them wholly to accept or reject; but they, France especially, often choose the latter alternative. Many nations, nominally Catholic, have very little regard for their religion, and endeavour to be liberal, without founding their liberty on the necessary basis of all durable freedom—universal consent and—the rights of conscience. The Latin races do not seem to understand either of these principles; authority with them stands instead of both, and when this authority exceeds its due limits, they have no other remedy than lawlessness and have recourse to revolutions, which by regular and inevitable stages bring them back to despotism.

12. The Congregations met every day from the 28th to the 31st of March. In these meetings, the greater part of the scheme, "De Fide," was voted without much difficulty, and almost unanimously for the reasons already stated, a result which gave rise to a joke on the scheme, to the effect that at the next Session it would be announced to the Catholic world, that the Vatican Council had almost unanimously decreed that God had created the universe.

13. An Exhibition of objects of Art applied to Catholic worship, was opened at this time, but proved a great failure. It was intended to be a sort of adjunct to the Council, and the Pope in his inaugural speech declared that Catholic feeling was the soul of art, but events almost proved the contrary. At any rate, it was evident that the originators of the Exhibition were not in sympathy with the modern world; and the Exhibition itself was only another argument to be added to those we brought forward in a former chapter when speaking on this subject. It was opened in the middle of February, but its popularity was of short duration; it attracted little notice, and the number of its visitors rarely equalled that of the gendarmes who guarded it.

14. Ancient art was ill represented when compared with the collections to be seen on all sides in the churches and palaces of Rome, and examples of modern art, though more numerous, were of indifferent quality. The sculpture was decidedly inferior to that usually seen in such exhibitions; the pictures were of ordinary merit. There was one fine painting by

Ceccarini, representing the administration of the Communion in both kinds, in the catacombs, to Christians preparatory to their martyrdom. This picture was full of feeling and of life, and its style was a happy combination of the historical and the "genre," which, joined with some romantic handling, is the fashion of the day, and most popular in the present century; it was bought by a German baron.

Passing on to the secondary and industrial arts, there was little worthy of praise. Of wood-carvings, though much used in churches, there were few examples, and still fewer bronzes; there were some sacred ornaments, but scarcely any musical instruments, such as are generally found in industrial exhibitions. Images and objects of painted terra-cotta abounded, but these are rather the vulgar expression of a material devotion than an artistic manifestation of high religious feeling, and the grand cloisters of the Certosa, which served as the Exhibition rooms, were filled with a multitude of other things of no value and of doubtful taste. Where are the days in which, from Giotto and Andrea Pisano to Michael Angelo and Cellini, from the art of the builder to the art of the weaver (Arte della Lana), all was animated and impelled by the Christian spirit? What subjects for contrast might not be found in art as we see it embodied in the Church of Santa Maria del Fiore, the Campanile of Giotto, the doors of the Baptistery, even in the Vatican itself, and art as shown forth by the Roman Exhibition of 1870! One cannot but feel that active Christian sentiment is manifested more worthily by the various specimens familiar to us in international exhibitions which are the work of an industrious and intelligent Christian society, than in the ostentation and pomp of a so-called special religious exhibition.

APRIL.

I.—THE SCHEME "DE FIDE" FOR THE SECOND TIME.

1. Cessation of diplomatic intervention.—2. Definitive voting on the scheme.—3. Result of the voting.—4. Easter festival.—5. The public Session fixed.—6. Third Session.—7. Impression it produced.

1. THE speech made by Visconti Venosta in the Chamber of Deputies at the end of March, in which he declared, in answer to some inquiry, that the policy of the Government with regard to the Council would be that of non-intervention, was very remarkable, not only in itself, but as an indication of the general opinion of Europe on the matter. The announcement of this policy of non-intervention by the Government the most interested in the Council, seemed to indicate the cessation of the action which the other Catholic Governments had taken at the request of the bishops in Opposition, and on the publication of the new Order. Count Daru, who was in favour of intervention, resigned just after he had addressed the despatch we have commented on, to the Italian Secretary of State, and had recalled M. de Banneville from Rome; and the latter shortly after returned to his post. There was no further diplomatic interference; in fact, it had been confined to the philosophical considerations of the French note, and a letter almost exactly like it emanating from the Austrian Cabinet. The Vatican resumed its course, feeling secure against all further interruption from that quarter, and as France was just then engrossed in the second plébiscite, ordered by the Emperor Napoleon as a means of strengthening a Government which, already tottering, urgently needed the support of all the proselytes it could gain; the Pope was able to convince himself that the fallibility of

the "plébiscite" might be an excellent argument for his own Infallibility.

2. During the early days of April, the Congregations worked with much assiduity to hasten the promulgation of the scheme "De Fide." On Friday, April 1st, and from the 4th to the 8th, the separate parts of the scheme were voted by "rising and sitting," and in one Congregation this mode of voting was used 100 times, to the great discomfort of the Fathers. The amendments to the scheme finally exceeded a hundred. Both parties, and especially the Opposition, made every endeavour to carry it through. The separate chapters, which were originally nine in number, were reduced to four, and on Tuesday, April 12th, the final and definitive vote by a call of names for the scheme "De Fide" took place. It was Tuesday in Holy Week, the last day on which a Congregation could be held before Easter, as the services of the Passion began on Wednesday.

3. Notwithstanding the good-will of both sides, out of the 592 bishops present, 83 gave dissentient votes, some with the formula "Non placet," others conditionally with the formula "Placet juxta modum." This result was very displeasing to the Pope, and to the Cardinal legates, who had hoped to give the foreigners present in Rome for Easter the grand spectacle of a public Session, as a testimony to the success of the Council, and as an adjunct to the festivities of the season. Another Congregation was announced for the earliest possible day, the Tuesday after Easter. There was a difference of opinion among the legates with regard to the scheme; some advising modifications for the sake of obtaining unanimity, but Capalti and Bizzarri would not hear of any change.

4. The Easter ceremonies were marked by no particular incident, and were less striking than usual, on account of the smaller number of strangers present, and also because the space occupied by the Council Hall diminished the size of the Church of St. Peter and detracted from its grand and imposing appearance.

Moreover, owing to the large number of bishops present in Rome, the ceremonies which usually take place in the Sistine Chapel, and which have a religious and artistic interest peculiar to themselves, were omitted for want of space.

5. The Congregation held on Easter Tuesday did not bring about any change of opinions, and the Pope, as a last resource, resolved to " force the situation," and to proceed with the scheme, reckoning that all who dissented under the formula " Juxta modum," and many of those who dissented absolutely would give way rather than cause scandal by a public resistance ; and that no one hardly would venture on repeating " Non placet " at the public session. This calculation was well founded, because the differences of opinion on the scheme in question were neither important nor remarkable, nor did they touch on subjects regarding which the Opposition were already compromised; so the result justified the Pope's anticipation.

6. The third public Session of the Vatican Council was held on the Sunday after Easter. The usual ceremonies being concluded, the scheme " De Fide," with its collateral Canons, was proposed, and all the Fathers present responded with " Placet." Those whose conscience remained inflexible and who would not give their consent, were to absent themselves from the Session. This course was adopted because it was found that only *one* prelate was in that position, Monsignor Strossmayer, Bishop of Bosnia and Sirmio. Strossmayer, being placed ·in the dilemma of either causing scandal by separating from his colleagues in Opposition, who had determined on pronouncing the " Placet," or of betraying his own convictions, preferred to absent himself altogether; and his protest, though almost unobserved at the time, subsequently acquired great value from his consistent conduct with regard to all the other and more important business of the Council.

7. It is impossible for a person not an eye-witness of the ceremony to understand the feeling it conveyed of the utter isolation of that grave assembly from the rest of the world, the very world, in fact, which it was intended to represent. The first Session had commanded some amount of attention, and had drawn many to witness its ceremonies from motives of curiosity, love of novelty, and perhaps even from the hope of a good result, but on this last occasion there were few people present in St. Peter's, and fewer still paid any attention to the proceedings of the Council. No one listened to the reading of these formidable precepts of the Church; no one knew what

was going on; to the public the Council Hall was merely a spectacle, and nothing more. It did not occur to the bystanders that, being Catholics, they would retire to rest that night with the obligation of a new set of declarations, and articles of faith weighing on their intellect and conscience. The only person whom I heard make an observation to this effect was a schismatical Greek, and the answer of the Catholic, to whom he addressed himself, did not indicate that the decrees would meet with much obedience. The curiosity felt at the first Session no longer prevailed, and the present ceremony was merely considered an addition to the long list of those observed at the Vatican. Indeed, at the time, very few were either aware of, or reflected on the decree thus promulgated, and those few agreed that the declarations of the scheme were, on the whole, mild and moderate. Its subjects were hardly such as could fix the wavering attention of society at the present day, and even for those who, from particular circumstances, are drawn to their consideration they are unimportant, because the matters they contain are for the most part no longer of interest, besides, the way in which they are treated is such as to render any practical results unlikely. The scheme (observed many people) can make rules for the Church, but "concerning those that are without," St. Paul himself says if I mistake not "quid ad nos?" To reiterate to those that are within the fold the primary foundations of their faith may seem at least superfluous.

As we remarked elsewhere, the condemnatory character of this scheme was, at the first, the reason for its being sent back; it was then reformed, but still retained its original defect. The Catholic Church had already condemned Pantheists, Rationalists, Materialists, and also Protestants; the latter, since they separated from the Church, the others ever since the Church existed, because those condemnations are embodied in all the successive explanations of faith that the Church has issued, and are therefore included substantially and absolutely in the belief of Catholics. But with regard to those who "are without," those who are neither Catholics nor Christians, such condemnations possess neither authority nor practical effect. To declare that a person is anathema, is to declare him out of the Church; but if he never was in it how can he be cast out?

how does this judgment affect him? Such were the observations generally made by those (and they were not many) who interested themselves in the matter. As the Vatican Council would not obey the mission which seemed to be imposed on it by the laws of the age, that is to introduce the reforms which the lapse of time renders necessary and which the conditions of the Church permit, it was compelled by the force of circumstances either to remain stationary and inactive,—a disposition which is exemplified in the scheme " De Fide,"—or to press forward in the road of absolute authority, as it endeavoured to do in the scheme " De Ecclesia."

II.—THE FIRST SCHEME " DE FIDE."

1. Comparison of the first and second schemes.—2. The same.—3. Description of first scheme.—4. The same.—5. The same.—6. Considerations.—7. Further reflections.—8. On faith.—9. The connection of faith and science.—10. Dogmatic theology.—11. Close of observations on first scheme.—12. Annotations.

1. In order to appreciate the mild and moderate character of the scheme as amended, it is necessary to compare it with the original text as at first drawn up, a comparison which was most useful at the time of its promulgation, as an evidence of the beneficent influence exercised by the Opposition and as affording ground for hope in the future.

2. We will first describe, as nearly as possible, the original form of the scheme. After a long preface, which indicated all the enemies to be combated, or the many antichrists who at the present day endeavour to subvert religion and reduce mankind to a state of unbelief, the scheme divided its subject into three parts. In the first, it condemned absolute Rationalism under its three manifestations, Materialism, Pantheism, and Rationalism, properly so called; in the second, it condemned semi-Rationalism, introduced into Catholic doctrines; and in the third it condemned, partially, various other errors which spring from Rationalism.

3. The first chapter began with the title, " Condemnatio Materialismi et Pantheismi," and after describing and condemning

these errors, it concludes with a profession of faith in God. "Una singularis, simplex omnino, et incommutabilis essentia, æternus et necessario existens intellectu ac voluntate, omnique perfectione infinitus :" who "profitendus est super omnia quæ præter ipsum sunt aut concipi possunt infinite exaltatus." The heading of the following chapter was "Condemnatio Rationalismi." In this the scheme first recognises the power of human reason to attain by itself to a knowledge of God, and then proceeds to assert that if God were pleased to manifest Himself only through revelation, in that case reason must subject itself entirely. It affirms that this hypothesis has by providential arrangement been actually confirmed, so that it forms the basis of the Christian religion, and concludes by condemning all those who exalt reason as a supreme law, and standard of good, above faith and revelation. This chapter ends by fervently exhorting rulers to preserve instruction free from such pestilential error, and warns them against that sort of secondary Rationalism which creeps into wholesome study, and by which *verbum veritatis non recte tractatur.*

These two last clauses really express the intention of the compilers of the scheme, just as the intention of a letter is very often revealed in its postscript. The systematic suspicion and the infinite precautions they contain against all that emanates from reason alone, and the insertion in such a document as the decree of a Council (which by right concerns only doctrinal and speculative matters), of an intemperate mandate to Governments to guard the faith by all the means in their power, characterise a party which leaves unmistakable traces on all it touches.

4. The third chapter bore the heading, "De divinæ revelationis fontibus in Sacra Scriptura et traditione." It affirmed the Divine inspiration of the Holy Scriptures, according to the text sanctioned by the Council of Trent and the truth of the interpretations contained in the traditions and infallible judgment of the Church.

The fourth chapter, "De supernaturalis revelationis necessitate," was on the necessity of a supernatural revelation, not only because by it might be accomplished the rapid and universal diffusion (impossible through any other means) of that which reason with all its powers often finds it hard to understand; but also because God, wishing to raise man above the order of nature, could not bring him to a knowledge of what is superior to reason, otherwise than through faith, reason being incapable of attaining of itself to the knowledge of supernatural dogmas which are beyond the reach of our natural faculties. From this argument, logically conducted, the scheme suddenly comes to the *postscript*, that is to say, to a conclusion like that of the second part, which by means of a few vague and undetermined phrases tends to further the constitution of an unlimited authority. The conclusion states the duty of recognising "supernaturalis revelationis maximum beneficium," even in those matters which are not "imperviæ" to human reason, that is to say, which can be treated of by reason, and the practical interpretation of this is simply that such matters are to be voluntarily subjected to the guidance of revelation. Every one can perceive the consequences which naturally result from such a doctrine, for those who are its depositaries and natural interpreters, and consequently for the Vatican.

5. The fifth chapter is entitled "De mysteriis fidei in divina revelatione propositis," and condemns all who say that it is possible by reason and philosophy to search out the mysteries of faith. At first sight this condemnation seems equivalent to a prohibition of seeing when it is dark. If, however, its real intention is to contemplate the case of a person endeavouring in this darkness to guide himself by the light of reason, leaving the result out of consideration, it is difficult to understand the grounds for the condemnation. We owe many works by the Fathers, such as the "De Trinitate" and the "De Opere sex dierum" of Saint Augustine, to just such a case, and not only does the Church acknowledge these writings, but she adopts them and regards them with great honour.

6. The sixth chapter is entitled "De fidei divinæ distinctione a scientia humana," and here again our first impression is, that an effort is made to distinguish between two things which could never be confounded. This chapter is a sort of sequel to the fifth, condemning those who do not distinguish between Divine faith and human science, and who believe, not because our belief is a

matter of Divine revelation, but because we can ourselves attain to it by natural means. It is difficult to see the meaning of this condemnation taken literally, and bearing in mind the subject indicated in the heading of the chapter, for every one is aware of the difference between faith and knowledge.

Who is not sensible that by faith we accept that which we do not know? We must look for the real object of the scheme in its explanation, which affirms that if any one should delude himself by trying to reconcile faith and reason, and by elucidating so far as he can the former by the latter, such a consolation is to be denied him, in order that the renunciation of reason may be absolute and entire, an act of sacrifice and not an act of homage. This conclusion reveals, in its obscure and mysterious language, the spirit of those who framed the scheme. Unceasing war to reason, on those points where it can properly be exercised, as much as on those where it must yield, and a systematic and constant mistrust of its guidance, are integral parts of that order of ideas which has long and persistently prevailed in the direction of Catholic institutions. Such guidance tends to weaken and often to confuse the natural judgment of men, it creates and favours unreasonable and superstitious habits, and is a bar to the progress of civilisation among those nations where the full and free action of this scheme has been felt.

7. Under the seventh heading, "De necessitate motivorum credibilitatis," the scheme (having in the previous chapter cautioned man against his own reason), condemns with an anathema all who deny that the truth may be rendered evident by external signs (miracles). As the Gospel contains many miracles, to begin to affirm their possibility after nineteen centuries seems inopportune and superfluous, and here again we must look for the real meaning of this condemnation elsewhere than in its actual words. While the sixth chapter teaches us to doubt what seems reasonable, the seventh condemns us if we hesitate to accept what actually appears unreasonable. The reproduction of the ideas of these two chapters, if taken literally, would have no aim; but the intention of thus combining them is to inculcate their practical application, and to favour their influence among Catholic populations. The frequent result of such teaching is this, that people finding themselves abandoned

in the darkness of the supernatural, without the safe guidance of reason, easily become a prey to that vague mystical feeling which is often superstitious, not infrequently fierce and sullen, always prejudicial, and always a serious obstacle to the acquisition of the energetic and useful habits of civilised life.

All these ideas and their practical results which we have now pointed out, are hidden and implied rather than openly expressed in the measured phrases of the above-mentioned chapter; their real meaning is shown by their order and connection with those that precede, still more so by the traditional use and constant application of their principles that have long prevailed in the economy of the Church.

The moderation in words is a concession, a sort of homage to the spirit of the age, which, unlike the scheme, worships the goddess of reason, and wages constant war against all supernatural events (at least against all those of a religious character) which it runs down; while at the same time it exalts reason by all the means in its power, especially invoking for the purpose the help of science and of public opinion.

8. The eighth chapter, "De supernaturali virtute fidei et de libertate voluntatis in fidei assensu," condemned all who do not acknowledge faith as a supernatural gift of God, rather than as a natural and necessary persuasion of reason. This again is so obvious in Catholic belief, that its repetition is useless, but the warnings on this subject are endless, and we are told to guard against reason, to repudiate the use of reason, not only when it attacks faith, but when it intervenes as a support and help to faith. The ninth chapter was in the same strain, " De necessitate et supernaturali firmitate fidei." This chapter, a very obscure one, condemned those who say that the condition of the faithful (or Catholics) is the same as that of those who have not yet come to the one true fold, so that it should be lawful for Catholics to doubt the faith received *sub Ecclesiæ Magisterio*, and to suspend their judgment until its credibility and veracity be demonstrated according to the rules of human science. This chapter was directed, as it seems, against the two particular tendencies of the present century, reciprocal tolerance, and the spirit of debate, and perhaps on that account its sentences were involved in obscurity; and like those of the sixth and seventh chapters,

L

were couched in terms of moderation that the compilers did not always adopt in other parts of this scheme, nor in the others, especially that " De Ecclesia."

9. The scheme having been occupied up to this point with faith in itself, began in the tenth chapter to regulate the connection between faith and science under the heading, " De recto ordine inter scientiam humanam et fidem divinam ;" and from the very beginning submitted all science to the judgment of the Church, with a course of reasoning which, apart from what it may contain that is just and true from a Catholic point of view, loses much of its force when one reflects that the practical application of these doctrines consisted for the most part in subjecting the laboured emanations of human intelligence, and even of human genius, to the narrow and ignorant tyranny of some obscure censor; who, endeavouring amid distrust and suspicion to reconcile the progress of science with the integrity of the faith, might end by producing a condition of intellectual culture similar to that which has prevailed in Spain, some parts of Italy, and in Mexico.

The eleventh chapter reverted to the argument, " De incommutabili veritate illius dogmatum sensus quem tenuit et tenet Ecclesia." Even here the scheme violently hurled its reproaches against those who hold that any intervention of reason and human philosophy is lawful in the explanation of dogmas. Reason again! nothing but reason! One might almost think that reason were the enemy, or, to adopt its own words, the most formidable of the antichrists against which this voluminous scheme contended.

10. In the twelfth chapter we seem to have gone back to the third century, " De unitate divinæ naturæ seu essentiæ in tribus distinctis personis." The thirteenth is headed " De divina operatione tribus personis communi, et de Dei libertate in creando." It was certainly time to leave some liberty to the Almighty, the acknowledgment of His retrospective power of creating the world was due to Him from the theologians of the Vatican, as a compensation for all the liberty in governing it, which they took away.

The fourteenth chapter is " De Jesu Christo una divina persona in duabus naturis, de redemptione et vicaria pro nobis satisfactione," &c. One would imagine we were living in the days of Nestorius, or some such period. Not content with having begun again at the work of redemption, the scheme in the fifteenth chapter goes back to the days of Adam. " De communi totius humani generis origine ab uno Adam, et de natura humana una composita ex anima rationali et corpore." It is certainly impossible to carry the question beyond this.

11. The sixteenth chapter affirmed the intervention of the supernatural, or Providence, in the world, not only in its events, but in the moral order of ideas that prevail in it, and declared that man without the aid of supernatural grace could not attain the heights of justice and virtue. All this is comprised under the heading " De ordine supernaturali et de supernaturali statu originalis justitiæ." The seventeenth heading is " De peccato originali et de pœna æterna destinata cuilibet mortali peccato," and from it one would imagine that the mysterious dogmas of original sin, and of eternal punishment, were now for the first time to be established in Catholicism.

The eighteenth was " De supernaturali ordine gratiæ quæ nobis per Christum redemptorem donatur." This chapter entered into the whole theory of grace as completing the Christian edifice, and condemned all who deny that Divine grace is a supernatural gift, permanent and inherent in the soul, or who think that they may attain to Christian justification by their own natural strength.

12. This was the last chapter, and it was followed by long annotations and comments. The first was on the inscription with which all the schemes opened—" Pius Episcopus sacro approbante Concilio." I ought, according to chronological order, to have spoken more fully of this title before, as it was debated in the assembly, where it gave great offence to the Opposition, and became the subject of grave remonstrance on the part of its leaders; but public opinion gave little heed to the matter at first; the petition against it was lost among the many others with which the Opposition filled the Vatican Hall, and thus I did not enter into the question when it first arose. The subject is, however, too important to be passed over without some observations, now that the annotations of the scheme which originally drew attention to it afford a suitable occasion for its consideration. We may really say that the whole significance of the Vatican

Council is expressed in the title of the schemes. The decrees of the Council of Trent bore the inscription, " Sacrosancta œcumenica et generalis Tridentina synodus in Spiritu Sancto legitime congregata præsidentibus apostolicæ sedis legatis." The decrees of the Vatican Council on the contrary are headed thus, " Pius Episcopus sacro approbante Concilio." The difference between these two formulas is such, that we cannot be surprised at the resistance made by the Opposition to the second ; or that Strossmayer very ably pointed out that the new title was not an innovation in form only, but that it substantially changed the standard of the authority of an Ecumenical Council. However, the Opposition obtained no redress, and the original title remained untouched. The reasons for this formula were given in the annotations on the scheme " De Fide," which declared it to be the most suitable in Councils presided over by the Pope in person ; in the same way that his representatives in the special Congregations of the Vatican Council, were called presidents instead of legates, which is their designation in ordinary Councils where the Pope is not present. To this Strossmayer replied that he wished the Pope did preside personally ; but that as he never was present at the discussions in which all the real work of the Council was carried on, the reason given, did not justify the great innovation in the inscription. The other side then urged that the Council must be considered under the presidency of the Pope, as he was in the Vatican, and was personally present at the public meetings, the only ones in which the Council passed authoritative decrees. In fact, Rome was firm on the point, and the title was carried like the Order, and all else which was desired, "*colà dove si puote.*" * The annotations of the scheme were twice as voluminous as the text, and contained the reasons and explanations of the same. Its form was so little in harmony with the habits of modern thought and science, so unscientifically expressed, in so dry a style, and in such pedantic language, that it will easily be believed that it met with little favour in the assembly. Every one may remember the lively assaults to which it was subjected, and the eloquent speeches by the Opposition against it ;

* " It is so willed there where is power to do
That which is willed."
—LONGFELLOW's Dante, *Inf.* iii. 95-96.

but reminiscences soon fade away, and as the discussion was then a purely verbal one, only a few reports of those speeches remain which were taken down by the shorthand writers, and now rest in eternal slumber among the secret archives of the Council.

III.—THE SECOND SCHEME "DE FIDE."

1. The scheme as a whole.—2. First and second chapters.—3. Third chapter.—4. Fourth chapter.—5. Observations of the bishops.—6. Their influence.—7. Continued observations.—8. Difficulties that beset the scheme.—9. Reasons for describing the scheme.—10. Note of the North-German Confederation.

1. When this scheme appeared for the second time, after all the events we have narrated, it was *heu quantum mutatus ab illo!* It only contained in the second edition an introduction and four chapters, in which part of the matter of the first scheme was condensed, the rest being either consigned to oblivion or temporarily laid aside. The four chapters of the second scheme are entitled:—1. "De Deo rerum Omnium Creatore." 2. "De Revelatione." 3. "De Fide." 4. "De Fide et Ratione." The entire bulk of the second scheme does not exceed thirty-one pages, whereas the first numbered more than one hundred and forty. The introduction to the second scheme is longer, and indicates its subjects more fully, pointing out Naturalism from the first as an enemy to be combated, in which term, Pantheism, Rationalism, Indifferentism, and Atheism are all included. There is no mention here, and very little afterwards, of the so-called semi-Rationalism so much made of in the first scheme.

2. The first chapter contains in summary all that was said in the first chapter of the former scheme, leaving out the nominal condemnations of Pantheism, Materialism, &c.; it contains likewise the confession of belief in God, with all His attributes, declaring that He is one in substance, distinct in nature and essence, *liberrimo consilio*, Creator of the world.

The second chapter contains a compendium of all that was said in the second, third, and fourth chapters of the first scheme on Revelation and on the books that contain it, which *Deum habent auctorem*, and are sanctioned by the Council of Trent and the tradition of the Church. With regard to Revelation, there is a notable difference in the text of the two schemes. The first contained a chapter with the heading, " On the necessity of Revelation." The new one omits that chapter entirely, almost as if it no longer considered Revelation to be essential.

3. The third chapter contains an abridgment of all the matters of the first scheme from Chapter 1st to 9th, that is to say, the subjection of reason to faith, not by an intellectual operation, but by the authority of revelation, the possibility of external signs, such as miracles, prophesies, &c.; the gift of grace, the supremacy of the Church, and her perfection when contrasted with other confessions and creeds, of which latter the present text affirms that they *falsam religionem sectantur*, whilst the old text was more moderate on the subject, saying only that, *ad fidem unice veram non pervenerunt*. The end of this chapter likewise asserts that it is impossible to doubt or to change the faith taught by the Church, and states all that was contained in the ninth chapter of the old scheme on this point.

4. The fourth chapter is on the relation between reason and faith; and here the difference between the two schemes is most apparent. This fourth chapter includes pretty nearly all the contents of the tenth and eleventh chapters of the old scheme, with the addition of the precepts on the connection between faith and science scattered through other chapters. The intolerable pedantry with which reason is denounced, under the name of semi-Rationalism in the first scheme, is here omitted; and the relation between reason and faith is treated of less absolutely.

In fact, all the doctrines of the second scheme are relatively moderate. And were it not that practical experience has shown how far the results of that *jus*, acknowledged in the Church as *divinitus falsi nominis scientiæ oppositiones proscribendi* extend, the same character of moderation might be accorded to some of its ideas on the great questions raised among Catholic societies by modern civilisation. There is no mention whatever in the new scheme, of the matter contained in the old one, between the twelfth and the last chapter. The doctrinal parts then follow, the Canons corresponding to each of the headings;

and last of all a sort of Appendix, which explains briefly the reason and the method of the emendation of the first scheme.

5. We have now described the scheme "De Fide" in its amended form, and prepared for the public Session, the changes made in it before its promulgation in the Session of April 24th being few and unimportant. Its consideration for the second time took place under the new Order, and consequently the observations on it were for the most part in writing, and distributed to the bishops, so that we have more records of them. It is curious and important to observe, as a means of estimating the final result of all these events, that most of the annotations made by the bishops on the second scheme (already amended in an Infallibilist sense) are in the direction of exaggeration and restriction. For instance, a bishop tries to introduce Infallibility into the scheme as an accessory, by saying that " licet omnibus Ecclesiæ necessitabus per ordinarium Summi Pontificis regimen et magisterium satis fuerit provisum, tamen," &c. Two or three other prelates proposed similar amendments. The introduction, in particular, was marked by their observations. The Infallibilists preferred writing, and the Opposition speaking, feeling that they had most eloquence on their side, and also that, being in the minority, speaking was the best means of gaining strength and of spreading their ideas. Still the great predominance of Infallibilist opinions in those annotations throws much light on the history of the Council. The introduction received various unimportant changes from the annotations. The observations on the first chapters, "De Deo rerum omnium creatore," were numerous, and entirely in an Infallibilist sense. There are a few remarks by independent and more liberal bishops; one proposing the suppression of Canons in the scheme, judging the decrees as quite sufficient; and another proposing to omit the anathema, and to condemn errors only, and never persons.

6. No notice was taken of these observations, and the first chapter re-appeared at the final publication of the scheme in almost the same form as at its promulgation. The only change was the addition of the last paragraph, and the omission of a word in the first, which was done at the instigation of the one bishop who had succeeded in carrying his emendations on this chapter.

One annotation proposed the substitution of " Sancta Catholica Ecclesia " for " Romana Catholica Ecclesia." Another, more modestly, proposed " Catholica et Romana ; " and, on failing to obtain the conjunctive particle, pleaded for the insertion of a comma only, between *Catholica* and *Romana*, but even this was in vain. The oral debate on this subject was much hotter than appears from the written observations, but it was unsuccessful.

The majority would not yield, and the only variation obtained in the formula was the change from " Sancta Romana Catholica Ecclesia," to " Sancta Catholica Apostolica Romana Ecclesia." The protesting bishop obtained a transposition of words instead of a comma, and the Church of Rome preserved its prerogatives untouched.

7. Of the many observations on the second chapter, those are worthy of notice which tended to allow more scope to the natural perception of God in the conscience of Catholics, otherwise this chapter underwent scarcely any change.

The annotations on the third chapter were numerous, but of slight consequence for the laity; the doctrinal part of the scheme was somewhat modified in form, but scarcely at all in substance. One remark frequently made by the bishops we also have alluded to, and it is this, that most of those condemnations concern persons out of the Church, but, as one of the prelates justly observes, *qui non credit, jam judicatus est*. Many observations are also made on the fact that the opening formula of the scheme is " Pius Episcopus," instead of " Sancta Synodus Ecumenica." These are the few traces of independent opinion, and of sincere concern for the dignity and liberty of the Church which we meet with in perusing the records of the time; and, owing to their small number, they are lost in the existing mass of obsequious testimony and theological subtleties. The Canons remained intact, excepting one on the connection between faith and reason, which was omitted in consequence of the remarks of the bishops. It condemned those who entertain opinions which, though not declared to be heretical, are yet contrary to the mind of the Church. With this exception the text, when finally promulgated, was almost identical with that sent back to the assembly after the first emendation.

8. In the debate on this scheme there were two subjects of

difficulty which divided the Fathers for some time, notwithstanding their good-will. The first was the addition of the word *Romana* added with an exclusive sense to *Catholica Ecclesia*, the second, the suppressed Canon.

On the first point there were many petitions for the elimination of the word *Romana*. One bishop very ingenuously recounted the fact that in his English diocese some land had been left by will to the "Catholic Church," and that the Anglicans had appropriated it on the plea that they were really the Catholic Church, the so-called Catholic Church being styled *Roman* Catholic. The Roman Church, for whom this designation was of great import, paid no regard to the land lost by the bishop, but maintained the title, only deigning to grant the wish of the more moderate among the Opposition, who begged for the addition of all the other titles as "Sancta Apostolica," &c. More explanation is needed on the second subject.

In the text of the scheme was a Canon (the 3rd I believe) which condemned those who held opinions contrary to the mind of the Church, even though not declared heretical. At the end of the scheme, after the Canons, came an Appendix, which contained a sort of indefinite injunction (*monemus*) to Catholics to observe all those constitutions and decrees of the Holy See, directed against errors which are not exactly heresies, but yet are akin to them.

These two parts of the text completed each other, because, as every one must see, the Appendix was contemplated and comprehended by the Canon in such a way that the simple *monemus* was in fact a decided condemnation referring to that in the third Canon. The resistance on this point was most serious, and nearly all the eighty-three members of the Opposition who had answered "Non placet," or "Placet juxta modum," at the voting of the scheme, turned their attention to the subject.

Although, as we have seen, the Canon was suppressed, the Appendix and the disputed paragraph remained unaltered, and the Opposition thought that, from what I might call their ambiguous wording, and the fact of their juxtaposition, they might easily, even without the Canon, be so construed as to indicate and establish the sole and absolute dominion, or, in other words, the personal Infallibility of the Pope.

9. We do not intend to follow in detail the progress of the other schemes, which would be entirely beyond the limits of the present work, but have dwelt at length upon this one, in order to convey to our readers a clear idea of the way in which the Council was managed, and of the spirit that guided its deliberations. We have considered the scheme " De Fide," as it appeared at the opening of the Council, and after its first amendment, and have seen that though the difference is great, the changes that it underwent in the debate between its second appearance and its final publication were of slight importance, and here we have an answer to the question which was asked at first on all sides as to the fate of the amended schemes.

10. The few changes actually made in the scheme on this second occasion were probably due in some measure to diplomatic intervention recently provoked by the insertion in it of certain strictures on Protestants. The North-German Minister, accredited to the Holy See, addressed a violent and menacing note on the subject to the Roman Secretary of State, either because really offended by these expressions, or in order to flatter the Opposition and the opinions prevailing in the Catholic provinces of Germany, and intimated that such words were likely to diminish the obedience due from those subjects to the King and to the Prussian authorities; he added, moreover, that should the Prussian bishops accept the document and become sharers in it, proceedings would be taken against them. This made a deep impression, the Prussian Cabinet not having shown such resentment against the Vatican before. The remonstrance had the greater effect owing to its novelty, and it was generally believed that the relative moderation of the scheme was owing in some degree to the note. We will not examine the particulars of the scheme as published on April 24th at the public Session, for every one can study it for himself.* When considered as a whole, and with regard to the circumstances of its production, one must give it credit for some degree of moderation ; and were it not for the last paragraph, which made such an advance towards Infallibility, even the Opposition might have been in great measure content, and many might have hoped that in future the decrees would bear the same temperate character.

* See Appendix, Document XVIII.

M A Y.

I.—THE SCHEME "DE ECCLESIA" FOR THE SECOND TIME.

1. The scheme "De parvo Catechismo" for the second time.—2. The scheme "De Ecclesia" sent back.—3. Returns modified.—4. The scheme "De parvo Catechismo" is voted.—5. Its amendments are voted and the scheme is laid aside.—6. The debate on the scheme "De Ecclesia" is opened.—7. It is continued.—8. Speech of the Pope on giving the prizes at the Exhibition of Catholic Art.—9. Speech against Infallibility.

1. THE public Session of April 24th was succeeded by a short recess, during which the scheme on the short Catechism was distributed for the second time, being the last of the four schemes published previous to the famous "De Ecclesia." It had been amended by the bishops like that "De Fide," but its spirit had, in reality, been subjected to very slight modification, the real intention of the scheme being to substitute one Catechism for all the various forms hitherto used by different churches in the Catholic world. The fact of the order of business being thus changed, and the two schemes, "De Episcopis" and "De Moribus Clericorum," which should, by rights, have followed that "De Fide," being put aside for "De Catechismo," the shortest and the last, clearly indicated the wish of the authorities to expedite matters as much as possible. People began to feel that the moment was approaching in which the truce would end and the strife recommence, a strife which this time would be decisive.

The first Congregation held after the recess was on Friday, the 29th of April, when, a short report having been read, the debate "De parvo Catechismo" began. It terminated the following day, although it met with deep and serious resistance, so great was the desire of hastening on. The *Giornale di Roma* of that day, perhaps unable to contain its impatience, by an exception to its usual practice, made the conclusion of the debate known to the public, who otherwise remained in complete ignorance of what passed in the Council. Thus, the famous scheme towards which all the business of the Vatican Council gravitated, after having been sent back and amended, now reappeared.

2. For the third time within six months was this question, so fundamental in the constitution of the Church, brought under discussion. The first time it was attempted to obtain the declaration of Infallibility by acclamation; the second time, in March, it was attempted to carry a petition suddenly in favour of Infallibility; and now, for the third time, the question was to be fought again with all the strength we cannot say of both parties, as the word strength is scarcely applicable in regard to the Opposition. Still connection and talent are always powerful, even when undisciplined, and we must remember that the favour of the day made up in some degree to the minority for their lack of numbers and of organisation.

3. The scheme " De Ecclesia " was not presented for discussion the second time in a complete form. By virtue of that impersonal and all-powerful authority which governed the Vatican Council, the scheme had been amended or rather mutilated without any discussion; and during this process the first part of it had remained in the laboratories of the Vatican, to be reproduced perhaps on some future occasion. This concession was probably due to the apprehensions of Foreign Powers, as the part of the scheme now omitted contained the famous Canons published by the *Augsburg Gazette*, which regulated the connection between Church and State. Foreign Powers, and France in particular, seem, strangely enough, to have been very suspicious as to these Canons, while they never troubled themselves on the question of Infallibility. Rome, on the other hand, was wisely content, for the moment, to sacrifice these Canons for the sake of the dogma of Infallibility, which virtually includes them all, and as many more besides as may spring from the sole and irresponsible will of an individual. If the statesmen who directed the policy of Europe had been more familiar with ecclesiastical matters and less distracted by other important interests, they would have seen that the dogma of Infallibility was a far more serious matter

than the Canons, because the effects and limits of these latter are known, whereas those of Infallibility are infinite and boundless, as was apparent on all occasions when they could be exercised. Rome, profiting by the prevailing state of opinion, in re-casting the scheme "De Ecclesia" entirely omitted the Canons, and only brought forward the part, entitled, "De Apostolici Primatus in beato Petro Institutione." In the fourth chapter, under the heading "De Romani Pontificis Infallibilitate," was inserted the petition of the bishops, so unexpectedly presented in the month of March, although even this, as we shall see, had undergone a slight change.

4. On Wednesday, May 4th, the nominal voting of the scheme "De parvo Catechismo" took place. There were about 100 "Non placet," as if the Opposition, aware of the coming battle, wished to show themselves fully prepared for resistance. The number of votes on that day was 591, fewer than in the winter. On this occasion, the observations in opposition to the scheme, and the consequent changes, were read, together with the original text, by the Commission which had made the amendments, and then the partial amendments and the entire text of the scheme were voted at the same sitting. The result was such as we have related, that is, there were 100 dissentient votes; nor is this surprising. If we consider the great difficulty of meddling with the Catechism, a religious formula familiar to whole populations from their earliest days, we shall rather wonder that the opposing votes were so few. To touch the Catechism at all is almost to touch the faith of a people, who, not being capable of comprehending the true value of words which habit has taught them to regard with veneration, remain faithful to the doctrines which those words convey, solely from respect for the familiar terms themselves. Why, said many of the bishops, should we cause this disturbance to Christian populations, in order to bring about a nominal agreement that cannot really increase the unity which consists in the belief which binds those people together in one faith and moral law, and not in the words or phrases by which that belief is expressed? No Congregations were held between the 4th, and Friday, May 13th, as it was necessary to confer on the resistance which now manifested itself.

5. The assembly was not induced by these deliberations to swerve a hair's-breadth from the course it had adopted. On the 13th it announced the amendments on the scheme " De parvo Catechismo," and proceeded no further that day, perhaps with the intention of adopting the same expedient with regard to this scheme which it had so successfully used for that " De Fide," and trusting that at the public Session the Opposition would overlook all they now objected to, for fear of creating a scandal, and in consequence of the attracting force of the majority.

6. For this reason, instead of dwelling longer on " De Catechismo," they proceeded at once to the discussion on the famous scheme " De Ecclesia Christi," now reduced to four chapters and three Canons. It bore the title " Constitutio Dogmatica Prima," perhaps in order to leave room for a second title, which should include the part now omitted, " De Ecclesia Christi reverendissimorum patrum examini proposita." Then follows the inscription, " Pius Episcopus, servus servorum Dei, sacro approbante Concilio, ad perpetuam rei memoriam," &c. After a short introduction comes the first chapter, " De Apostolici Primatus in beato Petro Institutione ;" the second, " De Perpetuitate Primatus Petri in Romanis Pontificibus ;" the third, " De vi et ratione Primatus Romani Pontificis." The fourth bears the dangerous heading, " De Romani Pontificis Infallibilitate," thus changed from the corresponding title in the first scheme, which was " De Ecclesiæ Infallibilitate." The three Canons follow.

The reporter of the Commission on Dogma opened the debate with a long speech, which, with its glowing pictures, inflamed the benevolent minds of the Infallibilists, but produced a very different effect on the Opposition. The theme of this discourse was a comparison between the martyrdom of St. Peter and that of St. Paul, great significance being attached to the mysterious dispensation of Providence, which, though it permitted the latter saint to be beheaded, had preserved the former from such treatment. It is easy to see the intention of this comparison with reference to the question at issue; every one will admit that, as an argument in favour of Infallibility, it was even more unworthy than as a rhetorical artifice, and will allow that the sarcastic smiles with which it was greeted by the Opposition, were more justifiable than the enthusiasm of the Infallibilists.

The reporter was the Bishop of Poitiers, especially noted of late years for his Ultramontane opinions, and of whom the story is told that he pronounced a solemn funeral oration for a Pontifical Zouave, reported to have fallen at Castelfidardo, but actually alive and well at the very time in France.

7. From that time forward the discussion was always on the same subject. Thirteen orators had inscribed their names on the 14th; but seven only spoke, and among them was the Cardinal-Vicar. One might almost have imagined oneself back at the Council of Florence while listening to their obsolete arguments and antiquated forms of discussion. On Monday there was no Congregation, that being the day fixed for the distribution of prizes at the Exhibition of Catholic Art, which had a share in the ceremonies of the Vatican Council.

8. On this occasion the Pope delivered a speech, in which he reiterated the remark he made at the opening of the Exhibition, that he considered it a proof of the beneficent influence of the Papacy on civilisation. A few days after, he included in the same category an Exhibition of Roman Agriculture, at which he likewise attended, seizing the occasion to speak on the present crisis. Fortunately for himself, the Pope had never seen the great Exhibitions of modern times, or it would have been difficult for him to develope his subject within the narrow limits, in which he desired to restrict it.

9. The sitting of Tuesday, May 17th, was short, three orators only speaking, and the battle on Infallibility may be said to have commenced on the following day, when the number of Fathers inscribed had reached seventy. Among these were three cardinals, Schwarzemberg, the Cardinal Archbishop of Vienna, and Cardinal Donnay. The Archbishop of Vienna was unable to make himself heard, and consequently his speech was read for him. Schwarzemberg was vehement on behalf of the Opposition, and created a profound impression. He made a most serious declaration, and a terrible threat for the future, in the words attributed to him on that occasion:—"It is said that you really believe in this dogma; but if that be true, you cannot pretend that I and my companions ought to acknowledge what seems to us absurd, and if you do so, be sure that schisms will arise and abjurations will follow within the Church of Rome."

On Thursday, the 19th, the Cardinal Archbishop of Dublin spoke for the first time, likewise Cardinal Moreau and the Chaldean Patriarch; on the 20th the Primate of Hungary, the Archbishop of Paris and two others. In Saturday's Congregation the speeches were in rapid succession; but nothing worthy of particular attention occurred.

II.—FOREIGN POLICY.

1. Despatch by Ollivier.—2. 'Ce qui se passe au Concile.'—3. Disquietude at the Vatican.—4. Speech by Monsignor Kettler.—5. Infallibility publicly promoted.—6. Address of the Roman parish priests.—7. Unfortunate position of affairs.—8. Duke of Saldanha.—9. Feast of St. Peter.

1. Meantime the Opposition seemed to have recovered from their stupor, and regained strength and boldness. A report was circulated that Ollivier, who then directed the policy of France released from the cares of the plébiscite, and from any particular consideration for the interests of the clergy, had turned his attention to Rome, and in consequence of the vacancy at the Foreign Office subsequent on the resignation of Daru, had himself written a new note to the Vatican, which he sent through M. de Banneville, strongly remonstrating against the promulgation of the dogma of Infallibility. It was said that this note threatened, in case of its counsels being rejected, a rupture of the Concordat and the withdrawal from Rome of the French army of occupation. This report was loudly denied by the Curia, which immediately published in the *Osservatore Romano* a dispatch according to which M. de Grammont, the new Minister of Foreign Affairs, instructed M. de Banneville to continue the same line of conduct as formerly, and to preserve a strict neutrality and careful abstention from all interference with the Council. Considering that the first note was signed by Ollivier, and was sent before M. de Grammont took office, and could issue the dispatch in question; and remembering also the frequent changes of French policy at that time, it is possible that both these reports were true. In fact, the matter was soon forgotten, and Ollivier's note was neither confirmed nor denied, until in the month of June the original document appeared in the newspapers. According to this publication the note sent to the ambassador at Rome

was harsh in tone and of uncertain import. It directs him to hold no further communications with the Court of Rome on the matter in question, the opinion of France being already sufficiently clear, while at the same time he is instructed to express to the bishops the sympathy of the Government, and its trust in their energy, and readiness to take the initiative. As two-thirds of the French bishops were Ultramontanes, and one-third of the Opposition, M. de Banneville had to consider to which side he should deliver the communication. This was the whole of the note so much exalted by one party, and so much decried by the other, according to their wishes and hopes. Everybody could read it in the newspapers, and learn the extent of the influence exercised by the Ollivier Ministry on the Vatican Council.

2. About the same time an anonymous work, 'Ce qui se passe au Concile,' appeared in France; it was short, but very important, and evidently written by some person of authority, so that it excited great attention. This work passed the most formidable judgments on the Vatican Council that could ever be inflicted by the severest criticisms of history. Its author pointed out that the real aim of the Council was to satisfy the exorbitant pretensions, and the old ambition of the Court of Rome; noticed the means used to this end, described the irregularities and innovations which might in days to come cause its validity to be questioned, and lastly foretold the fatal results to the Church of the fulfilment of so outrageous an attempt.

3. The Vatican now for the first time showed signs of disquietude, whether on account of the French note, though that was of little weight, or of this new demonstration on the part of the Opposition; and in its next meeting for amendments, the Commission on Faith endeavoured to frame such a formula on Infallibility, as should calm the irritation and displeasure of the Opposition, and win over some of its least determined members, without sacrificing in any respect the substance of the dogma.

4. The Congregations sat unweariedly, and on Monday 23rd, Monsignor Kettler spoke most strongly, pointing out to his colleagues what would remain to the episcopate after the proclamation of Infallibility. This argument, which he cleverly handled, had considerable effect, as it touched very nearly all

the Fathers in the assembly who exercised any jurisdiction, and it was said that (contrary to the usual result of the best speeches in the world), it really convinced some people, and attracted a few sheep from the Infallibilist flock to swell the forces of the Opposition. The sittings of the 24th, 25th, 28th, 30th, and 31st of May, were passed in the same way, that is to say, in a repetition of the arguments already well known on both sides. On the latter occasion eighty orators had inscribed their names, so that it almost seemed as if the desire of speaking grew as the speeches multiplied, much in the same way as appetite is said to grow by eating.

5. On the part of the Opposition, this increase of speakers was in accordance with the policy imposed on them by circumstances from the first, the desire to gain time, and the expectation of its benefits. On the part of the majority, it sprang from a desire to limit the chances of the Opposition as much as possible, by bringing every sort of pressure to bear upon them in the most minute particulars, as had been done from the beginning, and thus expecting and awaiting the moment when they could be entirely crushed without any great difficulty. The pamphlet 'Ce qui se passe au Concile,' gave an index of the briefs, the letters, and different works in the name of the Pope and other Authorities by which they encouraged personally and openly all who had in any way promoted Infallibility, or shown themselves in favour of it, and this fact produced a great impression. The instances cited by the pamphlet were, for the most part, collected beyond the limits of Italy, but some very curious examples were to be found in Rome itself. Whoever said or did anything in favour of Infallibility received acknowledgments, remunerations, and honours, the Pope himself condescending to act openly in this way. The papers published a Papal rescript approving and commending all those who fought for the good cause by means of the press (that press sometimes so much blamed). The newspapers even gave a formula of assent to Infallibility, a sort of plébiscite in its favour, drawn up by an ecclesiastic, and said to be sent from Rome through the bishops, to the clergy of their dioceses, with imperious commands that it should be accepted and signed.* The

* See Appendix, Document XIX.

author of the French pamphlet was not aware of the thanks and official encouragement given in the name of the Pope by the Nuncio at Paris to the French clergy who had assented to Infallibility, and made any demonstrations in its favour, conduct for which the said Nuncio was severely reprimanded by the French Government. By such a proceeding the Nuncio put into practice the principles of the scheme "De Ecclesia" before it was passed, and France, by her remonstrances, protested against the application of those doctrines.

These facts were not publicly known before the month of June, when the observations of the French Government were published, though they had been under preparation for some time. The crisis was provoked by the conduct of some of the clergy who manifested themselves openly in favour of Infallibility, while their bishops in Rome were speaking against the dogma from the benches of the Opposition. This conduct, however, was approved of at Rome, notwithstanding the complaints of the bishops interested in the matter, one of whom actually threatened to resign in consequence. Many examples of the like nature, both small and great, might be given. Nothing but the prestige inherent in all deep convictions could have so long sustained the Pope in the difficult position in which he was placed by his own followers; the position of a man who, living in the nineteenth century, was urged to proclaim his own apotheosis.

6. In order to have an idea of the pressure exercised to attain the declaration of Infallibility, we will mention an important incident, of which at the time very little notice was taken. At the beginning of March, in one of the parochial meetings held periodically in Rome for the transaction of business, a priest belonging to a religious order which had sent a legate to the Council, proposed to his colleagues to draw up an address in favour of Infallibility. Another priest immediately answered that it was no business of theirs to do anything of the kind; that they were not consulted on the matter, and that it would be inopportune and presumptuous for them to express any opinion on a question of so much gravity before the Church had decided on it. This rejoinder being approved of by the clergy present, the priest referred to saved his colleagues from entering into the stormy current of disputation from which, for

the better exercise of their ministry, they should endeavour to keep aloof.

By some chance, the newspapers got hold of this incident, which at once acquired weight from the fact that, as the parish priests are the best and most active among the clergy of Rome, the special diocese of the Pope, it was now apparent to the world that they were, if not actually adverse, but little inclined to Infallibility. The authorities immediately intervened with all the force which, in conformity with ecclesiastical law, they could exercise upon those subject to them; they intimated to the priests that they must repair the scandal, and *strongly advised* that an address should be framed. The parochial clergy accordingly drew up a form, which though apparently moderate, was to be understood by the public, who do not look narrowly into such matters, as favourable to Infallibility. Every one in Rome is acquainted with the history of that address. Some of the clergy evidently did violence to their own convictions; for as Infallibility was not yet declared, they were by no means bound to accept it from the duty of submission, but according to certain Ultramontane notions of discipline, authority has a conscience for all. This substitution of the dictates of an external authority for those of the individual conscience in all cases, is one of the chief causes of the evils that disturb Catholicism.

7. The Jesuits had originally brought forward the question of Infallibility in the month of February, when no one in the world was thinking of it, by their celebrated article in the *Civiltà Cattolica*, and now they adduced the fact of its discussion as a reason for its proclamation. The case of the parish priests was just the same; one of them proposed an address, a word which implies liberty and spontaneous action, but these characteristics are removed by the fact of the proposal, which is then used as an argument for the project being carried out, and so alternately a necessity is created and the desired advantage is taken of it. What will be the judgment of posterity on this phase of ecclesiastical history? what will be the opinion of those who view it with unprejudiced minds and full knowledge of the accompanying circumstances?

8. If very little forbearance is shown by Rome in the pursuit of her wishes, equally little is shown in her conduct when

those wishes are attained, and it almost seemed as if she were unwilling to leave those who voted for Infallibility under the slightest delusion as to the consequences that might follow. Although this prerogative is not supposed to extend beyond certain conditions, and to be exercised on certain matters only, yet it must inevitably add weight to the ordinary judgments of the individual invested with such virtue, and be reflected involuntarily in all his actions.

The news of the "Pronunciamento" in Portugal, by which the Duke of Saldanha had imposed by force on his King a new administration, of which he himself was the head, reached Rome about this time. "Pronunciamenti" are the worst form of revolution, because they disturb the highest expression of order, and violate the faith that binds soldiers to their flag. As soon as the news was received, the Pope paid a visit to the national Church of the Portuguese, and the same evening the *Osservatore Romano* announced the fact, and said that the Pope wished to inspect the restorations made in the Portuguese Church by order of the Duke of Saldanha when ambassador in Rome. The coincidence afforded ground for the belief that the Pope had hastened to give the Duke of Saldanha the only mark of approbation in his power, the rather that the Duke is of the clerical party, and on taking office had found some pretext for an assumed quarrel with the Italian Minister.

The effect of this conduct, whether intentional or fortuitous on the part of the Pope, was felt by all ; and the thoughts of those who remembered the 16th of November, 1848, went back to the moment in which he had found himself in the very same condition as that in which the Duke of Saldanha had placed his Sovereign, forced by violence to receive a minister from the rebels who directed their arms against his own palace ! Such persons wondered that the Pope, having been placed in that situation, did not perceive how dangerous might be even the mistaken presumption that his high sanction in any degree palliated acts of violence, or tended to render them familiar to the multitude, who are not all Excellencies like the Duke of Saldanha.

9. With these and similar events which, without adhering strictly to chronological order, I have brought together, as illus-

trating popular feeling, the work went on with the greatest activity and energy, June being fixed for the proclamation of Infallibility, as the feast of St. Peter and the anniversary of the Pope's accession are both celebrated in that month. We shall now see that the restless and imperious wishes of the majority were doomed to disappointment in carrying out this design, as they were in many other things.

JUNE.

I.—CLOSE OF THE GENERAL DISCUSSION.

1. Close of the general discussion on the scheme "De Ecclesia."—2. Speech of Monsignor Maret.—3. New protests.—4. Proposal for secret voting.—5. Resistance to be kept up to the last.—6. Feast of Pentecost.—7. Objections to proposal of the Archbishop of Malines.

1. THE congregations of June opened with an act which, though unexpected at the moment, was yet the legitimate consequence of the events we have described, and which will greatly influence the judgment, not only of the present day, but of future ages, on the Vatican Council, namely, the conclusion of the general debate on the scheme "De Ecclesia." It will be remembered that an article was inserted in the new Order, by which the power of proposing to vote the close of a debate was vested in any ten bishops. This proviso had caused great displeasure, for every one was aware that the legates, who could always be sure of inducing the majority to vote the closing, could with still greater certainty reckon on finding ten bishops to make the proposition. In fact, the article was considered as one of the means employed to crush and subdue the minority. The new Order on its first appearance had caused a great disturbance, but seemed to superficial observers to have now dropped into oblivion, those even who framed it making very little use of it; but when once its application seemed desirable, as in the present case, it reappeared in full force, and was employed with the utmost severity. The great numbers of orators inscribed for the scheme "De Ecclesia," the advance of the hot season, and the excitement manifested in the assembly, were the reasons for again applying the Order with much vigour, so as to bring about the results intended. On the 28th of May, the Bishops of Granvaradino, of Ratisbon, of

Savanah, and others, had spoken strongly in favour of the Opposition ; indeed the Bishop of Savanah said that it was sacrilege to make innovations in the Church, and to introduce the doctrine of the personal Infallibility of the Pope. The majority could not brook the application of the word sacrilege to their long-sought and cherished ideal ; the Presidents Capalti and De Angelis quite lost their temper, and a scene of anger and excitement ensued, very similar to that which occurred in March. The majority, confident in their own strength, then resolved to close the debate, and carried their intention into effect at the second Congregation, on June 3rd. On that occasion, towards the end of the sitting and without any suspicion on the part of most of the Fathers present, the legates produced a petition, signed by many bishops, praying that the debate should be closed, and immediately, without postponing the decision to the next meeting, the question was *in procinctu*—put to the vote by rising and sitting. There was a large majority in its favour, and the legates then announced that the general debate on the scheme " De Ecclesia " was ended.

2. The minority were painfully surprised at this proceeding, the more so as Strossmayer had spoken at the preceding meeting of June 1st with greater calmness and moderation than usual, pointing out that the reason of the continued opposition on his own part and that of his colleagues, was the serious consideration of the belief of their flocks, who would never accept the dogma of Infallibility. The Opposition had remained calm, even though Valerga, the Latin Patriarch of Jerusalem, one of the most ardent Infallibilists, had made a speech inveighing against them in unmeasured language, but their only reward was the unexpected closing of the debate by the presidents. Circumstances, in themselves unimportant, sometimes greatly change or aggravate the impression produced by an event. In the Congregation of June 3rd, the Fathers, unaware that the debate was to be stopped, had continued to speak as on former occasions, and the Bishop of Sens, Monsignor Maret, who had inaugurated the work of Opposition in France by the publication of his book on the Council, had made a long address.

He tried to make the assembly understand, that to render the personal Infallibility of the Pope co-existent with the Infallibility of the Church would be to introduce into the Catholic faith a new mystery, similar to that of the Trinity, a dogma teaching two Infallibilities in one. As he continued to dilate on this subject, he was stopped, and told to desist. Being rather deaf, he did not at once hear the command; but when he became aware of it, said, with dignity and energy, that his conscience and sense of honour impelled him to complete his speech, and he did so. A North American bishop, who then took up the question on practical grounds, and declared that the dogma was repugnant to his countrymen, and would prove a serious obstacle to the conversion of Protestants in America, was also subjected to the like treatment. And thus the close of the general debate on the scheme was brought about, the president announcing that at the next meeting on Whit-Monday, particular points, such as the Primacy, Infallibility, &c., would come under discussion.

3. The Opposition were much irritated by this new blow (as they considered it) on the part of the majority, this fresh attempt to urge them on to the hated declaration, and began seriously to consider what course they should adopt. Their several leaders held a meeting at once, and many opinions were circulated. Some advised an immediate departure from Rome; others, new protests; others, a line of abstention and indifference henceforward to all proceedings in the Council up to the day of voting, on which occasion they might once for all give openly and definitively the answer " Non placet."

The latter alternative involved a contradiction, for such indifference implied a refusal to recognise the validity of the Council, which would have been the only legitimate ground for disregarding its proceedings, and then, how was it possible to give even a negative vote in a Council possessed of no authority whatever? So great was the prevailing irritation, that some began to speculate on the course to be followed outside the Council, and when it was ended, alluding thereby to the resistance which might be manifested towards the Church of Rome.

As usually happens on such occasions, after the first explosion of wrath, the line of action adopted was a combination of all the plans that had been proposed. A strong protest against the closing of the debate, signed by about ninety bishops, was drawn up, and presented to the Pope. Meantime, some of the Opposition relaxed their attendance at the Congregations, and others took a short holiday under the pretext of visiting Naples or other neighbouring localities. Some of them were refused passports on applying for them at the office of the Secretary of State; but being for the most part foreigners, they could dispense with them, and travelled none the worse, meeting with no difficulties.

4. Among the many plans hatching in the heated minds of the Opposition was a petition that the vote on the delicate and anxious question of Infallibility should be secret, so as to relieve the sense of responsibility which would weigh heavily on many persons, and restore to them the moral liberty which they would be deprived of, in feeling that they were deciding the prerogative of the Pope, under his very eyes. The petition was drawn up, and obtained about eighty signatures. Its object was evident, and had it been successful it would have greatly assisted the Opposition, although no real difference in the final result could be expected. Owing to the general disregard of all the petitions and protests hitherto made by the minority, it was hardly probable that this request for an essential change in the arrangements of the Council would be granted, especially on account of its aim, and the occasion for which the favour was asked—the very moment of reaching the long wished for conclusion of the struggle.

5. The Opposition now numbered about 130, their body having increased rather than diminished since the opening of the Council, and they used every means in their power of protesting against the famous dogma. They did not quite agree among themselves on the matter, some deeming the time unsuitable for a declaration of Infallibility, though not averse to it in itself, and others being opposed to the substance of the dogma. This discrepancy, though not formidable in itself, as very often the belief of the first was only a milder and more practicable expression of the opinions of the second, was yet a serious hindrance to combined action; as the first were logically unable to combat the ideas of the majority with energy and success. Moreover, on account of the natural weakening of the individual will usually found among priests, it was impossible to tell how

many of the 130 in opposition would resist to the end, and dare to say " Non placet " at the public Session.

This was the root of the matter, on this depended the future of Catholicism, not so much on the convictions already shown, as on constancy in manifesting them, and maintaining them to the end. There was certainly every hope that as the opinions of the minority had been clearly made known (though without any official demonstration), the majority would be obliged to recognise them, for fear of losing in authority before the impartial tribunal of posterity all that by energetic and summary means they had gained in power with the view of overcoming and subduing their opponents.

6. Whitsuntide was approaching, and the Cardinal-Vicar ordered its celebration with special pomp. On Whit-Monday the whole Council, headed by the Pope, descended in solemn procession from the Sistine Chapel to the Church of St. Peter, to invoke the Holy Spirit. During the octave all the religious bodies in Rome went round the city in procession, imploring His aid — a proceeding which gave rise to a profane joke, with reference to the black habits of the monks, and the representation that they carried of the Holy Spirit,—that He would be rather driven away than attracted by such a cloud of wandering crows. The most singular among these processions was one comprising all the Jesuits in Rome, who very seldom manifest their numbers to the world at large.

7. Notwithstanding these demonstrations, the tenacious resistance of the Opposition caused considerable apprehension to the majority, who again tried to find some means of dividing and weakening them, the more thoughtful endeavouring to put forth a formula which might win over some of their opponents. But in this attempt, as often happens, the majority, instead of dividing their opponents, were very nearly divided themselves. The Archbishop of Malines, being opposed to all compromise, and dubious of the success of the means hitherto employed, proposed, instead, another formula, which should declare the whole of the Opposition excommunicate and out of the Church, and should anathematise all who held that the bishops shared the supreme authority vested in the Church; and as this was a favourite doctrine of the Opposition, it followed that the whole of their

number were consequently excommunicate. It seems that Manning shared the opinions of the Archbishop of Malines; but Monsignor Pie, Bishop of Poitiers, the same who had opened the debate with a speech on the decapitation of St. Paul, was of a contrary opinion, and refused to give his sanction to the summary decapitation of the episcopate. The bishops of the majority were divided on the matter, and this divergence threatened for a time to become serious, as there were said to be dissensions even among the legates. The firm conduct of Maret proved of great value in this conjecture. He declared to the Archbishop of Malines that as the proposal in question was *in odium* of himself and his colleagues, he should oppose it to the last by every means in his power.

The exorbitant nature of such a plan became apparent at length even to the Archbishop of Malines, and being warned by Maret of the results if he persisted in his intention, he finally withdrew the proposal himself, and no further mention was made of it.

In its place it seems that the majority agreed on another formula, to be issued at once. The details were not known as yet, but it was to admit of no concession to the wishes of the minority. This again was an innovation in the proceedings of the Council, for it implied the right of the presidents to substitute for documents already proposed, new ones which were without legal sanction, and were beyond Conciliar action. This familiar treatment of controversial matters took away a certain regularity, and consequently a certain security, from the debate. It was first adopted on discussing the introduction of the scheme " De Fide," and was substituted in various cases for the prudent traditions hitherto followed in conducting the business of the Council.

II.—SUMMARY OF THE QUESTION OF INFALLIBILITY.

1. Summary of the question.— 2. The scheme "De Ecclesia" is reduced.— 3. First and second chapters.—4. Third chapter, and its quotation from St. Gregory the Great.—5. Doctrines of the scheme "De Primatu."—6. The time for presenting observations upon personal Infallibility limited to ten days.— 7. Text inserted in the first draft of "De Ecclesia."—8. No special Canon for Infallibility.

1. Before the new formula appears, and while *sub judice lis est*, we will take a retrospective view of the whole subject, and consider all the documents which had hitherto appeared, as well as the present state of the question while its ultimate decision was still pending. Every one will remember what was said in the first scheme "De Ecclesia," which contained the famous Canons published in the *Augsburg Gazette*, and the sudden appearance of the declaration of Infallibility, under the form of an adjunct to the scheme "De Ecclesia," which was supported by many of the bishops, and caused such dismay to the Opposition in the month of March. The indignation excited by that surprise somewhat cooled the enthusiasm of its authors, or rather induced them to let the tempest pass over before they proceeded any further. The scheme, with its Appendix, disappeared in the dark recesses of the Secretary's office, and the scheme "De Fide" occupied public attention. When the prevailing agitation had calmed down with the reproduction of the scheme "De Fide" and "De parvo Catechismo," the scheme "De Ecclesia" reappeared modified, as circumstances required. In this process Infallibility had lost its character of a simple "postulatum," and had become an integral part of the scheme before the assembly had considered the matter. The object of the first appearance of the question in March was now apparent. It was plain that the Pope's part in the proposals submitted to the Council was of so direct a character that he could not spontaneously, and by his own initiative, embody in them the demand for the declaration of his own Infallibility, and therefore for the moment he was obliged to let it appear to emanate from the bishops. Neither could it be left isolated in a form which would give it less weight in the eyes of those in the assembly, who were accustomed to strict ecclesiastical discipline,

than it would possess if formally incorporated into the scheme itself; and therefore after its first appearance, Infallibility was inserted in the scheme from whence its authors had resolved that it should only emerge to become a dogma for the whole Church.

2. At the same time they sacrificed great part of the scheme "De Ecclesia," as they had part of that "De Fide," in deference to the remonstrances of diplomacy on the Canons regulating the connection between Church and State, thinking very justly that Infallibility virtually contained them all. Under these conditions the scheme that we mentioned last month, "Constitutio Dogmatica Prima de Ecclesia Christi" appeared in four chapters and three Canons, many fewer than those contained in the first draft.

3. In the first chapter, under the title " De Apostolici Primatus in Beato Petro Institutione," was contained the declaration of the primacy of St. Peter over the whole Church. In the second, " De Perpetuitate Primatus Petri in Romanis Pontificibus," is asserted the perpetual and uninterrupted continuation of that primacy in the bishops of Rome as successors of St. Peter in the Church he founded. In the third chapter, entitled, "De Vi et Ratione Primatus Romani Pontificis," are enumerated and described the effects of this primacy, and here commences the apotheosis of the Pope, terminating in the last chapter with personal Infallibility.

4. The third chapter affirms the supreme jurisdiction, ordinary and immediate, of the Pope, over all churches singly and collectively, over the pastors as well as the flocks; from which doctrine it follows that bishops, in exercising any jurisdiction, or authority, only do so as official delegates of the Pope.

It seems that, conscious of this logical inference, the compilers of the scheme tried to avoid it, and to defend themselves from the imputation of seeking to lessen the jurisdiction of the bishops; but in this endeavour, instead of exculpating themselves, they really admit the charge. The scheme cites the words of St. Gregory the Great, in a letter to Eulagius, Bishop of Alexandria, "Tum vero ego honoratus sum cum singulis quisquis honor debitus non negatur." But these words are contained in the following passage, with reference to the title of Universal Apostle assumed by the Patriarch of Constantinople. "Non dixi nec mihi vos nec cuiquam alteri tale aliquid scribere debere; et ecce in præfatione epistolæ quam ad me ipsum qui prohibui direxistis superbæ appellationis verbum universalem me Papam dicentes imprimere curastis. Quod peto dulcissima mihi Sanctitas vestra ultra non faciat, quia vobis subtrahitur quod alteri plus quam ratio exigit præbetur. Ego enim non verbis quæro prosperari sed moribus. Nec honorem esse reputo in quo fratres meos honorem meum perdere cognosco. Meus namque honor est honor Universalis Ecclesiæ. Meus honor est fratrum solidus vigor. Tum vero ego honoratus sum cum singulis quisque honor debitus non negatur. Si enim universalem me Papam vestra Sanctitas dicit negat se hoc esse quod me fatetur universum."

When the whole quotation is given the words bear a much clearer and more extended application. The extraction of one phrase only, omitting the rest of the passage, indicates a wish to restrict its real meaning. In a series of letters on the pretensions of the Patriarch of Constantinople, St. Gregory the Great speaks yet more clearly and decidedly. In writing to Eulagius of Alexandria on the matter,* he alludes to the fact that the title of Universality was offered to the See of Rome by the Council of Chalcedon, and says, " Sed nullus unquam decessorum meorum hoc tam profano vocabulo uti consensit, quia videlicet si unus Patriarca universalis dicitur Patriarcarum nomen cæteris derogatur. Sed absit hoc, absit a christiani mente id sibi velle quempiam arripere unde fratrum, suorum honorem imminuere in quantulacumque parte videatur."

In another letter to the Emperor Maurice,† on the same subject, he says, " Si igitur illud nomen in ea Ecclesia sibi quisque arripuit, quod apud bonorum omnium judicium fuit, universa ergo Ecclesia quod absit, a statu suo corruit quando is qui appellatur universalis cadit." And, after strongly reprobating the idea of universal supremacy being vested in one See, he says that the Church of Rome declined the offer, " Ne dum privatim aliquid daretur uni honore debito sacerdotes privarentur universi." In another letter to the Emperor,‡ his words on this matter are still stronger. From all these passages, taken in full, it is very clear what St. Gregory meant by " honor debitus ; " but in the scheme which has so isolated and, I might almost say,

* Lib. vii. cap. xxx.   † Lib. iv. cap. xxxvi.   ‡ Lib. iv. cap. xxxii.

retrenched them, what signification do they bear? The scheme itself does not explain the meaning, and only touches on it later in the fourth paragraph, where it vehemently condemns those who oppose the legitimate jurisdiction of the Pope over the bishops, or place any obstacle between them. The limits of this jurisdiction are explained and defined in the third chapter.

In the fourth paragraph, the scheme has two aims; that of distinctly affirming the unlimited jurisdiction of the bishops, and of defending it against all lay interference, renewing the old protests against the "Exequatur," the "Placet," and all other lay rights, which it collectively denounces and condemns.

5. Up to this point some power was left to the Episcopate, and there was still a considerable step to be made before reaching an absolute system of arbitrary power in the Church. Kings enjoy supreme jurisdiction, particularly when they are absolute monarchs, but even they must recognise the possibility of being in error.

There is always a great difference, and especially in the Church, in the jurisdiction which deals with facts, and legislation which regards principles. If the primacy be held in the full significance given it by Rome, the Pope can order and dispose matters at will, he is, in fact, omnipotent, while the episcopate does not as a body interfere with him; and the Pope can exercise full power, or even it may be dictatorship, while the Church, which is the depositary of the highest authority, does not meet in the most solemn manner and take measures to reassert and exercise it. This was precisely the point on which arose the different opinion and pretensions of the "Curiali Romani," and their supporters, and the resistance of particular schools and churches, which had hitherto been respected, and had succeeded in keeping the matter unsettled and open to discussion.

In the fourth paragraph of this chapter, before mentioning Infallibility, the scheme declares that no authority above that of the Pope exists in the Church; that there is no appeal from his judgment; that he can never be judged by any one, or in any case; and lastly, it formally condemns any who should presume to appeal from the decision of the Pope to that of an Ecumenical Council. The reason of this last condemnation does not proceed, as might be supposed, from prudence, and from the necessity of not allowing the judgment of an ordinary authority to be eluded, by transferring the cause to an uncertain and prospective Council, thereby upsetting ecclesiastical discipline; but it proceeds absolutely from the principle asserted by the scheme, that the authority of the Church, even when united with that of the Pope, is not superior to the authority of the Pope alone.

6. From a practical point of view, the declaration of Infallibility could add nothing to the weight of this paragraph, because, if the Pope is raised above human judgment, whatever consequences may ensue to the Church, he is, in fact, Infallible. But absolute ideas are seldom satisfied with asserting and re-asserting their own principles; and so, in the fourth chapter, under the heading, " De Romani Pontificis Infallibilitate," the Pope is specifically declared not only supreme judge, but supreme and Infallible ruler. The first petition for Infallibility, drawn up in March, after quoting the text on which the Roman primacy is founded, " Thou art Peter," &c., and the other, on which the present dogma is built up, " I have prayed for thee, that thy faith fail not," asserted that the Pope—" errare non possit "—in deciding questions of faith and morals ; and added, that the object of this Infallibility is the same as that to which the Infallibility of the Church extends. The document concluded with a *monitum*, limiting to ten days the time allowed to the bishops for presenting their observations. This was a fresh and exceptional restriction, which went beyond those introduced by the new Order. This clause—by which a small body of persons endeavoured to impose the brief space of ten days on the supreme assembly of the united Church, as the limit of time in which they should decide on a very grave matter, that of giving a perpetual vote of confidence to the person of the Pope, and of rendering his authority absolutely unlimited—this clause may be some day regretted by those who framed it. It remains as a testimony to the pressure they exercised in order to carry it, and will lessen the belief in their wisdom, not only in the minds of philosophers and of men of intelligence and energy, but also in the minds of moderate Christians capable of reasoning on the future.

7. The new text which was inserted in the Constitution "De Ecclesia Christi," recently published, gave as nearly as possible the same definition of the personal Infallibility of the Pope, only in a still more explicit form. It asserts that the acceptance of all his decisions in questions of faith and morals is obligatory, and reiterates even more strongly than the first text, that the same Infallibility is inherent in the Church and in the Pope, and applies in both to the same object. This was the declaration which gave rise to Maret's remark on the analogy created by its incomprehensible nature, between the new dogma and the mystery of the Trinity.

8. Both the schemes conclude by saying that he who (*quod Deus avertat*) contradicts this declaration, falls into error, and separates himself from the truth and unity of the Catholic Church. There is no Canon on Infallibility in either of the schemes. The three Canons of "De Ecclesia" answer to the three first chapters, namely, the Primacy of St. Peter, its perpetuity in his successors, and the supreme jurisdiction that flows from it; but the chapter on Infallibility contains merely the doctrinal matter, and in neither text is there a special Canon. All, therefore, which the resistance of so many bishops and Catholics to the dogma of Infallibility had been able to extract from the Vatican was that it should not be compiled in the form of a Canon, or have an anathema literally coupled with it. This is a distinction which may not be evident even to acute and elevated minds, but it has great significance in the obscure and subtle reasoning introduced into the Church of Rome by the Greek influences, which were prevalent at its first formation.

III.—DEBATE ON INFALLIBILITY.

1. Prognostications and state of parties.—2. Processions, prayers, and addresses. —3. Opening of the debate on Infallibility.—4. Approach of summer.— 5. Speech of the Pope on the Festival of Corpus Domini.—6. The fight begins. —7. History of the question of Infallibility.—8. The same.—9. The same.— 10. Continuation and ending.—11. Speech of Cardinal Guidi.—12. Speech of Valerga.—13. Speech of the Archbishop of Osimo.—14. Predictions.—15. A third party.—16. The Opposition pray for a prorogation of the Council.

1. All parties now looked eagerly for the promised formula, the plan of reconciliation which should emanate from the majority. Time wore on; it was already the middle of June; the feast of St. Peter, the date fixed by the Infallibilists for the promulgation of the new dogma was at hand, and the greatest anxiety was felt on both sides. Meanwhile as *motus in fine velocior* all sorts of conjectures were rife, especially with regard to the character of the formula, so long desired, and so much delayed, as well as the particular shade of Infallibilist opinion that would prevail in it. The general impression was, that coming from the majority it would be very absolute in tone, and would contain the most extreme Ultramontane opinions, hardly concealed, with the view of gaining over some few of the minority, and that it would insist on an unqualified declaration of Infallibility. The Opposition, on their part, had considered the expediency of putting forth a formula, by which both sides might come to an understanding, and Sant Antonio, Bishop of Florence, had suggested one which should affirm the Infallibility of the Pope, whenever he speaks with the advice of the episcopate and the assent of the Universal Church. All these movements were, however, more apparent than real, the actual state of the case being such as we have described. The majority declared, with more reason than was evident at the moment, that they could carry their measures in despite of the minority, while the minority thought themselves secure of from eighty to one hundred and thirty votes, to keep up the Opposition. Many, however, doubted that such a number would be found willing to pronounce the "Non placet," which must necessarily be given, not only in the private Congregations, but before the Pope at the last public Session; such people could not but see that it would

be a very difficult, if not an impossible matter to force the definitive promulgation of a dogma so disputed, while still opposed by such a number of Fathers as must (even if diminished) be considerable, and acquire great importance from the antecedents of the discussion, and the state of popular feeling. The minority, therefore, strained every nerve to hold back the majority, threatening them with a large number of adverse votes, while the majority retorted, asserting their firm resolution to carry out their intentions. Whichever party could first discover the weakness of the other seemed sure of victory, and as the means of authority and influence were all in the hands of the majority, it was likely that they would succeed in dividing, if not crushing, the minority, or would find some less dangerous way of oppressing them.

2. The Catholic party used all possible measures for bringing about this result, and attempted by public prayers and processions, in Rome and other places, to arouse the religious feelings of the people on the matter. The episode described in the month of May, regarding the parish priests, was utilised as a good example; their address was the first of a series of addresses imploring the declaration of Infallibility, obtained from the collegiate and religious bodies in the city, and even from the Roman University. In order to procure the greatest possible number of clerical assents, individual priests were invited to subscribe for the celebration of masses in favour of Infallibility, and to devote the alms collected to the "Obolo di San Pietro." All the demonstrations employed since the year '60 in furtherance of the temporal power were now renewed in favour of Infallibility. Religious enthusiasm was excited on all sides in favour of the new dogma; enticement and blandishments were tried on those who were independent, and very direct means of influence were brought to bear on the many in Rome—who, being in some way or other dependent on the Curia, are especially interested in finding it infallible—at the beginning of every month. Addresses were circulated in the country, where they had been hitherto strictly prohibited under heavy penalties; the people (though far from possessing sovereign power) were canvassed for a plébiscite; and owing to the state of fervid agitation which prevailed, anecdotes were circulated

which would sometimes have been comical, were it not that they might soon give place to something of a sad and serious character.

3. The partial discussion on the different chapters proceeded rapidly, as many bishops pretended to consider it of slight importance: towards the middle of June the three first were gone through; and on Wednesday, the 15th, the debate on Infallibility, the subject of the fourth chapter began. Eighty persons were prepared to speak, and as the discussion would thus inevitably extend beyond the feast of St. Peter, the majority were disappointed in their expectation of carrying the declaration of the dogma on that solemn festival. In fact, St. Peter's Day was so near, that even had the majority tried to bring the debate to a close by such another stroke (as they had employed on previous occasions), they had no time left to benefit by their success. That festival once passed, and the long, burning Roman summer begun, there seemed to be no special day which could afford a pretext for bringing the debate to a close, for undoubtedly recurring anniversaries exercise considerable influence in ancient establishments. Although the declaration of Infallibility, a dogma on which the fate of Christianity depended, was so important a matter, that no limit could be assigned to its consideration, some people deemed it necessary that the declaration should take place on a great festival, such as that of St. Peter, for if the devout public had learnt on an ordinary week-day that the Pope was Infallible, it seems that they would hardly have appreciated the fact, and therefore the triumph of the supporters of the dogma would have been incomplete.

4. The programme of the Opposition appeared well arranged, for it was likely that the slackness in the work of the Council might end in a prorogation, on account of the heat of summer, and thus they would be saved from the otherwise inevitable shipwreck that awaited them. But, as will be seen, this reckoning did not suit the other side. Every one felt the gravity of the situation, and consequently the new move on the part of the majority gave rise to all sorts of conjectures, and people wondered what effect would under these circumstances be produced on the Council by the trying and unhealthy season now fast approaching—would it overpower the Oppo-

sition or discourage the majority? The issue must soon be apparent, but though all the advantages appeared to be on the side of the majority, this fact was against them, that notwithstanding all which had been done in the six months the Council had been sitting, its deliberations had produced no definite results.

5. On Thursday, being the feast of Corpus Christi, no congregation was held, nor was there any on Friday, on account of the anniversary of the Pope's election. On the latter day it is customary for the Sacred College to offer their congratulations to the Pope through the Cardinal-Vicar, after the religious service is completed, and on this occasion their address was full of allusions to Infallibility, with prayers for its speedy definition, and of good wishes for the extension of the Pope's reign even beyond the years of St. Peter's.

The Pope displayed great dexterity in his answer; he avoided the open acknowledgment of the honour paid to him, but alluding to the bishops now assembled in Rome, he divided them into three classes. He said the first (*the Opposition*) were worldly, and cared more for popularity than for the truth, and prayed for their illumination. The second class, he said, were uncertain, and for them he implored decision from heaven. On the third (the Infallibilists) who were walking in the paths of the Lord, he simply bestowed his benediction. These judgments appeared, at the least, premature, for if one part were already condemned, what was the use of prolonging the discussion.

6. The sittings were resumed on Saturday, June 18th, when it was expected that the third chapter would be finally voted, but instead of that, the debate on Infallibility was opened. It was a memorable day, for it witnessed the commencement of the final combat in which (though pretty well settled by what had preceded) was to be irrevocably decided the fate of the Catholic Church, the most serious struggle in which she had ever been engaged, for it brought her into opposition with the institutions and civil society of the age. We have now arrived at the knot of the question which agitated the Vatican Council, a critical and decisive question, on which depended the constitution of the Catholic Church, and before proceeding further we

will turn back and consider briefly the history of the doctrine of Infallibility up to the present time.

7. The growth of the Papacy has been gradual; it began with the application of our Lord's words to St. Peter to his successors, the Bishops of Rome, and, being strengthened by the transfer of the seat of government brought about by Constantine, it naturally increased, as containing within itself the first principles of unlimited power, which were fostered by the growing favour of successive ages, and furthered by the wonderful talent and virtue of such men as Gregory VII., Innocent III., and Boniface VIII. The Church in general was occupied in the task of her own organisation, and in the laborious development of new forms of Christian life; and though she had on many occasions acknowledged the primacy of the See of Rome, she had never had the opportunity nor felt the need of determining à *priori* the character and conditions of their mutual relations, which varied according to circumstances, and were never made the subject of discussion, or accurately defined until the ninth century, when the study of Canon law sprang into existence. It was then that the jurists, seizing on the fact of the acknowledged primacy of the Roman See, constructed the syllogism which, with the aid of logic and dialectics (both powerful instruments of the intellectual movements referred to), would have led long since to the final result now under discussion but for the resistance constantly maintained by the energetic and practical working of the Church herself. The school that supported the theory of the unlimited power of the Pope arose with the appearance of the Decretals, or the formation of Canon law; but with regard to his Infallibility, that was not included in the science of law, but belonged to the region of dogma; therefore, however much the Papal school of canonists tried to amplify the prerogatives of the See of Rome, declaring it universal, above all other authority, and subject to no control, they could only open the way for Infallibility and facilitate its declaration, but could go no further. Infallibility, as a matter of discussion, and as a definite opinion of the Church, only appears at a later date with the advance of theological studies.

8. The age of St. Thomas Aquinas was fertile in canonical and theological controversy, and it is then that we meet with

the first mention of Infallibility as a dogma; it was taken up
from that time by the Roman "Curia," and was maintained by
the numerous mendicant orders who constitute the special
defenders of Roman doctrine; but even in those days it was resisted by many, and its nature was not accurately determined by
its own supporters. A question had already been raised as to
the case of a Pope falling into heresy, and the point was argued
whether such a one would *de facto* lose the Papal quality. The
Popes themselves carefully avoided giving any opinion on the
matter of Infallibility for a long time. Some, like St. Gregory
the Great, had declined the attribute indirectly, indeed, but most
warmly and repeatedly; and even those who, like Innocent III.,
were strongly in favour of Papal authority, had never ventured
on assuming such a quality. The University of Paris, the
earliest school of theology, and especially devoted to its study,
had constantly opposed the doctrine, and had inaugurated the
Gallican traditions, which were firmly maintained in France,
with varying success, until the end of the last century. The
jurisconsults and the canonists had indeed striven all this
time, unweariedly and with some degree of success, to extend
and enlarge the Papal authority, as is shown by the works on
Papal prerogative so common in the thirteenth and fourteenth
centuries—those of Martino di Tropau, of Tolomeo da Lucca,
for instance, and many others. By these means, and by the
increased authority acquired by the Roman See after the reigns
of Gregory VII. and Innocent III., the prerogatives of the Popes
and their Infallibility would have made rapid progress but for
the schism of the West, which occurred towards the end of the
fourteenth and the beginning of the fifteenth century. This
schism, by its long duration, by its disastrous consequences, and
by the perplexity experienced by the faithful in witnessing the
proceedings of the different Popes who contended for the Chair
of St. Peter, gave a shock to the Papal system, and greatly diminished the prestige of the school which supported it to the utmost.

9. In this crisis, people looked for help to the intervention of
the episcopate, and a Council met at Pisa, whose work was not
really completed until the Council of Constance. This latter
assembly, which was convened in consequence of the great strife
agitating the Church, checked the advancement of the Roman

Curia, of Papal authority, and, indirectly, the progress of the question of Infallibility.

The Council of Basle was held shortly after, during the Pontificate of Eugenius IV., and under much the same conditions as the Council of Constance, but was dissolved on the deposition of Eugenius and the accession of Felix V., though, when Eugenius was again in power, it re-assembled at Florence. This time Papal authority recovered its lost prestige, owing to the Council being held in Italy, to the favourable opportunity now afforded for the advancement of the Pope's authority by the reunion of the Latin and Greek Churches, and also on account of the mistakes committed at Basle.

The formula of the Council of Florence concerning the Pope, though the last hope of the Opposition at the Vatican Council, seemed a great gain to the Roman Curia after the Councils of Constance and of Basle, assisted its rising fortunes, and added to the prestige of the Papacy. The formula was to this effect: that the Pope is Vicar of Christ, Head of the Church, Father and Master of all Christians, and that he is endued by God with full power to rule the Church in the manner laid down by the Canons and the precepts of Ecumenical Councils. Ever since the Council of Constance, and especially since that of Basle, the promoters of absolute authority had urged their views within and without the Curia, and they became more active and energetic when, in consequence of those Councils, Papal authority was questioned and the dominion of the Curia threatened; in fact, we may say that Infallibility then, for the first time, acquired a scholastic or scientific form. The works of Cardinal Torquemada, theologian, and Master of the Sacred Palaces under Eugenius IV., which are the manual of the new school, appeared after the Council of Basle. They were followed by the writings of Cardinal Caetano and of Cano; and up to the time of Bellarmine, Infallibilist doctrines were steadily on the ascendant, though some protests against them were heard, even in Italy: as, for example, in the severe words addressed by St. Catherine of Siena to Gregory XI., with the view of arresting the growing absolutism of Rome. Many illustrious and able churchmen endeavoured to do the same, by raising the influence and authority of the bishops. Sadoleto,

Contarini, Caraffa, Pole, and others among the cardinals, whose opinions carried much weight from their learning and high position, in the famous Memorial of 1538 acknowledged the necessity of placing some limit to the Pope's authority, and tried to find one; but the fate of the Catholic Church in this respect was decided at the Council of Florence, where the triumph of the Papal system was inaugurated, the attempt to vindicate episcopal rights having failed at Basle. Torquemada and his school immediately resumed their efforts to further the movement towards Infallibility, which increased until its theory, though never universally accepted, and always opposed, was more or less explicitly admitted in the teaching and opinion of the adherents of the Roman "Curia." The doctrine of Infallibility was not, however, fully admitted for three centuries, as a storm far more violent than the schism of the West now arose, and produced an insurmountable barrier to its progress. The Roman "Curia," as often happens, feeling confident of success, would not moderate its pretensions; and from the beginning of the sixteenth century there reigned a series of Popes who employed, without any restraint, the unlimited authority, political and religious, which the Curia had assured to them; and thereby excited (especially among the German races, who were of a sterner cast than others) a profound reaction; and opened the door to the religious innovators who, for more than a century, had been agitating the minds of the newly-civilised populations of Europe.

When the great crisis burst forth which rent Western Christendom and threatened the foundations of the Christian religion, the rapid and unlooked-for success of the Reformation interrupted all those laborious efforts which since the Council of Florence had contributed greatly to further Papal ascendency both in theory and in practice, and to promote the authority of the Curia. The progress of the doctrine of Infallibility, which had been as rapid as possible in that corrupt and heretical century, was also arrested.

10. The discussion of the prerogatives of Rome was impossible at a moment when the very foundations of the Christian edifice were trembling beneath the shocks of the tempest of Reformation. That great event was attended by the same con-

sequences as had resulted from the schism of the West; when the crisis was past and Rome had triumphed at Trent (though with the loss of two flourishing countries), her one thought was how best to profit by the victory, and, as in the Protestant movement, the question of Papal authority was set in the front rank, so also a reaction in favour of that authority was manifested on the Catholic side. This reaction encountered but slight resistance and few obstacles, for the more energetic and vigorous populations had detached themselves definitively from the interests at issue, and those who did take part in it were already affected in some measure by that frivolous and sceptical spirit which prepared the way for the philosophy of Voltaire, and brought about a new crisis in the nineteenth century.

The famous Bull of Urban VIII., "In Cœna Domini," was the most solemn manifestation of the renewed vigour of Papal authority, and in it the Pope himself spoke. Boniface VIII., three hundred years before, had established the primacy of the Papacy on earth in the Bull "Unam Sanctam," and now the Bull "In Cœna Domini" confirmed those provisions, strongly reasserted ecclesiastical jurisdiction, and affirmed the unlimited power of the Pope in the Church. It is well to remark that the reaction against the independence and freedom of enquiry, introduced by the Reformation into Christianity, was characterised by an affected devotion and a blind and passive obedience to authority. One of the highest expressions of the tendencies of that period was the formation of the Order of the Jesuits, which adopted the qualities mentioned above as the rule of their conduct and as the very principle of their existence. For all these reasons Papal authority and the doctrine of Infallibility found themselves on favourable ground. Previous to the Reformation Infallibility had borne a vague and indefinite character. Torquemada and his companions had indeed striven to fix its application; but their theories had always been upset by one adverse argument, the possibility of a Pope proving to be a heretic. Here was a difficulty which they could not entirely overcome, though they endeavoured, by every possible means, to guard against it. It belongs to the character of passive reaction against mental freedom, which gave birth to the Order of the Jesuits, to advance the question of Infallibility, which had constantly progressed as a recoil from any independent movement manifested in the Church; and accordingly, in the period of repose and lassitude which succeeded the Council of Trent, the doctrine of Infallibility, with the assistance of casuistry, assumed more definite shape. Though obliged to contend with the incipient scepticism and pronounced cynicism of the age, it gained ground, and by means of the numerous writings and uncontested action of the Roman Curia, insinuated itself yet further into the feeble belief and lax practice of the Catholic populations, especially in Spain and Italy. There is, however, a considerable gap between Baronius, Orsi, and the apologists of that age and the present Infallibilists; and in reading the 'Annals' of the famous Baronius one can hardly understand, according to present ideas, how it was possible for a cardinal to use the language he often adopts, in writing the history of the Papacy. It remained for the storm of modern Revolution to drive into the widest antagonism the workings of absolute authority in opposition to those of uncontrolled license, and by the help of the latter, the promoters of absolutism, who are now represented by the so-called Catholic party, and led by the Jesuits (always its strongest promoters) have succeeded in passing the theory of the Pope's personal Infallibility in the clearest and most decided form, presenting it to a Council convoked for the express purpose of instituting it as a dogma of the Church on the 18th of June, 1870, about nineteen centuries after the foundation of Christianity, and about ten centuries after the theory had first become matter of debate.

11. Five cardinals, Rauscher, Di Pietro, Bonnechose, Cullen, and Guidi, spoke on the 18th. Rauscher was obliged to have his speech read for him, the weakness of his voice preventing his being heard: it was moderate and conciliatory, but did not produce much effect. The event of the day, was the speech of Cardinal Guidi, who, having begun in such a way as to please the majority, ended by showing himself favourable to, if not entirely in accordance with, the views of the minority. His conclusion was that the Pope could not define doctrine without the Council or the advice of the Church; for there was some uncertainty among his hearers as to whether his words were *sine consilio* or *sine concilio Ecclesiæ*.

He was so led on by his own eloquence, that in the peroration he passed the limits he had originally fixed, and proposed a Canon which should contain an anathema against all who hold that the Popes could define doctrine without the advice of the Church. According to this, the Pope himself was in some peril of being condemned as having several times distinctly professed his belief in Infallibility.

The effect of this speech was like that of a sudden thunder-clap in a cloudless sky. A Roman Cardinal actually the first, the only one, to side openly with the minority! If a shell had exploded amongst the majority, it could hardly have excited more commotion. The Infallibilist Fathers were much perturbed, and turned to Cardinal Guidi with violent gestures, and marks of extreme displeasure, while the bishops of the Opposition received him with the warmest demonstrations of pleasure and affection. The next day Cardinal Guidi was the universal subject of conversation, and was cruelly spoken of and reviled by those who do not follow the doctrine taught by St. John in the charitable exhortation, "Brethren, love one another." At the same time Guidi was summoned to the Vatican, and there it was reported he had to encounter many reproaches, which he received with perfect firmness and dignity. It was said that on this occasion the Pope adopted the well-known words of Louis XIV., turning their application to himself with regard to ecclesiastical tradition; but it was impossible to ascertain the truth of these reports which circulated in Rome, but were of no real importance, and neither added to nor detracted from the weight of the incident itself.

12. The number of inscribed orators on the 18th had risen to 108, and the presidents determined not to interrupt the discussion, but to leave it unchecked, as they did not wish again to incur the reproach of exercising pressure or violence on the minority. Perhaps they were assisted in this resolution by the expectation that the heat of summer would soon bring about the close of the discussion. When the Fathers met on Monday, the 20th, the legates addressed to them a *monitum* recommending brevity in their speeches; and the Patriarch Valerga, who in discussing Eastern affairs, expressed himself as violently as he had done on a former occasion, when he caused great offence to the French bishops,

was called to order. Valerga's vehement speech met with little favour, on account of the unfortunate position of Eastern affairs, in the direction of which he was a good deal concerned. The majority even were displeased, and he was obliged to descend from the ambo, although his party had looked to him to undo the effect produced on the previous day by the speech of Cardinal Guidi. On Tuesday no Congregation was held, that being the anniversary of the coronation of the Pope, and Pius IX. entered upon the twenty-fifth year of his reign under auspices not indeed devoid of sadness. For twenty-four years he had been applauded and made much of in every possible way, and now he was gradually approaching his apotheosis. All parties vied with each other in exalting him, and doing honour to his high and lofty station, until nothing remained but to ascribe to him the powers of Divinity, and, indeed, he was about to receive one of the Divine prerogatives. The twenty-fifth year of their reign seems to be a fatal one for the Popes; Pius IX. was no exception to this rule, for it was to be the occasion of his ceasing in some ways to be merely human and of his becoming something higher. The ultra-Catholic journals were full of observations and felicitations on the aupicious event.

13. On Wednesday the sittings were resumed, and the *monitum* ordering brevity in the speeches was put into practice. The legates adopted the expedient of ringing a bell in order to stop any orators who exceeded twenty minutes, and this plan answered very well, instead of closing the debate, a practice which was given up for the present. Only seven speeches were made on the 22nd, one of them by a bishop who warmly supported Infallibility, but even he was obliged to desist after twenty minutes. The Archbishop of Osimo then made a conciliatory speech, and in order to dispose the legates in his favour, began by stating that he would be so brief as to save them the trouble of stopping him. In attempting this he incurred the imputation of want of clearness; but notwithstanding the difficulty of treating matters so grave and complicated in a very short time, he managed to bring forward a project of reconciliation. This was not of so absolute a nature as the formula adopted by the Jesuits, but was a reproduction of the ancient formula, which ever since the Council of Trent had been used in Roman

theology, and much resembled that contained in the second address issued after the first petition of the Infallibilists. This formula, as we have already stated, by asserting that the Pope and the bishops together form, *de jure et de facto*, one Church, virtually sanctions the Infallibility of the Pope. The Bishop of Osimo, while rejecting the separation of the Pope from the bishops as a thesis and a hypothesis, both *de jure et de facto*, left the nature of their reciprocal influence and connection as indefinite as possible ; so as to avoid countenancing the Gallican system on the one hand, or admitting personal Infallibility on the other.

This proposal was quite as much as could be hoped for in an assembly known to be adverse to reform; and in which the Opposition ultimately showed itself unequal to making a serious resistance, or of entertaining a firm resolution. It was a last hope for those who saw no other chance of safety, and who, unwilling to prejudge the question, wished to leave matters as they were previous to the Council, postponing their decision till a happier moment should arise ; but this sensible opinion was not the general one, and the bishop's speech was lost with the many other ardent and generous voices *clamantium in deserto*. Other speeches succeeded that of the Bishop of Osimo, and the presence of Cardinal Guidi in the Council Hall was especially noted. On the 23rd seven orators spoke against Infallibility ; and in the next sitting, on the 25th, Strossmayer, the great champion of the Opposition, again came forward. So great was the desire of making progress, that a Congregation was held on Tuesday, the 28th, although the Vigil of St. Peter, and Monsignor Genuilhac, Primate of Gaul, spoke against Infallibility, but could scarcely be heard, on account of the murmurs of the majority. He was formerly Bishop of Grenoble, and had only been raised a few days since to his new dignity on the urgent request of the French Government, for the Holy See, knowing his opinions, would rather have chosen another candidate. Wednesday, the 29th, being the feast of St. Peter, no sitting was held, and next day the Pope gave up the usual ceremonies at the Ostian Basilica for the feast of St. Paul, in order that the Congregations might be resumed, and the happy moment of the declaration of Infallibility might be hastened.

14. Meantime the feast of St. Peter had passed, and the aspect

of affairs, far from improving, grew darker. As Cardinal Guidi, who was considered an able and intelligent man, had abandoned the majority in order to side with the Opposition, it could hardly be supposed that their position was as yet hopeless, at least, such was the opinion of many. Moreover, the history of the address of the parochial clergy, and many other incidents, made it evident that the Opposition were daily growing stronger, and signs of discontent were apparent very near the Papal throne. In Germany there were indications of a deep and increasing resistance; and the same spirit showed itself in France, where, according to the disposition of the people, it was expressed in a less serious manner, and found vent in many sharp and witty sayings, but certainly gained ground rather than decreased. The Opposition was no longer vague, isolated, and divided, as when first it sprang into existence, but was now an organised, and, to a certain extent, a disciplined body, representing a considerable portion of the Church, from the Catholics of America to the Cardinals of the Holy See. A person of great talent and of excellent judgment, in describing the state of affairs at this time, said that if Infallibility were accepted the Vatican Council would certainly not be accepted; and, indeed, in forming any opinion on the prevailing condition of affairs, which was at all reasonable, it was impossible to escape from this dilemma.

15. All who were acquainted with the course of Roman business saw that the Vatican could not stop halfway, and submit to a defeat which would be the more serious in proportion to the advance already made. At the same time it did not seem possible for the Vatican to insist on passing a dogma against the wish and convictions of an authoritative minority, whose numbers varied from 80 to 130, and if the timid and backward be included, reached 150. For if the whole of this number could not be reckoned upon for a definitive resistance, still the minority was too important to be overlooked. The majority were well aware of this, and though quite determined themselves, they never gave up seeking for a formula which should split the Opposition and win over some of its members, but as they were determined not to sacrifice the smallest part of the dogma of Infallibility, their search was a vain one.

The result of these attempts had been to found a sort of third party in the Council (though a third party in religious matters has a difficult position), the head of which, at this moment, was Cardinal Guidi; for when the first surprise occasioned by his conduct had subsided, it was evident that the step he had taken was rather with a view to reconciling conflicting parties than of joining the Opposition. Moreover, the fact of the Cardinal Archbishop of Bologna, a personal friend of the Pope, placing himself at the head of this attempt at reconciliation, was felt to be an indication of its vigour and suitability. We must allow that the endeavour was both liberal and courageous on the part of Cardinal Guidi; but, like many previous attempts of the same nature, it was fruitless, since nothing could induce the majority to make any concession on the matter of personal Infallibility, and the Opposition, having been subjected to so many vexations and delusions, were resolved not to put up with further equivocation, and had become mistrustful and stubborn. Moreover there was this technical difficulty to contend with, that the Popes, having gradually reached a position of unlimited authority by a constant though gradual system of expansion, and being endued with the rights of primacy and absolute jurisdiction in the Church, had already acquired all the accessories of Infallibility; and as in the long and disputed process all possible sophisms and verbal subtleties, and all the most ingenious combinations of phrases had been exhausted, there really remained nothing further to do in the way of discussion. It only remained now to say the word, and therefore the Council found itself inevitably in the dilemma of either declaring the dogma, or of leaving matters as they were; but they viewed this latter course in the light of a defeat, so that reconciliation seemed impossible, and the state of antagonism in which both parties had been placed for the last six months continued unchanged.

16. Towards the end of June the Opposition bethought themselves of another expedient, and offered to the Pope a means of escaping in a manner convenient both to himself and to them, from the difficult position in which he was placed from being both the judge and the party chiefly interested, in the same question. Several bishops of the Opposition signed a petition, in which they prayed for a prorogation of the Council, on account of the great heat now prevailing in Rome, which seriously affected

many of their number. Their petition met with the usual reception, and nothing further was known of its results save the inexorable determination of the Pope that the Congregations should proceed without interruption until all the business of the Council was completed. With these or similar tentative efforts on both sides, the month of June, the seventh since the Council had assembled, drew to a close, and though the grand question had not made any real advance since the first day, the Opposition had gained many adherents, had greatly extended its influence, and had spread considerably. This extension had drawn forth the expression of public opinion, which found vent in the saying we have alluded to, that " if the dogma of Infallibility were accepted, the Vatican Council would not be accepted," an opinion very generally entertained in the present serious state of affairs. Those who supported it did not suppose that if the Opposition were conquered, they would question the validity of the Council on account of the difficulties occasioned by the want of unanimity in its decisions, and other matters which they had often and earnestly lamented. Their intention was rather to point out that the world which had looked to the Council for the solution of the great political-religious and social-religious problems which had long troubled Catholic nations, and saw it occupied only in building up a perplexing and questionable apotheosis, would cease to regard it with attention, would lose all hope in it, and that in proportion as it endeavoured to render its action absolute and coercive, the influence of that action on society would be diminished.

JULY.

I.—CLOSE OF THE DEBATES.

1. Effects of the climate.—2. Weariness of the assembly.—3. The bishops begin to leave Rome.—4. The first heads of the scheme "De Ecclesia" are voted.—5. Close of the discussion.—6. Reasons of the Opposition for accepting it.—7. The same.—8. Discussion on the amendments.—9. The Opposition consider their future course.—10. Formula of Infallibility.—11. After the proposal.—12. The third chapter is voted.—13. The fourth chapter is voted.—14. The vote on Wednesday, July 13.

1. THE venerable assembly now began to experience the full heat of a Roman summer. The burning rays of the sun have not only a weakening effect on the constitution, but falling on the uncultivated and marshy Campagna occasion a state of atmosphere, if not always fatal, at least injurious to the natives themselves. Only those who have actually experienced the summer heat in Rome can understand the effect it produced on the bishops from northern countries, accustomed to the cool temperature, the bracing air, and the sparkling streams of Germany. At an advanced age, changes of temperature which would otherwise have no great effect, have serious and rapid results, and many of the bishops and their dependents fell ill. It is difficult to describe the lassitude and despondency which the hard and wearisome work of the Council produced in those sensitive natures, when the temperature was such as suited the Spaniards, Calabrians, and Mexicans. These latter had probably looked forward to the result produced on their northern brethren in Opposition, when the thermometer stood at 115° in the shade. The Opposition were influenced by the same consideration when they had prayed for the prorogation of the Council before proceeding to the definition of Infallibility ; but the south occupied

the seat of authority, and the north was unable to carry this or any other of its wishes.

2. Signs of this state of weariness had been apparent for some time. The Bishop of Ferentino had urged it in one of the recent Congregations as an argument against the Opposition, accusing its members of prolonging the sufferings of the Fathers, but he became himself the victim of his own accusation. While venting his displeasure against the minority in the well-known classical quotation, "quousque tandem abutere patientia nostra?" the legate remarked that his words were most apt, and invited him to set the example of the right course by himself descending from the tribune. The assembly, tired of him, as indeed it was of all the orators, cordially hailed the intervention of the legate, and those present asserted that the ringing of the bell which cut short the ardent speaker, was the most grateful sound which had ever yet reverberated through the Council Hall.

3. When the bishops learned that the Pope refused to listen to the just plea for a prorogation afforded by the tropical heat, their state of discouragement became one of deep vexation, and they began one by one to leave Rome for their own dioceses, partly from disgust at the want of kindness and generosity with which they had been treated, and partly from reasons of health and from mistrust of the future. The Vatican willingly granted leave of absence to all who then applied for it, with the hope, perhaps, of diminishing the strength of the Opposition by offering its members a safe means of retreat from the difficulties of their position. It was said that the authorities afterwards regretted not having obtained from those Fathers who left Rome, some guarantee or promise of submission to the decrees of the Council in the event of its proclaiming the dogma of Infallibility, a result which now seemed probable and near at hand. At any rate, the bishops in Opposition believed this, and several times feared that some such promise would be exacted from them, and this misgiving considerably affected their later deliberations.

4. The bishops of Savannah and Paderborn spoke on Friday, July 1st. The latter attempted to bring about a reconciliation between the two parties by conceding to the Pope the attribute

of Infallibility, without imposing its belief upon the consciences of the faithful as a dogma. This proposal was hailed with shouts of indignation, and the bishop who next came forward, proposed rather to extend the Infallibility of the Pope beyond the region of faith and morals, to all which is comprised in Catholic morality, as science, politics, &c. It does not appear that the assembly gave this second proposal as bad a reception as it had offered to the first. On the 2nd of July the Council clearly manifested their desire to bring the proceedings to a close. Some Fathers inscribed to speak, declared their intention of not doing so, and therefore in the course of one sitting, thirty-two names were cleared off the lists, of whom the greater number never entered the tribune at all. Several bishops proposed that two Congregations should be held daily as a means of shortening the discussion and gaining time, but this idea was unanimously rejected. The second and third chapters of the scheme were voted on this occasion, and the debate proceeded until brought to an end by the refusal of those who should have spoken, to come forward.

5. It was impossible to indulge any further illusions as to the intentions of the Vatican, which was evidently determined to carry through the plans approved by the majority, notwithstanding the resistance they might encounter. The patience of the Opposition had been already sorely tried by the heat of the climate and the wearisome delays in business, while the refusal of the Pope to agree to a prorogation of the Council after the festival of St. Peter had put the finishing stroke to their displeasure, and now the conviction that the Vatican was bent upon the declaration of Infallibility caused a real panic among them. On Sunday, July 3rd, their leaders held a meeting, in which they finally determined to desist from a combat henceforward useless, and possibly dangerous; the resolution was spontaneously adopted by nearly all present, and, in this frame of mind, the Fathers attended the Congregation on Monday. The history of the close of the debate has been told in many ways, but all admit that when one of the bishops belonging to the Opposition attempted to speak, he was greeted with impatient cries of "abstineas, renuncia," &c., from the majority; whereupon another member of the minority, supposed to

be Strossmayer, rose and declared his determination to be henceforward silent, an example which was soon followed by his colleagues. One of the majority then observed that the Opposition having announced their resolution not to speak further, the debates were ended, and invited his own party to express their agreement in this conclusion. Accordingly, all who had prepared to speak, announced their willingness to desist, excepting two or three of the Fathers, who still wished to be heard. Cardinal de Luca, one of the presidents, gladly availed himself of the occurrence, praised the assembly for its determination, thanked those who had originated the happy idea, and declared the debate, and the sitting to be concluded. In fact, it might be said that the war ended for lack of combatants to carry it on.

6. The intention of the Opposition in thus promoting the close of the debate was simply, as one of their members publicly declared, to avoid wasting time and arguments upon adversaries who were resolved to take no account of them, and to disregard the traditions and the future fate of the Church. The majority tried to set aside this reasoning and to explain the matter so as to suit their own wishes, but the result of the definitive vote soon vindicated the truth of the assertion, even without the declaration of the bishops in Opposition.

7. Many people have criticised the conduct of the Opposition on this occasion, but to form a correct judgment on the point all the facts of the case should be fully considered. Owing to the state of despondency prevailing in the minority, and the fact that many of the German, Hungarian, and French bishops had already left Rome, the Infallibilists had become more daring, and interrupted the speeches of their adversaries with signs of irony and disapprobation. It almost seemed that, like the Russians when their country was invaded by the French in 1812, they expected the climate to fight for them, and as soon as they felt its beneficial influences, they considered themselves masters of the field, and began to taste the sweets of victory. The Opposition were obliged by their own policy, and by the nature of the subject and length of the discussion, to repeat the same things very frequently, but this could not go on.

When it was once ascertained that the Pope was determined not to prorogue the Council, and that the dogma of Infallibility would be certainly declared, there was no use in further delay, and no hope but in the final vote. Prolonged discussion on a matter already settled could not influence the opinions of the Fathers, and, moreover, the attempt to continue the debate in a season of intense heat, far from bringing about a good result, was likely rather to prejudice their cause. Indeed, had the meetings of the Council been extended, the bishops would still have gone on leaving Rome, and the Opposition would in consequence have become daily weaker, as its members, being chiefly from northern latitudes, were especially sensitive to the effects of the Roman climate. The minority were most anxious to prevent this result, because the loss of votes, though not important to the majority, was a most serious one to them at the final and conclusive decision, when the whole matter would be settled. Every day, therefore, now wasted was a clear gain to the majority, and an equal loss to the minority, a result which the former had probably foreseen; when, once certain that the assembly would not be dissolved before their work was accomplished, they no longer demanded, or directly promoted the closing, but left the matter to be brought about by the state of general weariness prevailing among the Fathers, and the result soon justified their expectations. The Opposition were also induced by these considerations to join, though reluctantly, in furthering the desires of the majority, who were naturally delighted to end a discussion on which they had made up their minds before it ever began. It remained for the future, now so dark and stormy, and pregnant with most important events, to reveal whether the Opposition had been right or wrong in their policy, and whether, after all that can be said in their defence, it might not appear that by a chance which could not be foreseen their patience had suffered shipwreck when they were almost within the harbour. If succeeding events had not justified this latter conclusion, it would have been difficult to blame the Opposition for a policy which had been fatally guided by the natural course of events and the prevailing public opinion. Great astonishment was felt in the city on the day when the sitting of the Council terminated in the sudden manner we have described, and all sorts of rumours were circulated at the sight of the bishops leaving St. Peter's at an unwonted hour, many on foot, having sent away their carriages, and others crowded together in the public conveyances ; but none, perhaps, who witnessed the prelates thus returning quietly home, realised the influence their decrees would exercise on the civil and religious future, not only in Italy, but in Europe and the whole world !

8. Business proceeded rapidly after this. On Monday, July 5th, the amendments on the third chapter concerning the Primacy were discussed, and, the general resistance having ceased, no objections were made, although the Congregation was a very full one.

Some bishops proposed, in order to gain time, that this chapter, with the amendments agreed on, should be again printed and distributed to the Fathers, that they might examine its contents at leisure ; this occasioned a delay, and the vote on that chapter only took place on Monday the 11th. It was, if we may so consider it, the last concession granted by the president. It was said that on this chapter being presented to the Pope for his approbation, after it had been amended, though not definitively voted by the Council, he added something to it of his own accord, and when this became known to the assembly it aroused, on the part of the Opposition, the last demonstrations of an indignation which they well knew was hereafter unavailing and powerless. Everyone will understand that matters having reached this stage, such anecdotes are of little importance, and it is most difficult to arrive at a knowledge of their accuracy ; but one thing is certain—that the third chapter was passed in the assembly without serious resistance.

9. The majority, elated by this result, began to entertain hopes not only for the vote on the third chapter, but for the much questioned and important fourth chapter, and their expectations were strengthened by the knowledge that differences had arisen among the leaders of the Opposition.

When these latter had agreed at their meeting to give up speaking and to allow the debates to be closed, they had also reflected on the conduct to be pursued when the end, which their policy was now hastening, should arrive. It seems that the Bishop of Orleans, and most of the French prelates in Opposition, wished to make a solemn protest against the treatment they had met with, against the advantage taken of the hot season to weary them, the want of fairness shown towards them by the presidents all through the discussion, and, lastly, against the excesses, insults, and affronts of which the majority had been guilty with regard to them. Having made this protest, they proposed to leave Rome immediately. The Germans, with Monsignor Haynald at their head, were of a different opinion; they were adverse to the protest, and wished to remain in Rome till the end. Perhaps they were right; so many protests had been already made and disregarded, that to continue them seemed almost undignified; and, moreover, the subjects of complaint, though they might be just in themselves, were not of a nature easily susceptible of proof. In fact, the protest was never made. As to the question of leaving or remaining at Rome, time has perhaps shown that on this point the judgment of the Germans was the right one, for the most resolute and the clearest course is usually the best.

10. These divisions were a cause of hope to the Vatican, and therefore, whether in consequence of the encouragement thus gained, or as the logical and natural results of the policy adopted, it came about that the formula of Infallibility was finally produced under these auspices at the end of the discussion on the amendments to the fourth chapter, and in the very Congregation of the 4th of July in which the Fathers had announced their intention of not prolonging the debate. The formula was just what had been expected for some time, and what the majority had prepared with much care, though it had never assumed a definite shape before, and it now appeared as the final result, the consummation of the unanimous wish of the majority who had convoked the Vatican Council and guided the course of its deliberations. As this formula was produced by itself, before the close of the debate, it might be looked upon as a sort of amendment to the fourth chapter, an amendment to the new scheme " De Ecclesia " introduced during the discussion. This scheme had not been sent back to the Commission for revision, and thus the formula preserved that curt and unceremonious character appertaining to the *motus in fine velocior*, with which the later business of the Council proceeded. The formula was thus

worded, that the Pope "cum omnium Christianorum pastoris et doctoris munere fungens, pro suprema sua apostolica auctoritate, doctrinam de fide vel moribus ab universa Ecclesia tenendam definit, per assistentiam divinam ipsis in Beato Petro promissam ea infallibilitate pollere, qua Redemptor Ecclesiam suam institutam esse voluit."

This was the ultimatum which, at the close of a trying and stormy discussion, and after numerous protests, the Vatican offered to the bishops, now wearied out by the simultaneous weight of an unbending will, of ecclesiastical prestige, and of the torrid climate of Rome.

The formula itself was so clear and precise as to defy all comments. Some tried to persuade themselves that it was better than the preceding one; others thought it worse; in truth, it was difficult to draw fine distinctions where none really existed; when one has said that snow is white, it would be hard to make the assertion in better or worse terms, for having said it, one has stated all that there was to say. The terms of this formula, on minute examination, might perhaps be construed to indicate that Infallibility resides primarily in the Church, and is enjoyed by the Pope *ex derivato* when he makes definitions *ex cathedrâ*, &c. But of what practical value are these subtleties? In reality, any Pope wishing to extend this power to its logical consequences, has really the means of upsetting the whole world, or, at least, that part of it which recognises his authority, whenever he chooses. History presents us with the example of several Popes who virtually exercised this power before it was decreed to them by an Ecumenical Council, and we do not find that they acknowledged any limit to their dominion.

11. It seems that, having thus made the definitive stroke, the Vatican remained for a moment astonished, and uncertain as to the effect it had produced. The authorities took measures to ascertain from the bishops in Opposition through their colleagues, what course they intended to pursue in the event of the Pope disregarding their resistance and vote of "Non placet," and insisting on the promulgation of the dogma of Infallibility. The Secretary of State appeared very uneasy as to the opinion of Governments on this declaration. How would they receive the bishops, new Papal vicars, who would now represent in their

States no longer a national authority and local interests, but the authority of Rome, and consequently of a foreign prince, with a policy of his own, a prince to whom they owed an obedience superior to all national duties and obligations? With regard to the first doubt, the uncertainty as to the conduct of the Opposition, it was seriously proposed to present to the bishops, along with the definition of the dogma, a document to be signed by all those who had voted against it; by which they should promise either to accept the dogma, or resign their sees. The Opposition, rightly or wrongly, were much alarmed at this prospect, not possessing such unanimity of opinion or firmness of organisation as would insure their safety under the trial. They found themselves reduced to such a predicament, that to escape from it logically, they must impugn, not only the Infallibility of the Pope, but the validity of the Council, thus indicating the constraint under which they had been placed in forming their decisions, for if they acknowledged the validity of the Council without accepting Infallibility, the resignation of their sees was the logical result. It was not possible for them to assume the course of action first mentioned, as Rome was not the place for it, the time was not propitious, and they themselves not the men to do it; so to avoid the consequences of the second alternative was very difficult, and the uncertainty and perplexity they experienced greatly influenced their conduct in the public Session. With regard to the second doubt, the difficulty about Foreign Powers, although the most clear-sighted were far from being at ease, persons not possessed of great discrimination comforted themselves with the reflection that an undue pressure of authority is readily excused by those who exercise authority themselves, and thought that the Secretary of State might easily reassure Foreign Governments by some such note as he had already addressed to them. The so-called Catholic party trusted, with regard to public opinion, to the tolerance and freedom of thought which has everywhere triumphed in modern days, a liberty which that party never ceases to oppose, but which it knows how to convert to its own purposes, better even than the Liberals.

12. The third chapter was voted on Monday, July 11th. Thirty or forty votes of " Non placet " were irremediably lost by the return of so many German, Hungarian, and French bishops to

their own dioceses. On the same day the debate on the amendments to the fourth chapter—nearly 100 in number—was commenced, but it is clear from what we have already stated that no effectual discussion on the amendments could be undertaken, as the debate on the text itself had been abandoned. A last resistance was made to the word anathema, which was not originally inserted in the formula of Infallibility, nor in the text as read by the reporters, but was now unexpectedly brought forward in a new amendment by some Infallibilist bishops, who, being masters of the field, succeeded in affixing it to the statement as prepared for promulgation. The condemnatory clause may accordingly be read in the draft of the dogma, which was promulgated at the public Session, and takes the place of the circumlocutory phrases which had closed the other formulas presented to the assembly.

13. The greatest precipitation now characterised the proceedings of the assembly; formulas succeeded one another with such rapidity that they were no longer revised by the Commissions, but were substituted one for another and amended in the course of a single debate. So great was the haste, that the discussion on the amendments to the fourth chapter, numbering almost 100, which commenced on the 11th, was finished on the 13th, and put to the vote, with the alterations we have indicated. The latter day will be ever memorable in the annals of the Church for its influence on her future destiny. That day witnessed the voting on the Infallibility of the Pope, the fourth chapter of the scheme " De Ecclesia," with these results: bishops inscribed, 692; total number of votes, 601; "Placet," 451; "Non placet," 88; "Juxta modum," 62; among which latter were three cardinals; absent, 91, among whom was the Secretary of State. The number of Fathers absent from the Council on just grounds was about 30; so it might fairly be considered that the absence of the others was intentional, many of them being actually in Rome, and not choosing to appear, and others having left the city in order to avoid being present. From the absence of the Secretary of State it seems that up to that moment he was uncertain of the final result, and of the ultimate intention of the Pope.

14. Such is the history of the vote which expressed the

opinion of the assembly, on the personal Infallibility of the Pope. Notwithstanding all the efforts made to further the dogma, and all the pressure exercised by the authorities in its favour, between the votes of " Non placet," of " Placet juxta modum," those being conditional assents which in absolute matters become negative, and those who abstained from voting, we may dispassionately and equitably reckon the number of dissentients to be between 150 and 200.

We include in this number all the Fathers who in this Congregation rejected the proposed formula of the personal Infallibility of the Pope, more or less distinctly, and absolutely, as to the whole, or in part, either in word, or in deed. If we revert to the calculation made in the first chapters as to the number of the Fathers present at the Council, and recollect how many bishops *in partibus*, that is to say, holding no cure of souls, were there; how many cardinals in the same position, how many generals of religious orders, who constitute a sort of special army, and are trained under a peculiar and exceptional discipline, and if one remembers that all these form a class particularly dependent on the court of Rome, the sum of the dissentients, even taken at its lowest figure, acquires an importance greater than its amount would warrant in the proportions of the assembly. It must also be borne in mind that the episcopal sees of Italy and the Pontifical provinces, with regard to their size and number, are as five or six to one when compared with France and Germany; and as the Opposition came almost exclusively from the latter countries, the same number, taken as the expression of thought and power, gains still more in value. Finally, we must admit that the moral worth of the criterion afforded by this vote re-establishes, with less difference than appears from the figures in themselves, the relative position of the majority and the minority. Moreover, we should not forget the influence exercised, and that naturally produced by the august presence of the Pope in the Vatican, on the Fathers of the Assembly, and we should also remember human weakness, which must always be taken into account, in the presence of one who was the dispenser of ecclesiastical promotion, and the author of ecclesiastical rebuke; when all this is borne in mind, the reflections we have already made are strengthened, and the relative proportions of the majority and the minority are somewhat modified in the mind of the sagacious and impartial observer. There remains but one other test which, though an indirect one, cannot be overlooked in our estimate of the votes given on July 13th, and that is the moral and intellectual weight of the bishops and populations who in one way or other took no part in it. We have now pointed out all that is required for a just appreciation of this event, both in a civil and historical point of view, an event which is not and cannot be unimportant, to the credit and the future of the religion of the great majority of the Latin races.

II.—FOURTH SESSION.

1. Calculations well founded, but disappointed.—2. The Opposition send a message to the Pope.—3. Adjunct to the formula of Infallibility.—4. Protest of the assembly.—5. Last attempts of the Opposition.—6. Fourth Session.—7. Reflections on the vote.—8. Protests of the Opposition.—9. After the event.—10. Text of the Canons that promulgate Infallibility.—11. The future. —12. Mnemosynon.

1. The result of this vote, though it was not, and could not be contested according to the rules, we do not say of ancient Roman wisdom only, but even by those of common prudence, was yet such as ought to have withheld any Assembly from proceeding to further decisions on a matter of so much gravity. Indeed, owing to that vote, one side of the dilemma raised by the Opposition was brought into a clear and formidable light. According to general belief, especially at Rome, the Church never creates a dogma new in itself; but, in defining a dogma, simply attests some belief which has been always and universally professed.

It was consequently maintained that a declaration which, notwithstanding all the helps and furtherances described, was still opposed by about one-third of the legitimate representatives of Catholic opinion, could not by the strongest resolution in the world be carried into effect; because, as the universality of belief would be thus seriously impugned, not only in the past but in the present, the result would only be a futile endeavour to demonstrate at the same time what was and what was not.

Those who up to the last day believed that the work undertaken by the *Civiltà Cattolica* would be unsuccessful, cannot be accused of presumption, or wilful self-deception, when all these considerations are borne in mind. The vote had, on the whole, justified the estimate formed of the state of opinion in the Church, and left room for a reasonable belief that the definition would be certainly suspended, if it did not altogether fail. But the contrary to all this soon became apparent. The Vatican was indeed deeply agitated at so grave a resistance, but in its agitation, " ne mosse collo ne piegò sua costa."*

On the day of the final vote, the legates only announced to the Fathers that the votes of " Placet juxta modum " would be taken into consideration, and a special report drawn up in the next Congregation.

2. The minority, who had already suspected it, then discovered that, notwithstanding their votes, the business was at once to proceed, and that the public Session for the definitive promulgation of the dogma would be held as quickly as possible. The leaders of the Opposition of different nations held meetings on the 14th and 15th, in order to settle by common consent the line of action to be adopted in this dangerous crisis ; and it was proposed to nominate a Commission on behalf of the minority, who should implore the Pope to suspend the definition of the dogma, making known to his Holiness their number, and their determination, if the demand were not complied with, to repeat, though with much regret, the " Non placet "—already given in the private Congregation—before all the world in the public Session. The Commission was composed of Cardinal Schwarzemberg, and the Archbishops of Paris, of Lyons, of Milan, and of Halifax. They spoke most strongly to the Pope of the dangers now threatening the Church ; they earnestly prayed for some modification of the scheme ; and they acquainted him with the intention of the Opposition to repeat the " Non placet " in the public Session if obliged to do so.

They also informed him that to this end they could reckon confidently on about 120 Fathers, who fully concurred in their opinions. The Pope returned an ambiguous answer, and

* 'Neither his neck he moved nor bent his side.'—
LONGFELLOW, ' Dante,' *Inf.* x. 75.

showed himself ill-informed in the matter; but said he would confer with the legates, promised to consider, and received the petition of the Commission. By such behaviour, he admitted that he was still dubious as to the attitude the Opposition might assume, and would not, therefore, give any decided opinion himself, but the doubt, if he ever really entertained it, was soon dispelled.

3. This took place on the Friday; and in the Congregation held on Saturday the 16th, the following day, no other effect of all the opposition shown at the last vote and of the remonstrances made by the Commissions to the Pope was apparent, save the presentation of another amendment drawn up by the extreme Infallibilists. In this the formula of Monday, already recorded and amended, was embodied in its most concise expression, carefully and specifically eliminating the proviso that the consent of the bishops and their approbation, though in a less exclusive form, was necessary in order to render the Papal decrees infallible.

The fourth public Session of the Vatican Council was then definitively fixed for Monday, July 18th. The last amendment was, in the first place, so worded that the Pontifical decree *ex cathedrâ* should be "irreformabiles ex sese absque consensu Ecclesiæ;" but this formula, when proposed, was not accepted by the assembly, notwithstanding its favourable leaning towards Infallibility. It was requisite in order that this amendment should gain the vote of the majority, to modify it as follows: " Ex sese non autem ex consensu Ecclesiæ irreformabiles esse."

The addition of this new clause excluding the bishops from participating in the universal decrees of the Church was an incident similar to that which occurred on the introduction of the word "anathema" into the text in the Congregation of Monday, the 14th, that is to say, the clause was proposed and accepted by the assembly in the course of the discussion without any preparation whatever. We may infer this also, from the fact that the formula, as given by the *Giornale di Roma* and every other official document, even the draft of its promulgation read at the public Session, contained the very phrases which expressly excluded the necessity of the consent of the bishops, according to the result of Saturday's Congregation; whereas, the formula given a little while before by the *Unità Cattolica*, which received its communications direct from Rome, contained the definitive text that was to be published, but no mention of the exclusion of the bishops.* It is clear that the *Unità Cattolica* had received its information from Rome immediately after the voting of Wednesday, the 13th, and previous to the last addition made in the text in the meeting of Monday, which we have already described. Therefore, if up to the day of voting it had never entered into the heads of the Commission or of the presidents to express this idea, and if they had already published the formula which resulted from that vote as definitive, there is ample proof that the clause was not the consequence of a careful consideration by the majority, but simply a partial opinion presented after the final voting under the form of an amendment, and summarily carried through on the 16th, after the minority had retired from the debate.

But whose idea was it? at whose instigation was it proposed? The *Giornale di Roma* of the 26th of July, a few days after, repelled the accusation made by other newspapers, that the words excluding the consent of the bishops had been placed there by the Pope, and insisted, instead, that they were inserted by the Congregation of Saturday; but the *Giornale di Roma* did not add at whose request or instigation had been proposed, in the last Congregation, an addition which the Commission itself up to that time had never brought forward. It did not say by whose authoritative hand the vote of the 13th had been taken back, after being once published, in order to be so much modified; and therefore the *Giornale Ufficiale* failed to throw any light on a question which remained still open to the free judgment of commentators. This was all the answer given to the remonstrances of the Commission of bishops sent to the Pope after the last voting. Moreover, the public Session which was fixed, as we have seen, for Tuesday, was anticipated by twenty-four hours, and after the visit of the Commission, in the Congregation of Saturday, at which the new amendment was voted, it was settled for Monday, the 18th. Whether the Pope had

* "Ideo hujusmodi Romani Pontificis definitiones esse ex sese irreformabiles."
Unità Cattolica, Martedì, 19 Luglio.

ascertained that the minority would not continue their resistance till the public Session—whether the die being once cast, it was considered well to make as much as possible out of the chance, and at the same time, in order to avoid new difficulties, to proceed as quickly as possible towards the attainment of the object now become indispensable for the majority—whatever were the reasons that determined the conduct of the principal actors at the moment, one thing is certain, that, between Friday and Saturday a great change was observable in their disposition, and that, finally, every external sign of hesitation and moderation was given up. It was said that during the voting of the last new amendment some of the most dispassionate bishops displayed signs of deep emotion, called forth probably by the consideration of the rapidity and security with which their act would be accomplished, and carried to its ultimate results: an act which spread over the future of the Church a veil impenetrable to human eyes.

4. At the close of Saturday's Congregation, a protest, afterwards inserted in the *Giornale di Roma*, was read to the whole assembly on behalf of the presidents. It was very decided in style, and marked by that violence which has of late characterised the productions of the Roman Chancery. This protest denounces in general terms all that, without distinction, it characterises as " le calunnie putridissime " (putrid calumnies), " e le turpissime menzogne " (shameful lies), not only of the heterodox but of nominal Catholics, and even of consecrated ministers of religion, against the proceedings and the freedom of the Council; and especially condemned two pamphlets on the subject, 'Ce qui se passe au Concile,' which we have already noticed, and another recently published, entitled 'La dernière heure du Concile,' which pointed to the hope of a future Council, in the arrangements of which such liberty and justice should prevail as are requisite for effectually remedying the ills of the Church.

It was evident from a protest so solemn, signed by the presidents and Secretary of the Council, against anonymous pamphlets and newspaper articles, that assaults, which are usually disregarded by private individuals, were keenly felt at Rome; but instead of producing the desired effect, they seemed rather to show that the authorities experienced the need of self-defence.

Whatever may be thought of the substance of the protest, and the time of its appearance, the form in which it was drawn up met with much disfavour. Indeed, persons who try to prove too much, sometimes end by proving nothing. One may protest against a particular lie or several definite lies, but to protest against lies in general is a work of supererogation. Criticism can only be exercised on determinate facts, and consequently this sort of generic eloquence is unavailing, and of no historical value.

Two copies of the protest, signed by the presidents, were distributed to each of the Fathers, who were invited to preserve one, and to sign the other, consigning it to the archives of the Council as a perpetual memorial. This document accordingly bore the signatures of those who usually made up the majority, and who had, in fact, done the whole work, including the framing of the protest itself, which will descend to posterity in connection with the history of the Council, and will, with all other events, be only then rightly estimated when it has undergone the scrutiny of succeeding generations.

Before the close of the Congregation on Saturday, the legates announced to the Fathers that the Council would not be prorogued, but that the Sovereign Pontiff granted them a vacation during the summer months : they were invited to reassemble at the Vatican in the beginning of autumn, to continue their work ; which, by the way, was deprived of much of its importance and utility by the last declaration.

5. Every possible means of resistance was employed by the minority in the hours that remained between the Congregation of Saturday, and the Session announced for Monday; prayers and supplications, written and verbal, and entreaties of every sort were used. Some of the Fathers, seeing that they were not likely to obtain any redress, proposed simply the elimination of the word "anathema," by which the proposition would revert to its original form, but in vain. On the Sunday, the bishops of the Opposition, seeing that all was lost, began to consider whether they should assist at the public Session, and openly repeat the "Non placet," as the Germans wished from the

beginning, or whether, following the opinion expressed by the French, they should protest and leave Rome. The latter opinion prevailed, as being the more simple and easy course, and the one, as they themselves declared, most in accordance with filial duty. But it seems that before carrying this resolution into practice, one of the leaders of the Opposition, the Archbishop of Vienna, on that very Sunday went again to the Pope to repeat the prayer already made on behalf of himself and his colleagues, and to inform him of their determination in the event of its rejection, not to assist at the public Session. This time the message met with a very decided and downright denial with regard to the thing prayed for, and very scant courtesy as to the matter generally; so that on the return of the last messenger of reconciliation, the bishops of the Opposition at once signed the protest, and left Rome in great numbers, as quickly as possible, for fear of any strong measures being adopted towards them by the conquerors. They were afraid, also, if the dogma were once promulgated, of finding themselves under the difficult alternative suggested by the "anathema," namely, of being constrained either to submit or to abandon their sees, and possibly, of finding themselves cast out of the bosom of the Church as well. This fear was, along with the motive reason of filial duty, the strongest argument in favour of the French opinion for leaving the city. If the dogma were once proclaimed in the public Session—notwithstanding the "Non placet" which they could pronounce—and with the addition of the "anathema" levelled against those who dissented from the doctrines contained in the schemes, what could they do when, as was inevitable, they found themselves obliged either to submit or resign their sees? They had no wish to be caught in this dilemma in Rome, under the very eyes of the Pope, and preferred to await the result of their conduct among their own flocks, in their respective dioceses. Accordingly, sixty-three bishops, all diocesans and representatives of the most illustrious sees in Christendom, affixed their names to the document on that same Sunday, and by the evening most of them had left Rome, and the circumscribed limits of her terrestrial dominion.

6. Now all was over, and the day began to dawn which was to witness the fulfilment of the destinies of the Vatican.

On the morning of July 18th the sun rose amid threatening clouds, as it had done on the 6th of December, and a violent storm burst over the Eternal City during the fourth Session of the Council, just as incessant rain had accompanied its first meeting. Both the Council Hall and the city itself presented that cold and severe aspect, which seems naturally to accompany the consummation of great events fraught with momentous considerations. No representatives of the Christian powers assisted at the Session, save those from Brazil, Holland, Portugal, the Principality of Monaco, and some small states of no political importance. The bishops of many eminent sees, such as Paris, Vienna, Turin, and Milan, were absent from the Session, as also those who formed the Opposition. The number of bishops in the hall was 535, which as the Council numbered 692 showed 157 absent, and of these, with the exception of 38 whose absence was accounted for, and whose opinions were unknown, all had consistently opposed the dogma to the last. This computation agrees with the number reported to the Pope by the Commission on the preceding Friday, when they implored him on the part of the Opposition to suspend the definition.

Of the 535 present at the Session, 533 gave a favourable vote; those who said "Non placet" were only two, the Bishops of Caiazzo and of Little Rock in Arkansas, a Neapolitan and an American: extremes meet. In the excitement of mind which prevailed during the last six months among those who took an active part in the struggle, everything is possible.

Comments were made even on these two dissentients thus separated from the rest of the Opposition and left behind, and it was insinuated that their remaining in order to bear testimony to the liberty of the Council, was due to some contrivance of the majority. This idea arose from the fact that the Bishop of Caiazzo had been recently nominated to his see by the Pope; and the American, imagining himself the only dissentient, at first begged not to be called forward, but on hearing that one of his brethren was prepared to give a contrary vote, he resolved to do the same, and accordingly pronounced the "Non placet," which echoed through the Council Hall as the last protest against the definition of the dogma of Infallibility. In such a momentous crisis, and on such occasions as we have described, people may suppose and assert anything; but why should one imagine abstruse and unlikely reasons for the conduct of these two representatives of the Opposition, instead of acknowledging that they chose the regular form for expressing their opinions, and afforded a striking proof of moral courage by their conduct before the Council? No sooner had the Pope pronounced the formula, than the little crowd of monks, nuns, and the like, who pressed round the door of the hall, gave vent to such demonstrations of joy as were hardly consistent with the sacredness of the locality; and as soon as the noise had ceased, the Pope made a short speech, in which he acknowledged the greatness of the dignity assured to him by the present declaration, and declared that it would be reflected on the bishops, and become a source of advantage to them likewise. He concluded by saying that he trusted all those now absent, would give their adhesion to the dogma. Two or three houses in the city were decorated, but this and the applause at the door of the Council Hall, were the only signs of rejoicing at the declaration of Infallibility. In the evening the Government offices, the religious establishments, and a few private houses were illuminated, but the rest of the city remained in perfect silence and profound darkness. It seemed, however, as if the elements had conspired to disturb the terrestrial calm, for a hurricane broke over Rome during the ceremony, thunderbolts fell in two or three places while the service was proceeding between half-past eleven and twelve o'clock, and both the heavens and the city of Rome appeared to bear external evidence of the great events then taking place, events which in one sense closely concerned them both.

7. The result of the voting gives rise to considerations very important in the history of mankind, as well as in the records of the Council. On the first voting for Infallibility on Wednesday the 13th there were 451 in favour of the dogma, and in the public Session 533, an increase of 82. These must be taken from the 91 absent, and the 62 "juxta modum," but as the numbers voting on Wednesday amounted to 601, and at the public Session only to 535, the number of absentees, far from diminishing, had increased by about one-half, and thus one must look for those who adhered to the definition after Wednesday,

as far as the calculation admits, chiefly among the 62 conditional votes. What had induced these Fathers to change their opinion? The formula remained the same in substance as on the day that it was voted, with the exception of the amendments, which exaggerated without essentially altering it, and the greater part of the sixty-two who had voted "juxta modum," were known to be personally unfavourable, if not actually adverse, at least for the present, to the declaration of the dogma. What was the reason which induced them so quickly to change their opinion, and then supposing that they had actually done so, what could be the value historically of a double and conflicting testimony at the same time, and on the same subject? Among those who were absent from the Congregation of the 13th were Antonelli, Berardi, Grassellini and Hohenlohe; M. de Mérode, the warlike minister of Castelfidardo, and Count Ludovico de Besi, Bishop of Canopo, once Vicar-Apostolic in China, Padre Luigi da Trento, formerly Apostolic preacher, and at the present time Vicar of the Capitolo di San Pietro, were likewise wanting at the meeting. Padre Luigi da Trento was renowned for his scientific acquirements, but his opinions were known to be adverse to Infallibility, and the Pope having observed his absence at the public Session, remonstrated with him on the point. Cardinal Guidi had given up the triumphant position he held for a short time, and though he had voted "juxta modum" on Wednesday the 13th, on perceiving that resistance was vain, he retraced his steps at the final decision by giving the orthodox "Placet." It was said that when he came forward to vote on this occasion the Pope observed him attentively, and on hearing him give the answer "Placet," said, "buon uomo" (good man); others thought the words were "pover uomo" (poor man). It is quite possible that in Italian these observations might bear the same signification. Several prelates of the minority, the French especially, had at the last moment modified their opinion, and among them, if I mistake not, were the Bishops of Rheims, of Avignon, and of Salzburg; also the Archbishop of Pisa, whose vote was considered most important from his being a Cardinal and a person of great piety. Up to this time he had been reckoned among those who opposed personal Infallibility, but now he accepted the doctrine. He and the other dissentient cardinals drew their scarlet hats down over their eyes, and remained silent. Thus was obtained the number that voted favourably at the public session, and the difference between that and the number of favourable votes in the Congregation held on Wednesday is explained. Nearly 150 pastors of Catholic flocks were absent altogether, though they occupied some of the most important and illustrious sees in Christendom. Among them, as we have already observed, were the Archbishops of Paris, Vienna, Turin, and Milan. Also the Primate of Gaul, the Bishop of Orleans, the Primate of Hungary, the Archbishop of Prague, of Saint Louis, of Colocsza, and the Bishops of Mayence, of Trèves, of Bosnia and Sirmio, of Nice, of Marseilles, and many others; in fact, we may say that the absent prelates were not only men who occupied eminent positions, but men eminent in themselves, which means that at the present time in them lay the best and surest hopes of the Church.

8. The protest signed by sixty-three bishops of the Opposition before leaving Rome was written in a sober and respectful style, which forms a striking contrast with the address of the legates. We will give the document *in extenso*, on account of its importance both in itself and in regard to the occasion of its production :—

BEATISSIME PATER.

In congregatione generali die xiii hujus mensis habita, dedimus suffragia nostra super schemata primæ constitutionis dogmaticæ de Ecclesia Christi.

Notum est Sanctitati vestræ octoginta octo patres fuisse, qui conscientia urgente et amore sanctæ Ecclesiæ permoti, suffragium suum per verba non placet emiserunt: sexaginta duo alios, qui suffragati sunt per verba juxta modum, denique septuaginta circiter, qui a congregatione abfuerunt atque a suffragio emittendo abstinuerunt. His accedunt et alii, qui infirmitatibus aut aliis gravioribus rationibus ducti, ad suas diœceses reversi sunt. Hac ratione Sanctitati vestræ et toti mundo suffragia nostra nota atque manifestata fuere, patuitque quam multis episcopis sententia nostra probetur, atque hoc modo munus officiumque quod nobis incumbet persolvimus. Ab eo inde tempore nihil prorsus, evenit, quod sententiam nostram mutaret, quin imo multa eaque gravissima acciderunt, quæ nos in proposito confirmaverunt.

Atque ideo nostra jam edita suffragia nos renovare et confirmare declaramus. Confirmantes itaque per hanc scripturam, suffragia nostra a sessione publica die decimoctava hujus mensis habenda ut abesse liceat constituimus. Pietas enim filialis ac reverentia, quæ missos nostros superrime, ad pedes Sanctitatis vestræ, advexit, non sinunt nos in causa Sanctitatis vestræ personam adeo proxime concernente palam et in facie patris dicere non placet.

Et aliunde. suffragia in solemni sessione edenda repeterent dumtaxat suffragia in generali congregatione deprompta. Redimus itaque sine mora ad greges nostros, quibus post tam longam absentiam ob belli timores atque pressantissimas eorum spirituales indigentias summopere necessarii sumus, dolentes quod ob tristitiam in quibus versamur rerum adjunctam, etiam conscientiarum pacem et tranquillitatem turbatam inter fideles nostros reperturi sumus.

Interea Ecclesiam Dei et Sanctitatem vestram, cui intemeratam fidem et obedientiam profitemur Domini nostri Jesu Christi gratiæ et præsidio toto corde commendantes sumus Sanctitatis vestræ

Devotissimi et obedientissimi

(Here follow the signatures.)

The day after the protest had been signed by so many bishops, the *Giornale di Roma* gave an account of the public Session, in which it said that the dogma of Infallibility had been unanimously passed, with the exception of two votes of "Non placet," and that numbers of the absent bishops had sent their adhesion to it in writing, and all the members of the majority remaining in Rome repeated the same assertion. It is, of course, very difficult for outsiders to penetrate the mysteries of the secret retractations and mental compromises made by uncertain consciences within the hidden recesses of the Congregations and offices of Rome ; but though the *Giornale di Roma* might choose to say that the dogma had met with universal assent, such words could not avail to blot out the protests that had been made, to account for the voluntary absences, to cancel, in fact, the whole history of the last few months. Nothing can alter the final dilemma,— either those who publicly and formally protested, adhered to their protest—and then it is impossible to maintain the universal acceptance of the dogma, for whatever may be said of the favourable votes, the number of Fathers who signed the protest is much too considerable to be overlooked—or supposing those who protested to have afterwards retracted, then their assent to the dogma was more detrimental to the object they had in view, than the most ardent opposition.

9. From this first test it became apparent that the decided opinion of the German bishops who advocated the attendance of the Opposition at the public Session, in order to repeat the "Non placet" given at the preceding Congregation, was by far the best and surest course ; for the assertion of the *Giornale di Roma* gave them a foretaste of the false statements and judg-

ments they must in future expect from having followed milder counsels. If the individual who induced the minority to adopt this course acted in good faith, he will have ample cause to regret his advice, for the sake of his own party; if otherwise, upon him must rest the responsibility of the whole matter. Another phase of the question was opened by this article—a phase of "approbation." Now that the dogma is declared, it is evident that the same pressure used to bring about its promulgation will be exercised to secure its acceptance, and, without doubt, this policy will succeed. The constitution of the Church in the nineteenth century renders resistance impossible; it is like a machine worked by a single motive force which casts away all that it does not absorb within itself. The secondary wheels have no longer any controlling power, and as there is no repugnance to throw out more than is gathered in, there is no regular and lawful means of opposing the impulse from above: indeed, those who attempt it have always been themselves expelled. Consequently, the dissentients were nearly sure to give their approbation, and in the end they did give it, almost all; but whatever its theological or canonical value may be, it is certain that cotemporaries as well as posterity will have much difficulty in understanding how it is possible to retract an opinion once given, to say at the same time yes and no in a question of fact; a question whether the universal Church has held *ab initio*, and does hold at the present day, the doctrine of Infallibility. One can understand a change of determination from devotion, but to see white when the object contemplated is black, is beyond human power, and passes the limits of reasonable concession. In order to escape this contradiction we must detract from the value of the votes first given, but in doing so we diminish their worth as a testimony both in the first and second case, and with regard to the Opposition and the Majority. If the whole matter were not a question of fact, but an attempt to produce *ex novo* a development in the Church, how many difficulties arise and present themselves to the observer!

We will not, however, enter upon this view of the question, which rather concerns theologians and canonists, but confine ourselves to such considerations as best serve to guide public opinion; not that which is found in the newspapers or the passing politics of the day, but that which is based on conscientious conviction. This opinion, in the long run, is certain to ascribe to all events their just value and importance, and by means of it alone, can be rightly estimated the effects of the Vatican Council, on the religious and political condition of Catholicism.

10. It is unnecessary to insert here the scheme "De Ecclesia," which any one can study now that it is not only published, but has become a law common to all; those, however, who are anxious to peruse it, will find it in the Appendix.* Meantime it is well to call attention to the Canons, which contain the substance and last decisions of the scheme. In these three Canons, and the paragraph which answers to the fourth, are the words which serve as the key-note of the drama we have been considering, words which complete the work pursued for many centuries with wonderful constancy, and which secure for the Catholic Church the most absolute supremacy known upon earth.

They are as follows:—

CANON I.

Si quis dixerit, Beatum Petrum Apostolum non esse a Christo Domino constitutum Apostolorum omnium principem et totius Ecclesiæ militantis visibile caput, vel eumdem honoris tantum, non autem veræ propriæque jurisdictionis primatum ab eodem Domino nostro Jesu Christo directe et immediate accepisse, anathema sit.

CANON II.

Si quis dixerit, non esse ex ipsius Christi Domini institutione seu jure divino, ut Beatus Petrus in primatu super universam Ecclesiam habeat perpetuos successores, aut Romanum Pontificem non esse Beati Petri in eodem primatu successorem, anathema sit.

CANON III.

Si quis dixerit, Romanum Pontificem habere tantummodo officium inspectionis vel directionis, non autem plenam et supremam potestatem jurisdictionis in universam Ecclesiam, non solum in rebus quæ ad fidem et mores sed etiam in iis quæ ad disciplinam et regimen Ecclesiæ per totum orbem diffusæ pertinent aut eum habere tantum potiores partes, non vero totam plenitudinem hujus supremæ potestatis: aut hanc ejus potestatem non esse ordinariam et immediatam, sive in omnes et singulas Ecclesias, sive in omnes et singulos pastores et fideles, anathema sit.

* See Appendix, Document XX.

Paragraph that takes the place of the 4th Canon.

Itaque nos traditioni a fidei Christianæ exordio perceptæ fideliter inhærendo ad Dei Salvatoris nostri gloriam, religionis Catholicæ exaltationem et Christianorum populorum salutem, sacro approbante concilio, docemus et divinitus revelatum dogma esse definimus Romanum Pontificem cum ex cathedra loquitur, id est cum omnium Christianorum pastoris et doctoris munere fungens, pro suprema sua apostolica auctoritate, doctrinam de fide vel moribus ab universa Ecclesia tenendam definit per assistentiam divinam ipsi in Beato Petro promissam ea infallibilitate pollere, qua divinus Redemptor Ecclesiam suam in definienda doctrina de fide vel moribus instructam esse voluit, ideoque ejusmodi Romani Pontificis definitiones ex sese, non autem ex consensu Ecclesiæ irreformabiles esse. Si quis autem huic nostræ definitioni contradicere, quod Deus avertat, præsumpserit, anathema sit.

11. This, then, is the act for which during the last seven months a never varying combat has been waged, with the result that, on all points and in all ages, usually attends such struggles, namely, in the triumph of authority, whenever that authority is well organised, and possesses the constancy of purpose and the requisite means for carrying its wishes into effect. It is the formal and solemn act by which the Church assumes absolute power, in such a way that one man, by means of his subordinates, who are under the strictest obligations of obedience, and are deprived of all freedom of judgment, can govern the consciences of more than a hundred millions of persons who acknowledge his sway; consciences which must reflect the will and the ideas of their head, under the penalty of being deprived of the religious rites which direct and comfort them. Thus organised, the Roman Catholic religion is certainly easily guided by its superiors, and is well qualified for intervening in social or political strife, with its immense influence, while it also lends itself more surely to become an instrument of party. On the other hand, how does such a constitution promote that universality which is the characteristic of Christianity and is implied in the very name of Catholic? It is almost superfluous again to remind our readers that we have no desire to pass judgment on theological questions on which we are not competent to decide, but simply wish to place before them the social and civil aspects of the question, and the practical results to society of the influence of the Vatican Council. Weighing these considerations by past experience, it seems probable that

all that is intelligent, reasonable, and liberal in Catholicism, finding itself bound down within such narrow limits by external authority, will press forward with energy until it reaches a position of greater ease and freedom, a position in which the irresistible impulse of modern life may be able to attain its full development; and it will be a great thing if in this struggle those who wish to preserve their religion, and yet are unable to follow the novelties of the Vatican, will content themselves with the old news, the good news par excellence, and still find guidance and comfort in the Gospel. The most devout and well-disciplined portion of Catholicism will no doubt strive under the direction of the Pope to set itself against the spirit of the age—but where will its course end? That is a question which none can answer, and which will probably depend in great measure on the individual dispositions of the Popes who seek to make the experiment. Of course, it is possible that some Pope of large and liberal ideas may arise, but what could he do? Might not his best endeavours in a position of such unlimited power be attended by the same dangers as follow on a policy of reaction? Can a principle, illiberal by nature, ever produce real fruits of liberty? The very name of "Catholic party," which the devout Catholics of all countries have spontaneously assumed, seems to be a forecast of the future, and to indicate the opinion of those who have given up the universality of their kingdom, while it points out the probable condition of the Church of Rome in its laborious struggle with modern society. The world which previous to the Vatican Council was indiscriminately termed Catholic, will now inevitably split into two divisions; but between them there will remain a considerable number of persons, who, unable to follow the liberal ideas of the first party, and impatient of the yoke of the second, will be lost in the burning sands formed by the *detritus* of wasted religious beliefs and moral principles, which constitutes the interminable desert, stretching away into the distance along the borders of modern civilisation.

12. History is bound to award to the author and originator of every work the praise or blame which is due to him. All must remember the part taken by the Fathers of the *Civiltà Cattolica*, and Monsignor Manning, Archbishop of Westminster,

in promoting the dogma of the personal Infallibility of the Pope, and all know that it was their mind and their will that carried it. On the day of the promulgation of the dogma Monsignor Manning received as a gift, from the Society of the Jesuits, a portrait of Bellarmine with the following inscription—

> HENRICO EDWARDO MANNING,
> ARCHIEP. WESTMONAST.
> SODALES SOC. JESU,
> COLLEGII CIVILITATIS CATHOLICÆ,
> SESSIONIS IV. CONCILII VATICANI
> MNEMOSYNON.

CONCLUSION.

1. Two years have elapsed since the events we have recorded took place, a period which appears as nothing with reference to the history of human thought, but which affords sufficient space for measuring the results already effected by the Vatican Council, especially in the relations it has established with Catholic nations and with society in general. And this inquiry is the more opportune, because the Council being now prorogued, it is important accurately to estimate its results during this period of interruption and repose. They may be considered under three aspects, corresponding with the three modes in which the interests of all societies are affected, namely, the religious, the social, and the political.

2. Under the religious aspect, the immediate effect of the Vatican Council has been to cause a feeling of weariness, even among the most devoted Catholics ; and in those quarters where the new doctrines have been most favourably received, to leave an impression of the disproportion between the object longed for and the result obtained ; to produce in the human mind that sort of vacuity which usually accompanies the attainment of a wish, the *non plus ultra* of the reality itself, the possession of anything ardently longed for by an individual, a people or an institution. The calamities in which the policy of the Vatican have resulted, in respect to its own temporal condition and its international relations, have also contributed very materially to strengthen this feeling.

3. That portion of the Church which comprised the Opposition remains like the conquered after a battle, in a shattered and irresolute state; and we are unable yet to form any conjectures as to its sentiments, or as to the line of action which it may adopt. The bishops may be said to have universally

submitted; and although the individuals who held aloof preserve a distinct character, which may one day acquire more general importance, this does not alter the fact of the more or less spontaneous, but almost universal, acceptance on the part of the episcopate, of the work of the Vatican Council.

Among the inferior ranks of the hierarchy the case was different. A considerable number of clergy scattered in different countries, especially in Germany, and a still larger number of the laity, have laid the foundations of a state of separation, the importance and duration of which it would as yet be premature and speculative to foretell.

4. Besides, no conscientious or impartial observer can fail to discern in the submission of the bishops, and equally in the energetic resistance of the Old Catholics, an absence of enthusiasm and a forlorn resignation. This resignation almost assumes the character of a passive resistance, according to their disposition and temperament, among a considerable number of intelligent Catholics capable of exercising their individual judgment on the doctrines and policy which, gradually gaining ground in these latter years in the guidance of the Church, have finally brought about those conclusions which are their seal and natural consequence, or, we might rather say, the compendium and formula by means of which those doctrines have been converted from mere matters of opinion, into integral parts of the common law of the whole Catholic world.

5. A great part of the episcopate accepted the doctrines and policy that prevailed in the first phase of the Vatican Council from a feeling of duty, or a desire to choose the lesser evil, or other similar reasons, rather than from actual conviction, and the sincere and spontaneous testimony of their own conscience. This applies first to those who gave in their adhesion after having upheld the contrary, as undoubtedly in their case the primary and spontaneous decision of conscience must have essentially affected their mind and modified their external action in regard to the tenets they finally adopted; and it applies still more to all who, after evident hesitation, either held aloof or passively accepted, on account of their order and position in the hierarchy, doctrines which no opposition on their part could enable them to repel. Among the

inferior clergy the proportion of those who possess the consciousness and often the painful experience of the dangers and difficulties attending the application of those doctrines, and the tendency of that policy, is much greater than among the bishops; but an equal sentiment of order and discipline, and perhaps a lower degree of personal independence, keeps them in a state of obedience and of passive resignation, which paralyses their action, and renders them mechanical rather than intelligent members of the Church.

Among the laity, all who are contained between the two extremes, that is between the Rationalists, the real free-thinkers, and those who compose what is properly called the Catholic party—that multitude which includes the living working mass of the Catholic populations—feels more or less, with a perception varying with the intelligence and morality possessed by each individual, the practical difficulties, the perils and the misfortunes, resulting from the constant prosecution of such aims as we have described.

The spirit of resistance, moreover, manifests itself differently among the laity and among the clergy. The former, not being controlled by any special conditions or restraints, for the greater part break loose from the narrow circle which confines them; and temporarily cease to belong to their own Church (at least in externals), without feeling any deep or lasting convictions in the matter, or being supported by the deliberate approval of their own conscience.

Such desertions are readily and zealously noticed, by the very persons who actually promote them, and who prefer to see the number of the faithful constantly diminished, rather than to recognise as such any who are not completely and blindly submissive. A small part only accept the ungrateful and difficult task of resisting at the same time the oppressive and expulsive forces which assail them; and have in consequence the greatest difficulty in making themselves accepted "da Dio e da nemici suoi."

6. A decided school, or rather a party, stands forth in opposition to the various forms of resistance we have specified, and to the great multitude whose active powers are neutralised by the conflict between the pressure of ecclesiastical authority and

the reluctance of their feelings and interests, sometimes even of their reason and conscience, to submit to its demands. This party is ardent, impassioned, and fanatical, and is from character and education little familiar with the interests of daily life. Its programme is based on the freest interpretations of the old school of authority, and on the traditional absolutism of the Roman Curia; and it is bound together by the troubles and disappointments, hopes and regrets, to which our days of rapid and violent changes give such ample scope. This party, strong in the progressive development by which its purposes have been attained, has the advantage of possessing numerous traditions and writings which have all contributed to its success, and may all be quoted in its favour; and even more, it is strong in consequence of the preponderating influence exercised by its practices, and methods of teaching on the organisation of the Church, that wonderful organisation which has been matured by fifteen centuries of experience and of strife. Furnished with these formidable elements of power, it exercises an unquestioned supremacy over the multitudes that will not obey, but cannot resist it. Above this party, which by its movement imparts an impulse to the whole Catholic hierarchy, stands the Pope, as its highest expression and representative; indeed, I might almost say its real personification, for on him necessarily rests the whole responsibility of its progress, owing to the supreme authority with which he is endued, an authority which has recently attained its highest development.

7. In consequence of the informal nature of this book, we may here venture to make a slight digression. Great moral authorities ought to be impersonal, in order to resist the many violent and conflicting currents of interests which they must encounter on their path; and these latter must never be allowed to individualise or personify the obstacles they oppose, for there are combinations of power against which no isolated force or resistance can possibly prevail, just as there are responsibilities to which no human individual, however great, is equal. The will of an individual is a narrow passage, difficult of access for general interests. An individual will becomes the expression of the desires of those nearest to it, or of those who are instrumental in carrying out its own designs; and

who, having thus the advantage over others, impart to that will a character less universal and a disposition to become tyrannical. The greater the development attained by these tendencies towards isolation and concentration, the more serious are their consequences. The will of the Pope becoming of infinite importance in the Church, his responsibility, and the difficulties to be overcome in order to maintain its universal and uncontrolled exercise, are also infinitely increased. How much we might learn if only the mighty spirits of those Popes who ruled the Church in times of great conflict and violent passions, when their supreme authority, though not so explicitly affirmed as at present, was in reality far more effective and more widely respected, could appear again among us! If only we could freely study the precious documents of the Vatican archives, and find out the real connection between those great individualities and the important events of their respective ages, what part they took in them, and how they influenced them, we should be greatly enlightened on the subject, and be able accurately to appreciate the conditions of an authority so amazing, in its collision with the violent passions that oppose it. Critical works on ecclesiastical history, and the biographies of the great Popes which abound at the present day, have already begun to raise the veil from that period of history especially, which treats of the wonderful vicissitudes of the Reformation, the League, the English revolution, and of all, in short, that during the four last centuries has changed the face of Europe. We are now beginning to learn how to estimate the absolute will of individuals with regard to grave misfortunes, the sole responsibility of which is often attributed to them by the popular voice. But in the meanwhile how many persons attribute the massacre of St. Bartholomew, the assassination of Henry IV., and a thousand other horrors and crimes solely to the instigation of the Vatican?

The fact that Paul III. first accepted the dedication of the works of Copernicus has not availed to counterbalance the fact that the imprisonment of Galileo was due to the Papacy, while the resistance of the Lutherans to the new astronomical theories have been entirely lost sight of in the ever-widening waves of universal opinion; and in those days the work was not yet finished, the responsibility of the government of the Church had not yet been renounced by the whole ecclesiastical hierarchy, in order that it might reside in the head alone.

8. But to return to our subject from this brief digression, it will easily be understood that the action of the Church on Catholic society is retarded in its free development, by the reciprocal relations of its internal elements.

The condition of the Catholic Church is not satisfactory or hopeful with regard to her external relations, either from a purely religious view, or with respect to societies whose confession of faith differs from her own. The spirit of absolute and unlimited authority in Catholicism finds its counterpart in a spirit of equally absolute exclusiveness.

Catholicism has been more successful in the second tendency than in the first, and has practically succeeded in placing the faithful in a condition of almost hostile isolation, in real life, from the members of all other Christian confessions. On this point its success has been entire. Catholics at the present day very often neither have, nor profess, any religion whatever; but they rarely attempt, whether as individuals or as societies, to fraternise with others, or in the slightest degree to modify their views from contact with forms of religion the nearest, and most akin to their own.

On the contrary, this curious phenomenon may be observed among them in the matter, that they seem to draw closer to those confessions of faith which tend most towards rationalism, than to those that have kept the nearest to religion. The same results have been generated by the spirit of hostility and exclusiveness as by the spirit of authority, both these sentiments have increased and reached their culminating point, just in proportion as their practical application has been most at variance with the temper and habits of the age. Such exaggeration at the present day, when universal tolerance prevails, is a source of great difficulty for Catholics in their intercourse with persons of kindred confessions of faith, for though always obliged in such intercourse to submit to an outward appearance of equality, they never frankly accept it.

Again, from the overstrained application of the spirit of exclusiveness in practical life, Catholic institutions are unwilling to make any interchange with others; to give and accept at the same time any active co-operation on practical points of morals, or on grounds of common interest, but they keep up and create distrust and rancour where they ought rather to seek friends, or, at least, auxiliaries. These evil results are at variance both with the spirit of the Gospel and with true civilisation, and are as hurtful to the religious development as to the material progress of nations.

9. The situation that we have described is one of the principal hindrances to the progress of modern civilisation among Catholic nations, and a reason why it can only be attained by degrees, at the cost of much suffering and great revulsions. We see in this state of things an authority at once inflexible and incapable of carrying out its designs, bearing with all its weight on an unwilling and inert multitude, strong enough to overpower all resistance from its subjects, but incapable of assimilating them to itself, and making them partakers of its own spirit. It is an authority ever at war with the rest of the world; ready and eager to create difficulties in the civil society in which it moves, but unable to conquer in the battle it has provoked.

This authority is ever striving after the realisation of an ideal, which it seeks more ardently in proportion as that ideal eludes its grasp, and escapes from the region of human sympathies; and for this it wages a perpetual warfare with the science, the laws, the habits, and the wants of modern society—in short, with all that constitutes the present age. We see here the reason why religious institutions which, as we learn from the history of great nations, should be and are, when in harmony with civil life, a most effective element of order, of unity, and of force, prove too often just the reverse. Those institutions should offer to mankind repose from their conflicts, consolation under disappointment, and a neutral ground whereon they may meet in the pilgrimage of life; but their real action is too often very different. They become an inexhaustible source of divisions and of difficulties; a perpetual battle-field, on which none are indifferent spectators of the combat, but all, both friends and enemies, when engaged in the fight, may prove equally dangerous to social order. Perhaps the most marked sign of the times is to be found in the fact that, in the unceasing and deadly warfare in which the Church is engaged, her enemies if worsted, meet with only slight discomfiture, whereas her friends are often wholly vanquished. We have now considered the second, the social view of the question.

10. We must not deceive ourselves, the equipoise, or we might almost say the mechanical balance of the moral powers, is a law similar to that which, through the material forces, regulates the world ; it is therefore superior to all human laws, and cannot be disturbed without causing terrible confusion and violent reaction. An unnatural state of things outside of that equilibrium may be created and maintained by clever artificers, who, in so doing, demonstrate the power of human intellect ; but before long the inconvenience of such a position is manifested, and a reaction occurs sooner or later, becoming more violent in proportion as it is delayed, and most violent when it comes too late, and is powerless to restore the primitive order of things. Very often, in this latter case, reaction only seems to drag down to destruction the whole work, so painfully, and sometimes so wonderfully, built up and kept together.

Institutions prosper, and constitute the happiness of societies, according as not only in their foundation, but in their successive development, they conform and accommodate themselves to the rules of this great moral law, and keep the limits determined by this just equilibrium. In the precepts of the Gospel, and its full and comprehensive teaching, we find the highest expression of a law that meets all the needs and provides for all the conditions of humanity, and it was in the strength of this law alone that Christianity in four or five centuries conquered the whole of the known world. As Christian institutions have by degrees been developed, their application has become more minute and complicated (sometimes, it is true, with wonderful results), but they have lost in consequence much of their original simplicity and breadth, and much also of that character of universal adaptability which distinguished primitive Christianity.

"Brethren, love one another," was the doctrine taught as a synthetical precept, by one of the earliest and most illustrious preachers of Christianity. Dissensions grew as the tendency to define and particularise increased ; and the legal definitive elevation of the See of Rome was marked by the schism of the East.

The process of ordering, arranging, and defining continued until they produced a system, a policy, and a law, which awoke differences of opinions, passions, and interests in men's minds, divided them into friends and enemies, and gave rise to endless controversies. This phase was replete with active life in Christianity and in the Church ; and the vitality, movement and collision inherent in it, produced the greatest men and the most marvellous institutions. While it lasted, there were many obstacles and difficulties to be encountered, and much resistance, moral and material, to be overcome ; but yet men continued to legislate, to order, to govern, and to centralise, until, finally, after much transitory agitation and resistance, a great part of Christian Europe refused to bend any longer to the laws of Rome, and made laws for itself. Still the work of defining and particularising proceeded, until casuistry was constituted into a science, and the framing of decrees and canons went on till the 18th of July, 1870. The result of an infinite number of circumstances, which arose during this long development of an authority so unlimited as that potentially and effectively contained in the Roman Church, has been to evolve and perfect a system which, though founded on a law most pure and simple (that of the Gospel), has by degrees embodied a new code so full, so minute, so uniform, alike in principle and in application, in theory and in practice—applying to matters of greatest breadth, as well as to minute particulars ; pressing equally on all its subjects, with scarcely any or no distinction of race and nation ; so framed as to bring all people to a given end by certain means, in such a way, and by none other—that human nature, finding itself thus bound down by a rule which was invariable, not only in substance, but in its special application, began to react, first instinctively and submissively, and then consciously, openly and wildly.

11. Amidst all these explanations and definitions, this legislation preserved the character of the times and circumstances whence it derived its birth and expansion. Inflexible in its nature, the more it was enlarged and became minute, the greater also became the number of cases in which it applied, and to which that inflexibility extended. It followed in consequence

that in order to render its application possible, it was requisite to open or to enlarge a safety-valve, which might serve as a means of relief from such severe pressure, and thus the system of indulgence became widespread in the economy of the Church. Without this, very soon there would not have remained a single member who could be considered truly faithful according to her own rules, on account of the ever-increasing difficulties on the one side, and the weakening of religious belief and of individual character on the other. Meanwhile, time rolled on, customs changed, and both found themselves more than ever at variance with the laws that ruled them. The expedient we have noticed, already dangerous on account of its influence on individual character, no longer sufficed to meet the evil it was intended to obviate, neither could the patience and tolerance with which the Roman Curia prudently moderated its ecclesiastical policy, provide a commensurate remedy.

The time had come when the Curia, which claimed for itself the height of power and of learning, was constrained either to submit to the modifications demanded by the new character and exigencies of the age, or else to find itself in conflict with them. The authoritative nature of its constitution prevented its progressive modification, and rendered its affinity with advancement and science very difficult; equally so its relations with the feelings and habits gradually unfolded in the rest of mankind, and thus by little and little became visible the breach between Church and society, which had formerly been united. This separation increased daily; and the more apparent it was, the more the pressure of religious institutions in Catholic society became artificial on one side, and intolerable on the other.

The Church, on her part, multiplied laws, penalties, censures, inquisitions; framed new institutions, and founded new militant religious orders. She also originated, for one reason or another, new devotions, new associations, new signs of fellowship, and tried by every possible means to advance her own special institutions. Catholics became more than ever a separate class, living under an exceptional régime, which, though containing much that was good, was yet so peculiar and uniform as to render it little adapted for universal application, and in the end, owing to their numbers being restricted, obedient Catholics, and, as they are called,

" praticanti," became, what indeed at the present day they are, simply a party in the Church. The age was not propitious to religious discussions, nor to the outward exhibition of religious passions; and accordingly those who could not submit to the régime we have described, never thought of resorting to argument on the question, nor of separating themselves from the Church; they did not try to bring about a reform or to create a schism; but, with regard to thought, they simply gave up thinking; and, with regard to practical duties, they neglected them altogether; so that, by little and little, they fell into a state of indifferentism, and of habitual corruption. Such people, however, still hoped ultimately to obtain forgiveness; and so the Church was able to retain them in a second circle, wider than that which comprises her faithful children, but consisting, as it were, of honorary members for life, on the condition of their abstaining from argument on matters of principle; of observing a few external practices of religion, and promising a final repentance.

12. The unexpected awakening of thought in Europe, at the end of the last century, made the falsity of such a moral situation for Catholics keenly felt by all elevated minds and generous hearts; and provoked much irreverence and dislike to a régime which produced alternately, and sometimes contemporaneously, bigotry and immorality. Indeed, at that moment began the phase of fierce reaction which showed itself in the horrors of 1793, and has not yet come to a close with the misfortunes of 1871. The antagonism between religion and intellect being thus established, and the Church thrown back upon herself in consequence of so serious a breach with society, she still clung tenaciously to the system of inexorable and invariable pressure which had hitherto proved unsuccessful, and which now, far from helping her, was actually prejudicial to her interests, by rendering her difficult of access to mankind in general. Thus the condition of the Church in Catholic countries, with regard to the social question after the events we have described, is very much that of a refuge, the entrance to which is so rugged and difficult, that its proximity is a source of irritation rather than of succour to the people who dwell around it.

This state of discord does not arise from the inevitable obstacles that must be encountered in the pursuit of all that is right and just, but comes from the fact that a man who would be a good Catholic has so many difficulties to contend with, in regard to the external authority that guides him.

A good Catholic finds such a voluminous codex of what is relatively good and evil to be consulted, so many customs prescribed by time to be respected; so much of the learning of our age now familiar to us to be abandoned; so many things to be renounced; scientific opinions, political principles, and not rarely even one's country to be given up; so many difficulties to be overcome regarding the institutions that govern us, that it is requisite to have two consciences, one to judge on matters of religion, and the other on civil government. Intelligent minds, which are the first to feel the burden of such a trial as this, are driven to rebel; they are followed instinctively by the multitudes, and consequently both one and the other are deprived of the substantial benefits of religion, and remain embittered and forsaken, without guidance and without comfort. The Church is still before them—the Church that educates their children and guides their wives, but which denies to them that peace and equanimity, which is only possessed when all the feelings and faculties of the mind meet with their due recognition. The Church withholds from them this peace, because they profess some ideas or opinions which may not perhaps be faultless in themselves, but are yet of a nature that raises and ennobles the human mind; while she does not deny her blessings to souls stained with the greatest crimes when they implore her mercy. From this result naturally, war with the Church, and hatred towards the priests who represent her; and if the open enemies of religion profit largely thereby, it is because they find the ground so well prepared. To this state of antagonism are also due the terrible aberrations prevailing among Catholic populations, for the reaction has been proportioned to the action which had been provoked; and their rebellion has been fierce as the pressure upon them by the Church was inexorable; nor must we forget that one of the permanent causes of these evils is found exactly there where their chief remedy should be sought.

Hence it comes that, in our day, Catholicism has shown itself unequal to the difficulties it must face, and impotent against contemporaneous social evils. We see not only that *coups d'état*, but the most inhuman revolutions recur among Catholic nations; we see them have recourse to such violent measures as the axe, petroleum, brigandage, and summary executions; and the Church has nothing wherewith to calm their fury but vain declamations, and tardy lamentations; or, descending to practical efforts, her only remedies are such as Peter's pence, the French pilgrimages, mystical associations, and periodical religious demonstrations. Fighting itself, and unsuccessfully, among the combatants already so numerous, Catholicism has only become another element in the social war, which it is unable either to restrain or to bring to a victorious close.

Here we meet with another most discouraging phenomenon, so common that it cannot be overlooked, which is this.

Nearly all the Governments of Europe, both Liberal and Conservative, in accomplishing the task of keeping order (a difficult one at the present day), are often obliged to oppose at the same time the aggressions of revolution, and the demands of the Church. We are far from wishing to pronounce judgment on these facts individually; but their frequent recurrence in different conditions of life, reveals to us an organic phenomenon worthy of the deepest attention.

13. A second digression is necessary at this point, in order to take note of the argument of those who hold the doctrines of absolutism—viz., that it is not the part of the Church to accommodate herself to progress, to science, or to the habits of the age; but rather that it is the part of these to submit to the Church. This view of the question is one-sided, and can apply only to Catholics, as it takes no account of others; but even as regards them such an opinion is incorrect. Without making science and material progress responsible for all the mistakes, errors, and follies, that have sought refuge under their shield, and which are reproduced in every age and under every condition of human nature, it is clear that the change of customs, the advance of science, great social and political discoveries, all things, in fact, which are included under the term, "The progress of the age," are providential dispensations beyond the limit of human power; and thus, generally speaking, the responsibility of the

good or evil attaching to them does not fall, or cannot be rightly charged on any individual. The most eminent men only figure as instruments in these grand movements, and either sink or swim according as they use their little influence with equanimity and wisdom among those irresistible currents.

On the other hand, the organised and disciplined administration of the Church, though with regard to principles and to great questions founded on the faith, and grounded in the hearts of the faithful, is yet actually in the power of a small number; especially as to those matters which are not essential to its essence, but have been introduced by other ages, and for other necessities.

The same remark applies to points of discipline, which are neither integral parts of the Church's system, nor from their nature invariable, but which contain the principal subjects of dispute and of danger, and are exactly those points which enter most closely into the social and political life of nations. As the Church possesses full authority on these matters, she is likewise inevitably responsible for them; not only because the unlimited power which she exacts renders her so, but because her own great and exalted mission is one of good tidings and of peace—she herself being founded on the most wonderful sacrifice ever made for the salvation of humanity.

14. We have taken a broad view of the case, and considered from its origin the state of things which now meets us after the prorogation of the Vatican Council, because its aspect is not new, neither is it simply the result of the work of the Council. It is rather the consequence of a policy long since begun, constantly followed, with varying success, and especially manifested in these latter years in the Catholic direction; and it is a result of the spirit of absolutism which prevails in the guidance of the Church. The subject presents no new features; and the events of 1870 have had no other practical effect either on the religious or social side, save that of carrying with them, directly and indirectly, the seal and sanction of an Ecumenical Council in favour of the existing state of things. This it is that gives the deepest importance to the first period of the Vatican Council; its sanction of the past is of equal value with the new laws and regulations it has introduced. All that had taken

place in the Church from the Council of Trent to the present day, a period of more than 300 years, in which, owing to its great length, may be found most of the causes of the events we have briefly considered; all the laws and ecclesiastical customs which prevailed in those three centuries had never been brought under discussion, and had never received the solemn sanction of the Church. Consequently, a Council assembling for the first time, after that long interval, had a grand field before it; three centuries of experience, and no binding precedents during that long period. The fact that the Council did nothing to show its appreciation of the great advantages of this situation, and its desire to profit thereby; but, on the contrary, the fact that it made haste to pursue in the first Sessions what yet remained to be traversed of the road of dogmatism, and of absolutism, this it is that imparted so serious a character to the first period of its discussions, and at once determined the real position of the Church with regard to modern society, and the Catholic nations, in particular.

This position may be summed up in one word—immobility—absolute immobility, as opposed to the decided movement and progress of the age. In the present state of things, this immobility signifies strife; and we have been learning for nearly a century the evils which result from that strife; moreover, so far as human foresight can reach, there seems little hope of its cessation.

15. We now turn to the political situation, and find that, from this point of view, the position of the Church since the prorogation of the Council is, owing to extraneous circumstances, very much altered, and presents an entirely new aspect. The doctrine of Infallibility was proclaimed at Rome on the 18th of July, 1870; and at Berlin, on the 19th of July in the same year was received the intimation of that war which was to effect the ruin of the temporal power; and thus, by a singular disposition of Providence, the completion on one side of the edifice, reared with such perseverance through the lapse of centuries, was to coincide with the commencement of its demolition on the other. The clay feet of the Colossus were broken down and crumbled into dust, just as its head was surmounted with the last golden crown. At the very moment when the Papacy

had reached its utmost development of power, it lost its most effective and powerful instrument for exercising that power in the way, and with the intention, for which it had been raised so high. At the time when the Papacy was ready, solemnly to proclaim to the world its possession of the ascendency it had so long arrogated, but was as yet unable explicitly to assume, at that very moment the world with unwonted indifference saw it deprived of the modest and limited dominion it had hitherto enjoyed. A strange result, indeed, but one which might have been foreseen, though little expected by those who mainly brought it about, and who perhaps awaited a very different result of their labours.

16. The downfall of the temporal power is a great and real innovation in the economy of the Church, and it places the aspect of her political relations with Catholic nations in a new light; so new, indeed, that as yet one cannot estimate, and can only conjecture, the consequences which may be evolved.

The most important point in this new phase is this: that as the different aspects of a question are distinct, rather subjectively in regard to the mind of the observer, than in reality with reference to the actual essence of the question, since they mutually influence each other and are ultimately blended—so this novel and singular phase of the Church's political history cannot fail to react in some way or other, more perhaps than is now imagined, upon her own condition, and her religious and social affinities.

17. Every attempt has been made in past years, both within and without the Church, to reconcile her with the politics, the science, and the habits of the age; with all those elements, in short, which constitute the sum of modern civilisation, in the hope that she might no longer be compelled to stand aloof from civilisation in the position either of an enemy or a victim, but might remain at its side as one of its own agents, an element of strength and moral power. All such attempts have hitherto failed. Each of them has been marked in history by schisms, strife, or profound social perturbations; but society has not made a single step towards the solution of the problem, and the policy of the Church has proceeded tranquilly and unalterably on its own way. Although many, and not the

least among these Dante Alighieri, have been more discerning, society at large has not attached great importance to the influence that might be exercised on the constitution and character of the Church by such a centre of authority as the Roman Curia. The Roman Curia is furnished with infinite moral and material forces; and by the education of its members, its peculiar traditions and forms, it stands detached from the ordinary interests of life, while it is endowed with a wonderful hierarchical organisation, and possesses a boundless supremacy. The diminution of power which the Church has recently undergone, not in regard to her spiritual and speculative authority, but in regard to that practical and material power which has always been the special aim of what is properly called the Roman Curia, is a new phase in her history. Owing to this fact, the political element in the Church has diminished, while the purely ecclesiastical element has naturally resumed the upper hand; as the mechanical centralisation of a State ceases, the moral uniformity takes its place as a spontaneous effect of the concordance of feeling and of principles; force being suspended, conscience remains. This state of things must necessarily be modified by the opinions, the sentiments, and the requirements of the age. The bishops and clergy who living the ordinary life of citizens cannot but be to a certain degree influenced by that common life, naturally take the place occupied exclusively up to that time by the *Prelatura*, and by the ecclesiastical congregations which are composed of mixed elements, and the pressure of the Curia on the episcopate loses considerably thereby, both in prestige and in power.

These modifications are not the effect of a preconceived wish or design, but the notable result of the situation, and they are therefore the more deep and real. The essential transformation in the practical life of the Church which we have described, is coincident with, and balances the declaration of absolute power in her speculative life. What will be the result of such a clashing combination in the economy of the Church? How can these two different orders of things co-exist? Which of them will prevail? A transformation of this nature should be accomplished in the serene air of liberty in order to produce its full effects. The adverse pressure of the State, or of the violent currents of public opinion produced by political passions in times of revolution, may render the change unavailing, and may again rivet the fetters that liberty has unloosed ; and reproduce under the form of some hidden and powerful combination, the same phenomena that were apparent under the distinct and imposing form of the Curia when it was endued with temporal power. The problem consists in this very fact, and it is not easy of solution; at any rate, to determine it à priori is impossible, for our experience in the matter hitherto is too short, and cannot throw much light on the question. At any rate, in weighing the different results that have accrued to the Church from the proceedings of the last three years, no doubt can be entertained on the one hand, of the very great force exercised on all institutions by the principles that govern them, while on the other hand it is impossible to overlook the positive influence of the facts and interests which determine the conditions under which those institutions exist. Lastly, we must not forget the vital strength which animates a great organization like the Church, for she embodies the moral and religious sentiments of numerous and powerful races, sentiments which derive from the circumstances of the age the means necessary for their active and effectual development.

18. The present situation of the Church, as we have shortly described it, with regard to modern society and the religious condition of Catholic populations, is very discouraging, even to the least observant eyes and the most prejudiced judgment, for it presents many deplorable features. So far as to the Church herself. With regard to society, religion is one of its integral elements, it is one of the firmest bonds by which it is united, it is the foundation that sustains the social edifice.

Abstract theories, multiplied reasonings, and the experiments of philosophers and of statesmen, have never yet been able to change this condition of humanity in the least degree; on the contrary, if they have done anything they have rendered it more apparent. From the earliest age, a people is found to be religious in proportion as it is honest, laborious, moral, and strong ; and with disorder and decay come corruption and impiety : cotemporaneous history has in no way changed or added to this rule, and all the endeavours made by elevated minds and determined wills to confute it have utterly failed before the logical power of facts.

19. The religious sentiment, moreover, resembles the other faculties of the human mind; when kept within due limits and applied rationally, it helps to form great societies and strong nations; when hindered and turned out of its proper course, it prepares, or follows, the decay of a nation, and often perishes with it. All constituted societies and forms of civilisation have been animated by some religion which represented their mysterious tie with the Infinite, that is to say, with God. The small and degraded populations of central Africa have a religion that guides them, just as the cultivated Greek societies and the mighty Roman societies had theirs; and without doubt religion has governed and still controls, though many fail to recognise it, the marvellous civilisation of the present age.

Art, which so faithfully and indelibly represents the spirit of the times, has imprinted the character of this civilisation of which we are so justly proud in the 'Divina Commedia,' in the 'Disputa del Sacramento,' and in the glorious churches scattered over the face of the earth. The religious sentiment, which contains in itself the moral tie that binds society together, is at the same time cause and effect, it is an integral part of civilisation, its very germ and spirit. The birth and development of civilisation are alike marked by a strong and living faith. The religious sentiment grows with civilisation; feels the influence of expanding reason and tends itself to become rational; adapts itself to the refinements of civilisation, and inspires the arts and literature. These are the two stages which conduct civilisation to its culminating point. When society degenerates and becomes corrupt, religion does the same; and its downfall is marked by excessive devotion to outward forms, by the neglect of the inward reality, and by the growth of bigotry and indifference. That which happens on a large scale in the history of the world is reproduced in a minor degree in the life of separate nations. The principle is invariable, but its application is infinitely various. The offences of men do not subvert the principle, but only corrupt the societies in which they live. Societies that have become corrupt fall to pieces, but other communities may

R

adopt the principles they have lost, and carry them out more worthily. Society passes away, but the world must accomplish its destiny. The paganism of classical ages, with all its terrible corruptions, fell to rise no more, and at the present day not a single pagan exists on the face of the earth. Meanwhile, Jewish Monotheism, which was relatively obscure and hidden in a corner of the Roman empire, was, in its decay, transformed into Christianity, and spread through the whole world.

Christianity itself has gone through a reform by which it has given life to new societies, and new forms of modern civilisation. By reason of the vast area over which these transformations take place, much of their working is above the judgment of man, and cannot be affected in any way by the will of individuals, they resemble the great vicissitudes of the material world; we may confront them, but can neither advance nor retard their progress by a single second.

On the other hand, men are undoubtedly responsible for the part they take in promoting the development of national life, which accompanies an advanced state of civilisation. As society cannot exist without a religion, neither can it change that religion just as it pleases. The conditions under which religion exists, are beyond and above the ordinary action, and effective will of society, and surpass its calculable powers. It is of course possible for society by a process of self-training to modify its religion, to educate its religious as well as its civil sense. Society may, by cultivating simultaneously its feelings and reasoning powers, and improving at the same time its religious and civil institutions, be able to acquire gradually that harmony of reason and of will, that unity of action in all its faculties, which is requisite for the full development of its strength and greatness.

20. The examination and precise definition of the mystery of order, social and moral—the determination of the point at which individual responsibility for great revolutions ceases, and also where it begins—this examination is the *quia** at which "deve stare contenta la umana gente." Yet this mystery by no means releases any nation from the responsibility as to its own destiny which naturally belongs to it. The more a people seeks

* "State contenti, umana gente, al quia."—Dante, *Purg.* iii. 37.

to be, and actually does become, great and strong, the more that responsibility increases; as it gains in power it is more directly the arbiter of its own fate; and the unknown sum of general causes and influences which affect it, decreases in proportion as the certain and evident sum of its wisdom and virtue increases.

21. Three conclusions evidently result from this brief examination into the present state of Catholic populations, under the consideration of their religious, social, and political aspect. First, it appears that the relations between Church and State, and the religious and civil condition of the inhabitants of Catholic countries in our day, are universally considered to be uncomfortable, dangerous to public order, and obstructive to the diffusion of civilisation and religion. Secondly, it is the interest of the Church, for the sake of her own life, and for the fulfilment of her own mission, to modify this state of things so far as she can. Thirdly, it is essential for society, which can neither exist without a religion, nor can change its religion at will, to adapt itself to that form which it already possesses, endeavouring to improve or modify it in such a way as is most easily reconcilable with its nature and principles. This last condition must be especially observed, in order that the two interests may coalesce favourably, and also in order that the whole scheme of improvement may have a practical result, and not remain a dead letter. Reform in religious matters cannot satisfy reason in the abstract, but only in the relative sense, because faith and feeling are special faculties, having their own proper development. Hence appears the futility of the work of those rationalistic reformers who, having no religion to begin with, endeavour to construct one that may satisfy their own notions; and also of those statesmen who, not feeling any need of religion themselves, try to make one for others. The first class endeavour to produce faith by a process of reasoning; the second to create religious feeling out of scepticism, and both these errors, very common at the present day, spring from a profound ignorance of the origin of the matter. The religious sentiment is not fostered deliberately by a rational and symmetrical plan fixed à *priori*, but, like all other strong convictions, it is developed by education, by habit, and by example, and it is nourished by affections.

Philosophers and statesmen find a justification for religion in its effects rather than in its causes, which remain a mystery to them—a problem only understood by its results; and yet this problem is solved daily by the multitudes whose social condition is determined by the education and the habits they have acquired from religion. Moreover, these very multitudes, from their nature are accessible, more or less rapidly, to strong and profound convictions; they possess intuitively a perception of justice and uprightness, which often compensates for their lack of reasoning power, and are not so easily led away by paradoxes and imposition as might be supposed.

22. The three conclusions we have now stated might be reached by different ways, but they are unimpeachable, and indeed are unquestioned. Objections may be made to the last by those who believe in a society composed of philosophers. We have no wish, with ancient and modern history in our hands, to engage in a discussion on this subject. It is sufficient to state our conviction that those who profess this hazardous opinion seriously, and not merely as a matter of pretext or fashion, cannot, if grave and conscientious men, in the presence of so dangerous a responsibility, and in a matter so vital to society, but see the necessity of carefully testing their experiments in the region of speculation, before endeavouring to give them practical effect; time and liberty, render justice to every one, and everything. This being conceded, we believe that such persons will practically find little to change in the constitution of national life as we understand it, or in the guidance and direction of those interests which can never be successfully treated hypothetically, but must follow the rules that are implanted in the history, the habits, and the conscience of mankind.

23. From whatever side the question be considered, it is evident that to enable Catholic nations to come out of the abnormal and dangerous condition which now so severely tries them, and to proceed quietly on their road, they must be freed from the antagonism between the capital principles which govern them. They must be able to reconcile their religious and civil opinions under the ægis of liberty, in order to proceed without struggles and disturbance to the fulfilment of their

destiny, and to contemplate, without grave misgivings, the dark possibilities of the future.

24. Thus far we have pursued the road which we traced for ourselves. Were we to go further, we might be in danger of exceeding our limits, and of entering the labyrinth of questions which are raised by the conflict between Church and State.

We have been careful in this brief sketch not to touch on any arguments directly regarding canonical or theological matters, because it is better for the profane not to meddle with these questions. We have been content to consider the deep and essential affinity of the subjects under discussion, with social and political questions, because in such points the natural instinct of self-preservation asserts its rights in each of us. If sometimes we have transgressed these limits, it has been unintentionally, and owing to our being drawn on by the intimate connection that exists between all the various interests discussed. Keeping to our resolution, we have noticed the phenomena manifested in Catholic societies, and the breach between religion and civilisation daily widening within them; the substitution of two consciences, a religious and a civil, in opposition to each other, in place of the one conscience, to which all feelings and faculties should be subject, as supreme guide in the difficult road of virtue and of justice; and we have noticed the weakness and disorders that result to Catholic nations from this severance of moral responsibility.

The "free Church in a free State," which is, indeed, a wonderful political formula, an excellent expedient, according to official opinion, for ameliorating the present condition of Catholic populations, is socially an impracticability, especially for those nations that have one single form of religion, the influence of which is therefore dominant in their disposition, their habits, and their civilisation.

The only case in which this ideal could be carried out would be in the event of a great weakening of the religious sentiment among the people, and the entire absorption of the human conscience by the State; but the State in itself is a fact and not a conviction, and is unable to satisfy the human conscience, which cannot divide its allegiance. The power of man, who is, after all, physically speaking, but a weak creature, lies in his intelligence and conscience; by the first he is capable of acquiring the most profound knowledge; by the second, of attaining the highest moral grandeur.

Nations are only assemblages of men, and their power lies in their conscience. No great civilisation has ever been founded on scepticism; and no society has ever maintained its greatness, if the elements of which it is constituted, are in permanent and irreconcilable conflict.

We have considered all these subjects because they come within the range of the social investigation we undertook; but it is impossible to go further without entering into questions that we have avoided. We may, however, without infringing this rule, suggest a few general considerations tending to simplify the question which seems so difficult and intricate as to be almost insoluble, of the amicable co-existence of the Church with the State and with modern society, particularly in Catholic countries, the interests of which we have much at heart.

25. The principles of the Catholic Church are most simple; her mysteries represent dogma, and her commandments represent morals. The mysteries are in every religion above the reach of human reason; the commandments contain the one eternal universal moral law, the observance of which constitutes the life and prosperity of nations. The sum of both is expressed in the simple and comprehensive words :—" On these two commandments hang all the law," &c. And—" Thou shalt love the Lord thy God, and thy neighbour as thyself."

Is it so very difficult a matter to live in accordance with this precept? Or can a rule be found in any past or future system of legislation more suited to serve as the basis of civilisation than this? Is it likely that of all which has been accomplished in the Church by the work of man and the lapse of time, beyond the limits indicated by these two commandments, nothing will be modified or undone by the same agencies—man and time? or, again, is it likely that, as far as regards society, these same agencies will never constitute another, otherwise and elsewhere, than within the limits of these commandments?

26. Time and men, those two great factors in all institutions and forms of civilisation, carry out their work under different conditions. The work of time is necessarily irresistible; we

can but observe and submit to it. The work of man, on the other hand, is accomplished by successive acts, and of free will, and thus the responsibility falls on him alone. In those regions of elevated principle, where passion and party differences vanish, nations regain their generic character which is determined by the concurrent action of all their component elements ; and therefore it has been said that the destiny of a people is that which itself has merited. The truth of this axiom is proved by long experience, though it may be liable to special or temporary exceptions.

The customs, the laws, the religious type, the civil type of a nation are all its own work, the application, the emanation of itself ; and if they could not be modified by education and study, free-will would be an expression void of meaning, and the whole world would become the prey of a revolting and iniquitous fatalism. When a society falls into a state of decay and disorder, the blame is usually thrown upon any one, or anything, as is most convenient at the time, and people reciprocally accuse one another ; the Government, the Liberals, the clergy, the sects, the Church herself, are from time to time denounced as the cause of the evil. All these have, of course, in varying degrees, their own measure of responsibility, which is sometimes partial, sometimes exceptional, and sometimes very serious ; but we cannot look upon them as apart from ourselves, for, after all, we make up their numbers, we determine their opportunities of action ; we constitute their power and their strength. The moral state and the prevalent opinion of a people determine the morality and the power of those who rule it materially and morally, just as these, in their turn, guide and direct the opinion of their subjects.

Having thus settled the respective influences and the collective responsibility of all classes in a nation, with regard to its social condition and the development of its prosperity, we can more easily investigate the causes of the dangers and difficulties that disturb our own people ; determine the measure of responsibility attaching to them, and ascertain exactly the duty of each section of society, with the hope of supplying some remedy for the evils under which it is labouring. The opinions, the education, and the moral and intellectual condition of our people are such as to condemn them to a perpetual alternation between opposite and dangerous extremes. If, for instance, those races that we call the Latin races, which form a large proportion of the Catholic nations, be affected by the religious movement, it often conducts them, by a strictly logical process, to a state of theocracy and superstition. If, on the other hand, the spirit of liberty, and the exercise of reason be awakened among them, it often happens that by a similar process of logic their onward social and political march is only arrested when they have reached a state of anarchy and impiety; and a negation of all responsibility, is the effect of this second course. The law of reaction and of compensation originates and regulates these moral oscillations, giving to the first phase greater durability, and to the second greater force and intensity. Wherever the Latin races have settled and manifested their principles by their institutions and forms of government, they seem to forget that their strength can only consist in so ruling their faculties and sentiments as to render them practically useful, just as the economy of human life, social and individual, consists in a tempered moderation. A people whose life is passed between one phase of superstition and tyranny, and another of anarchy and impiety, resembles an individual who spends half his existence in habitual excess, and the rest in fasting, in both cases the result must be death.

27. Having already spoken of logic, we would here protest very strongly against the manner in which it is used. Owing to the scholastic form in which it has mingled with the traditions of the period of our intellectual development, logic has often proved a source of evil, and has led to disastrous conclusions. In the form in which it has passed into our method of reasoning and thinking, logic is an imperfect instrument, by which man endeavours to reach the truth; it is a machine to create truth. No doubt on many occasions this artificial process has been helpful to the weakness of the human mind, especially in the earlier ages; it was a means of eliciting the truth on testing a subject by two propositions, just as a spark is produced by two currents of electricity. But, granting all the services rendered us by logic, we must not forget that it is only an artifice, that the infinite can never be contained in

the finite; and that though all can aspire to the truth, and find it in some degree, it is not given to all to possess it, and possess it always. In all truth there is something above our comprehension, which must be supplied by faculties other than those of the intellect; faculties that we must educate and develop in order to use them efficaciously. This is the reason why nothing is more likely to lead us to absurd conclusions than the process of argument familiar to us from long habit, which we call logic; and it misleads us irremediably, because logically. Our mental errors all involve a syllogism, and therefore they last so long, and produce so much harm.

The religious principle, guided only by logic to its utmost development, often becomes abstract, mystical and intolerant; it loses its chief characteristic, that of being the companion, the creator and the soul of civilisation; it isolates itself, and becomes a great and sometimes an insuperable obstacle to real progress. If the human mind blindly follows logic it may lose religion, and being unable to appreciate subtle distinctions, but adhering to absolute deductions, may even cast it off entirely; and society, being thus set free from the ties which bind it together, loses its strength and prosperity, and falls into a state of anarchy. In each of these cases an inflexible logic has been followed out with a like result—that of arriving at an absurd conclusion.

28. We have been led by these considerations to a point where we may consider the Church and society as standing on common ground, where their respective interests meet, and where it is possible to form such judgments on the condition of both, as may help the practical solution of the social problem affecting Catholic nations. But here we have reached the proper limit of a book so moderate in compass, and of so general a character as the present work. It remains for individuals to form for themselves, according to their opportunities, the conclusions to be deduced from the facts we have indicated. It is not our business to settle in what way, or how far, the Church can, and ought to carry out the modifications demanded by the very existence of Catholic society; any more than we can determine the progress of human society, or limit its irresistible course. The Church and society have each a wide field open to

them, where their respective powers for good may be duly developed; the Gospel and liberty. Every civil law may be in harmony with the Gospel, and every religious institution may be in harmony with liberty. How best to ensure the simple and faithful observance of both our religious and civil obligations, is a secret never yet discovered on account of its very simplicity; and who knows if it will ever be discovered amid the distracting struggles and the absorbing passions that agitate humanity.

29. It is, indeed, most desirable that this secret, this happy solution of difficulties should be brought to light, though here we do not intend to enter upon the arduous question of the religious future of the age. Without doubt, religious convictions have on all sides received a violent shock; and none can foretell the results of the great social revolutions that have taken place; they may work the ruin of societies and institutions; they may derange the equilibrium of nations, and change the course of the world; but as these hypotheses are purely speculative, their consideration cannot conduce to any certain conclusion, or to any practical effect. Whatever the universal religious condition of the world may be, our duty is to attend to our own, to find out in what our difficulties and dangers consist, and to discover the essential difference between our social state, and that of other Christian populations.

Among those nations religion and civilisation have, with more or less harmony, marched in unison, supporting and at the same time correcting, each other; they are able to co-exist not indeed without some divergencies, but, at all events, without causing variance and enmity.

Among our people, on the contrary, there seems to be definitively established a mortal strife between the religious principle represented by an exclusive inflexible authority, embodied in a form absolute and immutable in all its parts; and that moral revolution, of which the latter must eventually feel the influence, which has itself a form equally concrete and organic, and which tends to become equally exclusive, inflexible and despotic. Our people, as well as other nations, obey the universal law, and follow their appointed destinies, but with very different results, for the latter attain their ends without catastrophes or great struggles; whereas, the path of the former is marked by terrible losses and ruin, owing to the violence of the current that sweeps them along. Such considerations are of the utmost importance to Catholic nations ; for their course has been hitherto marked by a brilliant light, which still shines upon their path, and forbids our indulging any disparaging estimates as to their moral and political inferiority.

30. Therefore, before bringing these reflections to a close, we would remind Catholic nations that though they may try to find the causes of their abnormal condition in their institutions, yet habits form laws as much, or perhaps more, than laws form habits ; and as the universal sentiment of a society is the element that nourishes its institutions, their life or their death depends upon the state of that element.

It is requisite for the well-being of Catholic nations, not only that their own vitality be preserved, but that they do not prove occasions of ruin to others, and it is necessary that they find their own moral equilibrium. They must learn, moreover, that they will no more attain this moral equilibrium, this essential condition of life, through the inexorable mysticism of the Catholic party, than they would through the utter dissolution of all principle. They will not find it in scepticism, because nothing can be created by negation, nor in new divisions, because these only give rise to anger and discord; and by separating the energetic and ardent part of society from the rest, renders the former weaker, and leaves the latter a prey to reaction and hatred. Catholic nations will find their wished-for peace only in a real modification of their principles, a work requiring time and thought, by which their religious and civil institutions, being in conformity with the eternal principles of morality and truth, may subsist in harmony and may assimilate with the various phases and developments of human nature.

31. If, on the other hand, we could prevail on those to whom is entrusted the direction of Catholic institutions, and of the exercise of their influence, to listen to our arguments with unprejudiced minds, we would point out that although the spirit of the age is not congenial to religious belief, yet that real resistance and active enmity are never attracted by movements of an exclusively religious or speculative character, nor even by those that directly concern faith and morals. Such resistance is evoked

by movements political rather than religious—material rather than spiritual, and touching discipline rather than morals or dogma. Nor is this unnatural, for morality in itself is one and eternal, whereas its legal expressions are variable and transitory. Consequently, it is evident and logical that these legal expressions may change, and be affected by social movements and the progress of the age ; whereas morality in itself can be assailed by no real opposition other than that eternal antagonism between right and wrong which must affect all institutions, and is inseparable from the history of the universe itself. Two truths cannot contradict one another. There cannot be one truth for the Church and another for the State, any more than there is one truth for religion and another for science. That which is good for one nation cannot be evil for another; and all those who maintain such antitheses are in error. A true and sublime religion, firmly rooted on the earth and reaching to heaven, can never be opposed to truth and goodness, for that opposition could only be directed against evil.

Therefore, when the conditions of the strife are such, that goodness and truth are on one side, and all the strength and energy of human nature rally round them ; evil diminishes and retreats to the position of impotence and subordination which it is intended to hold in the order of the universe. The nearer we approach this ideal, the more surely shall we attain that happy state of things on which the prosperity and grandeur of nations depends ; and the social and political problems which at first sight appeared inexplicable, will resolve themselves as naturally as the snow melts away beneath the genial rays of the sun.

32. We might sum up the principal wants of Catholic nations as follows : their sense of right and wrong should be simplified and rendered clearer, and they should be relieved from the burden of artificial evils that oppress them, in order that they may acquire the power of discerning what is really evil, and may be able to oppose it. They must learn to be guided in their struggle by the spirit, and not by the letter of the law, because the spirit teaches what is upright in practice, whereas the letter is incapable of amending what is wrong. " Quid leges sine moribus." Much is to be done before these results can be at-

tained; in the first place, it is requisite that the authorities by which Catholic nations are governed, and the principles by which they are led, should not be the production of absolute and exclusive ideas, isolated from the rest of the world; but should rest upon universal opinion, and express the mind of the whole Church, for only in this way can she adopt and assimilate the various forms of good which are now extraneous to her, but with which she should be in unison. To this end it is necessary that her hierarchy, instead of being only the exponent of supreme authority, should be, as it was originally, the impersonation of the loftiest virtue and self-sacrifice. In taking the first step, religion escapes the danger of being only the appendage or instrument of a party, and becomes, what in truth she ought to be, the originator and fosterer of social order, the friend and benefactor of humanity. In taking the second step, religion becomes active, and descends from the region of abstruse speculation to enter upon that of facts, a region in which self-abnegation and virtue are necessary elements of progress.

Having reached this point, religion has fulfilled her mission; the rest is beyond our power and responsibility, and the destiny of nations remains in the hands of Him who created the universe. But up to that point the responsibility is ours; and we must answer for the evil resulting from a state of things we ourselves have brought about, and jealously maintain, with an energy worthy of a better cause, in despite of evidence and reason.

33. Even if the facts which we have specified did not exist, the peculiar form in which the internal working and the external movement of the Church manifest themselves, are such as to prevent our undertaking a discussion respecting them, of laying down rules or making suggestions to the authorities that guide and direct her course. The foundation on which these authorities rest their power, the connection existing between them, and all their movements, depend upon special laws which are inaccessible to external considerations, and thus on practical grounds we have no language in which to interchange our ideas. Just as the State is obliged to provide for its necessities, so now the Church must herself seek the best means of reconciling the difficulties she encounters, of meeting the new conditions of life

brought about by the lapse of time and the experience of the past; this being the only way in which the word reconciliation can bear a real signification, as a point of meeting and not of departure. It remains for the Church to find the best means of reconciling the substance of religion, that is, faith and morality, with the great development of reason and with the new social and civil conditions of nations; harmonising the good she teaches with the good which may be learned from science, from legislation, and from the ever-varying and progressive movement of human society. It is the part of the Church to be a help rather than a hindrance to society in the tempest through which it is now passing; an anchor of safety rather than a dangerous rock on which split the efforts of those—who placed at the helm of State, with the duty of guiding the ships tossed about by the angry surges of the social deep—must either strive to keep clear of such obstacles, or falling upon them, be dashed to pieces, leaving at the mercy of the waves the broken fragments of a ruined and shipwrecked society.

34. At this very moment when the Church, distracted by the many and serious controversies that trouble her, called together her States General, and looked trustfully to her Ecumenical Assembly for the solution of her difficulties, it was specially incumbent on her to carry out the course of action indicated by the steps she had already taken. Preliminary events do not as yet point to the fulfilment of this obligation, but still it is *summa lex* for the Church, because essential for the general safety, to discover some means of escape from the prevailing dangers; to take some step towards the solution of the great problem that touches so nearly her own life and the very existence of Catholic nations. She may find that help in the marvellous strength of her own constitution, in her extensive authority, and well-proved ability in dealing with matters of difficult interpretation; or, what would be still more satisfactory, she may find in a full and free discussion, the best solution of her difficulties.

35. It is true that to modify in any way the religion of a people while a strong and independent Rationalism prevails in the world, is a work so hard and so full of difficulties impossible to express à *priori*, that it can never be accomplished either by a Canon of the Church or by a law of the State, but must be the

combined operation of time and human efforts. Still, if we have the right to look to any special agents for help in this great work, it is surely to those who received the injunction, " Go and bring forth fruit;"* and who were likewise reminded as a commentary on this mission, that " a good tree cannot bring forth corrupt fruit."† We look to those prophets and apostles of good tidings of whom it was said that they should be known by their fruits; not by their privileges or vestments, not by the wisdom of their laws or the harmony of their institutions, not by the possession of worldly goods, or by the power they had attained, but simply by the fruits they brought forth, " wherefore by their fruits ye shall know them."‡

* St. John, xv. 16.   † St. Matthew, vii. 18.   ‡ St. Matthew, vii. 20.

APPENDIX OF DOCUMENTS.

CONTENTS.

Documents.	Page
I. Bull of Convocation of the Council	259
II. French Correspondence from the 'Civiltà Cattolica'	262
III. Proclamation of the Bishops at Fulda	263
IV. Letter of Padre Giacinto	266
V. Pastoral of the Archbishop of Paris	268
VI. Pastoral of the Bishop of Orleans	273
VII. Promulgation of the Jubilee	294
VIII. Allocution of the Sistine Chapel	296
IX. Bull "Multiplices inter"	298
X. Allocution at the First Session	303
XI. Bull for the Pope's Election	304
XII. Bull for limiting Censures	306
XIII. The Canons published in the 'Allgemeine Zeitung' and the 'Süd-Deutsche Presse'	311
XIV. Statistical Extract from Franscini	320
XV. Last Letter of Montalembert	321
XVI. Address of the Catholics of Coblenz to the Bishop of Treves	321
XVII. New Order of the Council, etc. Article by Döllinger	326
XVIII. The Scheme "De Fide"	332
XIX. Formula of Adhesion to the Dogma of Infallibility given by the 'Italie,' at the end of June 1870	337
XX. The Scheme "De Ecclesia," from the 'Giornale di Roma'	337

DOCUMENTS.

DOCUMENT I.

SANCTISSIMI DOMINI NOSTRI
PII
DIVINA PROVIDENTIA
PAPAE IX.

LITTERAE APOSTOLICAE
QVIBVS
INDICITVR OECVMENICVM CONCILIVM
ROMAE HABENDVM
ET DIE IMMACVLATAE CONCEPTIONI
DEIPARAE VIRGINIS SACRO AN. MDCCCLXIX
INCIPIENDVM.

PIVS EPISCOPVS

SERVVS SERVORVM DEI

Ad futuram rei memoriam.

Aeterni Patris Unigenitus Filius propter nimiam, qua nos dilexit, caritatem, ut universum humanum genus a peccati iugo, ac daemonis captivitate, et errorum tenebris, quibus primi parentis culpa iamdiu misere premebatur, in plenitudine temporum vindicaret, de caelesti sede descendens, et a paterna gloria non recedens, mortalibus ex Immaculata Sanctissimaque Virgine Maria indutus exuviis, doctrinam, ac vivendi disciplinam e caelo delatam manifestavit, eamdemque tot admirandis operibus testatam fecit, ac semetipsum tradidit pro nobis, oblationem et hostiam Deo in odorem suavitatis. Antequam vero, devicta morte, triumphans in caelum consessurus ad dexteram Patris conscenderet, misit Apostolos in mundum universum, ut praedicarent evangelium omni creaturae, eisque potestatem dedit regendi Ecclesiam suo sanguine acquisitam, et constitutam, quae est *columna et firmamentum veritatis*, ac caelestibus ditata thesauris tutum salutis iter, ac verae doctrinae lucem omnibus populis ostendit, et instar *navis in altum*

saeculi huius ita natat, ut, pereunte mundo, omnes quos suscipit, servet illaesos.[1] Ut autem eiusdem Ecclesiae regimen recte semper, atque ex ordine procederet, et omnis christianus populus in una semper fide, doctrina, caritate, et communione persisteret, tum semetipsum perpetuo affuturum usque ad consummationem saeculi promisit, tum etiam ex omnibus unum selegit Petrum, quem Apostolorum Principem, suumque hic in terris Vicarium, Ecclesiaeque caput, fundamentum ac centrum constituit, ut cum ordinis et honoris gradu, tum praecipuae, plenissimaeque auctoritatis, potestatis, ac iurisdictionis amplitudine pasceret agnos, et oves, confirmaret fratres, universamque regeret Ecclesiam, et esset *caeli ianitor*, ac *ligandorum, solvendorumque arbiter, mansura etiam in caelis iudiciorum suorum definitione.*[2] Et quoniam Ecclesiae unitas, et integritas, eiusque regimen ab eodem Christo institutum perpetuo stabile permanere debet, iccirco in Romanis Pontificibus Petri successoribus, qui in hac eadem Romana Petri Cathedra sunt collocati, ipsissima suprema Petri in omnem Ecclesiam potestas, iurisdictio, Primatus plenissime perseverat, ac viget.

Itaque Romani Pontifices omnem Dominicum gregem pascendi potestate et cura ab ipso Christo Domino in persona Beati Petri divinitus sibi commissa utentes, nunquam intermiserunt omnes perferre labores, omnia suscipere consilia, ut a solis ortu usque ad occasum omnes populi, gentes, nationes evangelicam doctrinam agnoscerent, et in veritatis, ac iustitiae viis ambulantes vitam assequerentur aeternam. Omnes autem norunt quibus indefessis curis iidem Romani Pontifices fidei depositum, Cleri disciplinam, eiusque sanctam, doctamque institutionem, ac matrimonii sanctitatem dignitatemque tutari, et christianam utriusque sexus iuventutis educationem quotidie magis promovere, et populorum religionem, pietatem, morumque honestatem fovere, ac iustitiam defendere, et ipsius civilis socie-

[1] San. Max., Serm. 89. [2] San. Leo, Serm. II.

tatis tranquillitati, ordini, prosperitati, rationibus consulere studuerint.

Neque omiserunt ipsi Pontifices, ubi opportunum existimarunt, in gravissimis praesertim temporum perturbationibus, ac sanctissimae nostrae religionis, civilisque societatis calamitatibus generalia convocare Concilia, ut cum totius catholici orbis Episcopis, quos *Spiritus Sanctus posuit regere Ecclesiam Dei*, collatis consiliis, coniunctisque viribus ea omnia provido, sapienterque constituerent, quae ad fidei potissimum dogmata definienda, ad grassantes errores profligandos, ad catholicam propugnandam, illustrandam et evolvendam doctrinam, ad ecclesiasticam tuendam ac reparandam disciplinam, ad corruptos populorum mores corrigendos possent conducere.

Iam vero omnibus compertum, exploratumque est qua horribili tempestate nunc iactetur Ecclesia, et quibus quantisque malis civilis ipsa affligatur societas. Etenim ab acerrimis Dei hominumque hostibus catholica Ecclesia, eiusque salutaris doctrina, et veneranda potestas, ac suprema huius Apostolicae Sedis auctoritas oppugnata, proculcata, et sacra omnia despecta, et ecclesiastica bona direpta, ac Sacrorum Antistites, et spectatissimi viri divino ministerio addicti, hominesque catholicis sensibus praestantes modis omnibus divexati, et Religiosae Familiae extinctae, et impii omnis generis libri, ac pestiferae ephemerides, et multiformes perniciosissimae sectae undique diffusae, et miserae iuventutis institutio ubique fere a Clero amota, et quod peius est, non paucis in locis iniquitatis, et erroris magistris commissa. Hinc cum summo Nostro, et bonorum omnium moerore, et nunquam satis deplorando animarum damno ubique adeo propagata est impietas, morumque corruptio, et effrenata licentia, ac pravarum cuiusque generis opinionum, omniumque vitiorum, et scelerum contagio, divinarum, humanarumque legum violatio, ut non solum sanctissima nostra religio, verum etiam humana societas miserandum in modum perturbetur, ac divexetur.

In tanta igitur calamitatum, quibus cor Nostrum obruitur, mole supremum Pastorale ministerium Nobis divinitus commissum exigit, ut omnes Nostras magis magisque exeramus vires ad Ecclesiae reparandas ruinas, ad universi Dominici gregis salutem curandam, ad exitiales eorum impetus conatusque reprimendos, qui ipsam Ecclesiam, si fieri unquam posset, et civilem societatem funditus evertere conituntur. Nos quidem, Deo auxiliante, vel ab ipso supremi Nostri Pontificatus exordio nunquam pro gravissimi Nostri officii debito destitimus pluribus Nostris Consistorialibus Allocutionibus, et Apostolicis Litteris Nostram attollere vocem, ac Dei, ciusque sanctae Ecclesiae causam Nobis a Christo Domino concreditam omni studio constanter defendere, atque huius Apostolicae Sedis, et iustitiae, veritatisque iura propugnare, et inimicorum hominum insidias detegere, errores, falsasque doctrinas damnare, et impietatis sectas proscribere, ac universi Dominici gregis saluti advigilare et consulere.

Verum illustribus Praedecessorum Nostrorum vestigiis inhaerentes, opportunum propterea esse existimavimus, in Generale Concilium, quod iamdiu Nostris erat in votis, cogere omnes Venerabiles Fratres totius catholici orbis Sacrorum Antistites qui in sollicitudinis Nostrae partem vocati sunt. Qui quidem Venerabiles Fratres singulari in catholicam Ecclesiam amore incensi, eximiaque erga Nos, et Apostolicam hanc Sedem pietate et observantia spectati, ac de animarum salute anxii, et sapientia, doctrinae eruditione praestantes, et una Nobiscum tristissimam rei cum sacrae tum publicae conditionem maxime dolentes, nihil antiquius habent, quam sua Nobiscum communicare, et conferre consilia, ac salutaria tot calamitatibus adhibere remedia. In Oecumenico enim hoc Concilio ea omnia accuratissime examine sunt perpendenda, ac statuenda, quae hisce praesertim asperrimis temporibus maiorem Dei gloriam, et fidei integritatem, divinique cultus decorem, sempiternamque hominum salutem, et utriusque Cleri disciplinam, eiusque salutarem, solidamque culturam, atque ecclesiasticarum legum observantiam, morumque emendationem, et christianam iuventutis institutionem, et communem omnium pacem et concordiam in primis respiciunt. Atque etiam intentissimo studio curandum est, ut, Deo bene iuvante, omnia ab Ecclesia, et civili societate amoveantur mala, ut miseri errantes ad rectum veritatis, iustitiae, salutisque tramitem reducantur, ut vitiis, erroribusque eliminatis, augusta nostra religio eiusque salutifera doctrina ubique terrarum reviviscat, et quotidie magis propagetur, et dominetur, atque ita pietas, honestas, probitas, iustitia, caritas omnesque christianae virtutes cum maxima humanae societatis utilitate vigeant, et afflorescant. Nemo enim inficiari unquam poterit, catholicae Ecclesiae, eiusque doctrinae vim non solum aeternam hominum salutem spectare, verum etiam prodesse temporali populorum bono, eorumque verae prosperitati, ordini, ac tranquillitati, et humanarum quoque scientiarum progressui ac soliditati, veluti sacrae ac profanae historiae annales splendidissimis factis clare aperte-quo ostendunt, et constanter, evidenterque demonstrant. Et quoniam Christus Dominus illis verbis Nos mirifice recreat, reficit, et consolatur: *Ubi sunt duo vel tres congregati in nomine meo ibi sum in medio eorum*;[1] iccirco dubitare non possumus, quin Ipse in hoc Concilio Nobis in abundantia divinae suae gratiae praesto esse velit, quo ea omnia statuere possimus, quae ad maiorem Ecclesiae suae sanctae utilitatem quovis modo pertinent. Ferventissimis igitur ad Deum luminum Patrem in humilitate cordis Nostri dies noctesque fusis precibus hoc Concilium omnino cogendum esse censuimus.

Quamobrem Dei ipsius omnipotentis Patris, et Filii, et Spiritus Sancti, ac beatorum eius Apostolorum Petri et Pauli auctoritate, qua Nos quoque in terris fungimur, freti et innixi, de Venerabilium Fratrum Nostrorum S. R. E. Cardinalium consilio et assensu, sacrum Oecumenicum et Generale Concilium in hac alma Urbe Nostra Roma futuro anno millesimo octingentesimo sexagesimo nono, in Basilica Vaticana habendum, ac die octava mensis Decembris Immaculatae Deiparae Virginis Mariae Conceptioni sacra incipiendum, prosequendum, ac Domino adiuvante, ad ipsius gloriam, ad universi Christiani populi salutem absolvendum, et perficiendum hisce Litteris indicimus, annuntiamus, convocamus et statuimus. Ac proinde volumus, iubemus, omnes ex omnibus locis tam Venerabiles Fratres Patriarchas, Archiepiscopos, Episcopos, quam Dilectos Filios Abbates, omnesque alios, quibus iure, aut privilegio Conciliis Generalibus residendi, sententias in eis dicendi facta est potestas, ad hoc Oecumenicum Concilium a Nobis indictum venire debere, requirentes, hortantes, admonentes, ac nihilominus eis vi iurisiurandi, quod Nobis, et huic Sanctae Sedi praestiterunt, ac sanctae obedientiae virtute, et sub poenis iure, aut consuetudine in celebrationibus Conciliorum adversus non accedentes ferri, et proponi solitis, mandantes, arcteque praecipientes, ut ipsimet, nisi forte iusto detineantur impedimento, quod tamen per legitimos procuratores Synodo probare debebunt, Sacro huic Concilio omnino adesse, et interesse teneantur.

In eam autem spem erigimus fore, ut Deus, in cuius manu sunt hominum corda, Nostris votis propitius annuens ineffabili sua misericordia et gratia efficiat, ut omnes supremi omnium populorum Principes, et Moderatores praesertim catholici quotidie magis noscentes maxima bona in humanam societatem ex catholica Ecclesia redundare, ipsamque firmissimum esse Imperiorum, Regnorumque fundamentum, non solum minime

[1] Matth., cap. xviii, v. 20.

impediant, quominus Venerabiles Fratres Sacrorum Antistites, aliique omnes supra commemorati ad hoc Concilium veniant, verum etiam ipsis libenter faveant, opemque ferant, et studiosissime, uti decet Catholicos Principes, iis cooperentur, quae in maiorem Dei gloriam, eiusdemque Concilii bonum cedere queant.

Ut vero Nostrae hae Litterae, et quae in eis continentur ad notitiam omnium, quorum oportet, perveniant, neve quis illorum ignorantiae excusationem praetendat, cum praesertim etiam non ad omnes eos, quibus nominatim illae essent intimandae, tutus forsitan pateat accessus, volumus, et mandamus, ut in Patriarchalibus Basilicis Lateranensi, Vaticana, et Liberiana, cum ibi multitudo populi ad audiendam rem divinam congregari solita est, palam clara voce per Curiae Nostrae cursores, aut aliquos publicos notarios legantur, lectaeque in valvis dictarum Ecclesiarum, itemque Cancellariae Apostolicae portis, et Campi Florae solito loco, et in aliis consuetis locis affigantur, ubi ad lectionem et notitiam cunctorum aliquandiu expositae pendeant, cumque inde amovebuntur, earum nihilominus exempla in eiusdem locis remaneant affixa. Nos enim per huiusmodi lectionem, publicationem, affixionemque, omnes, et quoscumque, quos praedictae Nostrae Litterae comprehendunt, post spatium duorum mensium a die Litterarum publicationis et affixionis ita volumus obligatos esse et adstrictos, ac si ipsismet illae coram lectae et intimatae essent, transumptis quidem earum quae manu publici notarii scripta, aut subscripta, et sigillo personae alicuius Ecclesiasticae in dignitate constitutae munita fuerint, ut fides certa, et indubitata habeatur, mandamus ac decernimus.

Nulli ergo omnino hominum liceat hanc paginam Nostrae indictionis, annuntiationis, convocationis, statuti, decreti, mandati, praecepti, et obsecrationis infringere, vel ei ausu temerario contraire. Si quis autem hoc attentare praesumpserit, indignationem Omnipotentis Dei, ac Beatorum Petri et Pauli Apostolorum eius se noverit incursurum.

Datum Romae apud Sanctum Petrum Anno Incarnationis Dominicae millesimo octingentesimo sexagesimo octavo, tertio kalendas Iulias.

Pontificatus Nostri Anno Vicesimotertio

✠ EGO PIVS CATHOLICAE ECCLESIAE EPISCOPVS

Loco ✠ Signi

✠ Ego Marius Episc. Ostiensis et Veliternus Card. Decanus Mattei Prodatarius.

✠ Ego Constantinus Episc. Portuen. et S. Rufinae Card. Patrizi.

S

✠ Ego Aloisius Episc. Praenestinus Card. Amat S. R. E. Vice-Cancellarius.
✠ Ego Nicolaus Episc. Tusculanus Card. Paracciani Clarelli a Secretis Brevium.
✠ Ego Camillus Episc. Albanus Card. Di Pietro.
✠ Ego Carolus Augustus Episc. Sabinensis Card. De Reisach.
✠ Ego Philippus Tit. S. Laurentii in Lucina Proto-Prosb. Card. De Angelis Archiep. Firmanus, et S. R. E. Camerarius.
✠ Ego Fabius Maria Tit. S. Stephani in Monte Coelio Presb. Card. Asquini.
✠ Ego Alexander Tit. S. Susannae Presb. Card. Barnabo.
✠ Ego Ioseph Tit. S. Mariae in Ara Caeli Presb. Card. Milesi.
✠ Ego Petrus Tit. S. Marci Presb. Card. De Silvestri.
✠ Ego Carolus Tit. S. Mariae de Populo Presb. Card. Sacconi.
✠ Ego Angelus Tit. SS. Andreae et Gregorii in Monte Coelio Presb. Card. Quaglia.
✠ Ego Fr. Antonius Maria Tit. SS. XII Apost. Presb. Card. Panebianco Poenitentiarius Maior
✠ Ego Antoninus Tit. SS. Quatuor Coronator. Presb. Card. De Luca.
✠ Ego Ioseph Andreas Tit. S. Hieronymi Illyricorum Presb. Card. Bizzarri.
✠ Ego Ioannes Bapt. Tit. S. Callixti Presb. Card. Pitra.
✠ Ego Fr. Philippus Maria Tit. S. Xysti Presb. Card. Guidi Archiep. Bononiensis.
✠ Ego Gustavus Tit. S. Mariae in Transpontina Presb. Card. d'Hohenlohe.
✠ Ego Aloisius Tit. S. Laurentii in Pane Perna Presb. Card. Bilio.
✠ Ego Lucianus Tit. S. Pudentianae Presb. Card. Bonaparte.
✠ Ego Ioseph Tit. SS. Marcellini et Petri Presb. Card. Berardi.
✠ Ego Raphael Tit. SS. Crucis in Hierusalem Presb. Card. Monaco.
✠ Ego Iacobus S. Mariae in Via Lata Proto-Diac. Card. Antonelli.
✠ Ego Prosper S. Mariae Scalaris Diac. Card. Caterini.
✠ Ego Theodulphus S. Eustachii Diac. Card. Mertel.
✠ Ego Dominicus S. Mariae in Dominica Diac. Card. Consolini.
✠ Ego Eduardus SS. Viti et Modesti Diac. Card. Borromeo.

✠ Ego Hannibal S. Mariae in Aquiro Diac. Card. Capalti.

M. CARD. MATTEI, *Pro-Datarius*.
N. CARD. PARACCIANI CLARELLI.

Loco + Plumbi
Reg. in Secretaria Brevium.
Visa de Curia D. Bruti
I. Crugnionius.

(Dalla *Civiltà Cattolica*,
18 luglio 1868.)

DOCUMENT II.

CORRISPONDENZA DI FRANCIA.

5. Per ciò che riguarda la parte dommatica, già dissi che i cattolici desidererebbero che il futuro Concilio Ecumenico promulgasse le dottrine del *Syllabus*. Potrebbe darsi che il Concilio, enunciando con formole affermative e col necessario svolgimento le proposizioni stanziate nel *Syllabus*, sotto forma negativa, facesse compiutamente sparire il malinteso che sussiste non solo nelle sfere del potere, ma ben anco in un gran numero d'intelligenze per altro colte, ma non intendenti di stile teologico. Checchè ne sia, coll' andar del tempo i pregindizii si dilegueranno, gli occhi si avvezzeranno alla luce, e la verità, essendo immortale, trionferà colle sole sue forze.

I cattolici riceveranno con gioia la proclamazione del futuro Concilio sull' infallibilità dommatica del Sommo Pontefice. Essa riuscirebbe indirettamente ad annullare la famigerata Dichiarazione del 1682, senza che fosse necessaria una speciale discussione di quei malaugurati *quattro articoli*, che furono per sì gran tempo l'anima del Gallicanismo. Nessuno però si dissimula che il Sommo Pontefice, per un sentimento di augusta riserbatezza, non voglia da per sè prendere l' iniziativa d' una proposizione, che sembra riferirsi a lui direttamente. Ma si spera che la manifestazione unanime dello Spirito Santo per la bocca dei Padri del futuro Concilio Ecumenico la definirà per acclamazione.

Finalmente un gran numero di cattolici emettono il voto che il futuro Concilio chiuda il ciclo degli omaggi resi dalla Chiesa alla Vergine Immacolata, promulgando il dogma della *gloriosa Assunzione di lei*.

Siffatti sono i voti in ciò che riguarda il dogma. I bisogni della Chiesa di Francia, in ciò che spetta alla disciplina, sono molteplici ed esigono spiegazioni più estese, che io prendo la libertà di rimettere ad una prossima corrispondenza.

— E altrove:

Il presentimento delle traversie politiche, che forse potrebbero nascere, nell' animo di molti si combina con una non so quale confidenza di un esito fortunato. Bisogna altresì avvertire, come una nota caratteristica, la persuasione quasi direi universale, che trovasi nella più parte dei cattolici. Essi credono che il futuro Concilio sarà molto breve, o che rassomiglierà sotto questo rispetto a quello di Calcedonia. Questa idea non procede soltanto dalle difficoltà sentite di tenere ora lunga assemblea; ma rampolla anzi tutto dal sentimento che i Vescovi di tutto il mondo si troveranno d' accordo nelle questioni principali, in guisa che la minorità, per quanto eloquente esser possa, non potrà durarla in una lunga opposizione. Finalmente non potrebbero non vedersi senza un certo stupore delle lotte prolungate di opinioni o di discorsi nel seno del futuro Concilio.

(Dalla *Civiltà Cattolica*, 6 febbraio 1869.)

DOCUMENT III.

PASTORALE COLLETTIVA DEI VESCOVI TEDESCHI RIUNITI A FULDA.

Anche quest' anno noi Vescovi tedeschi, nello spirito di Gesù Cristo e della sua santa Chiesa, che anzitutto è spirito di unità e di comunione, ci siamo uniti a Fulda presso al sepolcro di San Bonifacio, in fraterna conferenza. Scopo di queste adunanze non è già quello di emanare decisioni obbligatorie in materie ecclesiastiche, il che secondo le leggi della Chiesa può farsi soltanto nelle assemblee ecclesiastiche propriamente tali e tenute nella dovuta forma (nei Sinodi o Concilii); ma esse hanno unicamente per iscopo di renderci, mediante vicendevoli colloqui, più atti ad adempiere nel modo migliore il nostro sacro ministero, e di coltivare fra noi quell' unione e carità, che è la madre e nutrice di ogni bene.

Naturalmente in quest' anno un oggetto principale della nostra conferenza fu di prepararci al Concilio Ecumenico, al quale il nostro Santo Padre Pio IX ha convocato tutti i Vescovi della terra.

A questo riguardo noi abbiamo giudicato cosa buona e salutare, prima di separarci, di rivolgere in comune ai nostri amati diocesani, ecclesiastici e secolari, alcune brevi parole.

Allorchè erasi fatta certa la convocazione di un Concilio Ecumenico, per una parte gli animi dei fedeli furono riempiti da pia aspettazione e lieta speranza, e migliaia di essi tengono rivolti con figliale fiducia i loro sguardi a Roma. Non quasi fosse il Concilio un mezzo magico per togliere da noi ogni male e pericolo, e per mutare d' un tratto la faccia della terra, ma perchè, secondo la costituzione data da Cristo nella sua divina sapienza alla Chiesa, l' unione dei successori degli Apostoli intorno al successore di San Pietro, in un Concilio Ecumenico, è il mezzo principale per mettere in più chiara luce la verità salutare del Cristianesimo, e per introdurre nella vita più efficacemente la sua santa legge. Ciò che il santo pontefice Gregorio Magno dice sì bellamente, che nel corso dei tempi le porte della divina verità e sapienza si aprono sempre di più alla cristianità, questo si effettua nel modo più grandioso mediante i Concilii Ecumenici. Dall' essere poi la dottrina di Cristo esattamente conosciuta e la sua legge più universalmente osservata dipende senza dubbio, come l' eterno, così pure il vero benessere temporale dell' umanità. Perciò i figli fedeli della Chiesa hanno salutato in ogni tempo i Concilii Ecumenici con gioia e con santa fiducia. Egli è nostro sacro dovere di nutrire in noi stessi e di diffondere negli altri cotali sentimenti anche riguardo all' imminente Concilio.

Tuttavia non possiamo dissimularci, che d' altra parte persino da membri fervorosi e fedeli della Chiesa si nutrono timori, atti a scemare la fiducia. Si aggiunge che dagli avversari della Chiesa vengono mosse accuse, le quali non hanno altro scopo, che di suscitare vastamente la diffidenza e l' avversione contro il Concilio, e di risvegliare persino il sospetto dei Governi. Così si sentono delle voci che il Concilio possa e voglia promulgare nuovi dogmi di fede, i quali non si contengono nella rivelazione di Dio e nella tradizione della Chiesa, e che esso possa e intenda stabilire dei principii che, pregiudicievoli agli interessi del Cristianesimo, sieno *incompatibili colle giuste pretese dello Stato, colla civiltà e colla scienza, come pure colla legitima libertà e colla prosperità temporale dei popoli*. Si va ancor più innanzi; si accusa il Santo Padre che egli, sotto l' influsso di un partito, voglia puramente usare del Concilio come di un mezzo per accrescere smodatamente il potere della Sede Apostolica, per cambiare l' antica e vera costituzione della Chiesa, per istabilire una signoria spirituale incompatibile colla cristiana libertà. Non si ha rossore di designare il Capo supremo della Chiesa e l' Episcopato con nomi di fazione, che noi finqui eravamo usi di sentire solamente dalla bocca dei più dichiarati nemici della Chiesa. Quindi non si ha alcun riguardo di far sentire il sospetto, che *non sarà concessa ai Vescovi la piena libertà di discussione*, o che mancherà anche agli stessi Vescovi la necessaria cognizione e il necessario coraggio per adempiere il loro dovere nel Concilio, e in conseguenza di ciò si pone persino in questione la validità stessa del Concilio e delle sue decisioni.

Da qualunque parte provengano questi e simili discorsi, essi non sono certamente dettati da fede viva, da fedele amore alla Chiesa, da un' incrollabile fiducia in quell' aiuto, che non mai il Signore alla sua Chiesa sottrae. Così non hanno mai pensato i nostri padri nella fede, non mai i santi di Dio; ciò, amati diocesani, è contrario senza dubbio anche al vostro intimo convincimento cristiano. Non pertanto noi vogliamo anche esplicitamente esortarvi a non vi lasciar sedurre da tali discorsi, e a non vacillare per cagione di essi nella vostra fede e nella vostra speranza.—*Giammai un Concilio Ecumenico pronuncierà nè può pronunciare una nuova dottrina, che non sia contenuta nella Sacra Scrittura o nella Tradizione Apostolica*; come in generale la Chiesa, quando pronuncia in cose di fede, non promulga nuove dottrine, ma svela l' antica e originaria verità in chiara luce e la difende contro nuovi errori.

Giammai un Concilio Ecumenico può promulgare o promulgherà dottrine, le quali sono in contraddizione coi principii della giustizia, col diritto dello Stato e delle sue autorità, colla moralità e coi veri interessi della scienza, o colla legittima libertà e col benessere dei popoli. In generale il Concilio non istabilirà nuovi principii, nè altri da quelli, che sono scritti dalla fede e dalla coscienza nel cuore di tutti voi, che furono sacri ai popoli cristiani di tutti i secoli, e sui quali ora e sempre riposa la prosperità degli Stati, l' autorità dei superiori, la libertà dei popoli, e che costituiscono la base di ogni vera scienza e moralità.—E perchè possiamo noi fare questa dichiarazione con tale precisione e fidanza? Perchè noi siamo accertati dalla fede, che Gesù Cristo è colla sua Chiesa i dì sino alla fine del mondo, che lo Spirito Santo non la abbandona mai, e le ricorda ogni cosa e la introduce in ogni verità, per modo che essa è e rimane la colonna e il sostegno della verità, cui le stesse porte dell' inferno non possono espugnare; finalmente perchè noi crediamo e sappiamo che, quando i successori di Pietro e degli Apostoli, il Papa e i Vescovi, adunati legittimamente in un Concilio Ecumenico, fanno delle decisioni in cose della fede e della legge morale, sono assicurati contro ogni errore della provvidenza e assistenza divina.

A quella maniera, che Cristo è il medesimo ieri e oggi e in eterno, e la sua parola dura sempre, quand' anche passino cielo e terra; così anche la sua Chiesa rimane la stessa in ogni tempo, e la verità di Cristo rimane in lei perpetua e immutabile. Anche il solo temere che un Concilio Ecumenico nelle sue decisioni dottrinali possa errare contro la verità della Tradizione, che esso possa in alcun modo alterare nella sua essenza la costituzione della Chiesa stabilita da Dio, è un disconoscere la virtù delle divine promesse fatte alla santa Chiesa, e l' efficacia dell' aiuto della divina grazia. *Egualmente nessuno ha ragione di temere, che il Concilio Ecumenico prenda inconsideratamente e con precipitazione delle risoluzioni, le quali senza necessità si oppongano ai vigenti rapporti e ai bisogni della presente età, oppure che esso, seguendo il fanatismo di umani pensamenti, voglia trapiantare nell' età presente costumi e istituzioni di tempi trascorsi*. E come si può anche solo ragionevolmente temere una tal cosa da un' adunanza dei Vescovi di tutto il mondo cattolico, i quali forniti delle più ricche esperienze della vita, famigliari alle condizioni dei più svariati paesi, aggravati dalla responsabilità della più santa missione, dal Capo supremo della Chiesa, vengono adunati principalmente allo scopo, *per deliberare con lui*, in quale modo migliore le eterne verità della religione debbansi attuare nella presente età, e come il beneficio del Cristianesimo si possa meglio conservare e trasmettere alle presenti e future generazioni?

Egli è con sì poco fondamento e con sì poca giustizia che si temerebbe di veder attentare alla libertà delle deliberazioni del Concilio. Quanto poco coloro che ciò pensano, conoscono i sentimenti del Papa, i sentimenti dei Vescovi e il modo di procedere della Chiesa! Noi sappiamo nel modo più certo che è volere formale e dichiarato del Santo Padre di non mettere alcun ostacolo alla libertà e alla durata delle deliberazioni, e ciò è nella natura stessa delle cose. Infatti in un Concilio della Chiesa i varii partiti non combattono con tutte le arti dell' eloquenza per ottenere la vittoria; i diversi membri dell' Assemblea non cercano di vincerla sui loro avversarii coll' acquisto di una maggioranza favorevole alle loro opinioni. E malgrado delle differenze di sentire, tutti sono anticipatamente d' accordo sui principii della fede, e non tendono che ad uno scopo, che è la salute delle anime e il bene del Cristianesimo. Le dicussioni non hanno dunque per oggetto di vincere un avversario o di far trionfare un interesse particolare; non si discute se non per fare risplendere la verità sotto ogni suo aspetto e per non decider nulla prima di aver risolto tutte le difficoltà o chiarito tutto ciò che è oscuro. In ciò che riguarda soprattutto le eterne verità della fede, il Concilio non deciderà nulla prima di aver esauriti tutti i mezzi della scienza e delle più mature deliberazioni.

E che direm noi a proposito degl' indegni sospetti che suppongono che i Vescovi potrebbero per considerazioni umane rinunciare nel Concilio alla libertà della parola, che è uno dei loro obblighi? Noi ricord indoci del comando del nostro Maestro non risponderemo con ingiurie a coloro che c'insultano, e ci contenteremo di dire semplicemente e lealmente: Quando i Vescovi della Chiesa Cattolica saranno riuniti in Concilio Ecumenico, non dimenticheranno mai *il più santo dei loro doveri, il dovere di rendere testimonianza alla verità*: si rammenteranno di quelle parole dell' Apostolo: *Chi vuol piacere agli uomini, non è servo di Cristo*; ricordandosi del conto che dovranno rendere quanto prima dinanzi al tribunale di Dio, penseranno ch' essi non hanno altra regola da seguire che quella della loro coscienza.

Non abbiam creduto che fosse indegno di noi il difendere l' Episcopato Cattolico e il Concilio Ecumenico contro questi tristi sospetti; noi sappiamo che lo stesso Apostolo dei Gentili non ha disdegnato, nell' interesse dell' Apostolico suo ministero e del suo amore per le anime e per la Chiesa, di respingerne in tal modo le accuse più insussistenti.

Ma quando si giunge persino ad incriminare ed oltraggiare le intenzioni del Santo Padre e la Santa Sede Apostolica stessa, dimenticando completamente il rispetto e l' affetto che dobbiamo alla Chiesa ed al suo capo, quando lo si rappresenta lui, che Cristo ha costituito pastore di tutti e di cui fece la pietra sulla quale riposa tutta la Chiesa, come un partito e come lo strumento d' un partito; quando gli si attribuiscono progetti di dominazione ed ambiziosi, assolutamente come coloro che davanti Ponzio Pilato accusarono altre volte Cristo, il fondatore della Chiesa, di essere un ribelle e di ammutinare il popolo, le parole ci mancano per esprimere il nostro dolore nell' udire simili discorsi, e per dichiararci contro lo spirito, da cui sono inspirati.

Nulla è tanto contrario ed estraneo all' essenza della Chiesa Cattolica quanto lo spirito di partito. Il divin Salvatore ed i suoi Apostoli non hanno condannato nulla più energicamente della scissione e della divisione in partiti, ed è precisamente per impedire ogni fatto di questo genere e conservare l' unità degli animi mediante il legame della pace, che Cristo ha scelto fra tutti gli Apostoli uno solo per fare di lui il centro dell' unità ed il pastore supremo, sottoporre tutti all' autorità paterna di quel pastore ed unire a lui tutti i vescovi, preti e fedeli del mondo intero col legame indissolubile dell' obbedienza, fondata sulla fede e sull' amore.

È vero che la Chiesa si compone di una immensa quantità di caratteri nazionali ed individuali. Essa abbraccia le associazioni, corporazioni e manifestazioni più diverse della vita religiosa; essa tollera e protegge persino la varietà delle dottrine teoriche e pratiche; ma non tollera ed approva mai i partiti, ed essa stessa non è mai un partito. Per un cuore cattolico, finchè la sua fede ed il suo amore non sono oscurati dalle passioni, è impossibile che sotto il rapporto religioso ed ecclesiastico sia mai penetrato dallo spirito di parte, poichè la sua fede lo induce a subordinare con umiltà, amore e fiducia illimitata, il suo proprio giudizio e più ancora i suoi interessi e le sue passioni alla Sede suprema, di cui Cristo s' impose di ascoltare gl' insegnamenti ed alla quale si applica eternamente la sua parola: " Chi vi ascolta, mi ascolta."

Al prossimo Concilio Ecumenico, questa Sede suprema ed infallibile della Chiesa parlerà a tutti, o piuttosto sarà Cristo ed il suo Spirito Santo, che parleranno mediante l' organo di quella Sede, e tutti gli uomini di buona volontà, tutti coloro che amano Iddio, udiranno la voce di Cristo: " La voce della verità, della giustizia, della pace di Cristo."

Come Pietro e i suoi Apostoli non avevano che una sola e stessa opinione al primo Concilio di Gerusalemme, e non parlavano che una sola lingua, così pure non vi sarà oggidì che una sola opinione ed una sola lingua, sarà rivelato a tutto il mondo che, come nella prima comunità cristiana, anche oggidì tutti gli aderenti della Chiesa Cattolica non hanno che un cuore ed un' anima sola.

È da questa fonte dell' unità che deriva nella Chiesa tutto ciò che v' ha di grande, di buono e di salutare; vi si riferiscono tutti i vantaggi del Cristianesimo e soltanto mediante questa unità noi partecipiamo alla luce ed alla vita di Cristo. Perciò Cristo nella sua preghiera dopo la Cena implorò dal suo Padre Celeste i benefizi di questa unità, poichè i benefizi di questa unità comprendono tutti gli altri beni di salute, la fede, l'amore, la forza, la pace e tutte le benedizioni.

All'opposto, dalla scissione e dalla secessione sono sòrti i mali peggiori, da cui siano mai stati afflitti il Cristianesimo ed il mondo, mentre che al contrario la salvezza dipende dalla conciliazione e dal ristabilimento dell'unità.

Se, all'epoca nostra, come dobbiamo riconoscerlo, grazie al Cielo, molti mali di passati tempi nefasti furono guariti; se la vita ecclesiastica e religiosa ha guadagnato forza, malgrado tutte le circostanze sfavorevoli, e so è stato fatto molto bene per la salute delle anime e la consolazione dei poveri e di coloro che soffrono; se il coraggio della fede e l'amore per la Chiesa sono divenuti più forti in tutti gli ecclesiastici ed i laici; se in tutto l'universo il regno di Dio cresce con novello vigore e porta frutti; se anche tutti gli attacchi contro la Chiesa e tutt'i suoi patimenti non si rivolgono che a suo vantaggio, noi non dubitiamo che ciò non sia soprattutto il risultato di quell'armonia intima e di quella unità di sentimento che, se si eccettuano alcune tristi ed insignificanti perturbazioni, regna in tutto il mondo cattolico.

Non è vana iattanza, ma rendere omaggio ad una verità evidente dire che tutti i Vescovi del mondo cattolico sono uniti fra loro e colla Sede Apostolica nella più perfetta unità, e che il clero ed il popolo sono pure d'accordo coi loro Vescovi; è così che l'unione più cordiale esiste generalmente fra i varii servi della Chiesa e che i cattolici di tutte le nazioni si sentono pure d'accordo ed uniti nella fede e nell'amore per la Chiesa; le calamità e le burrasche dei tempi non fecero che consolidare questa unità e specialmente l'affettuosa cooperazione di tutte le nazioni a proteggere il Santo Padre, gravemente minacciato, ha stretto sempre più i legami di questa unità.

Nello spirito di questa unità, come inviati da Cristo, in nome di Cristo e per il Suo Cuore, noi consigliamo, preghiamo e scongiuriamo tutti e particolarmente i nostri fratelli nel sacerdozio e nel santo ministero dell'insegnamento, di mantenere e sviluppare questa perfetta concordia, secondo la loro posizione, colle parole, gli scritti e l'esempio, facendo sparire completamente tutti i conflitti che potrebbero essere avvenuti precedentemente da una parte o dall'altra, ed astenendosi da tutto ciò che potrebbe servire d'alimento alla discordia o risvegliare le passioni umane.

Fra breve noi lasceremo per lungo tempo le nostre diocesi, ed i nostri cuori sono grandemente commossi, allorchè pensiamo ai gravi pericoli dell'età presente. In con-

seguenza abbiamo deciso ed ordinato che siano indirizzate preghiere durante tre giorni al Sacro Cuore di Gesù, incominciando dall'8 dicembre di quest'anno in tutte le parrocchie delle nostre diocesi. Noi ci riserbiamo di prendere ulteriori disposizioni intorno a queste preghiere.

La grazia e la pace di Gesù Cristo, l'intercessione della Santissima Vergine e di tutti i Santi, sia e rimanga con voi tutti.

Fatto a Fulda, il 6 settembre 1869.

✠ PAOLO, *Arcivescovo di Colonia.*
✠ GREGORIO, *Arciv. di Monaco e di Frisinga.*
✠ ENRICO, *Principe Vescovo di Breslavia.*
✠ G. ANTONIO, *Vescovo di Wurzborgo.*
✠ CRISTOFORO FIORENZO, *Vescovo di Fulda.*
✠ GUGLIELMO EM., *Vescovo di Magonza.*
✠ EDOARDO GIACOMO, *Vescovo d'Hildesheim.*
✠ LUIGI, *Vescovo di Leontopoli in* p. i. *Vicario Apostolico di Sassonia.*
✠ CORRADO, *Vescovo di Paderborna.*
✠ PANCRAZIO, *Vescovo di Augsborgo.*
✠ MATTIA, *Vescovo di Treveri.*
✠ NICOLÒ, *Vescovo d'Alicarnasso* p. i. *Vicario Apostolico di Lussemburgo.*
✠ GIO. ENRICO, *Vescovo d'Osnabruck e Provicario delle Missioni settentrionali tedesche e danesi.*
✠ FRANCESCO LEOPOLDO, *Vescovo di Eichstaedt.*
✠ LOTARIO, *Vescovo di Leuca in* p. i. e *Vic. cap. dell'Arcidiocesi di Friburgo.*
✠ FILIPPO, *Vescovo di Ermeland.*
✠ GIO. NEPOMUCENO, *Vescovo di Culm.*
✠ NICOLÒ, *Vescovo di Spira.*
✠ CARLO GIUSEPPE, *Vescovo eletto di Rottenbourg.*

(Dalla *Rivista Universale*, ottobre 1869, fasc. 84, vol. x.)

DOCUMENT IV.

LETTERA DI PADRE GIACINTO.

Au R. P. *Général des Carmes déchaussés.*

MON TRÈS-RÉV. PÈRE,

Depuis quelques années que dure mon ministère à Notre-Dame de Paris, et malgré les attaques ouvertes et les délations cachées dont j'ai été l'objet, votre estime et votre confiance ne m'ont pas fait un seul instant défaut. J'en conserve de nombreux témoigorges écrits de votre main, et qui s'adressent à mes prédications autant qu'à ma personne. Quoi qu'il arrive, j'en garderai un souvenir reconnaissant.

Aujourd'hui cependant, par un brusque changement dont je ne cherche pas la cause dans votre cœur, mais dans les menées d'un parti tout-puissant à Rome, vous accusez ce que vous encouragiez, vous blâmez ce que vous approuviez, et vous exigez que je parle un langage, ou que je garde un silence qui ne seraient plus l'entière et loyale expression de ma conscience.

Je n'hésite pas un instant. Avec une parole faussée par un mot d'ordre ou mutilée par des réticences je ne saurais remonter sur la chaire de Notre-Dame. J'en exprime mes regrets à l'intelligent et courageux archevêque qui me l'a ouverte, et m'y a maintenu contre le mauvais vouloir des hommes dont je parlais tout-à-l'heure. J'en exprime mes regrets à l'imposant auditoire qui m'y environnait de son attention, de ses sympathies, j'allais presque dire de son amitié. Je ne serais digne de l'auditoire, ni de l'évêque, ni de ma conscience, ni de Dieu, si je pouvais consentir à jouer devant eux un pareil rôle.

Je m'éloigne en même temps du couvent que j'habite, et qui, dans les circonstances nouvelles qui me sont faites, se change pour moi en une prison de l'âme. En agissant ainsi je ne suis point infidèle à mes vœux : j'ai promis l'obéissance monastique, mais dans les limites de l'honnêteté de ma conscience, de la dignité de ma personne et de mon ministère. Je l'ai promise sous le bénéfice de cette loi supérieure de justice et de *royale liberté* qui est, selon l'apôtre saint Jacques, la loi propre du chrétien.

C'est la pratique la plus parfaite de cette liberté sainte que je suis venu demander au cloître, voici plus de dix années, dans l'élan d'un enthousiasme pur de tout calcul humain, je n'ose pas ajouter dégagé de toute illusion de jeunesse. Si en échange de mes sacrifices on m'offre aujourd'hui des chaînes, je n'ai pas seulement le droit, j'ai le devoir de les rejeter.

L'heure présente est solennelle. L'Église traverse une des crises les plus violentes, les plus obscures et les plus décisives de son existence ici-bas. Pour la première fois depuis trois cents ans, un Concile Œcuménique est non-seulement convoqué, mais déclaré nécessaire : ce n'est pas selon les expressions du Saint-Père. Ce n'est pas dans un pareil moment qu'un prédicateur de l'Évangile, fût-il le dernier de tous, peut consentir à se taire, comme ces chiens muets d'Israël, gardiens infidèles, à qui le prophète reproche

de ne pouvoir point aboyer : *Canes muti non valentes latrare*. Les saints ne se sont jamais tus. Je ne suis pas l'un d'eux, mais toutefois je me sens de leur race, *filii sanctorum sumus*, et j'ai toujours ambitionné de mettre mes pas, mes larmes, et s'il le fallait, mon sang dans les traces où ils ont laissé les leurs.

J'élève donc devant le Saint-Père et devant le Concile ma protestation de chrétien et de prêtre contre ces doctrines et ces pratiques, qui se nomment romaines, mais ne sont pas chrétiennes, et qui dans leurs envahissements toujours plus audacieux et plus funestes, tendent à changer la constitution de l'Église, le fond comme la forme de son enseignement, et jusqu'à l'esprit de sa piété. Je proteste contre le divorce impie autant qu'insensé qu'on s'efforce d'accomplir entre l'Église, qui est notre mère selon l'éternité, et la société du dix-neuvième siècle, dont nous sommes les fils selon le temps, et envers qui nous avons aussi des devoirs et des tendresses.

Je proteste contre cette opposition plus radicale et plus effrayante encore avec la nature humaine atteinte et révoltée par ces faux docteurs dans ses aspirations les plus indestructibles et les plus saintes. Je proteste par-dessus tout contre la perversion sacrilége de l'Évangile du Fils de Dieu lui-même, dont l'esprit et la lettre sont également foulés aux pieds par le pharisaïsme de la loi nouvelle.

Ma conviction la plus profonde est que si la France en particulier et les races latines en général, sont livrées à l'anarchie sociale, morale et religieuse, la cause principale en est non pas sans doute dans le catholicisme lui-même, mais dans la manière dont le catholicisme est depuis longtemps compris et pratiqué.

J'en appelle au Concile qui va se réunir pour chercher des remèdes à l'excès de nos maux, et pour les appliquer avec autant de force que de douceur. Mais si des craintes que je ne veux point partager venaient à se réaliser, si l'auguste assemblée n'avait pas plus de liberté dans ses délibérations, qu'elle en a déjà dans sa préparation ; si en un mot elle était privée des caractères essentiels à un Concile Œcuménique, je crierais vers Dieu et vers les hommes pour en réclamer un autre véritablement réuni dans le Saint-Esprit, non dans l'esprit des partis, représentant réellement l'Église universelle, non le silence des uns, l'oppression des autres. —" Je souffre cruellement à cause de la souffrance de la fille de mon peuple ; je pousse des cris de douleur, et l'épouvante m'a saisi. N'est-il plus de baume à Galaad ?

et n'y a-t-il plus là de médecin ? Pourquoi donc n'est-elle pas fermée la blessure de la fille de mon peuple ?" (*Jérémie*, viii.)

Et enfin j'en appelle à votre tribunal, ô Seigneur Jésus, *Ad tuum Domine Jesu tribunal appello*. C'est en votre présence que j'écris ces lignes ; c'est à vos pieds, après avoir beaucoup prié, beaucoup réfléchi, beaucoup souffert, beaucoup attendu ; c'est à vos pieds que je les signe. J'en ai la confiance : si les hommes les condamnent sur la terre, vous les approuverez dans le ciel. Cela me suffit pour vivre et pour mourir.

Paris-Passy, le 20 septembre 1869.

Fr. Hyacinthe,

Supérieur des Carmes déchaussés de Paris, deuxième définiteur de l'Ordre dans la province d'Avignon.

(Dai Giornali contemporanei, come dall' *Italie*, n° 23, sett. 1869.)

DOCUMENT V.

Lettre Pastorale de Monseigneur l'Archevêque de Paris sur le prochain Concile.

Georges Darboy, par la grâce de Dieu et l'autorité du Saint-Siége apostolique, archevêque de Paris, grand aumônier de l'Empereur.

Au clergé et aux fidèles de notre diocèse, salut et bénédiction en Notre - Seigneur Jésus-Christ.

Nos très-chers Frères,

Il y a deux ans, le Souverain Pontife a manifesté aux évêques réunis à Rome autour de lui le vif désir de convoquer, aussitôt qu'il le pourrait, un Concile général pour rechercher avec eux les remèdes nécessaires aux maux présents de l'Église. Quelques mois après, il a publié la bulle d'indiction qui fixe l'ouverture du Concile au 8 décembre prochain, et un peu plus tard il a demandé à tous les fidèles, en leur accordant une indulgence plénière en forme de jubilé, d'appeler par leurs supplications les lumières et les grâces de Dieu sur les travaux de cette grande assemblée. Ainsi le moment approche où les évêques du monde catholique vont répondre à l'appel du Saint-Père, et où vous-mêmes, nos très-chers frères, devrez vous mêler à leur œuvre par vos prières et vos actes de piété. Il importe donc de vous exposer, au moins brièvement, ce qui va s'accomplir, et les motifs que vous avez d'y prendre un religieux intérêt.

Ce qui rend plausible et moralement nécessaire aujourd'hui la tenue d'un Concile, c'est l'état général du monde ; ce qui l'autorise, c'est la constitution même, le droit et le devoir de l'Église, divinement établie pour veiller au salut des âmes ; ce qui permet d'y rattacher de solides et consolantes espérances, c'est avec les dispositions de l'épiscopat la bénédiction d'en haut et l'assistance promise du Saint-Esprit.

L'état général du monde est tel qu'il préoccupe les moralistes et les politiques autant que les hommes de religion. Est-ce à dire que notre siècle, considéré dans l'ensemble de ses actes, soit plus mauvais que les siècles antérieurs, qu'il souffre de choses que le passé n'aurait pas connues et qu'il se présente avec une plus grande somme d'ignorances et de perversités ? Nous ne pouvons pas l'admettre : les erreurs et les crimes sont de toutes les époques ; le libre arbitre de la créature a ses défaillances et ses emportements inévitables, et l'imparfaite humanité marche vers son but et accomplit sa destinée, en traversant des vicissitudes pleines de grandeurs et de misères qui recommencent toujours et ne se ressemblent jamais. Elle cherche, sans parvenir à le réaliser parfaitement ni pour longtemps, l'équilibre des éléments dont se compose le monde : autorité et liberté, droit et devoir, intérêt et conscience, État et Église. Ce qu'elle règle se pratique mal ou ne dure pas. Dans les milieux complexes et si variables où elle se meut avec des forces et des faiblesses qui restent les mêmes, le bien et le mal prennent des aspects qui se modifient sans cesse ; et chaque génération semble avoir ses vertus et ses vices préférés. Dresser le tableau comparatif de ces évolutions morales, et faire la part de responsabilité qui revient aux divers âges et aux diverses régions, est une œuvre où l'on peut difficilement être et paraître impartial, une œuvre qui d'ailleurs ici ne serait pas à sa place. Tout ce que nous voulons dire, c'est que notre temps ne nous fait pas peur, et que nous l'aimons, malgré ses défauts ; car il a des défauts, et nous n'avons point envie de les dissimuler.

Personne en effet ne refusera de reconnaître que bien des choses se passent qui gênent l'action de l'Église et compromettent le salut des âmes, et qui du reste sont une cause de souffrance et une menace pour la société civile. Les vérités de la foi, l'autorité des saintes Écritures, la divinité du christianisme, l'existence même de Dieu ne sont-elles pas incessamment attaquées par une critique intempérante, ou par un scepticisme froid et railleur, qui prennent la négation pour de la force et le rire pour la hardiesse et de la raison? Les journaux, les livres et les discours publics ne sont-ils pas à toute heure dirigés contre ce qu'il y a de plus nécessaire et de plus sacré, la religion, la morale, la famille et la société? La liberté de parler et d'écrire ne va-t-elle pas jusqu'à l'extrême licence, ouvrant le chemin à la liberté de tout faire et de tout défaire? Car la logique n'est pas, autant qu'on le croit, absente des choses humaines. Si en effet les droits de Dieu sont contestés et méconnus, comment ceux de l'homme ne seraient-ils pas précaires et plus que discutables? Et comment y aurait-il des autorités sur la terre, si l'autorité n'est pas dans le ciel? Mais s'il n'existe de droits nulle part, il n'existe point de devoirs non plus; dès lors le respect n'a rien à faire dans le monde, la force seule y règne, et tout est en proie à tous. Ce n'est donc pas seulement la religion qui est en cause, c'est aussi l'ordre public et la tranquillité des États: les sophistes sèment le vent, et les nations moissonnent la tempête.

Telle est la situation morale de notre époque. Du reste, le Saint-Père, en y cherchant un remède, l'a décrite dans les termes suivants: "Depuis longtemps, dit-il, tout le monde sait et constate quelle horrible tempête subit aujourd'hui l'Église, et de quels maux immenses souffre elle-même la société civile. L'Église catholique et sa doctrine salutaire, sa puissance vénérable et la suprême autorité de ce Siége apostolique, sont attaquées et foulées aux pieds par des ennemis acharnés de Dieu et des hommes; toutes les choses sacrées sont vouées au mépris, et les biens ecclésiastiques dilapidés; les pontifes, les hommes les plus vénérables consacrés au divin ministère, les personnages éminents par leurs sentiments catholiques sont tourmentés de toutes manières; on anéantit les communautés religieuses; des livres impies de toute espèce et des journaux pestilentiels sont répandus de toutes parts; les sectes les plus pernicieuses se multiplient partout et sous toutes les formes: l'enseignement de la malheureuse jeunesse est presque partout retiré au clergé, et ce qui est encore pire, confié en beaucoup de lieux à des maîtres d'erreur et d'iniquité. Par suite de tous ces faits, pour notre désolation et la désolation de tous les gens de bien, pour la perte des âmes, on ne pourra jamais assez pleurer, l'impiété, la corruption des mœurs, la licence sans frein, la contagion des opinions perverses de tout genre, de tous les vices et de tous les crimes, la violation des lois divines et humaines, se sont partout propagées, à ce point que, non-seulement notre très-sainte religion, mais encore la société humaine sont misérablement dans le trouble et la confusion."

Cette peinture est triste, et de tels maux ont besoin d'être combattus avec zèle et vigueur. Non pas qu'il faille se flatter d'en avoir entièrement raison, quelque effort qu'on fasse; mais il est possible d'en arrêter le développement et d'en limiter les funestes conséquences; d'ailleurs le rôle des justes dans cette vie de luttes et d'épreuves, c'est de vouir en aide à la vertu. Or, tel est précisément le droit et le devoir de l'Église. Elle est instituée de Dieu pour éclairer, diriger et soutenir les âmes par la prédication de la vérité, par ses règles de discipline et par l'efficacité des sacrements. Cette mission de salut, Jésus-Christ l'a confiée aux apôtres et aux évêques leurs successeurs; ils la remplissent depuis dix-huit siècles, veillant sur tout le troupeau où le Saint-Esprit les a placés pour gouverner l'Église de Dieu, sous la commune houlette du Souverain Pontife, successeur de Pierre, chargé de paître les agneaux et les brebis. En conséquence, l'objet de leur travail est de se maintenir et de maintenir les fidèles dans l'unité, qui a pour signe public et permanent la communion avec le Pape, divinement investi d'une primauté d'honneur et de juridiction s'étendant à toute l'Église.

L'œuvre s'accomplit dans ces conditions; que les évêques soient dispersés ou réunis, ils instruisent et gouvernent avec autorité et succès. Les délibérations générales, les résolutions concertées ne sont donc pas absolument nécessaires dans l'Église; mais elles y ont toujours paru d'une force considérable et d'une grande efficacité. On n'a rien trouvé de meilleur que cette union des conseils et des sollicitudes pour faciliter la définition des dogmes de foi, pour réfuter et dissiper les erreurs les plus répandues, pour mettre en lumière et développer la doctrine religieuse, pour maintenir et relever la discipline ecclésiastique, pour corriger et perfectionner les mœurs. On n'a rien trouvé de meilleur non plus pour engager les chrétiens à recevoir avec promptitude et respect les décisions doctrinales et disciplinaires de l'Église, formulées et décrétées par les évêques du monde entier qui se prononcent qu'en tenant compte tout à la fois de la révélation dont ils sont les gardiens, et des sentiments, des habitudes et des besoins de leurs diocèses, dont ils sont les pasteurs et les guides.

Aussi le Saint-Père déclare-t-il opportune la réunion d'un Concile, où tous les évêques du monde catholique seront appelés à s'entendre sur le caractère et la portée des maux actuels, et sur les remèdes qu'il est expédient de leur appliquer. "Le Concile œcuménique, dit la Bulle d'indiction, devra donc examiner avec le plus grand soin et déterminer ce qu'il convient de faire, en ces temps si calamiteux, pour la plus grande gloire de Dieu, pour l'intégrité de la foi, pour la splendeur du culte, pour le salut éternel des hommes, pour la discipline et la solide instruction du clergé régulier et séculier, pour l'observation des lois ecclésiastiques, pour la réforme des mœurs, pour l'éducation chrétienne de la jeunesse, pour la paix générale et la concorde universelle. Il nous faudra travailler aussi de toutes les forces de notre esprit, et avec l'aide de Dieu, à délivrer de tout mal l'Église et la société civile, à ramener dans la voie de la vérité, de la justice et du salut les malheureux qui s'égarent. Enfin nous devons réprimer tout vice et repousser toute erreur, afin que notre auguste religion et sa doctrine salutaire reprennent partout une vigueur nouvelle, qu'elles se propagent de jour en jour, qu'elles reconquièrent leur légitime empire, et qu'ainsi la piété, l'honnêteté, la probité, la justice, la charité et toutes les vertus refleurissent pour le salut du monde. Non-seulement, en effet, la puissante influence de l'Église et de sa doctrine a pour objet direct le salut éternel des hommes, mais aussi, et personne ne le niera, le bonheur temporel des peuples, leur véritable prospérité, le maintien de la paix et de l'ordre, le progrès même et la solidité des sciences humaines : les faits les plus éclatants de l'histoire ne le prouvent-ils pas constamment, et de la manière la plus évidente ?"

Tel est donc, ainsi qu'on le voit par les paroles du Saint-Père, tel est l'objet général dont s'occupera l'assemblée des évêques. Naturellement il se décompose en divers points qui deviendront à leur tour l'objet de décisions spéciales, et donneront lieu sans doute à des mesures particulières. Mais cela ne peut se faire sans qu'on agisse par là même sur vos opinions et vos doctrines pour les fixer et peut-être les corriger, et sur certains détails de votre conduite privée ou sociale pour y apporter quelque heureuse modification. Cette perspective ne vous a pas toujours été présentée d'une manière satisfaisante, et plusieurs semblent avoir pris à tâche de vous inquiéter à ce sujet. Ils vous ont dit, par exemple, qu'on imposerait à votre foi catholique des articles que jusqu'ici vous n'étiez pas tenus de croire ; que des questions intéressant la société civile et les relations de l'Église et de l'État seraient traitées et décidées dans un esprit d'opposition aux lois et aux mœurs politiques du temps présent ; qu'on enlèverait certain vote par acclamation, qu'ainsi les évêques ne seraient pas libres, et que la minorité, fût-elle éloquente, serait traitée comme un parti d'opposition qu'étoufferait bientôt la majorité.

Mais rassurez-vous, nos très-chers frères. Ces plaintes, au moins prématurées, ne peuvent prendre leur source que dans une connaissance imparfaite des choses, et ces menaces offensantes viennent assurément d'hommes plus hardis qu'autorisés. L'Église n'est pas une école de désordre et de violence ; les évêques, ses représentants et ses interprètes au concile, ne voudront pas se départir du plus religieux respect pour la vérité et des plus grands égards pour les personnes, et ils traiteront leurs droits comme ceux des autres avec une conscience réfléchie et avec un profond sentiment de justice.

D'abord, en ce qui touche les définitions nouvelles, si le Concile œcuménique ordonne de croire explicitement des choses qu'on pouvait nier jusqu'ici sans être hérétique, c'est que ces choses seraient déjà certaines et généralement admises ; car en ces matières les évêques sont des témoins qui constatent, et non pas des auteurs qui inventent. Pour qu'une vérité devienne article de foi, il faut qu'elle ait été révélée de Dieu et qu'elle soit contenue dans le dépôt que les siècles chrétiens gardent fidèlement et se transmettent l'un à l'autre sans altération. Or, on n'en saurait douter, cinq ou six cents évêques n'attesteront pas, à la face de l'univers, avoir trouvé dans les croyances de leur Église respective ce qui n'y est pas. Si donc ils proposent, en concile, des vérités à croire, c'est qu'elles existent déjà dans les monuments de la tradition et dans le commun enseignement de la théologie, et qu'ainsi elles ne sont pas une nouveauté.

Il y a plus : les évêques auraient reçu des siècles antérieurs, par voie de tradition, certaines vérités considérables, qu'ils ne s'empresseraient pas pour cela de les déclarer articles de foi. Le pouvoir de l'enseignement ne leur a pas été donné pour la destruction, mais pour l'édification. Avant donc d'ajouter aux obligations du peuple chrétien et d'accroître peut-être les obstacles qui s'opposent au retour de nos frères dissidents, ils voudraient examiner sérieusement les dispositions générales du monde et rechercher si ces nouvelles définitions de foi sont opportunes et vraiment réclamées par l'état des esprits. C'est de la sorte que nos aînés ont procédé, comme le témoigne l'histoire des Conciles, et c'est de la sorte aussi que procédera la prochaine assemblée des évêques. Si donc elle ordonne, sous peine d'anathème, de croire désormais quelque vérité qui jusqu'à présent n'était pas de foi catholique, c'est que cette vérité se trouverait déjà dans la tradition léguée par vos ancêtres, et qu'elle serait d'ailleurs jugée utile au progrès du sentiment religieux et au triomphe de l'Église. Dans ces conditions, délibérés en concile par le Pape et les évêques, des décrets comme ceux que redoutent plusieurs personnes, n'auraient rien d'abusif ni de périlleux; ils seraient au contraire l'exercice régulier d'un droit et ne pourraient qu'avoir en définitive de salutaires effets. Il n'est pas loisible de penser autrement à qui veut rester catholique.

Ensuite, quant aux questions qui intéressent plus directement la société civile et les rapports de l'Église et de l'État, quelques-uns d'entre vous craignent qu'on ne les décide dans un sens opposé aux lois et aux mœurs politiques de l'Europe, et qu'on ne crée ainsi entre les devoirs du fidèle et du citoyen un antagonisme violent et douloureux. Il faut le reconnaître, bon nombre d'écrivains, quoique placés à des points de vue contraires, se sont accordés pour éveiller ces alarmes et ont tout fait pour les nourrir et les répandre. Mais peut-être n'y a-t-il là que des malentendus; en ce cas, des explications plus complètes comme le concile peut en fournir réussiront à les faire cesser.

Au fond, que peuvent vouloir les évêques rassemblés à Rome de toutes les parties du monde, sinon servir la cause de l'Église et de la société ? Quelle est leur doctrine sur les matières dont il s'agit ? En ce qui vous concerne, par exemple, ils diraient sans doute que vous êtes une nation baptisée et qu'ainsi vous appartenez à Jésus-Christ, que par conséquent vos lois et vos mœurs doivent être chrétiennes, et, comme elles ne le sont pas assez, qu'il y a donc lieu de les corriger, en les rendant plus conformes à l'Évangile, et par là même plus en rapport avec vos véritables intérêts du temps et de l'éternité. Partant de ces principes et de ces faits, ils ajouteraient probablement que la liberté de la presse, telle que vous l'avez faite, est un élément de dissolution universelle et qu'il importe de la contenir dans de plus justes bornes ; que la liberté des cultes, étant souvent prise pour le droit légal d'outrager tous les cultes et de n'en professer aucun, doit être autrement entendue et pratiquée ; que la morale n'est pas un vain mot, qu'il n'y en a pas deux, l'une privée et l'autre publique, mais une seule, laquelle nous oblige tous, individus et nations ; qu'enfin le nombre et la force ne suffisent pas à tout justifier, et qu'ainsi tous encore, princes et peuples, ont besoin d'avoir raison pour valider leurs actes. Ce sont là certainement des vérités que vous n'ignorez pas, et que déjà nous vous avons dites et répétées, sans vous blesser ni vous nuire. Mais cette fois, elles vous seront expliquées par le concile avec plus d'autorité et de vigueur, et sans doute aussi avec plus de précision. Qu'avez-vous donc à y perdre, puisque vous saurez mieux des choses dont la connaissance est pour vous un devoir et un intérêt de premier ordre ?

Mais, dites-vous, en appliquant ces principes aux détails de notre vie privée et sociale, on nous placera sous l'inspiration et la tutelle du clergé, et la théocratie est au bout d'une telle entreprise. Soyez sans peur, nos très-chers frères : vous ne mourrez pas de cette maladie ; vous n'en êtes pas atteints, et vous avez tout ce qu'il faut pour la prévenir. Bien des années s'écouleront avant que les soixante journaux que Paris voit éclore chaque matin, et les douze mille volumes qu'il publie par an, acceptent la censure ecclésiastique, et qu'ainsi la liberté de la presse vous soit ravie par vos archevêques ; peut-être penserez-vous qu'il ne faut pas se donner le tort de craindre un péril aussi lointain. Il en est de même pour la liberté des cultes : vous n'attendez pas de nous sans doute que nous les mettions tous sur un rang d'égalité, puisque nous tenons l'un d'eux pour le meilleur et le seul vrai. Or, telle étant notre conviction et notre foi au sujet du catholicisme, vous ne pouvez que nous trouver logiques, si nous vous pressons avec instance d'y adhérer et de vous y maintenir fidèlement. Est-ce donc à dire que nous allons combattre matériellement les autres cultes, en provoquant contre eux des mesures sévères et des décrets d'expulsion ? En vérité, vous ne le croyez pas : nous sommes assez de ce siècle pour ne pas réclamer de telles choses, et vous en êtes trop pour les faire. Après comme avant le Concile, à côté des catholiques il y aura des dissidents, on peut le prévoir. Ainsi tout ce que vous nommez vos conquêtes vous restera. Loin donc d'appréhender que le concile ne tranche violemment toutes ces questions délicates et ne règle tous ces détails épineux, plusieurs craignent au contraire qu'il ne trouve pas le moyen de vous aider efficacement à rendre sage la liberté de la presse et à rétablir en Europe l'unité si désirable des croyances religieuses.

Est-il besoin d'ajouter qu'en rappelant la règle et l'idéal, les évêques ne fermeront pas les yeux sur le côté positif et les exigences de la vie réelle, et qu'en traitant des sujets qui toucheraient à la politique, ils n'oublieront pas ce qu'ils doivent à leur pays? Nous n avons donné à personne le droit de suspecter notre patriotisme ; la religion, la voix du sang, l'intérêt même, tout nous commande la sympathie et le dévouement pour nos concitoyens, et tout nous engage à servir, dans la mesure de nos forces, leurs destinées terrestres. C'est un commun drapeau qui nous couvre, une commune loi qui nous protège ; nous vivons de la même vie et voulons être avec vous dans toutes les vicissitudes, à la peine encore plus qu'à la fortune. L'indépendance et la grandeur de la nation nous sont aussi chères qu'à vous : la France, c'est le sol que nos aïeux ont habité et qui garde leurs ossements avec leur souvenir et leur histoire ; c'est le coin de terre que vous honorez de vos travaux et de vos vertus, et où coulent, chaque jour, vos sueurs et vos larmes. Notre cœur y tient par toutes ses fibres. Le sentiment religieux nous y attache aussi, soit parce que Dieu même inspire aux hommes l'amour du sol natal et met le patriotisme au nombre de nos obligations, en nous prescrivant d'aimer nos semblables et surtout ceux qui nous sont plus proches, soit parce que nous trouvons dans notre pays une grande facilité pour pratiquer la religion et remplir les devoirs que la conscience nous impose. S'il est certains points où nous voudrions exprimer des regrets et des vœux, ce peut être l'objet de demandes et d'explications que vous ne refuserez pas d'entendre.

Du reste, nous ne l'ignorons pas plus que vous, dans le milieu complexe et tourmenté où nous vivons, tout est matière ou prétexte à des réclamations contradictoires et à des prétentions rivales, et nulle solution n'est entièrement satisfaisante ou durable. Aussi croyons-nous que, dans les affaires religieuses, il faut maintenir, malgré les imperfections qu'on y peut voir, les rapports de l'Église et de l'État tels que le concordat les a déterminés. Sans doute une mutuelle condescendance ne tranche pas les difficultés ; elle les assoupit, mais les laisse vivre, et l'on peut dire ainsi que la modération même a ses désavantages ; mais il n'est pas expédient non plus de tout surmener avec l'impuissant dessein de tout refaire, car l'âpreté du zèle aigrit les esprits et la violence ne finit rien. Ce qui est donc possible et plausible, c'est de s'en tenir à de sages transactions qui garantissent suffisamment tous les intérêts et tous les droits essentiels, et c'est là que tend le patriotisme des évêques. Ils sont disposés, autant que les hommes politiques peuvent l'être d'autre part, à ne point obéir à des ardeurs intempérantes, mais à mesurer leur action sur les circonstances et à faire prévaloir, dans le règlement des questions mixtes, ces tempéraments qui sont la condition de la marche correcte et prospère des choses humaines.

Enfin, nos très-chers frères, ce qu'on a dit de l'entraînement avec lequel certain dogme serait voté d'acclamation par la majorité des évêques, étouffant ainsi la liberté de leurs collègues dont la conscience ne se trouverait pas tout de suite pénétrée des mêmes lumières irrésistibles, mérite à peine qu'on s'y arrête pour le réfuter. Le bon sens et l'histoire protestent contre ces insinuations mal venues et vaines. Si, pour les plus graves motifs, l'Église juge qu'il faut vous imposer, sous peine de damnation éternelle, l'obligation de croire à l'avenir ce qu'elle ne vous avait pas demandé de croire jusqu'à présent, elle ne le fera point de manière à déconsidérer son acte, en le dépouillant des conditions qui peuvent le recommander à vos yeux. Elle n'édictera pas d'enthousiasme une peine aussi terrible que celle de l'anathème, et cinq ou six cents évêques, réunis pour délibérer sur des intérêts si graves, ne s'emporteront pas à les décider de haute lutte, en dédaignant d'écouter et de calmer, s'il y en a, des scrupules respectables et présentés avec modestie. Est-ce que l'Église a jamais manié les âmes avec ce sans-façon, et commencera-t-elle demain ?

Dans le concile de Jérusalem, qui fut le premier des Conciles et leur servit de modèle, on a délibéré, quoique tous les membres de cette auguste assemblée fussent personnellement infaillibles, et tous ont pu dire leur avis, même après l'avis du plus autorisé. Un Concile œcuménique s'est tenu trois siècles plus tard, où il s'agissait de définir et de formuler la foi de l'Église touchant la consubstantialité du Verbe, en d'autres termes d'affirmer la divinité de Jésus-Christ, le dogme fondamental du christianisme, un dogme pour lequel étaient morts plusieurs millions de martyrs, un dogme qui avait renversé les religions anciennes et fait la conquête du monde, malgré les légions romaines et les lois de l'empire. Certes, si jamais dogme devait échapper à toute délibération, c'était celui-là ; s'il y avait une erreur éclatante et absurde, au point de vue du christianisme, c'était celle d'Arius, et pourtant on délibéra dans le Concile de Nicée ; on entendit les raisons des contradicteurs, si infirmes qu'elles fussent ; on ne vota point par acclamation. Ce précédent, pour ne parler que de celui-là, nos très-chers frères, doit vous rassurer : on ne sera pas moins libre à Rome aujourd'hui qu'on ne l'était à Nicée il y a quinze siècles, et le prochain concile ne flétrira pas son œuvre en supprimant la discussion.

Vous le voyez donc, il n'y a rien de sérieux ni de fondé dans les alarmes que vous auraient fait concevoir, au sujet du concile, les paroles de quelques personnes prévenues ou simplement irréfléchies et maladroites. Le but de cette assemblée est élevé et d'une suprême importance ; ses travaux seront conduits avec une sagesse dont la présidence du Saint-Père est la garantie ; les évêques y porteront un égal souci de leur dignité, de vos intérêts et de vos droits. Pour vous, aidez-les par la prière et les bonnes œuvres ; et, afin qu'elles soient plus méritoires et plus efficaces, profitez de la grâce que le Souverain Pontife accorde sous la forme d'une indulgence plénière. Selon l'invitation qu'il adresse au monde entier, préparez-vous par de pieux exercices au jubilé qui va s'ouvrir ; et, en ce qui vous concerne, ramenez dans l'Église et faites-y régner la pureté des mœurs antiques, la sincérité et l'énergie de la foi, la pratique généreuse de la charité.

Permettez qu'en nous éloignant de vous pour quelque temps, nous sollicitions le secours de vos prières fraternelles, afin que Dieu soit avec nous dans nos travaux et qu'il bénisse le retour comme le départ. De notre côté, nous ne manquerons pas de porter votre souvenir devant lui, dans les sanctuaires privilégiés de Rome, et d'assurer de nouveau le Saint-Père de votre religieux et filial dévouement.

(*Seguono gli articoli riguardanti il Giubileo che omettiamo.*)

Donné à Paris, sous notre seing, le sceau de nos armes et le contre-seing du secrétaire général de notre Archevêché, le 28 octobre 1869.

✠ GEORGES,
Archevêque de Paris,
Grand Aumônier de l'Empereur.

Par Mandement de Monseigneur l'Archevêque :
E. PETIT, *Ch. hon. Secr. gén.*

DOCUMENT VI.

LETTRE DE MONSEIGNEUR L'ÉVÊQUE D'ORLÉANS AU CLERGÉ DE SON DIOCÈSE.

MESSIEURS,

En m'adressant vos adieux et vos vœux, avant mon départ pour Rome, vous m'avez dit les inquiétudes et le trouble que répandent autour de vous, parmi les fidèles, les violentes polémiques soulevées dans les journaux relativement au futur Concile, et en particulier touchant la définition de l'infaillibilité du Pape.

Ces inquiétudes, je les ai comprises. Il s'agit ici du Saint-Père et de ses priviléges, c'est-à-dire de ce qui parle le plus au cœur catholique. Il est naturel à la piété filiale de vouloir orner un père de tous les dons, de toutes les prérogatives ; et combien il est pénible à des fils d'entendre discuter, là où il leur serait doux, au contraire, de voir acclamer ce qu'ils considèrent comme l'honneur et la gloire de leur père.

Des polémiques sur l'infaillibilité du Souverain-Pontife devaient donc inévitablement susciter dans les âmes ces deux sentiments, tous deux respectables.

Mais, si douces et si chères que soient les suggestions de l'amour filial, il y a, Messieurs, vous le sentez, dans une question aussi délicate que la proclamation d'un dogme, autre chose à considérer et à écouter que les élans du sentiment. Il y a les raisons pour et contre, qui ont pu, dans une question non définie, partager de grands esprits : il y a de plus les intérêts même du Père vénéré et chéri qu'on voudrait exalter, et qu'on pourrait compromettre : il y a surtout les intérêts de l'Église, qui sont avant tout les siens : il y a enfin l'intérêt sacré des âmes, l'état des esprits contemporains, dont il faut bien aussi tenir compte : il y a, en un mot, à côté des avantages qu'on croirait voir, les inconvénients, qu'il convient de peser mûrement et gravement. Voilà, Messieurs, ce qui ne doit pas s'oublier, si on ne veut point s'exposer, malgré les meilleures intentions, à mêler, sans le vouloir, la querelle à l'amour, et faire d'une question de théologie une question d'enthousiasme ou de colère.

A Dieu ne plaise, Messieurs, que je veuille contrister un seul de mes vénérables Frères dans l'Épiscopat ! S'il n'y avait que des Évêques qui eussent exprimé ici leurs pensées d'après les inspirations de leur conscience, j'aurais gardé le silence, et écouté avec respect des discussions respectueuses, sans contredire, ni leurs doctrines pour ou contre la question, ni leurs vues pour ou contre l'opportunité. Sans vouloir juger ici aucune conduite, telle eût été la mienne. Et si, plus tard, au Concile, j'avais été appelé à me prononcer entre eux, je l'aurais fait, pour ma part, dans la simplicité de ma conscience, dans la vérité et la charité de mon âme.

Mais il n'en a pas été ainsi, il s'en faut ; et la question, jetée d'une tout autre manière dans le public, a produit dans les âmes les inquiétudes que vous m'avez exposées, et sur lesquelles, ainsi que je vous l'ai promis, je me fais un devoir de vous dire maintenant ma pensée.

Mais, auparavant, je dois rappeler ce qui s'est dit, ce qui s'est fait jusqu'ici, et où la question en est à ce moment.

I. Ce que je commencerai par vous faire remarquer, Messieurs, c'est qu'une telle question regardait le Concile, et aurait dû n'être traitée que par lui.

Malheureusement, des journalistes intempérants n'ont pas réservé ce soin à la future Assemblée de l'Église. Forçant les portes du Concile, avant même et longtemps avant qu'il pût être réuni, ils se sont hâtés d'ouvrir le débat sur un des sujets théologiques les plus délicats, et d'annoncer à l'avance en quel sens le Concile déciderait et devait décider. C'était un effort pour créer dans l'opinion un courant favorable à leurs désirs, et pour peser, de tout le poids de cette opinion préjudicielle, sur les Évêques assemblés.

Dois-je aller jusqu'à mentionner ici les pieuses industries qui ont été imaginées dans le même but? On a été jusqu'à distribuer dans les rues, je l'ai vu, il y a deux ans, et on n'a pas cessé de le faire depuis, des milliers de petites feuilles imprimées, contenant le vœu de croire à l'infaillibilité personnelle et séparée du Pape. On les faisait signer à de bons fidèles, dont beaucoup, assurément, n'étaient guère théologiens, et n'entendaient certes pas le premier mot de la question.[1]

Deux journaux surtout, la *Civiltà Cattolica* et l'*Univers*, ont pris ici la plus étonnante des initiatives. Tandis que le Saint-Père imposait un prudent et rigoureux silence aux Consulteurs des Congrégations romaines chargés des travaux préparatoires au Concile, ils n'ont pas craint de livrer au public les questions qui, selon eux, doivent être agitées et résolues par la future Assemblée. Ils ont annoncé, en particulier, que la question de l'infaillibilité personnelle du Pape y serait définie : bien plus, qu'elle serait définie par acclamation.

Cette délicate question ayant été ainsi soulevée, et jetée dans la rue et dans la presse, un prélat belge, mon saint ami, Mgr Dechamps, récemment nommé Archevêque de Malines, a publié un écrit spécial sous ce titre : *Est-il opportun de définir, dans le prochain Concile, l'infaillibilité du Pape?* et il a répondu affirmativement. Déjà, dans un premier écrit, le nouvel archevêque de Westminster, le pieux et éloquent Mgr Manning, avait traité la même question, au même point de vue, et en a traité depuis, plus expressément encore, dans une seconde lettre à ses diocésains. Les journaux anglais, catholiques et protestants, ont pris une part active à la controverse.

D'un autre côté les Évêques allemands réunis à Fulda, le *Mémorial diplomatique* l'annonçait il y a quelques jours, outre cette Lettre si pleine de mesure, d'élévation et de gravité, que toute l'Europe a admirée, ont adressé au Souverain-Pontife, mais sans le livrer à l'avide publicité des journaux, un Mémoire, pour lui demander de ne permettre pas que la question de son infaillibilité personnelle fût posée au prochain Concile.

Les choses en étaient là, quand la controverse s'est réveillée en France entre plusieurs de nos vénérés Collègues. Malheureusement les journaux s'en sont immédiatement emparés avec une ardeur extrême : la prompte et vive simultanéité des attaques a ému le public ; une certaine presse, sous les yeux de laquelle s'agitait ce débat, s'en est tristement égayée, et des publicistes connus se sont moqués de ce qu'ils appelaient *la guerre sainte*.

Enfin, d'autres écrivains, laïques ou ecclésiastiques, en France, en Angleterre et en Allemagne, suivant l'exemple qui leur avait été donné, ont rompu le silence et exprimé à leur tour leurs opinions et leurs craintes.

Il était difficile, devant ce spectacle, de ne pas se dire : si la question se traite déjà de la sorte devant le public, que sera-ce, si elle vient à être introduite au Concile ? Et il était impossible de ne pas sentir, une fois de plus, le tort grave des journalistes qui, les premiers, ont soulevé, avec une suprême indiscrétion, une question de cette nature.

La question, en effet, est très-grave. Car il s'agirait de proclamer un dogme nouveau, le dogme de l'infaillibilité personnelle et séparée du Pape.

Nous disons dogme nouveau, non pas en ce sens, vous le comprenez, Messieurs, qu'un dogme serait créé par le Concile : l'Église ne crée pas les dogmes, elle les déclare ; et il ne faut pas ici d'équivoque. Je dis dogme nouveau en ce sens que jamais, depuis dix-huit siècles, les fidèles ne furent tenus, sous peine de cesser d'être catholiques, à croire ainsi.

Il s'agirait donc d'obliger désormais tous les catholiques à croire, sous peine d'anathème, que le Pape est infaillible, même, je me sers des propres expressions de Mgr l'Archevêque de Westminster, quand il prononce seul, "EN DEHORS DU CORPS ÉPISCOPAL, RÉUNI OU DISPERSÉ ; " et qu'il peut définir les dogmes seul, "SÉPARÉMENT, INDÉPENDAM-

---

[1] Il y a certaines villes, où des laïcs ont pris l'initiative vis-à-vis de leurs curés, et sont allés leur demander de signer, soit le vœu de croire à l'infaillibilité, soit des pétitions sur ce sujet pour le Concile.

ment de l'épiscopat;"[1] sans aucun concours exprès ou tacite, antécédent ou subséquent, des Évêques.

Or ce n'est pas là, on le voit, un dogme spéculatif : c'est une prérogative qui aurait, dans la réalité pratique, les plus sérieuses conséquences.

Telle est la question que nous voyons chaque matin traitée et tranchée, par un journalisme téméraire, avec la plus étrange liberté.

Plusieurs du reste la traitent de telle sorte, qu'à leurs yeux il n'y a là aucune difficulté. Il suffit pour cela, dit l'un d'eux, de savoir son Catéchisme. Bossuet, apparemment, ne le savait pas ; ni Fénelon, qui entendait l'infaillibilité autrement que Bellarmin, qui ne s'accorde pas de tout point ici avec d'autres théologiens romains. A entendre ces journalistes, la proclamation du dogme de l'infaillibilité du Pape est si nécessaire, si facile, et si certaine, que le Concile n'aura même pas à examiner ; et douter un instant de sa décision, ce serait lui faire injure : ce serait aussi se montrer suspect, à tout le moins, d'un bien tiède dévouement pour l'Église et pour le Pape.

C'est ce qu'ils disent, et avec de tels outrages pour ceux qui ne pensent pas comme eux, qu'en vérité il n'y a plus de limites, et le débat s'envenime étrangement.

Cependant tout le monde ignore absolument ce que jugera bon de faire ou de ne pas faire sur ce point le Concile, qui n'existe pas encore.

Mais en attendant, Messieurs, ces excès de la controverse troublent les fidèles, et les jettent dans la situation évidemment dangereuse que vous m'avez dite. Car, si le Concile vient à juger convenable de ne pas suivre la ligne qu'on lui trace si impérativement, ne paraîtra-t-il pas à plusieurs avoir manqué à son devoir? On affirme, et avec raison, que les Évêques auront au Concile une pleine et entière liberté. Mais vraiment quelle liberté leur laissent, dès à présent, de telles discussions, menées de cette façon par le journalisme? A la manière dont ils poursuivent ce débat, ne semblent-ils pas dénoncer à l'avance comme des schismatiques ou des hérétiques, ceux qui se permettront d'être d'un sentiment contraire ?

Ce sont là, Messieurs, des réflexions de sens commun, qui m'ont été exposées, de vive voix et par écrit, non-seulement par vous-mêmes, mais bien des fois déjà par une

[1] Lettre pastorale de Monseigneur, sur le Concile œcuménique et l'infaillibilité du Pontife romain.— Postscriptum.

foule d'esprits, et des meilleurs, et des plus chrétiens, que ces polémiques, autour de moi ou loin de moi, préoccupent et agitent.

J'ai attendu beaucoup avant de me résoudre à prendre la parole sur un tel sujet. Vous m'y avez décidé, Messieurs. Je m'inquiétais en effet, non pas de savoir si certains hommes suspecteront plus ou moins et calomnieront mon zèle pour le Pape et pour l'Église, mais ce que j'avais à faire pour servir comme je le dois ces causes si chères.

J'ai examiné, longuement, sous toutes ses faces, et surtout au point de vue pratique, la question discutée dans les journaux. J'y ai vu, pour ma part, des difficultés de plus d'une sorte, et qui doivent, ce me semble, frapper ceux mêmes qui sont le plus convaincus, théologiquement, de l'infaillibilité pontificale.

Je n'ai certes aucun goût à me jeter dans une mêlée si violente. Je gémis de la controverse qui s'agite devant le public, et si j'écris, ce n'est pas pour l'irriter, mais plutôt pour la calmer, et même, s'il se pouvait, la supprimer ; car, pour moi, je la crois très-inopportune, très-regrettable pour le Saint-Siége lui-même, et les querelles qui viennent d'avoir lieu n'ont fait qu'ajouter à ma conviction, déjà ancienne, sur cette inopportunité.

Ce sont ces difficultés que,—sans toucher au fond même de la question théologique,— je voudrais exposer simplement dans cet écrit.

Je ne discute pas l'infaillibilité, mais l'opportunité. Et du reste, les vues que je vous présenterai ici ne me sont pas personnelles. Je m'en suis entretenu souvent avec un grand nombre de mes vénérés Collègues, de France et d'ailleurs, et ces raisons nous ont paru si graves, à eux comme à moi, qu'à tout le moins sont-elles de nature à faire réfléchir la presse religieuse, et à lui persuader enfin de réserver aux Évêques de si délicates discussions.

II. Ces débats, je vous l'ai dit, Messieurs, ne m'ont pas moins étonné qu'attristé. Car enfin, avant cette ingérence et ces éclats d'une certaine presse, la question n'était pas posée. Le silence s'était fait, grâce à Dieu, sur des querelles qu'il vaut mieux, je l'ai toujours pensé, oublier que raviver. Jamais l'autorité du Saint-Père n'avait été plus respectée dans l'Église, ni sa parole mieux écoutée. Jamais les Évêques n'avaient été plus empressés à se serrer autour de la chaire pontificale, accourant, non pas même sur un ordre, mais sur un simple désir du Pape, des extrémités du monde, au centre de la catholicité.

En quoi donc le Concile pouvait-il être une

occasion de provoquer des controverses sur les prérogatives pontificales ? Est-ce dans ce but, est-ce pour se faire déclarer infaillible, que le Saint-Père a voulu assembler les Évêques du monde entier ? La définition de l'infaillibilité personnelle est-elle entrée pour quelque chose dans les motifs et les causes de la convocation du Concile ? Pas le moins du monde.

Quand le Pape Pie IX annonça, dans deux allocutions célèbres, aux Évêques rassemblés à Rome en 1867, son projet de convoquer un Concile œcuménique, il ne dit pas un mot de la nécessité ou de l'utilité de faire ériger en dogme de foi par la future Assemblée son infaillibilité personnelle.

Et les cinq cents Évêques réunis alors à Rome, dans leur adresse au Saint-Père, en réponse à cette communication, ne dirent pas non plus un seul mot de cette question.

Enfin, dans la Bulle d'indiction, où le Saint-Père a tracé si largement, et avec un si grand langage, le programme du futur Concile, il ne fut de même nullement parlé de son infaillibilité personnelle.

Non, nulle part, dans aucun des actes du Saint-Père, cette préoccupation de grandir son autorité au moyen du Concile et à la faveur de ce respect dont le monde entoure ses vertus et ses malheurs, n'apparaît un seul instant.

Vous le savez, Messieurs, ce sont d'autres et bien grands buts que le Vicaire de Jésus-Christ assigne à l'Assemblée des représentants de l'Église catholique.

"Porter remède aux maux du siecle présent dans l'Église et la société," voilà pourquoi le Pape a convoqué le Concile ; et de là certes, que de questions posées par les temps nouveaux, et par la crise actuelle! On se demande de toutes parts avec anxiété si, à une époque aussi incertaine—où d'un moment à l'autre peuvent surgir des événements capables de dissoudre le Concile avant qu'il ait achevé son œuvre—les Évêques auront même le temps de les traiter.

Et c'est au milieu de tant d'urgentes et nécessaires questions qu'on voudrait tout à coup en jeter une nouvelle, imprévue, inattendue, d'une solution difficile assurément, et pleine d'orages ! Et que l'on s'exposerait, en suivant la voie tracée par les journalistes, au lieu de ce magnifique spectacle d'union que le monde attend de nous, à en donner un tout contraire !

Hélas ! on peut prévoir déjà, à l'âpreté de ces débats préliminaires, ce que cette question, si on l'y portait, pourrait soulever de discussions au sein du Concile !

Mais pourquoi l'y porter ? Est-ce que la nécessité y force ? Est-ce que les périls du temps l'imposent ?

Non. Mais j'entends dire qu'il s'agit ici d'un principe.

D'un principe ? Eh quoi ! répondrai-je à mon tour, ce principe, si c'en est un, est-il donc nécessaire à la vie de l'Église, qu'il devienne dogme de foi ? Comment alors expliquez-vous que l'Église ait vécu dix-huit siècles, sans que ce principe essentiel à sa vie ait été défini ? Comment expliquez-vous qu'elle ait formulé toute sa doctrine, produit tous ses docteurs, condamné toutes les hérésies, sans cette définition ? De nécessité il n'y en a évidemment aucune ici, et la solution de cette question n'est pas plus indispensable qu'elle n'était réclamée.

La raison, d'ailleurs, en est simple. L'Église est infaillible, et l'infaillibilité de l'Église suffit à tout jusqu'à cette heure. Craignez-vous qu'à l'avenir elle devienne insuffisante, et vous flatteriez-vous que ceux qui ne voudront pas croire à l'infaillibilité de l'Église unie au Pape, croiront plus facilement à l'infaillibilité personnelle et séparée du Pape ?

Est-ce qu'il y a dans l'Église catholique un doute sur l'infaillibilité de l'Église ? Est-ce qu'ici tous ne sont pas d'accord ? Est-ce que le moindre fidèle ne se sait pas en communion avec son pasteur, qui est en communion avec son Évêque, qui est en communion avec le Pape ? Est-ce que cela ne suffit pas pleinement à la sécurité de notre foi ? et dans cet accord merveilleux de témoignages, les fidèles n'ont-ils pas tous une sûre garantie contre l'erreur ?

Craignez-vous que l'Église ne puisse plus vivre à l'avenir sur les mêmes bases qui l'ont soutenue dans un passé de dix-neuf siècles ?

Que parlez-vous donc de la nécessité de faire dans un Concile une définition nouvelle sur la règle de la foi, et de constituer dogmatiquement une nouvelle règle de foi ? Quoi ! c'est en notre siècle qu'il devient nécessaire de venir mettre cela en question, de toucher à ce principe constitutif, à ce ressort principal de la vie de l'Église ! Nous aurions été constitués durant tant de siècles d'une façon défectueuse ou incomplète !

Après dix-huit cent soixante-dix années d'enseignement, il faut qu'on en vienne à se demander dans un Concile, qui a le droit d'enseigner infailliblement ! Et cela à la face du monde incrédule et protestant qui nous regarde ! Non, laissons-là ces questions que rien n'appelle. Que des publicistes téméraires n'aillent pas, avant l'heure, étonner et désorienter le bon sens des fidèles par des controverses violentes, qui semblent vouloir imposer d'avance ces questions aux

Évêques. Pour moi, Messieurs, ma pensée, en la soumettant à mes vénérés Collègues, est formelle sur ce point. Quand le chêne est vingt fois séculaire, creuser, pour chercher le gland originaire sous ses racines, c'est vouloir ébranler l'arbre entier !

III. Mais n'y-a-t-il pas déjà, Messieurs, des précédents décisifs pour cette question d'opportunité qui nous occupe ? Je rappellerai d'abord la sage conduite du Concile de Trente et du Pape Pie IV.

Au fond, du temps du Concile de Trente, la question qui passionna si vivement les esprits, et fut même sur le point d'amener la dissolution du Concile, c'était, sous une autre forme, car les questions ne reviennent jamais absolument sous les mêmes formes, celle-là même dont nous traitons ici.

Comment oublier avec quelle sagesse le Saint-Siège sut écarter le péril de ces controverses en écartant le débat ?

Pie IV, à la fin, voyant combien les esprits étaient émus, écrivit à ses légats pour leur ordonner de retirer le sujet du litige, et déclara qu'il ne fallait rien traiter qui pût provoquer des discussions orageuses et jeter de la division parmi les Évêques. Il posa cette règle si sage qu'il ne fallait rien décider que de leur consentement unanime : *Ne definirentur, nisi ea, de quibus inter Patres unanimi consensione constaret.*

Le Concile comprit qu'il avait autre chose à faire, devant les erreurs du temps, que d'ériger en dogmes des opinions, si respectables qu'elles fussent, mais controversées parmi les docteurs, et de flétrir des théologiens catholiques. Et la discussion fut mise de côté, sans dommage aucun pour l'Église.

Je me souviens très-bien, et plus d'un Évêque présent à Rome en 1867 peut se le rappeler, qu'une des plus sérieuses préoccupations de Pie IX, avant de se décider à convoquer le Concile du Vatican, c'était qu'il n'y surgît quelque question de nature à provoquer des discussions orageuses et des divisions dans l'Épiscopat. Mais le Pape se souvint de la conduite si sage du Concile de Trente et de Pie IV, et, sur l'espoir qu'on ne l'oublierait pas au futur Concile, il passa outre.

Est-ce qu'on penserait que, pour soulever et trancher une question aussi délicate que celle de la définition dogmatique annoncée, nous sommes aujourd'hui en des temps plus favorables que ceux du Concile de Trente; et que nous vivions à une époque de foi plus vive, et de plus grande soumission à l'Église !

¹ Voir ce récit dans *Pallavicini*, liv. XIX, ch. XV ; et ailleurs encore.

Un autre précédent de sagesse et de modération qu'il faut rappeler ici, c'est la conduite du Pape Innocent IX à l'égard de Bossuet. Quand Bossuet écrivit son *Exposition de la doctrine catholique*, après avoir, à l'article de l'autorité du Saint-Siége, établi fortement la primauté de droit divin, la primauté d'honneur et de juridiction de saint Pierre, et des Papes ses successeurs, il passa sous silence, expressément et à dessein, la question de l'infaillibilité pontificale.

"Quant aux choses dont on sait qu'on dispute dans les écoles, quoique les Ministres ne cessent pas de les alléguer *pour rendre cette puissance odieuse*, il n'est pas nécessaire d'en parler ici, puisqu'elles ne sont pas *de la foi catholique.*"

Ce silence réfléchi et calculé à l'endroit de l'infaillibilité du Pape empêcha-t-il Innocent XI d'approuver l'ouvrage ? Bien loin de là ; car ce saint Pape adressa à Bossuet deux brefs, dans lesquels *il le félicitait d'avoir écrit ce livre avec une méthode et une sagesse bien propres à ramener les hérétiques dans la voie du salut, et à procurer à l'Église les plus grands biens pour la propagation de la foi orthodoxe.*

Bossuet, d'ailleurs, en écartant avec soin, dans la pensée si sagement exprimée par Innocent XI, le point controversé, n'avait fait qu'imiter le Catéchisme du Concile de Trente. J'ai lu et relu ce grand Catéchisme, composé sur l'ordre du saint Concile et des Souverains Pontifes, par les plus célèbres théologiens romains : je l'ai lu, avec la pensée expresse de chercher s'il parlait, oui ou non, de l'infaillibilité du Pape, et j'ai constaté qu'il n'en dit pas un seul mot.—Et il n'en est pas question non plus dans la solennelle profession de foi, dressée par l'ordre de Pie IV et insérée au pontifical romain.

Enfin, pourquoi ne citerions-nous pas ici l'exemple du vénéré Pie IX lui-même ? On sait qu'il y a deux ans environ, en 1867, cent quatre-vingt-huit ministres anglicans lui écrivirent pour lui témoigner de leur bonne volonté, et lui demander les bases possibles de l'union. Que fit le Très-Saint Père ? Dans une réponse pleine de charité et de sagesse, il parla de l'autorité de l'Église, il parla de la suprématie du Pape ; mais il ne parla pas de son infaillibilité.

Et c'est quand le Saint-Père, dans l'inspiration de son noble et pacifique cœur, donne de tels exemples de modération et de sagesse, que des journalistes, en s'abritant derrière le nom vénéré qu'ils profanent dans de semblables luttes, ont entrepris, à force d'affirmations tranchantes, de peser sur l'opinion publique, tandis que, du même coup, comme s'ils voulaient intimider les Évêques et leur fermer la bouche, ils tiennent suspendues au-dessus de leurs têtes des insultes pleines de violence et de fiel !

Je puis leur dire : Vous ne connaissez ni Pie IX, ni l'Épiscopat.

IV. Nous parlions de nos frères des communions séparées. C'est en effet quand on se place à leur point de vue, que la question d'une définition de l'infaillibilité personnelle du Pape paraît surtout grave et périlleuse.

Qu'on y songe : il y a 75 millions de chrétiens orientaux séparés ; il y a près de 90 millions de protestants de toutes nuances. Certes, s'il est un intérêt suprême pour l'Église, un vœu ardent de tous les cœurs vraiment catholiques, c'est bien le retour à l'unité de tant de frères sortis du giron de la même mère, et aujourd'hui éloignés de nous. Voilà la grande cause pour laquelle il faudrait être prêts, tous, à donner son sang, et trembler à la seule pensée de ce qui pourrait la mettre en péril. Aussi quelles invitations pressantes du Saint-Père aux Églises orientales ! Quel appel aux communions protestantes !

Eh bien, qu'est-ce qui sépare de nous les Orientaux ? La suprématie du Pape. Ils ne veulent pas la reconnaître comme de droit divin. C'est le point sur lequel on n'a jamais pu, ni après Lyon, ni après Florence, les décider sérieusement, efficacement, et amener un retour durable.

Et voilà qu'à cette difficulté, insurmontable jusqu'à ce jour, qui les tient depuis neuf siècles séparés de l'Église et de nous, on voudrait ajouter une difficulté nouvelle et beaucoup plus grande, élever entre eux et nous une barrière qui n'a jamais existé, en un mot leur imposer un dogme dont on ne leur parla jamais, les menaçant, s'ils ne l'acceptent pas, d'un nouvel anathème !

Car, ce n'est plus seulement la primauté de juridiction qu'ils devront reconnaître, c'est l'infaillibilité personnelle du Pape, "EN DEHORS ET SÉPARÉMENT DU CORPS ÉPISCOPAL."[1]

Se pourrait-il, je le demande,—et ici je répète simplement ce que le bon sens a déjà inspiré à ceux qui ont voulu y réfléchir,—pourrait-il, vis-à-vis des Églises Orientales séparées, rien de plus contradictoire qu'une telle conduite, et de moins persuasif qu'un tel langage : "Nous vous invitons à profiter de la grande occasion du Concile œcuménique, pour vous expliquer et vous entendre avec nous. Mais voici auparavant ce que nous allons faire : élever un nouveau mur de séparation, une nouvelle et plus haute

[1] Monseigneur Manning.

barrière entre vous et nous. Un fossé nous sépare ; nous allons en faire un abîme. Vous vous êtes refusés jusqu'à présent à reconnaître la simple Primauté de juridiction du Pontife Romain ; nous allons vous obliger préalablement à croire bien autre chose, et à admettre ce que jusqu'ici des docteurs catholiques eux-mêmes n'ont pas admis : nous allons ériger en dogme une doctrine bien plus obscure, pour vous, dans l'Écriture et dans la Tradition, que le dogme même non encore accepté par vous, à savoir, l'infaillibilité personnelle du Pape, seul, INDÉPENDAMMENT ET SÉPARÉMENT DES ÉVÊQUES. Voilà dans quelles conditions nous venons vous proposer l'entente."

Parler ainsi, ne serait-ce pas vraiment une dérision ? Et ne serait-ce pas aussi un malheur ? appeler et éloigner en même temps ?

Ces considérations devront frapper encore plus, si l'on réfléchit à l'état d'esprit des chrétiens schismatiques de l'Orient. Lorsqu'on traite avec les hommes, il faut bien savoir où ils en sont. Or, sur ce point, où en sont nos frères séparés ?

Ils en sont restés précisément aux temps du schisme, au IX siècle. Ils n'ont pas marché depuis. Ils ne connaissent pas les controverses qui se sont agitées sur ces matières dans l'Église Occidentale. Ils n'ont lu ni Bossuet, ni Bellarmin, ni Melchior Cano. Et, quelque conviction personnelle qu'on puisse avoir sur l'infaillibilité du Pontife Romain, il faut bien reconnaître que le IX siècle était loin d'être disposé à la définition d'un tel dogme. En fait, jusque-là, les Conciles étaient la grande forme de la vie de l'Église ; il s'en assemblait sans cesse ; toutes les plus grandes définitions dogmatiques avaient été rendues en Concile. Les Grecs ne sont donc en rien préparés à la définition qu'on voudrait leur faire imposer par le Concile du Vatican. Ma conviction profonde est qu'un des effets certains, inévitables, d'une telle définition, serait de faire reculer bien loin la réunion des Églises Orientales. Une telle considération ne paraîtra légère à aucun de ceux qui savent le prix des âmes.

Un fait récent montre si la crainte que nous exprimons ici est sans fondement : c'est la réponse faite à l'envoyé du Souverain-Pontife par le vicaire général du Patriarche schismatique de Constantinople. Parmi les raisons alléguées par lui pour décliner l'invitation venue de Rome, se trouvait celle-ci : que "l'Église grecque ne peut reconnaître l'infaillibilité du Pape, et sa supériorité sur les Conciles œcuméniques."[1]

[1] *Civiltà Cattolica*, chronique du Concile.—Cité par Monseigneur l'Évêque de Grenoble.

Les schismatiques arméniens parlent le même langage, et j'ai eu sous les yeux un journal arménien qui prétend que si Rome les invite au Concile, c'est " pour leur imposer l'infaillibilité du l'ape."

On dira peut-être: Mais de quoi vous préoccupez-vous? Les Schismatiques ne veulent pas de l'union. Qu'importe entre eux et nous une barrière de plus!—Je suis loin, pour ma part, de perdre ainsi l'espérance, et sans connaître les desseins de Dieu sur les peuples, je ne me crois pas permis de sceller ainsi la tombe de ces antiques nations chrétiennes,—surtout quand je viens à penser que dans cette tombe, dans ce sol de l'Orient, reposent des cendres comme celles des Athanase, des Cyrille, des Basile, des Grégoire, des Chrysostôme, mêlées à celles des Paul, des Antoine, des Hilarion, des Pacôme, et de tant d'autres saints à jamais illustres.

Mais quand cela serait, quand aucun souffle de Dieu ni aucun effort des hommes ne devrait rappeler de l'erreur qui les a perdus ces vieux peuples de l'Orient, non, alors même je ne croirais pas qu'il fût de la charité de Jésus-Christ, et de la mission d'un grand Concile, de les éloigner davantage, et de leur rendre le retour plus difficile.

J'ai eu souvent l'heureuse occasion de m'entretenir longuement des intérêts de ces antiques Églises, avec les Évêques orientaux qu'il m'a été donné de rencontrer à Rome dans nos grandes réunions; et en outre, une correspondance particulière, active, avec plusieurs d'entre eux, m'a permis de connaître un peu l'état des choses.

Ce que j'ai appris d'eux, c'est ceci: un grand désir du rapprochement.—Oui, dans cet immobile Orient, beaucoup d'âmes sont travaillées par ces aspirations.—Et, en même temps, de vives susceptibilités, pour les moindres détails de leurs vieilles coutumes: à combien plus forte raison, pour ce qui est des grandes questions dogmatiques.

Certes, le Concile de Trente eut une tout autre conduite, et des ménagements bien autrement dignes de l'Église de Jésus-Christ vis-à-vis des Églises orientales, et cela, dans une question d'une capitale importance. Tout théologien sait comment, à la demande des ambassadeurs vénitiens, le fameux canon: *Si quis dixerit Ecclesiam* ERRARE, chef-d'œuvre de prudence théologique, et de charité, fut tempéré de manière, tout-à-la-fois, à maintenir la vérité et à ménager les Orientaux.

V. La question est plus délicate encore en ce qui touche le Protestantisme. Car le schisme oriental, du moins, admet l'autorité des Conciles œcuméniques—de ceux qu'il regarde comme tels—et l'autorité de l'Église, dont il se persuade faire toujours partie. Tandis que le Protestantisme n'admet pas cette autorité. Là, sur ce point précis et décisif, l'autorité de l'Église est la grande controverse entre lui et nous. Le Protestantisme est avant tout la négation de l'autorité de l'Église. Dans ce principe de division est son essence, sa plaie fatale. Et c'est ce que beaucoup de nos frères séparés commencent à entrevoir. Ils sentent qu'un principe qui permet la division à l'infini, qui permet même de n'être plus chrétien tout en demeurant toujours protestant, ne peut pas être le vrai principe chrétien. De là ce travail qui se fait au sein du Protestantisme, ces grands et consolants retours, dont surtout l'Angleterre et l'Amérique nous donnent le spectacle, et ces aspirations vers l'union, qui sont, je le sais, au cœur de tant de Protestants.

Qui, parmi nous, ne compatit à ce travail et à ces souffrances de tant d'âmes? Qui ne les appelle avec amour? Qui ne prie avec elles? car elles prient, je le sais encore, pour ce grand et suprême intérêt, l'union des Églises chrétiennes. "Nous sommes," me disait à Orléans même le docteur Pusey, il y a deux ans, " huit mille en Angleterre, qui prions, chaque jour, pour l'union."

Ah! si les rapprochements tant désirés parvenaient enfin à se faire! Si l'Angleterre surtout, la grande Angleterre, se retournait un jour vers nous! De toutes les réconciliations que le monde a vues, ce serait assurément la plus heureuse et la plus féconde. Je le disais, dans ce livre de *la Souveraineté pontificale*, écrit en quelque sorte sous le feu des luttes pour lo Saint-Siège, je le disais avec confiance aux Anglais maîtres d'eux-mêmes et de leurs préjugés: " Vous avez été, il y a trois siècles, les plus redoutables ennemis de l'unité: quel honneur il y aurait pour vous à ramener en Europe l'unité! Cet étendard de la Catholicité chrétienne, comme il siérait à vos mains de le relever, et à vos vaisseaux de le porter par-delà les mers sur toutes les terres que vous visitez! Heureux ceux à qui il sera donné de voir ces temps meilleurs, qui peut-être ne sont pas éloignés!"

Eh bien! le Concile a ranimé chez un grand nombre de nos frères séparés, et chez nous, ces espérances. Ah! sans doute, on doit le craindre, elles ne seront pas toutes réalisées. Mais au moins, des retours partiels peuvent se voir, et en grand nombre; surtout une puissante impulsion peut être donnée. Le temps, avec la grâce de Dieu, fera le reste.

Que du moins le Concile, pour ceux à qui

T 2

le Saint-Père adressait naguère ce pressant appel, ne devienne pas la plus dure des pierres d'achoppement!

Ne parlez donc plus de leur imposer préalablement, pour condition de retour, l'infaillibilité personnelle et séparée du Pape! Car ce serait l'oubli de toute prudence comme de toute charité.

Les nouveaux catholiques, ai-je ouï dire, sont pleins de ferveur pour ce dogme. Oui, certains nouveaux catholiques peut-être. Mais je connais, moi, d'autres convertis, que l'annonce d'une définition a troublés. Je connais certains protestants, désireux de venir à nous, que cela seul fait reculer. J'en connais que cette définition repoussera:t absolument.

Il faut être, ce me semble, bien peu ou bien mal renseigné sur les dispositions actuelles de nos frères séparés, pour ne pas voir qu'on élèverait là, infailliblement, une nouvelle barrière, peut-être à jamais infranchissable, entre eux et nous.

Mais attendez donc! dirai-je aux impatients: les schismes et les hérésies ne sont pas éternels. L'Église a bien attendu, sans cette définition, dix-huit siècles, et la vérité, gardée par elle, a été bien gardée.

VI. Il est d'autres périls, d'un autre ordre, et très-graves encore. Il faut calculer les conséquences que pourrait avoir un tel acte au point de vue des Gouvernements modernes: c'est là une politique, ou pour mieux dire, une sagesse dont l'Église ne peut se départir. Je sais que beaucoup d'Évêques, et des plus courageux, en sont préoccupés.

Et certes, non sans cause; car il y a de sérieuses raisons de craindre, à ce point de vue encore, que les inconvénients possibles de la définition ne soient très-considérables.

Voyons les faits; examinons l'état de l'Europe.

Sur les cinq grandes puissances européennes, trois ne sont pas catholiques: la Russie, la Prusse et l'Angleterre. Je ne parle pas ici de l'Amérique et des États-Unis. Et parmi les États secondaires de l'Europe, un grand nombre aussi appartiennent au schisme et à l'hérésie, la Saxe, la Suède, le Danemark, la Suisse, la Hollande, la Grèce. Qui ne sait quels ombrages tous ces Gouvernements nourrissent encore contre l'Église? Or, je pose simplement la très-grave question que voici: Croit-on qu'une définition de l'infaillibilité personnelle du Pape soit de nature à dissiper ces ombrages? Quand, par un préjugé invétéré, qu'on ne détruira pas en l'aggravant, ces gouvernements regardent le Pape comme un souverain étranger, croit-on, de bonne foi, que déclarer le Pape infaillible, ce sera rendre meilleure la position des catholiques dans tous ces pays? Croit-on que la Russie, que la Suède, que le Danemark en deviendront plus doux pour leurs sujets catholiques? Leurs haines contre Rome en seront-elles apaisées, et le rapprochement rendu plus facile?

Si quelqu'un était tenté de traiter à la légère, comme chimériques, ces craintes sur les dispositions des Gouvernements non catholiques, je rappellerais ici simplement les faits contemporains. Pourquoi donc, en 1826, les Archevêques et Évêques catholiques d'Irlande, et ceux d'Angleterre et d'Écosse, ont-ils été obligés de signer les deux déclarations que j'ai sous les yeux?

Dans l'une, les Archevêques et Évêques catholiques d'Angleterre et d'Écosse, placés en face de ce grief: "On accuse les catholiques de partager leur fidélité entre leur souverain temporel et le Pape," y répondent longuement; et dans l'autre, les Archevêques et Évêques catholiques d'Irlande sont forcés de venir à protester qu'ils ne croient pas "qu'il soit licite de tuer une personne quelconque, sous prétexte qu'elle serait hérétique:"—souvenir exagéré, mais évident et permanent des bulles lancées contre Henri VIII—et de plus—ceci est à remarquer—"qu'il n'est pas exigé d'eux de croire que le Pape est infaillible."

Qu'on se récrie tant qu'on voudra sur l'injustice de tous ombrages et de ces préventions, de telles déclarations solennelles imposées à l'Épiscopat d'un grand pays, démontrent assez quelle est la puissance de ces préventions. J'ai lu cette déclaration des Évêques d'Irlande, je dois le dire, la rougeur au front. Combien ils ont dû souffrir d'avoir à repousser, et de trouver vivantes dans leur pays, de pareilles défiances, qui s'attaquaient à tout ce qu'il y a de plus sacré dans la conscience, de plus délicat dans l'honneur!

En veut-on d'autres preuves encore? On sait les atroces qui restèrent si longtemps suspendues sur la tête des catholiques d'Angleterre et d'Irlande, et qu'ils ont eu tant de peine à faire abolir. Eh bien, quand le célèbre Pitt, à la fin du siècle dernier, dans une pensée politique que je veux croire généreuse, songea, pour la première fois, à délivrer de ce joug les catholiques, qu'est-ce qui obsédait et arrêtait tout court l'homme d'État anglais? La Puissance pontificale, les vieux souvenirs des démêlés des Papes avec les couronnes. C'est pourquoi, avant tout, il voulut savoir quelles étaient sur ce point les doctrines catholiques, et il s'adressa dans ce but à toutes les plus savantes Universités de France, de Belgique, d'Espagne et d'Allemagne.

J'ai sous les yeux les réponses des Universités de Paris, de Douai, de Louvain, d'Alcala, de Salamanque, de Valladolid : toutes, se plaçant au point de vue du droit divin, et laissant de côté, par conséquent, ce qui a pu être le droit public d'un autre âge, répondent expressément que, ni le Pape, ni les Cardinaux, ni aucun corps ou individu de l'Église romaine, n'ont, de par Jésus-Christ, aucune autorité civile sur l'Angleterre, aucun pouvoir de délier les sujets de S. M. Britannique de leur serment de fidélité.

Cette doctrine, professée alors par les plus grandes Universités de l'Église catholique, pouvait rassurer Pitt sur la doctrine contraire, professée, dans des bulles célèbres, il le faut dire, par plus d'un Pape. Mais supposez la Papauté déclarée infaillible : cette définition dogmatique de l'infaillibilité du Pape ne serait-elle pas de nature à raviver les vieilles défiances ? Certes, ou peut le craindre, et voici pourquoi :

Les Gouvernements non-catholiques, en effet, ne croiront pas à cette infaillibilité ; et ce pouvoir immense, reconnu dogmatiquement au Pape, le Pape, selon eux, en pourra abuser, en outrepasser les limites. Mais, ce qui sera grave à leurs yeux, leurs sujets catholiques y croiront, et seront obligés de se soumettre à toutes ses décisions, même les plus abusives au point de vue de ces Gouvernements non-catholiques : comment ne pas voir que dès lors le pouvoir pontifical leur semblera bien plus redoutable et plus odieux ? Ils ont déjà, ils conservent contre l'Église les défiances ombrageuses que chacun sait : combien plus suspecteront-ils le Pape infaillible, c'est-à-dire un seul homme, qui, à leur point de vue, leur offrira bien moins de garanties que l'Église, c'est-à-dire que les Évêques de leur pays et de tous les pays ?

VII. Et les Gouvernements des nations catholiques elles-mêmes, de quel œil verront-ils proclamer le dogme nouveau ? C'est ce qu'il faut se demander aussi. Car enfin, les Gouvernements ne se regarderont jamais comme désintéressés dans la question. Qui leur persuadera qu'elle ne les regarde pas ?

Ici encore, pour apprécier sans illusion et selon la vérité les conséquences de la définition dogmatique annoncée, et sollicitée avec tant de bruit par des journalistes — qui, certes, devraient cesser, l'heure en est venue, de se mêler dans les affaires les plus intimes, les plus graves, et les plus réservées de l'Église,—plaçons-nous dans la réalité des choses, dans les faits ; voyons ce qui est, et ce qui sera.

Le grand fait, malheureux, mais incontestable, et plus que jamais subsistant, le voici : c'est que les pouvoirs publics, même chez les nations catholiques, sont pleins d'ombrages contre l'Église. C'est ce que toute l'histoire proclame ; car l'histoire est pleine des conflits entre les deux puissances.

Mais que parlé-je du passé ? A l'heure même où j'écris ces lignes, est-ce que trois des quatre grandes puissances catholiques de l'Europe, l'Autriche, l'Italie et l'Espagne ne sont pas engagées plus ou moins dans de tristes luttes avec l'Église ? Et chez nous-mêmes, d'un moment à l'autre, ne peut-il pas surgir un litige ? Et ce mot ne serait-il pas encore trop doux, dans la terrible éventualité de telle révolution possible ?

Voilà la situation : les Gouvernements catholiques ont été, sont, ou peuvent se trouver de plus en plus en conflit avec l'Église.

Certes, nul plus que moi ne déplore ces redoutables conflits, quand ils se produisent ; et si peu de goût que j'aie pour ces luttes, peut-être ai-je montré, on me pardonnera de le rappeler, que je ne suis pas de ceux qui reculent alors et faiblissent ? Mais là n'est pas la question, et, que les Gouvernements soient, ou non, coupables, ce n'est pas non plus de cela qu'il s'agit. Il s'agit de savoir de quel œil, aujourd'hui, les Gouvernements verraient déclarer le Pape infaillible.

Est-ce là une timide préoccupation ? Et l'Église doit-elle, dans ses Conciles, ne consulter que les principes de sa pleine indépendance à l'égard des Gouvernements humains, agir, décréter, définir, même sur les questions pratiques les plus délicates, comme si les Gouvernements n'existaient pas, et sans s'inquiéter, en aucune sorte, de savoir si ses actes les blesseront, ou non, au vif ?

Telle n'est pas, telle ne fut jamais, dans les choses qui ne sont point de nécessité, la coutume de la sainte Église.

Ah ! si d'un coup, et par une simple proclamation dogmatique, on pouvait couper court aux conflits, supprimer les vieux ombrages, et rendre, par décret, les Gouvernements des nations catholiques dociles à l'Église et au Pape, comme des brebis ! Cela ou vaudrait la peine !

Mais s'en flatter, aujourd'hui surtout, serait la plus chimérique des illusions.

Quelqu'un peut-il douter qu'une définition

dogmatique de l'infaillibilité personnelle du Pape, loin de supprimer les défiances anciennes, ne ferait qu'en raviver les causes, ou, si l'on veut, les éternels prétextes, en leur donnant une apparence de plus?

Quels sont, en effet, ces prétextes? Certes, je ne prétends en rien justifier ici les Gouvernements : presque toujours, presque partout, ils ont voulu opprimer l'Église ; mais il faut voir les hommes et les choses comme ils sont.

Il y a d'abord ici les souvenirs du passé. En déclarant le Pape infaillible, pourront se demander les Souverains, le déclarera-t-on impeccable? Non. La déclaration qu'on provoque ne devant rien ajouter ni retrancher à ce qui est, à ce qui fut, ce qui s'est déjà vu se pourra voir encore. Or on a vu, il faut le dire avec respect et avec tristesse, mais il faut le dire,—car l'histoire y condamne, et Baronius lui-même, le grand historiographe de l'Église romaine, nous enseigne qu'il ne faut pas, en histoire, dissimuler la vérité ;[1] or, on a vu dans cette longue et incomparable série des Pontifes romains, quelques Papes, en petit nombre, mais enfin, il y en a eu, des Papes qui se sont montrés faibles, des Papes ambitieux, des Papes entreprenants, confondant le spirituel et le temporel, affectant des prétentions dominatrices sur les couronnes. On n'est pas assuré d'avoir, dans toute la suite des siècles, un Pie IX sur le trône pontifical.

N'est-il pas naturel de penser que, si le Pape est proclamé infaillible, ces réflexions se présenteront d'elles-mêmes aux Gouvernements d'aujourd'hui ? Et déjà, n'est-il pas inutile, et, je l'ajouterai, très-dangereux de réveiller de tels souvenirs? Certes, ce n'est pas moi qui les réveille! mais pourquoi d'imprudents avocats de la Papauté se donnent-ils tous les jours la triste mission de les réveiller, et de les envenimer ?

Mais, en outre, on se demandera sur quels objets s'exercera cette infaillibilité personnelle. Quand il n'y aurait que les matières mixtes, où les conflits furent toujours si fréquents, quelles sont ici les limites? Qui les déterminera? Le spirituel ne touche-t-il pas au temporel de tous côtés ? Qui persuadera aux Gouvernements que le Pape ne passera plus, jamais, dans aucun entraînement, du spirituel au temporel? Dès lors, la proclamation du nouveau dogme ne paraîtra-t-elle pas, non aux théologiens habiles, mais aux Gouvernements, qui ne sont pas théologiens, consacrer, dans le

[1] Et il suffit de lire dans ses *Annales* l'histoire du dixième siècle pour voir que lui-même ne la dissimule pas.

Pape, sur des matières peu définies et parfois non définissables, une puissance illimitée, souveraine, sur tous leurs sujets catholiques, et, pour eux Gouvernements, d'autant plus sujette aux ombrages, que l'abus leur paraîtra toujours possible ?

Alors on se souviendra des doctrines formulées, sinon définies, dans des Bulles célèbres.

Certes, ce n'est pas moi qui ai la moindre envie de défendre ici Philippe-le-Bel et ses imitateurs. Mais enfin, dans la Bulle *Unam sanctam*, par exemple, Boniface VIII ne déclare-t-il pas qu'il y a deux glaives, le spirituel et le temporel, que ce dernier aussi appartient à Pierre, et que le successeur de Pierre a le droit d'instituer et de juger les souverains? *Potestas spiritualis terrenam potestatem instituere habet et judicare.*

Et dans la Bulle *Ausculta fili*, il demandait au Roi d'envoyer à Rome les Archevêques et les Évêques de France, avec les abbés, etc., *pour y traiter de tout ce qui paraîtrait utile au bon gouvernement du royaume de France.*

Et après même que le protestantisme fut venu changer si profondément l'état de l'Europe, Paul III, dans la fameuse Bulle qui excommuniait Henri VIII, ne déliait-il pas de leur serment de fidélité les sujets du roi d'Angleterre, et n'offrait-il pas l'Angleterre à qui la voudrait conquérir, donnant, à ceux qui en feraient la conquête, tous les biens, meubles et immeubles, des Anglais devenus dissidents ?

Croit-on que cette Bulle soit oubliée en Angleterre? Et les déclarations, dont je citais tout à l'heure quelques mots, pense-t-on qu'elles n'ont pas été demandées aux Évêques catholiques d'Irlande par le souvenir, tout vivant encore, de cette Bulle? Me sera-t-il permis de dire ici toute ma pensée, et n'est-il pas permis de le demander après l'histoire : cette Bulle effrayante, à l'époque où elle fut publiée, n'était-elle pas de nature à précipiter, plutôt qu'à ramener, la nation anglaise? Est-il bien certain qu'elle n'a pas été pour la Chrétienté un grand malheur? Du moins, en pensant ainsi, on ne contredirait aucun dogme catholique, pas même celui de l'infaillibilité du Pape, si elle venait jamais à être érigée en dogme.

Je suis triste, et qui ne le serait? en rappelant ces grands et douloureux faits de l'histoire ; mais ils nous y forcent, ceux dont la légèreté et la témérité remuent ces questions brûlantes. Ils nous y forcent, et ma conviction profonde est que tout cela jette dans les meilleurs esprits un trouble déplorable, et que si on avait entrepris de rendre la puissance pontificale odieuse, on ne pourrait rien faire de mieux que de perpétuer de telles controverses.

Car, enfin, pourront encore se demander les Souverains, même catholiques, la proclamation dogmatique de l'infaillibilité du Pape rendra-t-elle, oui ou non, à l'avenir de telles Bulles impossibles ? Qui donc alors empêchera un nouveau Pape de définir ce que plusieurs de ses prédécesseurs ont enseigné : que le Vicaire de Jésus-Christ a un pouvoir *direct* sur le temporel des princes ; qu'il est dans ses attributions d'instituer et de déposer les souverains ; que les droits civils des rois et des peuples lui sont subordonnés ?[1]

Mais alors, et après la proclamation du dogme nouveau, nul clergé, nul évêque, nul catholique ne pourra récuser cette doctrine si odieuse aux Gouvernements ; c'est-à-dire qu'à leurs yeux tous les droits civils, politiques, comme toutes les croyances religieuses, seraient entre les mains d'un seul homme !

Et vous penseriez que les Gouvernements verraient avec indifférence l'Église s'assembler de tous les points du monde, pour proclamer un dogme qui, suivant eux, peut avoir de telles conséquences !

Et ils pourront être d'autant plus induits à considérer la définition de l'infaillibilité du Pape comme une consécration implicite de ces doctrines si redoutées, que ces doctrines sont loin d'être abandonnées. Sans cesse les journaux, qui se donnent parmi nous comme les purs représentants des principes romains, étalent ces théories dans leurs colonnes, les établissent à grand renfort d'arguments, et vont même jusqu'à signaler, comme entachée d'athéisme, la doctrine, à laquelle tiennent si fort les souverains, catholiques comme non catholiques, de l'indépendance des deux puissances chacune dans sa sphère.

Il y a très-peu de temps que nous lisions, citées avec éloge par un journal français, les paroles suivantes, où l'on compare aux manichéens ceux qui soutiennent que les deux glaives ne sont pas dans la même main :

" Y aurait-il donc deux sources d'autorité et de pouvoir, deux fins suprêmes pour les membres d'une même société, deux buts divers dans l'idée de l'être ordonnateur, et deux destinées distinctes chez un même homme qui est à la fois membre de l'Église et sujet de l'État ? Mais qui ne voit de suite l'absurdité d'un semblable système ? C'est le dualisme des manichéens, sinon l'athéisme."

[1] Ignore-t-on que Bellarmin lui-même fut mis à l'*index* pour n'avoir pas soutenu le pouvoir *direct* du Pape sur les couronnes ?

C'était là aussi ce que prétendait l'abbé de Lamennais, dans les emportements de sa logique ; et, contre le premier des quatre articles, il posait ce dilemme : *ultramontain* ou *athée*. Ces excès lui ont peu réussi. Et, au fond, sous ce rapport, les écrivains dont il s'agit ici sont de l'école de Lamennais. Mais plus ils reprocheront aux Gouvernements de ne pas admettre la doctrine de la Bulle *Unam sanctam*, et de tenir à cette indépendance des deux puissances, plus ils démontreront eux-mêmes la force des répugnances et l'universalité des répulsions que je redoute.

Et quand je parle de l'indépendance des deux puissances, loin de moi la pensée de mettre en doute un seul instant la divine et certaine autorité de l'Église, pour définir, proclamer, et rappeler, aux Gouvernements comme aux sujets, les saintes et éternelles règles du juste et de l'injuste ! Mais là n'est pas la question, on le sait bien, et c'est trop évident !

Non, les vieilles susceptibilités ne sont pas près de disparaître : un journalisme passionné a tout fait pour les ranimer ; et nulle part, on le peut affirmer avec certitude, ni en France, ni dans la catholique Autriche, ni dans la Bavière et sur les bords du Rhin, ni dans l'apostolique Espagne, ni dans ce Portugal, qui naguère chassait les Sœurs de charité, les dispositions des Gouvernements européens ne sont favorables à la proclamation du dogme annoncé.

L'heure vous paraît-elle donc venue de réveiller d'un bout de l'Europe à l'autre les haines contre le Saint-Siège ?

Ou plutôt, l'heure présente n'est-elle pas déjà pleine d'assez nombreux et d'assez grands périls ?

Veut-on mettre à l'ordre du jour, dans l'Europe entière, la séparation de l'Église et de l'État ?

Veut-on même faire courir au Concile d'autres chances ? Que faudrait-il, dans l'état actuel de l'Italie et de l'Europe, pour amener les plus grands malheurs ?

Il est impossible de se le dissimuler : il y a des esprits qui tiennent à pousser l'Église aux dernières extrémités !

Dans quel intérêt ?

VIII. J'arrive maintenant aux difficultés théologiques, non précisément de l'infaillibilité pontificale,—cette question, encore une fois, je ne la traite, ni dans un sens, ni dans un autre,—mais aux difficultés théologiques de la définition : car ces difficultés-là, si elles sont vraiment sérieuses, sont aussi une forte raison contre l'opportunité.

Les journalistes qui semblent vouloir enjoindre au Concile de définir l'infaillibilité du Pape, et de la définir par acclamation, se douteut-ils des conditions dans lesquelles le Concile aurait à faire cette définition ? Certes, on ne le dirait pas, à la manière dont ils en parlent ;—comme ils ne se doutent guères de ce qu'il y a d'étrange, de prodigieusement anormal, et de tout à fait impossible, dans le rôle qu'ils se donnent depuis six mois surtout, en s'ingérant au point où ils le font, dans les affaires les plus intimes du gouvernement de l'Église.

Je ne suis pas surpris d'ailleurs de leur extraordinaire imprudence. Ils ne sont pas théologiens. Vous, Messieurs, vous connaissez toutes les questions que je vais rappeler : elles vous sont enseignées dans vos écoles. Mais en même temps qu'on vous les enseigne, on vous apprend à ne pas en entretenir inutilement les fidèles. Prêtres, nous avons un double devoir, c'est d étudier les choses obscures et de ne prêcher que les choses claires. Quant aux laïques, encore une fois, je ne leur reproche pas d'ignorer, mais je leur reproche d'agiter et de trancher les questions qu'ils ignorent. Il ne savent pas à quelles difficultés ils touchent étourdiment, et je suis malheureusement obligé de les en avertir, en vous rappelant, à vous, Messieurs, ce que vous savez déjà.

"En matière si *grave*, si *délicate* et si *complexe*, dit avec une raison supérieure Mgr l'Évêque de Poitiers, on ne doit se laisser guider ni par l'enthousiasme, ni par le sentiment personnel ; tous les mots doivent être pesés et expliqués, toutes les faces de la question examinées, tous les cas prévus, toutes les fausses applications écartées, tous les inconvénients balancés avec les avantages."[1]

Au reste, Mgr l'Évêque de Poitiers n'est pas le seul à parler ainsi. Parmi les théologiens, les plus grands partisans de l'infaillibilité avouent eux-mêmes les prodigieuses difficultés pratiques qui peuvent se rencontrer ici. Ce sont, disent-ils, des difficultés inextricables, *intricatissimæ difficultates ;* et les plus habiles, ajoutent-ils, ont toute la peine du monde à s'en tirer ; *in quibus dissolvendis multum theologi peritiores laborant.*

1º Difficultés tirées de la nécessité de définir les conditions de l'acte *ex cathedrâ*, tous les actes pontificaux n'ayant pas ce caractère ;

2º Difficultés tirées du double caractère du Pape, considéré soit comme docteur privé, soit comme Pape ;

3º Difficultés tirées des multiples questions de fait qui se peuvent poser à propos de t ut acte *ex cathedrâ ;*

4º Difficultés tirées du passé et des faits historiques ;

5º Difficultés tirées du fond même de la question ;

6º Difficultés, enfin, tirées de l'état des esprits contemporains.

La première chose à faire par le Concile, avant de porter ici une définition dogmatique, ce serait donc de déterminer les conditions de l'infaillibilité ; car définir l'infaillibilité du Pape, sans préciser et définir les conditions de cette infaillibilité, ce serait ne rien définir, parce que ce serait définir trop, ou pas a-sez.

Mais comment déterminer ces conditions ? Les théologiens en disputent, soit en théorie, *in abstracto*, soit *in concreto*, et en fait. En un mot, quand et comment le Pape est-il infaillible ? Voilà ce qu'il faudra déterminer. Mais c'est ici que les difficultés ne sont pas médiocres.

Le Pape, toutes les fois qu'il parle, est-il infaillible ? Des théologiens l'ont pensé.— Ou bien ne l'est-il que quand il parle, comme on dit, *ex cathedrâ ?*

Mais, c'est précisément pour définir les conditions de la parole *ex cathedrâ*, que le Concile, s'il jugeait à propos d'entrer dans cette question, aurait fort à étudier et fort à faire.

Qu'est-ce, en effet, que la parole *ex cathedrâ ?* quelles en sont les conditions ? On discute là-dessus dans toutes les écoles : les uns exigent plus et les autres moins. Le Cardinal Orsi ne parle pas précisément comme le Cardinal Bellarmin, ni Bellarmin comme le Cardinal Capellari, qui fut depuis le Pape Grégoire XVI.

Mansi parle, soit de "Conciles assemblés préalablement," soit de "docteurs appelés," soit de "Congrégations instituées" et de "supplications publ ques." "*Sans cela*, dit-il, *que Bossuet le sache bien, nous ne reconnaissons plus le Pape comme infaillible.*"[1]

Bellarmin essaie de concilier ceux qui disent : *Pontifex consilium audiat pastorum,* avec ceux qui disent qu'il peut définir tout seul, *etiam solus.*[2]

Eh bien ! devant toutes ces divergences d'opinions, et je n'en cite ici que quelques-unes,—car on en compte un bien plus grand nombre, même parmi les théologiens ultramontains,—comment agira le Concile ? Il faudra donc qu'il entreprenne, approuvant les unes, réprouvant les autres, la rude tâche de faire, d'une façon dogmatique et absolue,

---

[1] Homélie prononcée dans la chapelle de son Grand-Séminaire.

[1] De Maistre, *du Pape*, liv. I, ch. x. v.
[2] *Disputationis Bellarmini.*

un choix parmi toutes ces opinions théologiques : mais sur quelles bases, certaines, claires et indiscutables, s'appuiera-t-il pour cela ?

Encore une fois, qu'est-ce donc exactement qu'un acte *ex cathedrâ* ?

Est-ce un simple bref ? Oui, disent les uns ; non, disent les autres. Est-ce un rescrit ? Même partage d'opinions. Est-ce une bulle, une allocution consistoriale, une encyclique ?

Faut-il, dans l'acte *ex cathedrâ*, que le Pape s'adresse à toute l'Église ? —Oui, disent la plupart.—Non, dit un Anglais, professeur laïque de théologie[1] et journaliste contemporain : quand il ne parlerait qu'à un seul Évêque, ou même à un simple laïque, il peut avoir voulu enseigner *ex cathedrâ*. Et c'est assez.

Eh bien, alors, faut-il au moins, comme plusieurs le réclament, pour qu'il n'y ait aucun doute sur son intention, que le Pape définisse la doctrine sous la sanction d'un anathème contre l'erreur ?

— Ou suffit-il, comme d'autres le prétendent, qu'il exprime, d'une manière quelconque, son intention de faire un dogme ?

— Ou bien enfin, comme le soutient encore le théologien laïque que je citais tout à l'heure, peut-il parler *ex cathedrâ*, même quand il n'exprimerait pas clairement son intention d'imposer la foi ? *Etiamsi obligatio assensum præstandi non diserte exprimatur*.[2]

— Ou bien, faut-il, comme certains autres le veulent, que le Pape ait consulté ? Et s'il le faut, qui doit-il consulter ? Quelques évêques ? ou, à défaut d'évêques, les cardinaux ? ou, à défaut des cardinaux, les congrégations romaines ? ou, à défaut des congrégations romaines, des théologiens, des docteurs, et combien ? Suffirait-il d'un décret qu'il aurait dressé seul dans son cabinet ? Pourquoi distinguer, disent quelques-uns, là où les paroles des promesses ne distinguent pas ?

Voici du reste un autre théologien contemporain, l'allemand Phillips, que cette difficulté n'arrête pas. Pour lui, la définition *ex cathedrâ* ne demande que le Pape consulte qui que ce soit : ni le Concile, ni l'Église romaine, ni le Collége des cardinaux. Le docteur allemand va plus loin encore : il n'est pas nécessaire, selon lui, que *le Pape réfléchisse mûrement* ;

Ni qu'il étudie soigneusement la question à

[1] M. Ward, *De infallibilitatis extensione, thesis duodecima*, p. 35.—M. Ward est un ancien ministre anglican converti, zélé catholique aujourd'hui, et qui a été, quoique laïque, professeur de théologie au Grand-Séminaire de l'archevêché de Westminster.

[2] Ibid. *Thesis duodecima*.

la lumière de la parole de Dieu écrite et traditionnelle :

Ni qu'il élève sa prière vers Dieu avant de prononcer.

Sans toutes ces conditions, sa décision n'en serait pas moins aussi valide, aussi valable, aussi obligatoire pour toute l'Église, que s'il avait observé toutes les précautions que dicte la foi, la piété, le bon sens.

Que faut-il donc, selon ce docteur, pour qu'une définition soit *ex cathedrâ* ? Le voici : " Il reste à dire d'après cela, pour défendre la valeur d'une décision *ex cathedrâ*, qu'elle existe, lorsque le Pape, dans un Concile ou hors d'un Concile, VERBALEMENT ou *par écrit*, donne à tous les fidèles chrétiens, comme Vicaire de Jésus-Christ, au nom des apôtres Pierre et Paul, ou en vertu de l'autorité du Saint-Siége, *ou en d'autres termes semblables, avec* ou *sans* la menace de l'anathème, une décision relative au dogme ou à la morale." (Phillips, dict. Goschlez, article *Pape*.)

D'après ce théologien, l'Église n'a pas le droit de mettre une restriction ni une condition quelconque, quant à la validité, à l'exercice de l'infaillibilité.

Un écrivain français, auteur d'un récent traité *De Papa*, ne dit guère autre chose, et ne demande, pour que le Pape, parlant à l'Église universelle, soit infaillible, qu'une condition, non pas qu'il ait prié, non pas qu'il ait délibéré, étudié, consulté, mais simplement qu'il ait eu l'intention de faire un dogme, et qu'il n'ait pas été violenté.

M. Ward, nous l'avons vu, ne demande même pas que le Pape s'adresse à l'Église : qu'il s'adresse à un seul Évêque ou à un seul laïque, cela suffit.

Voilà donc de quelle sorte quelques-uns ne craignent pas, aujourd'hui, de traiter ces immenses questions !

Je dis *quelques-uns*, et je prie qu'on veuille remarquer ce mot ; car, je ne voudrais pas que toutes les plus extrêmes théories parussent être, contre mon intention, mises au compte de toute la théologie catholique.

Eh bien ! en présence de toutes ces opinions, le Concile déclarera-t-il qu'il y a une forme nécessaire, sous laquelle le Pape SERA TENU d'exercer son infaillibilité ? ou bien la forme n'y ferait-elle rien ? et le Pape sera-t-il infaillible, quand et de la manière qu'il jugera bon de l'être, sans avoir ni prié, ni étudié, ni consulté, et s'adressant au premier fidèle venu ?

Et, puisque déterminer en quelles circonstances le Pape est infaillible, c'est déterminer aussi dans quelles conditions il ne l'est pas, il y aura donc à définir ici deux dogmes, au lieu d'un : le dogme de l'infaillibilité, et le dogme de la faillibilité ? On déclarera, comme de foi, non-seulement que le Pape est infaillible dans telles et telles conditions, mais qu'en dehors de ces conditions, il est faillible.

Et comment, encore une fois, s'y prendra-t-on pour fixer ces limites ? Où sont-elles clairement dans l'Écriture ? Où sont-elles dans l'enseignement, si varié et si contradictoire ici, des théologiens ? Quelles opinions va-t-on ériger en dogmes ? ou en hérésies ?

Et si on ne le fait pas, dans quel inconnu va-t-on jeter l'Église ?

IX. Mais ce n'est pas tout : outre la question de droit, il y aura encore la question de fait. Qui décidera, en fait, que telle décision du Pape remplit toutes les conditions d'un décret ex cathedrâ ? Ce discernement sera-t-il toujours facile ? Non.

C'est ce que reconnaissent de bonne foi les partisans les plus avancés de l'infaillibilité pontificale. Le théologien anglais Ward, par exemple, dit expressément : "Puisque toutes les allocutions pontificales, toutes les lettres apostoliques, même toutes les encycliques, ne contiennent pas des définitions ex cathedrâ, il faut regarder de près pour discerner d'une façon suffisante quels sont ceux de ces actes où le Souverain-Pontife doit être censé parler ex cathedrâ ; et il faut y regarder de près dans les actes mêmes ex cathedrâ, c'est-à-dire dans les actes infaillibles, pour bien discerner ce qu'il enseigne ex cathedrâ, c'est-à-dire infailliblement." [1]

Et ce discernement est si difficile parfois aux théologiens eux-mêmes, que M. Ward reconnaît, avec une modestie qui l'honore, avoir commis, et opiniâtrement soutenu une grave méprise, touchant la nature des actes pontificaux de diverses sortes, où avaient été flétries les propositions signalées plus tard dans une pièce récente émanée de Rome. Il avait cru, et il affirmait, que chacun des actes qui a fourni des propositions au recueil appelé Syllabus, devait être regardé par cela seul comme ayant le caractère d'un acte ex cathedrâ. Ce qu'il confesse maintenant avec franchise avoir été une grosse erreur.

L'histoire ecclésiastique, du reste, est pleine de faits semblables. Qu'on se rappelle certains actes considérables des Papes, dans les temps passés, sur lesquels les théologiens ont tant disputé, et disputent encore,

[1] Circa has igitur allocutiones et litteras apostolicas adlaborandum est, ut satis dignoscatur in quibusnam earum Pontifex ex cathedrâ loqui, et quidnam ex cathedrâ docere, jure censeatur.

pour savoir s'ils sont, oui ou non, ex cathedrâ.

Quand le Pape Étienne condamna saint Cyprien dans la question du baptême des hérétiques, a-t-il parlé ex cathedrâ ? Les uns affirment, les autres nient.

Quand le Pape Honorius, consulté sur la question du monothélisme par Sergius, Patriarche de Constantinople, et d'autres Évêques orientaux, écrivit ces fameuses lettres qui donnèrent lieu à tant de débats, a-t-il parlé ex cathedrâ ? Les théologiens ont encore là-dessus vivement discuté.

Qui décidera donc ? L'Église. Il faudra donc souvent en revenir, de fait, à une décision de l'Église.

Et en effet, outre les deux questions de fait dont parle M. Ward, et qui se doivent poser à propos de tout acte ex cathedrâ : — l'acte est-il ex cathedrâ ? — Et s'il l est, sur quoi porte précisément la définition ? — il y en a un autre, pas si simple dans la pratique qu'on pourrait le croire d'abord, et que voici :

Ne se peut-il jamais rencontrer, en effet, dans la suite des siècles, tel Pape de la liberté duquel on puisse légitimement douter ?

Les plus zélés sont bien forcés de le reconnaître, et d'admettre, en présence de l'histoire, qu'un Pape, sous l'influence de la crainte, peut définir l'erreur.

Voilà donc, dans certaines circonstances, une troisième question de fait, à constater : la pleine et entière liberté du Pape.

N'y en a-t-il pas une quatrième ? car, si un Pape, même déclaré infaillible, pourrait encore, même dans un acte ex cathedrâ, errer sous le coup de l'intimidation et de la crainte, ne le pourra-t-il jamais par entraînement, par passion, par imprudence ? — Les théologiens, partisans de l'infaillibilité, expliquent que non : Dieu, disent-ils, ne fera pas de miracle dans le premier cas, pour empêcher un Pape faible de céder à la crainte ; mais il en fera toujours un dans le second, pour empêcher un Pape passionné ou téméraire d'errer par imprudence ; — et cela, ajoutent quelques-uns, même quand le Pape n'aurait pris aucune des précautions qu'on apporte d'ordinaire dans une affaire sérieuse : ils savent qu'un Pape peut définir l'erreur par faiblesse, pas autrement.

Voilà l'explication de ces théologiens. Mais je pose ici cette question : Sera-t il toujours facile d'apprécier la contrainte qu'aura pu subir un Pape ? Non. Il peut se rencontrer des cas où une telle constatation soit chose fort délicate ; et " tous les cas doivent être prévus."

Comme aussi, " toutes les faits de la question examinées."

Croit-on que la solution de toutes ces difficultés serait une mince besogne pour le Concile ? Et ces écrivains quotidiens, qui en parlent si fort à leur aise, parce que les difficultés ne les inquiètent guère,—ils ne les voient seulement pas—sont-ils autorisés, comme ils le font, à prescrire aux Évêques de s'en charger ?

X. C'est bientôt fait de dire que la question, aujourd'hui, est jugée ; mais les vrais théologiens, les théologiens sérieux, savent bien qu'au fond il n'en est rien ; et que, si le Concile ici veut procéder avec la maturité et la gravité dont ces saintes assemblées de l'Église ne se sont jamais départies, lorsqu'il s'est agi de proclamer les dogmes, de bien longs labeurs peuvent être réservés à ses délibérations.

La tradition, quels que puissent être ses témoignages, est-elle donc ici unanime, et l'histoire sans embarras ? C'est sur ce terrain surtout que la définition de l'infaillibilité pontificale, si le Concile croyait devoir s'en occuper, l'entraînerait forcément dans les plus longues et les plus délicates recherches.

Par la définition, en effet, de l'infaillibilité personnelle du Pape, ce ne serait pas l'avenir seulement qu'on engagerait, ce serait aussi tout le passé. Car, si le Pape est infaillible, il l'a toujours été. La proclamation de ce dogme donnerait, d'un coup, le caractère de décisions infaillibles à tout ce que les Papes, depuis dix-huit siècles, ont jamais décidé, s'ils l'avaient fait dans les conditions et les formes que l'on aurait déterminées pour l'exercice de l'infaillibilité. Je dis que le Concile ne pourrait rien avoir à examiner de plus grave et de plus épineux.

Je rappelais, tout à l'heure, deux souvenirs historiques, la dispute du Pape saint Étienne avec saint Cyprien, et la réponse du Pape Honorius à Sergius au sujet du monothélisme. Eh bien, s'il était prouvé que saint Étienne avait prononcé *ex cathedrâ*, infailliblement, obligatoirement, saint Cyprien et les Évêques qui ont résisté ne croyaient donc pas à l'infaillibilité du Pape ?

Et saint Augustin, qui les excuse, parce que, dit-il, l'Église n'avait pas encore prononcé,[1] n'y croyait donc pas non plus ? Et quand il écrivait, au sujet des Donatistes : qu'après le jugement de Rome, il restait encore celui de l'Église universelle, *restabat adhuc plenarium universæ Ecclesiæ concilium*,[1] il croyait donc qu'après le jugement de Rome, le jugement de l'Église devait entrer pour quelque chose dans la définition de la foi ? Voilà un nouvel exemple des difficultés que l'examen des faits historiques peut soulever.

De même pour Honorius. On a écrit des volumes, pour prouver que les actes du 6° Concile, qui l'a condamné, avaient été altérés ; des volumes, pour prouver que ce Pape n'a pas réellement enseigné l'hérésie ; des volumes encore, pour prouver qu'Honorius n'a écrit qu'une lettre *privée*.

Quoi qu'il en soit de ces discussions, si fâcheuses à soulever,—qu'Honorius ait été hérétique et condamné justement comme tel par un Concile œcuménique, qui a prononcé, *Honorio hæretico anathema* ; ou qu'il ait été simplement un fauteur de l'hérésie, et réprouvé comme tel par les Papes ses successeurs, dans la formule de serment qu'ils prononçaient à leur sacre : *Qui pravis eorum assertionibus fomentum impendit ;*—c'est ainsi que s'exprime le *Liber diurnus pontificalis*, recueil des actes authentiques de la chancellerie romaine,—en dehors de ces points d'histoire incontestés, une autre question, fort sérieuse assurément, se présente ici.

Dans ce temps-là, le Concile œcuménique, l'Église par conséquent, considérait donc le Souverain-Pontife lui-même, adressant sur une question de foi à de grandes églises, des lettres dogmatiques, *Litteras dogmaticas*,[2] comme sujet à l'erreur ; et les Évêques réunis, comme compétents pour le condamner et lui dire anathème ?

Et le pape Léon II a confirmé la sentence du Concile ; les Églises d'Orient et d'Occident l'ont acceptée. Le pape Léon II et les Églises croyaient donc également qu'un pape, s'expliquant sur des questions de foi portées à son tribunal, peut mériter l'anathème ?

Voilà un point sur lequel le Concile aurait encore à se prononcer.

Je n'ai ni la pensée ni le temps de faire ici, ce qu'il serait nécessaire que le Concile fît pour procéder avec la circonspection accoutumée des Conciles, une revue complète de l'histoire. Je laisse les difficultés que peuvent soulever les Papes Vigile et Libère ; mais je demande permission de rappeler encore un seul fait. Au moyen âge, un Pape, Pascal II, fait à un empereur d'Allemagne, Henri V, une concession tellement exorbitante sur l'investiture des Évêques, qu'un Concile s'assemble à Vienne, et qu'un Archevêque, qui devait plus tard monter lui-même sur la chaire de Saint-

[1] Epist. ad Geor. Eleus. xlviii
[2] Conc. t. III, p. 1331.

---

[1] Saint Augustin, *De Baptismo*.

Pierre, sous le nom de Calixte II, déclare que la concession faite par le Pape implique une véritable hérésie, *hæresim esse judicavimus*, et condamne sa lettre à l'Empereur.

Et déjà le Pape lui-même, en plein Concile de Latran, en présence de plus de cent Évêques, était humilié de son propre mouvement, et le Concile avait cassé et annulé sa concession.

Quoi qu'il en soit de la faute de Pascal II, à tout le moins, ses contemporains et lui-même croyaient donc qu'un Pape peut tomber dans l'hérésie?

Dira-t-on qu'une hérésie implicite, et cependant digne d'anathème, dans un grand acte pontifical, ne prouve rien contre l'infaillibilité, quand cet acte n'est pas une définition *ex cathedrâ*? Mais comment faire comprendre à la foule ces distinctions?

Car voici un autre côté de la question, dont le Concile aurait encore à se préoccuper sérieusement : les conséquences de la définition au point de vue des hommes de ce temps.

XI. Il ne faut pas se faire d'illusion, non-seulement sur les esprits incrédules, mais encore sur la masse énorme des esprits chez qui la foi est faible. Pour ma part, je ne puis penser sans effroi au nombre de ceux que la définition demandée éloignerait peut-être de nous à jamais !

Mais pour les fidèles eux-mêmes, la définition serait-elle sans inconvénients ?

Je ne vois encore ici contraint de poser des questions qui me répugnent profondément. Mais je parle du passé et pour l'avenir. On nous contraint de réveiller le passé endormi, et nous avons à travailler pour les siècles futurs.

Voilà donc le Pape déclaré infaillible, qui, néanmoins, peut comme écrivain, comme docteur privé, faire un livre hérétique, et s'opiniâtrer dans l'hérésie. C'est l'opinion générale.

Bien plus, voilà le Pape qui, même comme Pape, quand il ne parle pas *ex cathedrâ*,—et même dans un acte où il parle *ex cathedrâ*, en ce qui n'est pas l'objet précis de la définition,—peut, de l'avis universel, errer, enseigner l'erreur ; et puis être jugé, condamné, déposé.

Eh bien ! supposons un Pape errant, ou accusé d'erreur : il faudra prouver que son enseignement, ou n'est pas *ex cathedrâ*, ou n'est pas erroné ; quelle difficulté nouvelle si le Pape a été déclaré infaillible ! En ne contestant qu'un fait, ne semblera-t-on pas contester un droit ? Et si le Pape s'obstine, quel désarroi dans les âmes! Il faudra donc faire le procès pour cause d'hérésie celui dont l'infaillibilité sera un dogme?

Qu'un nouvel Honorius dans l'avenir rencontre, qui, je ne dis pas définisse, mai par des lettres *dogmatiques*, adressées à grandes Églises, fomente l'hérésie,—la d claration d'infaillibilité ne l'empêchera pa mais se représente-t-on quel serait en parc cas le trouble des Églises et des cor sciences?

Sans doute, les théologiens distingueron ici les nuances et les délicatesses, et mon treront qu'il n'y a pas précisément déf nition ; mais la foule des esprits qui ne son pas théologiens, comment pourra-t-elle dis cerner que le Pape faillible, dans tel ou t acte, même comme Pape, ne l'est plus dan tel ou tel autre ? Comment comprendra t-elle qu'il puisse être infaillible, et *fomenter* par de grands actes pontificaux, *l'hérésie* ?

Aux yeux du public, ce sera toujour l'infaillibilité. De là, le trouble pour le consciences, qui se croiront toujours obligée de faire des actes de foi ; et, pour les enne mis de l'Église, l'occasion de décrier la doctrine catholique, en lui imputant comm dogme ce qui ne le serait pas.

Sans vouloir, encore une fois, toucher à la question de fond, à la question même de l'infaillibilité, nous ne pouvons cependant nous défendre ici, au point de vue des gens du monde, d'une réflexion. L'infaillibilité personnelle du Pape, non pas l'absurde infaillibilité, inconditionnelle et universelle, dont nous parlions tout à l'heure, mais seulement certains théologiens, mais l'infaillibilité, telle que Bellarmin, par exemple, l'entend, constitue une institution, non pas sans doute au-dessus du pouvoir du Tout-Puissant, mais assurément bien prodigieuse, et plus étonnante que l'infaillibilité de l'Église tout entière.

Comment se fait-il, c'est là ce qui étonnera les fidèles, que ce privilége immense se trouve être à la fois celui dont la définition est, à ce qu'il paraît par l'histoire, la moins nécessaire, puisque l'Église a pu s'en passer pendant dix-huit siècles ; et sa certitude, moins établie que ne l est l infaillibilité de l'Église elle-même, puisque celle-ci est et a toujours été article de foi, tandis que l'autre n'a jamais été professée dans l'Église comme un dogme ?

Au reste, les plus grands partisans de l'infaillibilité détaillent eux-mêmes les prodigieuses difficultés pratiques que ces deux manières d'être du Pape, faillible ou infaillible, suivant la différence des cas, peuvent entraîner. *Intricatissimæ dificultates ;* disent ils, *in quibus dissolvendis multum peritiores theologi laborant.*

Et voici, en effet, toujours selon eux, quelques-unes des questions—si pénibles—qui alors se posent :—Un Pape, par le fait de l'hérésie, cesse-t-il d'être Pape ?—Par qui et comment peut-il être déposé ?—Quand le Pape est-il censé agir comme Pape ou comme personne privée ? etc., etc. *An papa per hæresim a dignitate excidat ?—A quo et quomodo reniat deponendus ?—Quanmlonam it l'ontifex, aut ut privata persona, agere nseatur ?*

La déclaration d'infaillibilité rendra-t-elle toutes ces difficultés moins inextricables ? Tout au contraire, elle y ajouterait, dans la pratique, d'énormes embarras.

Aussi certains théologiens ultramontains[1] ne voient-ils qu'un moyen de se tirer de là : c'est, disent-ils, de proclamer l'infaillibilité absolue, inconditionnelle et universelle du Pape. Sans cela, et si on ne proclame qu'une infaillibilité conditionnelle,—l'infaillibilité *ex cathedrâ*,—on expose l'Église à un péril ÉVIDENT : *Ecclesia* EVIDENTI *periculo exponeretur.* Et ils le prouvent.

Le système, disent-ils, de l'infaillibilité du Pape dans certains cas, et de sa faillibilité dans les autres, implique une vraie contradiction. Ne pourra-t-il, en effet arriver que le Pape enseigne comme Pape, *ex cathedrâ,* l'erreur que, comme docteur privé, il aura cru la vérité, c'est-à-dire définisse dans un acte infaillible l'erreur et veuille l'imposer à l'Église ? *Posset namque ipse suum errorem definire et Ecclesiæ obtrudere.*

Ou répond que cette hypothèse, précisément parce qu'elle implique contradiction, ne se réalisera jamais.

Mais alors, répliquent-ils, vous êtes forcés d'avoir recours à un miracle : un Pape qui erre avec opiniâtreté, et qui naturellement fait tous ses efforts pour proposer son erreur à la foi de l'Église : *Potest Pontifex personaliter in fide d ficere, errorem suum pertinaciter tueri, et, quod amplius est, velle et conari eum Ecclesiæ obtrudere et proponere;* et qui, cependant, s'abstiendra toujours de la définir ; et ne peut pas arriver à faire une Bulle que nulle puissance humaine ne pont l'empêcher d'écrire ; ou bien, un Pape qui pense d'une façon, et qui définit de l'autre : *Aut certe grande miraculum esset, quod ipse definiendo contra mentem suam definiret.*

Et de plus, ajoutent-ils, n'y a-t-il pas, dans cette faillibilité et cette infaillibilité tout ensemble chez le même homme, une anomalie étrange, et profondément injurieuse à la divine Providence, qui pourrait si facilement rendre le Pape infaillible dans tous les

[1] Albert Pighius, et quelques autres, cités par Bannès, quæst. 1. dubit. 2.

cas aussi bien que dans quelques-uns : *Contra divinam Providentiam, quæ omnia suaviter disponit, pugnat Pontificem posse personaliter errare ?*

Et enfin, poursuivent-ils, pourquoi distinguer là où Jésus-Christ n'a pas distingué du tout : *Oravi pro te, Petre, ut non deficiat fides tua,* cela, disent-ils, s'entend de la foi de Pierre dans tous les sens ; DE FIDE PETRI TUM PERSONALI ET PRIVATA, *tum publica et pastorali, intelligitur ?*

Voilà donc des théologiens qui constatent, qui démontrent les périls de l'infaillibilité *ex cathedrâ,* et qui, logiques et résolus, vont jusqu'au bout, jusqu'à l'infaillibilité absolue, inconditionnelle et universelle du Pape : de telle sorte qu'un Pape, disent-ils, ne pourrait pas, *même quand il le voudrait,* tomber dans aucune erreur, soit publique, soit privée: *Ut non possit,* ETIAMSI VELIT, *in errorem* PRIVATIM *aut publice cadere!*

Un théologien français[1] exposa au long tous ces raisonnements, et lui, qui accable d'injures les plus grands hommes de son pays, se contente de présenter ce romanisme, véritablement inouï, comme une opinion parfaitement libre : *De* LIBERE *controversa opinione quæ tenet romanum Pontificem,* ETIAM QUATENUS DOCTOREM PRIVATUM, *esse infallibilem.*

Eh ! mon Dieu ! on est libre aussi de controverser, si cela plaît, la question de savoir si les hommes des antipodes marchent sur la tête ou sur les pieds. Il n'y a, que je sache, aucune définition qui dise le contraire, et on n'est justiciable ici que du bon sens.

Évidemment, il y a dans l'Église, en ce moment, bien des gens passionnés ; et qui poussent à d'étranges excès ! Mais le Concile, nous en sommes sûrs, ne se laissera pas entraîner sur une telle pente.

XII. Il y a plus d'un point encore où il est à craindre que la proclamation du nouveau dogme, si elle avait lieu, ne trouble et n'embarrasse, dans l'esprit des fidèles, ce qu'ils ont cru jusqu'ici.

Comment, par exemple, leur persuader que cette définition n'entraînera pas, sinon en droit, du moins en fait et dans la pratique, un amoindrissement de l'Épiscopat ?

Et d'abord, à ce point de vue, penseront-ils, que deviendront les Conciles ?

Les Conciles ont été jusqu'ici une des grandes formes de la vie de l'Église, un de ses plus puissants moyens d'action. Ils ont commencé dès l'origine de l'Église, dès les temps apostoliques ; tous les siècles chrétiens,

[1] *De l'ap*â, t. l, p. 257.

sauf les deux derniers, les ont connus. Il y a même de saints personnages, de grands esprits, des Conciles, qui ont réclamé ou décrété le retour périodique de ces saintes assemblées. Il est vrai, la politique ombrageuse d'un régime qui n'est plus, les avait rendues dans les siècles derniers plus difficiles ; mais les libertés modernes ont abaissé ces jalouses barrières ; les conquêtes de la science contemporaine, en abrégeant les distances, ont frayé partout des voies rapides aux Évêques du monde entier vers la Ville éternelle ; et ces assemblées délibérantes, en même temps qu'elles sont devenues plus faciles, se trouvent plus en harmonie aujourd'hui avec les vœux des peuples chrétiens. Ne peut-on pas voir en tout cela des coïncidences vraiment providentielles ?

Mais, si le prochain Concile définissait l'infaillibilité du Pape, les fidèles ne pourraient-ils pas penser et se dire : à quoi bon désormais les Conciles œcuméniques ? Puisque UN SEUL, le Pape, "EN DEHORS DES ÉVÊQUES," pourra tout décider infailliblement, même les questions de foi, à quoi bon réunir les Évêques ? A quoi bon les longueurs, les recherches, les discussions des Conciles ?

Il est évident en effet que si le dogme nouveau, une fois proclamé, ne supprime pas en droit ces grandes assemblées, à tout le moins, en fait, il en diminuera singulièrement l'importance.

Ainsi donc, on voudrait que le futur Concile fît un décret qui désormais supprimât ou amoindrît les Conciles !

Et que les Évêques décrétassent eux-mêmes pour ainsi dire leur abdication !

Mais ce n'est pas là le seul amoindrissement que l'Épiscopat semblerait subir aux yeux des fidèles. Ses plus essentielles prérogatives, sur lesquelles aucun catholique ne dispute, ne vont-elles pas, dans la pratique du moins, perdre singulièrement aussi de leur réalité ?

Et d'abord les Évêques sont JUGES DE LA FOI : juges avec le Pape, bien entendu ; mais vrais juges. Et toujours, jusqu'ici, ils ont eu une part effective dans les jugements et les définitions du dogme : toujours ils ont décidé dans les Conciles comme des juges réels : *Ego judicans, ego definiens, subscripsi*. Toujours ils ont été, comme le dit Benoît XIV, *co-judices*, juges de la foi avec le Pape.

Mais avec la nouvelle règle de foi, ne semblerait-il pas aux fidèles qu'il n'y a plus qu'un juge réel, et que les Évêques ne le sont plus sérieusement ? Leur coopération, antécédente ou subséquente, en effet, ne

sera plus en rien nécessaire. Le jugement infaillible du Pape, comme dit Monsignor Manning, sera complet et parfait en lui même, " EN DEHORS ET INDÉPENDAMMENT DE L'ÉPISCOPAT." Ils pourront ne plus entrer pour rien, si le Pape le veut ainsi, dans les jugements sur la foi. Alors il n'y aura plus en fait, qu'un seul juge, le Pape.

Comment en effet, lorsque le Pape aura proclamé, seul, en dehors de l'épiscopat et sans les Évêques, un dogme de foi, comment faire comprendre aux fidèles ces deux choses que la sentence du Pape a immédiatement par elle-même, indépendamment de toute adhésion épiscopale, la force de chose jugée et que les Évêques cependant restent vrais juges !

Quelle sentence peuvent-ils donc alors porter ?—Une sentence de simple adhésion dit-on.—Mais cette sentence du moins sera-t-elle libre ? Non ; elle n'est pas libre, car ils sont obligés d'adhérer.—Est-elle même requise ? Non, elle n'est requise d'aucune façon, car la sentence du Pape est obligatoire par elle-même, indépendamment de toute adhésion de l'Épiscopat.

Je me demande si, dans ces conditions les fidèles considéreront toujours les Évêques comme de vrais juges ?

Que serait en effet, à leurs yeux, un tribunal dont le président aurait le privilège de décider et de juger tout, tout seul de telle sorte que tous les autres juges seraient obligés de juger comme lui ? Le vote seul du président suffirait : la sentence des autres serait faite par la sienne, dictée par la sienne ; nul ne pourrait juger après lui autrement que lui ; et l'adhésion de ses collègues ne serait même pas requise pour la décision.

Évidemment un tel tribunal paraîtra dérisoire, et de juges, en réalité, on n'en verrait qu'un.

Les théologiens peuvent argumenter et distinguer ici. Mais les fidèles, ce grand public qui n'entend pas les distinctions théologiques, où en sera-t-il ?

Sans doute le Pape est le juge principal et son jugement est toujours indispensable. Non-seulement il préside le tribunal, mais il confirme le jugement des autres juges. Dans les tribunaux ordinaires, la voix du président est ordinairement prépondérante ; mais dans l'Église, la voix du Pape est ou plus nécessaire, et le jugement des Évêques même dans un Concile œcuménique, n'est définitif que quand celui du Pape s'y ajoute. En un mot, dans la définition de la foi, les Évêques et le Pape ont respectivement leur part nécessaire. Cela serait-il encore vrai pour les Évêques, aux yeux des fidèles quand le Pape, déclaré infaillible, jugerait seul ?

XIII. Continuons, Messieurs, en nous plaçant toujours au point de vue des fidèles, à rechercher et à examiner quels peuvent être les inconvénients probables de la définition dogmatique en question.

En même temps que JUGES, les Évêques sont DOCTEURS. Tous les catéchismes disent cela. Les paroles de Notre-Seigneur Jésus-Christ sont formelles. C'est aux Apôtres, et par conséquent aux Évêques, successeurs des Apôtres, qu il a été dit : *Euntes docete omnes gentes. . . . Ecce ego vobiscum sum omnibus diebus.* C'est aux Apôtres, et par conséquent aux Évêques successeurs des Apôtres, que Jésus-Christ a dit encore : *Accipite Spiritum Sanctum*, etc. Et enfin : *Qui vos audit, me audit.* Ce sont là autant de paroles que tous les fidèles savent par cœur.

C est pourquoi saint Paul dit : *Fundati estis super fundamentum Apostolorum.—Posuit Episcopos regere ecclesiam.*

Toute la tradition a constamment assimilé ici les Évêques aux Apôtres, et le Concile de Trente, résumant toute la tradition, dit expressément : *In locum Apostolorum successerunt*, en parlant des Évêques.

Ainsi donc, les Évêques ne sont pas seulement des échos, ils enseignent : ils constituent, avec le Pape, l'Église enseignante.

Mais avec l'infaillibilité personnelle du Pape, sans le concours des Évêques, " EN DEHORS, ET INDÉPENDAMMENT DU CORPS ÉPISCOPAL," c'est, aux yeux des fidèles, un seul qui définit, un seul qui enseigne, un seul qui est docteur, comme il est seul juge.

Et les Évêques ne semblent plus des voix dans l'Église, mais de simples échos.

L'adhésion du corps enseignant pouvant n'entrer pour rien dans ce qui est l'essence du jugement doctrinal, comment les fidèles comprendront-ils que ce corps enseignant enseigne ?

De plus, Messieurs, qu'est-ce que l'enseignement de l'Église ? Un témoignage. Ni le Pape, ni l'Église ne font le dogme : ils le constatent. La révélation est un fait ; les vérités révélées sont des faits. Et un jugement doctrinal n'est au fond que l'attestation d'un fait révélé. Or, quand c'est l'Église, assemblée ou dispersée, qui prononce le jugement, c'est là quelque chose que les fidèles conçoivent sans peine, quelque chose où l'assistance divine est requise, sans doute, mais tout à fait conforme à la nature des choses, à l'harmonie même de l'Église, telle que Jésus-Christ l'a constituée. C'est un témoignage, attesté par tous ceux qui sont les témoins ; ce sont les Églises particulières, attestant, par le fait même qu'elles témoignent, la foi de l'Église universelle. Quand toutes les Églises, quand le corps des pasteurs unis à leur chef, a parlé, par là-même, la foi de l'Église est constatée : ce qui n'était qu'implicite est devenu explicite, et le dogme est défini. Et la grande maxime catholique se réalise : *Quod ubique, quod semper, quod ab omnibus.* Les fidèles comprennent facilement cela.

Tandis qu'un jugement doctrinal du Pape seul, sans que l'adhésion de l'Épiscopat n'y fût à aucun point de vue requise, se présentera à eux sous un autre aspect. Ce sera, dans une question de témoignage, un témoin, qui pourra, quand il le voudra, remplacer tous les autres : un seul témoin, au lieu de tous : un témoin qui n'a aucun besoin, s'il le trouve bon, des autres témoins, ni de leur témoignage, pour savoir ce qui est la tradition et la foi de leurs Églises.

C'est-à-dire qu'à quelque chose de très-simple et de très-compréhensible, dans l'ordre spirituel, on substituerait, aux yeux des fidèles, quelque chose d'extraordinaire, d'anormal, un miracle perpétuel, et bien autre que celui de l'infaillibilité de l'Église.

Ici du moins, s'il y a encore miracle, les fidèles conçoivent que ce miracle est absolument nécessaire, et impliqué dans la notion même de l'Église : sans l'infaillibilité dans l'Église, pas d'Église. Mais ils conçoivent moins la nécessité de ce miracle pour le Pape seul, parce que sans l'infaillibilité personnelle et séparée du Pape, l'Église se comprend encore parfaitement : l'infaillibilité de l'Église pourra toujours suffire à tout, comme elle y a toujours suffi.

Les fidèles savent très-bien que, dans ce grand et universel témoignage de l'Église, le Pape est témoin, principal témoin, témoin de la principale et souveraine Église, de celle qui, placée au centre, communique avec toutes les autres, comme toutes les autres doivent communiquer avec elle.

Mais jusqu'ici les fidèles n'ont pas cru que le Pape fût dans l'Église le seul témoin.

Désormais, prononçant seul, il le serait quand il voudrait.

XIV. On dit bien, et il faut le dire : *Ubi Petrus, ibi Ecclesia.* C'est là un grand mot de saint Ambroise. Mais on abuse quelquefois de ce mot étrangement. A entendre certains écrivains, dont les exagérations assurément ne plaisent ni au Pape, ni guère à personne, on dirait que le Pape est à lui seul toute l'Église. Non, le Pape est le Chef de l'Église ; il n'est pas toute l'Église. Le mot Église est un mot collectif, qui ne peut s'entendre d'aucune individualité séparée, quelle qu'elle soit. L'Église de Jésus-Christ a pour chef nécessaire le Pape, et il n'y a pas d'Église de Jésus-Christ sans le Pape : ce serait un corps sans tête. Mais le Pape n'est pas et n'a jamais prétendu être toute l'Église. Le vrai et légitime usage pratique de ce mot célèbre, c'est que, dans les divisions produites, par les schismes et les hérésies, pour reconnaître où est l'Église, il faut regarder où est le Pape. C'est ainsi que nous sommes certains que l'Église russe, l'Église anglicane ne sont pas l'Église de Jésus-Christ, parce qu'elles n'ont pas le Pape avec elles ; et au contraire l'Église catholique romaine est la vraie Église, parce qu'elle reconnaît le successeur de Pierre pour Chef : *Ubi Petrus, ibi Ecclesia.*

Ne paraissons donc pas, Messieurs, séparer, aux yeux des fidèles, par une définition qui les troublerait, ce qui ne doit pas être séparé : le Pape et l'Épiscopat.

Certaines écoles théologiques ont eu longtemps ici le même tort, en sens contraire : les uns voulant séparer le Pape de l'Épiscopat, et les autres l'Épiscopat du Pape.

L'Église est un corps vivant : *Corpus.* C'est là le mot sans cesse répété par saint Paul, qui s'applique à montrer dans ce corps mystique les rapports de la tête et des membres, et l'harmonie de l'organisme tout entier.

Le Pape est la tête, le Chef visible de l'Église.

Mais si l'on met la tête d'un côté et le corps de l'autre, où sera la vie ?

L'Église est un édifice : *ædificabo Ecclesiam meam;* pourquoi vouloir isoler le fondement de l'édifice, et l'édifice du fondement ?

L'Église est bâtie sur la pierre : oui, mais au-dessus de la pierre il y a l'édifice, et la pierre n'est le fondement que par sa liaison avec l'édifice : *Super hanc petram ædificabo Ecclesiam meam.*

Certains disent : Pierre est tout. Évidemment non : le Chef n'est pas tout le corps.

Il est le fondement, il n'est pas tout l'édifice.

L'édifice sans le fondement croulerait ; le fondement sans l'édifice ne serait le fondement de rien.

Point donc de séparation, Messieurs, ni germaniste, ni romaniste, ni gallicane, ni ultramontaine, ni dans les définitions dogmatiques, ni autrement, Jésus-Christ a voulu autre chose : *Unum sint !*

Laissons-là les vieilles et vaines querelles !

Les fidèles ne comprennent que l'Église avec son Chef suprême, et le chef avec l'Église.

Cette conception de l'Église ne nuit en reste en rien à la divine autorité et l'initiative souveraine du Pontife romain.

Successeur de Pierre, Vicaire de Jésus-Christ, en qui réside la plénitude de la puissance apostolique, Chef de tous les Évêques, Pontife de la chaire principale, à laquelle toutes les autres gardent l'unité, Pasteur universel non-seulement des brebis mais aussi des Pasteurs, bouche de l'Église, clef de voûte de la catholicité :

Voilà le Pape, voilà la tête de l'Église enseignante.

Et voici les Évêques : Successeurs des apôtres, Juges et Docteurs, avec lesquels Jésus-Christ est chaque jour et jusqu'à la consommation des siècles ; Pasteurs des peuples, sous l'autorité supérieure et principale du Pontife souverain : *posés par l'Esprit Saint pour régir l'Église de Dieu, et enseigner toutes les nations :*

Telle est l'économie toute puissante de cette mystérieuse et vivante unité de l'Église où tout est divin, parce que tout est un, et où l'assemblage et la correspondance sont tels que chaque partie, quand elle est à sa place, participe à la force du tout.

Non, n'étonnons pas les fidèles en portant la critique sur cette divine constitution : ne creusons pas autour et au-dessus de ce fondements sacrés : que personne ne sépare ce que Jésus-Christ a fait pour demeurer éternellement uni.

Ah ! que plutôt, nous serrant tous plus que jamais avec vénération, obéissance et amour, autour du Souverain-Pontife, non éloignions de nous qu'à l'ombre même de la division ! Que tous, nous oubliant généreusement nous-mêmes, et sacrifiant à l'Église nos préoccupations personnelles, nous travaillions unanimement à la conservation de cette paix et de cette unité où Dieu habite ! C'est alors, mais alors seulement, que nous présenterons au monde le spectacle de cette *grande armée rangée en bataille,* dont parle l'Ecriture ; *invincible, parce qu'elle est rangée.* Et c'est alors aussi que, par l'exemple non moins que par la doctrine nous offrirons à la société en péril le secours de Dieu qu'elle attend, et cette dernière ressource de vie qu'elle appelle à grands cris.

XV. Voilà, Messieurs, bien des détails

de théologie que j'aurais voulu éviter ; je les destine au clergé, mais ils tomberont aussi sur le grand chemin, sur la pierre et parmi les ronces, au milieu des oiseaux moqueurs, des ennemis et des ignorants. Du reste, que nul ne s'étonne des opinions agitées dans nos écoles. Cette diversité, ces discussions entre théologiens, prouvent la liberté, *in dubiis libertas*, et aussi la charité, *in omnibus caritas*. Mais quand il faut arriver aux décisions nécessaires sur lesquelles l'accord doit se faire, *in necessariis unitas*, nous ne sommes pas alors des philosophes qui disputent, nous sommes des docteurs qui enseignent, et des témoins qui déposent.

Or nous devons nous consumer en réflexions, en distinctions, en scrupules, avant de donner quelque chose à porter à vos esprits ou à vos consciences, hommes légers qui vous moquez d'un labeur entrepris pour vous ! Vous ne vous plaignez pas des calculs minutieux des astronomes et des marins, avant de vous embarquer, ni des investigations du juge qui tient votre sort entre les mains. Les théologiens méritent aussi vos respects dans des recherches qui regardent vos âmes et la vérité. Ne vous moquez pas, et ne vous troublez pas. Au lieu d'écouter aux portes de nos écoles, entrez dans cet admirable temple de la vérité chrétienne, dont dix-neuf siècles n'ont pas arraché une pierre, là où l'on rencontre cette alliance unique de l'assistance de Dieu et de l'unanimité des témoignages, qui s'appelle l'Église : semblable en quelque sorte au système lumineux du monde, qui se compose d'un principal foyer, d'astres sans nombre et d'une seule et même lumière en tous lieux répandue. Dans l'éclat d'un midi tranquille, un seul foyer semble répandre la lumière ; mais si la nuit s'obscurcit, on voit au firmament des astres innombrables, afin que l'homme puisse toujours se conduire, mille rayons se fondant sur sa tête dans une seule clarté.

XVI. Je voudrais résumer toute cette longue série de questions, et exprimer clairement l'état de mon âme.

Nous avons bien des combats, et c'est la vie ! mais sur cette grande question de l'Église, nous avons la paix. Nul catholique ne doute de l'infaillibilité de l'Église ; comme nul ne doute de la Primauté du Pape, qui institue les Évêques, convoque les Conciles, propose les décrets, confirme les décisions ; nul ne doute de la perpétuité, de l'unanimité de la tradition sur tout cela, depuis dix-neuf siècles. Tous les fidèles, après avoir lu l'Évangile, consulté l'histoire,

écouté leurs pasteurs, récitent du fond du cœur : *Credo Ecclesiam, unam, sanctam, catholicam, apostolicam.* Et de fait, entre les témoignages des Évêques, des Papes, des Apôtres, et du Christ, depuis le commencement, il y a un accord infaillible, et Dieu même est dans cet accord.

Tout à coup, quelques-uns se sont mis à demander en qui réside originairement dans cette Église l'infaillibilité ? Et les yeux fixés sur un fait merveilleux, on se met à agiter des questions. Devant un fait, on se plaît à remuer des hypothèses. Devant une solution, les éléments du problème sont remis en doute, et un procès jugé, terminé par un accord admirable, est repris, ranimé, remis au feu ! Aussitôt, et à l'énoncé du problème, l'homme ennemi se réveille, et les fidèles sont déconcertés, l'Orient arrêté, les protestants refoulés, les gouvernements inquiets, les plus tristes pages de l'histoire du passé remises en lumière, les Évêques attristés, la paix des âmes compromise, et la voie du salut rendue plus difficile. Pourquoi ? dans quel intérêt ? avec quel profit ?

Demain, quelle que fût la conduite adoptée, qu'arriverait-il ? Ce qu'on ne discutait pas serait discuté, ce qu'on oubliait serait reproduit, et une fois l'habitude des discussions reprise, plus de paix !

Eh bien, non ! nous ne nous réunirons pas pour substituer la division à l'unanimité, la dispute à l'amour.

Par la grâce de Dieu, l'Église de France a, depuis deux siècles, largement mérité d'être affranchie de tous les ombrages surannés. Cette Église, j'ose le dire, a été, et elle le serait toujours, héroïne et martyre de l'Unité. Depuis cent années surtout, il n'est pas de branche de l'arbre divin qui ait été mieux unie au tronc et à la racine, en s'étendant plus loin, avec plus de zèle, par-delà toutes les frontières ; pas de branche plus catholique, pas de branche plus apostolique, pas de branche plus romaine. Nos prédécesseurs sont morts sur l'échafaud, pour ne pas rompre l'unité. Ils ont accepté l'exil et la confiscation sans céder, ni à l'oppression du peuple, ni à la tyrannie du maître absolu. Ils se sont rencontrés sur toutes les routes de l'exil avec Pie VI et Pie VII, dans la communion du martyre. C'est dans le Clergé français que Pie VII a trouvé ses plus vives consolations. Les Églises des États-Unis ont commencé par des Évêques français. Ce sont les Évêques français qui ont défendu, sans faiblir, la Pologne opprimée, l'Irlande affamée, l'Orient écrasé. Nous avons tous ensemble réclamé et obtenu la liberté des pères de famille

U

dans l'éducation de leurs enfants, tous ensemble défendu la liberté des associations religieuses, liberté de la charité, le développement des missions civilisatrices. L'Église entière doit à la France les Sœurs de charité, les Frères des écoles chrétiennes, l'Œuvre de la propagation de la foi dans les deux mondes, les Conférences de Saint-Vincent de Paul, les colléges des Jésuites et des Dominicains, les Petites-Sœurs des pauvres, et toute cette incomparable armée pacifique qui est, comme notre armée guerrière, la première du monde. Depuis vingt ans, le Siége pontifical a été attaqué, frappé, trahi, opprimé, livré à des adversaires implacables. Les Évêques français l'ont défendu, servi, assisté, aimé, exalté, consolé dans un magnifique mouvement que le temps n'a pas affaibli. Et ne sont-ce pas eux encore, dans les mauvais jours que nous traversons, qui ont donné la première impulsion à cette œuvre si touchante et aujourd'hui universelle du Denier de saint Pierre? Ah! j'ose dire que tant de dévouement à Rome et au monde catholique, donne à l'Église de France le droit d'être crue, le droit d'être entendue, quand elle parle de son attachement au Saint-Siége, et au Vicaire de Notre-Seigneur Jésus-Christ.

Que dis-je! Tel est l'entraînement de la France vers le centre de l'unité, que les doctrines exagérées passent les monts en venant de France, et c'est de Rome que part la modération, le tempérament, la sagesse; c'est Rome qui arrête la *furia francese*, et se refuse à mettre les excès dans les dogmes. Aussi mes frères, ne soyez pas inquiets! Hommes de foi, ne vous troublez pas!

Si je me suis décidé à entrer avec vous, Messieurs, et en public dans ces détails, c'est par un secret instinct que j'avais plutôt à calmer des émotions dans mon pays qu'à devancer des objections à Rome. J'en suis convaincu : à peine aurai-je touché la terre sacrée, à peine aurai-je baisé le tombeau des Apôtres, que je me sentirai dans la paix, hors de la bataille, au sein d'une assemblée présidée par un Père et composée de Frères. Là, tous les bruits expireront, toutes les ingérences téméraires cesseront, toutes les imprudences disparaîtront, les flots et les vents seront apaisés. Nous penserons aux âmes dont nous répondons devant Dieu, nous penserons au Dieu qui nous voit et nous jugera, nous penserons aux Apôtres, nous croirons les voir encore en face du monde à conquérir et du Maître à écouter ; et lorsqu'à la place de ce Maître souverain des esprits, son Vicaire sur la terre redira à chacun de nous : "Mon Frère, m'aimez-vous?" ah! croyez que votre vieil Évêque ne sera pas le dernier à répondre : "Père, vous savez si je vous aime! comme disait le doux Évêque de Genève : *Dans la contention d'amour pour le Vicaire de Jésus-Christ*, je ne me suis laissé vaincre par personne. Depuis vingt ans, mes cheveux ont blanchi, ma main s'est épuisée à votre service. O Saint-Père, Dieu sait que la dernière parole de mes lèvres et le dernier soupir de mon cœur appartiendront à l'Église et à vous."

Veuillez agréer, Messieurs et chers Coopérateurs, la nouvelle assurance de mon profond et religieux dévouement.

✠ FELIX, *Evêque d'Orléans*.

Orléans, ce 11 novembre, en la fête de saint Martin.

DOCUMENT VII.

PROMULGAZIONE DEL GIUBBILEO.

Omnibus Christifidelibus, praesentes litteras inspecturis, PIUS PP. IX salutem et apostolicam benedictionem.

Nemo certe ignorat, Oecumenicum Concilium a Nobis fuisse indictum in Basilica Nostra Vaticana, die 8 futuri mensis Decembris, Immaculatae Sanctissimaeque Deiparae Virginis Mariae Conceptioni sacro, inchoandum. Itaque hoc potissimum tempore nunquam desistimus in humilitate cordis Nostri ferventissimis precibus orare et obsecrare clementissimum luminum et misericordiarum Patrem, a quo omne datum optimum, et omne donum perfectum descendit,[1] ut mittat de caelis sedium suarum assistricem sapientiam, quae Nobiscum sit, et Nobiscum laboret, et sciamus quid acceptum sit apud eum.[2] Et quo facilius Deus Nostris annuat votis, et inclinet aures suas ad preces Nostras, omnium Christifidelium religionem, ac pietatem excitare decrevimus, ut conjunctis Nobiscum precibus, Omnipotentis dexterae auxilium, et caeleste lumen imploremus, quo in hoc Concilio ea omnia statuere valeamus, quae ad communem totius populi christiani salutem, utilitatemque, ac maiorem catholicae Ecclesiae gloriam et felicitatem, ac pacem maxime pertinent. Et quoniam compertum est, gratiores Deo esse hominum preces si mundo corde, hoc est animis ab omni scelere integris ad ipsum accedant, iccirco hac occasione caelestes Indulgentiarum thesauros dispensationi Nostrae commissos Apostolica liberalitate Christifidelibus reserare constituimus,

[1] Sanct. Jac., cap. i., v. 1, 17.
[2] Sapient., cap. ix., v. 4, 10.

ut inde ad veram poenitentiam inceusi, et per Poenitentiae Sacramentum a peccatorum maculis expiati, ad Thronum Dei fidentius accedant, eiusque misericordiam consequantur, et gratiam in auxilio opportuno.

Hoc nos consilio Indulgentiam ad instar Iubilaei Catholico Orbi denunciamus. Quamobrem de Omnipotentis Dei misericordia, ac Beatorum Petri et Pauli Apostolorum eius auctoritate confisi, ex illa ligandi ac solvendi potestate, quam Nobis Dominus, licet indignis, contulit, universis ac singulis utriusque sexus Christifidelibus in alma Urbe Nostra degentibus, vel ad eam advenientibus, qui a die primo futuri mensis Iunii usque ad diem, quo Oecumenica Synodus a Nobis indicta fuerit absoluta, S. Ioannis in Laterano, Principis Apostolorum, et Sanctae Mariae Maioris Basilicas, vel earum aliquam bis visitaverint, ibique per aliquot temporis spatium pro omnium misere errantium conversione, pro sanctissimae fidei propagatione, et pro catholicae Ecclesiae pace, tranquillitate, ac triumpho devote oraverint, et praeter consueta quatuor anni tempora tribus diebus, etiam non continuis, nempe quarta et sexta feria, et Sabbato iciunaverint, et intra commemoratum temporis spatium peccata sua confessi Sanctissimum Eucharistiae Sacramentum reverenter susceperint, et pauperibus aliquam eleemosynam, prout unicuique devotio suggerit, erogaverint; ceteris vero extra Urbem praedictam ubicumque degentibus, qui Ecclesias, ab Ordinariis locorum, vel eorum Vicariis, seu Officialibus, aut de illorum mandato, et, ipsis deficientibus, per eos, qui ibi curam animarum exercent, postquam ad illorum notitiam hae Nostrae Litterae pervenerint, de ignandas, vel earum aliquam praefiniti temporis spatio bis visitaverint, aliaque recensita opera devote peregerint, plenissimam omnium peccatorum suorum remissionem et Indulgentiam, sicut in anno Iubilaei visitantibus certas Ecclesias intra, et extra Urbem praedictam concedi consuevit, tenore praesentium misericorditer in Domino concedimus atque indulgemus: quae Indulgentia animabus etiam quae Deo in caritate coniunctae ex hac vita migraverint, per modum suffragii applicari poterit.

Concedimus etiam, ut navigantes atque iter agentes, quam primum ad sua se domicilia receperint, operibus suprascriptis, et bis visitata Ecclesia Cathedrali, vel Maiori, vel propria Parochiali loci ipsorum domicilii, eamdem Indulgentiam consequi possint, et valeant. Regularibus vero personis utriusque sexus etiam in claustris perpetuo degentibus, necnon aliis quibuscumque tam laicis, quam saecularibus, itemque in carcere, aut captivitate existentibus, vel aliqua corporis infirmitate, seu alio quocumque impedimento detentis, qui memorata opera, vel eorum aliqua praestare nequiverint, ut illa Confessarius ex actu approbatis a locorum Ordinariis in alia pietatis opera commutare, vel in aliud proximum tempus prorogare possit, eaque iniungere, quae ipsi poenitentes efficere possint cum facultate etiam dispensandi super Communione cum pueris, qui nondum ad primam Communionem admissi fuerint, pariter concedimus atque indulgemus.

Insuper omnibus et singulis Christifidelibus Saecularibus et Regularibus cuiusvis Ordinis et Instituti, etiam specialiter nominandi, licentiam concedimus, et facultatem, ut sibi ad hunc effectum eligere possint quemcumque Presbyterum Confessarium, tam Saecularem, quam Regularem ex actu approbatis a locorum Ordinariis (qua facultate uti possint etiam Moniales, Novitiae, aliaeque mulieres intra claustra degentes, dummodo Confessarius approbatus sit pro Monialibus), qui eos ab excommunicationis, suspensionis, aliisque ecclesiasticis sententiis, et censuris a iure vel ab homine quavis de causa latis vel inflictis praeter infra exceptas, necnon ab omnibus peccatis, excessibus, criminibus et delictis quantumvis gravibus et enormibus, etiam locorum Ordinariis, sive Nobis, et Sedi Apostolicae speciali licet forma reservatis, et quorum absolutio alias quantumvis ampla non intelligeretur concessa, in foro conscientiae, et hac vice tantum absolvere valeant; et insuper vota quaecumque etiam iurata, et Sedi Apostolicae reservata (castitatis, religionis, et obligationis, quae a tertio acceptata fuerit, seu in quibus agatur de praeiudicio tertii semper exceptis, quatenus ea vota sint perfecta et absoluta, necnon poenalibus, quae praeservativa a peccatis nuncupantur, nisi commutatio futura indicetur eiusmodi ut non minus a peccato committendo refraenet, quam prior voti materia), in alia pia et salutaria opera dispensando commutare, iniuncta tamen eis, et eorum cuilibet in supradictis omnibus poenitentia salutari, aliisque eiusdem Confessarii arbitrio iniungendis.

Concedimus insuper facultatem dispensandi super irregularitate ex violatione Censurarum contracta, quatenus ad forum externum non sit deducta, vel de facili deducenda. Non intendimus autem per praesentes super alia quavis irregularitate sive ex defectu, vel publica, vel occulta, aut nota, aliaque incapacitate, aut inhabilitate quoquomodo contracta dispensare, vel aliquam facultatem tribuere super praemissis dispensandi, seu habilitandi, et in pristinum statum restituendi, etiam in foro conscientiae neque etiam derogare Constitutioni cum appositis declarationibus editae a fel. rec. Benedicto XIV, Praedecessore Nostro *Sacramentum Poenitentiae*, quoad inhabilitatem absolvendi complicem, et quoad obligationem denunciationis ; neque easdem praesentes iis, qui a Nobis, et ab Apostolica Sede, vel aliquo Praelato, seu Iudice Ecclesiastico nominatim excommunicati, suspensi, interdicti, seu alias in sententias, et censuras incidisse declarati, vel publice denunciati fuerint, nisi intra tempus praefinitum satisfecerint, aut cum partibus concordaverint, nullomodo suffragari posse aut debere. Quod si intra praefinitum terminum iudicio Confessari satisfacere non potuerint, absolvi posse concedimus in foro conscientiae ad effectum dumtaxat assequendi Indulgentias Iubilaei, iniuncta obligatione satisfaciendi statim ac poterunt.

Quapropter in virtute sanctae obedientiae tenore praesentium districte praecipimus, atque mandamus omnibus, et quibuscumque Ordinariis locorum ubicumque existentibus, eorumque Vicariis et Officialibus, vel ipsis deficientibus, illis, qui curam animarum exercent, ut cum praesentium Litterarum transumpta, aut exempla etiam impressa acceperint, illa, ubi primum pro temporum ac locorum ratione satius in Domino censuerint, per suas Ecclesias ac Dioeceses, Provincias, Civitates, Oppida, Terras, et loca publicent, vel publicari faciant, populisque etiam Verbi Dei praedicatione, quoad fieri possit, rite praeparatis, Ecclesiam, seu Ecclesias visitandas pro praesenti Iubilaeo designent.

Non obstantibus Constitutionibus, et Ordinationibus Apostolicis, praesertim quibus facultas absolvendi in certis tunc expressis casibus ita romano Pontificis pro tempore existenti reservatur, ut nec etiam similes, vel dissimiles Indulgentiarum, et facultatum huiusmodi concessiones, nisi de illis expressa mentio, aut specialis derogatio fiat, cuiquam suffragari possint ; necnon regula de non concedendis Indulgentiis ad instar ; ac quorumcumque Ordinum, et Congregationum, sive Institutorum etiam iuramento, confirmatione Apostolica, vel quavis firmitate alia roboratis, statutis et consuetudinibus, privilegiis quoque, indultis, et Litteris Apostolicis eisdem Ordinibus, Congregationibus, et Institutis, illorumque personis quomodolibet concessis, approbatis, et innovatis: quibus omnibus et singulis etiamsi de illis, eorumque totis tenoribus, specialis,

specifica, expressa et individua, non autem per clausulas generales idem importantes, mentio, seu alia quaevis expressio habenda, aut ulia aliqua exquisita forma ad hoc servanda foret, illorum tenores praesentibus pro sufficienter expressis, ac formam in iis traditam pro servata habentes, hac vice specialiter, nominatim et expresse ad effectum praemissorum, derogamus, ceterisque contrariis quibuscumque.

Praecipimus autem, a commemorato die primo Iunii usque ad diem, quo Oecumenica Synodus finem habuerit, ab omnibus universis catholici Orbis utriusque Cleri Sacerdotibus quotidie addi in Missam Conventualem, Sacrificium fieri in omnibus huius Urbis Patriarchalibus, aliisque Basilicis, et Collegialibus et Collegiatis Ecclesiis in quarum Canonicis, atque etiam in singulis cuiusquo Religiosae Familiae Ecclesiis Regularium, qui Conventualem Missam celebrare tenentur, feria quinque quinta, qua festum duplex primae et secundae classis non agatur, quin tamen haec de Spiritu Sancto Missa ullam habeat applicationis obligationem.

Ut autem praesentes Nostrae, quae ad singula loca deferri non possunt, ad omnium notitiam facilius deveniant, volumus ut praesentium transumptis, vel exemplis etiam impressis, manu alicuius Notarii publici subscriptis, et sigillo personae in dignitate ecclesiastica constitutae munitis, ubicumque locorum et gentium, eadem prorsus fides habeatur, quae haberetur ipsis praesentibus, si forent exhibitae vel ostensae.

Datum Romae apud Sanctum Petrum sub Annulo Piscatoris, die 11 Aprilis anno 1869.

Pontificatus Nostri Anno Vicesimotertio.

N. *Card.* PARACCIANI CLARELLI.

(Dalla *Civiltà Cattolica*,
1° maggio 1869.)

DOCUMENT VIII.

Allocuzione tenuta nella Congregazione generale innanzi la prima sessione del Concilio Vaticano dal Santissimo nostro Signore per la divina Provvidenza PAPA PIO IX, il dì 2 dicembre dell' anno 1869 ai vescovi del mondo cattolico per lo stesso Concilio in Roma convenuti.

VENERABILES FRATRES.

Sacri oecumenici Vaticani Concilii Conventus post paucos hinc dies auspicaturi nihil opportunius Nobisque iucundius existimavimus, VV. FF., quam ut Vos universos hodierno die iuxta Nostra hic desideria congregatos alloqui, ac praecipuam caritatem, quam intimo corde alimus, Vobis aperire possemus. Cum enim de re maxima agatur, qualis est illa in qua de remediis comparandis agitur tot malis, quae Christianam et civilem societatem hoc tempore perturbant, putavimus Apostolica Nostra sollicitudine dignum esse, et tantae rei magnitudini consentaneum, ut antequam Conciliarium rerum actio initium habeat, in omnis gratiae auspicium Vobis caelestis benedictionis opem a Deo clementissimo precaremur; ac necessarium censuimus, Vobis eas tradere normas, Apostolicis Nostris litteris consignatus atque editas, quas ad omnia in Conciliaribus actionibus rite et ordine agenda, constituenda esse iudicavimus. Hoc autem illud est, VV. FF., quod Deo et immaculata Deipara votis Nostris annuente hodierno die in amplissimo hoc Vestro conventu peraginus; nec satis verbis explicare possumus ingentem eam consolationem, quam Vestra haec exoptata, et debita Apostolicae vocis obsequio frequentia Nobis ingerit, cum Vos tandem ex omnibus Catholici Orbis partibus in hanc almam Urbem, indicti a Nobis Concilii causa convenisse, et summa animorum consensione Nobiscum coniunctos aspicimus: quos eximia erga Nos et Apostolicam Sedem devotio, mirificus ad navandam Christo Regno operum ardor, et in pluribus etiam tribulationum pro Christo perpessio iure efficit cordi Nostro carissimos. Haec autem, VV. FF., haec Vestra Nobiscum coniunctio eo gratior Nobis accidit, quod in ea haerentes Apostolorum vestigiis insistimus, qui suae unanimae et constantis cum divino Magistro coniunctionis luculenta Nobis exempla reliquerunt. Nostis enim ex sacris litteris, cum Christus Dominus Palestinae regiones peragrans iter faceret per civitates et castella, praedicans et evangelizans regnum Dei, Eius lateri Apostolos pari omnes studio adhaesisse, et duodecim cum Illo, uti Sanctus Lucas [1] loquitur, fideliter quancumque iter haberet, esse versatos. Atque haec Apostolorum coniunctio splendidius etiam enituit eo tempore, cum caelestis Magister docens in Capharnaum, de divinae Eucharistiae mysterio coram Hebraeis fusiori sermone pertractavit: tunc enim cum eus illa carnalis et obtusioris sensus sibi de tantae caritatis opere persuadere non posset, utque ita Magistri pertaesum se ostendisset, ut multi discipulorum, Domine testante, abirent retro et [2] non cum Illo ambularent, Apostolorum tamen amor in Magistri veneratione et obsequio immotus perstitit, et Iesu Apostolos percunctante

num et ipsi vellent abire, graviter id ferens Petrus in eas voces erupit: "Domine ad quem ibimus?" ac rationem adiecit quare Dominum constanti fide sequi velle statueret: "Verba vitae aeternae habes." Haec nos animo recolentes, quid dulcius aut iucundius hac nostra coniunctione reputare, quid porro etiam firmius ac stabilius tueri debeamus? Non deerunt certe Nobis, una licet in Christi nomine coniunctis, non deerunt contradictiones ac dimicationes subeundae, nec inimicus homo segnis erit, nil magis cupiens quam superseminare zizania; at Nos memores Apostolicae firmitudinis et constantiae, quae Domini praeconio laudari meruit: "Vos estis qui permansistis mecum in tentationibus meis," [1] memores Redemptoris Nostri diserto denunciantis: "Qui mecum non est contra me est," officii pariter Nostri memores esse debebimus, omnique studio curare, ut inconcussa fide ac firmitate Christum sequamur, Illique omni tempore concordibus animis adhaereamus. In ea enim, VV. FF., conditione constituti sumus, ut in acie adversus multiplices eosdemque acerrimos hostes, diuturna iam contentione versemur. Utamur oportet spiritualibus militiae Nostrae armis, totumque certaminis vim, tum divina iunixi auctoritate, tum caritati, patientiae, precationis et constantiae clypeo sustineamus. Nihil autem metus est ne vires nobis in hac dimicatione deficiant, si in Auctorem et Consumatorem Fidei nostrae, oculos animosque coniicere voluerimus. Si enim Apostoli oculis et cogitatione in Christo Iesu defixi satis ex hoc animi viriumque sumpserunt, ut adversa quaeque strenue perferrent, Nos pariter Ipsum adspicientes in salutari pignore Redemptionis nostrae, ex hoc aspectu, unde divina manat virtus, Nos eam vim roburque inveniemus, quo calumnias, iniurias, inimicorum artes superemus, ac salutem Nobis, totque etiam miseris a via veritatis errantibus ex Christi Cruce haurire laetabimur. Neque vero Redemptorem Nostrum respicere contenti, eam quoque mentis docilitatem induamus necesse est, ut Eidem libenter toto cordis affectu audientes simus. Hoc est enim quod ipse Pater caelestis Maiestatis suae auctoritate praecepit, cum revelante Christo Domino gloriam suam in monte praecelso coram electis testibus: "Hic est, inquit, Filius meus dilectus in quo mihi bene complacui, Ipsum audite." Iesum igitur prono mentis obsequio audiamus utique in omni re, ut in ea praecipue quum Ipse ita cordi habuit, ut praenoscens difficultates quibus ipsa obnoxia futura esset in mundo, de illa ipsa Patrem suum obsecrare

[1] Luc., 8, 1.   [2] Ioann., 6, 67.   [1] Luc., 22, 28.

in novissima Coena effusis iteratisque votis non omiserit: "Pater Sancte, serva eos in nomine tuo quos dedisti mihi, ut sint unum sicut et nos."[1] Una itaque anima cum uno corde in Christo Iesu sit cunctis. Non aliud sane Nobis maiori consolationi futurum est quam si obsequentem Christi monitis aurem cordis iugiter praebuerimus, quo pacto et Nos esse cum Christo agnoscemus, et perspicuum aeternae salutis pignus inesse reperiemus in Nobis: "Qui enim ex Deo est, verba Dei audit."[2]

Has Pontificiae Nostrae cohortationis voces ex intimo corde depromptas, Omnipotens et Misericors Deus, Deipara Immaculata deprecante, potenti sua ope confirmet, officiatque propitius, ut uberibus fructibus augeantur. Convertat deinde faciem suam ad Vos, VV. FF., ac tum corpora tum animos Vestros benedictionis suae gratia prosequatur: corpora nempe, ut labores omnes, qui a Vestro sacro ministerio abesse non possunt, strenue alacriterque ferre valeatis; animos vero, ut caelestibus auxiliis abunde repleti, sacerdotalis vitae exemplis et virtutum omnium splendore in Christiani Gregis salutem praeluceatis. Huius autem benedictionis gratia Vobis contineuter adsit, atque omnibus vitae Vestrae diebus clementer adspiret, ut dies pleni inveniantur in Vobis, pleni sanctitatis et iustitiae, pleni sanctorum operum fructibus, in quibus verae nobis divitiae et gloria continetur. Atque ita Nobis continget feliciter ut expleto mortalis peregrinationis cursu, in novissimo illo vitae die dicere cum Propheta Rege non vereamur: "Laetatus sum in his quae dicta sunt mihi, in domum Domini ibimus;" atque aditum Nobis patere plano confidamus in Montem sanctum Sion, caelestem Hierusalem.

(Dalla *Civiltà Cattolica*, 18 decembre 1869.)

DOCUMENT IX.

Lettere Apostoliche della Santità di nostro Signore per divina Provvidenza PAPA PIO IX, colle quali si stabilisce l'ordine generale da osservarsi nella celebrazione del sacrosanto ecumenico Concilio Vaticano.

PIVS PAPA IX

AD FVTVRAM REI MEMORIAM.

Multiplices inter, quibus divexamur angustias, ad Divinae Clementiae, quae conso-

[1] Ioann., 17, 11. [2] Ioann., 8, 47.

latur *Nos in omni tribulatione Nostra*,[1] gratias persolvendas maxime excitamur, qua propitiante, illud celeriter Nobis continget, ut sacrosanctum generale et oecumenicum Concilium Vaticanum iam a Nobis ea adspirante indictum, feliciter auspicemur. Gaudium autem in Domino iure praecipimus, quod salutares Concilii eiusdem conventus solemni die Immaculatae Dei Matris Mariae semper Virginis Conceptioni sacro, atque adeo sub potentibus maternisque auspiciis eius aggressuri sumus. eosque in Vaticana Nostra Basilica inituri ante Beatissimi Petri cineres, qui *in accepta fortitudine Petrae perseverans suscepta Ecclesiae gubernacula non reliquit, et in quo omnium Pastorum sollicitudo, cum commendatarum sibi ovium custodia perseverat*.[2] Iamvero memores hoc oecumenicum Concilium a Nobis convocatum fuisse, ut extirpandis erroribus, quos praesertim huius saeculi conflavit impietas, removendis malis, quibus Ecclesia affligitur, emendandis moribus et utriusque Cleri disciplinae instaurandae, coniuncta Nobiscum sacrorum Ecclesiae Antistitum adhibeatur opera, ac probe noscentes, quo studio intentaque sollicitudine curare debeamus, ut ea omnia, quae ad rectam rationem tam salutaris negotii gerendi, tractandi ac perficiendi pertinent, ex sancta maiorum disciplina institutisque statuantur, idcirco Apostolica Nostra auctoritate ea quae sequuntur decernimus, atque ab omnibus in hoc Vaticano Concilio servanda esse praecipimus.

I.

De modo vivendi in Concilio.

Reputantes animo quod *omne datum optimum, et omne donum perfectum desursum est, descendens a Patre luminum*,[3] quodque nihil Caelestis Patris benignitati pronius est, quam ut *spiritum bonum petentibus se*,[4] iam Nos, dum Apostolicis Nostris Litteris,[5] die undecimo Aprilis hoc anno datis, Ecclesiae thesauros sacrosancti huius Concilii occasione Christifidelibus reseravimus, non solum eosdem Christifideles vehementer hortati sumus, ut emundantes *conscientiam ab operibus mortuis ad serviendum Deo viventi*[6] orationibus, obsecrationibus, ieiuniis aliisque pietatis actibus insistere velint: sed etiam Divini Spiritus lumen et opem in sacrosancto Missae sacrificio celebrando, quotidie in universo Orbe

[1] II. Corinth. i. 4.
[2] San. Leo P. Serm. 2, *in Anniver. Assumptionis suae*. [3] Iacob. i. 17.
[4] Luc., xi., 13. [5] Litt. Nost. 11 aprilis 1869.
[6] Ep. ad Hebraec., ix., 14.

Catholico implorari mandavimus, ad prosperum a Domino huic Concilio exitum, et salutares ex eo Ecclesiae sanctae fructus impetrandos.

Quas quidem adhortationes et praescriptiones modo renovantes et confirmantes, id praeterea iubemus, ut in huius almae Urbis Nostrae Ecclesiis, sacrosancta Synodo perdurante singulis diebus Dominicis hora, quae pro fideli populo magis congrua videatur, Litaniae aliaeque orationes ad hunc finem constitutae recitentur.

At longe his maius aliquid et excellentius ab Episcopis, aliisque qui in Sacerdotali Ordine censentur hoc Concilium concelebrantibus, praestandum est, quos, uti ministros Christi et dispensatores mysteriorum Dei oportet in omnibus seipsos praebere *exemplum bonorum operum in doctrina, in integritate, in gravitate, ve bum sanum, irreprehensibile, ut his qui ex adverso est vereatur nihil habens malum dicere de nobis.*[1] Quare veterum Conciliorum ac Tridentini nominatim vestigiis inhaerentes hortamur illos omnes in Domino, ut orationi, sacrae lectioni, caelestium rerum meditationibus pro sua cuiusque pietate studiose intendant : ut pure casteque sancto Missae sacrificio, quam fieri possit, frequenter operentur ; animum mentemque ab humanarum rerum curis immunem servent ; modestiam in moribus, in victu temperantiam, et in omni actione religionem retineant. Absint animorum dissidia, absit prava aemulatio et contentio, sed omnibus imperet, quae inter ceteras virtutes eminet charitas, ut illa dominante et in olumi, de hoc sacro Episcoporum Ecclesiae conventu dici possit : *Ecce quam bonum et quam iucundum habitare fratres in unum.*[2] Evigilent demum Patres in domesticorum suorum cura, et christianae ab eis sanctaeque vitae disciplina exigenda, memores quam gravibus verbis Paulus Apostolus praecipiat Episcopis, ut siut suae domui bene praepositi.[3]

II.

De iure et modo proponendi.

Licet ius et munus proponendi negotia, quae in sancta oecumenica Synodo tractari debebunt, de iisque Patrum sententias rogandi nonnisi ad Nos, et ad hanc Apostolicam Sedem pertineat, nihilominus non modo opamur, sed etiam hortamur, ut si qui inter Concilii Patres aliquid proponendum habuerint, quod ad publicam utilitatem conferre posse existiment, id libere exequi velint. Cum vero probe perspiciamus

[1] Ep. ad Tit., ii, 7.   [2] Ps. cxxxii. 8.
[3] I. Timoth. iii, 4.

hanc ipsam rem, nisi congruo tempore et modo perficiatur, non parum necessario Conciliarium actionum ordini officere posse, idcirco statuimus eiusmodi propositiones ita fieri debere, ut earum quaelibet 1. scripto mandetur, ac peculiari Congregationi nonnullorum, tum VV. FF. NN. S. R. E. Cardinalium, tum Synodi Patrum a Nobis deputandae privatim exhibeatur : 2. publicum rei christianae bonum vere respiciat, non singularem dumtaxat unius vel alterius Dioecesis utilitatem : 3. rationes contineat, ob quas utilis et opportuna censetur : 4. nihil praeseferat, quod a constanti Ecclesiae sensu, eiusque inviolabilibus traditionibus alienum sit.

Peculiaris praedicta Congregatio propositiones sibi exhibitas diligenter expendet, suumque circa earum admissionem vel exclusionem consilium Nostro iudicio submittet, ut Nos deinde matura consideratione de iis statuamus, utrum ad Synodalem deliberationem deferri debeant.

III.

De secreto servando in Concilio.

Prudentiae hic ratio Nos admonet, ut secreti fidem, quae in superioribus Conciliis non semel, adiunctorum gravitate exigente, indicenda fuit, in universa huius Concilii actione servandam iubeamus. Si enim unquam alias, hoc maxime tempore haec cautio necessaria visa est, quo in omnem occasionem excubat invidiae conflandae contra Catholicam Ecclesiam eiusque doctrinam, pluribus nocendi opibus pollens impietas. Quapropter praecipimus omnibus et singulis Patribus, Officialibus Concilii, Theologis, Sacrorum Canonum Peritis, ceterisque, qui operam suam Patribus vel Officialibus praedictis quovis modo in rebus huius Concilii praebent, ut decreta et alia quaecumque, quae iis examinanda proponentur, necnon discussiones et singulorum sententias non evulgent, nec alicui extra gremium Concilii pandant, praecipimus pariter ut Officiales Concilii, qui episcopali dignitate praediti non sunt, aliique omnes, qui ratione cuiusvis demandati a Nobis ministerii Conciliaribus disceptationibus inservire debent, iuramentum emittere teneantur de munere fideliter obeundo, et de secreti fide servanda circa ea omnia quae supra praescripta sunt, necnon super iis rebus, quae specialiter ipsis committentur.

IV.

De ordine sedendi, et de non inferendo alicui praeiudicio.

Cum ad tranquillitatem concordiamque animorum tuendam non parum momenti habeat, si in quibuslibet Conciliaribus actibus, unusquisque suae dignitatis ordinem fideliter ac modeste custodiat: hinc ad offensionum occasiones, quoad eius fieri possit, praecidendas, infrascriptum ordinem inter diversas dignitates servari praescribimus.

Primum locum obtinebunt VV. FF. NN. S. R. E. Cardinales Episcopi, Presbyteri, Diaconi; secundum Patriarchae; tertium, ex speciali Nostra indulgentia, Primates, iuxta ordinem suae promotionis ad Primatialem gradum. Id autem pro hac vice tantum indulgemus, atque ita, ut ex hac Nostra concessione nullum ius vel ipsis Primatibus datum, vel aliis imminutum censeri debeat. Quartum locum tenebunt Archiepiscopi, iuxta suite ad Archiepiscopatum promotionis ordinem; quintum Episcopi, pariter iuxta ordinem promotionis suae; sextum Abbates Nullius Dioecesis; septimum Abbates Generales, aliique Generales Moderatores Ordinum Religiosorum, in quibus solemnia vota nuncupantur, etiamsi Vicarii Generalis titulo appellentur, dum tamen re ipsa cum omnibus supremi moderatoris iuribus et privilegiis, universo suo Ordini legitime praesunt.

Ceterum ex superiorum Conciliorum disciplina institutoque decernimus, quod, si forte contigerit, aliquos debito in loco non sedere, et sententiae etiam sub verbo *placet* proferre, Congregationibus interesse, et alios quoscumque actus facere, Concilio durante, nulli propterea praeiudicium generetur, nullique novum ius acquiratur.[1]

V.

De Iudicibus excusationum et querelarum.

Quo graviorum rerum pertractatio, quae in hac sacrosancta Synodo agi gerive debent, minus quam fieri possit, impediatur, aut retardetur ob cognitionem causarum, quae singulos respiciunt: statuimus ut ipsa Synodus per schedulas secretas quinque ex Concilii Patribus eligat in *Iudices excusationum*, quorum erit procurationes et excusationes Praelatorum absentium, necnon eorum postulata, qui, Concilio nondum dimisso, iustam discedendi causam se habere putaverint, excipere, atque ad normam conciliaris disciplinae et SS. Canonum expendere: quod cum fecerint, non quidquam de hisce rebus decernent, sed de omnibus ad Congregationem generalem ordine referent. Praeterea statuimus, ut eadem Synodus pariter per schedulas secretas,

[1] Conc. Trid. Sess. 2. Decret. *De modo viv.* § *Insuper.*

alios quinque ex Patribus eligat, in *Iudices querelarum et controversiarum*.

Hi porro controversias omnes circa ordinem sedendi, vel ius praecedendi, aliasque, si quae forte inter congregatos oriantur, iudicio summario atque *oeconomice*, ut aiunt, ita componere studebunt, ut nulli praeiudicium inferatur: et quatenus componere nequeant, eas Congregationis generalis auctoritati subiicient.

VI.

De Officialibus Concilii.

Quo vero et illud magni refert, ut necessarii ac idonei ministri et officiales, iuxta conciliorem consuetudinem et disciplinam, omnibus in hac Synodo actibus rite et legitime perficiendis designentur, Nos huiusmodi ministeriorum rationem habentes, infrascriptos viros ad ea deligemus et nominamus, scilicet:

1. Generales Concilii custodes, dilectos filios Ioannem Columna et Dominicum Orsini romanos Principes Pontificio Nostro solio Adsistentes.

2. Concilii Secretarium, Venerabilem Fratrem Iosephum Episcopum S. Hippolyti, eique adiic'mus cum officio et titulo Subsecretarii, dilectum filium Ludovicum Iacobini e Nostris et huius Apostolicae Sedis Protonotariis, necnon adiutores, dilectos filios Canonicos Camillum Santori et Angelum Iacobini.

3. Concilii Notarios, dilectos filios Lucam Pacifici, Aloisium Colombo, Ioannem Simeoni, Aloisium Pericoli, et Dominicum Bartolini Nostros et huius Apostolicae Sedis Protonotarios, eisque adiungimus dilectos filios Salvatorem Pallottini et Franciscum Santi Advocatos; qui Notariis eisdem adiutricem operam navent.

4. Scrutatores Suffragiorum, dilectos filios Aloisium Serafini et Franciscum Nardi causarum Palatii Nostri Apostolici Auditores; Aloisium Pellegrini et Leouardum Dialti Nostrae Camerae Apostolicae Clericos; Carolum Cristofori et Alexandrum Montani Signaturae Iustitiae votantes; Fridericum de Falloux du Coudray Nostrae Cancellariae Apostolicae Regentem, et Laurentium Nina Abbreviatorem ex maiori Parco. Hi autem octo scruta'ores in quatuor distincta paria distributi, ita ad excipienda suffragia procedent, ut bina paria unum Conciliaris Aulae latus totidemque alterum obeant; ac praeterea singula paria singulos ex Notariis secum habere debebunt, dum in munere fungendo versantur.

5. Promotores Concilii, dilectos filios Ioan-

nem Baptistam de Dominicis-Tosti, et Philippum Ralli S. Consistorii Advocatos.

6. Magistros Caeremoniarum Concilii, dilectos filios Aloisium Ferrari Antistitem Nostrum domesticum Praefectum, et Pium Martinucci, Camillum Balestra, Remigium Ricci, Iosephum Romagnoli, Petrum Iosephum Rinaldi-Bucci, Antonium Cataldi, Alexandrum Tortoli, Augustinum Accoramboni, Aloisium Sinistri, Franciscum Riggi, Antonium Gattoni, Balthasarem Baccinetti, Caesarem Togni, Rochum Massi, Nostros, et huius Apostolicae Sedis Caeremoniarios.

7. Assignatores locorum, dilectos filios Henricum Folchi Praefectum, ac Aloisium Naselli, Edmundum Stonor, Paulum Bastide, Aloisium Pallotti intimos Nostros Cubicularios, et dilectos filios Scipionem Perilli, Gustavum Gallot, Franciscum Rognani, Nicolaum Vorsak, et Philippum Silvestri Cubicularios Nostros honorarios.

VII.

De Congregationibus generalibus Patrum.

Ad ea modo curam convertentes, quae Congregationum generalium ordinem respiciunt, statuimus ac decernimus, ut iisdem Patrum Congregationibus, quae publicis sessionibus praemittuntur quinque ex VV. FF. NN. S. R. E. Cardinalibus Nostro Nomine et Auctoritate praesint, et ad hoc munus eligimus et nominamus, Venerabilem Fratrem Nostrum Carolum S. R. E. Cardinalem Episcopum Sabinensem De Reisach nuncupatum, dilectos filios Nostros S. R. E. Presbyteros Cardinales Antoninum titulo SS. Quatuor Coronatorum De Luca nuncupatum ; Iosephum Andream titulo S. Hieronymi Illyricorum Bizzarri nuncupatum, et dilectum filium Nostrum Hannibalem S. R. E. Cardinalem Diaconum S. Mariae in Aquiro Capalti nuncupatum.

Hi autem Praesides, praeter alia, quae ad aptam horum Conventuum moderationem spectant, curabunt ut in rebus pertractandis initium fiat a disceptatione eorum, quae ad fidem pertinent; deinde integrum ipsis erit consultationes in fidei vel disciplinae capite conferre, prout opportunum iudicaverint.

Cum vero Nos, iam inde a tempore, quo Apostolicas Litteras ad hoc Concilium indicendum dedimus, Viros Theologos et ecclesiastici iuris Consultos, ex variis Catholici orbis regionibus in hanc almam Urbem Nostram evocandos curaverimus, ut una cum aliis huius Urbis, et earumdem disciplinarum peritis viris, rebus apparandis darent operam, quae ad huius generalis Synodi scopum pertinent, atque ita expeditior via in rerum tractatione Patribus

patere posset; hinc volumus et mandamus, ut *schemata* decretorum et canonum ab iisdem viris expressa et redacta, quae Nos, nulla Nostra approbatione munita, integra integre Patrum cognitioni reservavimus, iisdem Patribus in Congregationem generalem collectis ad examen et iudicium subiiciantur. Itaque, curantibus memoratis Praesidibus, aliquot ante dies quam Congregatio generalis habeatur, decretorum et canonum schemata, de quibus in Congregatione indicta agendum erit, typis impressa singulis Patribus distribuentur, quo interim illa diligenti consideratione in omnem partem expendant, et quid sibi sententiae esse debeat accurate pervideant. Si quis Patrum de schemate proposito sermonem in Congregatione ipsa habere voluerit, ad debitum inter oratores ordinem pro cuiusque dignitatis gradu servandum, opus erit, ut saltem pridie diei Congregationis ipsius, Praesidibus suum disserendi propositum significandum curet. Auditis autem istorum Patrum sermonibus, si alii etiam post eos in conventu ipso disserere voluerint, hoc iisdem fas erit, obtenta prius a Praesidibus dicendi venia, et eo ordine, quem dicentium dignitas postulaverit.

Iamvero si in ea quae habetur Congregatione exhibitum schema vel nullas, vel nonnisi leves difficultates in ipso congressu facile expediendas obtulerit, tunc nihil morae erit, quominus, disceptationibus compositis, decreti vel canonis Conciliaris, de quo agitur, formula, rogatis Patrum suffragiis, statuatur. Sin autem circa schema praedictum huiusmodi oriantur difficultates, ut, sententiis in contraria conversis, via non suppetat, qua in ipso conventu componi possiut, tum ea ratio ineunda erit, quam heic infra statuimus, ut stabili et opportuno modo huic rei provideatur. Volumus itaque, ut ab ipso Concilii exordio quatuor speciales ac distinctae Patrum Congregationes seu *Deputationes* instituantur, quarum prima de rebus ad fidem pertinentibus, altera de rebus disciplinae ecclesiasticae, tertia de rebus Ordinum Regularium, quarta demum de rebus ritus Orientalis, Concilio perdurante, cognoscere et tractare debebit. Quaevis ex praedictis Congregationibus seu Deputationibus numero Patrum quatuor et viginti constabit, qui a Conciliii Patribus per schedulas secretas eligentur. Unicuique ex iisdem Congregationibus seu Deputationibus praeerit unus ex VV. FF. NN. S. R. E. Cardinalibus a Nobis designandus, qui ex Conciliaribus Theologis vel Iuris Canonici peritis, unum aut plures in commodum suae Congregationis seu Deputationis adsciscet, atque ex iis unum constituet, qui Secretarii munere eidem Congregationi seu Deputationi operam navet. Igitur si illud contigerit, quod supra innuimus, ut nimirum in generali Congregatione quaestio de proposito schemate exorta dirimi non potuerit, tum Cardinales eiusdem generalis Congregationis Praesides curabunt ut schema, de quo agitur, una cum obiectis difficultatibus examini subiiciatur illius ex specialibus Deputationibus, ad quam, iuxta assignata cuique rerum tractandarum genera pertinere intelligitur. Quae in hac peculiari Deputatione deliberata fuerint, eorum relatio typis edita Patribus dirigenda erit, iuxta met. odum a Nobis superius praescriptam, ut deinde in proxima Congregatione generali, si nihil amplius obstiterit, rogatis Patrum suffragiis, decreti vel canonis Conciliaris formula condatur. Suffragia autem a Patribus oretenus edentur, ita tamen, ut ipsis integrum sit etiam de scripto illa pronuntiare.

VIII.

De Sessionibus publicis.

Publicarum nunc Sessionum celebratio exigit, ut rebus et actionibus iu ea rite dirigendis, congrua ratione consulamus. Itaque in unaquaque publica Sessione, considentibus suo loco et ordine Patribus, servatisque adamussim caeremoniis, quae in rituali instructione iisdem Patribus de mandato Nostro tradenda continentur, de suggestu decretorum et canonum formulae in superioribus Congregationibus generalibus conditae, voce sublata et clara iussu Nostro recitabuntur, eo ordine, ut primum canones de dogmatibus Fidei, deinde decreta de disciplina pronuncientur, et ea adhibita solemni tituli praefatione, qua Praedecessores Nostri in eiusmodi Conciliari actione uti consueverunt, nempe: *Pius Episcopus Servus Servorum Dei, sacro approbante Concilio, ad perpetuam rei memoriam.* Tunc vero rogabuntur Patres, an placeant canones et decreta perlecta; ac statim procedent scrutatores suffragiorum, iuxta methodum superius constitutam, ad suffragia singillatim et ordine excipienda, eaque accurate describent. Hac autem in re declaramus suffragia pronunciari debere in haec verba, *placet* aut *non placet :* ac simul edicimus, minime fas esse a Sessione absentibus quavis de causa, suffragium suum scripto consignatum ad Concilium mittere. Iamvero suffragiis collectis, Concilii Secretarius una cum supradictis scrutatoribus penes Pontificalem Nostram Cathedram, iis accurate dirimendis ac numerandis operam dabunt, ac de ipsis ad Nos referent: Nos deinde supremam Nostram sententiam edicemus, eamque enunciari et promulgari mandabimus, hac adhibita solemni formula: "*Decreta modo lecta placuerunt omnibus Patribus, nemine dissentiente ;* vel (si qui forte dissenserint) *tot numero exceptis ; Nosque, sacro approbante Concilio, i la ita decernimus statuimus atque sancimus, ut lecta sunt.*" Hisce autem omnibus expletis, erit Promotorum, Concilii rogabo Protonotarios praesentes, ut de omnibus et singulis in Sessione peractis, unum vel plura, instrumentum vel instrumenta conficiantur. Denique die proximae Sessionis de mandato Nostro indicta, Sessionis conventus dimittetur.

IX.

De non discedendo a Concilio.

Universis porro Concilii Patribus, aliisque qui eidem interesse debent praecipimus sub poenis per SS. Canones indictis, ut ne quis eorum, antequam Sacrosanctum hoc generale et Oecumenicum Concilium Vaticanum rite absolutum et a Nobis dimissum sit, discedat, nisi discessionis causa iuxta normam superius definitam cognita et probata fuerit, ac impetrata a Nobis abeundi facultas.

X.

Indultum Apostolicum de non residentia pro iis qui Concilio intersunt.

Cum ii omnes qui Conciliaribus actionibus interesse tenentur, ea in re universali Ecclesiae deserviant ; Praedecessorum Nostrorum etiam exemplum sequuti [1] Apostolica benignitate indulgemus, ut tum Praesules aliique suffragii ius in hoc Concilio habentes, tum ceteri omnes eidem Concilio operam quovis titulo impendentes, suorum beneficiorum fructus, reditus, proventus ac distributiones quotidianas percipere possint, iis tantum distributionibus exceptis, quae *inter praesentes* fieri dicuntur ; idque concedimus Synodo perdurante, et donec quisque eidem adsit aut inserviat.

Haec vero volumus atque mandamus, decernentes has Nostras Litteras et in eis contenta quaecumque, in proximo sacrosancto generali et Oecumenico Concilio Vaticano, ab omnibus et singulis ad quos spectat, respective et inviolabiliter observari debere. Non obstantibus, quamvis speciali atque individua mentione ac derogatione dignis, in contrarium facientibus quibuscumque.

Datum Romae apud S. Petrum sub Annulo Piscatoris, die XXVII Novembris

---

[1] Paulus III, Brev. I, Januarii 1546; Pius IV. Brev. 25, Nov. 1561.

anno MDCCCLXIX. Pontificatus Nostri
anno Vigesimo quarto.

N. CARD. PARACCIANI-CLARELLI.

(Dalla *Civiltà Cattolica*, 18 decembre 1869.)

DOCUMENT X.

Allocuzione che il Santissimo nostro Signore per divina Provvidenza PAPA PIO IX, per dare principio al sacro Concilio ecumenico il dì 8 decembre dell' anno 1869, tenne nella Basilica vaticana ai vescovi del mondo cattolico convenuti allo stesso Concilio.

VENERABILES FRATRES.

Quod votis omnibus ac precibus ab Deo petebamus, ut Oecumenicum Concilium a Nobis indictum concelebrare possemus, id insigni ac singulari Dei ipsius beneficio, datum Nobis esse summopere laetamur. Itaque exultat cor Nostrum in Domino et incredibili consolatione perfunditur, quod auspicatissimo hoc die Immaculatae Dei Genitricis Virginis Mariae Conceptioni sacro, Vos qui in partem sollicitudinis Nostrae vocati estis, iterum maiori quam alias frequentia, in hac catholicae Religionis arce praesentes intuemur, aspectuque Vestro perfruimur iucundissimo.

Vos autem nunc, Venerabiles Fratres, in nomine Christi congregati[1] molestis, ut Nobiscum testimonium perhibeatis Verbo Dei et testimonium Iesu Christi,[2] viamque Dei in veritate omnes homines Nobiscum doceatis,[3] et de oppositionibus falsi nominis scientiae,[4] Nobiscum Spiritu Sancto duce iudicetis.[5]

Si enim unquam alias hoc maxime tempore, quo vere luxit et defluxit terra infecta ab habitatoribus suis,[6] divinae gloriae zelus, et Dominici gregis salus a Nobis postulat, ut circumdemus Sion et complectamur eam, narremus in turribus eius, et ponamus corda Nostra in virtute eius.[7]

Videtis enim, Venerabiles Fratres, quanto impetu antiquus humani generis hostis Domum Dei, quam decet sanctitudo, aggressus sit et usque aggrediatur. Eo auctore funesta illa impiorum coniuratio late grassatur, quae coniunctione fortis, opibus potens, munita institutis, et velamen habens malitiae libertatem,[8] acerrimum adversus Sanctam Christi Ecclesiam bellum, omni

scelere imbutum urgere non desinit. Huius belli genus, vim, arma, progressus, consilia non ignoratis. Versatur Vobis continenter ante oculos sanarum doctrinarum, quibus humanae res in suis quaeque ordinibus innituntur, perturbatio et confusio, luctuosa iuris cuiusque perversio, multiplices mentiendi audacter et corrumpendi artes, quibus iustitiae, honestatis et auctoritatis salutaria vincula solvuntur, pessimae quaeque cupiditates inflammantur, Christiana Fides ab animis funditus convellitur, ita ut certum hoc tempore Ecclesiae Dei metuendum esset exitium, si ullis hominum machinationibus et conatibus exscindi posset. At nihil Ecclesia potentius, inquiebat sanctus Ioannes Chrysostomus: Ecclesia est ipso caelo fortior. Caelum et terra transibunt; verba autem mea non transibunt. Quae verba? Tu es Petrus, et super hanc Petram aedificabo Ecclesiam meam, et portae inferi non prevalebunt adversus eam.[1]

Quamquam vero Civitas Domini virtutum, Civitas Dei Nostri inexpugnabili fundamento nitatur, tamen agnoscentes ac intimo corde dolentes tantam malorum congeriem animarumque ruinam, ad quam avertendam vel vitam p nere parati essemus, Nos qui aeterni Pastoris Vicaria in Terris procumtione fungentes, zelo domus Dei prae caeteris incendamur necesse est, eam viam et rationem ineundam Nobis esse duximus, quae ad tot Ecclesiae detrimenta sarcienda utilior et opportunior videretur. Ac illud Isaiae saepe animo revolventes: "Ini consilium, coge concilium," et reputantes huiusmodi remedium in gravissimis rei christianae temporibus a Praedecessoribus Nostris salutariter esse usurpatum, post diuturnas preces, post collata cum Venerabilibus Fratribus Nostris Sanctae Romanae Ecclesiae Cardinalibus consilia, post expetita etiam plurium Sacrorum Antistitum suffragia, Vos, Venerabiles Fratres, qui estis sal terrae, Custodes Dominici Grogis et Pastores, apud hanc Petri Cathedram consuimus evocandos; atque hodie, divina benignitate favente, quae tantae rei impedimenta sustulit, sanctae Congregationis initia, solemni maiorum ritu celebramus. Tot autem sunt, tamque uberes caritatis sensus, quibus hoc tempore afficimur, Venerabiles Fratres, ut eos in sinu continere non valeamus. Videmus enim in Vestro Conspectu universam Catholicae gentis familiam, carissimos Nobis Filios praesentes intueri: cogitamus tot amoris pign ra, tot ferventis animi opera, quibus Vestro impulsu, ductu et exemplo suam pietatem erga observantiam Nobis et huic Apo-

[1] Matt., 18, 20.   [2] Apoc., 1, 2.   [3] Matth. 22, 16.
[4] I. Tim., 6, 20.   [5] Act. Apost. 15, 19.
[6] Isai., 21, 4, 5.   [7] Psalm xlvii., 13, 14.
[8] I. Pet., 2, 16.

[1] Homil. ante exil. n. 1.

stolicae Sedi mirifice probarunt, ac porro probant; atque hac cogitatione Nobis temperare non possumus, quin in vestro amplissimo coetu, Nostram erga eos omnes gratissimam voluntatem, solemni et publica significatione profitentes, Deum enixe adprecemur, ut probatio eorum fidei multo pretiosior auro, inveniatur in laudem et gloriam et honorem, in revelatione Iesu Christi.[1] Miseram deinde etiam tot hominum conditionem cogitamus, qui a via veritatis et iustitiae, ideoque verae felicitatis decepti aberrant, eorumque saluti opem afferre desiderio desideramus, memores Divini Redemptoris et Magistri Nostri Iesu, qui venit quaerere et salvum facere quod perierat.[2] Intendimus praeterea oculos in hoc Principis Apostolorum Trophaeum apud quod consistimus, in hanc almam Urbem, quae Dei munere tradita non fuit in direptionem gentium, in Romanum hunc Populum Nobis dilectissimum, cuius constanti amore, fide, obsequio circumdamur, atque ad Dei benignitatem extollendam vocamur, qui divini sui praesidii spem in Nobis hoc tempore, magis magisque fulcire et confirmare voluerit. At praecipue Vos cogitatione complectimur, Venerabiles Fratres, in quorum sollicitudine, zelo et concordia, magnum momentum ad Dei gloriam operandam positum nunc esse intelligimus; agnoscimus flagrans studium, quod ad Vestrum munus implendum attulistis, ac praesertim praeclaram et arctissimam illam Vestrum omnium cum Nobis, et hac Apostolica Sede coniunctionem, qua, ut semper alias in maximis Nostris acerbitatibus, ita potissimum hoc tempore nihil Nobis iucundius, nihil Ecclesiae utilius esse potest; ac vehementer gaudemus in Domino Vos ita esse animo comparatos, ut ad certam solidamque spem uberrimorum fructuum et maxime optabilium, ex Synodali hac Vestra editione concipiendam impellamur. Ut nullum fortasse aliud infestius et callidius bellum in Christi Regnum exarsit, sic nullum fuit tempus in quo magis Sacerdotum Domini cum Supremo Gregis Eius Pastore unio, a qua in Ecclesiam mira vis manat, postularetur; quae quidem unio, singulari divinae providentiae munere et spectata virtute Vestra, ita iugiter reipsa constitit, ut spectaculum facta sit, et futurum magis confidamus in dies, mundo et angelis et hominibus.

Agite igitur, Venerabiles Fratres, confortamini in Domino: ac in nomine ipsius Trinitatis Augustae, sanctificati in veritate,[2] induti arma lucis, docete Nobiscum viam, veritatem et vitam, ad quam tot agitata aerumnis gens humana iam non adspirare

[1] I. Pet., 1, 7.   [2] Ioann., 17, 19.

non potest, date Nobiscum operam, ut pa: regnis, lex barbaris, monasteriis quies Ecclesiis ordo, clericis disciplina, Deo populus acceptabilis restitui possit.[1] Stat Deus in loco sancto suo, Nostris interest consilii et actibus, suos Ipse ministros et adiutores in tam eximio misericordiae suae opere No: adlegit, atque huic ministerio ita Nos in servire oportet, ut illi unice hoc tempore mentes, corda, vires consecremus.

Sed nostrae infirmitatis conscii, Nostris diffisi viribus, ad Te levamus cum fiducia oculos, precesque convertimus, o Divine Spiritus, Tu fons verae lucis et sapientiae, divinae Tuae gratiae lumen praefer mentibus Nostris, ut ea quae recta, quae salutaria, quae optima sunt videamus; Corda rege, fove, dirige, ut huius Concilii actiones rite inchoentur, prospere promoveantur, salubriter perficiantur.

Tu vero Mater Pulchrae dilectionis, agnitionis et sanctae spei, Ecclesiae Regina et propugnatrix, Tu Nos, consultationes, labores Nostros in Tuam maternam fidem tutelamque recipias, ac Tuis age apud Deum precibus, ut in uno semper spiritu maneamus et corde.

Vos quoque Nostris adeste votis, Angeli et Archangeli, Tuque Apostolorum Princeps, Beatissime Petre, Tuque Coapostole Eius, Paule, doctor gentium, et praedicator veritatis in universo mundo, Vosque omnes, Sancti caelites, et praecipue, quorum cineres hic veneramur, potenti Vos deprecatione efficite, ut omnes, ministerium Nostrum fideliter implentes, suscipiamus misericordiam Dei in medio Templi Eius, Cui honor et gloria in saecula saeculorum.

(Dalla *Civiltà Cattolica*, 18 dicembre 1869.)

DOCUMENT XI.

SANCTISSIMI DOMINI NOSTRI

PII DIVINA PROVIDENTIA PAPAE IX.

CONSTITUTIO DE ELECTIONE ROMANI
PONTIFICIS
SI CONTINGAT SEDEM APOSTOLICAM
VACARE DURANTE CONCILIO OECUMENICO.

PIUS EPISCOPUS

SERVUS SERVORUM DEI

Ad perpetuam rei memoriam.

Cum Romanis Pontificibus in B. Petro Apostolorum Principe pascendi, regendi et

[1] San. Bern., *De Con.*, l. 4, c. 4.

THE VATICAN COUNCIL.

gubernandi universalem Ecclesiam a Domino Nostro Iesu Christo plena potestas tradita fuerit; pax et unitas ipsius Ecclesiae in grave discrimen facile adducerentur si, Apostolica Sede vacante, in electione novi Pontificis quidquam fieri contingeret, quod eam incertam, ac dubiam reddere posset.

Ad tam funestum periculum avertendum plures a Romanis Pontificibus Decessoribus Nostris, ac praesertim a fel. record. Alexandro III in generali Concilio Lateranensi III,[1] a B. Gregorio X in generali Concilio Lugdunensi II,[2] a Clemente V,[3] a Gregorio XV,[4] ab Urbano VIII[5] et a Clemente XII[6] editae sunt Constitutiones, quibus dum multa alia praescribuntur, ut negotium tanti momenti rite recteque expediatur, generatim et absque ulla exceptione declaratur ac decernitur electionem Summi Pontificis ad S. R. E. Cardinalium Collegium unice et exclusive spectare.

Haec Nos animo recolentes, cum Oecumenicum et Generale Concilium Vaticanum per Apostolicas Litteras quae incipiunt *Aeternis Patris* III kal. Iulias anno 1868, a Nobis in dictum, in eo iam sit ut solemniter initietur, Apostolici Nostri muneris esse ducimus, quamcumque occasionem discordiarum et dissensionum circa electionem Summi Pontificis praevenire ac praecidere, si Divinae voluntati placuerit Nos, eodem Concilio perdurante, ex hac mortali vita migrare.

Quapropter exemplo permoti fel. record. Iulii II, Decessoris Nostri, de quo, compertum ex historia est[7] tempore generalis Concilii Lateranensis V lethali morbo correptum Cardinales coram se convocasse, ac de legitima Successoris Sui electione sollicitum, illis adstantibus edixisse hanc non a praedicto Concilio, sed ab eorum tantum Collegio esse perficiendam, prout reapse, memorato Iulii sequuta morte, factum fuisse constat, atque exemplo insuper excitati aliorum Decessorum Nostrorum item fel. rec. Pauli III et Pii IV, quorum primus Apostolicis Litteris datis III kal. Decembris an. 1544, alter vero similibus Litteris datis X kal. Octobris 1561, casum mortis suae praevidentes cum Tridentina Synodus celebraretur, decreverunt, eiusmodi casu occurrente, electionem novi Pontificis nonnisi a S. R. E. Cardinalibus esse faciendam, exclusa prorsus quacumque memoratae Synodi participatione : atque insuper de his habita cum nonnullis Venerabilibus Fratribus Nostris eiusdem S. R. E. Cardinalibus matura deliberatione et diligenti examine, ex certa scientia Nostra, Motu proprio ac de Apostolicae potestatis plenitudine declaramus, decernimus atque statuimus quod, si placuerit Deo mortali Nostrae peregrinationi, praedicto generali Concilio Vaticano perdurante, finem imponere, electio novi Summi Pontificis, in quibuscumque statu et terminis Concilium ipsum subsistat, nonnisi per S. R. E. Cardinales fieri debeat, minime vero per ipsum Concilium, atque etiam omnino exclusis ab eadem electione peragenda quibuscumque aliis personis cuiusvis, licet ipsius Concilii auctoritate forte deputandis, praeter Cardinales praedictos.

Quin imo ut in eiusmodi electione memorati Cardinales, omni prorsus impedimento submoto, et quavis perturbationum et dissidiorum occasione sublata, liberius et expeditius procedere queant, de eadem scientia et Apostolicae potestatis plenitudine, illud praeterea decernimus atque statuimus ut si, praedicto Vaticano Concilio perdurante, Nos decedere contigerit, idem Concilium in quibuscumque statu et terminis existat, illico et immediate suspensum ac dilatum intelligatur, quemadmodum per Nostras has litteras illud nunc pro tunc suspendere atque in tempus infra notandum differre intendimus, adeo ut nulla prorsus interiecta mora, cessare statim debeat a quibuscumque conventibus, congregationibus et sessionibus, et a quibusvis decretis seu canonibus conficiendis, nec ob qualemcumque causam, etiamsi gravissima et speciali mentione digna videatur, ulterius progredi, donec novus Pontifex a Sacro Cardinalium Collegio canonice electus supremam sua auctoritate Concilii ipsius reassumptionem et prosequutionem duxerit intimandam.

Opportunum autem censentes, ut quae occasione praedicti Concilii Vaticani hactenus ordinavimus tum quoad Summi Pontificis electionem, tum quoad eiusdem Concilii suspensionem, certam stabilemque normam in simili rerum eventu perpetuo servandam suppeditent, pari scientia et potestate decernimus atque statuimus, ut futuris quibuscumque temporibus, quandocumque contigerit Romanum Pontificem decedere, perdurante celebratione alicuius Concilii Oecumenici sive Romae illud habeatur, sive in alio quovis orbis loco, electio novi Pontificis ab uno S. R. E. Cardinalium Collegio semper et exclusive iuxta modum superius definitum fieri debeat, atque ipsum Concilium, pariter iuxta regulam superius sancitam, statim ab accepto certo nuntio de

---

[1] Cap. *Licet de Electione*.
[2] Cap. *Ubi de Electione* in 6.
[3] Clement. 2 de Electione.
[4] Constit. *Decet Romanum Pontificem*.
[5] Constit. *Ad Romani Pontificis*, V kal. februarii 1625.
[6] Constit. *Apostolatus*, IV. nonas octobris 1732.
[7] RAYNALD, *Annal. Eccles.* ad annum 1513, n. VII.

mortui Pontificis suspensum ipso iure intelligatur, et tamdiu dilatum, donec novus Pontifex canonice electus illud reassumi et continuari iusserit.

Praesentes autem litteras semper validas, firmas et efficaces existere et fore, suosque plenarios et integros effectus sortiri et obtinere, ac nullo unquam tempore ex quocumque capite, aut qualibet causa de subreptionis, vel obreptionis seu nullitatis vitio, vel intentionis Nostrae, vel alio quopiam, quantumvis substantiali inexcogitato et inexcogitabili ac specificam et individuam mentionem aut expressionem requirente, defectu, aut ex quocumque alio capite a iure statuto, vel quocumque praetextu, ratione, aut causa quantumvis tali, quae ad effectum validitatis praemissorum necessario exprimenda foret, notari, impugnari, redargui, invalidari, retractari, in ius vel controversiam revocari posse; neque easdem praesentes sub quibusvis similium vel dissimilium dispositionum revocationibus, limitationibus, modificationibus, derogationibus, sub quibuscumque verborum tenoribus et formis, ac cum quibusvis clausulis et decretis, etiamsi in eis de hisce praesentibus, earumque toto tenore ac data specialis mentio fieret, pro tempore factis et concessis ac faciendis et concedendis comprehendi; sed semper et omnino ab illis excipi debere atque ex nunc quidquid contra praemissa, Apostolica Sede vacante, quavis auctoritate etiam memorati Concilii Vaticani, vel alterius cuiuscumque futuris temporibus Concilii Oecumenici, licet de unanimi consensu hodiernorum, seu pro tempore exsistentium S. R. E. Cardinalium scienter vel ignoranter fuerit attentatum, irritum et inane ac nullius roboris decernimus.

Non obstantibus quatenus opus sit, felicis recordationis Alexandri · Papae III Decessoris Nostri in Concilio Lateranensi edita, quae incipit "Licet de vitanda" et quibuscumque aliis etiam in universalibus Conciliis latis specialibus vel generalibus Constitutionibus Apostolicis, quamvis in corpore iuris clausis, et sub quibuscumque tenoribus et formis ac quibusvis etiam derogatoriarum derogatoriis, aliisque efficacioribus, et insolitis clausulis, irritantibusque et aliis decretis in genere vel in specie, etiam Motu pari ac consistorialiter statutis, quibus omnibus et singulis quatenus pariter opus sit eorumque omnium tenoribus perinde ac si praesentibus de verbo ad verbum exprimantur, pro insertis et expressis habentes, in ea tantum parte, quae praesentibus adversatur illis alias in suo robore permansuris, ad praemissorum omnium et singulorum validissimum effectum hac vice dumtaxat latissime et plenissime ac sufficienter necnon specialiter et expresse harum quoque serie derogamus, ceterisque contrariis quibuscumque.

Nulli ergo omnino hominum liceat hanc paginam Nostrae declarationis, ordinationis, statuti, decreti, derogationis et voluntatis infringere, vel illis ausu temerario contraire. Si quis autem hoc attentare praesumpserit, indignationem Omnipotentis Dei ac Beatorum Petri et Pauli Apostolorum eius se noverit incursurum.

Datum Romae apud S. Petrum Anno Incarnationis Dominicae millesimo octingentesimo sexagesimo nono. Pridie Nonas Decembris. Pontificatus Nostri anno vigesimoquarto.

M. Card. MATTEI Pro-Datarius.
N. Card. PARACCIANI CLARELLI.
Visa de Curia
Loco ✠ plumbi.   DOMINICUS BRUTI
I. CUGNONI.

(Dalla *Civiltà Cattolica*, 1° gennaio 1870.)

DOCUMENT XII.

SS. D. N. PII

DIVINA PROVIDENTIA

PAPAE IX

CONSTITUTIO

QUA CENSURAE LATAE SENTENTIAE
LIMITANTUR.

PIUS EPISCOPUS

SERVUS SERVORUM DEI

Ad perpetuam rei memoriam.

Apostolicae Sedis moderationi convenit, quae salubriter veterum canonum auctoritate constituta sunt, sic retinere, ut si temporum rerumque mutatio quidpiam esse temperandum prudenti dispensatione suadeat, eadem Apostolica Sedes congruum supremae suae potestatis remedium ac providentiam impendat. Quamobrem cum animo Nostro iampridem revolveremus, ecclesiasticas censuras, quae per modum latae sententiae, ipsoque facto incurrendae ad incolumitatem ac disciplinam ipsius Ecclesiae tutandam, effrenemque improborum licentiam coercendam et emendandam sancte per singulas aetates indictae ac promulgatae sunt, magnum ad numerum sensim excrevisse; quasdam etiam, temporibus moribusque mutatis, a fine atque causis, ob quas impositae fuerant, vel a pristina utilitate, opportunitate excidisse; eamque ob rem non infrequentes oriri sive in iis, quibus animarum cura commissa est, sive in ipsis fidelibus dubietates, anxietates, angoresque conscientiae; Nos eiusmodi incommodis occurrere volentes, plenam earumdem recensionem fieri, Nobisque proponi iussimus, ut diligenti adhibita consideratione, statueremus, quaenam ex illis servare ac retinere oporteret, quas vero moderari aut abrogare congrueret. Ea igitur recensione peracta, ac Venerabilibus Fratribus Nostris S. R. E. Cardinalibus in negotiis Fidei Generalibus Inquisitoribus per universam Christianam Rempublicam deputatis in consilium adscitis, reque diu ac mature perpensa, motu proprio, certa scientia, matura deliberatione nostra, deque Apostolicae Nostrae potestatis plenitudine hac perpetuo valitura Constitutione decernimus, ut ex quibuscumque censuris sive excommunicationis, sive suspensionis, sive interdicti, quae per modum latae sententiae, ipsoque facto incurrendae hactenus impositae sunt, nonnisi illae, quas in hac ipsa Constitutione inserimus, eoque modo, quo inserimus, robur exinde habeant; simul declarantes easdem non modo ex veterum canonum auctoritate, quatenus cum hac Nostra Constitutione conveniunt, verum etiam ex hac ipsa Constitutione Nostra, non secus ac si primum editae ab ea fuerint, vim suam prorsus accipere debere.

Excommunicationes latae sententiae speciali modo Romano Pontifici reservatae.

Itaque excommunicationi latae sententiae speciali modo Romano Pontifici reservatae subiacere declaramus:

1. Omnes a christiana fide apostatas, et omnes ac singulos haereticos, quocumque nomine censeantur, et cuiuscumque sectae existant, eisque credentes, eorumque receptores, fautores, ac generaliter quoslibet illorum defensores.

2. Omnes et singulos scienter legentes sine auctoritate Sedis Apostolicae libros eorumdem apostatarum et haereticorum haeresim propugnantes, necnon libros cuiusvis auctoris per Apostolicas litteras nominatim prohibitos, eosdemque libros retinentes, imprimentes et quomodolibet defendentes.

3. Schismaticos et eos qui a Romani Pontificis pro tempore existentis obedientia pertinaciter se subtrahunt, vel recedunt.

4. Omnes et singulos, cuiuscumque status, gradus seu conditionis fuerint, ab ordinationibus seu mandatis Romanorum Pontificum pro tempore existentium ad universale futurum Concilium appellantes, nec-

non eos, quorum auxilio, consilio vel favore appellatum fuerit.

5. Omnes interficientes, mutilantes, percutientes, capientes, carcerantes, detinentes, vel hostiliter insequentes S. R. E. Cardinales, Patriarchas, Archiepiscopos, Episcopos, Sedisque Apostolicae Legatos, vel Nuncios, aut eos a suis Dioecesibus, Territoriis, Terris, seu Dominiis eiicientes, necnon ea mandantes, vel rata habentes, seu praestantes in eis auxilium, consilium vel favorem.

6. Impedientes directe vel indirecte exercitium iurisdictionis ecclesiasticae sive interni sive externi fori, et ad hoc recurrentes ad forum saeculare eiusque mandata procurantes, edentes, aut auxilium, consilium vel favorem praestantes.

7. Cogentes sive directe, sive indirecte iudices laicos ad trahendum ad suum tribunal personas ecclesiasticas praeter canonicas dispositiones: item edentes leges vel decreta contra libertatem aut iura Ecclesiae.

8. Recurrentes ad laicam potestatem ad impediendas litteras vel acta quaelibet a Sede Apostolica, vel ab eiusdem Legatis aut Delegatis quibuscumque profecta, eorumque promulgationem vel executionem directe vel indirecte prohibentes, vel eorum causa sive ipsas partes, sive alios laedentes, vel perterrefacientes.

9. Omnes falsarios litterarum Apostolicarum, etiam in forma Brevis ac supplicationum gratiam vel iustitiam concernentium, per Romanum Pontificem, vel S. R. E. Vice-Cancellarios seu Gerentes vices eorum aut de mandato eiusdem Romani Pontificis signatarum: necnon falso publicantes Litteras Apostolicas, etiam in forma Brevis, et etiam falso signantes supplicationes huiusmodi sub nomine Romani Pontificis, seu Vice-Cancellarii aut Gerentis vices praedictorum.

10. Absolventes complicem in peccato turpi etiam in mortis articulo, si alius Sacerdos licet non adprobatus ad confessiones, sine gravi aliqua exoritura infamia et scandalo, possit excipere morientis confessionem.

11. Usurpantes aut sequestrantes iurisdictionem, bona, reditus ad personas ecclesiasticas ratione suarum Ecclesiarum aut beneficiorum pertinentes.

12. Invadentes, destruentes, detinentes per se vel per alios Civitates, Terras, loca aut iura ad Ecclesiam Romanam pertinentia; vel usurpantes, perturbantes, retinentes supremam iurisdictionem in eis; necnon ad singula praedicta auxilium, consilium, favorem praebentes.

A quibus omnibus excommunicationibus huc usque recensitis absolutionem Romano Pontifici pro tempore speciali modo reservatam esse et reservari: et pro ea generalem concessionem absolvendi a casibus et censuris, sive excommunicationibus Romano Pontifici reservatis nullo pacto sufficere declaramus, revocatis insuper earumdem respectu quibuscumque indultis concessis sub quavis forma et quibusvis personis etiam Regularibus cuiuscumque Ordinis, Congregationis, Societatis et Instituti, etiam speciali mentione dignis et in quavis dignitate constitutis. Absolvere autem praesumentes sine debita facultate, etiam quovis praetextu, excommunicationis vinculo Romano Pontifici reservatos se sciant, dummodo non agatur de mortis articulo, in quo tamen firma sit quoad absolutos obligatio standi mandatis Ecclesiae, si convaluerint.

Excommunicationes latae sententiae Romano Pontifici reservatae.

Excommunicationi latae sententiae Romano Pontifici reservatae subiacere declaramus:

1. Docentes vel defendentes sive publice, sive privatim propositiones ab Apostolica Sede damnatas sub excommunicationis poena latae sententiae: item docentes vel defendentes tamquam licitam praxim inquirendi a poenitente nomen complicis, prouti damnata est a Benedicto XIV in Const. *Suprema* 7 Iulii 1745; *Ubi primum* 2 Iunii 1746; *Ad eradicandum* 28 Septembris 1746.

2. Violentas manus, suadente diabolo, injicientes in Clericos, vel utriusque sexus Monachos, exceptis quoad reservationem casibus et personis, de quibus iure vel privilegio permittitur, ut Episcopus aut alius absolvat.

3. Duellum perpetrantes, aut simpliciter ad illud provocantes, vel ipsum acceptantes; et quoslibet complices, vel qualemcumque operam aut favorem praebentes, necnon de industria spectantes, illudque permittentes, vel quantum in illis est, non prohibentes, cuiuscumque dignitatis sint, etiam regalis vel imperialis.

4. Nomen dantes sectae *Massonicae*, aut *Carbonariae*, aut aliis eiusdem generis sectis quae contra Ecclesiam vel legitimas potestates seu palam, seu clandestine machinantur, necnon iisdem sectis favorem qualemcumque praestantes; earumve occultos coriphaeos ac duces non denunciantes, donec non denunciaverint.

5. Immunitatem asyli ecclesiastici violare iubentes, aut ausu temerario violantes.

6. Violantes clausuram Monialum, cuiuscumque generis aut conditionis, sexus vel aetatis fuerint, in earum monasteria absque legitima licentia ingrediendo; pariterque eos introducentes vel admittentes; itemque Moniales ab illa excuntes extra casus ac formam a S. Pio V in Constit. *Decori* praescriptam.

7. Mulieres violantes Regularium virorum clausuram, et Superiores aliosve eas admittentes.

8. Reos simoniae realis in beneficiis quibuscumque, eorumque complices.

9. Reos simoniae confidentialis in beneficiis quibuslibet, cuiuscumque sint dignitatis.

10. Reos simoniae realis ob ingressum in Religionem.

11. Omnes qui quaestum facientes ex indulgenitis aliisque gratiis spiritualibus excommunicationis censura plectuntur Constitutione S. Pii V. *Quam plenum* 2 Ianuarii 1569.

12. Colligentes eleemosynas maioris pretii pro missis, et ex iis lucrum captantes, faciendo eas celebrari in locis ubi missarum stipendia minoris pretii esse solent.

13. Omnes qui excommunicatione mulctantur in Constitutionibus S. Pii V. *Admonet nos* quartó Kalendas Aprilis 1567, Innocentii IX. *Quae ab hac Sede* pridie nonas Novembris 1591, Clementis VIII. *Ad Romani Pontificis curam* 26 Iunii 1592, et Alexandri VII. *Inter ceteras* nono Kalendas Novembris 1660, alienationem et infeudationem Civitatum et locorum S. R. E. respicientibus.

14. Religiosos praesumentes clericis aut laicis extra casum necessitatis Sacramentum extremae unctionis aut Eucharistiae per viaticum ministrare absque Parochi licentia.

15. Extrahentes absque legitima venia reliquias ex Sacris Coemeteriis sive Catacumbis Urbis Romae eiusque territorii, eisque auxilium vel favorem praebentes.

16. Communicantes cum excommunicato nominatim a Papa in crimine criminoso, ei scilicet impendendo auxilium vel favorem.

17. Clericos scienter et sponte communicantes in divinis cum personis a Romano Pontifice nominatim excommunicatis et ipsos in officiis recipientes.

Excommunicationes latae sententiae Episcopis sive Ordinariis reservatae.

Excommunicationi latae sententiae Episcopis sive Ordinariis reservatae subiacere declaramus:

1. Clericos in Sacris constitutos vel Regulares aut Moniales post votum solenne castitatis matrimonium contrahere praesumentes; necnon omnes cum aliqua ex prae-

dictis personis matrimonium contrahere praesumentes.
2. Procurantes abortum, effectu secuuto.
3. Litteris apostolicis falsis scienter utentes, vel crimini ea in re cooperantes.

Excommunicationes latae sententiae nemini reservatae.

Excommunicationi latae sententiae nemini reservatae subiacere declaramus:
1. Mandantes seu cogentes tradi Ecclesiasticae Sepulturae haereticos notorios aut nominatim excommunicatos vel interdictos.
2. Laedentes aut perterrefacientes Inquisitores, denuntiantes, testes, aliosve ministros S. Officii, eiusve Sacri Tribunalis scripturas diripientes, aut comburentes, vel praedictis quibuslibet auxilium, consilium, favorem praestantes.
3. Alienantes et recipere praesumentes bona ecclesiastica absque Beneplacito Apostolico, ad formam Extravagantis *Ambitiosae* De Reb. Ecc. non alienandis.
4. Negligentes sive culpabiliter omittentes denunciare infra mensem Confessarios sive Sacerdotes a quibus sollicitati fuerint ad turpia in quibuslibet casibus expressis a Praedecess. Nostris Gregorio XV Constit. *Universi* 20 Augusti 1622, et Benedicto XIV Constit. *Sacramentum poenitentiae* 1 Iunii 1741.
Praeter hos hactenus recensitos, eos quoque quos Sacrosanctum Concilium Tridentinum, sive reservata Summo Pontifici aut Ordinariis absolutione, sive absque ulla reservatione excommunicavit, Nos pariter ita excommunicatos esse declaramus; excepta anathematis poena in Decreto Sess. IV *De editione et usu Sacrorum Librorum* constituta, cui illos tantum subiacere volumus; qui libros de rebus sacris tractantes sine Ordinarii approbatione imprimunt, aut imprimi faciunt.

Suspensiones latae sententiae Summo Pontifici reservatae.

1. Suspensionem ipso facto incurrunt a suorum Beneficiorum perceptione ad beneplacitum S. Sedis Capitula et Conventus Ecclesiarum et Monasteriorum aliique omnes, qui ad illarum seu illorum regimen et administrationem recipiunt Episcopos aliosve Praelatos de praedictis Ecclesiis seu Monasteriis apud eamdem S. Sedem quovis modo proviso, antequam ipsi exhibuerint Litteras Apostolicas de sua promotione.
2. Suspensionem per triennium a collatione Ordinum ipso iure incurrunt aliquem Ordinantes absque titulo beneficii, vel patrimonii cum pacto ut ordinatus non petat ab ipsis alimenta.
3. Suspensionem per annum ab Ordinum administratione ipso iure incurrunt Ordinantes alienum subditum etiam sub praetextu beneficii statim conferendi, aut iam collati, sed minime sufficientis, absque eius Episcopi litteris dimissorialibus, vel etiam subditum proprium, qui alibi tanto tempore moratus sit, ut canonicum impedimentum contrahere ibi potuerit, absque Ordinarii eius loci litteris testimonialibus.
4. Suspensionem per annum a collatione Ordinum ipso iure incurrit, qui excepto casu legitimi privilegii, ordinem sacrum contulerit absque titulo beneficii vel patrimonii clerico in aliqua Congregatione viventi, in qua solemnis professio non emittitur, vel etiam religioso nondum professo.
5. Suspensionem perpetuam ab exercitio ordinum ipso iure incurrunt Religiosi eiecti, extra Religionem degentes.
6. Suspensionem ab Ordine suscepto ipso iure incurrunt, qui eumdem ordinem recipere praesumpserunt ab excommunicato vel suspenso, vel interdicto nominatim denunciatis, aut ab haeretico vel schismatico notorio: cum vero qui bona fide a quopiam eorum est ordinatus, exercitium non habere ordinis sic suscepti, donec dispensetur, declaramus.
7. Clerici saeculares exteri ultra quatuor menses in Urbe commorantes ordinati ab alio quam ab ipso suo Ordinario absque licentia Card. Urbis Vicarii, vel absque praevio examine coram eodem peracto, vel etiam a proprio Ordinario postenquam in praedicto examine reiecti fuerint; necnon clerici pertinentes ad aliquem e sex Episcopatibus suburbicariis, si ordinentur extra suam dioecesim, dimissorialibus sui Ordinarii ad alium directis quam ad Card. Urbis Vicarium; vel non praemissis ante Ordinem Sacrum suscipiendum exercitiis spiritualibus per decem dies in domo urbana Sacerdotum a Missione nuncupatorum, suspensionem ab ordinibus sic susceptis ad beneplacitum S. Sedis ipso iure incurrunt; Episcopi vero ordinantes ab usu Pontificalium per annum.

Interdicta latae sententiae reservata.

1. Interdictum Romano Pontifici speciali modo reservatum ipso iure incurrunt Universitates, Collegia et Capitula quocumque nomine nuncupentur, ab ordinationibus seu mandatis eiusdem Romani Pontificis pro tempore existentis ad universale futurum Concilium appellantia.
2. Scienter celebrantes vel celebrari facientes divina in locis ab Ordinario, vel

x

delegato Iudice, vel a iure interdictis, aut nominatim excommunicatos ad divina officia, seu ecclesiastica Sacramenta, vel ecclesiasticam sepulturam admittentes, interdictum ab ingressu Ecclesiae ipso iure incurrunt, donec ad arbitrium eius, cuius sententiam contempserunt, competenter satisfecerint.

Denique quoscumque alios Sacrosanctum Concilium Tridentinum suspensos aut interdictos ipso iure esse decrevit, Nos pari modo suspensioni vel interdicto eosdem obnoxios esse volumus et declaramus.

Quae vero censurae sive excommunicationis, sive suspensionis, sive interdicti Nostris, aut Predecessorum Nostrorum Constitutionibus aut sacris canonibus praeter eas, quas recensuimus, latae sunt, atque hactenus in suo vigore perstiterunt sive pro R. Pontificis electione, sive pro interno regimine quorumcumque Ordinum et Institutorum Regularium, necnon quorumcumque Collegiorum, Congregationum, coetuum locorumque piorum cuiuscumque nominis aut generis sint, eas omnes firmas esse, et in suo robore permanere volumus et declaramus.

Ceterum decernimus, in novis quibuscumque concessionibus ac privilegiis, quae ab Apostolica Sede concedi cuivis contigerit, nullo modo ac ratione intelligi unquam debere, aut posse comprehendi facultatem absolvendi a casibus, et censuris quibuslibet Romano Pontifici reservatis, nisi de iis formalis, explicita, ac individua mentio facta fuerit: quae vero privilegia aut facultates sive a Praedecessoribus Nostris, sive etiam a Nobis cuilibet Coetui, Ordini, Congregationi, Societati et Instituto, etiam regulari cuiusvis speciei, etsi titulo peculiari praedito, atque etiam speciali mentione digno a quovis unquam tempore huc usque concessae fuerint, ea omnia, easque omnes Nostra hac Constitutione revocatas, suppressas et abolitas esse volumus, prout reapse revocamus, supprimimus, et abolemus, minime refragantibus aut obstantibus privilegiis quibuscumque, etiam specialibus comprehensis, vel non in corpore iuris, aut Apostolicis Constitutionibus, et quavis confirmatione Apostolica, vel immemorabili etiam consuetudine, aut alia quacumque firmitate roboratis, quibuslibet etiam formis ac tenoribus, et cum quibusvis derogatoriarum derogatoriis, aliisque officacioribus et insolitis clausulis, quibus omnibus, quatenus opus sit, derogare intendimus, et derogamus.

Firmam tamen esse volumus absolvendi facultatem a Tridentina Synodo Episcopis concessam *Sess. XXIV, cap. VI de Reform.* in quibuscumque censuris Apostolicae Sedi hac Nostra Constitutione reservatis, iis tantum exceptis, quas eidem Apostolicae Sedi speciali modo reservatas declaravimus.

Decernentes has Litteras atque omnia et singula, quae in eis constituta ac decreta sunt, omnesque et singulas, quae in eisdem factae sunt ex anterioribus Constitutionibus Praedecessorum Nostrorum atque etiam Nostris, aut ex aliis sacris Canonibus quibuscumque, etiam Conciliorum Generalium, et ipsius Tridentini, mutationes, derogationes, suppressiones atque abrogationes ratas et firmas ac respective rata atque firma esse et fore, suosque plenarios et integros effectus obtinere debere, ac reapse obtinere; sicque et non aliter in praemissis per quoscumque Iudices Ordinarios, et Delegatos, etiam Causarum Palatii Apostolici Auditores, ac S. R. E. Cardinales, etiam de Latere Legatos, ac Apostolicae Sedis Nuntios, ac quosvis alios quacumque praeminentia, ac potestate fungentes, et functuros, sublata eis, et eorum cuilibet quavis aliter iudicandi et interpretandi facultate, et auctoritate, iudicari, ac definiri debere; et irritum atque inane esse ac fore quidquid super his a quoquam quavis auctoritate, etiam praetextu cuiuslibet privilegii, aut consuetudinis vel inducendae, quam abusum esse declaramus, scienter vel ignoranter contigerit attentari.

Non obstantibus praemissis, aliisque quibuslibet ordinationibus, constitutionibus, privilegiis, etiam speciali et individua mentione dignis, necnon consuetudinibus quibusvis etiam immemorabilibus, ceterisque contrariis quibuscumque.

Nulli ergo omnino hominum liceat hanc paginam Nostrae Constitutionis, Ordinationis, limitationis, suppressionis, derogationis, voluntatis infringere, vel ei ausu temerario contraire. Si qui autem hoc attentare praesumpserit, indignationem Omnipotentis Dei et Beatorum Petri et Pauli Apostolorum eius, se noverit incursurum.

Datum Romae apud S. Petrum, anno Incarnationis Dominicae Millesimo Octingentesimo Sexagesimo Nono, Quarto Idus octobris, Pontificatus Nostri anno vigesimo quarto.

M. Card. MATTEI Pro-Datarius.
    N. Card. PARACCIANI CLARELLI
      Visa de Curia DOMINICUS BRUT
Loco ✠ plumbi.   I. GUGNONI.

(Dalla *Civiltà Cattolica*, 15 gennaio 1870.)

DOCUMENT XIII.

SCHEMA CONSTITUTIONIS DOGMATICAE DE ECCLESIA CHRISTI PATRUM EXAMINI PROPOSITUM.

Pius episcopus servus servorum Dei sacro approbante concilio ad perpetuam rei memoriam.

Supremi pastoris apostolicum ministerium, in quo Dei ineffabili providentia et misericordia positi sumus, sollicite ac continuo Nos urget, ut nihil praetermittamus, quo via, quae ad vitam et salutem ducit aeternam, omnibus hominibus pateat, et qui in tenebris et in umbra mortis sedent, ad lucem et agnitionem veritatis perveniant. Cum igitur Deus ac Salvator noster totius salutiferae doctrinae veritatem, et mediorum salutis thesauros, in Ecclesiam suam quasi in depositorium dives contulerit, ut omnes sumant ex ea potum vitae:[1] in primis ipsa vera Ecclesia et errantibus indicanda et fidelibus instantius commendanda est, ut illi ad viam salutis adducantur, hi autem in ea confirmentur et crescant. Quare Nostri muneris esse ducimus, potiora capita verae et catholicae doctrinae, de Ecclesiae natura, proprietatibus, ac potestate exponere, et grassantes oppositos errores subiectis Canonum articulis condemnare.

CAPUT I.

Ecclesiam esse Corpus Christi mysticum.

Unigenitus Dei Filius, qui illuminat omnem hominem venientem in hunc mundum, quique nulla unquam aetate miseris Adae filiis ope sua defuit, in ea plenitudine temporis, quae sempiterno consilio fuerat praestituta,[2] in similitudinem hominum factus[3] visibilis apparuit in assumpta nostri corporis forma, ut terreni homines atque carnales novum hominem induentes, qui secundum Deum creatus est in iustitia et sanctitate veritatis,[4] corpus efformarent mysticum, cuius ipse existeret caput. Ad hanc vero mystici corporis unionem efficiendam, Christus Dominus sacrum regenerationis et renovationis instituit lavacrum, quo filii hominum tot nominibus inter se divisi, maxime vero peccatis dilapsi, ab omni culparum sorde mundati membra essent ad invicem,[5] suoque divino capiti

[1] Cf. S. Iren. adv. Haer. 1. iii. c. 4.
[2] S. Ambros. de fid. ad. b. Hieron. presbyt. ap. Mai. vv. Scriptt. tom. vii. par. i. p. 159.
[3] Ep. ad Philipp. ii. 7.
[4] Ep. ad Ephes. iv. 24.
[5] Cf. ep. ad Ephes. iv. 4-25 coll. ep. i. ad Cor. xii. 12-14.

fide, spe, et caritate coniuncti, uno eius spiritu omnes vivificarentur, ac coelestium gratiarum et charismatum dona cumulate reciperent. Atque haec est, quae, ut fidelium mentibus obiiciatur alteque defixa haereat, satis nunquam commendari potest, praecellens Ecclesiae species, cuius caput est Christus[1] ex quo totum corpus compactum, et connexum per omnem iuncturam subministrationis, secundum operationem in mensuram uniuscuiusque membri, augmentum corporis facit, in aedificationem sui in caritate.[2]

CAPUT II.

Christianam religionem nonnisi in Ecclesia et per Ecclesiam a Christo fundatam excoli posse.

Hanc Ecclesiam, quam acquisivit sanguine suo, et tanquam sponsam unice electam aeternam dilexit, auctor fidei et consummator Iesus ipsa fundavit atque instituit, et per Apostolos suos eorumque successores iugiter usque ad consummationem saeculi in universo mundo et ex omni creatura colligendam, docendam, moderandamque praecepit, ut una esset gens sancta, unus populus acceptabilis, sectator bonorum operum.[3] Neque enim evangelicae legis ea ratio est, ut exclusο quovis societatis vinculo veri adoratores singuli seorsum Patrem adorent in spiritu et veritate; sed religionem suam ita societati a se institutae vivificarentem Redemptor noster voluit, ut cum ea penitus conserta ac veluti concreta maneret, et extra illam vera Christi religio nulla est.

CAPUT III.

Ecclesiam esse societatem veram, perfectam, spiritualem et supernaturalem.

Docemus autem ac declaramus, Ecclesiae inesse omnes verae societatis qualitates. Neque societas haec indefinita vel informis a Christo relicta est; sed quemadmodum ab ipso suam exsistentiam habet: ita eiusdem voluntate ac lege exsistendi formam suamque constitutionem accepit. Neque eadem membrum est sive pars alterius cuiuslibet societatis, nec cum alia quavis confusa aut commiscenda; sed adeo in semetipsa perfecta, ut dum ab omnibus humanis societatibus distinguitur, supra eas tamen quam maxime evehatur. Ab inexhausto enim misericordiae Dei Patris fonte profecta, per

[1] Ep. ad Coloss. i. 18.
[2] Ep. ad Ephes. iv. 16.
[3] Ep. ad Tit. ii. 14.

incarnati ipsius Verbi ministerium operamque fundata, in Spiritu sancto constituta est, qui in Apostolos primum largissime effusus, abunde etiam iugiter diffunditur in filios adoptionis, ut iidem lumine eius collustrati una mentium fide et Deo adhaereant et inter se cohaereant; ut pignus haereditatis in cordibus suis circumferentes, carnis desideria ab eius, quae in mundo est, concupiscentiae corruptione avellant, et beata una communique spe firmati, concupiscant promissam aeternam Dei gloriam, atque adeo per bona opera certam suam vocationem et electionem faciant.[1] Quum autem his bonorum divitiis in Ecclesia homines per Spiritum sanctum augeantur, atque his eiusdem sancti Spiritus nexibus in unitate cohaereant: Ecclesia ipsa spiritualis societas est, atque ordinis omnino supernaturalis.

CAPUT IV.

Ecclesiam esse societatem visibilem.

Absit tamen, ut quis credat, Ecclesiae membra nonnisi internis ac latentibus vinculis iungi, et abditam inde societatem ac prorsus invisibilem fieri. Aeterna siquidem Dei sapientia ac virtus voluit, spiritualibus et invisibilibus vinculis, quibus fideles supremo ac invisibili Ecclesiae capiti per Spiritum sanctum adhaerent, externa quoque ac visibilia respondere, ut spiritualis illa ac supernaturalis societas extrinsecus appareret, et conspicua patesceret. Hinc visibile magisterium, a quo credenda interius exteriusque profitenda fides[2] publice proponatur; visibile quoque ministerium, quod visibilia Dei mysteria, quibus interior sanctificatio hominibus et debitus Deo cultus comparatur, munere publico moderatur ac curat; visibile regimen, quod membrorum inter se communionem ordinat, externamque omnem et publicam fidelium in Ecclesia vitam disponit ac dirigit; visibile domum totum Ecclesiae corpus, ad quod non iusti tantum aut praedestinati pertinent, sed etiam peccatores, professione tamen fidei et communione cum eo coniuncti. Quibus fit, ut Christi Ecclesia in terris nec invisibilis nec latens sit; sed in manifestatione posita,[3] veluti civitas excelsa et illustris in monte,[4] quae abscondi non potest, ac veluti lucerna super candelabrum.[5]

[1] Ep. II. b. Pet. Ap. i. 10.
[2] Cf. ep. ad Rom. x. 10.
[3] St. Augustin. in Ps. xviii. enarrat. ii. n. b. coll. de unit. Eccl. l. un. c. 16, n. 40, con. Crescon. Donatist. l. ii. c. 36, n. 45, con. litt. Petil. l. ii. c. 32, n. 74, c. 104, n. 239.
[4] S. Cyrill. alex. com. in. Is. l. iii. c. 25, n. 4.
[5] Cf. Matth. v. 15.

CAPUT V.

De visibili Ecclesiae unitate.

Cum ciusmodi sit vera Christi Ecclesia, declaramus, hanc visibilem conspicuamque societatem, esse illam ipsam divinarum promissionum ac misericordiarum Ecclesiam quam Christus tot praerogativis ac privilegiis distinguere et exornare voluit; eandemque ita plane in sua constitutione esse determinatam, ut quaecumque societates a fidei unitate vel a communione huius corporis seiunctae nullo modo pars eius aut membrum dici possint; neque per varias christiani nominis consociationes dispersam atque diffusam, sed totam in se collectam penitusque cohaerentem, in sua conspicua unitate indivisam ac indivisibile corpus praeferre, quod est ipsum corpus mysticum Christi. De quo Apostolus inquit, unum corpus, et unus spiritus, sicut vocati estis in una spe vocationis vestrae. Unus Dominus, una fides, unum baptisma. Unus Deus et Pater omnium, qui est super omnes, et per omnia et in omnibus nobis.[1]

CAPUT VI.

Ecclesiam esse societatem ad salutem consequendam omnino necessariam.

Hinc omnes intelligant, quam necessaria ad salutem obtinendam societas sit Ecclesia Christi. Tantae nimirum necessitatis, quantae consortium et coniunctio est cum Christo capite et mystico eius corpore, praeter quod nullam aliam communionem ipse nutrit et fovet tanquam Ecclesiam suam, quam solam dilexit et seipsum tradidit pro ea, ut illam sanctificaret, mundans lavacro aquae in verbo vitae: ut exhiberet ipse sibi gloriosam Ecclesiam, non habentem maculam, aut rugam, aut aliquid huiusmodi, sed ut sit sancta et immaculata.[2] Idcirco docemus, Ecclesiam non liberam societatem esse, quasi indifferens sit ad salutem, cum sive nosse sive ignorare sive ingredi sive relinquere; sed esse omnino necessariam, et quidem necessitate non tantum praecepti dominici, quo Salvator omnibus gentibus eam ingrediendam praescripsit; verum etiam medii, quia in instituto salutaris providentiae ordine communicatio sancti Spiritus, participatio veritatis et vitae non obtinetur, nisi in Ecclesia et per Ecclesiam, cuius caput est Christus.

[1] Ep. ad Ephes. iv. 4–6.
[2] Cf. ep. ad Ephes. v. 29, et 25–27.

Caput VII.

Extra Ecclesiam salvari neminem posse.

Porro dogma fidei est, extra Ecclesiam salvari neminem posse. Neque tamen, qui circa Christum eiusque Ecclesiam invincibili ignorantia laborant, propter hanc ignorantiam poenis aeternis damnandi sunt, cum nulla obstringantur huiusce rei culpa ante oculos Domini, qui vult omnes homines salvos fieri et ad agnitionem veritatis venire, quique facienti quod in se est non denegat gratiam, ut iustificationem et vitam aeternam consequi possit; sed hanc nullus consequitur, qui a fidei unitate vel ab Ecclesiae communione culpabiliter seiunctus ex hac vita decedit. Si quis in hac arca non fuerit, peribit regnante diluvio. Quare reprobamus et detestamur impiam aeque ac ipsi rationi repugnantem do religionum indifferentia doctrinam, qua filii huius saeculi, veritatis et erroris sublato discrimine, dicunt, omnibus aeternae vitae portum ex qualibet religione patere: aut contendunt de veritate religionis opiniones tantum plus minusve probabiles, non autem certitudinem haberi posse. Pariterque reprobamus impietatem illorum, qui claudunt regnum coelorum ante homines, falsis praetextibus affirmantes, indecorum vel ad salutem minimo necessarium esse, deserere religionem, etsi falsam, in qua quis natus vel educatus ac institutus est; necnon Ecclesiam ipsam, quae se religionem esse unice veram profitetur, omnes autem religiones et sectas a sua communione separatas proscribit et damnat criminantur, perinde ac si ulla unquam esse posset participatio iustitiae cum iniquitate, aut societas lucis ad tenebras, et conventio Christi ad Belial.

Caput VIII.

De Ecclesiae indefectibilitate.

Declaramus insuper, Christi Ecclesiam, sive exsistentia sive constitutio eius spectetur, societatem esse perennem atque indefectibilem, nullamque post illam neque pleniorem neque perfectiorem salutis oeconomiam in hoc saeculo exspectandam esse. Etenim cum ad finem usque mundi qui in terris peregrinantur mortales Christo auctore salvandi sint: Ecclesia ipsius, quae sola est salutis societas, ad finem usque mundi in sua constitutione immutabilis semper et immota persistet. Licet igitur Ecclesia crescat, et utinam augentur igitur fide et caritate, ut Christi corpus aedificetur; licet pro varia aetate sua, et pro diversitate adiunctorum, inter quae constanter militando versatur, vario sese explicet; eadem tamen in se suaque a Christo accepta constitutione immutabilis perseverat. Quare Christi Ecclesia nunquam potest excidere suis proprietatibus et dotibus, sacro suo magisterio, ministerio et regimine, ut Christus per corpus suum visibile perpetuo sit omnibus hominibus via, veritas et vita.

Caput IX.

De Ecclesiae infallibilitate.

Excideret porro Ecclesia Christi a sua immutabilitate et dignitate, et desineret esse societas vitae ac necessariae salutis medium, si eadem a salutari fidei morumque veritate aberrare, ac in ea praedicanda atque exponenda falli vel fallere posset. At columna et firmamentum veritatis [1] est; ideoque ab omni erroris falsitatisque periculo libera et immunis. Sacro autem et universali approbante Concilio docemus atque declaramus, dotem infallibilitatis, quae tanquam perpetua Ecclesiae Christi praerogativa revelata est, quaeque nec cum inspirationis charismate confundi debet, neque eo spectat, ut Ecclesia novis revelationibus ditescat, collatam ad hoc esse, ut verbum Dei, sive id scriptum sive traditum sit, in universali Christi Ecclesia integrum, et a quavis novitatis immutationisque corruptela immune asseratur et custodiatur, secundum illud Apostoli mandatum: O Timothee, depositum custodi, devitans profanas vocum novitates, et oppositiones falsi nominis scientiae, quam quidam promittentes, circa fidem exciderunt.[2] Quod idem Apostolus iterum inculcat scribens: Formam habe sanorum verborum, quae a me audisti in fide et in dilectione in Christo Jesu. Bonum depositum custodi per Spiritum sanctum, qui habitat in nobis.[3] Obiectum igitur infallibilitatis tantum patere docemus, quantum fidei patet depositum, et eius custodiendi officium postulat; adeoque praerogativam infallibilitatis, qua Christi Ecclesia pollet, ambitu suo complecti tum universum Dei verbum revelatum, tum id omne, quod licet si ve revelatum non sit, eo tamen eiusmodi, sine quo illud tuto conservari, certo ac definitive ad credendum proponi et explicari, aut contra errores hominum ac falsi nominis scientiae oppositiones valide asseri defendique non possit. Haec autem infallibilitas, cuius finis est fidelium societatis in doctrina fidei et morum intemerata veritas, magisterio inest, quod Christus Ecclesia sua perpetuum instituit cum ad Apostolos dixit: Euntes

[1] Ep. I. ad Timoth. iii. 15.
[2] Ep. I. ad Timoth. vi. 20.
[3] Ep. II. ad Timoth. i. 13, 14.

ergo docete omnes gentes, baptizantes eos in nomine Patris, et Filii, et Spiritus sancti: docentes eos servare omnia quaecumque mandavi vobis; et ecce ego vobiscum sum omnibus diebus, usque ad consummationem saeculi.[1] Et iisdem promisit Christus veritatis suae Spiritum, qui maneret cum eis in aeternum, in eis esset, eosque omnem veritatem doceret.[2]

CAPUT X.

De Ecclesiae Potestate.

Christi autem Ecclesia non est societas aequalium, acsi omnes in ea fideles eadem iura haberent; verum est societas inaequalis, et hoc non ideo tantum, quia fidelium alii clerici sunt, alii laici; sed propterea maxime, quod in Ecclesia est potestas divinitus instituta, qua alii ad sanctificandum, docendum et regendum praediti sunt, alii destituuntur. Cum vero Ecclesiae potestas alia sit et dicatur ordinis, alia iurisdictionis; de hac altera speciatim docemus, eam non solum esse fori interni et sacramentalis; sed etiam fori exterui ac publici, absolutam atque omnino plenam, nimirum legiferam, iudiciariam, et coercitivam. Potestatis autem huiusmodi subiectum sunt Pastores et Doctores a Christo dati, qui eam libere et a quavis saeculari dominatione independenter exercent; adeoque cum omni imperio[3] regunt Ecclesiam Dei tum necessariis et conscientiam quoque obligantibus legibus, tum decretoriis iudiciis, tum denique salutaribus poenis in sontes etiam invitos, nec solum in iis, quae fidem et mores, cultum et sanctificationem, sed in iis etiam, quae externam Ecclesiae disciplinam et administrationem respiciunt. Unde Ecclesia Christi perfecta societas credenda est. Haec autem vera et tam felix Christi Ecclesia alia non est, praeter unam, sanctam, catholicam, et apostolicam Romanam.

CAPUT XI.

De Romani Pontificis primatu.

Pastor aeternus et episcopus animarum nostrarum, qui priusquam clarificaretur rogavit Patrem, ut credentes in ipsum omnes unum essent, sicut Pater et Filius unum sunt,[4] ad catholicae fidei et communionis unitatem in sua Ecclesia iugiter conservandam, in beato Petro Apostolo instituit perpetuum utriusque unitatis principium ac visibile fundamentum, dum iuxta evangelii testimonia Petro Apostolo primatum iuris-

dictionis in universam Dei Ecclesiam immediate et directe promisit atque contulit. Ad unum namque Petrum Christus Filius Dei vivi dixit: Tu es Petrus et super hanc petram aedificabo Ecclesiam meam, et portae inferi non praevalebunt adversus eam; et tibi dabo claves regni coelorum: et quodcumque ligaveris super terram, erit ligatum et in coelis: et quodcumque solveris super terram, erit solutum et in coelis.[1] Atque uni Simoni Petro contulit Jesus post suam resurrectionem summi pastoris et rectoris iurisdictionem in totum ipsius ovile dicens: Pasce agnos meos. Pasce oves meas.[2] Unde condemnamus atque reiicimus huic tam manifestae sacrarum Scripturarum doctrinae, ut ab Ecclesia catholica semper intellecta est, contrarias eorum sententias, qui constitutam a Christo Domino in sua Ecclesia regiminis formam pervertentes negant, solum Petrum prae omnibus Apostolis sive seorsum singulis sive omnibus simul vero proprioque iurisdictionis primatu fuisse a Christo instructum; aut qui affirmant, eundem primatum non immediate directeque ipsi beato Petro, sed Ecclesiae, et per hanc illi ut suo ministro delatum fuisse.

Quod autem in beato Apostolo Petro princeps pastorum et pastor magnus ovium Dominus Christus Jesus[3] in perpetuum salutem ac perenne bonum Ecclesiae instituit, id eodem auctore in Ecclesia, quae fundata super petram ad finem saeculorum usque firmiter stabit, iugiter durare necesse est. Manet ergo dispositio veritatis, et beatus Petrus suscepta Ecclesiae gubernacula non reliquit.[4] Semper enim in suis successoribus, episcopis sanctae Romanae Sedis, ab ipso primum fundatae, eiusque consecratae sanguine, vivit et praesidet et iudicium exercet, ita ut, quicumque in hac cathedra Petro succedit, is iuxta Christi ipsius institutionem primatum Petri in universam Ecclesiam obtineat. Hinc innovantes atque in omnibus sequentes tum praedecessorum Nostrorum Romanorum Pontificum decreta, tum praecedentium Conciliorum generalium disertas perspicuasque definitiones, docemus et declaramus, credendum ab omnibus Christi fidelibus esse, hanc sanctam Apostolicam Sedem, et Romanum Pontificem, in universum orbem tenere primatum, et ipsum Pontificem Romanum successorem esse beati Petri principis Apostolorum, et verum Christi Vicarium, totiusque Ecclesiae caput, et

---

[1] Matth. xxviii. 19, 20.
[2] Cf. Joann. xiv. 16, 17, coll. xvi. 13.
[3] Cf. ep. ad Tit. ii. 15, coll. ep. i. ad Cor. vii. 6.
[4] Cf. Joann. xvii. 1, 21, sq.

[1] Matth xvi. 18, 19.
[2] Joann. xxi. 16, 17.
[3] Ep. 1. Pet. iv. 4, coll. ep. ad Hebr. xiii. 20.
[4] S. Leo. M. ser. 3 (al. 2), n. 3.

omnium christianorum patrem, doctorem et iudicem supremum existere ; et ipso in beato Petro pascendi, regendi ac gubernandi universalem Ecclesiam a Domino nostro Jesu Christo plenam potestatem traditam esse; et hanc, quae propria est iurisdictionis potestas, ordinariam esse et immediatam, erga quam particularium ecclesiarum pastores atque fideles tam seorsum singuli quam simul omnes officio hierarchicae subordinationis veraeque obedientiae obstringuntur,[1] ut custodita cum Romano Pontifice tam communionis quam eiusdem fidei professionis unitate, Ecclesia Christi sit unus grex sub uno summo pastore. Haec est catholicae veritatis doctrina, a qua deviare salva fide atque salute nemo potest. Quare damnamus atque reprobamus eorum sententias, qui a fide discedentes et attendentes spiritibus erroris[2] negant, primatus potestatem a Christo Domino fuisse in beato Petro ita institutam, ut eundem oporteat perpetuos in collata sibi primatus potestate successores habere; aut affirmant, Romanorum Pontificum iurisdictionem ordinariam et immediatam non esse tam in omnes simul quam in singulas seorsum particularium pastorum ecclesias; aut etiam contendunt, licere ab iudiciis Romanorum Pontificum ad futurum generale Concilium tanquam ad auctoritatem Romano Pontifice superiorem appellare.

Ex hac autem suprema, ordinaria et immediata tum in Ecclesiam universalem, tum in omnes et singulos particularium Ecclesiarum pastores et fideles potestate iurisdictionis consequitur, Romano Pontifici necessarium ius esse, in huius sui muneris exercitio libere communicandi cum pastoribus et gregibus totius Ecclesiae, ut iidem ab ipso in via salutis doceri ac regi possint. Quare damnamus ac reprobamus perniciosas illorum sententias, qui hanc supremi capitis cum pastoribus et gregibus communicationem impediendam dicunt, aut eandem reddunt saeculari potestati obnoxiam, ita ut contendant, quae ab Apostolica Sede vel eius auctoritate ad regimen Ecclesiae constituuntur, vim ac valorem non habere, nisi potestatis saecularis placito confirmentur.

CAPUT XII.

De temporali Sanctae Sedis Dominio.

Ut autem Romanus Pontifex primatus sibi divinitus collati munus, uti par est, adimpleret, iis indigebat praesidiis, quae temporum conditioni et necessitati congrue-

[1] Expressa ad formulas fidei Conc. Lugdunens. ii. Conc. Florentin., et Pii VI. Brev. "Super soliditate."
[2] Ep. I. ad Tim. iv. 1.

rent. Unde singulari divinae providentiae consilio factum est, ut in tanta saecularium principum multitudine et varietate, Romana quoque Ecclesia temporalem dominationem haberet : quo Romanus Pontifex, summus totius Ecclesiae pastor, nulli principi subiectus, supremam universi dominici gregis pascendi regendique potestatem auctoritatemque ab ipso Christo Domino acceptam per universum orbem plenissima libertate exercere, ac simul facilius divinam religionem magis in dies augere, et quae pro re se tempore ad maiorem totius christianae reipublicae utilitatem pertinere ipso cognosceret, efficacius peragere posset.

Cum vero impii homines, qui omne in terris ius mutare conantur, hunc civilem Sanctae Romanae Ecclesiae principatum, in rei christianae bonum et utilitatem ordinatum, et ab ea omnibus iuris titulis legitime tot saeculorum decursu possessum, quovis insidiarum et violentiarum genere labefactare ac convellere adnitantur: sacro approbante Concilio innovantes huius Apostolicae Sedis ac praecedentium Conciliorum iudicia ac decreta, damnamus atque proscribimus tum eorum haereticam doctrinam, qui affirmant, repugnare iuri divino, ut cum spirituali potestate in Romanis Pontificibus principatus civilis coniungatur, tum perversam eorum sententiam, qui contendunt, Ecclesiae non esse, de huius principatus civilis ad generale christianae reipublicae bonum relatione quidpiam cum auctoritate constituere; adeoque licere catholicis hominibus, ab illius decisionibus hac de re editis recedere aliterque sentire.

CAPUT XIII.

De concordia inter Ecclesiam ac societatem civilem.

Perfecta haec civitas, quam sacrae litterae regnum Dei appellant, superna quidem est, si, unde orta sit et quo tendat, cogitatur, descendens quasi Christi sponsa de coelo et transitura in coelestem illam, quae sursum est Jerusalem consummatorum, cum Christus tradiderit regnum Deo et Patri, ut sit Deus omnia in omnibus.[1] Nunc vero Ecclesia usque ad finem saeculorum in terris atque inter terrenas civitates adhuc militans, ex divini fundatoris sui omniumque Redemptoris mandato in sinum suum maternum colligit omnes gentes, quae sicut indole ac moribus inter se diversae, ita etiam multiplici et varia civilis societatis forma sunt constitutae. Qui enim homines, ad sui conservationem et congruam rationi

[1] Cf. Heb. xii. 22, 23; 1 Cor. xv. 24, 2:.

felicitatem temporalem, natura duce et Dei creatoris ordinatione in civilem societatem coierunt, iidem ut aeternum salventur, in sanctam illam societatem, quae est Ecclesia, gratia Dei Salvatoris vocantur. Cum igitur utriusque societatis, licet modo diverso pro diverso earum ordine ac fine, Deus infinito sanctus et sapiens sit auctor: ex ipsa natura inter Ecclesiam et societatem civilem vel inter potestates, quibus utraque regitur, non sane pugna est aut oppositio.

Quin immo Ecclesia rempublicam maximo munimento firmat ac tuetur, eiusque securitati prospicit. Illa enim instituta ad sanctificandos homines, ipsa virtute et pietate christiana bonos etiam cives facit, qui si tales sint, quales esse praecipit doctrina catholica, sine dubio magna erunt salus reipublicae.[1] Praeterea cum terrena potestas in temporali utilitate et poenarum metu suam observandarum legum sanctionem positam habeat, vera religio, cuius et custos et magistra est Ecclesia catholica, auctoritatem imperantium validius doctrina legibusque divinis confirmat. Praecipit enim religio catholica sua auctoritate divina, ut homines legitimae potestati subditi sint non solum propter iram, sed etiam propter conscientiam.[2]

Quodsi Ecclesia monet ac iubet subditos secundum mandatum divinitus acceptum obedire regibus, non minus reges quoque docet prospicere populis, ut intelligant et erudiantur, qui iudicant terram, non ad dominandi cupiditatem, sed ad officium providendi sibi datum esse a Domino potestatem et virtutem ab Altissimo, ut tamquam ministri regni eius recte iudicent, et custodiant legem iustitiae; quoniam pusillum et magnum ipse fecit et aequaliter cura est illi de omnibus.[3]

Ecclesia igitur catholica regum et populorum, atque in his singulorum omnis conditionis hominum religione divina tum iura tuetur tum officia docet ac praecipit, atque ita legibus humanis sanctius fundamentum ponit et fideliorem conciliat obedientiam. Quare cum haec civitas Dei tantum conferat ad securitatem et felicitatem civitatis terrenae, vel ex hoc uno omnes intelligant, quanta sapientia ac bonitate Deus auctor naturae et gratiae atque utriusque civitatis ordinator potestates sacerdotii et imperii non inimicas sed vinculo pacis coniungendas disposuerit. Haec autem utriusque civitatis coniunctio ex qua in ipsam civilem societatem tanta bona promanant, non liberae hominum optioni permissa sed Dei lege praecepta est. Quoniam enim non solum

[1] Cf. Aug. ad Marcellin. ep. 138, n. 15.
[2] Rom. xiii. 5. [3] Cf. Sap. vi. 4–8.

singuli privatim homines sed etiam omnes in vita publica ipsaque societas ad veram religionem erga Deum tenentur religionisque legibus obstringuntur, hinc ipsa publica societas, cuius cives simul fideles sint, magnis necessariis officiis obligatur erga Dei Ecclesiam, quae vera religionis doctrinam et leges et iura ex divino mandato custodit ac tuetur.

Quapropter nemo dicere praesumat, non posse auctoritatem et iura Ecclesiae cum saecularis potestatis iuribus et auctoritate consistere; atque ideo ad optimam societatis publicae rationem necessariam esse civilis reipublicae ab Ecclesia separationem, ita ut imperio negetur ius et officium coercendi sancitis poenis violatores catholicae religionis, nisi quatenus pax publica postulet; vel omnino ita, ut humana societas constituatur et gubernetur nullo habito ad religionem respectu, ac si ea non existeret, vel saltem nullo facto veram inter falsasque religiones discrimine.

Quod inter sacerdotium et imperium dissidia orta sunt et in dies oriuntur, id nemo audeat asserere ex ipsa indole ac natura potestatis ecclesiasticae provenire. Pax vera inter utramque potestatem et concordia, quam Ecclesia semper optat et humili supplicatione postulat a Deo, servari nunquam potest, si libertas sponsae Jesu Christi opprimitur et violantur iura, quae Ecclesia exercere atque integra servare non solum potest sed etiam debet, quia simul cum officiis cohaerent, quae ipsi a divino suo fundatore iniuncta sunt ad salutem animarum.

Huiusmodi bella iniquissima, qui volunt esse Ecclesiae filii, matri suae nunquam inferrent, si imperantium et populorum mentibus constanter obversaretur veritas a Christo Domino severissimis verbis inculcata, nihil prodesse homini mundum universum lucrari, si animae suae detrimentum patiatur,[1] atque adeo supra illam felicitatem vitae humanae, ad quam civilis potestas per se ordinatur, esse finem sublimiorem et unice necessarium beatitudinis aeternae, ad quam homines per Ecclesiam sunt deducendi; ideoque habita vel sola ratione finis, qui utrique praestituitur, reipublicae civili Ecclesiam Jesu Christi tantum praecellere, quantum huius vitae commoda ac bona superat salus animarum non auro vel argento, sed pretioso sanguine Christi redemptarum, et vitae aeternae felicitas.

Quamvis igitur civilis societatis dispositio per se et directe non ad supernaturalem felicitatem, sed ad temporale communitatis

[1] Cf. Matth. xvi. 26.

bonum pertineat, christianis tamen hominibus non in hoc solummodo sistendum est; sed postulatur ab eis, ut temporali bono praeferant sempiternum, atque ideo non minus in publicis rebus, quam in privatis negotiis, finem inferiorem non ita respiciant, ut finem hominis ultimum et necessarium ab oculis dimittant; unde si quando videantur utilia regno temporali, quae bonis sublimioribus Ecclesiae et aeternae saluti repugnent, ea nunquam habebunt pro veris bonis, sed sincere consequi studebunt, quod aiebat magnus ille Gregorius, ut terrestre regnum coelesti regno famuletur.

Caput XIV.

De iure et usu potestatis civilis secundum Ecclesiae catholicae doctrinam.

Spreta Ecclesiae catholicae doctrina et auctoritate, eiusque circa humanam societatem iuribus conculcatis, subintroierunt nostris temporibus magistri mendaces, qui non solum Ecclesiae, sed etiam omnis humani consortii hostes, dominationem contemnunt,[1] ita ut nulla lege, nisi quam ipsi sponte susceperint, obligari se posse dicant, omnemque sublimiorem potestatem ab ipsis independentem pro iniusto dominatu habeant, quem pro lubitu abiicere atque evertere liceat: immo etiam contra manifestam Dei legem affirmant, omnes homines ex lege naturae ita aequales iuribus esse, ut tum privata possessionum proprietas tum alia quaevis unius prae reliquis praerogativa iniusta censeri et abrogari debeat.

Alii autem falsam civilis societatis speciem ac formam animo suo effingentes statum politicum, quem vocant, constituunt fontem omnis inter homines auctoritatis omnisque iuris, ita ut ab eodem statu politico ciusque lege tum ius proprietatis privatae unice derivari, tum societatem domesticam seu familiam suae existentiae totam rationem mutuari, omniaque parentum in filios iura dimanare ac pendere affirment, tum in eius lege vel in maioris numeri civium placitis et in publica, ut dicunt, opinione positam esse velint supremam normam conscientiae et officiorum pro publicis et socialibus sive imperantium sive subditorum actionibus. Quin et eo usque non paucos progressos esse videmus, ut fortunatis eventibus vim iuris tribuentes audeant dicere, id quod ex lege morali esset iniustum, si felicem habeat exitum, eo ipso in publicis rebus ac negotiis ex lege politica iustum credere et honestum, quasi vero lex moralis ad sociales et politicos

[1] Cf. II. Pet. II. 10.

actus non aeque ac ad privatos sese porrigeret. At haec humanae superbiae figmenta non alio tendunt, quam ut incommutabilis sanctitas et iustitia aeterni Dei auferatur a recordatione filiorum hominum, in eorum animis sensus extinguatur iusti et iniusti, et inficiatur terra ab habitatoribus suis, quia transgressi sunt leges, mutaverunt ius, dissipaverunt foedus sempiternum.[1]

Contra huiusmodi errores, qui etiam inter catholicos populos serpere coeperunt, omnibus in mentem revocandam statuimus doctrinam catholicam, ut ea integra et inviolata custoditatur. Docemus igitur, quod ab Apostolo traditum semper docuit Ecclesia, omnem legitimam potestatem, ideoque etiam civilem, Deum habere auctorem. "Omnis anima, scribit Apostolus,[2] potestatibus sublimioribus subdita sit, non est enim potestas nisi a Deo, quae autem sunt, a Deo ordinatae sunt;" et ex ciusdem Apostoli sententia, qui hanc potestatem tenet, Dei minister est sive bonum facientibus in bonum, sive malum agentibus vindex in iram,[3] atque ideo subditorum obedientiam iure suo postulat. Nemo itaque docere audeat, licitum esse huic legitimae potestati vi resistere, aut per detestandum facinus eam coniurationibus ac rebellione evertere, qui enim resistit potestati, Dei ordinationi resistit; qui autem resistunt, ipsi sibi damnationem acquirunt.[4]

Pari ratione docemus, imperantibus in suae potestatis usu eandem normam divinae legis esse sequendam. Lex enim moralis sive lumine rationis sive per supernaturalem revelationem manifestata sicut pro hominibus actionibusque privatis, ita n on minus pro iis qui praesunt, et pro publicorum munerum administratione actibusque socialibus ac politicis posita est. Norma itaque agendi non in utilitate, aut in multitudinis opinione ac voluntate constitui potest, quando ad illicita ac Dei legi repugnantia impellunt; sed necessaria morum regula sicut pro subditis ita pro imperantibus etiam in ipsorum muneribus administrandis est lex Dei iubentis aut vetantis, secundum quam omnes in supremo iudicio communi Domino aut stabunt aut cadent. De ipsa autem agendi norma iudicium, quatenus de morum honestate, de licito vel illicito statuendum est, pro civili etiam societate publicisque negotiis ad supremum Ecclesiae magisterium pertinet. Sane in via salutis aeternae omnibus tam subditis quam principibus Ecclesia a Deo constituta est dux et magistra. Neque de imperantibus minus verum est: qui Ecclesiam matrem non habet, Deum patrem habere non potest.

[1] Cf. Is. xxiv. 5. [2] Rom. xiii. 1.
[3] Cf. Ib. vers. 3, 4. [4] Rom. xiii. 2.

Ut igitur Regem regum patrem ac propitium habere possint, Ecclesiam se matrem habere re et opere comprobare studeant; neque licere sibi existiment sive in privatis sive in publicis negotiis ob politicas rationes Dei et sanctae matris Ecclesiae leges ac iura violare.

CAPUT XV.

De specialibus quibusdam Ecclesiae iuribus ¡ in relatione ad societatem civilem.

Inter sanctissimorum iurium violationes, quae nostra aetate ad nationes erroribus inficiendas corrumpendosque in eis mores christianos perpetrantur, illa est vel maxime perniciosa, qua fraudulenti homines contendunt, scholas omnes directioni ac arbitrio solius potestatis laicae subiiciendas esse, ita ut auctoritas Ecclesiae ad providendum religiosae institutioni et educationi iuventutis christianae omnino impediatur. Quin eo usque progressi sunt, ut ipsam catholicam religionem a publica educatione arcere, atque universim scholas nullius professionis religiosae, sed litterarias tantummodo esse debere dicant. Contra huiusmodi sanae doctrinae morumque corruptelas ex ipso fine Ecclesiae a Christo Salvatore fundatae, ut homines per salutarem fidem ac disciplinam docendo regendoque ad vitam aeternam adducat, ab omnibus agnoscendum est ius et officium, quo ipsa pervigilat, ut iuventus catholica in primis vera fide et sanctis moribus rite instituatur.

Hanc iniquitatem cumularunt alia usurpatione. Ipsam enim Clericorum educationem ac institutionem in disciplinis ecclesiasticis tum in aliis publicis scholis tum in ipsis Seminariis efficaci directioni ac vigilantiae Ecclesiae subducere et potestati laicae mancipare praesumunt contra ius proprium Ecclesiae, quo maxime in suis ministris sanitati catholicae doctrinae et sanctitati vitae ecclesiasticae providere debet. Quin etiam eos ipsos, qui in sortem Domini vocantur, a sancta sua vocatione per vim avellere et iniquissima lege subiicere militiae saeculari alicubi veriti non sunt, atque ita quantum in ipsis est, Ecclesiam necessariis ad docendum, regendum et sanctificandum populum Dei ministris privare conantur. Quare declaramus et docemus, iura praedicta atque officia ad Ecclesiam pertinere, et esse cum eius magisterio divinitus instituto, cum ipsius constitutione ac fine intime coniuncta, adeoque humanis legibus non posse auferri.

Alia gravis iniuria sanctae Ecclesiae infertur ab illis, qui professionem perfectionis evangelicae in Ordinibus Institutisque religiosis ab eadem Ecclesia approbatis iniqua oppugnatione persequuntur, atque affirmare audent, professionem religiosam iuribus naturae libertatisque humanae contrariam, vel ex regnis et civitatibus nostrae aetatis eliminandam esse, quod illa profectui ac felicitati populorum opponatur; eoque magis dolendum, quod inter ipsos legum latores, qui se catholicos profitentur, non desint, qui in hac re Ecclesiae ius conculcare et iniquis legibus, quantum valent, irritum reddere non vereantur.

Quoniam vero sponsa Iesu Christi ipsam divini sponsi sui vitam et exemplum in se suisque membris exprimere, atque ingiter sanctitatis praerogativa fulgere debet, idem Dominus Noster Iesus Christus non solum sancta dedit mandata omnibus, si volunt ad vitam ingredi, necessario servanda; sed etiam pro Ecclesia praemonstravit in suo evangelio statum perfectionis, quo ii, qui Deo vocante capiunt verbum istud, relictis omnibus, ut thesaurum habeant in coelis, ipsum Iesum Christum propinquiori imitatione sequantur.[1] Consilia haec Iesu Christi ad Ecclesiam sponsam ac reginam ornandam varietatibus[2] non potuerunt manere irrita; unde operante divina gratia omnibus Ecclesiae aetatibus plurimi utriusque sexus crucis Christi sectatores in hac via ipsum Dominum ducem ac magistrum secuti sunt. Ut sic vocatis evangelicam perfectionem consectandi media non deessent, providentissima mater Ecclesia semper sedulo curavit. Legis enim pro summa auctoritate vel ipsa tulit vel a sanctissimis viris propositas probavit, quibus religiosa vita et professio firma ac tuta consisteret, et ad sanctum suum finem dirigeretur. Quamvis igitur non omnes vocati sint ad hanc vitae rationem in consiliis evangelicis voluntariae ac perpetuae paupertatis, continentiae, et obedientiae sequendam: attamen ex constanti Ecclesiae declaratione atque usu omnibus necesse est aestimare, eam apostolicae doctrinae consentaneam esse et ad christianam perfectionem conducere. Ii vero, quibus datum est a Patre Christum vocantem audire et sequi, ultra praeceptorum observationem consilia quoque evangelica in institutis religiosis non solum activo sed etiam contemplativae vitae secundum modum ab Ecclesia approbatum pie et laudabiliter amplectuntur, ac divina gratia opitulante possunt et tenentur, quae voverunt, reddere Domino Deo. Quare tum haec Ecclesiae et fidelium iura tum suscepta votis religiosis officia in supernaturali Dei lege ac ordinatione fundantur, qua Christus

[1] Cf. Matth. xix. 11, 12, 17-29.
[2] Cf. Ps. xliv. 10-16.

sapientia aeterna in sancta Ecclesia sua viam perfectionis evangelicae monstravit ac disposuit; nec illa politicis legibus sive dirigi sive doleri possunt.

Damnamus igitur tum doctrinam, qua professio religiosa illicita vel vero profectui populorum noxia, ac propterea eliminanda esse dicitur, tum impios hominum conatus, qui commemorata Ecclesiae ac fidelium iura invadunt, et tantam·ipsi Deo ac sanctae religioni catholicae irrogant iniuriam.

Hic porro aliam sacrilegam iniustitiam, qua contra matrem Ecclesiam crudeliter et in dies latius grassatur, iterum damnare et perniciosissimas fallacias, quibus homines mendaces illam obvelare student, proscribere necesse Nobis est. Dicunt nimirum, ius Ecclesiae, acquirendi et possidendi bona temporalia, esse subiectum arbitrio status politici, et ab eius libera concessione iugiter pendere, ita ut potestas politica vi suae suprema auctoritatis possit illud ius abolere, latisque legibus sibi vindicare velut bona domino vacua, quae legitimo proprietatis titulo sunt in possessione Ecclesiae; aut affirmant, dispositionem ac distributionem bonorum ecclesiasticorum non secus ac eorum, quae publica sunt totius nationis, pertinere ad nativum ius supremae potestatis politicae. Huiusmodi autem perversis doctrinis impugnantur iura Ecclesiae certissima, quae ex ipsa eius divinitus data constitutione promanant. Ecclesia namque cum sit perfecta societas divino iure constituta, supernaturalis quidem, sed eadem societas visibilis ex hominibus et ad hominum salutem in terris consistens, propterea rebus etiam visibilibus et externis atque inter haec bonis quoque temporalibus utitur et iuvatur tamquam mediis ad divinam suam missionem adimplendam et ad finem sibi a Christo Salvatore propositum assequendum. Ad hanc enim suam missionem Ecclesia visibilis ex natura sua et ex divina institutione ministros proprios habet ex hominibus assumptos et pro hominibus constitutos, qui non potestati saeculari subordinati, sed ab ea independentes sacris muneribus fungantur: atque ideo iure suo .Ecclesia eis prospicit, ut iuxta ordinationem Domini qui evangelium annuntiant, de evangelio vivant:[1] ciusdemque Ecclesiae sicut officium ita proprium ius est, providendi tum decori externi divini cultus, tum multiplicibus indigentium membrorum Christi necessitatibus, tum aliis, quae opportuna iudicaverit, christianae caritatis et pietatis operibus. His vero muneribus Ecclesiae atque officiis exsequendis cum secundum ordinem divinae providentiae bona

temporalia subserviant, sane illud ius acquirendi ac possidendi titulo proprietatis, quod mere humanis societatibus legitime con-titutis competere potest, in Ecclesia non deficit, sed in ea, ut in societate divinitus et ad altiorem finem instituta et ad imperiis mundanis independente, etiam sanctius est ac superioris ordinis, quia bona huiusmodi mystico corpori Christi, et per hoc ipsi Christo Deo specialius dicata sunt.

Quare docemus, Ecclesiae, ut societati visibili a Deo inter homines constitutae, ius esse, bona temporalia acquirendi et possidendi, neque hoc iure eam a quavis potestate saeculari privari posse; ac propterea praedictos errores damnamus, et leges quibus status politicus tanquam ex supremo iure sibi inhaerente bona ecclesiastica usurpat, iniustas spoliationes esse declaramus.

Haec sunt, quae generatim visum Nobis est, Christi fideles circa Ecclesiam Christi docere: his autem contraria certis et propriis Canonibus in hunc qui sequitur modum damnare, ut omnes, adiuvante Christo fidei regula utentes, catholicam veritatem facilius agnoscere et tenere possint.

De Ecclesia Christi.

CANON I.—Si quis dixerit, Christi religionem in nulla peculiari societate ab ipso Christo fundata exstantem et expressam esse, sed a singulis seorsum, non habita ratione ad ullam societatem quae vera ipsius Ecclesia sit, rite observari et excoli posse; anathema sit.

CANON II.—Si quis dixerit Ecclesiam a Christo Domino nullam certam ac immutabilem constitutionis formam accepisse, sed aeque ac reliquas hominum societates, pro temporum diversitate vicissitudinibus et transformationibus subiectam fuisse, aut subiici posse; anathema sit.

CANON III.—Si quis dixerit, divinarum promissionum Ecclesiam non esse societatem externam ac conspicuam, sed totam internam ac invisibilem; anathema sit.

CANON IV.—Si quis dixerit, veram Ecclesiam non esse unum in se corpus, sed ex variis dissitisque christiani nominis societatibus constare, per easque diffusam esse; aut varias societates ab invicem fidei professione dissidentes atque communione seiunctas, tanquam membra vel partes unam et universalem constituere Christi Ecclesiam; anathema sit.

CANON V.—Si quis dixerit, Ecclesiam Christi non esse societatem ad aeternam salutem consequendam omnino necessariam; aut homines per cuiusvis religionis cultum salvari posse; anathema sit.

[1] Cf. 1 Cor. ix. 14.

CANON VI.—Si quis dixerit, intolerantiam illam, qua Ecclesia catholica omnes religiosas sectas a sua communione separatas proscribit et damnat, divino iure non praecipi; aut de veritate religionis opiniones tantum non autem certitudinem haberi posse; ideoque omnes sectas religiosas ab Ecclesia tolerandas esse; anathema sit.

CANON VII.—Si quis dixerit, eandem Christi Ecclesiam posse offundi tenebris, aut infici malis, quibus a salutari fidei morumque veritate aberret, ab originali sua institutione deviet, aut depravata et corrupta tandem desinat esse; anathema sit.

CANON VIII.—Si quis dixerit, praesentem Christi Ecclesiam non esse ultimam ac supremam consequendae salutis oeconomiam, sed exspectandam esse aliam, per novam vel pleniorem divini Spiritus effusionem; anathema sit.

CANON IX.—Si quis dixerit, Ecclesiae infallibilitatem ad ea tantum restringi, quae divina revelatione continentur, nec ad alias etiam veritates extendi, quae necessario requiruntur, ut revelationis depositum integrum custodiatur; anathema sit.

CANON X.—Si quis dixerit, Ecclesiam non esse societatem perfectam, sed collegium; aut ita in civili seu in statu esse, ut saeculari dominationi subiiciatur; anathema sit.

CANON XI.—Si quis dixerit, Ecclesiam institutam divinitus esse tanquam societatem aequalium; ab episcopis vero haberi quidem officium et ministerium, non autem propriam regiminis potestatem, quae ipsis divina ordinatione competat, quaeque ab iisdem sit libere exercenda; anathema sit.

CANON XII.—Si quis dixerit, a Christo Domino et Salvatore nostro Ecclesiae suae collatam tantam fuisse potestatem dirigendi per consilia et suasiones, non vero etiam iubendi per leges, ac devios contumacesque exteriori iudicio ac salubribus poenis coercendi atque cogendi; anathema sit.

CANON XIII.—Si quis dixerit, veram Christi Ecclesiam, extra quam nemo salvus esse potest, aliam esse praeter unam, sanctam, catholicam, et apostolicam Romanam; anathema sit.

CANON XIV.—Si quis dixerit, beatum Petrum Apostolorum a Christo Domino constitutum non esse Apostolorum omnium principem et totius Ecclesiae militantis visibile caput; vel cum tantum honoris, non autem verae proprineque iurisdictionis primatum accepisse; anathema sit.

CANON XV.—Si quis dixerit, non esse ex ipsius Christi Domini institutione, ut beatus Petrus in primatu super universam Ecclesiam habeat perpetuos successores; aut Romanum Pontificem non esse iure divino Petri in eodem primatu successorem; anathema sit.

CANON XVI.—Si quis dixerit, Romanum Pontificem habere tantummodo officium inspectionis vel directionis, non autem plenam et supremam potestatem iurisdictionis in universam Ecclesiam; aut hanc eius potestatem non esse ordinariam et immediatam in omnes ac singulas ecclesias; anathema sit.

CANON XVII.—Si quis dixerit, potestatem ecclesiasticam independentem, quam Ecclesia catholica sibi a Christo tributam esse docet, supremamque potestatem, civilem non posse simul consistere, ita ut iura utriusque salva sint; anathema sit.

CANON XVIII.—Si quis dixerit, potestatem, quae ad regendam civilem societatem necessaria est, non esse a Deo; aut eidem ex ipsa Dei lege subiectionem non deberi; aut eam naturali hominis libertati repugnare; anathema sit.

CANON XIX.—Si dixerit, omnia inter homines iura derivari a statu politico; aut nullam nisi ab ipso communicatam dari auctoritatem; anathema sit.

CANON XX.—Si quis dixerit, in lege status politici vel in publica hominum opinione constitutam esse pro publicis ac socialibus actionibus supremam conscientiae normam; aut ad easdem non extendi Ecclesiae iudicia, quibus ea de licito et illicito pronuntiat; aut vi iuris civilis fieri licitum, quod iure divino vel ecclesiastico est illicitum; anathema sit.

CANON XXI.—Si quis dixerit, leges Ecclesiae vim obligandi non habere, nisi quatenus civilis potestatis sanctione firmentur; aut eidem civili potestati vi suae supremae auctoritatis competere, in causis religionis iudicare et decernere; anathema sit.

DOCUMENT XIV.

Apparisce da questo prospetto, e consta dalle relazioni unanimi di quanti hanno percorsa la Svizzera, che i Protestanti vi godono di maggior prosperità che i Cattolici. Se cercassimo di ascrivere un tal fatto alla differenza del territorio, mostreremmo ignorare che più Cantoni cattolici (per esempio, Lucerna, Friburgo, Solera, Ticino) hanno suolo più fertile di quello dei Protestanti di Ginevra, Neuchatel, ec., che dove i Cattolici si trovano misti ai Riformati su terreno di egual indole, ivi sono questi non poco superiori a quelli in benessere, e ciò si tocca con mano nei Cantoni di Glarona, Friburgo, Appenzello, Grigioni, San Gallo, ec. Adunque molti dei Protestanti vanno dicendo esser la religione riformata migliore della cattolica, ma essi la discorrono alla peggio, perchè in ciò l' essenza della religione non ha parte; ma dicesi dunque, perchè sonosi i Cattolici lasciati sorpassare in prosperità dai Riformati? Chi adduce una causa, e chi un' altra. I prudenti sono d'avviso concorrero insieme parecchie ragioni, ec.

(*Statistica della Svizzera* di Stefano Franscini, ticinese. Lugano, 1827.)

DOCUMENT XV.

LETTRE DU COMTE DE MONTALEMBERT.

"Paris, juillet 1869.

"MONSIEUR,

"... Deux fois, depuis quelques semaines, j'ai touché au bord de la tombe, sans pouvoir y trouver la délivrance après laquelle je soupire et que le bon Dieu me fait attendre si longtemps.... Toutefois, la fin de mes maux ne peut tarder; et dès à présent il me semble que je puis juger des choses et des personnes d'ici bas avec un désintéressement et une indépendance dont la mort seule a le privilége.

"Au milieu de cette ruine du corps, mon âme me semble avoir conservé encore une certaine vigueur, et c'est avec une intime et profonde jouissance que mon cœur et mon esprit vont se réfugier sur ces bords du Rhin où se sont développées mes premières impressions d'étudiant, et où je retrouve aujourd'hui les seules consolations qu'il me soit donné de rencontrer dans la sphère des préoccupations du polémiste politique et religieux.

"Ces consolations, c'est à vous, Monsieur, que je les dois, à vous et à vos amis, à votre excellent journal les Kœlnische Blætter, à la savante et courageuse Feuille théologique de Bonn, mais surtout à l'admirable Adresse de certains laïques de Coblence à l'évêque de Trèves sur le futur concile, dont vous avez publié lo texte et dont vous avez eu l'extrême bonté de m'envoyer un exemplaire.

"Je ne saurais vous dire à quel point j'ai été ému et charmé par ce glorieux Manifeste de la conscience et de la raison des catholiques.... J'ai cru voir luire un éclair au milieu des ténèbres, et entendre enfin un accent viril et chrétien au milieu des déclamations et des adulations écœurantes dont nous sommes assourdis....

"Tout m'y a paru irréprochable dans la forme comme dans le fond. J'en aurais volontiers signé chaque ligne.

"Vous me permettrez d'ajouter que je me sens un peu humilié par la pensée que vous autres, Allemands du Rhin, vous avez eu cette fois l'initiative d'une démonstration qui convenait si bien aux antécédents des catholiques français, comme aux convictions qui, pendant la première moitié du dix-neuvième siècle, nous ont valu l'honneur d'inaugurer la défense de la liberté religieuse sur le continent...

"Agréez, etc.,

"CH. DE MONTALEMBERT."

DOCUMENT XVI.

COBLENZER LAIEN.—ADRESSE AN DEN B. V. TRIER.

Hochwürdigster Herr! Ew. Bischöflichen Gnaden als unserem geistlichen Hirten und Bischofe nahen wir, die unterzeichneten Gläubigen der Diöcese Trier, in einer hochwichtigen, ernsten, unsere h. Kirche und damit unsere tiefsten Lebensinteressen unmittelbar berührenden Sache, von unserem Gewissen gedrungen, eine ehrfurchtsvolle, offene und freimüthige Erklärung vor Ihnen und der ganzen Kirche abzugeben.

Hochwürdigster Herr! In Ihrem diesjährigen Fastenhirtenbriefe, in welchem Sie die Gläubigen auf die Bedeutung des bevorstehenden allgemeinen Concils hinwiesen, erwähnten Sie, dass in einem allgemeinen Concil zwar nur die Bischöfe als die Nachfolger der Apostel entscheidendes Stimmrecht haben, dass aber nicht bloss ihre, sondern aller Glieder der Kirche Erfahrung und Einsicht dort gehört und beachtet werde, dass nicht nur Priester, auch Laien, selbst in wichtigen Fragen, Einfluss auf die Beschlüsse der Concilien zu üben berufen sein könnten. In der That sehen wir demgemäss auch heute eine Anzahl von Gläubigen, deren lauteste Stimmführer nicht Bischöfe, sondern Ordensmänner und Laien sind, eifrigst bemüht, der Wirksamkeit des künftigen Concils gleichsam eine bestimmte Richtung anzuweisen, und hören, wie sie, ihre Wünsche und Lieblingsmeinungen mit dem Glauben und den Bedürfnissen der Kirche verwechselnd, alle diejenigen im Gegensatze zu den "eigentlichen" für "liberale" Katholiken erklären, welche ihre Lehrsätze als Dogmen anzuerkennen und ihre Bestrebungen als heilbringend zu betrachten ausser

Stande sind. Diese Gläubigen haben im Mittelpunkte der Kirche, in Rom selbst, ein Pressorgan, die *Civiltà Cattolica*, in welchem sie vor Kurzem in Form einer Correspondenz aus Frankreich folgende auch in einer Zeitschrift deutscher Ordensmänner reproducirte, durch spätere Erklärungen nicht wesentlich abgeschwächte Sätze veröffentlichten:

"Die liberalen Katholiken fürchten, das künftige Concilium möchte etwa die Doctrin des Syllabus und die dogmatische Unfehlbarkeit des Papstes proklamiren, hoffen jedoch wieder andererseits das Concilium könne etwa einige von den Sätzen des Syllabus modificiren oder in einem ihnen günstigen Sinne erläutern. Ebenso hegen sie die Erwartung das Concilium werde die Unfehlbarkeit des Papstes gar nicht behandeln, oder doch wenigstens nicht erledigen...

"Die eigentlichen Katholiken aber, das heisst die grosse Mehrheit der Gläubigen, nähren ganz andere Hoffnungen.

"Ziemlich allgemein findet man die Ueberzeugung verbreitet, dass das künftige Concil ein kurzes, etwa wie das von Chalcedon, sein werde, denn man fühlt die Schwierigkeit, unter den gegenwärtigen Umständen eine langdauernde Versammlung zu halten, und vor Allem erwartet man von den Bischöfen, dass sie in den Hauptfragen einig sein werden, so dass die Minorität nicht lange wird opponiren können, so beredt sie auch sein mag...

"Die Katholiken wünschen, wie schon gesagt, dass das ökumenische Concil die Doctrinen des Syllabus proklamire...

"Die Katholiken werden die Proclamation der dogmatischen Unfehlbarkeit des Papstes mit Jubel aufnehmen.... Natürlich wird der Papst in dieser Frage, welche ihn direct zu berühren scheint, die Initiative nicht ergreifen, sondern schweigsam und zurückhaltend sein. Aber man hofft, dass die einstimmige Kundgebung d. h. Geistes durch den Mund der Väter des ökumenischen Concils das Dogma der Unfehlbarkeit des Papstes per acclamationem definiren wird.

"Endlich giebt es in Frankreich auch noch eine Menge Katholiken welche den Wunsch aussprechen, das künftige Concilium möge den vielen von der Kirche der unbefleckten Jungfrau Maria dargebrachten Huldigungen durch das Dogma von der glorreichen Aufnahme Mariä in den Himmel die Krone aufsetzen!"

Hochwürdigster Herr! Wären das Acusserungen irgend einer beliebigen, vereinzelten, durch keinerlei Gunstbezeugungen von Seiten einer kirchlichen Autorität aufgemunterten katholischen Zeitung, wir dürften wohl schwerlich uns veranlasst gesehen haben, aus unserer Zurückhaltung hervorzutreten. Nun aber ist es nicht unbekannt, dass jene Gläubigen mit der Zuneigung kirchlicher Autoritäten und des heil. Stuhles selbst sich schmeicheln, und hat es den Anschein, als ob ein grosser Orden mit der ganzen Wucht einheitlicher Organisation nach denselben Zielen dränge; es wäre demnach leicht erklärlich, wenn ein so planmässiges und energisches, die allgemeinste Zustimmung beanspruchendes Vorgehen, falls es von keiner Seite offenen Widerspruch erfahren sollte, über die Gesinnungen der Katholiken bedeutende, unter den gegenwärtigen Umständen doppelt beklagenswerthe Irrthümer veranlasste. Angesichts einer solchen Lage aber dürfen und können auch wir nicht im Schweigen verharren, die wir nicht minder treue, gläubige und für das Wohl unserer gemeinsamen Mutter ohne Rückhalt begeisterte Kinder der Kirche zu sein bestrebt sind, als jene; wir müssen vielmehr unsere Stimme erheben und vor Ihnen, unserem Bischofe, es laut aussprechen:

Wir theilen jene Ansichten, Hoffnungen und Wünsche der sogenannten eigentlichen Katholiken nicht, verwahren uns vielmehr gegen dieselben auf das entschiedenste,—uns sind im Hinblick auf die vom heil. Vater in seiner Berufungsbulle erläuterte Bedeutung des bevorstehenden Concils Gedanken anderer Art vor die Seele getreten, die Ew. Bischöflichen Gnaden in Kürze darzulegen uns vergönnt sein möge.

Ueberschauen wir die Verhältnisse, unter denen das allgemeine Concil zusammenzutreten im Begriffe ist, so sehen wir in neuerer Zeit nirgendwo eine häretische Punkte des Glaubensbekenntnisses berührende Spaltung, wie sie frühere Concilien zur Formulirung kirchlicher Lehren veranlasste, hervortreten. Der uns rings umgebende Unglaube stützt sich auf philosophische Meinungen, deren Falschheit längst durch die grossen christlichen Wahrheiten in helles Licht gesetzt ist, und eine Vereinigung mit unsern im Glauben getrennten christlichen Brüdern möchte kaum dadurch erleichtert werden, dass man die Summe der uns trennenden Glaubenssätze noch um einige neu formulirte vermehrte.

Hochwürdigster Herr! Unsere Zeit hat, wenn auch nicht in der eben bezeichneten Richtung, in der That eigenthümliche, auch von uns lebhaft gefühlte Bedürfnisse, denen gerecht zu werden die Kirche, die Allen Alles zu sein bestimmt ist, aus dem unerschöpflichen Born ihrer göttlichen Kraft die Mittel zu schöpfen vermag. In der Befreiung der Kirche von der Staatsgewalt, in der Herstellung einer selbstständigen und harmonischen Bewegung der beiden Ordnungen, in denen nach Gottes Willen das Leben der Menschheit sich entfalten soll, in der organischen Regelung der Theilnahme der Gläubigen an der Gestaltung der kirchlichen Lebensbeziehungen, in der Zurückführung der getrennten Brüder zur Kirche, in der Bewältigung des socialen Elendes, im Aufsuchen der richtigen Stellung des Klerus und des einzelnen Christen zur allgemeinen Bildung und zur Wissenschaft: an diesen das kirchliche Leben im weitesten Sinne umfassenden Aufgaben müht die Gegenwart in geistigem Ringen sich ab, und für ihre Lösung scheint sie sehnsuchtsvoll Hülfe und Beistand von dem vom göttlichem Geiste geleiteten, von der Einsicht der ganzen Kirche getragenen bevorstehenden Concil zu erwarten.

Wir verhehlen uns nicht, dass ein näheres, Einzelheiten bestimmendes Eingehen auf alle diese in dem vielgestaltigen und reichgegliederten Leben der Kirche wurzelnden Bedürfnisse einem allgemeinen Concil kaum möglich sein würde. Der Organismus der Kirche selbst wird in seinen einzelnen Theilen die Formen hervorzubringen haben, in denen die Schäden Heilung finden, die gesunden Kräfte sich in segensreicher Wirkung entfalten können. Zunächst und vor Allem würden wir es daher als sichere Bürgschaft segensreicher Entwicklung mit Freude begrüssen, wenn vom bevorstehenden Concil eine Neubelebung des grossen kirchlichen Organismus durch allgemeine Wiedereinführung jener durch Jahrhunderte erprobten regelmässigen National-, Provinzial- und Diöcesansynoden ausginge. Solche Synoden, wenn ihre Beschlüsse aus wahrhaft freier und gründlicher Berathung geschöpft und auf die Forderungen des wirklichen Lebens gerichtet waren, sind von jeher ein Quell des Heiles für die Kirche gewesen, ihr Aufhören war fast überall Beginn oder Zeichen der Erstarrung und des Hinwelkens, von ihrer Herstellung, nicht bloss der äusseren Form, sondern dem Geiste und Wesen nach, dürfen wir daher die Erfüllung derjenigen Wünsche hoffen, die wir in Bezug auf die kirchlichen Verhältnisse in unserem Vaterlande so manchen betrübenden und bedenklichen Erscheinungen der Gegenwart gegenüber Ew. Bischöflichen Gnaden ans Herz zu legen vertrauensvoll wagen werden.

Richten wir vorher noch unsere Aufmerksamkeit auf das allgemeine Verhältniss der Kirche zum Staate und zur modernen Gesellschaft überhaupt, so scheint es uns im Interesse der Freiheit und Selbstständigkeit der Kirche aufs dringendste gerathen, dass das bevorstehende Concil keinen Zweifel darüber lasse, die Kirche habe mit dem Wunsche, die theokratischen Staatsformen des Mittelalters herzustellen, vollständig gebrochen. Denn das ist es vorzüglich, was die Geister heute der Kirche entfremdet, dass man fürchtet, jene Zeiten möchten wiederkehren, wo die Staatsgewalt mit weltlichen Zwangsmitteln für die Dogmen und Gesetze eines bestimmten auf übernatürliche Offenbarung zurückgeführten religiösen Bekenntnisses eintrat, wo demnach das Gewissen gebunden und die Würde der Religion selbst, welche ohne die von staatlichem Zwange freie Hingebung der Gläubigen nicht zu bestehen vermag, geschädigt wurde. Wir verkennen nicht, dass auch das Staatsleben eine religiöse Grundlage hat, insofern die Ordnung des Staates und die obrigkeitliche Gewalt auf der Anerkennung eines lebendigen persönlichen Gottes und des von ihm der Seele eingepflanzten Sittengesetzes beruhen; aber wir sind uns auch mit voller Ueberzeugung bewusst, dass die Sphäre des Staates, der in gleicher Weise, wie die Kirche, auf dem ihm eigenthümlichen Gebiete in voller Selbstständigkeit sich bewegt, innerhalb jener geistigen Erkenntnisse und sittlichen natürlichen Kräfte des Menschen erfasst werden. Gerade der Staat wird unserer Meinung nach der christlichste sein, der diese seine Schranken am gewissenhaftesten achtet, und während er der übernatürlichen Religion, der Kirche und den Confessionen, welche seine eigene religiös-sittliche Grundlage anerkennen, die freieste und selbstständigste Bewegung auf ihrem Gebiete und den Schutz ihrer Rechte sichert, seinerseits freiwillig, soweit es ohne Verletzung der Rechtsgleichheit geschehen kann, auf die religiöse Sitte des Volkes Rücksicht nimmt und die höhere Einsicht der durch das Christenthum erzogenen Bürger gern benutzt, um das natürliche Gesetz immer tiefer zu erfassen und in seinen Ordnungen immer reiner zum Ausdruck zu bringen. Auf diesem Wege wird sich eine vollkommnere Harmonie, eine fruchtbarere Wirksamkeit, eine idealere Ausgestaltung von Staat und Kirche erreichen lassen, als die Geschichte sie bis jetzt gesehen hat; und wenn dennoch im Leben der Einzelnen Conflicte zwischen beiden Ordnungen eintreten, so werden es doch nur solche sein, die einerseits aus dem durch das Christenthum zuerst klar ausgesprochenen Unterschiede der Kirche und des Staates, andererseits aus der Schwäche und Fehlerhaftigkeit alles Menschlichen sich mehr oder weniger nothwendig ergeben.

Hochwürdigster Herr! Noch peinlicher und drückender, als die Störung der Harmonie zwischen Kirche und Staat, müsste es von uns empfunden werden, wenn das Band, welches Clerus und Laien, Seelsorger und Gemeinde umschlingen soll, gelockert würde oder gar eine tiefgreifende Disharmonie zwischen ihnen entstände. Mit schmerzlichem Bedauern würden wir daher jeden Versuch betrachten, die gemeinsame Bildungsgrundlage zu zerstören, welche bisher in Deutschland, wenigstens im Allgemeinen noch, den Clerus und die durch akademische Studien vorbereiteten weltlichen Berufsstände einigte. Wenn es schon an sich den Interessen der Kirche als der ersten Culturmacht widerspricht, an den grossen Bildungsstätten unserer Nation, um die alle Nachbarn uns beneiden, nicht vertreten zu sein, so genügt ein Blick auf das Verhältniss, in welchem der Clerus mehrerer romanischen Länder zu den gebildeten Laien steht, uns vor den Folgen einseitiger Erziehung und Bildung der künftigen Seelsorger zurückschrecken zu lassen. Würde man aber gar die theologische Bildung der angehenden Geistlichen beschränken, wollte man Studirenden der Theologie, wie es in öffentlichen Blättern heisst, von denjenigen Disciplinen ausschliessen, welche in die unmittelbaren Quellen des Glaubens und der kirchlichen Entwicklung einführen, so müssten wir darin gerade zu eine unheilvolle Schädigung der kirchlichen Wissenschaft wie des kirchlichen Lebens erblicken. Wir sprechen daher den Wunsch aus, das bevorstehende allgemeine Concil möge, falls es die Bildung des Clerus zum Gegenstande der Berathung machen sollte, auf die eigenthümlichen Verhältnisse unseres Vaterlandes vorsorglich Rücksicht nehmen, oder die entgültige Festsetzung dieses Gegenstandes nationalen Synoden überlassen.

Hochwürdigster Herr! Die Gefahren, welche der Kirche in unseren Tagen durch den uns von allen Seiten bekämpfenden Unglauben drohen, die bedeutenden Anforderungen, welche die socialen Uebel der Zeit an die christiche Liebesthätigkeit stellen, lassen es mehr als je nothwendig erscheinen, dass alle Gläubigen im engsten Verbande mit ihren Seelsorgern am kirchlichen Leben theilnehmend und in einmüthiger Gemeindethätigkeit die ganze Fülle christlichen Wirkens entfalten. Als in ähnlicher Lage die alte Kirche dereinst die heidnische Welt überwand, da war diese Einmüthigkeit vollkommen, da war der Gemeindeverband so innig und fest, dass die Stimme des Volkes bei der Wahl des Bischofs gehört wurde. Die zeitgemässe Herstellung auch dieser Einrichtung wird freilich wohl erst einer ferneren Zukunft vorbehalten und von einer freundlichen Auseinandersetzung zwischen Kirche und Staat abhängig sein; schon jetzt aber scheint uns eine allgemeinere organisch geregelte Betheiligung der Laien am christlichsocialen Leben der Pfarrgemeinde höchst wünschenswerth. Denn heute gibt es kaum noch einen lebendigen regelmässigen christlich-socialen Verkehr der ganzen Gemeinde als solcher mit ihrem Seelsorger, dem Pfarrer. Fast nur im Gotteshause oder bei den Cultushandlungen steht der Pfarrer der ganzen Gemeinde gegenüber; die christlichen Liebeswerke sind religiösen Orden, Einzelnen, endlich freien Genossenschaften überlassen, in die einzutreten sehr viele durch Gleichgültigkeit, viele andere durch eine nicht unberechtigte Scheu sich hindern lassen. Die Gemeinde hat fast überall kein Organ, denn die Kirchenvorstände unserer Tage sind auf ein sehr kleines Gebiet beschränkt und kaum der Schatten einer wirklichen Vertretung. Und doch müsste nicht nur die Verwaltung des kirchlichen Vermögens, sondern auch die Sorge für Arme, Kranke und Elende aller Art und für die christliche Erziehung der Jugend; es müsste die Begutachtung der Niederlassung religiöser auf Unterstützung durch die Gläubigen oder öffentliche Wirksamkeit innerhalb der Gemeinde angewiesener Orden, die Theilnahme an der Missionsthätigkeit und den allgemeinen Angelegenheiten der Kirche, das Alles müsste der Idee nach Sache der ganzen mit ihrem Seelsorger auch mit Rücksicht auf diese Verhältnisse in zeitgemässen Formen organisch verbundenen Gemeinde sein. Der freien Liebesthätigkeit Einzelner, der rühmlichen Aufopferung und Hingebung religiöser Orden und dem Hirtenwalten des Seelsorgers auf diese Weise beengende Schranken zu ziehen kann um so weniger unsere Absicht sein, als kirchliche Organe der bezeichneten Art ihrer Natur nach zwingende Entscheidungen nicht zu treffen hätten, wohl aber scheint uns die Hoffnung begründet, dass mit Hülfe solcher Organe, welche nicht nur eine allgemeinere Heranziehung der Laien, sondern auch eine angemessene Verbindung und planvolle Leitung aller betheiligten Kräfte ermöglichen würden, den socialen Uebeln der

Gegenwart von der Kirche mit durchgreifendem Erfolge begegnet, die Einwirkung des Klerus auf das Volk, die Durchdringung des Lebens mit christlichen Grundsätzen sicherer erzielt, religiöse Gleichgültigkeit eher gehoben, einseitige Richtungen besser hintangehalten, dass durch sie namentlich jene von Tage zu Tage sich erweiternde Kluft zwischen sogenannten guten und gewöhnlichen Katholiken am ersten überbrückt werden könnte.

Hochwürdigster Herr! Der heisse Wunsch, der den h. Vater, den ganzen hochwürdigen Episcopat, jeden gläubigen Katholiken und vor Allen uns deutsche Katholiken, beseelt, der Wunsch, die Versöhnung der von uns getrennten protestantischen Confessionen mit der Kirche zu erleben, hat wohl nur dann Aussicht auf Erfolg, wenn von unserer Seite Entscheidendes geschieht, um die Furcht und das Misstrauen bei unsern Brüdern zu beseitigen, Vorurtheile zu überwinden und Vertrauen zu erwecken. Wie viele ihrer Vorurtheile aber würden nicht mit einem Male schwinden, wenn sie bei uns die grossen Organe der Kirche wieder lebendig thätig, wenn sie auch ein wahres, die socialen Aufgaben des Christenthums erfüllendes Gemeindeleben bei uns wieder blühen sähen, und daher unmöglich länger die misstrauische Furcht zu hegen überredet werden könnten, dass eine herrschsüchtige Hierarchie in der Kirche die Gläubigen ausbeute und die Geister gewaltsam in falsche Richtungen lenke oder niederdrücke. Was das Eintreten der Kirchenspaltung wahrscheinlich verhindert hätte, das wird auch wohl am besten sie aufzuheben vermögen; nun aber hat die Verzweiflung an der Hierarchie, welcher man den Verfall des kirchlichen Lebens Schuld gab, diese in jenen Tagen erklärliche, wenn auch kleingläubige Verzweiflung im Grunde jene Lehren geboren, welche die Hierarchie überflüssig machen sollten. Die altchristliche Kirche, das altchristliche Gemeindeleben wollte man herstellen; es gelang nicht, weil man das priesterliche verworfen hatte, auf welches allein die kirchliche Gemeinde sich erbauen lässt: wir aber, die wir die festen Säulen uns bewahrt haben, können unschwer auf den unzerstörten Fundamenten die nur lose geschichteten Steine zum herrlichen Tempel zusammenfügen, in dessen weit geöffnete Pforten nach Gottes gnädiger Fügung die heimkehrenden Brüder freudig wieder einziehen.

Eine andere nicht unwichtige Frage endlich, welche wir Ew. Bischöflichen Gnaden und des ganzen zum allgemeinen Concil eingeladenen Episcopats Erwägung unterbreiten möchten, betrifft die Einrichtung des Index librorum prohibitorum.

Wir wissen, dass es der kirchlichen Autoritäten heilige Pflicht ist, über die Reinheit der Lehre zu wachen, Irrthümer zu bezeichnen und zu verbessern, Irrende auf den rechten Weg zu leiten. Allein das Verfahren, welches man in den letzten Jahrhunderten in Ausübung dieses Berufs eingeschlagen hat, die Eintragung solcher Schriften, die irrige oder bedenkliche und unsittliche Darstellungen enthalten, in einem demnächst veröffentlichten Katalog und das Verbot, solche Bücher ohne besondere Erlaubniss der kirchlichen Obern zu lesen, dieses Verfahren scheint uns weder seinem eigentlichen Zwecke zu entsprechen, noch dem Geiste und der Würde der Kirche vollkommen angemessen, noch für die Entwicklung der Wissenschaften heilsam. Es erfüllt seinen Zweck nicht, weil unmöglich alle Schriften mit irrigen und bedenklichen Sätzen katalogisirt werden können und es daher oft von Zufälligkeiten, etwa von Denunciationen, abhangen muss, welche Bücher eingetragen werden, welche nicht; weil ferner nicht die irrigen und bedenklichen Lehren selbst, sondern nur die Bücher, deren Lectüre nicht gestattet sei, und deren Autoren bezeichnet werden; weil das Verbot, solche Bücher zu lesen, von der Mehrzahl der gebildeten Katholiken in sehr vielen Fällen gar nicht beachtet werden kann und, wie Ew. Bischöflichen Gnaden gewiss recht wohl bekannt ist, auch ganz allgemein nicht beachtet wird; es ist der Würde und dem Geiste der Kirche nicht vollkommen angemessen, weil öfter gläubige katholische Verfasser, die in der besten Absicht geirrt oder auch nur Missfälliges geäussert haben, durch Notirung ihres Namens, mitunter unmittelbar neben den Verfassern wahrer Schandschriften, als gefährlich gekennzeichnet und für alle Zeit mit einem Makel behaftet werden, während Wissenschaft und Kirche ihnen für bedeutende Leistungen eher Dank schuldig wären; es ist endlich für den wissenschaftlichen Fortschritt nicht heilsam, weil die Furcht, durch irgend einen unwillkürlichen Fehltritt oder Missgriff, vielleicht gar in Folge der unberufenen Dienstfertigkeit eines Gegners, sich eine solche diffamirende Strafe zuzuziehen, sich wie ein Bleigewicht an die Forschungen der katholischen Gelehrten hängt. Wir hegen daher den Wunsch es möge dem bevorstehenden allgemeinen Concil gefallen, den Index librorum prohibitorum aufzuheben. Es ist das Recht der kirchlichen Autorität, uns durch den Mund unserer Seelsorger vor irrigen Lehren und unsittlichen Büchern zu warnen, wann und so oft sie es für nöthig hält; die unfreiwillig irrende Person aber darf von der christlichen Liebe der kirchlichen Obern Schonung ihres Namens und Rufes erwarten, so lange sie in gläubiger Demuth bereit ist, den Irrthum aufzugeben, und nicht eine äusserste Gefahr für das Seelenheil der Gläubigen Warnung vor dem Irrlehrer erheischt.

Das sind, hochwürdigster Herr, die Ueberzeugungen und Wünsche, welche vor Ihnen auszusprechen unser Gewissen uns gedrängt hat. Sie verdienen, dünkt uns, gehört zu werden, so gut wie alle andern, die von treuer Anhänglichkeit an unsere heilige Kirche, von aufrichtiger Besorgniss für deren Wohl eingegeben und in langjährigem Nachdenken gebildet sind. Uns hat nichts anderes veranlasst, öffentlich mit unserm Namen hervorzutreten, als das Gefühl der Pflicht, lebhaft erregt durch die Wahrnehmung zunächst der weitverbreiteten Abneigung mit der man in katholischen Kreisen die oben mitgetheilten Auslassungen der *Civiltà* aufgenommen, sodann der beklagenswerthen Bedenklichkeit, mit der so manche, die es nicht sollten, vor freimüthigem Widerspruch zurückschrecken. Auch der traurigen Kirchenspaltung des 16. Jahrhunderts ging ein allgemeines Concil unmittelbar voraus, ohne auf die Entwicklung der Dinge einen günstigen Einfluss auszuüben. Sollen heute die christlichen Völker durch das für die Kirche wirklich wiedergewonnen werden, so muss einseitig absprechenden Behauptungen gegenüber die lehrende und regierende Kirche durch bestimmte und klare Bekenntnisse von dem Zustande der Geister vollkommen unterrichtet, den wahren Bedürfnissen der Zeit entgegenzukommen in den Stand gesetzt sein, und dazu nach Kräften beizutragen fühlten auch wir uns verpflichtet, die wir als treue Söhne der Kirche in der Einheit mit ihr und ihrem Mittelpunkte, dem Stuhle zu Rom. und in kindlichem Gehorsam gegen Ew. Bischöflichen Gnaden mit Gottes Hülfe zu leben und zu sterben entschlossen sind.

DOCUMENT XVII.

Die neue Geschäftsordnung des Concils und ihre theologische Bedeutung.

Die neue Geschäftsordnung, welche dem Concil durch die fünf Cardinal-Legaten auferlegt worden, ist völlig verschieden von allem, was sonst auf Concilien gebräuchlich war, und zugleich massgebend und entscheidend für den ferneren Verlauf dieser Versammlung, und für die zahlreichen Decrete, welche durch sie zu Stande gebracht werden sollen. Sie verdient daher die sorgfältigste Beachtung. Zur geschichtlichen Orientirung mag nur in der Kürze erwähnt werden, dass für die allgemeinen Concilien der alten Kirche im ersten Jahrtausend eine bestimmte Geschäftsordnung nicht existirte. Nur für römische und spanische Provincial-Concilien gab es ein liturgisches Ceremoniell.[1] Alles wurde in voller Versammlung vorgetragen; jeder Bischof konnte Anträge stellen, welche er wollte, und die Präsidenten, die weltlichen sowohl, welche die Kaiser sandten, als die geistlichen, sorgten für Ordnung und leiteten die Verhandlungen in einfachster Weise. Die grossen Concilien zu Konstanz und Basel machten sich eine eigene Ordnung, da die Theilung und Abstimmung nach Nationen eingeführt wurden. In Trient wurde diese Einrichtung wieder verlassen, aber die Legaten, welche präsidirten, vereinbarten die Geschäftsordnung mit den Bischöfen, der Cardinal de Monte liess darüber abstimmen, und alle genehmigten sie.[2] Von keiner Seite erfolgte ein Widerspruch. So ist denn die heutige römische Synode die erste in der Geschichte der Kirche, in welcher den versammelten Vätern ohne jede Theilnahme von ihrer Seite die Procedur vorgeschrieben worden ist. Das erste *Regolamento* erwies sich so hemmend und unpraktisch, dass wiederholte Gesuche um Abänderung und Gestattung freierer Bewegung von verschiedenen Fractionen des Episkopats an den Papst gerichtet wurden. Dies war vergeblich; aber nach dritthalb Monaten fanden die fünf Legaten endlich 'selber, dass, wenn das Concil nicht ins Stocken gerathen solle, eine Aenderung und Ergänzung dringend nothwendig sei. Auf die Petitionen der Bischöfe ist indess in der neuen Einrichtung keine Rücksicht dabei genommen worden.

Zwei Züge treten darin vor allem hervor. Einmal ist alle Macht und aller Einfluss auf den Gang des Concils in die Hände der präsidirenden Legaten und der Deputationen gelegt, so dass das Concil selbst ihnen gegenüber machtlos und willenlos erscheint. Sodann sollen die gewichtigsten Fragen des Glaubens und der Lehre durch einfache

[1] Aufgenommen von Pseudoisidor, und abgedruckt bei Mansi, *Conc. Coll.* i. 10.
[2] Le Plat, *Monumenta*, iii. 418 : " Dicunt Patres, utrum hic modus procedendi eis placeat." Worauf abgestimmt wurde.

Mehrheit der Kopfzahl, durch Aufstehen und Sitzenbleiben, entschieden werden.

Man hat bekanntlich, in den zwei Jahren, welche der Eröffnung des Concils vorhergegangen, eine Menge von Abhandlungen mit dazu gehörigen Decreten und Canones ausarbeiten lassen; diese sollen nun von dem Concil angenommen und dann vom Papst "approbante Concilio" als Gesetze, als Lehr- und Glaubensnormen für die ganze katholische Christenheit verkündigt werden. Es sind im ganzen einundfünfzig solcher Schemate, von welchen bis jetzt erst fünf discutirt sind.

Das Verfahren welches bei der Berathung und Abstimmung stattfinden soll, ist nun folgendes:

1. Das Schema wird mehrere (zehn) Tage vor der Berathung den Vätern des Concils ausgetheilt, welche dann schriftliche Erinnerungen, Ausstellungen, Verbesserungsanträge machen können.

2. In diesem Fall müssen sie sogleich eine neue Formel oder Fassung des betreffenden Artikels statt des von ihnen beanstandeten in Vorschlag bringen.

3. Solche Anträge werden durch den Secretär der einschlägigen Deputation (es sind deren vier) übergeben, welche dann nach ihrem Ermessen davon Gebrauch macht, indem sie das Schema, wenn sie es für zweckmässig hält, reformirt und dann in einem, aber nur *summarisch* gehaltenen, Berichte dem Concil von den gestellten Anträgen eine Notiz gibt.

4. Die Präsidenten können jedes Schema entweder bloss im Ganzen oder auch in Abschnitte getheilt der Berathung unterstellen.

5. Bei der Berathung können die Präsidenten jeden Redner unterbrechen, wenn es ihnen scheint, dass er nicht bei der Sache bleibe.

6. Die Bischöfe der Deputationen können in jedem Moment das Wort ergreifen, um den Bischöfen, welche den Wortlaut des Schema beanstanden, zu erwiedern.

7. Zehn Väter reichen hin, um den Schluss der Discussion zu beantragen, worüber dann mit einfacher Mehrheit durch Aufstehen oder Sitzenbleiben entschieden wird.

8. Bei der Abstimmung über die einzelnen Theile des Schema wird zuerst über die vorgeschlagenen Veränderungen, dann über den von der Deputation vorgelegten Text durch Aufstehen oder Sitzenbleiben abgestimmt, so dass die einfache Mehrheit entscheidet.

9. Hierauf wird über das ganze Schema mit Namensaufruf abgestimmt, wobei jeder der Väter mit *placet* oder *non placet* antwortet. Ob auch hier die blosse Mehrheit der Kopfzahl entscheiden solle, ist nicht angegeben. Es scheint aber nach der Analogie bejaht werden zu müssen, denn das ganze Schema ist ja doch nur wieder ein Stück oder Theil von einem grössern Ganzen, und es liegt durchaus kein Grund vor, mit dem grössern Stück anders zu verfahren als mit dem kleinern. Würde das Princip der schlechthinigen Mehrheit hier verlassen, so würden wohl gerade die wichtigern, tiefer einschneidenden, Schemate verloren gehen.

Man sieht nun wohl, dass einige parlamentarische Formen in diese Geschäftsordnung herübergenommen sind. Aber wenn in politischen Versammlungen gewisse den hier gegebenen ähnliche Einrichtungen bestehen, so sollen sie gewöhnlich zum Schutze der Minderheit gegen Majorisirung dienen, während sie hier umgekehrt zu dem Zwecke gegeben zu sein scheinen, die Mehrheit noch mächtiger und unwiderstehlich zu machen, wie sich dies besonders in dem ihr eingeräumten Rechte zeigt, die Discussion, sobald es ihr gefällt, abzuschneiden und also der Minderheit das Wort zu entziehen; dies wird um so peinlicher wirken, als bekanntlich auch die Möglichkeit, sich in gedruckten Gutachten oder Aufklärungen den übrigen Mitgliedern des Concils mitzutheilen, weder für einzelne noch für ganze Gruppen von Bischöfen gegeben ist.

In politischen Versammlungen können Beschlüsse gefasst, selbst Gesetze gegeben werden durch einfache Mehrheit, da keine der folgenden Parlamente oder Kammern durch die Beschlüsse und Gesetze der früheren gebunden ist. Jede kann zu jeder Zeit eine Satzung ihrer Vorgängerinnen ändern oder abrogiren. Aber die dogmatischen Beschlüsse eines Concils sollen, wenn es wirklich ein ökumenisches ist, für alle Zeiten unantastbar und unwiderruflich gelten.

Voraussichtlich wird bei den nun folgenden Abstimmungen die Mehrheit dieses Concils nicht etwa eine flüssige, auf- und abwogende sein, sie wird nicht wechseln mit den zu fassenden Beschlüssen, sondern sie wird sich, mit geringen Schwankungen der Zahl, in ihrer Zusammensetzung wesentlich gleich bleiben. Denn es ist bekannt, dass die Theilung der Bischöfe in eine Mehrheit und eine Minderheit sich gleich von Anfang an schon bei der Wahl der Deputationen, und die noch eine einzige Abstimmung stattgefunden, scharf und entschieden herausgestellt hat. So musste es kommen, weil in der Frage von der päpstlichen Unfehlbarkeit sich alsbald ein durchgreifender und principieller Gegensatz ergab, und man sofort erkannte, dass diese Frage die Hauptangelegenheit der Versammlung bilde, und alle andern von ihr beherrscht würden. Es steht zu erwarten, dass die Anhänger der Unfehlbarkeitstheorie die Vorlagen, sowie sie aus den Händen der Deputationen hervorgehen, auch unbedenklich votiren werden ; denn für sie ist ganz folgerichtig alles massgebend, was vom römischen Stuhle ausgeht, und dafür ist ausreichend gesorgt, dass in den Deputationen, welchen jetzt über alle auf die Verbesserung der Schemata bezüglichen Anträge die umfassendste und inappellable Gewalt übertragen ist, nur *eine* Ansicht sich geltend machen kann. Ein Blick auf das Personal der wichtigsten Deputation. " de fide," genügt. Vor allem findet sich da der Römer Cardoni, der schon in der Vorbereitungs-Commission das Dogma der päpstlichen Unfehlbarkeit in einer eigenen Denkschrift empfohlen und in seiner Commission hat annehmen lassen. Neben ihm der Jesuit Steins, sodann die bereiten Namen Dechamps von Mecheln, Spalding von Baltimore, Pie von Poitiers, Ledochowski. Hassun der Armenier, de Preux von Sitten, von Deutschen Martin, Senestrey, Gasser von Brixen, zwei Spanier, drei Südamerikaner, drei Italiener, ein Irländer, endlich Simor Regnier und Sharpman.

Seit 1800 Jahren hat es in der Kirche als Grundsatz gegolten, dass Decrete über den Glauben und die Lehre nur mit einer wenigstens moralischen Stimmeneinhelligkeit votirt werden sollten. Dieser Grundsatz steht mit dem ganzen System der katholischen Kirche im engsten Zusammenhang. Es ist kein Beispiel eines Dogma bekannt. welches durch eine einfache Stimmenmehrheit unter dem Widerspruche einer Minderheit beschlossen und darauf hin eingeführt worden wäre.

Um dies klar zu machen, muss ich mir Raum für eine kurze theologische, aber hoffentlich allgemein verständliche, Erörterung erbitten.

Die Kirche hat ein ihr von Anfang an übergebenes Depositum geoffenbarter Lehre zu bewahren und zu verwalten.[1] Sie empfängt keine neuen Offenbarungen, und sie macht keine neuen Glaubensartikel. Und wie mit der Kirche selbst, so ist es auch

[1] Die Theologie hat sich in der Entwicklung dieser Fragen angeschlossen an die allgemein als classisch und völlig correct angenommene Schrift des Vincentius von Lerins, das *Commonitorium*, das schon um das Jahr 434 erschien. Auf diese beziehe ich mich daher in dem folgenden.

mit dem allgemeinen Concil.[1] Das Concil ist die Repräsentation, die Zusammenfassung der ganzen Kirche ; die Bischöfe auf demselben sind die Gesandten und Geschäftsträger aller Kirchen der katholischen Welt : sie haben im Namen der Gesammtheit zu erklären, was diese Gesammtheit der Gläubigen über eine religiöse Frage denkt und glaubt, was sie als Ueberlieferung empfangen hat. Sie sind also als Procuratoren anzusehen, welche die ihnen gegebene Vollmacht durchaus nicht überschreiten dürfen.[2] Thäten sie es, so würde die Kirche, deren Vertreter sie sind, die von ihnen aufgestellte Lehre und Definition nicht bestätigen, vielmehr als etwas ihrem gläubigen Bewusstsein fremdes zurückweisen.

Die Bischöfe auf dem Concil sind also vor allem *Zeugen* , sie sagen aus und constatiren, was sie und ihre Gemeinden als Glaubenslehre empfangen und bisher bekannt haben; sie sind aber auch *Richter*, nur dass ihre richterliche Gewalt über den Glauben nicht über den Bereich ihres Zeugenthums hinausgehen darf, vielmehr durch dieses fortwährend bedingt und umschrieben ist. Als Richter haben sie das Gesetz (die Glaubenslehre) nicht erst zu machen,

[1] So sagt der Bischof Fisher von Rochester, der für den Primat des Papstes sein Leben opferte, in seiner Streitschrift gegen Luther (*Opera*, ed. Wirceburg, 1597, p. 592), mit Berufung auf den gleichen Ausspruch des Duns Scotus: " In eorum " (des Concils mit dem Papste) " arbitrio non est situm, ut quicquam tale vel non tale faciant, sed spiritu potius veritatis edocti, id quod revera pridem de substantia fidei fuerat jam declarant, esse de substantia fidei." Und der Minorit Davenport, *Systema fidei*, p. 140: " Secundum receptam, tum veterum, quam modernorum doctorum sententiam ecclesia non potest agere ultra revelationes antiquas, nihil potest hodie declarari de fide, quod non habet talem identitatem cum prius revelatis , . . Unde semper docet Scotus: Quod illae conclusiones solum possunt infallibiliter declarari et determinari per ecclesiam, quae sunt *necessario inclusae in articulis creditis*. Si igitur per accidens conjunguntur, vel si solum probabiliter sequuntur ex articulis, fidem non attingent per quascunque determinationes, quia Concilia non possunt identificare, quae sunt ex objecto diversa, nec necessario inferre ea, quae solum apparenter, seu probabiliter sunt inclusa in articulis creditis."

[2] " Concilium non est ipsamet ecclesia, sed ipsam tantum repraesentat; . . . id est episcopi illi qui concilio adsunt, legati mittuntur ab omnibus omnium gentium catholicorum ecclesiis, qui, ex nomine totius universitatis, declarent, quid ipsa universitas sentiat et quid traditum acceperit. Itaque ejusmodi legati omnium ecclesiarum sunt veluti procuratores, quibus nefas esset procurationem sibi creditam tantillum excedere. Unde constat, quod si quingenti episcopi, videre est in exemplis Ariminensis, et Constantinopolitanae contra imagines coactae synodi, suam de fide communi declaranda procurationem tantillum excederent, universa ecclesia, cujus sunt tantummodo procuratores et simplex repraesentanti, definitionem factam ab illis ratam non haberet, imo repudiaret."—*Œuvres de Fénelon*, Versailles, 1820, ii. 361.

sondern nur zu interpretiren und anzuwenden. Sie stehen unter dem öffentlichen Rechte der Kirche, an welchem sie nichts zu ändern vermögen. Sie üben ihr Richteramt, erstens: indem sie die von ihnen abgelegten Zeugnisse unter einander prüfen und vergleichen und deren Tragweite erwägen; zweitens, indem sie nach gewissenhafter Prüfung: ob an einer Lehre die drei unentbehrlichen Bedingungen der Universalität, der Perpetuität und des Consensus (" ubique, semper, ab omnibus ") zutreffen, ob also die Lehre als die allgemeine Lehre der ganzen Kirche, als wirklicher Bestandtheil des göttlichen Depositums, allen gezeigt und ihr Bekenntniss jedem Christen auferlegt werden könne.[1] Ihre Prüfung hat sich demnach sowohl über die Vergangenheit als die Gegenwart zu erstrecken. So ist von dem Amte der Bischöfe auf Concilien jede Willkür, jedes bloss subjective Gutdünken ausgeschlossen. Es würde da frevelhaft und verderblich sein, denn da die Kirche keine neuen Offenbarungen empfängt, keine neuen Glaubensartikel macht, so kann und darf auch ein Concil die Substanz des Glaubens nicht ändern, nichts davon wegnehmen und nichts hinzufügen. Ein Concilium macht also dogmatische Decrete nur über Dinge, welche schon in der Kirche, als durch Schrift und Tradition bezeugt, allgemein geglaubt wurden,[2] oder welche als evidente und klare Folgerungen in den bereits geglaubten und gelehrten Grundsätzen enthalten sind. Wenn aber eine Meinung Jahrhunderte lang stets auf Widerspruch gestossen und mit allen theologischen Waffen bestritten worden, also stets mindestens unsicher gewesen ist, so kann sie nie, auch durch ein Concilium nicht, zur Gewissheit, das heisst zur Dignität einer göttlich geoffenbarten Lehre, erhoben werden. Daher der gewöhnliche Ruf der Väter auf den Concilien nach der Annahme und Verständigung eines dogmatischen Decrets: " haec fides Patrum."

Soll also z. B. an die Stelle der früher geglaubten und gelehrten Irrthumsfreiheit der ganzen Kirche die Unfehlbarkeit eines Einzigen gesetzt werden, so ist das keine Entwicklung, keine Explication des vorher implicit Geglaubten, keine mit logischer Folgerichtigkeit sich ergebende Consequenz, sondern einfach das gerade Gegentheil der früheren Lehre, die damit auf den Kopf gestellt würde. Gerade wie es im politischen Leben keine Fortbildung oder Entwicklung, sondern einfach ein Umsturz, eine Revolution wäre, wenn ein bisher freies Gemeinwesen plötzlich unter das Joch eines absolut herrschenden Monarchen gebracht würde.

Die Zeit, in welcher ein ökumenisches Concil über den Glauben der Christen beräth, ist also stets eine Zeit der lebhaftesten Erweckung des religiösen Bewusstseins, eine Zeit der abzulegenden Zeugnisse und der offenen Erklärungen für alle treuen Söhne der Kirche, Geistliche wie Laien, gewesen. Man glaubte, wie die Geschichte der Kirche beweist, allgemein, dass man gerade durch solche Kundgebungen dem Concil seine Aufgabe erleichtere, und nicht die Väter dadurch störe oder hemme. Zeugniss ablegen, Wünsche aussprechen, auf die Bedürfnisse der Kirche hinweisen, kann und darf jeder, auch der Laie.[1]

---

[1] So der Jesuit Bagot in seiner *Institutio Theologica de vera Religione*, Paris, 1645, p. 385: "Universitas sine duabus aliis, nimirum antiquitate et consensione stare non potest. Quod autem triplici illa probatione confirmatur, et haud dubie ecclesiasticum et catholicum. Quod si universitatis nota deficit et nova aliqua quaestio exoritur, novaque contagio ecclesiam communicare incipit, tunc hac universitate praesentium ecclesiarum deficiente recurrendum est ad antiquitatem. Notat enim Vincent. posse aliquam haereseos contagionem occupare multas ecclesias, sicut constat de Ariana; adeo ut aliquando plures ecclesiae et episcopi diversarum nationum Ariani quam Catholici reperirentur. Et quantumvis doctrina aliqua latissime pateat, si tamen novam esse constat, haud dubie erronea est, nec enim est apostolica, nec per successionem et traditionem ad nos usque pervenit. Deinde, ut notat idem Vincentius, antiquitas non potest jam seduci. Verum cuimvero quia et ipse error antiquus esse potest: idcirco cum consulitur vetustas, in ea quaerenda est consensio."

[2] So Vincentius: "Hoc semper nec *quidquam aliud* Conciliorum decretis catholica perfecit ecclesia, nisi ut quod a majoribus sola traditione susceperat, hoc deinde posteris per scripturae chirographum consignaret."— *Commonit*. cap. 32. Der Tridentinische Theologe Vega, *ap.* Davenport, p. 9: "Concilia generalia hoc tantum habent, ut veritates jam alias, vel in seipsis, vel in suis principiis a Deo, ecclesiae vel SS. Patribus revelatas vel per scripturas vel traditionum prophetarum et apostolorum tum declarent, tum confirment et sua auctoritate clarius et apertas et absque ulla ambiguitate ab omnibus Catholicis tenendas tradant. Addit: et ad hoc dico: Praesentia Spiritus sancti illustrantur,

---

[1] primo ut infallibiles declarent veritates ecclesiae revelatas, et secundo, ut ad terminanda dubia in ecclesia suborta, extirpandosque errores et abusus infallibiliter etiam ex revelatis colligant populo Christiano credenda et usurpanda in fide et moribus."

[1] So sagt der Cardinal Reginald Pole, einer der Präsidenten des Tridentinischen Concils, in seinem Buche, *De Concilio*, 1562, fol. 11: " Patet quidem locus omnibus et singulis exponendi, si quid vel sibi vel ecclesiae opus esse censeant, sed decernendi non omnibus patet, verum iis tantum, quibus pastorali et maritali ipse unicus pastor et rector dedit." Papst Nikolaus I. bemerkt dass die Kaiser an den Concilien theilgenommen haben, wenn vom Glauben gehandelt worden sei. " Ubinam legistis, Imperatores antecessores vestros synodalibus conventibus interfuisse? nisi forsitan in quibus de fide tractatum est, quae universalis est, quae omnium communis est, quae non solum ad clericos, verum etiam ad Laicos et ad omnes omnino pertinet Christianos." Diese Stelle find auch in Gratians Decret Aufnahme

Ganz besonders wenn es sich um die Einführung eines neuen Dogma handelt, welches etwa, von einer Seite her gefordert, dem Bewusstsein der Gläubigen fremd ist und ihnen als eine Neuerung erscheint, dann ist der sich erhebende Protest der Laien ein ebenso gerechter als nothwendiger, und unvermeidliches Zeugniss der Anhänglichkeit an den ihnen überlieferten Glauben, und sie erfüllen damit eine Pflicht gegen die Kirche.

Auf dem Concil selbst aber beweist der Widerspruch, den eine Anzahl der Bischöfe gegen eine als Dogma zu verkündende Meinung erhebt, dass in den von ihnen repräsentirten Theilkirchen diese Meinung nicht für wahr, nicht für göttlich geoffenbart gehalten worden ist, und auch jetzt nicht dafür gehalten wird. Damit ist aber schon entschieden, dass dieser Lehre oder Meinung die drei wesentlichen Erfordernisse der Universalität, der Perpetuität und des Consensus abgehen, dass sie also auch nicht der ganzen Kirche als göttliche Offenbarung aufgedrungen werden darf.

Darum hat man es in der Kirche stets für nothwendig erachtet, dass, sobald eine nur einigermassen beträchtliche Anzahl von Bischöfen einem von der Mehrheit etwa vorgeschlagenen oder beabsichtigten Decret widersprach, dieses Decret beiseite gelegt ward, die Definition unterblieb. Die wahrhafte Katholicität einer Lehre soll evident und unzweifelhaft sein; sie ist es aber nicht, sobald das Zeugniss wenn auch einer Minderzahl den Beweis liefert, dass ganze Abtheilungen der Kirche diese Lehre nicht glauben und nicht bekennen.

Darum war bei jedem Concil die Hauptfrage: "Sind die Glaubensdecrete von allen Mitgliedern genehmigt worden?" Sogleich auf dem ersten allgemeinen Concil zu Nicäa, wo unter 318 Bischöfen zuletzt nur zwei sich der Unterschrift weigerten. Zu Chalcedon zögerte man so lange mit den Entscheidungen, liess sich immer wieder auf neue Erörterungen ein, bis endlich alle Bedenken, welche besonders die illyrischen und die palästinensischen Bischöfe gegen das Schreiben Leo's anfänglich hegten, gehoben waren. Noch ehe Kaiser Marcian die Synode entliess, drang er auf eine Erklärung: ob wirklich alle Bisc öfe (es waren über 600) der Glaubensdefinition zustimmten, was denn auch alle bereitwilligst bejahten, und worauf Papst Leo selbst Gott dankte, dass sein Schreiben "nach allen Zweifeln und Bedenken doch endlich durch die unwiderlegliche Zustimmung des gesammten Episkopats" bestätigt worden sei. So versicherten auch auf dem sechsten allgemeinen

Concil die Bischöfe auf die Frage des Kaisers: dass die dogmatische Entscheidung unter Zustimmung aller aufgestellt worden sei. Dasselbe geschah auf dem siebenten im Jahr 787. Und wiederum meldete Karl der Grosse von dem Concil zu Frankfort 794 den spanischen Bischöfen: alles sei geschehen, "quatenus Sancta omnium unanimitas decerneret," etc. In Trient gab Papst Pius IV den Legaten die Weisung: nichts entscheiden zu lassen, was nicht allen Vätern genehm sei. Einer der dort befindlichen Theologen, Payva de Andrada, berichtet: mehrmals habe man ein Decret Wochen, Monate lang unentschieden gelassen, weil einige wenige Bischöfe widerstrebten oder Bedenken äusserten; erst dann, wenn endlich nach langen und sorgfältigen Berathungen Einstimmigkeit der Väter erzielt worden, habe man das Decret publicirt. Payva führt mehrere Beispiele davon an.[1] Und Bossuet bemerkt über die Vorschrift Pius IV: dies sei eine treffliche Regel, um das Wahre vom Zweifelhaften zu scheiden.

Alle Theologen machen es zur Bedingung der Oekumenicität eines Concils, dass völlige *Freiheit* auf demselben herrsche. Freiheit des Redens, Freiheit des Stimmens. Niemand, sagt Tournely, darf zurückgewiesen werden, der gehört werden will. Nicht bloss physischer Zwang würde die Beschlüsse eines Concils kraftlos und werthlos machen. Die Freiheit, diese Lebensluft eines wahren Concils, wird auch durch die gar mannigfaltigen Formen, in denen moralischer Zwang eintritt, oder der Mensch sich willig knechten lässt (z. B. durch die verschiedenen Arten der Simonie), zerstört, und die Legitimität des Concils dadurch aufgehoben. Tournely nennt als die auf Synoden wirksamen und die conciliarische Freiheit aufhebenden Leidenschaften Furcht, Stellengier, Geldgeiz und Habsucht.[2]

Als der grosse Abfall zu Seleucia und Rimini gleichzeitig stattfand, als an sechshundert Bischöfe das gemeinsame Bekenntniss verläugneten und preisgaben, da war es "Geistesschwäche und Scheu vor einer mühseligen Reise" ("partim imbecillitate

[1] *Defensio Fidei Tridentinae*, f. 17: "Cum quindecim fere aut viginti dubitare se alebant, ne vero quicquam praeter Conciliorum vetu-tum morem concinderetur, horum paucorum dubitatio plurimorum impetum retardavit, atque effecit, ut res in allam sessionem dilata, omnium fere calculis tandem definiretur." Man vergleiche dort das Weitere. Man sieht, dass zu Trient die Ueberzeugung herrschte, es müsse alles in der Weise der *alten* Concilien behandelt und entschieden, wenigstens die wesentliche Form derselben beibehalten werden.

[2] *De Ecclesia*, 1. 3ᵃ⁴.

ingenii, partim taedio peregrinationis evicti," Sulp. Sever. 2, 43), was sie überwand.

Die blosse Thatsache einer wenn auch noch so zahlreichen, bischöflichen Versammlung ist also noch lange kein Beweis der wirklichen Oekumenicität eines Concils; oder, wie die Theologen, z. B. Tournely, sich ausdrücken, es kann wohl ökumenisch der Berufung nach sein, ob es dies aber auch dem Verlauf und Ausgang nach sei, darüber kann das Concil selbst nicht entscheiden, kann nicht selber sich Zeugniss geben; da muss erst die doch auch noch über jedem Concil stehende Autorität, oder das Zeugniss der ganzen Kirche, als entscheidend und bestätigend hinzutreten. Die Concilien als solche haben keine Verheissung— auch in den gewöhnlich angeführten Worten des Herrn von den "zwei oder drei" kommt el en alles auf das "in seinem Namen Versammeltsein" an, und dies enthält, wie alle Theologen unnehmen, mehrere Bedingungen, die z. B. Tournely aufführt.¹ Aber die Kirche hat die Verheissungen, und sie muss erst sich überzeugen, oder die Gewissheit besitzen, dass physischer oder moralischer Zwang, Furcht, Leidenschaften, Verführungskünste—Dinge wie sie zu Rimini und noch gar oft gewirkt haben—nicht auf dem Concil übermächtig geworden sind, dass also die wahre Freiheit dort geherrscht habe. In diesem Sinn sagt Bossuet von einem ökumenischen Concil: der Bischöfe auf demselben müssten so viele und aus so verschiedenen Ländern, *und die Zustimmung der übrigen so evident sein*, dass man klar sehe, es sei nichts anderes da geschehen, als dass die Ansicht der ganzen Welt zusammengetragen worden.¹ Sollte sich also zeigen, dass auf dem Concil keineswegs "die Ansicht der ganzen katholischen Welt zusammengetragen" worden, dass vielmehr Mehrheitsbeschlüsse gefasst worden seien, welche mit dem Glauben eines beträchtlichen Theils der Kirche im Widerspruch stehen, dann würden gewiss in der katholischen Welt die Fragen aufgeworfen werden: Haben unsere Bischöfe richtig Zeugniss gegeben von dem Glauben ihrer Diöcesen? und wenn nicht, sind sie wahrhaft frei gewesen? Oder wie kommt es, dass ihr Zeugniss nicht beachtet worden ist? dass sie majorisirt worden sind? Von den Antworten, die auf diese Fragen ertheilt werden, werden dann die ferneren Ereignisse in der Kirche bedingt sein. Und darum ist auch in der ganzen Kirche die vollste Publicität stets als zu einem Concil gehörig gewährt worden; denn es liegt der gesammten christlichen Welt höchlich daran, nicht nur zu wissen, *dass* etwas dort beschlossen wird, sondern auch zu wissen, *wie* es beschlossen wird. An diesem *Wie* hängt zuletzt alles, wie die denkwürdigen Jahre 359, 449, 754 u. s. w. beweisen. Auf das Concil von Trient hätte man sich bezüglich des zwangsweise auferlegten Schweigens nicht berufen sollen; denn erstens wurde dort bloss eine Mahnung gegeben, und zweitens betraf die Erinnerung nur die Bekanntmachung von Entwürfen, welche, was heutzutage bei dem Stand der Presse nicht` mehr möglich wäre, damals in der Ferne mit wirklichen Decreten verwechselt wurden.

Den 9 März 1870.

I. V. Döllinger.

---

¹ Quaeres: quibus conditionibus promisit Christus se conciliis adfuturum? Resp. Ista generali: Si in nomine suo congregata fuerint; hoc est servata suffragiorum libertate; invocato coelesti auxilio; adhibita humana industria et diligentia in conquirenda veritate. . . . Deus scilicet, qui omnia suaviter disponit ac moderatur, via supernaturali aperta et manifesta non adest conciliis, sed occulta Spiritus subministratione (Deus) permittit, episcopos omnibus humanae infirmitatis periculis subjacere et aliquando succumbere; neque enim unquam promisit, se a conciliis ejusmodi pericula certo semper propulsaturum; sed hoc unum, se iis semper adfuturum, qui in suo nomine congregarentur. Congregari autem in suo nomine censentur, quoties eas observant leges et conditiones, quas voluit observari. Tournely, *Praelectiones theologicae de Deo et divinis attributis*, l. 165. Tournely führt denselben Gedanken in seinen *Praelectiones theologicae de ecclesia Christi*, l. 384, noch weiter aus: "(Deus) episcopos permittit omnibus humanae infirmitatis periculis obnoxios esse, metus scilicet, ambitionis, avaritiae, cupiditatis," &c.

¹ "Et que les autres consentent si évidemment à leur assemblée, qu'il sera clair, qu'on n'y ait fait qu'apporter le sentiment de toute la terre." (*Histoire de Variations*, l. 15, n. 1000.) Und darum fordert der Papst Gelasius zu einer " bene gesta synodus " nicht nur, dass sie nach Schrift und Tradition und nach den kirchlichen Regeln ihre Entscheidungen gefasst habe, sondern auch, dass sie von der ganzen Kirche angenommen sei: "quam cuncta recepit ecclesia" (Epist. 13 bei Labbe, *Concil.* iv., 1200 und 1203). Und Nicole bemerkt gegen die Calvinisten: "Ils ont une marque évidente que le Concile qui s'dit Universel doit être reçu pour tel, dans l'acceptation qu'en fait l'Eglise." (*Prétendus Réformés convaincus de schisme*, 2, 7, p. 289.) Die Kirche gibt den Concilien Zeugniss (nicht erst Autorität), sowie sie durch ihren biblischen Canon den einzelnen Büchern der Bibel Zeugniss gibt, während natürlich die innere Autorität derselben nicht von der Kirche ausfliesst. Sie ist auch da " testis, non autor fidei."

DOCUMENT XVIII.

PIUS EPISCOPUS

SERVUS SERVORUM DEI

SACRO APPROBANTE CONCILIO

AD PERPETUAM REI MEMORIAM.

Dei Filius et generis humani Redemptor Dominus noster Jesus Christus, ad Patrem coelestem rediturus, cum Ecclesia sua in terris militante, omnibus diebus usque ad consummationem saeculi futurum se esse promisit. Quare dilectae sponsae praesto esse, adsistere docenti, operanti benedicere, periclitanti opem ferre nullo unquam tempore destitit. Haec vero salutaris eius providentia, cum ex aliis beneficiis innumeris continenter apparuit, tum iis manifestissimae comperta est fructibus, qui orbi christiano e Conciliis Œcumenicis ac nominatim e Tridentino, iniquis licet temporibus celebrato, amplissimi provenerunt. Hinc enim sanctissima religionis dogmata pressius definita uberiusque exposita, errores damnati atque cohibiti; hinc ecclesiastica disciplina restituta firmiusque sancita, promotum in Clero scientiae et pietatis studium, parata adolescentibus ad sacram militiam educandis collegia, christiani denique populi mores et accuratiore fidelium eruditione et frequentiore sacramentorum usu instaurati. Hinc praeterea arctior membrorum cum visibili Capite communio, universoque Corpori Christi mystico additus vigor; hinc religiosae multiplicatae familiae, aliaque christianae pietatis instituta; hinc ille etiam assiduus et usque ad sanguinis effusionem constans ardor in Christi regno late per orbem propagando.

Verumtamen haec aliaque insignia emolumenta, quae per ultimam maxime oecumenicam Synodum divina clementia Ecclesiae largita est, dum grato, quo par est, animo recolimus; acerbum compescere haud possumus dolorem ob mala gravissima, inde potissimum orta, quod eiusdem sacrosanctae Synodi apud permultos vel auctoritas contempta, vel sapientissima neglecta fuero decreta.

Nemo enim ignorat, haereses, quas Tridentini Patres proscripserunt, num reiecto divino Ecclesiae magisterio, res ad religionem spectantes privati cuiusvis iudicio permitterentur, in sectas paullatim dissolutas esse multiplices, quibus inter se dissentientibus et concertantibus, omnis tandem in Christum fides apud non paucos labefactata est. Itaque ipsa sacra Biblia, quae antea christianae doctrinae unicus fons et iudex asserebantur, iam non pro divinis haberi, imo mythicis commentis accenseri coeperunt.

Tum nata est et late nimis per orbem vagata illa rationalismi seu naturalismi doctrina, quae religioni christianae utpote supernaturali instituto per omnia adversans, summo studio molitur, ut Christo, qui solus Dominus et Salvator noster est, a mentibus humanis, a vita et moribus populorum excluso, merae quod vocant rationis vel naturae regnum stabiliatur. Relicta autem proiectaque christiana religione, negato vero Deo et Christo eius, prolapsa tandem est multorum mens in pantheismi, materialismi, atheismi barathrum, ut iam ipsam rationalem naturam, omnemque iusti rectique normam negantes, ima humanae societatis fundamenta diruere connitantur.

Hac porro impietate circumquaque grassante, infeliciter contigit, ut plures etiam catholicae Ecclesiae filiis a via verae pietatis aberrarent, in iisque, diminutis paullatim veritatibus, sensus catholicus attenuaretur. Variis enim ac peregrinis doctrinis abducti, naturam et gratiam, scientiam humanam et fidem divinam perperam commiscentes, genuinum sensum dogmatum, quem tenet ac docet Sancta Mater Ecclesia, depravare, integritatemque et sinceritatem fidei in periculum adducere comperiuntur.

Quibus omnibus perspectis, fieri qui potest, ut non commoveantur intima Ecclesiae viscera? Quemadmodum enim Deus vult omnes homines salvos fieri, et ad agnitionem veritatis venire; quemadmodum Christus venit, ut salvum faceret, quod perierat, et filios Dei, qui erant dispersi, congregaret in unum, ita Ecclesia, a Deo populorum mater et magistra constituta: omnibus debitricem se novit, ac lapsos erigere, labantes sustinere, revertentes amplecti, confirmare bonos et ad meliora provehere parata semper et intenta est. Quapropter nullo tempore a Dei veritate, quae sanat omnia, testanda et praedicanda quiescere potest, sibi dictum esse non ignorans: Spiritus meus, qui est in te, et verba mea, quae posui in ore tuo, non recedent de ore tuo amodo et usque in sempiternum.[1]

Nos itaque, inhaerentes Praedecessorum Nostrorum vestigiis, pro supremo Nostro Apostolico munere veritatem catholicam docere ac tueri, perversasque doctrinas reprobare nunquam intermisimus. Nunc autem sedentibus Nobiscum et iudicantibus universi orbis Episcopis, in hanc oecumeni-

[1] Is. lix. 21.

cam Synodum auctoritate Nostra in Spiritu Sancto congregatis, innixi Dei verbo scripto et tradito, prout ab Ecclesia catholica sancte custoditum et genuine expositum accepimus, ex hac Petri Cathedra in conspectu omnium salutarem Christi doctrinam profiteri et declarare constituimus, adversis erroribus potestate nobis a Deo tradita proscriptis atque damnatis.

Caput I.
De Deo rerum omnium Creatore.

Sancta Catholica Apostolica Romana Ecclesia credit et confitetur, unum esse Deum verum et vivum, Creatorem ac Dominum coeli et terrae, omnipotentem, aeternum, immensum, incomprehensibilem, intellectu ac voluntate omnique perfectione infinitum ; qui cum sit una singularis, simplex omnino et incommutabilis substantia spiritualis, praedicandus re et essentia a mundo distinctus, in se et ex-beatissimus, et super omnia, quae praeter ipsum sunt et concipi possunt, ineffabiliter excelsus.

Hic solus verus Deus bonitate sua et omnipotenti virtute non ad augendam suam beatitudinem, nec ad acquirendam, sed ad manifestandam perfectionem suam per bona, quae creaturis impertiur, liberrimo consilio simul ab initio temporis utramque de nihilo condidit creaturam, spiritualem et corporalem, angelicam videlicet et mundanam, ac deinde humanam quasi communem ex spiritu et corpore constitutam.[1]

Universa vero, quae condidit, Deus providentia sua tuetur atque gubernat, attingens a fine usque ad finem fortiter, et disponens omnia suaviter.[2] Omnia enim nuda et aperta sunt oculis eius,[3] ea etiam, quae libera creaturarum actione futura sunt.

Caput II.
De revelatione.

Eadem Sancta Mater Ecclesia tenet et docet, Deum, rerum omnium principium et finem, naturali humanae rationis lumine e rebus creatis certo cognosci posse; invisibilia enim ipsius, a creatura mundi per ea quae facta sunt intellecta, conspiciuntur :[4] attamen placuisse eius sapientiae et bonitati, alia, eaque supernaturali via se ipsum ac aeterna voluntatis suae decreta humano generi revelare, dicente Apostolo : Multifariam, multisque modis olim Deus loquens patribus in Prophetis : novissime, diebus istis locutus est nobis in Filio.[5] Huic divinae revelationis tribuendum

quidem est, ut ea, quae in rebus divinis humanae rationi per se impervia non sunt, in praesenti quoque generis humani conditione ab omnibus expedite, firma certitudine et nullo admixto errore cognosci possint. Non hac tamen de causa revelatio absolute necessaria dicenda est, sed quia Deus ex infinita bonitate sua ordinavit hominem ad finem supernaturalem, ad participanda scilicet bona divina, quae humanae mentis intelligentiam omnino superant; siquidem oculus non vidit, nec auris audivit, nec in cor hominis ascendit, quae praeparavit Deus iis, qui diligunt illum.[1]

Haec porro supernaturalis revelatio, secundum universalis Ecclesiae fidem, a sancta Tridentina Synodo declaratam, continetur in libris scriptis et sine scripto traditionibus, quae ipsius Christi ore ab Apostolis acceptae, aut ab ipsis Apostolis Spiritu Sancto dictante quasi per manus traditae, ad nos usque pervenerunt.[2] Qui quidem veteris et novi Testamenti libri integri cum omnibus suis partibus, prout in eiusdem Concilii decreto recensentur, et in vetere vulgata latina editione habentur, pro sacris et canonicis suscipiendi sunt. Eos vero Ecclesia pro sacris et canonicis habet, non ideo quod sola humana industria concinnati, sua deinde auctoritate sint approbati; nec ideo dumtaxat, quod revelationem sine errore contineant; sed propterea quod Spiritu Sancto inspirante conscripti Deum habent auctorem, atque ut tales ipsi Ecclesiae traditi sunt.

Quoniam vero, quae sancta Tridentina Synodus de interpretatione divinae Scripturae ad coërcenda petulantia ingenia salubriter decrevit, a quibusdam hominibus prave exponuntur, Nos, idem decretum renovantes, hanc illius mentem esse declaramus, ut in rebus fidei et morum, ad aedificationem doctrinae Christianae pertinentium, is pro vero sensu sacrae Scripturae habendus sit, quem tenuit ac tenet Sancta Mater Ecclesia, cuius est iudicare de vero sensu et interpretatione Scripturarum sanctarum : atque ideo nemini licere contra hunc sensum, aut etiam contra unanimem consensum Patrum ipsam Scripturam sacram interpretari.

Caput III.
De fide.

Quum homo a Deo tanquam Creatore et Domino suo totus dependeat, et ratio creata increatae Veritati penitus subiecta sit, plenum revelanti Deo intellectus et voluntatis obsequium fide praestare tenemur.

---

[1] Conc. Later. lv. c. 1. *Firmiter.*
[2] Sap. viii. 1.   [3] Cf. Heb. vi. 13.
[4] Rom. i. 20.   [5] Heb. i. 1, 2.

[1] Cor. ii. 9.
[2] Conc. Trid., sess. iv. Decr. *de Can. Script.*

Hanc vero fidem, quae humanae salutis initium est, Ecclesia catholica profitetur, virtutem esse supernaturalem, qua, Dei aspirante et adiuvante gratia, ab eo revelata vera esse credimus, non propter intrinsecam rerum veritatem naturali rationis lumine perspectam, sed propter auctoritatem ipsius Dei revelantis, qui nec falli nec fallere potest. Est enim fides, testante Apostolo, sperandarum substantia rerum, argumentum non apparentium.[1]

Ut nihilominus fidei nostrae obsequium rationi consentaneum esset, voluit Deus cum internis Spiritus Sancti auxiliis externa iungi revelationis suae argumenta, facta scilicet divina, atque imprimis miracula et prophetias, quae cum Dei omnipotentiam et infinitam scientiam luculenter commonstrent, divinae revelationis signa sunt certissima et omnium intelligentiae accommodata. Quare tum Moyses et Prophetae, tum ipse maxime Christus Dominus multa et manifestissima miracula et prophetias ediderunt; et de Apostolis legimus: Illi autem profecti praedicaverunt ubique, Domino cooperante, et sermonem confirmante, sequentibus signis.[2] Et rursum scriptum est: Habemus firmiorem propheticum sermonem, cui bene facitis attendentes quasi lucernae lucenti in caliginoso loco.[3]

Licet autem fidei assensus nequaquam sit motus animi caecus: nemo tamen evangelicae praedicationi consentire potest, sicut oportet ad salutem consequendam, absque illuminatione et inspiratione Spiritus Sancti, qui dat omnibus suavitatem in consentiendo et credendo veritati.[4] Quare fides ipsa in se, etiamsi per charitatem non operetur, donum Dei est, et actus eius est opus ad salutem pertinens, quo homo liberam praestat ipsi Deo obedientiam, gratiae eius, cui resistere posset, consentiendo et cooperando.

Porro fide divina et catholica ea omnia credenda sunt, quae in verbo Dei scripto vel tradito, continentur, et ab Ecclesia sive solemni iudicio sive ordinario et universali magisterio tamquam divinitus revelata credenda proponuntur.

Quoniam vero sine fide impossibile est placere Deo, et ad filiorum eius consortium pervenire; ideo nemini unquam sine illa contigit iustificatio, nec ullus, nisi in ea perseveraverit usque in finem, vitam aeternam assequetur. Ut autem officio veram fidem amplectendi, in eaque constanter perseverandi satisfacere possemus, Deus per Filium suum unigenitum Ecclesiam instituit, suaeque institutionis manifestis notis instruxit, ut ea tamquam custos et magistra verbi revelati ab omnibus posset agnosci. Ad solam enim catholicam Ecclesiam ea pertinent omnia, quae ad evidentem fidei christianae credibilitatem tam multa et tam mira divinitus sunt disposita. Quin etiam Ecclesia per se ipsa, ob suam nempe admirabilem propagationem, eximiam sanctitatem et inexhaustam in omnibus bonis foecunditatem, ob catholicam unitatem, invictamque stabilitatem, magnum quoddam et perpetuum est motivum credibilitatis et divinae suae legationis testimonium irrefragabile.

Quo fit, ut ipsa veluti signum levatum in nationes,[1] et ad se invitet, qui nondum crediderunt, et filios suos certiores faciat, firmissimo niti fundamento fidem, quam profitentur. Cui quidem testimonio efficax subsidium accedit ex superna virtute. Etenim benignissimus Dominus et errantes gratia sua excitat atque adiuvat, ut ad agnitionem veritatis venire possint; et eos, quos de tenebris transtulit in admirabile lumen suum, in hoc eodem lumine ut perseverent, gratia sua confirmat, non deserens, nisi deseratur. Quocirca minime par est conditio eorum, qui per coeleste fidei donum catholicae veritati adhaeserunt; atque eorum qui ducti opinionibus humanis, falsam religionem sectantur; illi enim, qui fidem sub Ecclesiae magisterio susceperunt, nullam unquam habere possunt iustam causam mutandi, aut in dubium fidem eamdem revocandi. Quae cum ita sint, gratias agentes Deo Patri, qui dignos nos fecit in partem sortis sanctorum in lumine, tantam ne negligamus salutem, sed aspicientes in auctorem fidei et consummatorem Iesum, teneamus spei nostrae confessionem indeclinabilem.

Caput IV.

De fide et ratione.

Hoc quoque perpetuus Ecclesiae catholicae consensus tenuit et tenet, duplicem esse ordinem cognitionis, non solum principio, sed obiecto etiam distinctum : principio quidem, quia in altero naturali ratione, in altero fide divina cognoscimus : obiecto autem, quia praeter ea, ad quae naturalis ratio pertingere potest, credenda nobis proponuntur mysteria in Deo abscondita, quae, nisi revelata divinitus, innotescere non possunt. Quocirca Apostolus, qui a gentibus Deum per ea, quae facta sunt, cognitum esse testatur, disserens tamen de gratia et veritate, quae per Iesum Christum facta

[1] Heb. xi. 1. [2] Marc. xvi. 20.
[3] 2 Petr. i. 19. [4] Syn. Araus. ii. can. 7.

[1] Is. xi. 12.

est,[1] pronuntiat: Loquimur Dei sapientiam in mysterio, quae abscondita est, quam praedestinavit Deus ante saecula in gloriam nostram, quam nemo principum huius saeculi cognovit :—nobis autem revelavit Deus per Spiritum suum: Spiritus enim omnia scrutatur, etiam profunda Dei.[2] Et ipse Unigenitus confitetur Patri, quia abscondit haec a sapientibus, et prudentibus, et revelavit ea parvulis.[3]

Ac ratio quidem, fide illustrata, cum sedulo, pie et sobrie quaerit, aliquam, Deo dante, mysteriorum intelligentiam eamque fructuosissimam assequitur, tum ex eorum, quae naturaliter cognoscit, analogia, tum e mysteriorum ipsorum nexu inter se et cum fine hominis ultimo; nunquam tamen idonea redditur ad ea perspicienda instar veritatum, quae propriam ipsius obiectum constituunt. Divina enim mysteria suapte natura intellectum creatum sic excedunt, ut etiam revelatione tradita et fide suscepta, ipsius tamen fidei velamine contecta et quadam quasi caligine obvoluta maneant, quamdiu in hac mortali vita peregrinamur a Domino: per fidem enim ambulamus, et non per speciem.[4]

Verum etsi fides sit supra rationem, nulla tamen unquam inter fidem et rationem vera dissensio esse potest: cum idem Deus, qui mysteria revelat et fidem infundit, animo humano rationis lumen indiderit; Deus autem negare seipsum non possit, nec verum vero unquam contradicere. Inanis autem huius contradictionis species inde potissimum oritur, quod vel fidei dogmata ad mentem Ecclesiae intellecta et exposita non fuerint, vel opinionum commenta pro rationis effatis habeantur. Omnem igitur assertionem veritati illuminatae fidei contrariam omnino falsam esse definimus.[5] Porro Ecclesia, quae una cum apostolico munere docendi, mandatum accepit, fidei depositum custodiendi, ius et officium divinitus habet falsi nominis scientiam proscribendi, ne quis decipiatur per philosophiam, et inanem fallaciam.[6] Quapropter omnes christiani fideles huiusmodi opiniones, quae fidei doctrinae contrariae esse cognoscuntur, maxime si ab Ecclesia reprobatae fuerint, non solum prohibentur tanquam legitimas scientiae conclusiones defendere, sed pro erroribus potius, qui fallacem veritatis speciem prae se ferant habere, tenentur omnino.

Neque solum fides et ratio inter se dissidere nunquam possunt, sed opem quoque

[1] Ioan. i. 17. [2] 1 Cor. ii. 7–9.
[3] Math. xi. 25. [4] 2 Cor. v. 7.
[5] Conc. Lat. V. Bulla *Apostolici regiminis*.
[6] Coloss. ii. 8.

sibi mutuam ferunt, cum recta ratio fidei fundamenta demonstret, eiusque lumine illustrata rerum divinarum scientiam excolat; fides vero rationem ab erroribus liberet ac tueatur, eamque multiplici cognitione instruat. Quapropter tantum abest, ut Ecclesia humanarum artium et disciplinarum culturae obsistat, ut hanc multis modis iuvet atque promoveat. Non enim commoda ab iis ad hominum vitam dimanantia aut ignorat aut despicit; fatetur imo, eas, quemadmodum a Deo, scientiarum Domino, profectae sunt, ita si rite pertractentur, ad Deum, iuvante eius gratia, perducere. Nec sane ipsa vetat, ne huiusmodi disciplinae in suo quaeque ambitu propriis utantur principiis et propria methodo; sed iustam hanc libertatem agnoscens, id sedulo cavet, ne divinae doctrinae repugnando errores in se suscipiant, aut fines proprios transgressae, ea, quae sunt fidei, occupent et perturbent.

Neque enim fidei doctrina, quam Deus revelavit, velut philosophicum inventum proposita est humanis ingeniis perficienda, sed tamquam divinum depositum Christi Sponsae tradita, fideliter custodienda et infallibiliter declaranda. Hinc sacrorum quoque dogmatum is sensus perpetuo est retinendus, quem semel declaravit Sancta Mater Ecclesia, nec unquam ab eo sensu, altioris intelligentiae specie et nomine, recedendum. Crescat igitur et multum vehementerque proficiat, tam singulorum, quam omnium, tam unius hominis, quam totius Ecclesiae, aetatum ac saeculorum gradibus, intelligentia, scientia, sapientia: sed in suo dumtaxat genere, in eodem scilicet dogmate, eodem sensu, eademque sententia.[1]

CANONES.

I.

De Deo rerum omnium Creatore.

1. Si quis unum verum Deum visibilium et invisibilium Creatorem et Dominum negaverit; anathema sit.

2. Si quis praeter materiam nihil esse affirmare non erubuerit; anathema sit.

3. Si quis dixerit, unam eandemque esse Dei et rerum omnium substantiam vel essentiam; anathema sit.

4. Si quis dixerit, res finitas, tum corporeas tum spirituales, aut saltem spirituales, e divina substantia emanasse;

[1] Vinc. Lir. *Common.* n. 2³.

aut divinam essentiam sui manifestatione vel evolutione fieri omnia; aut denique Deum esse ens universale seu indefinitum, quod sese determinando constituat rerum universitatem in genera, species et individua distinctam; anathema sit.

5. Si quis non confiteatur, mundum, resque omnes, quae in eo continentur, et spirituales et materiales, secundum totam suam substantiam a Deo ex nihilo esse productas;

aut Deum dixerit non voluntate ab omni necessitate libera, sed tam necessario creasse, quam necessario amat seipsum;

aut mundum ad Dei gloriam conditum esse negaverit; anathema sit.

II.

De revelatione.

1. Si quis dixerit, Deum unum et verum, Creatorem et Dominum nostrum, per ea, quae facta sunt, naturali rationis humanae lumine certo cognosci non posse; anathema sit.

2. Si quis dixerit, fieri non posse, aut non expedire, ut per revelationem divinam homo de Deo, cultuque ei exhibendo edoceatur; anathema sit.

3. Si quis dixerit, hominem ad cognitionem et perfectionem, quae naturalem superet, divinitus evehi non posse, sed ex scipso ad omnis tandem veri et boni possessionem iugi profectu pertingere posse et debere; anathema sit.

4. Si quis sacrae Scripturae libros integros cum omnibus suis partibus, prout illos sancta Tridentina Synodus recensuit, pro sacris et canonicis non susceperit, aut eos divinitus inspiratos esse negaverit; anathema sit.

III.

De fide.

1. Si quis dixerit, rationem humanam ita independentem esse, ut fides ei a Deo imperari non possit; anathema sit.

2. Si quis dixerit, fidem divinam a naturali de Deo et rebus moralibus scientia non distingui, ac propterea ad fidem divinam non requiri, ut revelata veritas propter auctoritatem Dei revelantis credatur; anathema sit.

3. Si quis dixerit, revelationem divinam externis signis credibilem fieri non posse, ideoque sola interna cuiusque experientia aut inspiratione privata homines ad fidem moveri debere; anathema sit.

4. Si quis dixerit, miracula nulla fieri posse, proindeque omnes de iis narrationes, etiam in sacra Scriptura contentas, inter fabulas vel mythos ablegandas esse, aut miracula certo cognosci nunquam posse, nec iis divinam religionis christianae originem rite probari; anathema sit.

5. Si quis dixerit, assensum fidei christianae non esse liberum, sed argumentis humanae rationis necessario produci; aut ad solam fidem vivam, quae per charitatem operatur gratiam Dei necessarium esse; anathema sit.

6. Si quis dixerit, parem esse conditionem fidelium atque eorum, qui ad fidem unice veram nondum pervenerunt, ita ut catholici iustam causam habere possint, fidem, quam sub Ecclesiae magisterio iam susceperunt, assensu suspenso in dubium vocandi, donec demonstrationem scientificam credibilitatis et veritatis fidei suae absolverint; anathema sit.

IV.

De fide et ratione.

1. Si quis dixerit, in revelatione divina nulla vera et proprie dicta mysteria contineri, sed universa fidei dogmata posse per rationem rite excultam e naturalibus principiis intelligi et demonstrari; anathema sit.

2. Si quis dixerit, disciplinas humanas ea cum libertate tractandas esse, ut earum assertiones, etsi doctrinae revelatae adversentur, tanquam verae retineri, neque ab Ecclesia proscribi possint; anathema sit.

3. Si quis dixerit, fieri posse, ut dogmatibus ab Ecclesia propositis, aliquando secundum progressum scientiae sensus tribuendus sit alius ab eo, quem intellexit et intelligit Ecclesia; anathema sit.

Itaque supremi pastoralis Nostri officii debitum exequentes, omnes Christi fideles, maxime vero eos, qui praesunt vel docendi munere funguntur, per viscera Iesu Christi obtestamur, necnon eiusdem Dei et Salvatoris nostri auctoritate iubemus, ut ad hos errores a Sancta Ecclesia arcendos et eliminandos, atque purissimae fidei lucem pandendam studium et operam conferant.

Quoniam vero satis non est, haereticam pravitatem devitare, nisi ii quoque errores diligenter fugiantur, qui ad illam plus minusve accedunt; omnes officii monemus, servandi etiam Constitutiones et Decreta, quibus pravae ciusmodi opiniones, quae isthic diserte non enumerantur, ab hac Sancta Sede proscriptae et prohibitae sunt.

Datum Romae in publica Sessione in Vaticana Basilica solemniter celebrata, anno

Incarnationis Dominicae millesimo octingentesimo septuagesimo, die vigesima quarta Aprilis.
Pontificatus Nostri anno vigesimo quarto.
Ita est.

IOSEPHUS Episcopus S. Hippolyti,
Secretarius Concilii Vaticani.

(Dalla *Civiltà Cattolica*, 7 maggio 1870.)

DOCUMENT XIX.

Formule.[1]

Les soussignés prêtres et clercs du diocèse de Florence, répondant à l'invitation faite au Clergé italien, offrent au Concile Œcuménique leur modeste obole pour le soulagement de l'auguste pauvreté du Vicaire de Jésus-Christ, et saisissent avec empressement cette occasion nouvelle d'affirmer leur dévouement à sa Personne sacrée, leur zèle pour ses droits sacrosaints et leur foi inébranlable à son infaillible autorité.

(*Suivent les signatures du Clergé.*)

(De *L'Italie*, 4 juillet 1870.)

DOCUMENT XX.

CONSTITUTIO DOGMATICA

PRIMA

DE ECCLESIA CHRISTI

EDITA IN SESSIONE QUARTA

SACROSANCTI OECUMENICI CONCILII VATICANI.

PIUS EPISCOPUS

SERVUS SERVORUM DEI

SACRO APPROBANTE CONCILIO

Ad perpetuam rei memoriam.

Pastor aeternus et episcopus animarum nostrarum, ut salutiferum redemptionis opus perenne redderet, sanctam aedificare Ecclesiam decrevit, in qua veluti in domo Dei viventis fideles omnes unius fidei et charitatis vinculo continerentur. Qua-

[1] Le présent modèle de souscription devra être remis, en même temps que les offrandes recueillies, à l'Ill. et Rév. chanoine N. au Séminaire florentin, pas plus tard que le 24 juin.

propter, priusquam clarificaretur, rogavit Patrem non pro Apostolis tantum, sed et pro eis, qui credituri erant per verbum eorum in ipsum, ut omnes unum essent, sicut ipse Filius et Pater unum sunt. Quemadmodum igitur Apostolos, quos sibi de mundo elegerat, misit, sicut ipse missus erat a Patre; ita in Ecclesia sua Pastores et Doctores usque ad consummationem saeculi esse voluit. Ut vero Episcopatus ipse unus et indivisus esset, et per cohaerentes sibi invicem sacerdotes credentium multitudo universa in fidei et communionis unitate conservaretur, beatum Petrum caeteris Apostolis praeponens in ipso instituit perpetuum utriusque unitatis principium ac visibile fundamentum, super cuius fortitudinem aeternum exstrueretur templum, et Ecclesiae coelo inferenda sublimitas in huius fidei firmitate consurgeret.[1] Et quoniam portae inferi ad evertendam, si fieri posset, Ecclesiam contra eius fundamentum divinitus positum maiori in dies odio undique insurgunt; Nos ad catholici gregis custodiam, incolumitatem, augmentum, necessarium esse iudicamus, sacro approbante Concilio, doctrinam de institutione, perpetuitate, ac natura sacri Apostolici primatus, in quo totius Ecclesiae vis ac soliditas consistit, cunctis fidelibus credendam et tenendam, secundum antiquam atque constantem universalis Ecclesiae fidem, proponere, atque contrarios, dominico gregi adeo perniciosos, errores proscribere et condemnare.

CAPUT I.

De apostolici primatus in Beato Petro institutione.

Docemus itaque et declaramus, iuxta Evangelii testimonia primatum iurisdictionis in universam Dei Ecclesiam immediate et directe beato Petro Apostolo promissum atque collatum a Christo Domino fuisse. Unum enim Simonem, cui iam pridem dixerat: Tu vocaberis Cephas,[2] postquam ille suam edidit confessionem inquiens: Tu es Christus, Filius Dei vivi, solemnibus his verbis allocutus est Dominus: Beatus es Simon Barjona, quia caro, et sanguis non revelavit tibi, sed Pater meus, qui in coelis est: et ego dico tibi, quia tu es Petrus, et super hanc petram aedificabo Ecclesiam meam, et portae inferi non praevalebunt adversus eam: et tibi dabo claves regni coelorum: et quodcumque ligaveris super terram, erit ligatum et in coelis: et quodcumque solveris super terram, erit solutum

[1] St. Leo M. Serm. iv. (al. iii), cap. 2, *in diem Natalis sui.*   [2] Ioan. i. 42.

et in coelis.[1] Atque uni Simoni Petro contulit Iesus post suam resurrectionem summi pastoris et rectoris iurisdictionem in totum suum ovile dicens : Pasce agnos meos : Pasce oves meas.[2] Huic tam manifestae sacrarum Scripturarum doctrinae, ut ab Ecclesia catholica semper intellecta est, aperte opponuntur pravae eorum sententiae, qui constitutam a Christo Domino in sua Ecclesia regiminis formam pervertentes, negant solum Petrum prae ceteris Apostolis, sive seorsum singulis sive omnibus simul, vero proprioque iurisdictionis primatu fuisse a Christo instructum ; aut qui affirmant eundem primatum non immediate, directeque ipsi beato Petro, sed Ecclesiae, et per hanc illi, ut ipsius Ecclesiae ministro, delatum fuisse.

Si quis igitur dixerit, beatum Petrum Apostolum non esse a Christo Domino constitutum Apostolorum omnium principem et totius Ecclesiae militantis visibile caput ; vel eundem honoris tantum ; non autem verae propriaeque iurisdictionis primatum ab eodem Domino Nostro Iesu Christo directe et immediate accepisse ; anathema sit.

CAPUT II.

De perpetuitate primatus Beati Petri in Romanis Pontificibus.

Quod autem in beato Apostolo Petro, princeps pastorum et pastor magnus ovium Dominus Christus Iesus in perpetuam salutem ac perenne bonum Ecclesiae instituit, id eodem auctore in Ecclesia, quae fundata super petram ad finem saeculorum usque firma stabit, iugiter durare necesse est. Nulli sane dubium, imo saeculis omnibus notum est, quod sanctus beatissimusque Petrus, Apostolorum princeps et caput, fideique columna, et Ecclesiae catholicae fundamentum, a Domino Nostro Iesu Christo, Salvatore humani generis ac Redemptore, claves regni accepit : qui ad hoc usque tempus et semper in suis successoribus, episcopis Sanctae Romanae Sedis, ab ipso fundatae eiusque consecratae sanguine, vivit et praesidet et iudicium exercet.[3] Unde quicumque in hac Cathedra Petro succedit, is secundum Christi ipsius institutionem primatum Petri in universam Ecclesiam obtinet. Manet ergo dispositio veritatis, et beatus Petrus in accepta fortitudine petrae perseverans suscepta Ecclesiae gubernacula non reliquit.[4] Hac de causa ad Romanam Ecclesiam propter potentiorem principalitatem necesse semper fuit

omnem convenire Ecclesiam, hoc est, eos, qui sunt undique fideles, ut in ea Sede, e qua venerandae communionis iura in omnes dimanant, tamquam membra in capite consociata, in unam corporis compagem coalescerent.[1]

Si quis ergo dixerit, non esse ex ipsius Christi Domini institutione, seu iure divino, ut beatus Petrus in primatu super universam Ecclesiam habeat perpetuos successores ; aut Romanum Pontificem non esse beati Petri in eodem primatu successorem ; anathema sit.

CAPUT III.

De vi et ratione primatus Romani Pontificis.

Quapropter apertis innixi sacrarum litterarum testimoniis, et inhaerentes tum Praedecessorum Nostrorum, Romanorum Pontificum, tum Conciliorum generalium disertis, perspicuisque decretis, innovamus Œcumenici Concilii Florentini definitionem, qua credendum ab omnibus Christi fidelibus est, Sanctam Apostolicam Sedem, et Romanum Pontificem in universum orbem tenere primatum, et ipsum Pontificem Romanum successorem esse beati Petri principis Apostolorum, et verum Christi Vicarium, totiusque Ecclesiae caput, et omnium Christianorum patrem ac doctorem existere ; et ipsi in beato Petro pascendi, regendi et gubernandi universalem Ecclesiam a Domino Nostro Iesu Christo plenam potestatem traditam esse ; quemadmodum etiam in gestis Œcumenicorum Conciliorum et sacris canonibus continetur.

Docemus proinde et declaramus, Ecclesiam Romanam, disponente Domino, super omnes alias ordinariae potestatis obtinere principatum, et hanc Romani Pontificis iurisdictionis potestatem, quae vere episcopalis est, immediatam esse ; erga quam cuiuscumque ritus et dignitatis pastores atque fideles, tam seorsum singuli quam simul omnes, officio hierarchicae subordinationis, veraeque obedientiae obstringuntur, non solum in rebus, quae ad fidem et mores, sed etiam in iis, quae ad disciplinam et regimen Ecclesiae per totum orbem diffusae pertinent ; ita ut custodita cum Romano Pontifice tam communionis, quam eiusdem fidei professionis unitate, Ecclesiae Christi sit unus grex sub uno summo pastore. Haec est catholicae veritatis doctrina, a qua deviare salva fide atque salute nemo potest.

Tantum autem abest, ut haec Summi Pontificis potestas officiat ordinariae ac

---

[1] Matth. xvi. 16-19.   [2] Ioan. xxi. 15-17.
[3] Cf. Ephesini Concilii, Act. III.
[4] St. Leo M., Serm. iii. (al. ii.), cap. 3.

[1] S. Iren. Adv. haer. l. iii. c. 3, et Conc. Aquilei, a 381 inter epp. S. Ambros. ep. xi.

immediatae illi episcopali iurisdictionis potestati, qua Episcopi, qui positi a Spiritu Sancto in Apostolorum locum successerunt, tamquam veri pastores assignatos sibi greges, singuli singulos, pascunt et regunt, ut eadem a supremo et universali Pastore asserantur, roboretur ac vindicetur, secundum illud sancti Gregorii Magni : Meus honor est honor universalis Ecclesiae.. Meus honor est fratrum meorum solidus vigor. Tum ego vero honoratus sum, cum singulis quibusque honor debitus non negatur.[1]

Porro ex suprema illa Romani Pontificis potestate gubernandi universam Ecclesiam ius eidem esse consequitur, in huius sui muneris exercitio libere communicandi cum pastoribus et gregibus totius Ecclesiae, ut iidem ab ipso in via salutis doceri ac regi possint. Quare damnamus ac reprobamus illorum sententias, qui hanc supremi capitis cum pastoribus et gregibus communicationem licite impediri posse dicunt, aut eandem reddunt saeculari potestati obnoxiam, ita ut contendant, quae ab Apostolica Sede vel eius auctoritate ad regimen Ecclesiae constituuntur, vim ac valorem non habere, nisi potestatis saecularis placito confirmentur.

Et quoniam divino Apostolici primatus iure Romanus Pontifex universae Ecclesiae praeest, docemus etiam et declaramus, eum esse iudicem supremum fidelium,[2] et in omnibus causis ad examen ecclesiasticum spectantibus ad ipsius posse iudicium recurri.[3] Sedis vero Apostolicae, cuius auctoritate maior non est, iudicium a nemine fore retractandum, neque cuiquam de eius licere iudicare iudicio.[4] Quare a recto veritatis tramite aberrant, qui affirmant, licere ab iudiciis Romanorum Pontificum ad Œcumenicum Concilium tamquam ad auctoritatem Romano Pontifice superiorem appellare.

Si quis itaque dixerit, Romanum Pontificem habere tantummodo officium inspectionis vel directionis, non autem plenam et supremam potestatem iurisdictionis in universam Ecclesiam, non solum in rebus, quae ad fidem et mores, sed etiam in iis, quae ad disciplinam et regimen Ecclesiae per totum orbem diffusae pertinent ; aut eum habere tantum potiores partes, non vero totam plenitudinem huius supremae potestatis ; aut hanc eius potestatem non esse ordinariam et immediatam sive in omnes ac singulas Ecclesias, sive in omnes et singulos pastores et fideles ; anathema sit.

[1] Ep. ad Eulog. Alexandrin. l. viii. ep. xxx.
[2] Pii P. VI. Breve *Super soliditate*, d. 28 nov. 1786.
[3] Concil. Oecum. Lugdun. II.
[4] Ep. Nicolai I, *ad Michaelem Imperatorem*.

CAPUT IV.

De Romani Pontificis infallibili magisterio.

Ipso autem Apostolico primatu, quem Romanus Pontifex, tamquam Petri principis Apostolorum successor, in universam Ecclesiam obtinet, supremam quoque magisterii potestatem comprehendi, haec Sancta Sedes semper tenuit, perpetuus Ecclesiae usus comprobat, ipsaque Œcumenica Concilia, ea imprimis, in quibus Oriens cum Occidente in fidei charitatisque unionem conveniebat, declaraverunt. Patres enim Concilii Constantinopolitani quarti maiorum vestigiis inhaerentes, hanc solemnem ediderunt professionem : Prima salus est, rectae fidei regulam custodire. Et quia non potest Domini Nostri Iesu Christi praetermitti sententia dicentis : Tu es Petrus, et super hanc petram aedificabo Ecclesiam meam, haec, quae dicta sunt, rerum probantur effectibus, quia in Sede Apostolica immaculata est semper catholica reservata religio, et sancta celebrata doctrina. Ab huius ergo fide et doctrina separari minime cupientes, speramus, ut in una communione, quam Sedes Apostolica praedicat, esse mereamur, in qua est integra et vera Christianae religionis soliditas.[1] Approbante vero Lugdunensi Concilio secundo, Graeci professi sunt : Sanctam Romanam Ecclesiam summum et plenum primatum et principatum super universam Ecclesiam catholicam obtinere, quem se ab ipso Domino in beato Petro Apostolorum principe sive vertice, cuius Romanus Pontifex est successor, cum potestatis plenitudine recepisse veraciter et humiliter recognoscit, et sicut prae caeteris tenetur fidei veritatem defendere, sic et, si quae de fide subortae fuerint quaestiones, suo debent iudicio definiri. Florentinum denique Concilium definivit : Pontificem Romanum, verum Christi Vicarium, totiusque Ecclesiae caput et omnium Christianorum patrem ac doctorem existere ; et ipsi in beato Petro pascendi, regendi ac gubernandi universalem Ecclesiam a Domino Nostro Iesu Christo plenam potestatem traditam esse.

Huic pastorali muneri ut satisfacerent, Praedecessores Nostri indefessam semper operam dederunt, ut salutaris Christi doctrina apud omnes terrae populos propagaretur, parique cura vigilarunt, ut, ubi recepta esset, sincera et pura conservaretur. Quocirca totius orbis Antistites, nunc sin-

[1] Ex formula S. Hormisdae Papae, prout ab Hadriano II. Patribus Concilii (Fcumenici VIII, Constantinopolitani IV, proposita et ab iisdem subscripta est.

guli, nunc in Synodis congregati, longam Ecclesiarum consuetudinem, et antiquae regulae formam sequentes, ea praesertim pericula, quae in negotiis fidei emergebant, ad hanc Sedem Apostolicam retulerunt, ut ibi potissimum resarcirentur damna fidei, ubi fides non potest sentire defectum.[1] Romani autem Pontifices, prout temporum et rerum conditio suadebat, nunc convocatis Œcumenicis Conciliis, aut explorata Ecclesiae per orbem dispersae sententia, nunc per Synodos particulares, nunc aliis, quae divina suppeditabat providentia, adhibitis auxiliis, ea tenenda definiverunt, quae sacris Scripturis et apostolicis Traditionibus consentanea, Deo adiutore, cognoverant. Neque enim Petri successoribus Spiritus Sanctus promissus est, ut eo revelante novam doctrinam patefacerent, sed ut eo assistente traditam per Apostolos revelationem seu fidei depositum sancte custodirent et fideliter exponerent. Quorum quidem apostolicam doctrinam omnes venerabiles Patres amplexi et sancti Doctores orthodoxi venerati atque secuti sunt; plenissime scientes, hanc sancti Petri Sedem ab omni semper errore illibatam permanere, secundum Domini Salvatoris Nostri divinam pollicitationem discipulorum suorum principi factam: Ego rogavi pro te, ut non deficiat fides tua, et tu aliquando conversus confirma fratres tuos.

Hoc igitur veritatis et fidei numquam deficientis charisma Petro eiusque in hac Cathedra successoribus divinitus collatum est, ut excelso suo munere in omnium salutem fungerentur, ut universus Christi grex per eos ab erroris venenosa esca aversus, coelestis doctrinae pabulo nutriretur, ut sublata schismatis occasione Ecclesia tota una conservaretur, atque suo fundamento innixa firma adversus inferi portas consisteret.

At vero cum hac ipsa aetate, qua salutifera Apostolici muneris efficacia vel maxime requiritur, non pauci inveniantur, qui illius auctoritati obtrectant; necessarium omnino esse censemus, praerogativam, quam uni-

[1] Cf. S. Bern., Epist. cxc.

genitus Dei Filius cum summo pastorali officio coniungere dignatus est, solemniter asserere. Itaque Nos traditioni a fidei Christianae exordio perceptae fideliter inhaerendo, ad Dei Salvatoris Nostri gloriam, religionis Catholicae exaltationem, et Christianorum populorum salutem, sacro approbante Concilio, docemus, et divinitus revelatum dogma esse definimus: Romanum Pontificem, cum ex Cathedra loquitur, id est, cum omnium Christianorum Pastoris et Doctoris munere fungens, pro suprema sua Apostolica auctoritate doctrinam de fide vel moribus ab universa Ecclesia tenendam definit, per assistentiam divinam, ipsi in beato Petro promissam, ea infallibilitate pollere, qua divinus Redemptor Ecclesiam suam in definienda doctrina de fide vel moribus instructam esse voluit; ideoque eiusmodi Romani Pontificis definitiones ex sese, non autem ex consensu Ecclesiae irreformabiles esse.

Si quis autem huic Nostrae definitioni contradicere, quod Deus avertat, praesumpserit; anathema sit.

Datum Romae, in publica Sessione in Vaticana Basilica solemniter celebrata, anno Incarnationis Dominicae millesimo octingentesimo septuagesimo, die decima octava Iulii.

Pontificatus Nostri anno vigesimo quinto.

Ita est.

Josephus Episcopus S. Hippolyti,
Secretarius Concilii Vaticani.

De mandato SS.mi in Christo Patris et Domini Nostri Domini divina Providentia Pii PP. IX., anno a Nativitate Domini MDCCCLXX., Indict. xiii., die vero xviii. Julii, Pontificatus eiusdem SS.mi Domini Nostri Anno xxv., praesens Constitutio Apostolica affixa et publicata fuit ad valvas Basilicarum S. Ioannis in Laterano, Principis Apostolorum, et S. Mariae Maioris, Cancellariae Apostolicae, ac Magnae Curiae Innocentianae, atque in Acie Campi Florae per me Aloisium Serafini Apost. Curs.

Philippus Ossani, *Magist. Curs.*

(Dal *Giornale di Roma*, 19 luglio 1870.)

ALBEMARLE STREET,
November, 1875.

MR. MURRAY'S
LIST OF FORTHCOMING WORKS.

MR. FORSTER'S LIFE OF SWIFT.
To be completed in 3 vols.

LIFE OF JONATHAN SWIFT.
By JOHN FORSTER.

With an Etching by RAJON *from the Portrait by* JERVAS, *and Facsimiles.*
Vol. I. 8vo. 15s.

"Swift's later time, when he was governing Ireland as well as his deanery, and the world was filled with the fame of *Gulliver*, is broadly and intelligibly written. But as to all the rest, it is a work unfinished; to which no one has brought the minute examination indispensably necessary, where the whole of a career has to be considered to get at the proper comprehension of single parts of it. The writers accepted as authorities for the obscurer years are found to be practically worthless, and the defect is not supplied by the later and greater biographers. Johnson did him no kind of justice because of too little liking for him; and Scott, with much hearty liking as well as a generous admiration, had too much other work to do. Thus, notwithstanding noble passages in both memoirs, and Scott's pervading tone of healthy manly wisdom, it is left to an inferior hand to attempt to complete the tribute begun by those distinguished men."—*Author's Preface.*

A THIRD SERIES OF

LECTURES ON THE HISTORY OF THE JEWISH CHURCH.
FROM THE CAPTIVITY TO THE DESTRUCTION OF JERUSALEM.
By A. P. STANLEY, D.D., Dean of Westminster.
8vo.

MEMOIR AND CORRESPONDENCE OF CAROLINE HERSCHEL,
SISTER OF SIR WILLIAM AND AUNT OF SIR JOHN HERSCHEL.
BY MRS. JOHN HERSCHEL.
With Portraits. Crown 8vo, uniform with "Mrs. Somerville's Memoirs."

LIFE IN FAITH.
SERMONS PREACHED AT CHELTENHAM AND RUGBY.
BY T. W. JEX-BLAKE, D.D.,
Head Master of Rugby.

Small 8vo.

A NATURAL HISTORY OF MAMMALS, INCLUDING MAN.
BEING THE FIRST PART OF AN INTRODUCTION TO ZOOLOGY AND BIOLOGY.
BY ST. GEORGE MIVART, F.R.S.
With numerous Illustrations on Wood. 2 vols. 8vo.

The object of this work is to present to ordinary readers and to medical and other students who have no special acquaintance with Zoology, a general view of the structure, physiology, habits, geographical and geological distribution, affinities and classification of the groups (of the rank of families and sub-families) which compose the highest class of animals.

It is also intended to serve as an introduction to Zoology and to Biology generally, and will therefore explain in simple language the various ways in which living bodies may be considered, giving the elementary facts and principles of Histology, Physiology, and the other sciences subordinate to Biology.

THE ST. JAMES' LECTURES.
COMPANIONS FOR THE DEVOUT LIFE;
SIX LECTURES ON THE FOLLOWING AUTHORS, DELIVERED IN ST. JAMES'S CHURCH, PICCADILLY.
WITH A PREFACE BY REV. J. E. KEMPE, M.A., RECTOR.

THE IMITATION OF CHRIST. *F. W. FARRAR, D.D., Marlborough College.*
PASCAL'S PENSÉES. *R. W. CHURCH, M.A., Dean of St. Paul's.*
S. FRANÇOIS DE SALES. *E. M. GOULBOURN, D.D., Dean of Norwich.*
BAXTER AND THE SAINTS' REST. *R. C. TRENCH, D.D., Archbishop of Dublin.*
S. AUGUSTINE'S CONFESSIONS. *WM. ALEXANDER, D.D., Bishop of Derry.*
JEREMY TAYLOR'S HOLY LIVING AND DYING. *WM. G. HUMPHRY, B.D., Prebendary of St. Paul's.*

8vo.

TRAVELS IN THE CAUCASUS, PERSIA, AND TURKEY IN ASIA.
INCLUDING A JOURNEY DOWN THE TIGRIS AND EUPHRATES TO NINEVEH AND BABYLON, AND ACROSS THE DESERT TO PALMYRA.
BY BARON MAX VON THIELMANN.
TRANSLATED FROM THE GERMAN BY CHAS. HENEAGE, F.R.G.S.
Map and Illustrations. 2 Vols. Post 8vo. 18s.

THE LETTERS OF SARAH DUCHESS OF MARLBOROUGH.

NOW FIRST PUBLISHED FROM THE ORIGINAL MSS. IN THE POSSESSION OF EARL BEAUCHAMP AT MADRESFIELD COURT.

With an Introduction. 8vo. 10s. 6d.

DICTIONARY OF CHRISTIAN ANTIQUITIES.

COMPRISING THE HISTORY, INSTITUTIONS, AND ANTIQUITIES OF

THE CHRISTIAN CHURCH.

BY VARIOUS WRITERS.

Edited by DR. WM. SMITH and PROF. CHEETHAM, M.A.

With Illustrations. Vol. I. Medium 8vo. 31s. 6d.

ALBERT DURER: HIS LIFE AND WORKS.

BY DR. TAUSSING,
Keeper of Archduke Albert's Art Collections at Vienna.

Translated, with the Author's sanction, from the German.

With Portrait and other Illustrations. Medium 8vo.

THRIFT.

BY SAMUEL SMILES, Author of "Self-help," "Character," &c.

Post 8vo. 6s.

CONTENTS:

INDUSTRY.	LIFE ASSURANCE.	LIVING ABOVE THE MEANS.
HABITS OF THRIFT.	SAVINGS BANKS.	GREAT DEBTORS.
IMPROVIDENCE.	LITTLE THINGS.	RICHES AND CHARITY.
MEANS OF SAVING.	MASTERS AND MEN.	HEALTHY HOMES.
EXAMPLES OF THRIFT.	THE CROSSLEYS.	ART OF LIVING.
METHODS OF ECONOMY.		

THE MOVEMENTS AND HABITS OF CLIMBING PLANTS.

BY CHARLES DARWIN, M.A., F.R.S.

Second Edition, revised. With Illustrations. Post 8vo. 6s.

THE VAUX-DE-VIRE OF MAISTRE JEAN LE HOUX, ADVOCATE, OF VIRE.

Translated and Edited by JAMES PATRICK MUIRHEAD, M.A.

With Portrait and Illustrations. 8vo.

RUSSIAN TARTARY, EASTERN SIBERIA, JAPAN, AND FORMOSA.

BEING A NARRATIVE OF A CRUISE IN THE EASTERN SEAS, FROM THE COREA TO THE RIVER AMUR.

BY CAPTAIN B. W. BAX, R.N.

With Map and Illustrations. Crown 8vo. 12s.

SPORT IN ABYSSINIA;
OR, THE MAREB AND TACKAZZEE.

BY LIEUT. THE EARL OF MAYO.
Grenadier Guards.

With Illustrations. Post 8vo.

AN ARTIST'S PORTFOLIO.

BEING A SELECTION FROM SKETCHES MADE DURING TOURS IN HOLLAND, GERMANY, ITALY, EGYPT, ETC.

BY E. W. COOKE, R.A.

50 Plates. Sm. folio.

LESSONS FROM NATURE
AS MANIFESTED IN MIND AND MATTER.

BY ST. GEORGE MIVART, F.R.S., Secretary to the Linnæan Society, Professor of Biology at University College, Kensington, and Lecturer on Zoology and Comparative Anatomy at St. Mary's Hospital.

8vo.

A SHORT HISTORY OF NATURAL SCIENCE;
AND THE PROGRESS OF DISCOVERY FROM THE TIME OF THE GREEKS TO THE PRESENT DAY.

FOR SCHOOLS AND YOUNG PERSONS.

BY ARABELLA BUCKLEY.

With 60 Illustrations. Post 8vo.

SPORT AND WAR.
RECOLLECTIONS OF FIGHTING AND HUNTING IN SOUTH AFRICA.
FROM 1834 TO 1867.
WITH A NARRATIVE OF THE VISIT OF H.R.H. THE DUKE OF EDINBURGH.
BY MAJOR-GENERAL BISSET, C.B.
With Map and Illustrations. Crown 8vo.

BIBLE LANDS; THEIR MODERN CUSTOMS AND MANNERS.
IN ILLUSTRATION OF SCRIPTURE.
BY HENRY VAN LENNEP, D.D.,
Author of "Travels in Asia Minor."
With Maps and Illustrations. 8vo.

FRAGMENTS ON ETHICAL SUBJECTS.
BY THE LATE GEORGE GROTE, F.R.S.
BEING A SELECTION FROM HIS POSTHUMOUS PAPERS. WITH AN INTRODUCTION,
BY ALEXANDER BAIN, M.A.
8vo.

PILGRIMAGES TO ST. MARY OF WALSINGHAM AND ST. THOMAS OF CANTERBURY.
WITH THE COLLOQUY OF RASH VOWS, AND THE CHARACTERS OF
ARCHBISHOP WARHAM AND DEAN COLET.
BY DESIDERIUS ERASMUS.
TRANSLATED, WITH AN INTRODUCTION AND ILLUSTRATIVE NOTES,
BY JOHN GOUGH NICHOLS, F.S.A.
Second Edition, Revised and Corrected. With Woodcuts. Post 8vo.

THE
CITIES AND CEMETERIES OF ETRURIA.
BY GEORGE DENNIS.
New Edition, Revised and Condensed. With Illustrations. 8vo.

EIGHT MONTHS AT ROME DURING THE VATICAN COUNCIL.
CONTAINING A DAILY ACCOUNT OF THE PROCEEDINGS.

BY POMPONIO LETO.

Translated from the Italian, with the Original Documents.

8vo.

BLACKSTONE'S COMMENTARIES,
New and Revised Edition.

ADAPTED TO THE PRESENT STATE OF THE LAW.
INCLUDING ALL THE RECENT CHANGES IN THE LAW TO 1875.

BY R. MALCOLM KERR, LL.D.,

Judge of the City of London Court, and one of the Commissioners of the Central Criminal Court.

4 Vols. 8vo.

A MEMOIR OF FRANCES, LADY CREWE.
FORMING

A SECOND VOLUME OF MONOGRAPHS SOCIAL AND LITERARY.

BY LORD HOUGHTON.

Portrait. Post 8vo.

THE

STUDENT'S MANUAL OF ECCLESIASTICAL HISTORY.

A HISTORY OF THE CHRISTIAN CHURCH FROM ITS FOUNDATION TO THE EVE OF THE PROTESTANT REFORMATION.

BY PHILIP SMITH, B.A.

Author of "The Student's Old and New Testament Histories."

With Illustrations. Post 8vo.

FOUNDATIONS OF RELIGION IN THE MIND AND HEART OF MAN.

BY THE RIGHT HON. SIR. JOHN BARNARD BYLES,

Late one of the Judges of Her Majesty's Court of Common Pleas at Westminster.

Post 8vo.

THE HISTORY OF HERODOTUS;
A NEW ENGLISH VERSION.

Edited, with copious *Notes* and *Essays*, from the most recent sources of information, Historical and Ethnographical, which have been obtained in the progress of Cuneiform and Hieroglyphical Discovery.

BY REV. GEORGE RAWLINSON, M.A.,
Canon of Canterbury, and Camden Professor of Ancient History at Oxford.

Assisted by SIR HENRY RAWLINSON and SIR J. GARDNER WILKINSON.

Third Edition, Revised. With Maps and 350 Woodcuts. 4 vols. 8vo.

POETICAL REMAINS,
INCLUDING TRANSLATIONS & IMITATIONS, OF THE LATE
EDWARD CHURTON, M.A.
ARCHDEACON OF CLEVELAND.

Post 8vo.

THE PRINCIPLES OF GEOLOGY;
OR, THE MODERN CHANGES OF THE EARTH AND ITS INHABITANTS, CONSIDERED AS ILLUSTRATIVE OF GEOLOGY.

BY SIR CHARLES LYELL, F.R.S.
12th *Edition*. With Illustrations. 2 vols. 8vo.

POETICAL WORKS OF RICHARD MONCKTON MILNES (LORD HOUGHTON).
Collected Edition. 2 vols. Fcap. 8vo.

A POPULAR EDITION OF

MR. MOTLEY'S LIFE AND DEATH OF JOHN OF BARNEVELD.
With Illustrations. 2 vols. Post 8vo.
Uniform with "History of the Dutch Republic."

THE

POETICAL WORKS OF ALEXANDER POPE.
VOL. III., CONTAINING THE SATIRES, &c.
EDITED BY REV. WHITWELL ELWIN, B.A.
8vo.

THE VARIATION OF ANIMALS AND PLANTS UNDER DOMESTICATION.
BY CHARLES DARWIN, F.R.S.
Revised Edition. With Illustrations. 2 vols. Crown 8vo.

HISTORY OF ANCIENT EGYPT.
DERIVED FROM MONUMENTS AND INSCRIPTIONS.
BY PROFESSOR BRUGSCH, OF GOTTINGEN.
Translated from the German by H. DANBY SEYMOUR, F.R.G.S.
8vo.

HISTORY OF INDIAN AND EASTERN ARCHITECTURE.
BY JAMES FERGUSSON, F.R.S.
With 400 Illustrations. Medium 8vo.
Uniform with the "History of Ancient and Mediæval Architecture."

DR. LIVINGSTONE'S SECOND EXPEDITION TO AFRICA.
A POPULAR ACCOUNT OF THE EXPEDITION TO THE ZAMBESI, LAKES SHIRWA, AND NYASSA.
Abridged from the larger work.
With Map and Illustrations. Post 8vo.

PORTRAITS OF THE MOST BEAUTIFUL ALPINE FLOWERS.
IN A SERIES OF COLOURED PICTURES, SELECTED
BY WM. ROBINSON, F.L.S.
50 Plates. Crown 8vo.
A Companion Volume to "Robinson's Alpine Flowers for English Gardens."

DICTIONARY OF CHRISTIAN BIOGRAPHY AND DOCTRINES.
FROM THE TIMES OF THE APOSTLES TO THE AGE OF CHARLEMAGNE.
BY VARIOUS WRITERS.
EDITED BY WM. SMITH, D.C.L., & REV. HENRY WACE, M.A.
Medium 8vo.

A MEDIÆVAL LATIN DICTIONARY.
Based on the Work of DUCANGE.
Translated into English and Edited, with many Additions and Corrections,
BY E. A. DAYMAN, B.D.,
Prebendary of Sarum, formerly Fellow and Tutor of Exeter College, Oxford.
Small 4to.

THE EPISTLES OF ST. PAUL TO THE CORINTHIANS;
WITH CRITICAL NOTES AND DISSERTATIONS.
BY A. P. STANLEY, D.D.,
Dean of Westminster.
Fourth Edition, Revised. 8vo.

A SCHOOL MANUAL OF MODERN GEOGRAPHY.
EDITED BY WM. SMITH, D.C.L.
Forming a New Volume of "Dr. Wm. Smith's English Course." 12mo.

LITTLE ARTHUR'S HISTORY OF ROME.
FROM THE EARLIEST TIMES TO THE ESTABLISHMENT OF THE EMPIRE.
Woodcuts. 16mo.

BOSWELL'S LIFE OF DR. JOHNSON.
EDITED BY THE LATE RIGHT HON. J. W. CROKER.
WITH NOTES BY LORD STOWELL, SIR WALTER SCOTT, SIR JAMES MACKINTOSH, DISRAELI, MARKLAND, LOCKHART, &c.
A New, Revised, Library Edition. With Portraits. 4 vols. 8vo.

THE SIXTH VOLUME OF

THE SPEAKER'S COMMENTARY ON THE HOLY BIBLE;
COMPLETING THE OLD TESTAMENT.

CONTENTS.

EZEKIEL—Rev. Dr. Currey.

DANIEL { Archdeacon Rose.
{ Rev. I. Fuller.

THE MINOR PROPHETS { Rev. E. Huxtable.
{ Professor Gandell.
{ Rev. F. Meyrick.
{ Canon Cook.
{ Rev. W. Drake.

Medium 8vo.

A NEW DICTIONARY OF THE ENGLISH LANGUAGE.

FOR PRACTICAL REFERENCE, METHODICALLY ARRANGED, AND BASED UPON THE BEST PHILOLOGIC AUTHORITIES.

Medium 8vo.

∗ Also, A STUDENT'S ENGLISH DICTIONARY.

Square 12mo.

THE FRENCH PRINCIPIA, PART II.

A READING BOOK; CONTAINING FABLES, STORIES, AND ANECDOTES, NATURAL HISTORY, AND SCENES FROM THE HISTORY OF FRANCE. WITH GRAMMATICAL QUESTIONS, NOTES, AND A DICTIONARY.

On the Plan of Dr. William Smith's "Principia Latina."

12mo.

THE FRENCH PRINCIPIA, PART III.

AN INTRODUCTION TO FRENCH PROSE COMPOSITION; CONTAINING A SYSTEMATIC COURSE OF EXERCISES ON THE SYNTAX, WITH THE PRINCIPAL RULES OF SYNTAX.

12mo.

THE GERMAN PRINCIPIA, PART I.

FIRST GERMAN COURSE, CONTAINING GRAMMAR, DELECTUS, EXERCISES, AND VOCABULARY.

On the Plan of Dr. Wm. Smith's "Principia Latina."

12mo.

THE GERMAN PRINCIPIA, PART II.

A READING BOOK; CONTAINING FABLES, STORIES, AND ANECDOTES, NATURAL HISTORY, AND SCENES FROM THE HISTORY OF FRANCE. WITH GRAMMATICAL QUESTIONS AND NOTES.

12mo.

THE GERMAN PRINCIPIA, PART III.

AN INTRODUCTION TO GERMAN PROSE COMPOSITION; CONTAINING A SYSTEMATIC COURSE OF EXERCISES ON THE SYNTAX, WITH THE PRINCIPAL RULES OF SYNTAX.

12mo.

50, ALBEMARLE STREET,
November, 1875.

MR. MURRAY'S
List of New Works, Now Ready

Rome
AND THE NEWEST FASHIONS IN RELIGION.
THREE TRACTS.
BY RIGHT HON. W. E. GLADSTONE, M.P.
Collected Edition. With a New Preface.
8vo. 7s. 6d.

Troy and its Remains.
A NARRATIVE OF DISCOVERIES AND RESEARCHES MADE ON THE SITE OF ILIUM, AND IN THE TROJAN PLAIN.
BY DR. HENRY SCHLIEMANN.
EDITED BY PHILIP SMITH, B.A.,
Author of "Ancient History from the Earliest Records," &c.
With Maps, and 500 Illustrations. Royal 8vo. 42s.

Insectivorous Plants.
BY CHARLES DARWIN, F.R.S.,
Author of "Origin of Species."
Third Thousand. With Illustrations. Crown 8vo. 14s.

The Papers of a Critic.
Including Articles on POPE, LADY MARY WORTLEY MONTAGU, SWIFT, JUNIUS, WILKES, GRENVILLE, BURKE, &c.
Selected from the Writings of the late CHARLES WENTWORTH DILKE.
WITH A BIOGRAPHICAL SKETCH BY HIS GRANDSON,
SIR CHARLES W. DILKE, Bart., M.P.,
Author of "Greater Britain," and of "The Fall of Prince Florestan of Monaco."
2 Vols. 8vo. 24s.

Protestantism and Catholicism.
IN THEIR BEARINGS UPON THE LIBERTY AND PROSPERITY OF NATIONS.
A STUDY OF SOCIAL ECONOMY.

BY EMILE DE LAVELAYE.

With INTRODUCTORY LETTER by MR. GLADSTONE.

Third Edition. 8vo. 2s. 6d.

The Travels of Marco Polo, the Venetian,
CONCERNING THE KINGDOMS AND MARVELS OF THE EAST.

A NEW ENGLISH VERSION.

Illustrated by the Light of Oriental Writers and Modern Travels.

BY COL. HENRY YULE, C.B.
Late Royal Engineers (Bengal).

Second Edition, Revised and Enlarged.

With 19 Maps and 130 Illustrations. 2 Vols. Medium 8vo. 63s.

Metallurgy;
THE ART OF EXTRACTING METALS FROM THEIR ORE.

BY JOHN PERCY, M.D., F.R.S.,
Lecturer on Metallurgy at the Government School of Mines, Honorary Member of the Institution of Civil Engineers, &c.

FIRST DIVISION.—FUEL, including

INTRODUCTION,	FIRE BRICKS,	COAL,
REFRACTORY METALS,	FUEL,	CHARCOAL,
FIRE CLAYS,	WOOD,	COKE,
CRUCIBLES,	PEAT,	GAS FURNACES, &c.

Revised and Enlarged Edition. With Lithographs and 112 Illustrations. 8vo. 30s.

A Popular Edition of Mr. Smiles' Lives of the Engineers,
FROM THE EARLIEST TIMES TO THE DEATH OF THE STEPHENSONS,
WITH AN ACCOUNT OF THEIR PRINCIPAL WORKS:

Comprising a History of Inland Communication in Britain, and the Invention and Introduction of the Steam Engine and Locomotive.

Revised Edition. With Portraits and 340 Woodcuts. 5 vols. Crown 8vo. 7s. 6d. each.

England and Russia in the East.

A SERIES OF PAPERS ON THE POLITICAL AND GEOGRAPHICAL CONDITION OF CENTRAL ASIA.

BY MAJOR-GEN. SIR HENRY RAWLINSON, K.C.B., F.R.S.,

President of the Royal Geographical Society, and Member of the Council of India.

Second Edition, Revised. With Map. 8vo. 12s.

The Hawaiian Archipelago.

SIX MONTHS AMONG THE PALM GROVES, CORAL REEFS, AND VOLCANOES OF THE SANDWICH ISLANDS.

BY ISABELLA BIRD,

Author of the "Englishwoman in America."

With Illustrations. Crown 8vo. 12s.

The Land of the North Wind,

OR TRAVELS AMONG THE LAPLANDERS AND SAMOYEDES, AND ALONG THE SHORES OF THE WHITE SEA.

BY EDWARD RAE.

With Map and Woodcuts. Post 8vo. 10s. 6d.

Last Journals of Dr. Livingstone in Central Africa,

FROM 1865 TO WITHIN A FEW DAYS OF HIS DEATH.

Continued by a Narrative of his last moments and sufferings.

BY REV. HORACE WALLER, M.A., F.R.G.S.,

Rector of Twywell, Northampton.

With Portrait, Maps, and Illustrations. 2 Vols. 8vo. 28s.

Memoir of Sir Roderick Murchison.

INCLUDING EXTRACTS FROM HIS JOURNALS AND LETTERS.

WITH NOTICES OF HIS SCIENTIFIC CONTEMPORARIES, ETC.

BY ARCHIBALD GEIKIE, LL.D., F.R.S.

Murchison-Professor of Geology and Mineralogy in the University of Edinburgh, and Director of the Geological Survey of Scotland.

With Portraits, &c. 2 vols. 8vo. 30s.

Old Times and Distant Places.

A SERIES OF SKETCHES.
BY THE LATE ARCHDEACON SINCLAIR, M.A.,
Vicar of Kensington.
Crown 8vo. 9s.

Handbook to the History of Painting.

THE ITALIAN, GERMAN, FLEMISH, AND DUTCH SCHOOLS.
BASED ON THE WORK OF KUGLER.
New and Revised Edition. With 200 Illustrations. 4 vols. Crown 8vo. 54s.

The Gothic Architecture of Italy.—Chiefly in Brick and Marble.

WITH NOTES OF RECENT VISITS TO AQUILEIA, UDINE, VICENZA, FERRARA, BOLOGNA, MODENA, AND VERCELLI.

BY GEORGE EDMUND STREET, R.A.

Revised Edition. With 130 Illustrations. Royal 8vo. 26s.

The Gnostic Heresies of the First and Second Centuries.

BY DEAN MANSEL, D.D.,
Late Professor of Ecclesiastical History at Oxford.

WITH A SKETCH OF HIS LIFE AND CHARACTER, BY LORD CARNARVON.

EDITED WITH A PREFACE BY CANON LIGHTFOOT.

8vo. 10s. 6d.

Principles of Greek Etymology.

VOL. I. INTRODUCTION; REGULAR SUBSTITUTION OF SOUNDS.

BY PROFESSOR GEORG CURTIUS.

TRANSLATED FROM THE GERMAN BY A. S. WILKINS, M.A.,
Professor of Latin and Comparative Philology, and

E. B. ENGLAND, M.A.,
Assistant-Lecturer in Classics, Owens College, Manchester.

8vo. 15s.

The Early History of Institutions.

IN CONTINUATION OF "THE HISTORY OF ANCIENT LAW."

BY SIR H. SUMNER MAINE, K.S.C.I., LL.D.,

Corpus Professor of Jurisprudence at Oxford, and Member of the Indian Council.

Second Edition. 8vo. 12s.

The Diary of the Shah of Persia,

DURING HIS TOUR THROUGH EUROPE IN 1873.

TRANSLATED BY J. W. REDHOUSE, F.R.A.S.

With Portrait and Coloured Title. Crown 8vo. 12s.

A Grammar of the English Language.

BY PROFESSOR MAETZNER, of Berlin.

TRANSLATED BY CLAIR J. GRECE, LL.B.

3 vols. 8vo. 36s.

POPULAR SELECTIONS FROM

Mr. Beresford Hope's Work on Worship in the Church of England.

8vo. 2s. 6d.

⁎ Copies of the LARGER WORK may still be had. 8vo. 9s.

School Board Architecture:

BEING PRACTICAL INFORMATION ON THE PLANNING, DESIGNING, BUILDING, AND FURNISHING OF SCHOOLHOUSES.

BY E. R. ROBSON, F.R.I.B.A.,

ARCHITECT TO THE SCHOOL BOARD FOR LONDON.

With 300 Illustrations. Medium 8vo. 31s. 6d.

Alpine Flowers For English Gardens.

HOW THEY MAY BE GROWN IN ALL PARTS OF THE BRITISH ISLANDS.

BY W. ROBINSON, F.L.S.

New and Revised Edition. Many additional Woodcuts. Crown 8vo. 12s.

Elucidations of the Student's Greek Grammar.

BY PROFESSOR CURTIUS.

TRANSLATED FROM THE GERMAN BY EVELYN ABBOTT, M.A.

Second Edition, Revised. Post 8vo. 7s. 6d.

The Nicene and Apostles' Creeds.

THEIR LITERARY HISTORY; TOGETHER WITH SOME ACCOUNT OF THE GROWTH AND RECEPTION OF THE SERMON ON THE FAITH, COMMONLY CALLED "*THE CREED OF ST. ATHANASIUS.*"

BY C. A. SWAINSON, D.D.,
Canon of Chichester and Norrisian Professor of Divinity at Cambridge.

With Facsimile. 8vo. 16s.

The Student's Edition of Austin's Lectures on Jurisprudence:

OR, THE PHILOSOPHY OF POSITIVE LAW.

COMPILED FROM THE LARGER WORK.

BY ROBERT CAMPBELL,
of Lincoln's Inn, Barrister-at-Law.

Post 8vo. 12s.

Sonnets and Songs.

BY PROTEUS.

Fcap. 8vo. 3s. 6d.

Pastoral Colloquies on the South Downs— Prophecy and Miracles.

By the late CANON SELWYN, D.D., Margaret Professor, Cambridge.

With Photographs. Crown 8vo. 6s.

Archæology, Art and Travel:

BEING SKETCHES AND STUDIES; HISTORICAL AND DESCRIPTIVE.

BY RICHARD J. KING, B.A.,

Late of Exeter College, Oxford.

8vo. 12s.

Hortensius;

AN HISTORICAL ESSAY ON THE OFFICE AND DUTIES OF AN ADVOCATE.

BY WILLIAM FORSYTH, Q.C., LL.D., M.P.,

Late Fellow of Trinity College, Cambridge.

Second Edition. With Illustrations. 8vo. 12s.

The Moon:

CONSIDERED AS A PLANET, A WORLD, AND A SATELLITE.

BY JAMES NASMYTH, C.E., AND JAMES CARPENTER, F.R.A.S.,

With 24 Illustrations of Lunar Objects, Phenomena, and Scenery.

Second Edition. 4to. 30s.

The Constitution and Practice of Courts Martial.

BY CAPT. T. F. SIMMONS, R.A.

Seventh Edition, Revised. 8vo. 15s.

Etchings from the Loire and the South of France.

IN A SERIES OF TWENTY PLATES. ' With Descriptive Text.

BY ERNEST GEORGE.

Folio. 42s.

Uniform with Mr. GEORGE'S "Etchings on the Mosel."

History of the Christian Church.
FROM THE APOSTOLIC AGE TO THE REFORMATION, 1517.

By REV. JAMES C. ROBERTSON, M.A.,
Canon of Canterbury.

Revised Edition. 8 Vols., with Index. Post 8vo. 6s. each.

The Origin and History of the Grenadier Guards.
From Original Documents in the State Paper Office, Rolls' Records, War Office, Horse Guards, Contemporary Histories, and Regimental Records.

BY LIEUT.-GEN. SIR FREDERICK W. HAMILTON, K.C.B.

With Portraits and Illustrations. 3 vols. 8vo. 63s.

The Sonnet;
ITS ORIGIN, STRUCTURE, AND PLACE IN POETRY.

WITH ORIGINAL TRANSLATIONS FROM THE SONNETS OF DANTE, PETRARCH, &c.

With Remarks on the Art of Translating.

BY CHARLES TOMLINSON, F.R.S.

Post 8vo. 9s.

The Naturalist in Nicaragua.
A NARRATIVE OF JOURNEYS IN THE SAVANNAHS AND FORESTS;
WITH OBSERVATIONS ON ANIMALS AND PLANTS.

BY THOMAS BELT, F.G.S.

With Illustrations. Post 8vo. 12s.

The Effects of Observation of India on Modern European Thought.
THE REDE LECTURE, delivered at CAMBRIDGE, 1875.

By SIR H. SUMNER MAINE, K.C.S.I.

8vo. 2s.

The Shadows of a Sick Room.
Second Edition. With a Preface by CANON LIDDON.
Post 8vo. 2s. 6d.

Forty Years' Service in India.
INCLUDING DISASTERS AND CAPTIVITIES IN CABUL, AFFGHANISTAN, AND THE PUNJAUB. WITH A NARRATIVE OF MUTINIES IN RAJPUTANA.

BY LIEUT.-GEN. SIR GEORGE LAWRENCE, K.C.S.I., C.B.
Second Edition. Crown 8vo. 10s. 6d.

HISTORY OF
Ancient and Mediæval Architecture.
BY JAMES FERGUSSON, F.R.S.
Revised Edition. With 1000 Illustrations. 2 Vols. 8vo. 63s.

Perils of the Polar Seas:
TRUE STORIES OF ARCTIC ADVENTURE AND DISCOVERY.
BY MRS. CHISHOLM.
With Maps and Illustrations. Post 8vo. 6s.

Personal Recollections from Early Life to Old Age.
BY MARY SOMERVILLE.
WITH SELECTIONS FROM HER CORRESPONDENCE.
Fourth Thousand. Portrait. Crown 8vo. 12s.

History of the Royal Artillery.
COMPILED FROM THE ORIGINAL RECORDS.
BY MAJOR FRANCIS DUNCAN, R.A.,
Superintendent of the Regimental Records.
Second Edition. With Portraits. 2 vols. 8vo. 30s.

The Communistic Societies of the United States.

From Personal Visits and Observations; including Detailed Accounts of the SHAKERS, the AMANA, ONEIDA, BETHELL, AURORA, ICARIAN, and other Societies; their Religious Creeds, Social Practices, Industries, and Present Condition.

BY CHARLES NORDHOFF.

With 40 Illustrations. 8vo. 15s.

An Atlas of Ancient Geography.

BIBLICAL AND CLASSICAL.

Intended to illustrate Smith's Classical Dictionaries, and especially the "Dictionary of the Bible." Compiled under the superintendence of

DR. WM. SMITH and MR. GEORGE GROVE.

With Descriptive Text, giving the Sources and Authorities, Indices, &c.

43 Maps. Folio, half-bound. £6 6s.

The Holy Bible;

WITH AN EXPLANATORY AND CRITICAL COMMENTARY AND A REVISION OF THE TRANSLATION.

BY BISHOPS AND CLERGY OF THE ANGLICAN CHURCH.

EDITED BY F. C. COOK, M.A.,

Canon of Exeter, and Preacher at Lincoln's Inn, and Chaplain in Ordinary to the Queen.

THE OLD TESTAMENT.

Vol. I.—(*Two Parts*) 30s.
GENESIS—Bishop of Ely.
EXODUS—Canon Cook & Rev. Samuel Clark.
LEVITICUS—Rev. Samuel Clark.
NUMBERS—Canon Espin and Rev. J. F. Thrupp.
DEUTERONOMY—Canon Espin.

Vols. II. and III.—36s.
JOSHUA—Canon Espin.
JUDGES, RUTH, SAMUEL—Bishop of Bath and Wells.
KINGS, CHRONICLES, EZRA, NEHEMIAH, ESTHER—Canon Rawlinson.

Vol. IV.—24s.
PSALMS—Dean of Wells and Rev. C. J. Elliott.
JOB—Canon Cook.
PROVERBS—Rev. E. H. Plumptre.
ECCLESIASTES—Rev. W. T. Bullock.
SONG OF SOLOMON—Rev. T. Kingsbury.

Vol. V.—20s.
ISAIAH—Rev. Dr. Kay.
JEREMIAH, LAMENTATIONS—Dean of Canterbury.

www.ingramcontent.com/pod-product-compliance
Lightning Source LLC
Chambersburg PA
CBHW030350230426
43664CB00007BB/602